A Companion to Latin American Legal History

Legal History Library

VOLUME 64

The titles published in this series are listed at *brill.com/lhl*

A Companion to Latin American Legal History

Edited by

M.C. Mirow and Victor M. Uribe-Uran

BRILL | NIJHOFF

LEIDEN | BOSTON

Cover illustration: Valparaíso II, Gregory Mirow (2010).

Library of Congress Cataloging-in-Publication Data

Names: Mirow, Matthew C. (Matthew Campbell), 1962- editor. | Uribe Urán, Victor, editor.
Title: A companion to Latin American legal history / edited by M.C. Mirow and Victor M. Uribe-Uran.
Description: Leiden ; Boston : Brill/Nijhoff, 2024. | Series: Legal history library; vol. 64 | Includes index.
Identifiers: LCCN 2023031328 (print) | LCCN 2023031329 (ebook) | ISBN 9789004370203 (hardback) | ISBN 9789004436091 (ebook)
Subjects: LCSH: Law–Latin America–History.
Classification: LCC KG76 .C66 2024 (print) | LCC KG76 (ebook) | DDC 349.8–dc23/eng/20230710
LC record available at https://lccn.loc.gov/2023031328
LC ebook record available at https://lccn.loc.gov/2023031329

Typeface for the Latin, Greek, and Cyrillic scripts: "Brill". See and download: brill.com/brill-typeface.

ISSN 1874-1793
ISBN 978-90-04-37020-3 (hardback)
ISBN 978-90-04-43609-1 (e-book)
DOI 10.1163/9789004436091

To the memory of Alejandro Guzmán Brito
M.C.M.

•••

To Ana Luna, Antonia, and Sebastián, my force and inspiration
V.M.U.

Contents

Figures and Tables

Figures

Tables

Contributors

Diego Acosta
is Professor of European and Migration Law, University of Bristol, U.K.

Alejandro Agüero
is Professor of Legal History, National University of Cordoba, Argentina.

Sarah C. Chambers
is Professor of History, University of Minnesota – Twin Cities, U.S.A.

Robert J. Cottrol
is the Harold Paul Green Research Professor of Law and Professor of History and Sociology at the George Washington University, Washington, District of Columbia, U.S.A.

Óscar Cruz Barney
is Researcher at the Instituto de Investigaciones Jurídicas of the National Autonomous University of Mexico, Mexico City, Mexico.

Mariana Dias Paes
is Head of a Research Group at the Max Planck Institute for Legal History and Legal Theory, Frankfurt, Germany.

Tamar Herzog
is Monroe Gutman Professor of Latin American Affairs and Professor of Spanish and Portuguese History, Harvard University, Cambridge, Massachusetts, U.S.A.

Marta Lorente Sariñena
is Chaired Professor of Legal History and Institutions, Autonomous University of Madrid, Madrid, Spain.

M.C. Mirow
is Professor of Law, Florida International University, Miami, Florida, U.S.A.

Jerome A. Offner
is Associate Curator, Northern Mesoamerica, Houston Museum of Natural Science, Houston, Texas, U.S.A.

Brian P. Owensby
is Professor of History, University of Virginia, Charlottesville, Virginia, U.S.A.

Juan Manuel Palacio
is Professor of Latin American History, National University of San Martin, Buenos Aires, Argentina.

Agustín Parise
is Associate Professor of Law, Maastricht University, The Netherlands.

Rogelio Pérez-Perdomo
is Professor of Law, Metropolitan University, Caracas, Venezuela.

Heikki Pihlajamäki
is Professor of Comparative Legal History and Academy Professor, University of Helsinki, Finland.

Susan Elizabeth Ramírez
is Neville G. Penrose Endowed Chair Emerita of History and Latin American Studies, Texas Christian University, Fort Worth, Texas, U.S.A.

Timo H. Schaefer
is currently Lecturer in Latin American History at the University of Edinburgh, Scotland.

William Suárez-Potts
is Associate Professor of History, Rice University, Houston, Texas, U.S.A.

Victor M. Uribe-Uran
is Professor of History and Law, Florida International University, Miami, Florida, U.S.A.

Cristián Villalonga
is Assistant Professor of Law, Pontifical Catholic University of Chile, Santiago, Chile.

Alex L. Wisnoski III
is Associate Professor of History, University of North Georgia, Gainesville, Georgia, U.S.A.

Eduardo Zimmermann
is Professor of History, University of San Andres, Buenos Aires, Argentina.

Introduction

M.C. Mirow and Victor M. Uribe-Uran

This volume seeks to provide a resource for those interested in the legal history of Latin America, a field that has undergone a veritable historiographical renaissance in American academic circles over the past two to three decades. Like other volumes in the *Brill Companion* series related to law, it presents an overview and analysis of current scholarship, debates, and trajectories of a dynamic and changing field for students, scholars, policymakers, and lawyers. The materials found here fill several gaps in the presently available literature. First, students of American legal history, English legal history, and European legal history have several recent multi-authored companions, handbooks, or guides to consult for introductory treatments and bibliography in their fields.[1] Until the publication of this volume there has been no such work available for students of Latin American legal history. Second, Latin American legal historians for periods other than the colonial era are still bound to mostly national treatments of their areas of interest. A comprehensive treatment such as this has been missing. Third, by publishing this inclusive volume in English, we hope to open this flourishing field to students who may be limited by their abilities in Spanish or Portuguese. Thus, the co-editors delight in bringing the complexities, sophistication, and dissonances of the law and the legal history of this region to readers who are new to the field or already have developed an expertise in the subject. Despite the goal of providing an introductory and readable, yet detailed, snapshot of present literature and debates, many authors have advanced their areas substantially in these chapters so that the final products can be read as both useful summaries and elaborated analyses of evolving questions.

Although all chronologies are problematic, the history of Latin America has been traditionally divided into several basic periods. These are, in chronological order, a period before European contact, the colonial period (sometimes further divided into early, middle, and later subperiods), the independence period, a long nineteenth century, and the twentieth century and beyond. This volume seeks to address these various stages of legal change. It provides valuable information on law in the region before contact with European societies; examines several dimensions of law from the early sixteenth century to the

1 Examples may be found in the references section of this Introduction.

 | DOI:10.1163/9789004436091_002

early nineteenth century, that is during the colonial era; looks at legal changes during independence, especially in the 1810s and 1820s, and brings the discussion of the modern period of Latin American law up to the twenty-first century.

1 A Brief Historiography of Latin American Law

Writing the history of law in the region and its constituent countries is a vast undertaking. This brief presentation of the literature of Latin American legal history is meant to touch on the highlights of this field and does not by any means purport to be comprehensive. Modern academic study of this topic reaches back to the latter part of the nineteenth century with various changes and shifts in emphases and methodologies to the present day. The investigations cited below are representative of the kind of studies we have in mind. We also hope to provide illustrative works and approaches that mark new vectors in the historiography. With our intended readership in mind, we have tried to include as much of the scholarship in English as possible and sought to mark the most important contributions or trends in Spanish and Portuguese that still may not be available in English.

Legal history as a discipline in Latin America arose during the late nineteenth and early twentieth centuries. At first, some studies took on a specific area of interest and explored it in great depth. For example, in 1890 Colombian jurist Fernando Vélez co-authored an annotated edition of the *Colombian Mining Code*. The first part of this work was an historical summary of mining laws from Spanish colonial times to the present, with a chapter exclusively devoted to the history of mining laws of his native region, Antioquia.[2] To give another example, at the beginning of the century, Domingo Amunátegui Solar published three volumes on *mayorazgos* and estates in Chile.[3]

As part of national explorations of culture and history, several countries produced broader individual histories of their national law. These were sporadic, variable in coverage, and of differing quality. Many works focused on the history of areas traditionally considered private law such as laws and institutions related to land and topics usually found in civil codes. In 1891, Fernando Vélez authored a book modestly titled *Datos para la Historia del Derecho Nacional*, a

2 Fernando Vélez and Antonio José Uribe, *Código de Minas Colombiano: Concordado y Anotado* (Medellín: Imprenta del Departamento, 1890).

3 Domingo Amunátegui Solar, *La sociedad chilena del sigo XVIII: mayorazgos i titulos de Castilla*, 3 vols. (Santiago: Imprenta Barcelona, 1901, 1902, 1904). See also, Guillermo S. Fernández de Recas, *Mayorazgos de la Nueva España* (México: Instituto Bibliográfico Mexicano, 1965).

standard reference material legal historians of Colombia have used widely over the years.[4] Despite the alleged limitations of his text, which Vélez intended to 'gather and order' basic documents for the benefit of those qualified to write the history of Colombian law in the future, he suggested that his book could serve in the meantime as a basic manual to teach Colombian legal history. In 1900, Mexican jurist Jorge Vera Estañol published a short text entitled *La evolución jurídica*. It addressed historical aspects of the law of persons, family and successions, property, contracts, and criminal law in his country.[5] In 1916, David Peña produced an encyclopedic digest of Argentine legislation tied to the nation's history. Covering materials from 1810 to 1916, this work provides historical material on law with the goal of deeper study and possible reform. The history of law was seen as the tool to understand and to improve law.[6] Yet more ambitious was the undertaking of his compatriot, Ricardo Levene, who between 1945 and 1949 published a multi-volume book on the history of Argentine law, addressing both colonial and early modern legal institutions and sources of law.[7]

A field drawing Spanish-speaking scholars from around the world, *derecho indiano* (the law of the Indies or Spanish colonial law) was the product of several scholars of legal history in the first decades of the twentieth century. If national legal histories focused on areas traditionally related to private law, then *derecho indiano*'s main concern was the public law side of imperial incorporation and control of the Americas. Argentine historian Ricardo Levene published his introduction to the subject in 1916, and subsequently *derecho indiano* drew scholars from Argentina, Chile, Mexico, Spain, and elsewhere. For example, Mexican legal historian Silvio Zavala made numerous contributions to

---

4 See references, some of them critical, in Miguel Aguilera, *La legislación y el derecho en Colombia: sinopsis histórica desde la conquista hasta el presente*, in *Historia Extensa de Colombia*, vol. 14 (Bogotá: Ediciones Lerner, 1965), prologue; Robert Charles Means, *Underdevelopment and the Development of Law: Corporations and Corporation Law in Nineteenth-Century Colombia* (Chapel Hill: University of North Carolina Press, 1980), 278–279; M.C. Mirow, *Latin American Law: A History of Private Law and Institutions in Spanish America* (Austin: University of Texas Press, 2004), 130, 195. See also Diego López Medina, *Teoria impura del derecho: La transformación de la cultura jurídica latinoamericana* (Bogotá: Legis, 2009), 119, 131.

5 Jorge Vera Estañol, *La evolución jurídica* (México: UNAM, 1994, reprint of 1900 edition).

6 David Peña, *Historia de las Leyes de la Nación Argentina*, 2 vols. (Buenos Aires: Ateneo Nacional, 1916).

7 Ricardo Levene, *Historia del derecho argentino*, 5 vols. (Buenos Aires: Editorial Guillermo Kraft, 1945–1949).

this field beginning in the 1930s.[8] Spanish historian and jurist Rafael Altamira y Crevea contributed various volumes on the subject, even methodological pieces, as early as the 1930s and 1940s.[9] Ricardo Levene co-authored a classical manual with Spanish historian José María Ots Capdequi, a towering figure in the field.[10] And, to cite just one more, Chilean Alamiro de Ávila Martel authored a piece on *derecho indiano*'s criminal dimension in 1946.[11] The list of examples could go on and on. Norberto C. Dagrossa published an important and useful bibliography of *derecho indiano* in 2000.[12] Heikki Pihlajamäki discusses the rise of this field, its historians, and its accomplishments and limitations beautifully in Chapter 3 of this volume. Scholars working in this field to this day often become members of the *Instituto Internacional de Historia del Derecho Indiano* founded in 1966 by Chilean Alamiro de Ávila Martel, Argentine Ricardo Zorraquín Becú, and Spaniard Alfonso García-Gallo. The Institute continues to produce proceedings of its congresses.[13] Several important introductory manuals or general guides remain available in this field.[14]

While both sides of the Atlantic were discovering the complexities and sophistication of *derecho indiano*, even noticing its continuity with the European *ius commune*,[15] individual countries produced a series of descriptive works on doctrine and institutions closely tied to the instruction of lawyers.

---

8 E.g., Silvio A. Zavala, *Las instituciones jurídicas en la Conquista de América* (Madrid: Centro de Estudios Históricos, 1935); Silvio A. Zavala, *La encomienda indiana* (Madrid: Centro de Estudios Históricos, 1935); Silvio A. Zavala, *De encomienda y propiedad territorial en algunas regiones de la América Española* (México: Porrúa, 1940).

9 Rafael Altamira, *Técnica de investigación en la historia del derecho indiano* (México: Porrúa, 1939); Rafael Altamira, *Manual de investigación de la historia del derecho indiano* (México: Talleres Editorial Stylo, 1948). For later works along the same lines see Alfonso García Gallo, *Metodología de la historia del derecho indiano* (Santiago: Editorial Jurídica de Chile, 1970).

10 Ricardo Levene and José María Ots Capdequi, *Manual de historia del derecho español en las Indias y del derecho propiamente indiano* (Buenos Aires: Losada, 1945).

11 Alamiro de Ávila Martel, *Aspectos del derecho penal indiano* (Buenos Aires: Imprenta de la Universidad, 1946).

12 Norberto C. Dagrossa, 'Bibliografía de historia del derecho indiano' in *Nuevas aportaciones a la historia jurídica de Iberoamérica*, coord. José Andrés-Gallego (Madrid: Digibus, 2000).

13 See Chapter 3 of this volume.

14 Antonio Dougnac Rodríguez, *Manual de Historia del Derecho Indiano* (México: UNAM, 1994); José María Ots Capdequí, *España en América*, 2nd ed. (Bogotá, Universidad Nacional de Colombia, 1952); Victor Tau Anzoátegui, *¿Qué fue el Derecho Indiano?*, 2nd ed. (Buenos Aires: Abeledo-Perrot, 1982); Victor Tau Anzoátegui, *La Ley en América Hispana: Del Descubrimiento a la Emancipación* (Buenos Aires: Academia Nacional de la Historia, 1992).

15 See Javier Barriento Grandón, *La cultura jurídica en la Nueva España* (México: UNAM, 1993).

Some of the most respected legal historians produced these introductory yet often fully researched works for students.[16] These works often ran into several editions and provide essential entry points for those interested in national developments and the doctrinal history of law. Many of these works tie their country's legal history to earlier developments in European law especially Roman law, canon law, and the *ius commune*.

For consumption by scholars rather than students, legal historians turned to deeper study of their national legal systems and developments. Several studies were produced to explore the work of important codifiers. In the late 1930s, Abel Cháneton published two volumes on the drafter of the Argentine Civil Code.[17] Alejandro Guzmán Brito's magisterial treatment of Andrés Bello is well known.[18] And several other scholars have been drawn to this foundational thinker of Latin American law.[19] Numerous other scholars have analyzed individual countries' civil or commercial legislation and codes.[20] The legal history of crime and criminal jurisdictions has also attracted significant attention.[21]

---

16 Humberto Bello Lozano, *Historia de las fuentes e instituciones jurídicas venezolanas*, 6th ed. (Caracas: Librería La Lógica, 1983); Óscar Cruz Barney, *Historia del Derecho en México*, 2nd ed. (México: Oxford University Press, 2004); Abelardo Levaggi, *Manual de historia del derecho argentino*, 3 vols. (Buenos Aires: Depalma, 1986, 1987, 1991); Ricardo Levene, *Manual de historia del derecho argentino*, 5th ed. (Buenos Aires: Depalma, 1985); Guillermo Floris Magardant S., *Introducción a la historia del derecho mexicano*, 9th ed. (Naucalpan: Editorial Esfinge, 1990); Victor Tau Anzoátegui and Eduardo Martiré, *Manual de historia de las instituciones argentinas*, 7th ed. (Buenos Aires: Librería Histórica, 2005).

17 Abel Cháneton, *Historia de Vélez Sarsfield*, 2nd ed., 2 vols. (Buenos Aires: Bernabé, 1938). Followed by Abelardo Levaggi, *Dalmacio Vélez Sarsfield y el derecho eclesiástico* (Buenos Aires: Depalma, 1969).

18 Alejandro Guzmán Brito, *Andrés Bello codificador: historia de la fijación y codificación del derecho civil en Chile*, 2 vols. (Santiago: Universidad de Chile, 1982); Alejandro Guzmán Brito, *Historia de la codificación civil en Iberoamérica* (Madrid: Fundación Histórico Tavera, 2000); Alejandro Guzmán Brito, *Vida y obra de Andrés Bello* (Santiago: Globo Editores, 2009).

19 Alamiro de Ávila Martel, *Estudios sobre la vida y obra de Andrés Bello* (Santiago: Editorial de la Universidad de Chile, 1973); Iván Jaksić, *Andrés Bello: Scholarship and Nation Building in Nineteenth-Century Latin America* (Cambridge: Cambridge University Press, 2001).

20 Fernando Vélez, *Estudio sobre el derecho civil colombiano*, 9 vols. (Medellín: Imprenta del Departamento, 1898–1911); Armando Braun Menéndez, *José Gabriel Ocampo y el Código de Comercio de Chile* (Buenos Aires: Instituto de Historia del Derecho, 1951); Victor Tau Anzoátegui, *La codificación en Argentina, 1810–1870: mentalidad social e ideas jurídicas* (Buenos Aires: Imprenta de la Universidad, 1977); Carlos Ramos Núñez, *El código Napoleónico y su recepción en América Latina* (Lima: Pontificia Universidad Católica del Perú, 1997); María del Refugio González, *Estudios sobre la historia del derecho civil en México durante el siglo xix* (México: UNAM, 1981).

21 Listed chronologically: Colin MacLachlan, *Criminal Justice in Eighteenth-Century Mexico: A Study of the Tribunal of the Acordada* (Berkeley: University of California Press,

Various authors turned their attention to the legal history of family relations, law and institutions, with a natural emphasis on gender conflicts and feminist struggles.[22] Still other scholars focused on relatively unexplored periods, legal institutions, or topics, with many studies addressing Mexico.[23] The changes

---

1974); Ricardo D. Salvatore, Carlos Aguirre, and Gilbert Joseph, eds, *Crime and Punishment in Latin America: Law and Society since Late Colonial Times* (Durham: Duke University Press, 2001); Tamar Herzog, *Upholding Justice: Society, the State and the Penal System in Quito (1650–1750)* (Ann Arbor: University of Michigan Press, 2004); Osvaldo Barreneche, *Crime and the Administration of Justice in Buenos Aires, 1785–1853* (Lincoln: University of Nebraska Press, 2006); Pablo Piccato, *A History of Infamy: Crime, Truth and Justice in Mexico* (Berkeley: University of California Press, 2017).

22 Listed chronologically: Asunción Lavrin, *Women, Feminism and Social Change in Argentina, Chile and Uruguay, 1890–1940* (Lincoln: University of Nebraska Press, 1995); Christine Hunefeldt, *Liberalism in the Bedroom: Quarreling Spouses in Nineteenth Century Lima* (University Park: Pennsylvania State University Press, 2000); Kimberly Gauderman, *Women's Lives in Colonial Quito: Gender, Law and Economy in Spanish America* (Austin: University of Texas Press, 2003); Linda Lewin, *Suprise Heirs I: Illegitimacy, Patrimonial Rights, and Legal Nationalism in Luso-Brazilian Inheritance, 1750–1821* (Stanford: Stanford University Press, 2003); Linda Lewin, *Surprise Heirs II: Illegitimacy, Inheritance Rights, and Public Power in the Formation of Imperial Brazil, 1822–1889* (Stanford: Stanford University Press, 2003); Nara Milanich, *Children of Fate: Childhood, Class and the State in Chile, 1850–1930* (Durham: Duke University Press, 2010). Precursor works in this field include Daisy Rípodas Ardanaz, *El matrimonio en Indias: realidad social y regulación jurídica* (Buenos Aires: Fundación para la Educación, la Ciencia y la Cultura, 1977); Maria Beatriz Nizza da Silva, *Sistema de Casamento no Brasil Colonial* (Sao Paulo: Editora Edusp, 1984); Patricia Seed, *To Love, Honor, and Obey in Colonial Mexico: Conflicts over Marriage Choice, 1574–1821* (Stanford: Stanford University Press, 1988).

23 Listed chronologically: J.H. Parry, *The Audiencia of New Galicia in the Sixteenth Century: A Study in Spanish Colonial Government* (Cambridge: Cambridge University Press, 1948); Fernando de Trazegnies Granda, *La idea del derecho en el Perú republicano del siglo xix* (Lima: Universidad Católica del Perú, 1979); Robert Charles Means, *Underdevelopment and the Development of Law: Corporations and Corporation Law in Nineteenth-Century Colombia* (Chapel Hill: University of North Carolina, 1980); José Luis Soberanes Fernández, *Los tribunales de la Nueva España* (México: UNAM, 1980); Alamiro de Ávila Martel, *La pena de excomunión en las fuentes canónicas del Reino de Chile* (Quito: Corporación de Estudios y Publicaciones, 1980); Woodrow Borah, *Justice by Insurance: The General Indian Court of Colonial Mexico and the Legal Aides of the Half-Real* (Berkeley: University of California Press, 1983); Jerome A. Offner, *Law and Politics in Aztec Texcoco* (Cambridge: Cambridge University Press, 1983); Charles R. Cutter, *The Legal Culture of Northern New Spain 1700–1810* (Albuquerque: University of New Mexico Press, 1995); Susan Kellogg, *Law and the Transformation of Aztec Culture, 1500–1800* (Norman: University of Oklahoma Press, 1995); Peter Lester Reich, *Mexico's Hidden Revolution: The Catholic Church in Law and Politics since 1929* (Notre Dame: University of Notre Dame Press, 1995); Susan Kellogg and Matthew Restall, eds, *Dead Giveaway: Indigenous Testaments of Colonial Mesoamerica and the Andes* (Salt Lake City: University of Utah Press, 1998); Eduardo Zimmermann, ed., *Judicial Institutions in Nineteenth-Century Latin America* (London: Institute of Latin

and growth of the legal profession, lawyers, and judges have been another fruitful area of scholarly work.[24] The history of legal education has attracted various studies as well.[25]

While histories tied to the colonial and modern legal profession have remained important to this day, new methodological debates continue to occur in the field of *derecho indiano*. These debates would also extend later to modern legal history. For example, since 1997, the publication of Victor Tau Anzoátegui's *Nuevos horizontes en el estudio histórico del derecho indiano*, has served as an intellectual fulcrum upon which the lever of academic debate about Spanish colonial law rises and falls. Drawing on research by European legal historians such as Paolo Grossi, António Manuel Hespanha, and Bartolomé Clavero, Tau noted the emphasis placed on sources, institutions, and public law by established scholars in the field and called for transcending

---

American Studies, 1999); William J. Suarez-Potts, *The Making of Law: The Supreme Court and Labor Legislation in Mexico, 1875–1931* (Stanford: Stanford University Press, 2012).

24 Listed chronologically: José María Restrepo Sáenz, *Biografías de los mandatorios y ministros de la Real Audiencia* (Bogotá: Cromos, 1952); Guillermo Lohmann Villena, *Los ministros de la Audiencia de Lima en el reinado de los Borbones (1700–1821)* (Sevilla: EEHA, 1974); Mark A. Burkholder, *Politics of a Colonial Career: José Baquíjano and the Audiencia of Lima* (Albuquerque: University of New Mexico Press, 1980); Rogelio Pérez-Perdomo, *Los abogados en Venezuela: Una elite intelectual y política 1780–1980* (Caracas: Monte Ávila, 1981); Dennis O. Lynch, *Legal Roles in Colombia* (Uppsala: Scandinavian Institute of African Studies, 1981); Vicente Oddo, *Abogados de Santiago de Estero durante el primer siglo de existencia de la ciudad (1553–1663)* (Santiago de Estero: Herca, 1981); Mark A. Burkholder, *Biographical Dictionary of Audiencia Ministers in the Americas, 1687–1821* (Westport: Greenwood Press, 1982); Alí Enrique López Bohórquez, *Los ministros de la Audienca de Caracas (1786–1810)* (Caracas: Academia Nacional de la Historia, 1984); Ralph Vigil, *Alonzo Zorita: Royal Judge and Christian Humanist, 1512–1585* (Norman: University of Oklahoma Press, 1987); Tamar Herzog, *Los ministros de la audiencia de Quito (1650–1750)* (Bogotá: Libri-Mundi, 1995); Francisco de Icaza Dufour, *La Abogacía en el Reino de Nueva España* (México: Porrúa, 1998); Javier Barrientos Grandón, 'Guía prosopográfica de la judicatura letrada indiana (1505–1898)' in *Nuevas aportaciones a la historia jurídica de Iberoamérica*, coord. José Andrés-Gallego (Madrid: Digibus, 2000); Alejandro Mayagoitia Hagelstein, *El ingreso al Ilustre y Real Colegio de Abogados de México: historia, derecho y genealogía* (México: Ilustre Colegio de Abogados de México, 1999); Victor M. Uribe-Uran, *Honorable Lives: Lawyers, Family, and Politics in Colombia, 1780–1850* (Pittsburgh: University of Pittsburgh Press, 2000); Rodolfo Aguirre Salvador, *Carrera, linaje y patronazgo: clérigos y juristas en Nueva España, Chile y Perú, siglos XVI–XVIII* (México: UNAM, 2004); Rogelio Pérez-Perdomo, *Latin American Lawyers: A Historical Introduction* (Stanford: Stanford University Press, 2006); Clément Thibaud, *La Academia Carolina y la independencia de América: los abogados de Chuquisaca, 1776–1809* (Sucre: Editorial Charcas, 2010).

25 Juan Vicente Ugarte del Pino, *Historia de la facultad de derecho* (Lima: Universidad Nacional Mayor de San Marcos, 1968); Lucio Mendieta y Núñez, *Historia de la facultad de derecho*, 2nd ed. (México: UNAM, 1975).

the old conception of legal history as the history of legal norms produced by a hegemonic state. The work suggested the exploration of private law and methodology rooted in sociological and newer historical approaches. Thus, *derecho indiano* should be viewed considering the prevailing social system and related legal culture. This led Tau to illustrate this new approach by offering studies of the social dimension of legal practice, provincial and local variations in *derecho indiano*, the relationship between *derecho indiano* and Indigenous communities, and the continuity of *derecho indiano* after the colonial period. The book also tackled the difficult and lasting question of defining *derecho indiano*, a debate that continues to surface at every gathering of students of this area of law.[26]

Tau's extensive contribution to *derecho indiano* has earned his recognition, in Ezequiel Abásolo's observation, as an intellectual leader of the 'third generation of great experts in the history of the Law of the Indies.'[27] Tau's expansive view of *derecho indiano* and his incorporation of local and regional American, rather than peninsular, sources reframed the field for legal historians. Tau's gentle insistence on understanding law in its social, political, and cultural contexts is a signal contribution to the history of *derecho indiano* and Latin American law. Established European trends in tracing legislation and treatises into the lawyer's daily work and forensic practice were introduced to *derecho indiano* by Tau's reorientation and expansion of the questions that may be brought to its sources.[28] Thomas Duve and Heikki Pihlajamäki followed up and broadened

26 Victor Tau Anzoátegui, *Nuevos horizontes en el estudio histórico del Derecho Indiano* (Buenos Aires: Instituto de Investigaciones de Historia del Derecho, 1997).

27 Ezequiel Abásolo, 'Victor Tau Anzoátegui and the Legal Historiography of the Indies' in *New Horizons in Spanish Colonial Law: Contributions to Transnational Early Modern Legal History*, eds Thomas Duve and Heikki Pihlajamäki (Frankfurt: Max Planck Institute for European Legal History, 2015), 152.

28 Mirroring the local emphasis of Tau's reconceptualization of *derecho indiano*, some scholars had tackled earlier sources from the peripheries of the Spanish colonial world. Charles Cutter advanced the idea of a *derecho vulgar* as applied in criminal cases in northern New Spain. Charles R. Cutter, *The Legal Culture of Northern New Spain, 1700–1810* (Albuquerque: University of New Mexico Press, 1995). Later, examining records of civil causes in St. Augustine during the second Spanish Period (1784–1821), Mirow found a higher degree of compliance to *derecho indiano* in his sources. M.C. Mirow, 'Causas civiles en la Florida Oriental, 1785–1821' in *Historia del Derecho: Décadas de Investigación y de Docencia Homenaje a Abelardo Levaggi*, eds Ricardo Rabinovich-Berkman and Agustín Parise (Buenos Aires: Editorial Universitaria de Buenos Aires, 2016), 305–315; M.C. Mirow 'Testamentary Proceedings in Spanish East Florida, 1783–1821' in *Studies in Honor of Richard H. Helmholz*, ed. Troy L. Harris (Berkeley: The Robbins Collection, 2015), 281–301; M.C. Mirow, 'Law in East Florida 1783–1821' (2015) 55 American Journal of Legal History 89–118.

the conversation on the 'new horizons' in Spanish colonial law highlighting a richer transnational and global turn in the discipline over the decade and a half after Tau's seminal work, a turn to which the Frankfurt-based Max Planck Institute for Legal History and Legal Theory has contributed greatly.[29]

As mentioned earlier, a participant in this important turn was Portuguese professor António Manuel Hespanha, a towering and extremely prolific European scholar who initially made major contributions to the institutional history of Portuguese and Brazilian colonial law, somewhat along the lines of works on Spanish *derecho indiano* but with the eye of a social historian. His research stays at the Max Planck Institute enriched his focus on the social history of jurists, the lineage of the early modern state, and the *ancien régime*'s transition to a liberal political system.[30] Eventually, Hespanha embraced an anthropological approach that informed his exploration of the interplay between erudite and popular law and the role of grace.[31] He was influenced by Foucault and adopted postcolonial notions that allowed him to problematize his perspectives on the circulation of ideas and juridical practices, highlighting deep cultural translations taking place along the way. Such notions permeated his critical approach to legal discourses and texts of various kinds, non-juridical normative sources, his emphasis on legal and judicial pluralism more generally, and his formulation of the 'jurisdictional paradigm.'[32]

The global turn and pluralism also became central to the work of Lauren Benton, another influential historian who forged the notion of 'jurisdictional

29 Thomas Duve and Heikki Pihlajamäki, 'Introduction: New Horizons of Derecho Indiano' in *New Horizons in Spanish Colonial Law: Contributions to Transnational Early Modern Legal History*, eds Thomas Duve and Heikki Pihlajamäki (Frankfurt: Max Planck Institute for European Legal History, 2015), 1–8.

30 António Manuel Hespanha, *História das instituições: épocas medieval e moderna* (Coimbra: Almedina, 1982); António Manuel Hespanha, *Poder e instituições na Europa do antigo regime: colecânea de textos* (Lisbon: Fundação Calouste Gulbenkian, 1984); António Manuel Hespanha, *As Vésperas do Leviathan: instituições e poder político: Portugal séc. XVII* (Lisbon: sn, 1986); António Manuel Hespanha, *Justiça e administração entre o Atigo Regime e a revolução* (Milan: Giuffrè, 1990).

31 António Manuel Hespanha, 'Da iustitia a disciplina' (1984) n. especial 2 Boletin da Facultade de Direito da Universidade de Coimbra 139–232; António Manuel Hespanha, *La gracia del derecho: economía de la cultura en la edad moderna* (Madrid: Centro de Estudios Constitucionales, 1993); António Manuel Hespanha, *Justiça e litigiosidade: história e prospectiva* (Lisbon: Fundação Calouste Gulbenkian, 1993).

32 António Manuel Hespanha, 'Uncommon Laws: Law in the Extreme Peripheries of an Early Modern Empire' (2013) 130(1) Zeitschrift der Savigny-Stitung für Rechtsgeschichte: Germanistische Abteilung 180–204; António Manuel Hespanha, *Como os juristas viam o mondo, 1550–1750: Direitos, estados, pessoas, coisas, contratos, ações e crimes* (Lisbon: CreateSpace Independent Publishing Platform, 2015).

politics' and in the process considerably transformed the study of international law, colonial legal cultures, and world history overall.[33] Benton's innovative perspective on colonial rule and the international order prompted research by a number of legal historians of Latin America and beyond who embraced, in particular, her views on the significance of Indigenous legal agency.[34]

Legal agency became the focus of an exciting body of work around the same time. Responding to the concern that doctrinal and institutional histories were limited by their reliance on 'law in the books' and a well-known and even officially recognized 'gap' between law and application, scholars increasingly examined the nexus between law and society.[35] They sought answers to how the law played out in the everyday lives of people. Simultaneously, new methods and questions enriched the broader legal history of colonial Latin America, beyond *derecho indiano* as such, opening refreshing debates and perspectives. Perhaps the most exciting ones have concerned different dimensions of subaltern litigation and administrative petitioning as mechanisms of social contestation. Such contestation involved Indigenous people, women, and enslaved humans struggling over property, land, village autonomy, physical safety, social mobility, or various dimensions of freedom.[36]

---

33 Lauren A. Benton, *Law and Colonial Cultures: Legal Regimes in World History, 1400–1900* (Cambridge: Cambridge University Press, 2002).

34 See, for instance, Brian Owensby, *Empire of Law and Indian Justice in Colonial Mexico* (Stanford: Stanford University Press, 2006); Saliha Belmessous, *Native Claims: Indigenous Law against Empire, 1500–1920* (Oxford: Oxford University Press, 2011). Owensby contributed to an ambitious anthology on the subject edited by Benton over a decade after the publication of her seminal *Law and Colonial Cultures*. See *Legal Pluralism and Empires, 1500–1850*, eds Lauren Benton and Richard Ross (New York: New York University Press, 2013).

35 On the 'gap' see M.C. Mirow, *Latin American Law: A History of Private Law and Institutions in Spanish America* (Austin: University of Texas Press, 2004), 235–238.

36 Listed chronologically: Ann Twinam, *Public Lives, Private Secrets: Honor, Gender, Sexuality and Illegitimacy in Colonial Latin America* (Stanford: Stanford University Press, 1999); Brian Owensby, *Empire of Law and Indian Justice in Colonial Mexico* (Stanford: Stanford University Press, 2006); Camillia Cowling, *Conceiving of Freedom: Women of Color, Gender, and the Abolition of Slavery in Havana and Rio de Janeiro* (Chapel Hill: University of North Carolina Press, 2013); Ann Twinam, *Purchasing Whiteness: Pardos, Mulattoes and the Quest for Social Mobility in the Spanish Indies* (Stanford: Stanford University Press, 2015); Victor Uribe-Uran, *Fatal Love: Spousal Killers, Law and Punishment in the Late Colonial Spanish Atlantic* (Stanford: Stanford University Press, 2016); Mauricio Novoa, *Protectors of Indians in the Royal Audience of Lima* (Leiden: Brill, 2016); Michelle A. McKinley, *Fractional Freedoms, Slavery, Intimacy, and Legal Mobilization in Colonial Lima* (Cambridge: Cambridge University Press, 2016); Bianca Premo, *The Enlightenment on Trial: Ordinary Litigants and Colonialism in the Spanish Empire* (Oxford: Oxford University Press, 2017); Alejandro de la Fuente and Ariela Gross, *Becoming Free, Becoming Black: Race,*

With an eye towards the rule of law and civil and human rights, scholars have also begun to consider the varied and complex constitutional history of the region and its countries.[37] Mirow has argued that the Spanish Constitution of 1812, the Constitution of Cádiz, provided a foundational moment in the region's constitutional development and many of the issues presented in this document have remained contested and unresolved.[38] Questions of national sovereignty, representation, citizenship, the franchise, the separation of powers, states of emergency or siege, and the relative power of the executive, and 'constitutional entrenchment' (to employ Miguel Schor's term) were present in the early nineteenth century and continue to the present day.[39] Indeed, the Constitution of Cádiz has received extensive study as a pivotal document in European and Latin American constitutionalism.[40] The influence of foreign

Freedom and Law in Cuba, Virginia and Louisiana (Cambridge: Cambridge University Press, 2020). Some of the works on slaves' pursuit of freedom built on the pioneering contribution of Rebecca Scott, *Slave Emancipation in Cuba: The Transition to Free Labor* (Princeton: Princeton University Press, 1985). See also Fernando de Trazegnies, *Ciriaco de Urtecho, Litigante por amor: Reflexiones sobre la polivalencia táctica del razonamiento jurídico* (Lima: Pontificia Universidad Católica del Perú, 1981); Carlos Aguirre, *Los esclavos de Lima y la desintegración de la esclavitud, 1821–1854* (Lima: Pontifica Universidad Católica del Perú, 1993); Christine Hunefeld, *Paying the Price of Freedom: Family and Labor among Lima's Slaves, 1800–1854* (Berkeley: University of California Press, 1994).

37 Bernardino Bravo Lira, *El estado constitucional en Hispanoamérica 1811–1991: Ventura y desventura de un ideal Europeo de gobierno en el Nuevo Mundo* (México: Escuela Libre de Derecho, 1992); Humberto Nogueira Alcalá, ed., *La evolución político-constitucional de América del Sur 1976–2005* (Santiago: Librotecnia, 2009); Antonio Colomer Viadel, *Introducción al constitucionalismo iberoamericano* (Madrid: Ediciones de Cultura Hispánica, 1990); Ernesto de la Torre Villar and Jorge Mario García Laguardia, *Desarrollo histórico del constitucionalismo hispanoamericano* (México: UNAM, 1976); Gabriel L. Negretto, *Making Constitutions: Presidents, Parties and Institutional Choice in Latin America* (Cambridge: Cambridge University Press, 2013); María Núñez Martínez, *Los orígenes del constitucionalismo hispanoamericano* (Madrid: Universitas Internacional, 2008); Hernán A. Olano García, *Constitucionalismo histórico: La historia de Colombia a través de sus constituciones y reformas*, 2nd ed. (Bogotá: Ediciones Doctrina y Ley, 2007).

38 M.C. Mirow, *Latin American Constitutions: The Constitution of Cádiz and Its Legacy in Spanish America* (Cambridge: Cambridge University Press, 2015).

39 For 'constitutional entrenchment' see Miguel Schor, 'Constitutionalism through the Looking Glass of Latin America' (2006) 41 Texas International Law Journal 1–37. For general themes in this sentence see Brian Loveman, *The Constitution of Tyranny: Regimes of Exception in Spanish America* (Pittsburgh: University of Pittsburgh Press, 1993).

40 To name just a few of the excellent studies available: Miguel Artola and Rafael Flaquer Montequi eds, *La Constitución de 1812* (Madrid: Iustel, 2008); María Teresa Berruezo, *La participación americana en las Cortes de Cádiz* (Madrid: Centro de Estudios Constitucionales, 1986); Manuel Chust, *América en las Cortes de Cádiz* (Madrid: Fundación Mapfe, 2010); Manuel Chust, *La cuestión nacional americana en las Cortes de Cádiz* (Alzira: Centro Francisco Tomás y Valiente, 1999); Rafael Estrada Michel, *Monarquía y Nación entre Cádiz*

constitutions and especially of the United States Constitution of 1787 in Latin American constitutional drafting has been explored to reveal the important place these constitutions had in shaping Latin American documents.[41] In some instances in Mexico and Argentina, scholars and judges have turned to United States treatises and case law to interpret and to understand parallel provisions and structures in their own constitutions.[42]

Just as the intellectual and legal influences on the drafters of codes captured the attention of legal historians, the perspectives and processes of constitutional drafters and committees have received study on the national and regional level. For example, Eduardo Herrera Andrade has examined the life and thought of conservative jurist Miguel Antonio Caro, the drafter of Colombia's Constitution of 1886.[43] There have been several recent studies of Argentine jurist and constitutional drafter Juan Bautista Alberdi, intellectual author of the Argentine Constitution of 1853/1860.[44]

---

y Nueva España: El problema de la articulación política de las Españas ante la revolución liberal y la emancipación americana (México: Porrúa, 2006); Ivana Frasquet, *Las caras del águila: Del liberalismo gaditano a la república Federal Mexicana (1820–1824)* (Castelló de la Plana: Publicacions de la Universitat Jaume I, 2008); Carlos Garriga and Marta Lorente Sariñera, *Cádiz, 1812: La Constitución jurisdiccional* (Madrid: Centro de Estudios Políticos y Constitucionales, 2007); Marta Lorente Sariñera, *La Nación y Las Españas: Representación y territorio en el constitucionalismo Gaditano* (Madrid: Universidad Autónoma de Madrid, 2010); Marie Laure Rieu-Millan, *Los diputados americanos en las Cortes de Cádiz: Igualdad o Independencia* (Madrid: Consejo Superior de Investigaciones Científicas, 1990); Mario Rodríguez, *The Cádiz Experiment in Central America* (Berkeley: University of California Press, 1978).

41 George Athan Billias, *American Constitutionalism Heard Round the World, 1776–1989* (New York: NYU Press, 1989); Thomas Buergenthal, Jorge Mario García Laguardia, and Rodolfo Piza Rocafort, *La constitución americana y su influencia en latinoamérica (200 años 1787–1987)* (San José: CAPEL, 1987); Alonso Lujambio, *La influencia del constitucionalismo anglosajón en el pensamiento de Emilio Rabasa* (México: Escuela Libre de Derecho, 2009).

42 Jonathan M. Miller, 'The Authority of a Foreign Talisman: A Study of U.S. Constitutional Practice as Authority in Nineteenth-Century Argentina and the Argentine Elite's Leap of Faith' (1997) 46 American University Law Review 1483–1572; Jonathan M. Miller, 'Judicial Review and Constitutional Stability: A Sociology of the U.S. Model and Its Collapse in Argentina' (1997) 21 Hastings International and Comparative Law Review 77–176; M.C. Mirow, '*Marbury* in Mexico: Judicial Review's Precocious Southern Migration' (2007) 35 Hastings Constitutional Law Quarterly 41–117.

43 Eduardo Herrera, *Miguel Antonio Caro: Pensamiento y Acción* (Cochabamba: Editorial Javeriana, 2011); Eduardo Herrera and M.C. Mirow, 'Miguel Antonio Caro Tobar (Colombia, 1843–1909)' in *Law and Christianity in Latin America: The Work of Great Jurists*, eds M.C. Mirow and Rafael Domingo (London: Routledge, 2021), 325–341.

44 Ezequiel Abásolo, 'Juan Bautista Alberdi (Argentina, 1810–84)' in *Law and Christianity*, 175–187; Jeremy Adelman, 'Between Order and Liberty: Juan Bautista Alberdi and the Intellectual Origins of Argentine Constitutionalism' (2007) 42 Latin American Research

From the texts of constitutions, scholars have looked at the institutions and legal actors, courts and judges, that implement the important shifts in legality found in a constitutionalized Latin America.[45] For the mid-twentieth century, scholars have charted the implementation of social doctrines and theories found in constitutions and applied in courts.[46] Themes of dictatorship and rule of law arise.[47] Concerns about the appearance of dictatorships, autocracies, military governments, and non-democratic transitions have led to careful studies of these events and periods. For example, Pinochet's regime in Chile and its constitutional aspects are the subjects of several studies.[48] Furthermore, the overlap of constitutionalism and private property has merited close analysis. For example, Jeremy Adelman has examined this issue within Argentina's economic development and challenges.[49] The Law and Development Movement of U.S. intervention in Latin American legal education, methodologies, substantive law, and institutions has been well chronicled.[50]

This cursory and selective description of the historiography of Latin American law indicates that the editors and contributors are influenced and informed by various approaches to the field and various ways of writing about law, history, and legal history. Although at the same institution, the co-editors

---

Review 86–110; Natalio R. Botana, *La tradición republicana: Alberdi, Sarmiento y las ideas políticas de su tiempo* (Buenos Aires: Editorial Sudamericana, 1997); M.C. Mirow, 'Bases y puntos de partida para la organización política de la República Argentina' in *The Formation and Transmission of Western Legal Culture: 150 Books that Made the Law in the Age of Printing*, eds Serge Dauchy, Georges Martyn, Anthony Musson, Heikki Pihlajamäki, and Alain Wijffels (Cham: Springer, 2016), 367–370.

45 Carlos Ramos Núñez, *Historia de la Corte Suprema de Justicia del Perú* (Lima: Fondo Editorial del Poder Judicial, 2008).

46 Timothy J. James, *Mexico's Supreme Court: Between Liberal Individual and Revolutionary Social Rights, 1867–1934* (Albuquerque: University of New Mexico Press, 2013); William J. Suarez-Potts, *The Making of Law: The Supreme Court and Labor Legislation in Mexico, 1875–1931* (Stanford: Stanford University Press, 2012).

47 Javier Couso, Alexandra Huneeus, and Rachel Sieder, eds, *Cultures of Legality: Judicialization and Political Activism in Latin America* (Cambridge: Cambridge University Press, 2010); Lisa Hilbink, *Judges beyond Politics in Democracy and Dictatorship: Lessons from Chile* (Cambridge: Cambridge University Press, 2007); William C. Prillaman, *The Judiciary and Democratic Decay in Latin America: Declining Confidence in the Rule of Law* (Westport: Praeger, 2000).

48 Robert Barros, *Constitutionalism and Dictatorship: Pinochet, the Junta, and the 1980 Constitution* (Cambridge: Cambridge University Press, 2002).

49 Jeremy Adelman, *Republic of Capital: Buenos Aires and the Legal Transformation of the Atlantic World* (Stanford: Stanford University Press, 1999).

50 James A. Gardner, *Legal Imperialism: American Lawyers and Foreign Aid in Latin America* (Madison: University of Wisconsin Press, 1980).

brought different perspectives to this project as legal historians. Uribe-Uran, whose academic home is in a history faculty, is predominantly a social and political historian who uses legal records, arguments, and materials to explore the human experience over time.[51] Mirow, housed in a law faculty, has focused more on doctrinal developments in private and public law and the intellectual and political forces that have shaped them.[52] This means that we are familiar with separate but overlapping bodies of scholarship, approaches, and authors; we were fortunately able to structure this volume in light of these varying perspectives and attracted scholars with a variety of approaches. We assert that there is no one way or correct school of legal history; different scholars with different interests contribute to the field in different ways. Our selection of authors and topics reflects this openness to all who work in the same field as they bring different tools to the task and seek different fruits of their labor.

2 Overview of Chapters

The authors of chapters were asked to address various time periods, concepts, actors, or institutions with a focus on presenting the essential material, modern scholarly debates, and most recent scholarship. Harsh space constraints on authors forced them to winnow their work to what they believed were the core aspects of the topic presented. Authors were given substantial liberty to construct their presentations of the topics as they saw fit. No chapter was subject to a matrix or forced structure. We thought it best to select experts in particular fields and let them present their subjects with scholarly freedom following the general guidelines and goals of the overall project.

This means that there is, of course, variation and some overlap amongst the chapters. We think that this is fine and indeed beneficial. The historian's task is illuminated by variation in perspective, and readers will be enriched by the way the same material may arise in different chapters. We hope the extensive index provided will aid readers in finding materials associated with their interests throughout the book.

While we understood that some periods and topics had to be addressed, the final selection of chapters and their order were neither obvious nor entirely voluntary. For example, we regrettably had to omit chapters dealing with international or global aspects of the history of Latin American law. These decisions

51 E.g. Uribe-Uran, *Honorable Lives*; Uribe-Uran, *Fatal Love*.

52 E.g. Mirow, *Latin American Law*; Mirow, *Latin American Constitutions*.

were based on the availability of authors and the forthcoming treatments of these topics in other companions, handbooks, or guides. We could not include either a chapter on notarial law, an area that would have made it possible to show the intersection and integration of various legal fields in the Latin American civil law system, something particularly useful for readers familiar with and operating in common law societies. Whilst somewhat scattered, references to notarial law are fortunately embedded in many of this companion's chapters.

As for the volume's order of presentation, as we finish our compilation the arrangement whose description follows next made perfect sense to us and we felt it was pedagogically sound. Still, as indicated above, there clearly is overlap between chapters grouped in a particular part of the volume and those in the same or other parts. This is for instance the case of Wisnoski's Chapter 11 in Part 1, and Uribe-Uran's Chapter 18, in Part 2, narratives in both of which women are central protagonists; or Suarez-Potts's Chapter 13, in the volume's Part 2, and Palacio's Chapter 16, in Part 3, both addressing labor issues; or, to mention but one more example, there is intersection too between Chambers's Chapter 4, in Part 1, and Herzog's Chapter 23, in the volume's Part 3, legal pluralism appearing to be an important common issue to the both of them. More significant than logical and beneficial overlaps such as these, though, is the fact that the order of the chapters could have been profitably altered, the best example perhaps being the fact that Tamar Herzog's insightful closing essay could have easily been the volume's first one instead. In any case, we are confident the following arrangement is sound and hope readers will benefit from commonalities and be able to connect the various analytical dots and critically evaluate the proposed sequence of essays imagining alternative arrangements to make better sense of things.

This book is divided into three parts. The first part offers six chapters that present the legal development of the region chronologically. Two chapters address law before European contact in the areas where most is known about social and legal developments. Jerome Offner addresses Mesoamerica with a focus on the Aztecs in Chapter 1. Relying mostly on Indigenous graphic manuscripts and Spanish colonial texts, Offner undertakes a remarkable reconstruction of precontact law and jurisprudence in Mesoamerica. His work with these sources leads to important and new observations on family, labor, contract, slavery, land, and institutional structures related to law.

Susan Ramírez explores Incan legal culture in Chapter 2. She places the creation and application of legal norms into their religious and political contexts. For example, aspects of family law and crime, particularly murder and theft were enforced by a hierarchy of officials who served as judges. Extracting law and legal actors from Andean manuscripts, Ramirez fully describes this legal system governed by the mandates of the Sun.

Three subsequent chapters in the chronological part address the colonial period to the early twentieth century. In Chapter 3, Heikki Pihlajamäki describes legal developments and institutions in the early colonial world. While Spain imposed relatively complex and efficient systems of legal institutions and sources, Portugal's essentially economic interests in the region led to comparatively less legal infrastructure. Pihlajamäki not only surveys important aspects of legal justifications for conquest, the sources and substance of colonial law, and administrative structures, but also presents us with telling observations about the historiography of colonial law, or *derecho indiano*, from the most recent thinkers on this debated topic.

Sarah Chambers addresses legal changes and continuities from the late colonial world to the early republic era in Chapter 4. Charting a shift from pluralistic systems of justice to positive law and the influence of Enlightenment thought during this period, Chambers emphasizes the importance of law during the independence period that brought wars, new constitutions, and the relative continuity of many areas of private law only later reconceptualized into codes. Legal changes related to crime, women, servants, and enslaved people provide telling foci for the changes she describes.

In Chapter 5, Timo Schaefer examines the long nineteenth century of national consolidation and liberalism. Liberalizing and illiberal tendencies vied from the 1830s to the 1930s, and Schaefer skillfully plots changes in law related to property, family, personal status, and housing as illustrative topics. His study incorporates the discussion of various institutions and legal actors that effected shifts in one direction or the other.

This part of the book is completed by Cristián Villalonga's analysis of Latin American law from the 1930s to the present in Chapter 6. Viewing law as a participant in various state projects of 'modernization,' Villalonga selects three important political streams over the past one hundred years as examples of the environments in which legal reform takes place. These are populist governments, structures arising from the Cold War, and recent moves towards liberalization in the economic and social spheres. Important trends are the socialization of law, the Law and Development Movement, Socialist revolutions, authoritarian reform, neoliberal modernization, and democratic reform. We purposefully selected periods and chronologies to provide porous interfaces between some very general moments of consolidation or change; overlap of materials and strands from one chapter to another naturally reach in both temporal directions.

The second part looks at people. In these seven chapters, we were drawn to the kinds of actors and subjects that have received significant attention in the legal history of Latin America. This part begins with Rogelio Pérez-Perdomo's discussion of lawyers and their education in Chapter 7. Focusing on the most populous countries, Pérez-Perdomo interrogates the knowledge and skills needed by lawyers, the relationship of their training to university education, and their roles in society. For example, he notes the educational and professional institutions of the colonial period, the structure of legal education in the early nineteenth century, and more recent trends of the globalization of the Latin American bar.

In Chapter 8, Brian Owensby tackles a large body of new learning about Indigenous people and the law. Seeking an understanding of how law shaped Indigenous action after 1492, Owensby argues that law was central to Indigenous lived experiences from the moment of contact. The chapter provides clear guidance on the methodological and historiographical issues associated with the study of Indigenous peoples and law over the past century, followed by an exploration of the rise of the global Indigenous movement and its relationship to law.

In an equally active field of Latin American legal history, the status and agency of African and Afro-descendants are analyzed by Robert Cottrol in Chapter 9. Cottrol discusses the arrival of enslaved humans to the Americas under colonial practices and presents the legal regimes established for slavery. Iberian racial categories were transplanted and modified in the Americas, while enslaved humans asserted some kinds of agency within colonial legal institutions. Cottrol reminds us that the legal status and activities of free people of color are part of the broader picture that must be incorporated into this topic. In the national period and with the eventual enactment of emancipation, countries adopted explicit and implicit forms of racial discrimination internally through policies and externally through laws regulating immigration. Such practices and legal norms provide the backdrop for recent efforts to remedy these entrenched social and legal patterns of unequal treatment and status.

In a related field receiving substantial scholarly attention, Mariana Dias Paes focuses exclusively on the law of enslaved humans in Chapter 10. She notes that the legal statuses of either 'free' or 'enslaved' were often in dispute in relation to any particular individual. Under legal systems that provided for contingent manumission, freedom was precarious and was often subject to continued ties of dependence or labor. Illegal enslavement was a reality that constantly threatened people of color. Abuse and violence were inherent aspects of slavery, and its gendered aspects are complex and compelling facets of the topic receiving substantial study. Courts often served as the locus of perhaps fleeting legal determinations of such issues.

In Chapter 11, Alex Wisnoski discusses women's legal status and challenges from the colonial era to the present. He explores legal categories and provisions as the base upon which women employed and resisted legal systems. Underscoring the heterogeneity of women's experience and legal interactions, Wisnoski asks us to consider women in the family, enslaved women, and mystics as examples of the varied lives of women and legal rules and institutions associated with them. Law not only created inequality for women but also provided avenues for women's agency and resultant legal reform. His presentation of the topic includes discussions of marriage, the Inquisition, property and commerce, suffrage, sex work, reproduction, and violence against women.

Diego Acosta addresses a relatively new area of study, immigrants, and outsiders, in Chapter 12. His work in this chapter tackles the complex tasks of understanding the legal categories that create inclusion and exclusion. Particularly within the context of new nations, legal texts such as constitutions and political immigration policies delineated who was welcomed into polity and who was not, as countries sought to increase their population or exclude foreigners from entry. Aspects of race, class, wealth, and geographic origin informed such decisions. In recent decades, this area of law has been influenced by international human rights standards, attempts at regional integration, and the plight of politically and economically displaced individuals.

The final chapter in the part on people, Chapter 13, is William Suárez-Potts's presentation of peasants and workers. This chapter addresses the areas of labor legislation, agrarian reform, and industrial relations in the context of the legal regimes related to agricultural and industrial workers. Issues of colonial institutions for the organization and exploitation of labor, the distribution of wealth, the ownership of land by Indigenous people and elite families, social legislation, land reform, and neoliberalism are presented in this cogent analysis of workers and the law.

The third part turns to specific areas of the law and institutions in nine chapters. In Chapter 14, Agustín Parise plumbs legal changes related to land and property. Parise frames property with several paradigms. The first paradigm, the allocation paradigm associated with the colonial period, served the primary function of allocating land and property to different claimants through individual or communal ownership. Within national governments, codes encapsulated a new liberal paradigm of absolute ownership in the nineteenth century. At the beginning of the twentieth century, this second paradigm gave way to a social function paradigm of property reflected in constitutions and codes. The social function paradigm notably gave a theoretical basis for land reform in the region.

Óscar Cruz Barney addresses commercial law in Chapter 15. Part of a tradition reaching back to European sources on trade from the Middle Ages, the development of commercial laws and practices was advanced by consulates in Spain and later in the Americas. Several jurists in Spain and the Americas turned their attention to this body of law and supplied treatises to guide colonial practice. After independence, nations of the region codified commercial law from approximately the mid-nineteenth century to the present, and Cruz Barney provides details of these efforts for several countries.

Legal developments related to labor and labor rights are the topic of Juan Manuel Palacio's Chapter 16. He addresses the legal regulation of work during the colonial period to the present with particular emphasis on the first half of the twentieth century, a period of rapid growth in the field. The chapter discusses slavery, the regulation of work under *derecho indiano*, changes brought about by independence, the rise of the social, social constitutionalism, labor rights, labor tribunals, industrial relations, unions, and working conditions.

Alejandro Agüero treats criminal law in Chapter 17. In the colonial period, a justice-centered system produced a legal culture that included criminal laws, institutional punishments, and governmental authorities charged with such activities. This system transformed into a law-centered system effected in the nineteenth century in many of the new republics. With independence, the institutionalization of Enlightenment values on the national level, and the growth of constitutional cultures, countries codified their criminal law in accordance with newer thought in the nineteenth century. The twentieth century brought new scientific approaches to the field as criminal law was appropriated to political ends, and advances in human rights challenged such actions and more traditional notions of criminal process and punishment.

The co-editors contribute to the volume in the next two chapters. In Chapter 18, Victor Uribe-Uran explores family, divorce, and domestic violence under the historical and legal centrality of patriarchy. Uribe-Uran examines the law and effect of marriage in relation to the legitimacy of children and the status of family members. He also considers domestic conflicts and the legal norms and institutions established to minimize their effects. The discussion highlights various forces influencing the direction of such changes including colonial powers, the church, scholarship, and women's agency. The chapter also notes the impact of the global feminist movement and international organizations in recent developments.

In Chapter 19, M.C. Mirow describes the place of the church in legal development in the region. In the colonial period, theological and canonical arguments provided intellectual and political justification for the actions of colonial powers. The church conceded significant ecclesiastical authority and much of the daily operations of the church to colonial powers under the Royal Patronage. The transfer of these powers to newly independent countries was hotly contested. By the nineteenth century, debates between liberalism, and its anticlericalism, and conservatism, and its privileging of the church, led to disputes about marriage, public records, cemeteries, church property, and the place of the church in society and government.

The final three chapters address broad areas of legal development. In Chapter 20, Eduardo Zimmermann discusses the legal history of the welfare state as part of the general development of 'social states' in Latin America. His focus is on the transnational circulation of doctrines, mechanisms, and experts that led to the rise of the welfare state in the region. An outgrowth of the 'social question' of the early twentieth century, a 'truncated welfare state' in which benefits were distributed to individuals better situated in the labor force formed. Social constitutionalism and the reconceptualization of property as a social function led to expanded forms of the welfare state. These new forms of the welfare state led to new structures and new intellectual approaches that produced profound shifts in the way law was perceived and applied.

Marta Lorente contributes Chapter 21 on constitutions, rights, and governments. Broadly examining constitutionalism from 1808 to the present, Lorente uses constitutions' approaches to individual rights and freedoms to characterize the region's constitutions as 'Catholic,' 'liberal,' 'revolutionary corporatist,' and 'new Latin American.' She also addresses the relationship between constitutions and authoritarian and military regimes.

The final chapter, Chapter 22, is Tamar Herzog's fascinating view of legal pluralism in the region. Noting the wide presence of legal pluralism in the colonial and early modern world, Herzog chronicles the diminution of pluralism after independence and the rise of national legal systems. Nonetheless, recent attention to human rights and discrimination inflicted on Indigenous peoples, Afro-nationals, and others, has led to the resurgence of pluralism through constitutional thought, new jurisdictions, and state institutions.

2.1 *Concluding Reflections*

To finish, and at the risk of leaving out several more that may be worth addressing, we would like to highlight a few common issues and themes that run through the various chapters. At least three must be considered briefly – namely, the long and complex impact of colonialism; the intriguing nature and significance of collective and individual agency at various levels; and the magnitude and persistence of pluralism and related jurisdictional jockeying.

The impact of colonialism is not only the obvious result of its direct presence and practice for more than four centuries (five in some cases!) during which – as especially discussed in the essays by Pihlajamäki, Owensby, Pérez-Perdomo, Cottrol, Dias Paes, Wisnoski, Parise, Cruz Barney, Agüero, Uribe-Uran, and Mirow – the Spanish and Portuguese empires forcibly shaped legal institutions concerning labor, land and other property, commerce, mining, family, crime and punishment, education, religion, and government in the region of our interest. It also extends to the way in which, as explicitly discussed by Chambers and detectable in several of the chapters just listed, and some others such as the pieces by Palacio and Suárez-Potts, post-independent nations went about extending the operation of colonial institutions. The transition to a new legal framework was thus, as Chambers establishes, 'gradual, uneven, and … incomplete.' This lengthening was done out of expediency to temporarily fill normative gaps in hopes of securing social, political, and economic stability amid the turbulent 'modern' era the region was entering. Even when one leaves such intriguing extension of colonial law and its immediate consequences aside, the long shadow colonialism casts remains visible to this day in the form of a deeply rooted civil law system and tradition all over the region. These were perpetuated through related code-centered legal education and notarial norms and practices rendering all sorts of legal relations and transactions extremely formalistic and bureaucratic.[53] This all constitutes a visible colonial legacy setting Latin America quite apart from its biggest northern neighbor which, in turn, followed its own colonial heritage, a radically different one, the common law. Colonialism and its legacies can of course be felt in myriad other ways in Latin America, including a corporatist approach to social relations and politics, the harsh treatment of the labor force, skewed land distribution, and deeply hierarchical ethnic and race relations, to mention but a few aspects each of which, as discussed in the essays by Palacio, Parise, Suárez-Potts, Paes Dias, and Cottrol, corresponds to specific legal orders. Still, these various faces of colonialism were tempered by various forms of agency and contestation.

As for agency, many chapters, including all the essays in Part 2, reflect various modalities of it involving, on one hand, Indigenous, free, and enslaved peoples of African descent, peasants and workers, women, immigrants, and outsiders; and on the other hand, lawyers and justice officials, landowners

---

53 See John Henry Merryman and Rogelio Pérez-Perdomo, *The Civil Law Tradition: An Introduction to the Legal Systems of Europe and Latin America*, 3rd ed. (Stanford: Stanford University Press, 2007); and Rogelio Pérez-Perdomo, *Educación Jurídica en Occidente: una Historia Cultural* (Valencia: Tirant lo Blanche, 2022).

and other proprietors, merchants, priests, and government officials, to provide some examples. Various contributors highlight, for instance, the significance of '*caciques* [who] had become "avid litigators" over labor, tribute, and land' (Owensby); 'the ability of slaves to make legally enforceable contracts for their freedom ... slaves in certain settings were often successful in using the courts of the Spanish Empire to vindicate claims of freedom under Spanish law' (Cottrol); 'the role enslaved and freed persons had in framing Latin America law' (Dias Paes); the fact that 'legal agency and subjecthood was not limited to elite women, and that marginalized women of lower racial statuses adeptly navigated these legal regimes ... enslaved women, married or divorced, fought for reunification with their families. Indigenous women, in turn, fought for traditional rights and negotiated within the Spanish legal system' (Wisnoski); and the visibility of 'peasants who individually – and collectively – litigated extensively against the privatization of communal property' (Suárez-Potts). It seems clear that legal relations and justice in the region were thus far from preordained and predictable but became the dynamic and somewhat contingent product of interactions, conflictive and otherwise, involving these and other social actors. Their efforts benefitted greatly from liminality, pluralism, and related 'forum shopping.'

Finally, as far as pluralism and related jurisdictional jockeying go, it is apparent that in both colonial and modern times, the region of our focus was made up of different and competing legal regimes, authorities, and courts. The volume's early essays, by Offner and Ramírez, for instance, established the significance and intriguing religio-political contexts of law and justice before European contact in Mesoamerica and the Andes. Then, we are reminded that if they were not contrary to Spanish law and morality 'Indigenous communities received judicial autonomy to settle their affairs according to their "laws and good customs"'(Herzog). Although clarifying that it was not entirely the product of empire and that it was murkier than described by previous scholars because a specific law regime and the jurisdiction supposed to go along with it did not always coincide, Herzog shows that colonial pluralism nevertheless allowed the Indigenous communities, enslaved and free Africans and their descendants, among others, to seek differential treatment whenever beneficial. Various legal regimes could also correspond to and benefit one's religious, gender, professional, residential, status, or familial classification or membership.

To be sure, as illustrated by Schaefer or Lorente, under the influx of liberalism, nineteenth-century legislation and constitutions eventually challenged the enduring colonial legal order and related privileges pushing forward a republican legal culture and thus trying to limit claims by autonomous communities and corporations to have the right to their own jurisdiction and distinctive privileges. But constitutionalism and law in general did not cease to display great hybridity because, as Lorente shows, traces of deep Catholicism, corporatism, and caudillism continued to accompany liberal and individualistic elements. Further, even as late as the twentieth century as insightfully discussed by Villalonga, Mirow, or Zimmerman, state- or church-led legal reforms and initiatives to modernize Latin America or, conversely, to respond to allegedly damaging dimensions of liberal modernity, were in place. They made the region embrace populist constitutional regimes and policies, economically protectionist, social and welfare legislation, pro-worker labor policies, and pro-clerical and socially minded reforms with a religious touch. In the end, as Herzog demonstrates, pluralism never died but just transformed itself through the years. Legal equality and the state's central monopoly over justice and legislation were, as she puts it, 'merely orienting principles.' Since the 1980s until today, ethnic and cultural plurality, and even gender diversity, have been embraced in numerous constitutions and laws throughout Latin America thus upending 'the idea of a single citizen led by a single authority and subjected to a single legal regime.' This is where we find ourselves now and we hope that this volume will allow readers understand the many dimensions of this complex, conflictive, and intriguing historical process.

2.2 *Gracias*

We thank Brill and our authors for their patience in these difficult times. The editors of *Brill's Companion* and the anonymous reviewers suggested many useful changes. At Brill, Alessandra Giliberto and Petra Stiglmayer have been thoughtful and wonderfully supportive editors. We also thank Thalien Colenbrander who prepared the work for production. We thank Tim Barnwell for his proofreading and providing editorial comments during production.

We thank our deans, Antony Page, Florida International University College of Law, and the late John F. Stack, Jr., Florida International University Stephen J. Green School of International and Public Affairs, for their support of our scholarship and for truly valuing these sorts of efforts.

We thank Angela B. Mirow who translated several chapters, revised the entire text, checked citations, provided extensive editorial comments, and managed many aspects of the preparation of this volume. This book would not exist but for her careful and almost daily work over the past several years.

Although this project began before the appearance of Covid-19, the book you hold was created amidst this horrific pandemic. For various reasons, some authors were unable to fulfil their original commitments, and several chapters were good-naturedly adopted by expert authors who stepped in towards the end of the project to ensure that essential topics were covered adequately. This took longer than we expected. With apologies for the delay, we are very pleased with what we have been able to accomplish under these strained conditions.

References

Adelman, Jeremy. *Republic of Capital: Buenos Aires and the Legal Transformation of the Atlantic World.* Stanford: Stanford University Press, 1999.

Benton, Lauren A. *Law and Colonial Cultures: Legal Regimes in World History, 1400–1900.* Cambridge: Cambridge University Press, 2002.

Borah, Woodrow. *Justice by Insurance: The General Indian Court of Colonial Mexico and the Legal Aides of the Half-Real.* Berkeley: University of California Press, 1983.

Burkholder, Mark A. *Politics of a Colonial Career: José Baquíjano and the Audiencia of Lima.* Albuquerque: University of New Mexico Press, 1980.

Cutter, Charles R. *The Legal Culture of Northern New Spain 1700–1810.* Albuquerque: University of New Mexico Press, 1995.

de la Fuente, Alejandro and Ariela Gross. *Becoming Free, Becoming Black: Race, Freedom and Law in Cuba, Virginia and Louisiana.* Cambridge: Cambridge University Press, 2020.

Duve, Thomas and Heikki Pihlajamäki, eds. *New Horizons in Spanish Colonial Law: Contributions to Transnational Early Modern Legal History.* Frankfurt: Max Planck Institute for European Legal History, 2015.

Gardner, James A. *Legal Imperialism: American Lawyers and Foreign Aid in Latin America.* Madison: University of Wisconsin Press, 1980.

Grossberg, Michael and Christopher Tomlins, eds. *The Cambridge History of Law in America,* 3 vols. Cambridge: Cambridge University Press, 2008.

Hadden, Sally E. and Alfred L. Brophy, eds. *A Companion to American Legal History.* Chichester: John Wiley & Sons, 2013.

James, Timothy J. *Mexico's Supreme Court: Between Liberal Individual and Revolutionary Social Rights, 1867–1934.* Albuquerque: University of New Mexico Press, 2013.

Katz, Stanley N., ed. *The Oxford International Encyclopedia of Legal History,* 6 vols. Oxford: Oxford University Press, 2009.

Kellogg, Susan. *Law and the Transformation of Aztec Culture, 1500–1800.* Norman: University of Oklahoma Press, 1995.

Kellogg, Susan and Matthew Restall, eds. *Dead Giveaways: Indigenous Testaments of Colonial Mesoamerica and the Andes.* Salt Lake City: University of Utah Press, 1998.

Loveman, Brian. *The Constitution of Tyranny: Regimes of Exception in Spanish America.* Pittsburgh: University of Pittsburgh Press, 1993.

McKinley, Michelle A. *Fractional Freedoms, Slavery, Intimacy, and Legal Mobilization in Colonial Lima.* Cambridge: Cambridge University Press, 2016.

Means, Robert Charles. *Underdevelopment and the Development of Law: Corporations and Corporation Law in Nineteenth-Century Colombia.* Chapel Hill: University of North Carolina, 1980.

Mirow, M.C. *Latin American Constitutions: The Constitution of Cádiz and Its Legacy in Spanish America.* Cambridge: Cambridge University Press, 2015.

Mirow, M.C. *Latin American Law: A History of Private Law and Institutions in Spanish America.* Austin: University of Texas Press, 2004.

Mirow, M.C. and Rafael Domingo, eds. *Law and Christianity in Latin America: The Work of Great Jurists.* London: Routledge, 2021.

Novoa, Mauricio. *Protectors of Indians in the Royal Audience of Lima.* Leiden: Brill, 2016.

Offner, Jerome A. *Law and Politics in Aztec Texcoco.* Cambridge: Cambridge University Press, 1983.

Pérez-Perdomo, Rogelio. *Latin American Lawyers: A Historical Introduction.* Stanford: Stanford University Press, 2006.

Pihlajamäki, Heikki, Markus Dubber, and Mark Godfrey, eds. *The Oxford Handbook of European Legal History.* Oxford: Oxford University Press, 2018.

Premo, Bianca. *The Enlightenment on Trial: Ordinary Litigants and Colonialism in the Spanish Empire.* Oxford: Oxford University Press, 2017.

Reich, Peter Lester. *Mexico's Hidden Revolution: The Catholic Church in Law and Politics since 1929.* Notre Dame: University of Notre Dame Press, 1995.

Scott, Rebecca. *Slave Emancipation in Cuba: The Transition to Free Labor.* Princeton: Princeton University Press, 1985.

Suárez-Potts, William J. *The Making of Law: The Supreme Court and Labor Legislation in Mexico, 1875–1931.* Stanford: Stanford University Press, 2012.

Uribe-Uran, Victor M. *Fatal Love: Spousal Killers, Law and Punishment in the Late Colonial Spanish Atlantic.* Stanford: Stanford University Press, 2015.

Uribe-Uran, Victor M. *Honorable Lives: Lawyers, Family, and Politics in Colombia 1780–1850.* Pittsburgh: University of Pittsburgh Press, 2000.

Zimmermann, Eduardo, ed. *Judicial Institutions in Nineteenth-Century Latin America.* London: Institute of Latin American Studies, 1999.

PART 1

Chronology

CHAPTER 1

Law before European Contact: Mesoamerica

Jerome A. Offner

Colonial Latin America researchers encounter mentions of Indigenous law in alphabetic sources and, less commonly, in Indigenous graphic manuscripts. This article is intended to assist with critical examination, evaluation, and contextualization of such data to optimize understanding of precontact law and therefore legal change after contact. Specific examples of Indigenous graphic expression and both Indigenous language and Spanish alphabetic texts will be employed. Along the way, important aspects of the best documented precontact system of Mesoamerica – Texcoco, Mexico – will be presented.

Contact commenced with Spanish invaders in the early sixteenth century and only the colonizers' limited technology, incompetence, disinterest, and intolerance in recording Indigenous legal systems makes it possible to write an article-length treatment of a region of such great civilizational complexity as Mesoamerica. This cultural area includes portions of current Mexico, Guatemala, Belize, Honduras, El Salvador, Nicaragua, and Costa Rica. Among numerous archaeological, historical, and contemporary cultures, the more familiar are the Aztec, Maya, Mixtec, Olmec, Totonac, and Zapotec. Linguistic and ethnic diversity remains immense, with continuous cultures stretching back centuries into millennia, and millions continuing to speak Indigenous languages.[1] The precontact economy was complex with maize, squash, beans, and amaranth agriculture at its base along with an ancient constellation of well-developed markets and local and long-distance market networks, providing a broad range of foodstuffs, raw materials, and manufactured goods. Urbanization was a recurring characteristic of this area with cities exceeding those of medieval Europe in size and complexity. The wheel was not used for transportation or industry, and transportation in its often mountainous and heavily dissected terrain was by footpath and waterway.

1 Moisés Bailón Corres and Carlos Brokmann Haro, *Los pueblos indígenas de México y sus derechos: una breve mirada*, 1st ed. (México: Comisión Nacional de los Derechos Humanos, 2011), 10–11 present useful data for Mexico.

 | DOI:10.1163/9789004436091_003

1 Challenges in Understanding Mesoamerican Cultural Concepts and Categories

Isolation of the Americas from the rest of the world for more than fifteen thousand years has led to scant overlap among Indigenous and Western concepts and categories. Investigators of Mesoamerican gender, performance, historiography, and writing and graphic communication, for example, continue to discover such differences and have only recently begun entering them accurately into worldwide comparative conversations. Precontact legal documentation is essentially non-existent, despite centuries-old precontact writing and graphic communication systems, leaving us to deal with data often severely limited and damaged by transmission through postcontact sources. Spanish administrative documents now situated throughout Mexico in local and parish archives, down to the level of community *baúles* passed from town president to president, constitute the great bulk of evidence, with the largest, higher-level collections located at the Archivo General de la Nación, Mexico City, and the Archivo General de Indias, Sevilla. These date to the late 1520s and expand in vast numbers into the colonial period. Nevertheless, the rapid decapitation of the Indigenous ruling apparatus renders even the earliest documents suspect as accurate reports of Mesoamerican law: contesting parties at all levels were situated differently after contact. Further, Spanish courts lacked the interest and expertise to understand Indigenous law: the blunt instrument of Spanish legal process was unable to discern even the basics, much less the subtleties, of Indigenous disputes. These disputes often included generations of competing claims from before contact, documented by Indigenous graphic manuscripts whose complexity, far beyond mere alphabetic text, the Spanish failed to comprehend. Additionally, many lawsuits became little more than competing choruses of orchestrated perjury by either side, as counseled by their Spanish advocates, to optimize victory in notoriously corrupt courts. Often only through serendipity, indirection, and ethnographic observation of this process (with the subjects including the Spanish as well as the Indigenous people) can we discern authentic glimpses of precontact Indigenous jurisprudence. There are occasional bright lights in Spanish administration such as Alonso de Zorita,[2] but his valuable analyses, already past the mid-sixteenth century, describe societies altered by political, economic, and demographic change.

2 J. Benedict Warren, 'An Introductory Survey of Secular Writings in the European Tradition on Colonial Middle America, 1503–1818' in *Handbook of Middle American Indians*, ed. Howard F. Cline (Austin: University of Texas Press, 1973), vol. 13, 73–74. See also references.

Missionaries, who believed in biblical creation and related Western foundation myths, as well as in a living and active devil expressing himself through Indigenous religion, custom, and behavior, provided additional reports on Indigenous law. They investigated these phenomena to suppress them, leading efforts to destroy Indigenous manuscripts, literacy, and images. They also exhibited a typical missionary preoccupation with sexuality and reproduction, so family-level law is better reported than most. Friars seized elite Indigenous youth and educated them away from their parents, asking them to inform on them. The Inquisition was for a time unleashed on the population culminating in the public burning of the Indigenous lord Don Carlos Ometochtzin, in Texcoco near Mexico City in late 1539. In other words, the usual, if still astonishing, catalogue of colonial atrocities must constantly be borne in mind when evaluating reports from these sources.

An essential source of information is the corpus of Indigenous graphic manuscripts, often in screen fold form.[3] Some screen folds and other manuscripts are precontact but none of these contain legal content beyond records of succession, although many of religious and divinatory nature contain a great deal regarding morality.[4] We are thus left with postcontact graphic content that nevertheless presents significant challenges to the Western mind which relies on and gives primacy to glottographic texts written alphabetically, while marginalizing images to residual Western categories of art and iconography.[5] Additionally, Western thought on text enshrines false beliefs as to its lack of ambiguity, its purported ability to record the spoken chain of speech, and its durability of meaning across space, time, languages, and cultures.[6] Mesoamerican graphic communication systems, in contrast, were intimately tied to oral and other performance. There was no original 'text' and no two performances would have been the same. With the exception of the Maya

3 These were probably never in codex form in precontact times, although almost any scrap of Indigenous or European paper or animal skin with Indigenous graphic content, including the screen folds, has come to be called a 'codex.'

4 Louise M. Burkhart, *The Slippery Earth: Nahua-Christian Moral Dialogue in Sixteenth-Century Mexico* (Tucson: University of Arizona Press, 1989) provides the best insights into precontact Aztec or Nahua morality.

5 This is so even as texts become increasingly involved with iconic and notational graphic content in the modern world (public signage, graphic user interfaces, etc.). Katarzyna Mikulska, 'The System of Graphic Communication in the Central Mexican Divinatory Codices from the Functional Perspective' in *Indigenous Graphic Communication Systems: A Theoretical Approach*, eds Katarzyna Mikulska and Jerome A. Offner (Louisville: University Press of Colorado, 2019), 41–92.

6 Jerome A. Offner, 'What Lies Beneath. Generating Mesoamerican Media Surfaces' in *Indigenous Graphic Communication Systems*, 180–203.

and a limited number of other cultures who left occasionally lengthy glottographic texts in both stone and paper form, the rest of Mesoamerican peoples relied on iconic and notational principles,[7] relegating the glottographic principle (expressed in Western culture through the alphabet) to a minor role. The Aztec[8] culture, well excavated with abundant contact-era documentation, has left no known precontact texts exhibiting grammar or syntax: even postcontact clusters of glyphs in linear array are beyond rare[9] and they, along with individual postcontact glyph composition, were influenced by the alphabetized hegemonic colonial culture. Although difficult to grasp, these differences are essential to understanding Mesoamerican jurisprudence in every aspect, including modes of argumentation and reasoning, legal process, and reports of legal rules. Neither text-centric Western preferences nor anthropological reports on law in entirely oral cultures provide reliable frameworks for understanding Mesoamerican law. Overall, scarcity of contact-era documentation, heavily filtered sources, and formidable conceptual challenges constitute the fascination and challenge of understanding Mesoamerican law.

2 Aztec Jurisprudential Graphic Expression: The Famous Example from Texcoco, Mexico

The best precontact Mesoamerican legal data emanate from the Aztec second city, Texcoco. Scholars reporting on other cultures find they have little to report.[10] Certainly, the *Relaciones Geográficas* from the later sixteenth century[11] occasionally provide, through a Spanish administrative questionnaire, interesting aspects of local legal systems throughout Mesoamerica, but from

7 Katarzyna Mikulska, 'On Numbers, Tables and Calendars: When Writing Appeared' (2014) 7 Contributions in New World Archaeology 47–72; Mikulska, 'The System of Graphic Communication.'

8 Aztec refers to the contact-era society involving multiple ethnic groups and languages, governed for the most part by the Nahua, speakers of Nahuatl. The largest city at contact was Tenochtitlan, now central Mexico City.

9 Gordon Whittaker, 'The Principles of Nahuatl Writing' (2009) 16 Göttinger Beiträge zur Sprachwissenschaft 47–81.

10 E.g. Ronald Spores, *The Mixtec Kings and Their People* (Norman: University of Oklahoma Press, 1967); Michael D. Coe and Rex Koontz, *Mexico: From the Olmecs to the Aztecs* (London: Thames & Hudson, 2013); Michael D. Coe and Stephen D. Houston, *The Maya* (New York: Thames & Hudson, 2015).

11 For *Relaciones Geográficas* c. 1579–c. 1585 see Howard F. Cline, 'A Census of the *Relaciones Geográficas*, 1579–1612' in *Handbook of Middle American Indians*, 12: 324–69.

already changed societies.[12] This article therefore focuses on the legal system of Texcoco, whose governing elite had themselves spoken other languages only a few generations before contact.[13]

Leaves 2 and 3 of the *Mapa Quinatzin*,[14] created by the Texcocan court by 1542, provide our best insights into Texcocan, Nahua, and Aztec jurisprudence. Leaving aside some conquest and tribute information along the top of leaf 3 (Figure 1.1), there are four columns of legal vignettes. The first and third columns specify common circumstances and punishments for theft and adultery, while the second column depicts diverse crimes committed against the state or rulership perhaps only by members of the ruling *pilli* class.[15] The fourth column specifies the circumstances and punishments for specific cases of judicial corruption during the reigns of the city's two most famous rulers, Nezahualcoyotl (1431–1472) and Nezahualpilli (1472–1515). This clearly Indigenous production using Indigenous paper, pigments, and techniques but already exhibiting European graphic influence, including Latin alphabetic glosses added in Nahuatl, may have been for internal court use or for presentation to colonial authorities. We know that this method of graphic presentation of legal vignettes is not dissimilar to precontact compositions.[16] The manuscript has a loss of uncertain extent at the bottom.

In conjunction with related alphabetic missionary and Indigenous/Spanish alphabetic reports, which partly derive from and constitute our only, if poor, substitute for now lost related oral performances, this composition provides pathways into Nahua jurisprudence. For example, columns 1 and 3 may be interpreted as codified law for theft and adultery. The first row of column 1 depicts a thief, shown strangled, digging into a house with a sleeping

12 Bailón Corres and Brokmann Haro, *Los pueblos indígenas*, navigate this uncertain analytical landscape with better discernment than most.

13 Regarding earlier modern studies of Aztec law, only J. Kohler's work merits mention (*El derecho de los aztecas*, Carlos Rovalo y Fernández, translator (México: Edición de la Revista Jurídica de la Escuela Libre de Derecho, 1924)). See Jerome A. Offner *Law and Politics in Aztec Texcoco* (Cambridge: Cambridge University Press, 1983), XIII–XIV for further commentary.

14 *Mapa Quinatzin. Códice Mapa Quinatzin: justicia y derechos humanos en el México antiguo*, ed. Luz María Mohar Betancourt (México: Comisión Nacional de los Derechos Humanos. CIESAS. Miguel Angel Porrúa Grupo, 2004). Although this edition contains the best recent photographs it is replete with errors. Jerome A. Offner, 'Review of Códice Mapa Quinatzin. Justicia y derechos humanos en el México antiguo' (2004) 52(3) Ethnohistory 659–662.

15 The class structure of Texcoco is detailed in Offner, *Law and Politics*, 124–147. Most commoners were often called *macehualtin*.

16 Jerome A. Offner, 'The Future of Aztec Law' (2016) 2(2) The Medieval Globe 1–32.

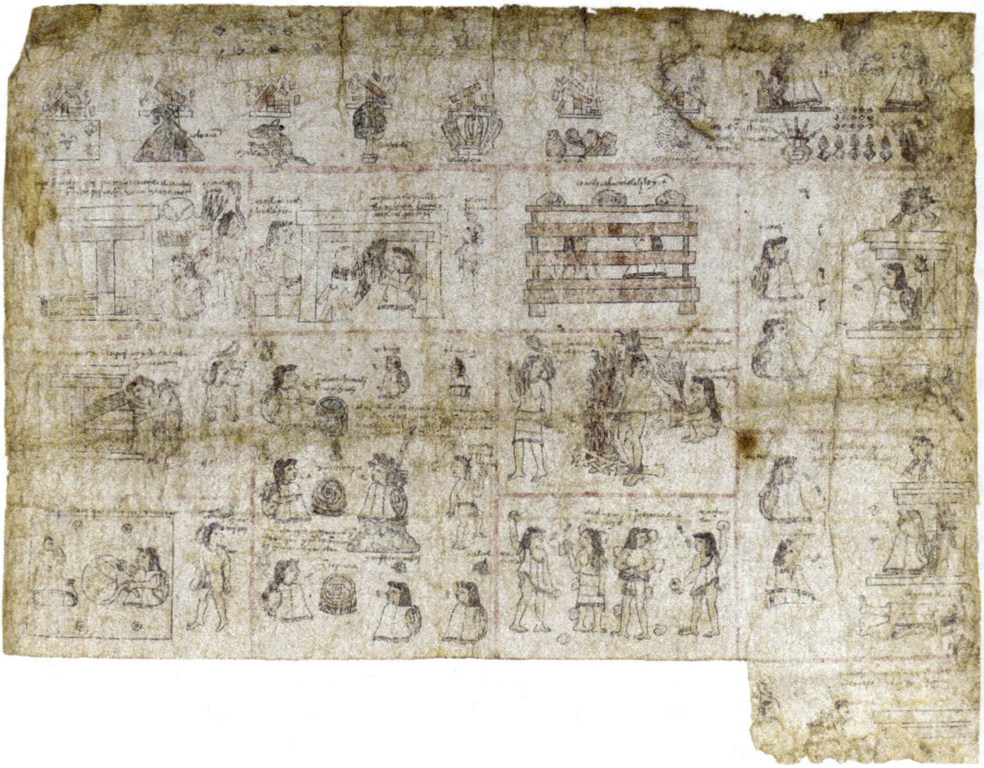

FIGURE 1.1 *Mapa Quinatzin*, leaf 3. Fonds Mexicain 396, Bibliothèque nationale de France

occupant. In the second row, another thief steals valuables from a reed box and is strangled. A theft of a bundle from a distracted market woman at night constitutes the third row, with the perpetrator again strangled. An adulterous pair kept in an open wooden holding cell awaiting further disposition leads off column 3. In the second row, the man is burned alive with saltwater splashed on him; the woman is merely strangled. From alphabetic reports, we know that these punishments were imposed when the adulteress's husband had been killed by the adulterer. In the third row, both adulterers are stoned to death after being convicted by direct evidence, perhaps being apprehended *in flagrante delicto*.

Colonial sources contain several lists of legal rules; the two most relevant for the *Mapa Quinatzin* are in the works of the castizo writer Ixtlilxochitl and the entirety of the short document 'Estas son las leyes.'[17] We also know that Nezahualcoyotl of Texcoco was regarded as a great legislator well before contact times. He promulgated eighty laws for his court's four supreme councils.[18] These reports of legal rules, however, are best regarded as poorly described pieces of decontextualized jurisprudence; they were neither as simple nor as uncoordinated as presented to us through colonial filters.[19] Nevertheless, the Texcocan legal system placed strong emphasis on adherence to legal rules in adjudication. For common offenses, such as theft, adultery, and drunkenness, specific circumstances led to specific punishments. Elsewhere,[20] I have shown that this policy of legalism, rare in world legal perspective, arose as imperial statecraft during a period of political consolidation following extended disorder among small warring states, each composed of a variety of ethnic groups.

The Texcocan government had four supreme councils whose composition and jurisdiction exhibit a dynamic balancing of power instead of the conventional image of a monolithic state led by an all-powerful ruler.[21] A close kinsman of the ruler led each council. The Supreme Legal Council was composed of at least twelve judges, at least half drawn from the ruling or *pilli* class, with six and/or twelve territorial jurisdictions. Their decisions could be appealed to two higher judges who sentenced only with the ruler's approval. The other three councils were made up at least in part of members of powerful groups in Texcoco's small empire, both commoners and *pipiltin* (pl. of *pilli*). Merchants as well as tribute collectors were members of the Treasury Council, and warriors were members of the War Council. Priests and craftsmen were among the members of the Council of Music, Arts, and Sciences.

17 Fernando de Alva Ixtlilxochitl, *Obras históricas*, 2 vols. (México: Universidad Nacional Autónoma de México, Instituto de Investigaciones Históricas, 1975–1977). 'Estas son leyes que tenían los indios de la Nueva España, Anáhuac o México' in *Nueva colección de documentos para la historia de México*, ed. Joaquín García Icazbalceta (México: Andrade y Morales, 1886–1892), vol. 3, 308–315.

18 The Nahua counting system is vigesimal, therefore four sets of twenty.

19 Offner, 'The Future of Aztec Law.'

20 Jerome A. Offner, 'Aztec Legal Process: The Case of Texcoco' in *Proceedings of the Conference on Late Post-classic Central Mexican Iconography*, ed. Elizabeth Hill Boone (Washington, DC: Center for Mesoamerican Studies, Dumbarton Oaks, 1982), 141–157; Offner, *Law and Politics*, 66–86.

21 Recently, I have mentioned the mapping of the Aztec imperial system onto the contemporary Mexican political system. 'Improving Western Historiography of Texcoco' in *Texcoco: Prehispanic and Colonial Perspectives*, eds Jongsoo Lee and Galen Brokaw (Boulder: University Press of Colorado, 2014), 25–61.

Reports in alphabetic sources detail legal rules ascribed to each council although fewer than twenty remain in each instance. In an earlier article,[22] I detailed much of the substantive law and the jurisdiction that may be discerned for each council, and how these related to economic and political dynamics within the Texcocan empire. Here some representative rules for the War Council (*tequihuacalli*, warrior house) can be mentioned. (1) Soldiers who disobeyed or inadequately fulfilled orders were beheaded. (2) A soldier who took another's prisoner or booty or who gave the prisoner to another was strangled. (3) Noble captives who escaped and returned to their homes were strangled, whereas commoners who did the same were rewarded. (4) The captains and soldiers of a ruler's, royal son's or prince's guard were strangled if their charge was taken by the enemy. Although each rule appears simple, more context is needed for full understanding. Explication of the significance of prisoner-taking, and a *pilli*'s obligation to remain with the enemy and accept his mortal ritual fate, for example, emanate from the still incompletely understood cultural concept of Flowery War (*xochiyaoyotl*) and would each go well beyond the scope of this article.

The most difficult entity to understand was the Council of Music, Arts, and Sciences. Its Nahuatl name remains unknown and it was involved with what the alphabetic sources report as poetry, rhetoric, astrology, and both good and evil magic and sorcery. Some legal rules and matters within its jurisdiction again bear mention. (1) Magic or witchcraft against a city was punished by heart extraction. (2) A magician who used his art to rob and abuse members of a household was strangled (cf. the first description of theft in the *Mapa Quinatzin* above), as were (3) highway robbers, (4) poisoners, and (5) travelers on roads impersonating the ruler's messengers. The different categorization of orality, performance, magic, craft, technology, and liminal spaces such as footpaths is immediately obvious and is only suggested but not captured by the reported rules. Aztec jurisprudence was evidently quite complex.

The alphabetic documents provide incidental details of jurisprudential thinking. Theft from granaries, for example, necessarily involved two persons. The one entering the granary and throwing grain to the other on the ground was assumed to be the instigator of the crime and was punished more severely. In the case of adultery, adultery only involved married women. A husband could have sex with other unmarried women without committing adultery.

22 Jerome A. Offner, 'The Distribution of Jurisdiction and Political Power in Aztec Texcoco: Subgroups in Conflict' in *Five Centuries of Law and Politics in Central Mexico*, eds Ronald Spores and Ross Hassig (Nashville: Vanderbilt University Publications in Anthropology, 1984), 5–14.

Recently, some Mexican scholars have claimed this as evidence that the wife was the man's property. Instead, eschewing the imported patriarchal tendencies of the region postcontact, which trace back to Roman times, the better perspective considers the interests of the two groups of kinsmen joined through the two spouses. The dominant organizing principle in precontact Nahua and Aztec culture was the personal kindred (*tlacamecayotl*). These were bilateral and ego-centered networks concatenated through parent–child ties providing access to kinship, social, political, and economic rights and duties – they were key to obtaining resources and building influence and power. Parent–child ties, whether from a mother or father, were valued in Aztec society. Women, for example, inherited, produced, and held property, held office, and dissolved marriages, although reportedly with the loss of any children. Kinsmen of both spouses therefore proceeded from the indisputable proof of birth from the wife and relied on her situation in a small, controlled community along with fearsome fatal punishments for adultery, for men as well as women, to assure paternity and to admit, jointly, a new person into this web of rights and obligations. Adultery law, therefore, was designed to promote overall social stability rather than to assert a perceived patriarchal property right.

Legalism entails a robust legal process and Nezahualcoyotl of Texcoco was renowned as a great 'justiciero.' The Texcocan alphabetic sources Pomar[23] and Ixtlilxochitl emphasize that the legal rules had to be applied without remission and without exception.[24] From the second leaf of the *Mapa Quinatzin* (Figure 1.2) we see mention of the *nauhpohuallahtolli*, or eighty-day legal council during which all important cases in the empire were to be discussed.

There were also councils every ten or twelve days. Punishment was intended to be rapid, usually public, and occasionally participatory. Judges were provided with support from the state and were expected to hear cases only in public in their official courts. Gifts from parties were not permitted. Aggravated judicial corruption was a capital offense and three instances are shown in column 4 of the *Mapa Quinatzin* (Figure 1.1). In the two fully depicted cases, strangulation was the punishment for the judges who are also forever shamed through the inclusion of their name glyphs. Although the intended audience for the *Mapa Quinatzin* remains unknown, the second and fourth columns, with requirements of proper behavior for the *pilli* class, may be a commentary

---

23 Juan Bautista Pomar, 'Relación de Tezcoco' in *Nueva colección de documentos para la historia de México*, ed. Joaquín García Icazbalceta (México: Impr. De Francisco Díaz de León, 1891).

24 Offner, *Law and* Politics, 66–69.

FIGURE 1.2 *Mapa Quinatzin*, leaf 2, detail. Fonds Mexicain 12, Bibliothèque nationale de France. Two judges converse in court during the *nauhpohuallahtolli*. The hand gesture appears to indicate the decision maker in the discussion

on perceived shortcomings of the intrusive Spanish and their inadequate legal system.

Another interesting aspect of the Texcocan legal process were two courts in the important cities of Teotihuacan and Otompan.[25] They appear to have been for *pipiltin* and commoners respectively. Separate courts for these two classes of people were common at various legal levels although the overall picture

25 Post-classic Teotihuacan was not located at the great Classic Period site but nearby, and the historian Ixtlilxochitl was a member of its colonial ruling family. Otompan was named after the empire's second most populous ethnic group, the Otomi. On *Mapa Quinatzin*, leaf 2, a red line (not included in Figure 1.2 due to manuscript damage) connects Teotihuacan and Otompan to the depiction of the *nauhpohuallahtolli*.

remains incomplete, with higher levels handling all cases at the ten or twelve and eighty-day intervals mentioned above.

Dictionary entries,[26] although decontextualized, help illuminate Nahua jurisprudential categories and thought. *Nahuatia* means 'to give orders to someone' and legal rules are *nahuatilli*.[27] Hunting metaphors were associated with the law – it was regarded metaphorically as a wild beast and a trap or snare.[28] The verb *yahualoa* meant both to surround and to be the first to bring a complaint. A person who committed a crime was called *matoyahuiani*, 'he who throws himself into the river.' Although justice of the facts and justice in adjudication were important in Aztec legal process, justice, *melahuacayotl*, from *melahua*, 'to walk straight,' was not etymologically related to law. Witnesses did perform a ritual act of earth-eating, to solemnize their testimony, and a good witness was a 'straight-walker' (*temelahuani*). According to the sources, good law benefited the entire community.

Nahuatl terminology recognized four steps in the legal process: (1) the bringing of an accusation, (2) the investigation of the facts of the case, (3) deciding and sentencing, and (4) punishment. The concept of *ixpan*, in front of face or eye was important as cases began – before the public as well as the sharp eye of an experienced and fierce-faced judge. *Ilhuia* 'to say' is also involved with expressions for accusation. A tribunal was a *tlacacoyan* or place where cases are heard. *Tzontequi* could mean both 'to judge' and 'to sentence': its roots are *tzon-* 'hair, top, or head' and *tequi-* 'to cut.'

For punishment, there were several groups of expressions. One group came from *nonotza* and embraced a broad range of meanings including 'to converse,' 'to consult,' 'to agree,' 'to admonish,' and 'to correct.' Another verb *tzacua*, and its causative form, *tzacuiltia* were more involved with physical punishment, further described in common expression such as 'to press down with bone and

26 Frances Karttunen has produced the best modern Nahuatl–English dictionary. Frances E. Karttunen *An Analytical Dictionary of Nahuatl* (Norman: University of Oklahoma Press, 2nd ed., 1992). Stephanie Wood (editor, 2000–2019) has long led the development of the best online *Nahuatl Dictionary*, https://nahuatl.uoregon.edu/content/welcome-nahuatl-dictionary. Etymologies and meanings in this article are largely drawn from these sources.

27 *Nahuatiā* is different from *nāhuat(i)* 'to be speak clearly' which is the root of the language name *Nāhuatl*, because of differences in the length of the vowel 'a' (ā is longer than a). This article, for a general audience, does not mark vowel length and employs English verb infinitive and unpossessed noun forms as translations for convenience. See Frances E. Karttunen, 'Introduction' in Karttunen, *An Analytical Dictionary*, XVII–XXXIV for conventions used in more specialized settings.

28 Offner, *Law and* Politics, 243–244.

nettle,' 'to cover someone with cold water' and to beat someone with sticks and stones. Suspected criminals might find themselves referred to in public by the punishment they were fit to receive, e.g., 'needs sticks and stones.' Nevertheless, as indicated by the *nonotza* terms (and other evidence), not all punishments were physical. They also involved public shaming and economic loss. Nahuatl terms for judicial corruption included covering the judge's mouth and a judge hiding or putting something under, including under his mat and seat, that is, his symbols of office.

Court personnel could include bailiffs (*achcauhtin*, literally 'older brothers') and other ill-defined minor personnel. Of paramount importance were the *tlacuiloque*[29] who recorded, in the Aztec system of graphic expression, the parties and witnesses in, and the substance, determination, and sentence of legal cases. These records on Indigenous paper were kept in a royal archive in Texcoco but were burned during the early conflicts with the Spanish and their allies. These allies knew well that such a catastrophic loss would foment disorder within Texcoco as well as vitiate its claims to resources and labor in disputes with other cities.

It is vital not to let emphases in the sources limit our understanding of Aztec law. Legal rules cannot encompass all that happens in society and precedent must have played a role in the Texcocan legal system, although specific examples remain scarce.[30] We cannot determine, for example, whether the rulers' and judges' names shown in the cases of judicial corruption mentioned above were reports of precedent, or new legal rules based on precedent. They were likely both. Nor should the sources' emphasis on capital punishment be accepted at face value: there is abundant evidence of lesser punishments[31] as

29 'Scribes' would be an inadequate English translation because these masters of graphic expression in a non-alphabetic, largely oral culture were necessarily well educated in art, language, oral presentation, history, culture, and other matters, and did far more than copy or write texts letter by letter.

30 Brokmann Haro, *La estera y la silla: Individuo, comunidad, estado e instituciones jurídicas nahuas* (México: Comisión Nacional de Derechos Humanos, 2006), 93–95 provides a brief but useful discussion of the roles of precedent and custom in the Aztec legal system. Unfortunately, following aspects of my work too closely, he considers that emphasis on rules in adjudication meant the Aztecs did not develop 'true' jurisprudence, with which I emphatically disagree. 'True' is often a gateway word for lapses into ethnocentricity and assumed inferiority of other cultures, neither of which are characteristic of Brokmann Haro's thought.

31 Motolinía, for example, reports lesser punishments for theft than are shown in the *Mapa Quinatzin*. Toribio de Benavente Motolinía, *Memoriales; o, Libro de las cosas de la Nueva España y de los naturales de ella*, ed. Edmundo O'Gorman (México D.F.: Universidad Nacional Autónoma de México, 1971), 309, 321. See also Offner, *Law and Politics*, 275–276.

well as non-criminal proceedings and cases between contesting parties, even to the extent that petty disputing by commoners over lands and houses was compared, in a common saying, to guarding turkeys squabbling among themselves. Litigiousness does not appear to have been a postcontact import.

There are no known Nahuatl terms differentiating between criminal and civil law. Commercial law must have been quite complex, but little is known of it because of the parallel development of Spanish hegemonic business practices. We can, however, employ reports of 'slavery' among the Aztecs as evidence of sophisticated, durable contract law. There were various sorts of slaves (*tlatlacohtin*, singular *tlacohtli*), including people captured during war, those made slaves as legal punishment or to make restitution, and those who entered into labor contracts with others. These comments pertain to the last group. In the sources, such people are often described as having sold themselves into slavery. More precisely, people were free to contract to sell their labor to others because of a gambling habit, or reckless lifestyle, or basic necessities of daily life, including food. They reportedly enjoyed the proceeds or consideration from the contracted sale before entering service. Parents could also contract with another for their child's labor, although a solemn ceremony and at least four witnesses were required for the transaction. Labor contracts could be bought back by returning the consideration given but this reportedly seldom happened.

The terms and conditions of labor contracts varied. Essentially, they were to provide a certain amount of service and those who held their contracts could not interfere in their lives beyond the provision of such services. *Tlatlacohtin* could have families and possess properties and other *tlatlacohtin*. They worked for only a set time and had to be treated humanely. Children of *tlatlacohtin* were not *tlatlacohtin*. The service contract was inheritable although it often ended at death, and there are reports of *tlatlacohtin* marrying the contract holder's wife and becoming head of household.[32] Parents who had contracted for their children's labor could replace one child with another and the contract holders were reportedly pleased with the change and offered gifts.[33] The contracts of well-behaved labor providers could not be resold.

Groups of people could also enter into joint labor agreements called *huehuetlatlacolli* in which one or several households agreed to provide labor in perpetuity across generations to another household in return for a one-time financial consideration. *Huehuetlatlacolli* had certain protective features: the

32 In most circumstances, a brother of the deceased husband was expected to marry the widow.

33 This substitution option may have only applied to the *huehuetlatlacolli* contract.

contract was cancelled if the service provider died in the household being served, or if that household tried to take what that person had acquired for himself or herself.

The state was intensely interested in these labor contracts and their enforcement. A person who found a lost child and sold that child's labor was enslaved. The fraudulent seller's estate was then divided between the victimized child and the deceived buyer.[34] If a person entered into two different labor contracts, the buyer of the first contract (or the buyer who could produce witnesses according to one source), prevailed. The buyer of the second contract saw it voided but kept his consideration. The slave who had sold his labor twice was also punished in an unspecified manner. *Tlatlacohtin* judged difficult by their contract holder could be forced to wear a large wooden collar after two or three warnings and their contract could then be sold. This was an escalation with risk on both sides. If the labor provider's contract was sold two or three times, the last contract holder could sell the service provider for ritual sacrifice. At the same time, if a collared slave escaped from the marketplace into the ruler's palace, he would become free and the ruler would pay the contract holder a consideration. Only the contract holder and his children could interfere with this flight into the palace – anyone else would be condemned to slavery.

Finally, *tlatlacohtin* may not have paid tribute to the political apparatus, although the data are not definitive. Perhaps for that reason, Nezahualpilli of Texcoco reportedly ended the entire practice of *huehuetlatlacolli* but we are not assured as to the motive for, or success of, this prohibition. The prevalence and concentration of well-regulated labor contracts – important assets – is a testimony to the complexity of the Aztec economy and makes little sense without accumulations of additional types of assets or capital by various groups in Texcoco.

The content of Aztec legal rules of land tenure was dictated in the twentieth century largely by European followers of nineteenth- and twentieth-century political-economic ideologies (Marxism and Polanyism). These belief systems require that societies pass through certain defined stages or transformations before reaching our contemporary and assumed dysphoric state. These writers assigned, and therefore exoticized, Aztec society to one or another of these prior stages or formations. Given that these ideologically defined prior stages or formations typically involve despotic, monolithic power as well as command or directed economies, and given the top-down, ruler-oriented information that typically survives from past societies, it was a simple matter to recruit

34 This may have applied to sale of a child into any form of servitude.

data to match the requirements of these belief systems. Archaeological theory, with the same materialist roots and derivative stage-bound, often evolutionary schemes, has largely contented itself within such frameworks and with such results. In contesting the resulting ethnocentric portrayals of Aztec land tenure and society, it is important not to be drawn into the false choices built into the differences between the stages posited by these belief systems (e.g., private/not private property; redistribution/market-integration). Instead, it is better to study the bundles of rights and duties attached to the different types of land and to compare those with similar, corrective analyses of other ancient societies[35] to build more accurate comparisons between cultures.

In 1983,[36] I presented the land tenure system of Texcoco with extensive commentary regarding relevant data from nearby regions and then emerging findings regarding great inequities in lands worked by households. I also included evidence of land sales by individuals rather than corporations such as rulerships (*tlahtohcayotl*) and palaces (*tecpan*). The conventional view of land tenure at the time allowed no individual ownership or sale of land, and claimed that at the lowest levels, *calpullis* (*capolli*, plural *capoltin* or wards, *barrios*, etc., now recently relabeled but scarcely better understood as *tlaxilacalli*),[37] distributed usufruct rights to land according to need. Texcocan studies benefit from an unusual density of documentation in the area. Two lengthy postcontact graphic manuscripts, the *Códice Vergara* and the *Códice de Santa María Asunción*, detail the household composition and landholdings of several *tlaxilacalli* in Tepetlaoztoc, near Texcoco (see for example, Figure 1.3). The information, reformatted for the European page and adapted in unknown ways from town-level archives, includes individual plot boundary and surface area measurements in a vigesimal Indigenous numerical system (including the zero) along with symbols indicating soil quality. Discrepancies

35 There was another effort to recruit reports of sumptuary laws to fit the requirements of these belief systems, but it has not prospered. Offner, 'The Future of Aztec Law.'

36 Offner, *Law and Politics*, 24–139. See also Jerome A. Offner, 'On the Inapplicability of "Oriental Despotism" and the "Asiatic Mode of Production" to the Aztecs of Texcoco' (1981) 46(1) American Antiquity 43–61; Jerome A. Offner, 'On Carrasco's Use of Theoretical "First Principles"' (1981) 46(1) American Antiquity 69–74.

37 See Benjamin Johnson, *Pueblos within Pueblos:* Tlaxilacalli *Communities in Acolhuacan, Mexico, ca. 1272–1692* (Boulder: University Press of Colorado, 2017) for discussions of legal and political structure at the lower legal levels of the Texcocan polity, largely in postcontact times. Vital details of the *tlaxilacalli* concept, and how it changed over time, however, continue to be absent, nor can we assume this concept was the unique method of local organization in the region.

in landholding are large and previously unknown evidence of rights to house lots appears.[38]

In a recent publication,[39] I pointed out the indirect mention in a major source from the largest Aztec city, Tenochtitlan, of the sale of *calpolli* land (and other types of land) by a commoner in precontact times. He needed funds to maintain his ambitious ritual status as a 'receiver' of Huitzilopochtli (the most important god of the Nahua of Tenochtitlan). A Nahua informant reports: 'he sold his land' (*quinamaca itlal*) or 'somewhere he arranged a loan' on it (*canah netlacujlli quichioa*). He did this with various types of land, including *calpolli* land (*quichioa in calpollali*). The informant went on to name other types of land this commoner might sell or on which he might get loans: 'the enclosed land, the marshy land, the dusty land' (*in chinamitl, in chiauhtlalli, in teuhtlalli*). Thus, this brief passage, offered as an aside by one of the sixteenth-century missionary Sahagún's informants, is full of evidence of the complexity and sophistication of precontact land tenure, including individual commoner land tenure and sale. It is not surprising then, that Ixtlilxochitl reports a legal rule parallel in structure to a rule governing the sale of labor contracts cited above: the second purchaser of the same piece of land lost the land and his purchase price, and the fraudulent seller was punished.[40]

3 Conclusions

A few available Indigenous graphic manuscripts, in conjunction with related alphabetic missionary and Indigenous or Spanish alphabetic sources, provide only limited evidence about precontact law in Mesoamerica. Through such evidence, we have learned especially about Texcocan, Nahua, and Aztec law.

---

38 Jerome A. Offner, 'Household Organization in the Texcocan Heartland' in *Explorations in Ethnohistory*, eds H.R. Harvey and Hanns J. Prem (Albuquerque: University of New Mexico Press, 1984), 127–146; Offner, *Law and Politics*, Appendix 2; *El Códice Vergara: edición facsimilar con comentario: pintura indígena de casas, campos y organización social de Tepetlaoztoc a mediados del siglo XVI*, eds Barbara J. Williams and Frederic Hicks (México: Universidad Nacional Autónoma de México: Apoyo al Desarrollo de Archivos y Bibliotecas de México, A.C., 2011); *The* Códice de Santa María Asunción*: Facsimile and Commentary: Households and Lands in Sixteenth-Century Tepetlaoztoc*, eds Barbara J. Williams and H.R. Harvey (Salt Lake City: University of Utah Press, 1997).

39 Offner, 'The Future of Aztec Law.'

40 Alva Ixtlilxochitl, *Obras históricas*, 1: 386.

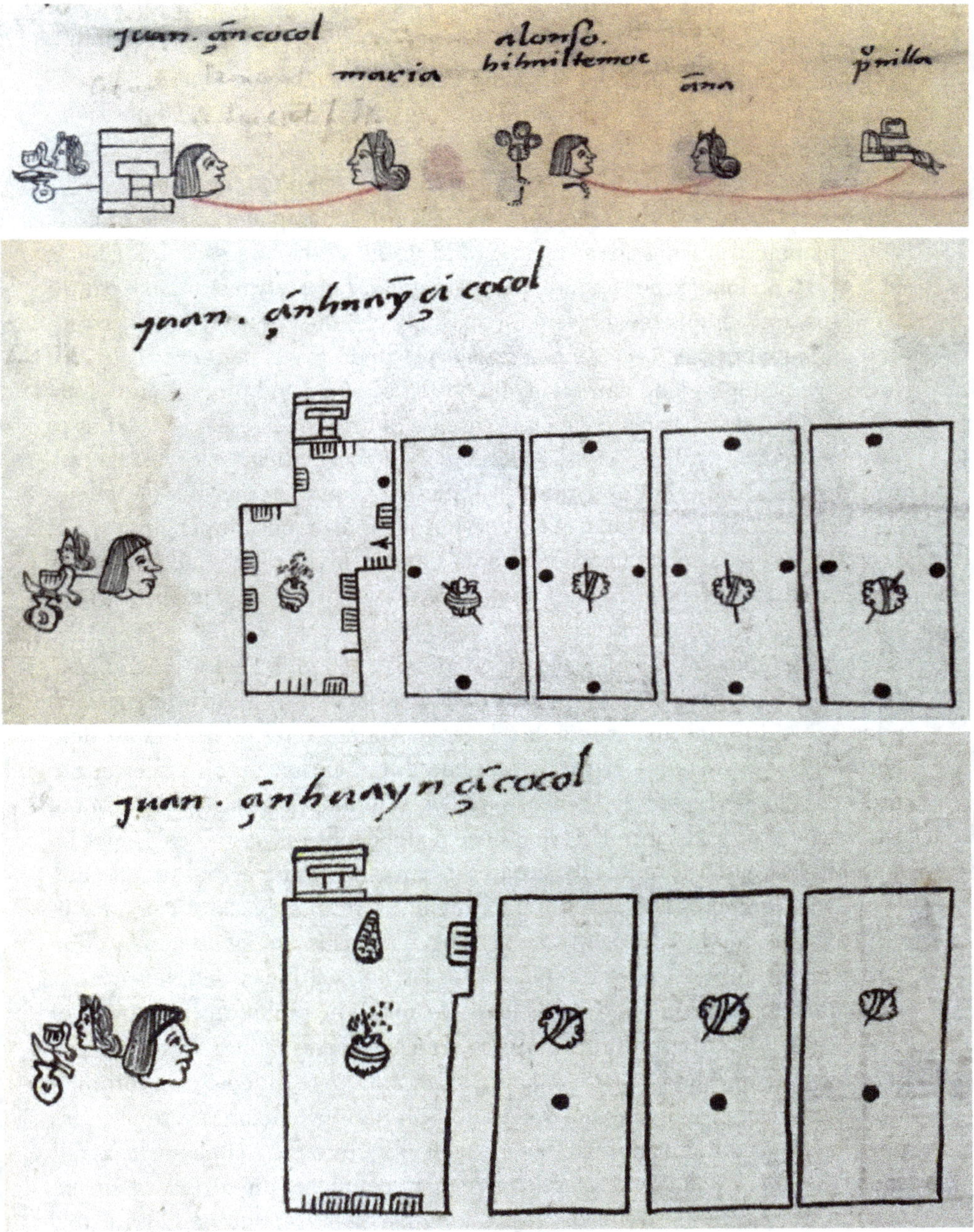

FIGURE 1.3 *Códice Vergara, Document cadastral ou codex Vergara,* folios 2r, 6v, 14r. Fonds Mexicain 37–39, Bibliothèque nationale de France. (a) Juan Çinhuanynçicocol, with name in glyph and gloss form, with his wife, an immigrant man (relationship unknown) with wife and infant daughter; (b) house lot's and additional fields' dimensions; (c) area calculations, along with soil quality glyphs again in the middle. For Spanish administrative purposes, all lands seem assigned to Juan

Some of the dominant evidence sheds light on aspects of criminal and family-related law and allows us to understand the general structure and function of government including the Supreme Legal Council. There is also evidence about contract law, some of it related to slavery. The details of land tenure continue to emerge.

Precontact Mesoamerican law was not well recorded by the intrusive Spanish. Most mentions in colonial sources are incomplete, heavily filtered, and emanate from missionaries with odd agendas, dispossessed Indigenous elites with no longer relevant abilities or roles, and scarcely restrained Spanish colonists. Indigenous towns were increasingly circumscribed and their strongest arguments, when they could afford legal standing, were often for common town ownership of land and town absorption of office and private lands associated with the former elite. The former elite in turn made excessive claims to ownership of town land. Thus, what is left is a fascinating history of culture contact and change, but one markedly different from the processes of precontact culture contact and change among various Indigenous ethnic groups. Not even Nahua law is adequately documented, and even the relative abundance of evidence from Texcoco can only produce windows into Nahua jurisprudential thought.

The tendency of ideological proponents to declare, rather than to investigate, the content of Mesoamerican political economy (and thereby law) adds an additional historiographic layer of source filtering and distortion. Fortunately, persistent portrayals of monolithic, authoritarian state formations entailing directed and redistributive economies and solely institutional land ownership and control of labor need no longer be taken seriously. Instead, students of the law are ideally situated to investigate the actual functioning of the law (and political economy) of ancient states. The lack of evidence in critical areas perennially proves frustrating, but this is true of documentation remaining from most ancient states. One lesson clearly learned, however, is that the better documented states least resemble the ambitious ideologies of the nineteenth and twentieth centuries. As a legal code cannot encompass all that happens in human society, neither can antiquated ideological formulations involving progressions of stages and formations encompass, much less adequately account for, human history in all its variety and richness. This is not to say that underlying principles do not generate much of the surface complexity that we perceive:[41] we need only to identify such principles and how they develop over time more fully and accurately.

41 Jerome A. Offner, 'Dueling Rulers and Strange Attractors: Some Patterns of Disorder and Killing in Aztec Society' (1993) 16(2) Political and Legal Anthropology Review 65–73.

References

Bailón Corres, Moisés J. and Carlos Brokmann Haro, *Los pueblos indígenas de México y sus derechos: una breve mirada*. 1st ed. México: Comisión Nacional de los Derechos Humanos, 2011.

Brokmann Haro, Carlos. *La estera y la silla: individuo, comunidad, estado e instituciones jurídicas nahuas*. México: Comisión Nacional de Derechos Humanos, 2006.

Burkhart, Louise M. *The Slippery Earth: Nahua-Christian Moral Dialogue in Sixteenth-Century Mexico*. Tucson: University of Arizona Press, 1989.

Códice de Santa María Asunción: Facsimile and Commentary; Households and Lands in Sixteenth-Century Tepetlaoztoc, edited by Barbara J. Williams and H.R. Harvey. Salt Lake City: University of Utah Press, 1997. (This work provides an intricately detailed Indigenous graphic record of family composition and landholding a few decades after contact).

Códice Vergara: edición facsimilar con comentario; pintura indígena de casas, campos y organización social de Tepetlaoztoc a mediados del siglo XVI, edited by Barbara J. Williams and Frederic Hicks. México: Universidad Nacional Autónoma de México, 2011. (This is similar to the *Códice de Santa María Asunción*).

'Estas son leyes que tenían los indios de la Nueva España, Anáhuac o México.' In *Nueva colección de documentos para la historia de México*, edited by Joaquín García Icazbalceta, 3: 308–315. México: Andrade y Morales, 1886–1892.

Ixtlilxochitl, Fernando de Alva. *Obras históricas*, edited by Edmundo O'Gorman. México: Universidad Nacional Autónoma de México, Instituto de Investigaciones Históricas, 2 vols., 1975–1977. (This is the principal early historian of Texcoco, Mexico).

Johnson, Benjamin. *Pueblos within Pueblos: Tlaxilacalli Communities in Acolhuacan, Mexico, ca. 1272–1692*. Boulder: University Press of Colorado, 2017.

Kohler, J. *El derecho de los aztecas*. Translated by Carlos Rovalo y Fernández. México: Edición de la Revista Jurídica de la Escuela Libre de Derecho, 1924. (This is the best of the pre-1950 studies of Aztec law, but see Offner, *Law and Politics*, XIII–XIV for discussion and cautions).

Motolinía, Toribio de Benavente. *Memoriales; o, Libro de las cosas de la Nueva España y de los naturales de ella*, edited by Edmundo O'Gorman. México D.F.: Universidad Nacional Autónoma de México, 1971.

Offner, Jerome A. 'Aztec Legal Process: the Case of Texcoco.' In *Proceedings of the Conference on Late Post-classic Central Mexican Iconography*, edited by Elizabeth Hill Boone, 141–157. Washington, DC: Center for Mesoamerican Studies, Dumbarton Oaks, 1982.

Offner, Jerome A. *Law and Politics in Aztec Texcoco*. Cambridge: Cambridge University Press, 1983.

Offner, Jerome A. 'The Distribution of Jurisdiction and Political Power in Aztec Texcoco: Subgroups in Conflict.' In *Five Centuries of Law and Politics in Central Mexico*, edited by Ronald Spores and Ross Hassig, 5–14. Nashville: Vanderbilt University, 1984.

Offner, Jerome A. 'Household Organization in the Texcocan Heartland.' In *Explorations in Ethnohistory*, edited by H.R. Harvey and Hanns J. Prem, 127–146. Albuquerque: University of New Mexico Press, 1984.

Offner, Jerome A. 'The Future of Aztec Law.' *The Medieval Globe*, 2(2) (2016): 1–32.

Zorita, Alonso de. *Breve y sumaria relación de los señores de la Nueva España: Life and Labor in Ancient Mexico; The Brief and Summary Relation of the Lords of New Spain*. Translated and with an introduction by Benjamin Keen. Norman: University of Oklahoma Press, 1994. (This is a good translation, but the precision of legal studies requires the original language version below).

Zorita, Alonso de. Breve y sumaria relación de los señores, y maneras y diferencias que habia de ellos en la Nueva España. In *Nueva colección de documentos para la historia de México: Códice Mendieta: Documentos Franciscanos, siglos XVI y XVII*, edited by Joaquín García Icazbalceta, 3: 71–227. México: Andrade y Morales, 1892.

CHAPTER 2

The Sun's Mandates: Customary Law in the Andes

Susan Elizabeth Ramírez

The dramatic execution of the Inca Atahualpa in the plaza of the highland ceremonial center of Cajamarca by the Spanish invader Francisco Pizarro and his men marked the beginning of the end of the system of customary law elaborated by the native regime. Surviving ethnic lords became suddenly free to interpret imperial rules that were believed to have been sanctioned by the gods in a manner that benefited them and their people. Only through the systematic imposition of the Spanish colonial legal regime which began seriously in the 1540s did European notions of justice and right replace the native sanctions relayed in oral traditions.

The Inca legal system is a controversial and difficult topic. For Horacio Urteaga, a Peruvian historian and archaeologist, the Incas enjoyed a system that was elaborate and functioned well. In his opinion, a corpus of laws that was orally transmitted from generation to generation served as the basis of a hierarchical judiciary organization. Ethnic lords acted as judges and, at the highest level, appointed functionaries sat on a Tribunal of Twelve, akin to a high court.[1]

His overly Western interpretation is challenged by other legal scholars who question whether or not a pre-Hispanic legal system even existed. On the one hand, Fernando de Trazegnies Granda, a lawyer and professor of philosophy, reviews the literature, focusing, in part, on semantics. In a final consideration, he notes that under the Inca regime there were no rights, only obligations, i.e., the regime was a tyranny, with no formal juridical system of laws. He concludes, then, that a pre-Hispanic legal system did not exist.[2] On the other, Jorge Basadre, a famous historian of republican Peru, mentions norms and religious sanctions that were different than Roman traditions, but served the same function of ordering society.[3] Hermann Trimborn, a German student of American

1 Horacio Urteaga, *La organización judicial en el imperio de los Incas* (Lima: Librería e Imprenta Gil, 1928); *El imperio incaico, en el que se incluye la historia del Ayllo y familia de los Incas* (Lima: Librería e Imprenta Gil, 1931), 204.

2 Fernando de Trazegnies Granda, '¿Hay un "Derecho" prehispánico?' (1992) 3(4) Ius et Veritas 46, 48.

3 Jorge Basadre, *Los fundamentos de la historia del derecho* (Lima: Librería Internacional del Perú, 1956).

 | DOI:10.1163/9789004436091_004

FIGURE 2.1 *Quipu*(*s*): native Andean counting device made of colored wool or cotton. Catalog number 41.2/7679
SOURCE: COURTESY OF THE DIVISION OF ANTHROPOLOGY, AMERICAN MUSEUM OF NATURAL HISTORY

anthropology, writes that it is difficult to separate Andean custom from law and judicial principles from morals.[4] Franklin Pease, a well-known ethnohistorian, supports this stand writing of taboos that were encoded in religion.[5] My analysis favors the latter interpretations. Andean rules for appropriate human behavior cannot be separated from their moral and religious universe.

Complicating the study of the topic is the fact that Andean peoples had no autochthonous system of writing. Chroniclers report that natives recorded their customs in a series of colored and knotted strings, called *quipus*, but their interpretation today is not completely understood.

So, this chapter depends largely on the participant-observations of a few literate Spanish men who described the Andes in the sixteenth and early seventeenth centuries. Some, like the chroniclers Juan de Betanzos and Garcilaso de la Vega, were bilingual – Spanish-Quechua, but some, such as Pedro Cieza de Leon, were not. Regardless of their linguistic capabilities, all their accounts are colored by their prejudicial views and the difficulties of understanding the exotic through a language that was not their own. What is more, systematic descriptions were not written for about another twenty years after first contact,

4 Hermann Trimborn, *El delito en las altas culturas de América* (Lima: Universidad Nacional Mayor de San Marcos, 1936/1968), 19–22.

5 Franklin Pease, 'Aproximación al delito entre los Incas' (1971) 29 Revista Derecho 52–62.

giving ample time for the natives, especially those who frequented large cities like Cuzco and Lima or who were in regular contact with the Europeans (such as priests or *encomenderos*, holders of a grant of native labor in return for service to the king) to learn Spanish rules and ways. They no doubt answered chroniclers' questions as they presumed the Spanish expected. Thus, throughout this analysis, although I try to discriminate between what is Andean and what is not, I cannot guarantee that the laws as described in the early Spanish sources reflect pre-Hispanic theory and practice or are Andean norms already tinged with what would become accepted colonial rules.[6]

I focus here on Indigenous usages to the extent possible, rather than colonial laws. My remarks are divided into three parts. The first provides an overview of the Inca state as the context in which native laws ordered society. The second presents the rules for communal living, as penned by a bilingual priest who spent years living among the Andeans. The third offers a distillation of specific norms as relayed by both Spanish and native writers. Throughout, I provide commentary on actual practices as evidenced in the sixteenth-century judicial and administrative ethnic records.

1 An Empire of One Law and One Birth

The famous mestizo writer of the early seventeenth century, Inca Garcilaso de la Vega, himself a native of the Andes and fluent in Quechua, reminds readers of the religio-political context of what Andeans considered right and wrong. The native peoples believed that their kings, starting with one named Manco Capac, descended from the union of the father Sun and the mother Moon. According to their oral traditions, the Sun conveyed to him all the laws he was to promulgate for the common benefit of the population. Garcilaso de la Vega elaborates that this Manco Capac drew up and put into practice some commands, while leaving others outlined so that his descendants, such as individuals with the names Inca Roca, Topa Inca Yupanqui, and Pachacutec, could dictate them later. By the time that Garcilaso de la Vega wrote (in the early seventeenth century, seventy or more years after the end of the pre-Hispanic regime), no one could say with certainty which of the kings made any particular law. Some decreed new ones; some reiterated or revised old ones, according

6 For a thoughtful and concise essay on the intersection of Spanish and native law, see Woodrow Borah, 'The Spanish and Indian Law: New Spain' in *Aztec and Inca States, 1400–1800: Anthropology and History*, eds George A. Collier, Renato I. Rosaldo, and John D. Wirth (New York: Academic Press, 1982), 265–288.

FIGURE 2.2 The *Quipu* and its Keeper and Interpreter (*Quipucamayoc*, in Quechua): A native specialist who fabricated a *quipu* and read it to interested parties. Each string recorded a different category of items, such as population, commodities, and cattle. The Royal Danish Library, Copenhagen, GKS 2232 4°: Guaman Poma, *Nueva corónica y buen gobierno* (1615), p. 360, Drawing 142, The Inka's council

to the needs of the times. But the laws were regarded as divine and were kept with love and respect, as emanating from their paramount god, the Sun. Thus, the populous considered any ordinary command of the king to be a divine commandment and lawbreaking was held to be sacrilegious and anathema, even if the misdeed were committed in ignorance. Such a divine origin legitimized Inca rule and the common understandings about right and wrong to the extent that they were unquestioned and rarely challenged – at least in theory.[7]

These norms for proper conduct spread as the empire increased in extent. The Inca domain by the date of the arrival of the Spanish in 1532 encompassed dozens of ethnic groups living in what is today southern Colombia, Ecuador, Peru, Bolivia, northern Chile, and northwestern Argentina. A native Huarochirí described it fittingly as a dominion of one birth, under one law. This saying aptly summarizes the Inca plans and goals for expansion. Inca leaders incorporated the various ethnic groups either by diplomacy and persuasion or by force. In the first case, the Inca ruler sent ambassadors bearing rich gifts with an invitation to ethnic groups on the frontier to ally with him and his people to enjoy friendship and a measure of security. The Incas promised peace and help in times of trouble. They would fight their common enemies or provide food and clothing in years of scarcity. Roads would be maintained and bridges built. In return, the people would have to learn the Quechua language if they did not already speak it, to accept and worship the Sun as their principal god above in status and strength to their own ethnic ancestral gods, and to work for the Inca when requested. All these ancestral gods were believed to have power to influence the course of a believer's life, adding at times a conditionality to the implementation of rules. If neglected or displeased, the ancestors could send misfortunes such as defeat, illness, death, famine, drought, floods, or blight.[8]

Upon accepting alliance, women were exchanged. The Inca took ethnic brides as secondary wives. The emperor rewarded some ethnic lords with his own daughters and sisters. The children of such unions guaranteed blood ties in the coming generations and eventually a congregation of one birth that shared a language, a bloodline, and the veneration of the Sun who inspired the one law by which all lived.

Those who chose to resist faced brutal force and defeat with the attendant humiliation of being labeled '*atisqa*' (abandoned by their less powerful ancestors and conquered), which came with the obligation of working for the victor;

7 Garcilaso de la Vega, Inca, *Royal Commentaries of the Incas* (Austin: University of Texas Press, 1609/1966/1987, hereafter GV), 88–89, 97, 226–227, 393, 396; Felipe Guaman Poma de Ayala, *El primer nueva corónica y buen gobierno*, eds John V. Murra and Rolena Adorno, 3 vols. (México: Siglo Veintiuno Editores, 1613/1980, hereafter GPA), 182 [184], 192 [194].

8 GV, *Royal Commentaries*, 97, 393.

with the potential division of the population and exile of some; and the possible loss of their traditional leaders. Once subjugated, though, ethnic groups were often treated with leniency, but made to accept the same conditions imposed on those who chose alliance.

All but a few served alike, required to provide tribute labor to the state. Anyone with a large family and following was considered 'rich,' because together they could finish the task quickly. Anyone with no children or family was considered 'poor,' because he had no one to help him finish his work. Those who were rich, finishing their tasks quickly, helped the poor for a day or two. Exempted from such tasks were those of royal blood; generals, captains, and soldiers on active duty; chieftains and their closely related kinsmen; youth under the age of twenty-five[9] who still served their parents; old men (aged over fifty); and all women, whether married or maidens, spinsters or widows. The sick until completely recovered, and all the disabled, were also exempt; although the deaf and mute were allotted chores for which they did not need to hear or speak. Priests and certain chosen women (*acllas*) did not serve. Commoners who held imperial posts were exempt while acting as officials.[10]

The rules governing tribute labor included the injunction that no one could be compelled to perform or undertake any craft but his own, unless it was the tilling of the soil or military service, two duties to which all were generally liable. All the craftsmen who worked for the Inca or his chiefs were furnished with everything necessary for their work; thus, for example, the smith was given ore and the weaver wool or cotton. The craftsman had to provide only his skills and the time to finish a task.

Tribute tasks and the items produced were recorded on *quipus* and the goods, after royal expenses, were devoted to the general well-being and placed in the common storehouses against times of need. Royal expenses included what was required to satisfy the needs of the royal household and its service and the items that were given as a reward to the captains and lords who had brought them, for even though their followers produced these objects, they were not allowed to use them except as a privilege with the Inca's permission.[11]

Ethnic lords were required to report births and deaths. The Incas used these numbers to apportion the labor obligations for public works, such as bridges, roads, and royal buildings. Demographics also determined the number of men who went to war, either as soldiers or as porters. If anyone returned from the war without permission, his presiding officer blamed him or his immediate

9 The Incas did not use years to gauge a person's age.

10 GV, *Royal Commentaries*, 272–274; GPA, *Primer nueva corónica*, 186 [188], 190 [192].

11 GV, *Royal Commentaries*, 275.

authority in his place, and he was punished with death for desertion and treachery in having disloyally abandoned his comrades, his relatives, his commander, and, finally, the Inca or the general who represented his person. The demographic reports also helped the Inca assess the existing abundance or want among each ethnic group, so that the quantity of supplies necessary to succor them in years of scarcity and bad harvests might be known and addressed. The ruler thought that in case of need there should be no delay in meeting the wants of his subjects.[12]

To facilitate administration, the Inca appointed officials who served him directly. Near the top of the managing structure sat four governors, one for each part of the empire. These consulted with two persons of royal blood on an advisory board to counsel the emperor on affairs of peace and war. They also collected reports about all that happened in the kingdom of concern. The Inca gave commands to this council on what to do in important situations that then passed to officials along the administrative hierarchy from rank to rank, down to the lowest. Under these were officials with various responsibilities: a counsellor, from the noble class; a second-in-charge, chosen from the elite; and high-level magistrates who each carried a staff as identity, specifically to arrest nobles. There were also a host of minor officials, including sheriffs, accountants, and scribes.

Guaman Poma de Ayala describes another imperial official called a *tocricoc* (literally, 'he who looks at everything'), which he equates with itinerant governors and specially commissioned judges. These inspectors and investigators secretly visited the ethnic groups to see what an official did wrong and to report it to superiors whose duty it was to punish their subordinates. All these officials, says Guaman Poma, were named to govern and bring good justice and well-being to the empire.[13]

At the level of the ethnic group, the state organized a decimally based hierarchy of authorities to rule the population (Table 2.1). The decurion of ten, for example, had the responsibility of being aware of any need of any household under his jurisdiction and reporting any offence, however slight, which had to be referred to the official above him, whose duty it was to apply a punishment. If any case of more importance or greater atrocity than usual occurred for which a higher judge was required, lower level lords informed the official above them in rank. These authorities acted as judges, one superior to another, and settled cases, ideally within five days, according to the seriousness of the

12 Ibid., 100–101.

13 GPA, *Primer nueva corónica*, 183 [185]–185 [187], 307 [309], 311 [313].

TABLE 2.1 Demographic basis of a lord's title and status

Lord	Jurisdiction by households
Hunu	10,000
Pisca guaranga	5,000
Guaranga	1,000
Pisca pachaca	500
Pachaca	100
Pisca chunga	50
Chunga	10

SOURCE: GV, *ROYAL COMMENTARIES*, 94

crime. The Incas held that delay in punishment encouraged delinquency. These authorities with administrative control and judicial jurisdiction were the very ones that Urteaga named as de-facto judges.[14]

These ethnic judges had no discretion about the penalties. Since the origin of the laws was thought to be divine, breaking any of them was sacrilege and punished accordingly. Officials were obliged to apply penalties in their integrity, under pain of death for infringement of the divine command. Any use of discretion, they thought, would make judges venal and open the door to a manipulation of the system, as, in theory, the severity and consistency of punishment resulted in little crime.[15]

The lower judges reported the sentences they gave each month to superior judges, and these reported to yet higher judges, according to the kind and seriousness of the business. The reports were made to show that due diligence had been administered so that the lower judges should not neglect it. If they disregarded it, they faced a more or less severe penalty, according to the need he failed to meet by his negligence. These penalties for injustice or fault were harsher than any a private person faced for a similar crime and more severe the higher the office. Anyone, for example, who did not inform on the transgression of a subject, even though it was only an unjustifiable delay of a day, made the fault his own, and was punished on two accounts: for neglecting his

14 GV, *Royal Commentaries*, 94.

15 Ibid., 97.

own duty and for the other's transgression, which he had made his own by not reporting it. And as each officer had another to watch over him the first tried hard to do his duty and fulfill his obligation conscientiously. For they said that it was intolerable that any who had been chosen to give justice should do wrong or that one sent to punish faults should commit them. Such wrongs were considered an offence to the Sun and to the Inca who had chosen him to be better than all his subjects.[16]

Such harsh dealings with transgressors in the service of the Inca were based on the ideal that governors should attend to two things with great attention: the first, that they and their subjects should observe and fulfil perfectly the Sun's mandates; and the second, that they should consider with great vigilance and care the common and particular interests of their followers.[17]

Examples of punishments of powerful lords and nobles who broke conventions and abused their authority were confinement in a jail called the *zancay* (discussed below) or exile to areas inhabited by the dreaded Chuncho Indians who were said to eat human flesh. Malfeasance of most other judges, whatever their rank, was confinement in the *pinas* jail (described below), and, if found guilty, death or an exemplary punishment. One such punishment was dropping a hard stone about the size of half of an adobe brick from a height of 2 *varas* (about 6 feet) onto his back. This killed some immediately. Those who survived and could be cured, recovered, although they were often left crippled.[18] There was one variation. A 'protector' existed for those who were close to the Inca, like the highest officials: lords of 10,000 households (the *huno apo*) and captains. The Inca helped them, while they were held in a special complex with food and services.[19]

Garcilaso de la Vega reminds his readers that there was a judge for every ethnicity with powers to give a final decision in suits between the inhabitants except those between one group and another, for which the Incas sent a special judge of the royal blood. These judges, after an inquiry, tried to reconcile what the two parties claimed. They rendered decisions in the Inca's name that became inviolable law, as if pronounced by the emperor himself. If the judge failed to reconcile the parties, he reported what had happened to the Inca with his recommendation about the claims of each party and the obstacles to settling the dispute. The Inca then pronounced sentence; or if the judge's report

16 Ibid., 98, 101.

17 Ibid., 397.

18 GPA, *Primer nueva corónica*, 312 [314]–313 [315].

19 Ibid., 305 [307].

did not satisfy him, he ordered the case to be suspended until he should next visit the ethnic groups so that he could see for himself and decide accordingly.[20]

In general, there were few offenders for none dared do what he ought not, for his accuser was near and his punishment set. This was generally a sentence of death, however slight the crime, for the punishment was not for the crime done nor for the wrong caused but for breaking the commandment and word of the Inca who must be respected as a direct descendant of a god. Even though the aggrieved person desisted from a complaint, justice was applied by obligation as part of the ordinary duties of the officers, and they applied the full penalty prescribed by the law in each case according to the degree of the crime, which might be death, whipping, exile, or the like.[21]

As mentioned above, when applied, confinement was in one of two types of jails. The *zancay* or perpetual jail was for traitors and major criminals. It extended below ground and was very dark. Poisonous snakes, lions, tigers, bears, foxes, dogs, mountain lions, vultures, eagles, owls, frogs, and lizards populated the space. In theory, these animals attacked and consumed the wrongdoers. Those who survived two days in the *zancay* were removed, by order of the Inca, and declared innocent and pardoned. The fear of the *zancay*, wrote Guaman Poma, kept rebellions from occurring. Lords, descendants of ancient kings who were 'more than the Inca,' kept quiet for fear of perishing among the wild beasts.[22]

The second type of jail was called the *pinas*, designed for ethnic lords and commoners. Prisoners were not jailed long, for they were promptly tortured so they confessed. Then, they were sentenced to death, given a physical punishment such as lashes, exile to the mines or the tropical lowlands, or assigned to another occupation. Exiled natives were forced to work hard as punishment and as an example of their blame.[23]

2 Commonly Understood Customs for Communal Living

Among the various chroniclers' accounts, the writings of the bilingual and very curious mestizo priest Blas Valera are the most representative of the rules at the ethnic group level. These laws were said to date back some 600 years from the time of Valera's writing; thus, some were still being observed in the second

20 GV, *Royal Commentaries*, 94–95, 98–99.

21 Ibid., 95.

22 GPA, *Primer nueva corónica*, 303 [305].

23 Ibid., 187 [189]; 305 [307].

FIGURE 2.3 The *zancay*, a subterranean prison filled with dangerous animals where violators of customary law were placed to indicate guilt or innocence. The Royal Danish Library, Copenhagen, GKS 2232 4°: Guaman Poma, *Nueva corónica y buen gobierno* (1615), p. 302, Drawing 118, Punishment and justice

half of the sixteenth century.[24] Valera's eight laws, though sometimes reflecting his own times (late sixteenth century) and not the reality of pre-Hispanic society (as will be noted below), included:

(1) the 'municipal law' – This granted each ethnic group the preservation of its own customs, presumably only if they did not contradict imperial law.

(2) an 'agrarian law' – Valera wrote that officials periodically distributed lands to household heads. The land measure they used was the '*tupu*' (also *topo*), which he equated with the *fanega* (a unit of dry measure equal to 1.5 bushels of corn in Mexico before 1580). More commonly, a *tupu*, according to other chronicles, was an area of land sufficient to provide subsistence to a couple. It was not a fixed measure, because it varied by type of seed, quality of soil, and climatic conditions. For example, a *tupu* for planting potatoes in a cold highland location was necessarily larger than a *tupu* for planting corn in a well-watered plot in a warmer clime. This portion of his writings reflected the practice after the Spanish mandated that the dispersed rural population be resettled in Spanish-style towns, called *reducciones*, in the 1560s and 1570s, and not pre-Hispanic practice. Valera's assertions that Inca laws held that every ethnicity or lineage should have definite limits enclosing heath, pasture, woods, rivers, lakes, and fields were also Spanish introductions that were still being unevenly implemented at the start of the seventeenth century.[25]

In fact, before the *reducciones*, all farmland was considered *sapçi*, translated as that which is common to all. A lineage member and his family could use as much abandoned land as they could productively work for as long as it remained fertile. Once depleted, the peasants moved to another empty plot, leaving the first fallow to regenerate and revert to a wild state, at which point another was free to use it.[26]

(3) a 'common law' – This mandated that all members of a community, except the elderly, the young and the ill, work together on common projects, such as building of temples, maintaining roads, and the like.

24 GV, *Royal Commentaries*, 262.

25 Ibid., 242, 394; María Rostworowski de Diez Canseco, 'Mediciones y cómputos en el antiguo Perú' in *La tecnología en el mundo Andino*, eds Heather Lechtman and Ana María Soldi (México: Universidad Nacional Autónoma de México, 1982), vol. 1, 379–405.

26 Susan Elizabeth Ramírez, 'Land and Tenure in Early Colonial Peru: Individualizing the *Sapci*, "That Which Is Common to All"' (2016) 2(2) The Medieval Globe 33–71.

(4) a 'humanitarian or brotherhood law' – This prescribed that the members of an ethnic group help each other to prepare, to plant, and to harvest a field; or to build a house; without providing payment of any kind. The third and fourth laws involved the ancient practice of collective labor. According to Garcilaso de la Vega who describes the practice for planting, the whole population would assemble, working in common and helping one another, to till the lands assigned to produce tribute for the king, the Sun, and their paramount lord. Then, they planted the lands of the widows and orphans and those who were unable to work owing to age or ill health. They followed the same practice in harvesting and transferring the crops to the royal or common storehouses. They built their houses in the same fashion. The native who needed a house would go to the ethnic authorities to appoint a day for it to be built. The population assembled with one accord to supply their kinsman's want and soon the house was finished.[27]

(5) a '*mitacanácuy* law' – This was a custom that men take turns working on common projects. Consequently, members of each ethnic group, lineage, and family took a turn, not to be repeated until all others had rotated through the task. *Mita* labor, as it was commonly called, was used to clear roads; and to decorate, to repair, or to reconstruct the temples of the Sun and other sanctuaries of their faith. They constructed public buildings, such as granaries; repaired roads and bridges; acted as messengers (*chasquis*); cleaned irrigation canals; grazed camelids; and served at lodging houses (*tambos*) to accommodate travelers.[28]

(6) a 'law of ordinary expenditure' – This law prohibited sumptuous clothing, covered with gold, silver, precious gems, or colored plumage for all but royalty or as a special privilege granted by the king; and excesses in banquets and feasting. The sumptuary rule was relaxed on the first day of the month and other days of festivals or solemnities, so that the people could dress better, but always with moderation. Elsewhere, Garcilaso de la Vega noted that people were to eat with frugality, though they had more liberty in drinking. Yet, in the latter regard, there were well-understood limits. Punishment for drunkards might include the indignity of having members of the immediate family step on his stomach so that he would vomit or cough up the beer that he had imbibed.[29]

27 GV, *Royal Commentaries*, 242–244, 394–395.

28 Ibid., 275–276.

29 Ibid., 291, 394; GPA, *Primer nueva corónica*, 313 [315].

But lest the population should weary by continuous toil, the Inca mandated that there should be a holiday of three days every lunar month. At these times, which ideally coincided with another ritual occasion, all lineage members, adults and children, the poor and orphaned, widows, sick, old, the blind and crippled, pilgrims and hikers, and shepherds and farm hands, ate together with their leaders in the plaza of their ceremonial centers. They also were to play military or popular games to reconcile with their enemies, to preserve the peace, and to share in the merriment. At these feasts, they would also see and hear whatever the Inca or his Council ordained.[30]

(7) a law 'of the poor' – The poor included the blind, the deaf and mute, the lame, crippled, the decrepit elderly, the long-term ill and other handicapped persons who could not farm, clothe, or eat by themselves. It mandated that they should be maintained from the common storehouses. A subsidiary law ordered that guests, strangers, pilgrims and hikers be provided for from the same stores.

(8) a 'ley *casera*' or 'domestic law' – This held that no one be lazy. The able-bodied had to work at something whether it be making ropes and sandals or tanning hides. Everyone should busy himself at his trade to serve his family or masters or work for the good of the commonwealth. Artisans, shepherds, weavers, cooks, administrators, scribes, singers and musicians, soldiers, and many other specialists were punished if idle. Even children of five, six, or seven were given a task suitable for their years. The blind, the lame, and the mute who could work with their hands were given tasks. The old were required to scare birds off the planted fields. Idleness was considered a breeder of discontent and penalized. People regarded punishment for sloth as a most degrading and dishonorable thing. Garcilaso de la Vega notes that there were special judges to suppress idleness who annually accounted for the work done.[31]

A second part of the same law required that natives eat with their doors open so that officials could visit them to make sure that they were taking care of their house and family and teaching their children obedience, solicitude, and a work ethic. They were to be either publicly praised or punished, according to the inspector's findings.[32]

---

30 GV, *Royal Commentaries*, 262–263, 294, 394; GPA, *Primer nueva corónica*, 192 [194].

31 GPA, *Primer nueva corónica*, 191 [193], 314 [316]; GV, *Royal Commentaries*, 248, 263, 394.

32 GV, *Royal Commentaries*, 263; Urteaga, *La organización judicial*, 47–50.

3 Other Crimes and Punishments

Additional crimes and punishments appear in these pages and those of other chroniclers.[33] Among the most serious crimes were irreligiosity, treason, and rebellion; murder; and theft.

3.1 *Irreligiosity, Treason, and Rebellion*

There were multitudes of commands and prohibitions dealing with the Inca religious practices, beginning with the most affronting, any attack on the person of the Inca or his officials. Even swearing at the father Sun or mother Moon, at the stars (e.g., Venus), ethnic divinities or ancestral gods, or the Inca or his wife, or the authorities was prohibited and punished severely.[34]

Rebellion was the ultimate treason and sacrilege. It was especially commonplace among newly incorporated groups. If an ethnic lord rebelled against the Inca, a powerful lord, or the Sun, he was put to death without appeal. There was no discretion in punishment, it was swift and severe. The guilty could be quartered and given to the animals in the *zancay* for food or, in other cases, the skin of the rebel or traitor was made into a drum; his bones were carved into flutes; his teeth were strung and made into necklaces, and his skull became a beaker to drink maize beer. The Inca once boasted: 'We will drink from the skull of the enemy, we will wear the necklaces of [his] teeth; we will play the flute of the bones; the drum of the skin and so we will dance.'[35]

The king also ordered that the calendar of rituals and sacrifices should be kept on pain of death of the individual and his family and relatives. In extraordinary times of ice or sleet or in times when the corn dried because it had not rained, all should walk about the hills crying and asking their gods for relief, dressed in mourning, with their face tinted black with sour plums.[36] Furthermore, in times of pestilence, tempests, or the death of an Inca or of a high-ranking lord, or rebellion, no one was to have a party nor dance nor sing nor play a flute. Men were prohibited from sleeping with their women. In times of fasting and penitence, no one was to eat salt or chili pepper or meat or fruit or drink maize beer or even cooked food. Only white, uncooked corn was consumed as atonement.[37]

---

33 For a comprehensive list, see Sally Falk Moore, *Power and Property in Inca Peru* (New York: Columbia University Press, 1958), Appendix.

34 GPA, *Primer nueva corónica*, 185 [187]; GV, *Royal Commentaries*, 102.

35 GV, *Royal Commentaries*, 96 and 548; GPA, *Primer nueva corónica*, 187 [189]–188 [190], 311 [313], 314 [316]. Elsewhere GPA said that traitors were condemned to life in jail (305 [307]).

36 GPA, *Primer nueva corónica*, 182–183 [184–185], 190–192 [191–193].

37 Ibid., 190 [192].

FIGURE 2.4 Penitence: Procession of penitents. The Royal Danish Library, Copenhagen, GKS 2232 4°: Guaman Poma, *Nueva corónica y buen gobierno* (1615), p. 284, Drawing 111, Processions, fasts, and penitence

Punishments for liars and perjurers and those who bore false witness against the Sun and other gods and sacred things were punished with twenty lashes from a rope that had large endings and ruined the innards. Garcilaso de la Vega adds that most people were humble and devout in their beliefs, and they knew if their lies were detected they would be punished brutally and often with death if the case were serious. Additionally, a witness knew that to speak to any judge was to address the Inca himself, whom they adored as a god, and it was chiefly out of regard for this, as well as for other reasons, that they told no lies.[38]

3.2 *Murder*

In general, given the importance of numbers of followers to a man's rank and status, the populous was enjoined from killing each other. The Inca ordered that a murderer should die by the same manner that he killed if with stones or with a beating. But there were various scenarios for murder. If someone was killed while being robbed, the guilty was put in jail, tortured, and later killed. For killings in a brawl, a judge would find out who had started the fight. If the dead person was at fault, the judge exiled the murderer to sickly and unoccupied lands; if the killer was the cause of the problem, he was immediately executed.[39]

In another instance, the principal lord who killed someone without getting permission from the Inca was publicly punished by dropping heavy stones on his back. This was the punishment for the first offence. If it happened again, he was condemned to death, and, if by pleading, he was granted his life, he was deprived of his position and jurisdiction and exiled to distant lands. This was one of the mandates that disappeared after the Spanish arrival. Paramount lords of the ethnicities killed their own subjects for various reasons with impunity until Spanish justice arrived in the countryside in the mid-1560s.[40]

Murder by sorcery also brought the death penalty. For these who they called healers; herbalists; prognosticators; and those who guarded the secrets of medicines, snakes, frogs, and objects that killed people, execution was mandatory. Not only was the sorcerer condemned to death but also his family (including children and grandchildren) so that no one was left who knew the spells. Nursing babies escaped death because they did not know the trade. The others

38 GPA, *Primer nueva corónica*, 313 [315]; GV, *Royal Commentaries*, 74.

39 GPA, *Primer nueva corónica*, 188 [190]; GV, *Royal Commentaries*, 397; Urteaga, *La organización judicial*, 40.

40 Urteaga, *La organización judicial*, 40; GV, *Royal Commentaries*, 226–227, 397; Ramírez, 'Land and Tenure.'

were all destined to a disgusting death, for example by quartering, in a field with their children and peers. They were left unburied as food for the condors and other birds of prey and foxes of the field. Poisoners were treated in the same way.[41] Related to this was the law that if someone received a non-life-threatening wound such as a broken bone, the responsible person would receive the same punishment as the aggrieved and nothing more.[42]

3.3 *Theft*

The great material equality for most of the population meant that theft was not a grand problem. According to Garcilaso de la Vega, those caught were subject to 500 lashes for the first offence and for the second they would be stoned to death or hanged. Their body was to go unburied so that foxes and condors would consume the remains.[43] But those who found something and returned it right away were not punished as thieves. A special case was for individuals accompanying the court on trips around the empire. If anyone traveling with the Inca entered the sown fields or houses of the commoners, even though they did little harm, he was killed. Likewise, soldiers were never allowed to rob or sack ethnic populations that were reduced by force of arms.[44]

4 Other Norms

4.1 *Succession*

Succession was a principal concern at all levels of Andean society. Usually, the most apt was chosen, subject to successfully completing an ordeal and oracular indications. The chroniclers wrote that, preferably, the oldest son of the Inca by a sister inherit the position; if not him, the eldest son considered as legitimate by blood; followed by the next oldest. If there were no sons, the nearest male relative succeeded. Administrative records show succession within ethnic groups varied. Successors could be brothers or nephews.[45] Garcilaso de la Vega indicates that the Inca rarely deprived of their powers those who inherited a chiefdom by birth. If one of them committed a crime requiring deprivation of his office, the Inca entrusted the chiefdom to one of his children or brothers

41 Urteaga, *La organización judicial*, 40; GPA, *Primer nueva corónica*, 311 [313].

42 GPA, *Primer nueva corónica*, 314 [316].

43 Ibid., 187 [189].

44 GV, *Royal Commentaries*, 102, 115–127, 266, 397.

45 Ibid., 208–209; María Rostworowski de Diez Canseco, *Curacas y sucesiones* (Lima: Librería Imp. Minerva, 1961).

FIGURE 2.5 Chief Priest and Witchdoctor, a prejudiced Europeanized depiction of native priest and healer worshipping the devil. The Royal Danish Library, Copenhagen, GKS 2232 4°: Guaman Poma, *Nueva corónica y buen gobierno* (1615), p. 277, Drawing 108, High priests

and commanded the rest to obey him. According to Pedro Cieza de Leon, the same principle was observed in time of war: ethnic captains from the various ethnicities from whence they recruited their troops were never displaced from command. They kept their posts even as field commanders and other generals of the royal blood were set over them.[46]

4.2 *Domestic Laws*

The rules of religiously sanctioned behavior extended down to familial and lineal units. Men were incentivized to have large families. The Inca maintained that some take multiple wives for his service and the increase in numbers in the realm. A paramount lord, ideally, had fifty wives; a lord of a thousand households had twenty; and a commoner had two. A corollary to this schedule was that women were punished for aborting. If the woman aborted a female baby who died, for instance, the woman received 200 lashes and was exiled.[47]

In addition, it was thought that he who engendered a child should be honored. The father of two or three children should be rewarded. He who had four children should be exempted from tribute labor and those who had five children should be named a *mandoncillo* (lower official, overseer) of his children and their families. And, he who had ten children should be a named a higher lord and those who had thirty, forty, or fifty children should be allowed to settle on unoccupied land and be named the lord of a lineage.[48]

The Inca also ordered that the youth and children should serve their parents until age twenty-five and be obedient to their fathers and mothers, the elderly, lords, and other siblings. A child was punished for the crimes he committed like anyone else, according to the gravity of the offence, even though it was no more than childish naughtiness. The penalty was increased or lessened according to the age and innocence of the person. For disobedience, the really young would be scratched from ear-to-ear until the child screamed and cried. Older children would be whipped for the first offence; and for the second, they were exiled to the silver and gold mines. Fathers were severely punished for not having instructed and corrected their children from an early age so that they should not grow up naughty or acquire bad habits. The official policed such duties, so that parents brought up children with care lest they should be guilty

46 GV, *Royal Commentaries*, 96.

47 GPA *Primer nueva corónica*, 188 [190]–189 [191].

48 Ibid., 188 [190]–189 [191].

of wanton acts. These punishments for the young were accepted as a guarantee that good order and honor reigned.[49]

Marriage was also regulated. Imperial authorities ruled that no one marry his sister or his mother, cousin, aunt, niece, or godmother on pain of punishment and the removal of both eyes and being quartered and left as an exhibit in the hills, because the Inca alone could marry his blood sister. John H. Rowe, long a student of Inca society, writes that the only exceptions were the nobles who were allowed to marry their half-sisters. Furthermore, marriage outside the lineage (*ayllu*) was forbidden. And, no native could change his lineage or ethnic dress, on pain of 100 lashes.[50] There were also rules about what Christians call morals, although those documented in the seventeenth century already had a thick veneer of Catholicism by the date they were recorded. Adulterers who destroyed the reputation and rank of others and took away their peace and happiness were considered thieves, and therefore condemned to death without any reprieve. If the two consented to adultery, both were punished alike to death, by stoning. They were not to be buried so that the vultures and foxes ate them, and the bones would be dispersed on the ground.[51]

For cases of rape, if the man forced the woman, the man alone was sentenced to death and the woman received 200 lashes and a life sentence to serve the Inca's women. If the woman forced the man, they sentenced the woman to death and the man to lashes and exile to the jungle to live with the Chunchos so as to never be seen again. Guaman Poma describes another punishment as lashes with a rope with a stone at its end that harmed the entrails. Just fifty lashes left a male or female half-alive.[52]

Finally, inspectors even assessed the cleanliness of a household and hamlet. All houses, clothes, pots, and almost anything that had been made, including the planted fields and the pens of guinea pig raisers, were to be inspected for cleanliness twice a year. Personal hygiene was also assessed and punishments levied for dirty hair, a stinking mouth, and unwashed hands and feet. Reprimands could be up to 100 lashes, besides being given all the dirt of the body to drink. An account was also kept of the manure that had been applied to the fields and whether or not each house kept a store of wood, straw, and

49 GPA, *Primer nueva corónica*, 186 [188]–187 [189], 314 [316]; GV, *Royal Commentaries*, 95, 226–227.

50 GPA, *Primer nueva corónica*, 190 [192], 192 [194]; John H. Rowe, 'Inca Culture at the Time of the Spanish Conquest' in *Handbook of South American Indians*, ed. Julian H. Steward (Washington, DC: U.S. Government Printing Office, 1946), vol. 2, 251–252, 254.

51 GV, *Royal Commentaries*, 397; GPA, *Primer nueva corónica*, 307 [309], 311 [313].

52 GPA, *Primer nueva corónica*, 188 [190], 309 [311], 312 [314].

FIGURE 2.6 Stoning, an example of one of the native mandated punishments for infractions of traditional law, here represented as stoning a couple for adultery. The Royal Danish Library, Copenhagen, GKS 2232 4°: Guaman Poma, *Nueva corónica y buen gobierno* (1615), p. 306, Drawing 120, Capital punishment by stoning of adulterers

potatoes for the family and for the runners on the royal highway. Finally, households were ordered not to bury their dead in their house on pain of exile.

They were to bury their dead, instead, in vaults and funerary constructions with their possessions and food and drink.[53]

5 The Sun's Will and Divine Retribution

The Andean norms for right and wrong cannot be understood without the benefit of their religio-political context. A hierarchy of officials doubled as judges to implement the will of the Sun as interpreted by the reigning king. Punishment for breaking the rules was usually swift and unforgiving. Yet the system offered a small number of attenuating features: the use of trial by ordeal (such as the *zancay*) to determine blame or innocence and separate considerations for nobles and high-ranking officials. The efficacy of the system allowed the native chronicler Guaman Poma, perhaps with some exaggeration in his attempt to portray the Inca regime as superior to Spanish colonial rule, to write that the people were obedient to Inca righteousness. Consequently, he concluded that their system did not allow for conflicts nor lies nor thieves, only truth and good justice and law. What cannot be determined from this vantage point is the extent to which the commands and prohibitions of the Sun were put into practice and implemented.[54]

References

Basadre, Jorge. *Los fundamentos de la historia del derecho*. Lima: Librería Internacional del Perú, 1956.

Borah, Woodrow. 'The Spanish and Indian Law: New Spain.' In *The Inca and Aztec States*, edited by George A. Collier, R.I. Rosaldo, and John D. Wirth, 165–188. New York: Academic Press, 1982.

Garcilaso de la Vega, Inca. *Royal Commentaries of the Incas*. Austin: University of Texas Press, 1609/1966/1987.

Guaman Poma de Ayala, Felipe. *El primer nueva corónica y buen gobierno*, edited by John V. Murra and Rolena Adorno, 3 vols. México: Siglo Veintiuno Editores, 1613/1980.

Moore, Sally Falk. *Power and Property in Inca Peru*. New York: Columbia University Press, 1958.

53 Ibid., 186 [188], 189 [191], 191 [193]–192 [194], 313 [315]–314 [316].

54 Ibid., 307 [309].

Pease, Franklin. 'Aproximación al delito entre los Incas.' *Revista Derecho* 29 (1971): 52–62.

Ramírez, Susan Elizabeth. 'Land and Tenure in Early Colonial Peru: Individualizing the Sapci, "That Which Is Common to All."' *The Medieval Globe* 2:(2) (2016): 33–71.

Ramírez, Susan Elizabeth. 'Amores prohibidos: The Consequences of the Clash of Juridical Norms in Sixteenth Century Peru.' *The Americas* 62(1) (2005): 47–63.

Rostworowski de Diez Canseco, María. 'Mediciones y cómputos en el antiguo Perú.' In *La tecnología en el mundo Andino*, edited by Heather Lechtman and Ana María Soldi, vol. 1, 379–405. México: Instituto de Investigaciones Antropológicas, Universidad Nacional Autónoma de México, 1982.

Rostworowski de Diez Canseco, María. *Curacas y sucesiones*. Lima: Librería Imp. Minerva, 1961.

Rowe, John H. 'Inca Culture at the Time of the Spanish Conquest.' In *Handbook of South American Indians*, edited by Julian H. Steward, vol. 2, 183–330. Washington, D.C.: U.S. Government Printing Office, 1946.

Trazegnies Granda, Fernando de. '¿Hay un 'Derecho' prehispánico?' *Ius et Veritas* 3(4) (1992): 44–49.

Trimborn, Hermann. *El delito en las altas culturas de América*. Lima: Universidad Nacional Mayor de San Marcos, 1936/1968.

Urteaga, Horacio. *La organización judicial en el imperio de los Incas*. Lima: Librería e Imprenta Gil, 1928.

Urteaga, Horacio. *El imperio Incaico, en el que se incluye la historia del ayllo y familia de los Incas*. Lima: Librería e Imprenta Gil, 1931.

CHAPTER 3

Law in Spanish and Portuguese America: The Early Colonial Period

Heikki Pihlajamäki

1 Introduction

After the Spanish and Portuguese conquest, the social and demographic conditions of the continent changed dramatically. Preconquest figures have been difficult to assess, but scholars have estimated that, for example, the population of Central Mexico dropped from 25 million in 1519 to 2.65 million in 1568, and that of Peru plummeted from nine million in 1532 to 1.3 million in 1570. The decrease in population was mainly due to diseases such as smallpox, tuberculosis, and measles brought by the Europeans.[1]

Not only were political and demographic transformations immense. The European conquerors dramatically changed the law of the Americas as well. Before this, the conquest needed an internationally recognized legal framework. Upon receiving information of the newly discovered lands in America in 1493, the Castilian rulers Ferdinand and Isabella asked the Spanish-born Pope Alexander VI to confirm the discoveries in their name and thus ward off the Portuguese and other European powers. The Pope, asserting his universal rule, issued bulls establishing a demarcation line at 100 miles west of the Cape Verde Islands and reaching from the North Pole to the South Pole. The lands west of this line, discovered or undiscovered, were to belong to the Castilian dominion. The rights of the Portuguese were restricted to the east of the line. The Portuguese – not to speak of other European powers, which by the late fifteenth century had trouble acknowledging such wide-reaching papal powers – were not content with the papal disposition and demanded new limitations. The Treaty of Tordesillas (1494) then moved the demarcation line to 370 leagues west of Cape Verde (about 46° 40' west of Greenwich), enabling the Portuguese to claim Brazil, which Pedro Álvarez Cabral had discovered in

1 J.H. Elliott, 'The Spanish Conquest and Settlement of America' in *The Cambridge History of Latin America: Vol. 1, Colonial Latin America*, ed. Leslie Bethell (Cambridge: Cambridge University Press, 1984), 202.

 | DOI:10.1163/9789004436091_005

1500, and to establish profitable maritime routes between Europe, Africa, and America.

This chapter starts with an outline of the legal justification of the conquest. We then proceed to a brief overview of the legal historiography of the Spanish colonies in the sixteenth and seventeenth centuries. Spanish colonial law as a specialized research area emerged in Spain and Argentina in the early twentieth century, and has remained viable ever since. It is worth noting that no corresponding research branch ever appeared on the Portuguese side. We should also acknowledge the fact that legal historians have almost exclusively dealt with (written) law with European origins, whereas Indigenous law has received much less attention. The same applies to this chapter, and not just because of the European biases that have largely dominated legal history. European learned laws wiped off much of the Indigenous laws, just as the conquest wiped out most of the Indigenous political, cultural, and social structures. Much the same, of course, happened in medieval and early modern Europe, where unwritten customary law could only partially find its way into the array of accepted legal sources in the early modern period and, finally into the nineteenth-century legal codes.

The following parts of the chapter will explain the sources of early Spanish colonial law, which were partly similar as in Europe, but partly distinctive. The chapter then moves on to the administrative institutions of Spanish America after which, albeit briefly, we examine some of the substance of the law itself. Before conclusion, a subchapter will explain the historiography and law of colonial Brazil.

This chapter emphasizes the Spanish colonies for two reasons. First, the Spanish conquerors used law more effectively than the Portuguese as a tool of colonial governance; and second, the secondary literature on Spanish colonial law is far greater than the information we have on law in Portuguese America in the early colonial period. Fortunately, the material available still allows for some comparative conclusions.

The periodization is mostly practical and follows from the fact that the next chapter of this volume continues from the late colonial period onwards. As in Europe, so in the Americas; the eighteenth century brought changes, which speak for its separate treatment, together with the early nineteenth century.

2 The Justification of the Conquest

The conquest of America was not the first that Europeans embarked upon. Therefore, they had legal arguments prepared for the colonization. The legal discourse justifying the war against non-Christians, their conversion, and eventual colonization, had already developed in the Middle Ages in connection to the Crusades to the Holy Land. The most famous of the legal discourses developed in the thirteenth century, when the jurist-pope Innocent IV wrote a commentary on the bull *Quod super his*, which his predecessor Innocent III had issued. The discussion, upon which leading early modern theorists on human rights such as Francisco de Vitoria and Hugo Grotius later commented, was about the rights and duties of pagans under natural law. The question was: when was the conqueror entitled lawfully to dispossess pagan people from their *dominium*, or lordship and property. According to Innocent IV, under normal circumstances and in natural law, pagan people were allowed to possess property and to choose their own leaders. However, the so-called Petrine mandate justified an exception. Christ had entrusted the first Pope, St. Peter, the duty of taking care of the souls and spiritual well-being of the entire humankind, pagans and infidels included. This led Innocent IV to the conclusion that the Pope could at times intervene in all secular affairs. All people belonged to the papal jurisdiction if not de facto at least de iure, because 'all men, faithful and infidels, are Christ's sheep by creation even though they are not of the fold of the church.'[2] In practice, however, this universal papal jurisdiction needed to be limited to situations where pagans clearly violated natural law. Cases of idolatry, for instance, created circumstances in which violation of natural law required papal intervention, because 'it is natural for man to worship the one and only God.'[3] The Pope – and only the Pope – could thus authorize war against infidels.[4]

The conversion of barbaric tribes in both western and eastern Europe, the Norman conquest of Britain, and the Crusades to the Holy Land are examples of missions fueled and justified by the legal framework that the thirteenth-century lawyer-pope had helped to create. Innocent IV's ideas were further tested in the so-called Lithuanian Controversy, which took place at the Council of Constance (1414–1418), when Poland contested the right of the Teutonic Knights to convert forcefully pagan Lithuanians.

The Crusades were not the only practical experience in conquests that the Portuguese and Spaniards had gained. The *Reconquista*, taking back the Iberian Peninsula from the Muslim rule was an important basis, and the conquest

2 Brian Tierney, *The Crisis of Church & State 1050–1300* (Eaglewood Cliffs: Prentice-Hall, 1964), 155–156.
3 James Muldoon, *Popes, Lawyers, and Infidels* (Philadelphia: University of Pennsylvania Press, 1979), 109.
4 Williams, Jr., *The American Indian*, 13–14.

of the Canaries in the late fifteenth century was important as well. Both the Portuguese and the Spanish showed increasing interest toward the strategically and commercially important North African region. From the fourteenth century onwards, Portuguese expeditions set off to western Africa (Upper Niger, Senegal, and the Gold Coast) and the island groups of Azores, Madeira, and the Canaries. In the legal controversy that followed from the Spanish rejection of the Portuguese activities in the Canaries, Pope Nicholas V took sides with the Portuguese. His bull *Romanus Pontifex* (1453–1454) was again an elaboration of the basic arguments, which Innocent IV had presented two centuries earlier. It confirmed the Portuguese right to the African 'provinces, islands, ports, districts, and seas [...] which have already been acquired and which shall be acquired in the future.'[5]

Once the first colonizers had reached America, the Spanish crown had two legal problems. First, they had no prior decree from the Pope to legitimize Columbus's expedition. Second, the expedition 'to the Indies' had to be related somehow to the title that the Pope had awarded Portugal. Papal authorization was extremely significant considering how quickly the Spanish crown sent its ambassadors to Rome to petition authorization from the new Aragon-born Pope, Alexander VI (Rodrigo de Borja, 1492–1503). Owing personal favors to the Spanish crown, the Pope soon issued bulls temporarily solving both Spanish legal problems regarding the colonization of America. The first bull, *Inter caetera* (1493), declared that since Columbus had now encountered people 'undiscovered by others,' and which were 'well disposed to embraced Christian faith,' all of the newly discovered lands and those that would be discovered would belong to the Castilian rulers. Generous as *Inter caetera* may seem from the Spanish point of view, Ferdinand and Isabel's jurists were not satisfied with it. The bull seemed still to leave open the question as to who owned the lands possibly to be discovered. There was also the risk that Portuguese and others might read the bull as referring only to some of the Caribbean islands close to Columbus's first discovery, Hispaniola. At the request of the Spanish crown, the Pope issued an updated version of the bull, *Inter caetera II*, which established the demarcation line between the Portuguese and Spanish spheres at 100 leagues west of the Azores. In the Treaty of Tordesillas (1494), the line was extended to 370 leagues west of the Cape Verde Islands.

In *Inter caetera II*, the Pope granted Ferdinand and Isabel 'full, free, and integral power, authority, and jurisdiction' in the newly conquered territories. On pain of excommunication, any competing power was prohibited from

5 As quoted in Williams, *The American Indian*, 72.

approaching Spain's possession whether it be for reasons of trade or for other reasons. Securing the geographical extension of the conquest, however, was only the beginning of legal discussions that followed in subsequent centuries. The rights of the pagan population, which had been on the agenda since Innocent IV, soon became the focal point of discussion. It started with the arrival of Dominicans in America in 1510. They soon noted that, as a result of recently introduced infectious diseases, the number of Indigenous people was rapidly declining. St. Thomas Aquinas's religious order, the Dominicans, felt responsible for upholding his natural law theories and, suspicious of the arguments propounded by Innocent IV, soon began to criticize the way Spaniards treated the Indigenous population. Friar Antonio de Montesinos started a campaign of criticism in 1511, when he, directing his words to the Spaniards gathered in his church, declared that they lived in mortal sin, 'for the cruelty and tyranny' they used in dealing with the Indians. Outraged but at the same time afraid that the Dominican critique might find resonance in Rome, Ferdinand organized a top-level conference with like-minded lawyers and theologians in Burgos to ponder on the matter. The meeting produced a legal document called the Laws of Burgos (1512). These laws reaffirmed Indigenous people's right to humane treatment under natural law, but also claimed that the subjugation of the Indians was necessary to save them from idleness and then to Christianize and civilize them. In addition, the Laws of Burgos regulated the life of the Indians and the responsibilities of the *encomenderos* in detail.[6]

Spaniards did not cease using the law to justify their colonial enterprise. Besides internal critique coming from Spain and the colonies themselves, external critique from other European nations not satisfied with Spain monopolizing large tracts of potential colonial lands prompted Spanish rulers to justify their enterprise. King Francis I of France, for instance, declared: 'The sun shines on me as well as on others. I should be very happy to see the clause in Adam's will which excluded me from my share when the world was being divided.'[7] To provide valid legal reasoning on the contested points, Ferdinand asked two prominent professors of the University of Salamanca, Spain's most renowned intellectual hub of the sixteenth and seventeenth centuries, to draft

6 The literature on this theme is large. See, for instance, Lewis Hanke, *The Spanish Struggle for Justice in the Conquest of America* (Philadelphia: University of Pennsylvania Press, 1949), 24–25; M.C. Mirow, *Latin American Law: A History of Private Law and Institutions in Spanish America* (Austin: University of Texas Press, 2004), 85–86; Silvio A. Zavala, *La encomienda indiana* (Madrid: Centro de Estudios Históricos, 1935), 15–20; Silvio A. Zavala, *Las instituciones jurídicas en la conquista de América* (México: Porrúa, 1971), 260–318.

7 Hanke, *The Spanish Struggle*, 148.

expert opinions on the disputed matter of the treatment of Indians. Matías de Paz, a theologian, and the law professor Juan López de Palacios Rubios wrote commentaries strongly supporting the crown's position. Paz's commentary relied on the idea of the Pope as holding temporal jurisdiction, delegated by Christ, over the whole world. Since Pope Alexander VI had in turn delegated this jurisdiction to the temporal ruler of Castile, his *dominium* of the New World was lawful. López recycled the old arguments of Innocent IV. In natural law, infidels possessed *dominium* over their lands, but the Pope could withdraw this right because of his temporal jurisdiction. He could then rightfully delegate the *dominium* to a temporal prince (such as the Spanish crown) who might subjugate infidels if necessary.

As the next step in his campaign to justify the treatment of the Indians in America, Ferdinand asked Juan López de Palacios Rubios to draw a charter of conquest. In 1513, the crown issued the *Requerimiento* ('Requirement'), 'a most remarkable document' as historian Lewis Hanke called it.[8] It was not a theoretical tract but instead a simple text to be read aloud to any group of local habitants encountered in America, before a war could lawfully commence against them. According to the *Requerimiento,* the Indians had to comply with two obligations. The first was to accept the church and the Pope as the superior ruler of world, and the Spanish kings, by virtue of the papal donation 'in his stead as superiors, lords, and kings of these islands and of this Tierra Firme.'[9] The second obligation Indians were to accept was to be preached the Christian religion. Denial meant war, the preparations of which were often well under way while the document was being read to the Indians.[10]

Although formally abolished in 1566, the *Requerimiento* and the colonial policy behind it had already given rise to mounting critique. Basing their judgment on Thomistic-Humanist philosophy, the critics claimed that all humans were rational beings. Therefore, they had the right to self-government and autonomy. The Spanish colonization had effectively denied them this right. Many of the critics belonged to the Dominican Order, which had become the backbone of the Spanish Inquisition and was therefore not an easy opponent to the crown. Many of the Dominican friars openly questioned Spanish colonial practices on both theoretical and practical grounds. The controversy caused the Spanish crown to allow a series of experiments during the first half

---

8 Ibid., 31.

9 Ibid., 33.

10 On the historical genealogy and centrality of the *requerimiento* as a means to justify the Spanish conquest see Patricia Seed, *Ceremonies of Possession in Europe's Conquest of the New World, 1492–1640* (Cambridge: Cambridge University Press, 1995), Chapter 3.

of century to find out whether Indians were truly capable of being civilized and to live like Christian Spaniards or whether Indians were slaves by nature. One such experiment was conducted by three Hieronymite monks under the leadership of Bartolomé de las Casas, one of the most famous critics of Spanish colonization.[11] In 1518, de las Casas (now appointed as 'Protector of Indians') received a royal order to establish free Indian villages in the New World. The experiments largely failed to show that Indians would have been able to be converted into an American version of the Spanish farmer. They revealed the resistance of the Indians themselves, their deeply different tribal customs, and insurmountable cultural differences.[12]

The Dominicans not only criticized Spanish colonialism from the practical point of view. Some of the sharpest theoretical critics were also Dominican friars. The Spanish scholars no longer believed in universal temporal jurisdiction of the Pope; instead, they continued in the Thomistic tradition of natural law, now to be applied to all human relations and those between nations. These scholars fit well together with the common struggle of both the Spanish crown and the Spanish church to free themselves of papal authority that, over the years, repeatedly had attempted to establish itself within the Spanish empire.

Regarded as the founder of the School of Salamanca and 'the father of international law,' Francisco de Vitoria (ca. 1483–1546) is the brightest example of a systematic critic of Spanish colonial practices. He was one of the most influential scholars of his time and a frequent consultant to the crown. Although Vitoria never went to America, his opinions on the legal situation of Spanish America carried great weight. Vitoria denied the Pope's universal power. Because the Pope possessed no such power, his delegation to temporal rulers was unlawful as well. Indians were free and rational, and they possessed natural rights. A refusal of the Indians to recognize papal *dominium* and their denial to subdue to the Spanish rule could not justify war against them.[13]

It would be a mistake, however, to read Vitoria or his fellow critics as modern human-rights champions. The inhabitants of America were entitled to the natural rights, but Indians were bound by the universal norms of the profoundly Eurocentric Law of Nations. Just war against the Indians was possible

---

11 See generally, Kenneth Pennington, 'Bartolomé de las Casas' in *Great Christian Jurists in Spanish History*, eds. Rafael Domingo and Javier Martínez-Torrón (Cambridge: Cambridge University Press, 2018), 98–115.

12 Williams, *The American Indian*, 96.

13 See generally, Andreas Wagner, 'Francisco de Vitoria' in *Great Christian Jurists*, eds Rafael Domingo and Javier Martínez-Torrón (Cambridge: Cambridge University Press, 2018), 84–97.

if the Indians transgressed those norms, regardless of how aware they were of their contents. In such circumstances, their lands could be conquered and colonized. Spaniards had the right to settle in America, and they had the right to practice trade freely. If Indians tried to prevent them from engaging in these activities, Spaniards could wage war against them. Furthermore, Indians had to accept that Spaniards could preach the Christian faith to them. If Indians attempted to prevent this, a war could again lawfully follow. As Richard Williams asserts, 'whether with the best of intentions, and whether through policies of extermination or forced conversion, the Spaniards who brought the burdens of European civilization to the Indians ultimately succeeded only in erasing a multiplicity of cultures and beliefs from the New World.'[14] To be sure, other cultures were soon added.

The Spaniards and the Portuguese brought slavery with them. During the early modern period, approximately 1.3 million Africans were brought, for the most part in the ships of Portuguese merchants, to Spanish America, and approximately five million to the Portuguese colonies. Slavery had been common on the Iberian Peninsula even before the conquest of America, and enslaved humans were used both as domestic servants and industrial workers. Spanish law, however, saw slavery as undesirable, and the *Siete Partidas* provided for comparably generous means of manumission. Jews and Muslims could not enslave Christians, masters could set slaves free, and slaves could buy themselves free, for example. Even though the *Siete Partidas* in principle condemned slavery, Spanish law accommodated enslaving people.

In America, various statutes prohibited the enslavement of Indians. The prohibition of enslavement had much to do with the clerical campaign for the Indigenous people explained above. Bartolomé de las Casas, for instance, was strictly against the enslavement of Indians. Even though nominally free, Indians became the backbone of systems of forced labor called *encomienda* (to which we will return further below) and *mita*. Africans, in turn, were classified as inferior to the Indigenous people and could be enslaved. Race matters, however, could be complex. For example, despite their low status (and unlike Indians) Black enslaved humans were part of the Spanish community (*República de los españoles*). They often learned Spanish and had better ways of integrating into the Spanish society than Indians. Black slaves were even used as overseers (*mayordomos*) of the supposedly free Indian *encomienda* laborers. Compared to those in North America, enslaved humans in Spanish and Portuguese America had better chances of being freed and integrated into

14 Williams, *The American Indian*, 96.

colonial society. Many scholars explain this by the fact that Roman law manumission became part of the Spanish and Portuguese legal orders, which did not happen in the North American system based on English common law. This may have contributed to a relatively rapid decline of slavery in most parts of Spanish and Portuguese America.[15]

2.1 *Historiography of Spanish Colonial Law*

For the past century, a sub-discipline of legal history called *derecho indiano* has dominated the study of law in Spain's American colonies. The term means literally 'the law of the Indies' but will here be used synonymously with 'Spanish colonial law.' *Derecho indiano* was essentially a creation of the Argentine historian Ricardo Levene (1885–1938). Levene's first publication on the subject, *Introducción al estudio del derecho indiano* (1916) became the foundational work of the research field. Levene was himself influenced by some of his teachers, including the legal sociologist, Ernesto Quesada. In the 1930s and 1940s, other scholars such as Rafael Altamira, Jorge Basadre, Manuel Ots Capdequi, and Manuel Belaunde Guinassi followed suit and further developed the notion of *derecho indiano*. From the 1950s onwards, the Spanish legal historian Alfonso García-Gallo emerged as the leading figure in the field. In his various works, such as *Problemas metodológicos del derecho indiano* (1967), García-Gallo set up the research agenda for subsequent decades. As António Manuel Hespanha once wrote, Levene identified and in fact created Spanish colonial law as an extension of Castilian law, and gave it the name *derecho indiano*, whereas García-Gallo reconstructed it as a legal system with its own system of sources.[16]

To ensure their continuity, research fields need institutional frameworks. Together with the Chilean Alamiro Ávila-Martel and the Argentinian Ricardo Zorraquín Becú, García-Gallo founded the *Instituto Internacional de Historia del Derecho Indiano* in 1966. The *Instituto* held its first international meeting that year and has been organizing them ever since on both sides of the Atlantic.

15 Robert J. Cottrol, *The Long Lingering Shadow: Slavery, Race and Law* (Athens: University of Georgia Press, 2013); Alejandro de la Fuente and Ariela J. Gross, *Becoming Free, Becoming Black: Race, Freedom and Law in Cuba, Virginia, and Louisiana* (Cambridge: Cambridge University Press, 2020).

16 António Manuel Hespanha, 'O 'direito de Índias' no contexto da historiografia das colonizações ibéricas' in *Actas del XIX Congreso del Instituto Internacional de História del Derecho Indiano* (Madrid: Dykinson, 2017), 42–83, 50.

The conference proceedings are published, and the *Instituto* publishes works as well.[17]

Spanish colonial law has always mirrored developments of general legal history. Born in the 1920s, *derecho indiano* was one of the first research areas in law to break out from the purely nationalist paradigm, which had developed in the late nineteenth-century law throughout the Western world. This escape, however, was only partial and superficial. *Derecho indiano* was at the same time an expression of *hispanoamericanismo*, or Hispanic-Americanism. This variant of pan-nationalism was popular among Latin American and Spanish intellectuals during the three first decades of the twentieth century and had its roots in the early nineteenth-century ideas of *Hispanidad*, or Hispanicity. Hispanic-Americanism saw the Castilian-speaking nations that had previously formed the Spanish Empire in Spain and America as a cultural entity. Among the most influential representatives of the movement were the historian and philologist Marcelino Menéndez Pelayo, the novelist Miguel de Unamuno, and the historian Rafael Altamira, one of the founding fathers of *derecho indiano*. The *hispanoamericanistas* wished to replace the foregone glory of Spanish colonialism with a new, cultural variant, exalting the common values of the Iberoamerican nations. Not all representatives of *hispanoamericanismo* were politically alike. Although Altamira was a liberal, the movement later came to be associated with the government of General Francisco Franco and his followers, the *franquistas*.[18]

The study of Spanish colonial law was predominantly positivistic and even legalistic until the 1970s, when methods of social science began to influence legal history everywhere in the West. The *Methodenstreit* in Germany and the rise of Critical Legal Studies are good examples of how the old positivist legal history was starting to shake. One would surely be hard-pressed to associate the leftist political thinking linked to the *Methodenstreit* or Critical Legal Studies with the research community of *derecho indiano*,[19] but reforms were demanded and began to occur in *derecho indiano* as well.

17 Thomas Duve and Heikki Pihlajamäki, 'Introduction: New Horizons of *Derecho indiano*' in *New Horizons of Spanish Colonial Law: Contributions to Transnational Early Modern Legal History*, eds Thomas Duve and Heikki Pihlajamäki (Frankfurt: Max Planck Institute for European Legal History, 2015), 1–2.

18 Hespanha, 'Direito de Índias,' 45–49; Xosé Núñez Seixas, *Suspiros de España: El nacionalismo español, 1808–2018* (Barcelona: Crítica, 2018), 53–54.

19 The Spanish legal historians Francisco Tomás y Valiente, Bartolomé Clavero, and their Portuguese colleague António Manuel Hespanha joined their western European radical colleagues in other Western countries by looking at legal history increasingly through the lenses of social science. However, their interests have only to a small part been directed to *derecho indiano*.

The Argentine legal historian Víctor Tau Anzoátegui has been the leading figure in the field of *derecho indiano* for many decades. In a programmatic text of 1997, he wished to see the scholarship of Spanish colonial law as related less to the 'rational and statutory state of law,' and more to different levels and modes of normativity, to the position of the jurist, and to casuistry as a character of legal decision making. Tau Anzoátegui then identified certain areas of Spanish colonial law, which needed more attention than they had received. These included the jurist, or *letrado*, as a legal actor, book history, local and provincial varieties of *derecho indiano*, as well as 'continuities and ruptures' of colonial legal heritage in the nineteenth century. All these phenomena needed study, according to Tau Anzoátegui, within their social, political, and economic contexts.[20]

The scholarship of Spanish colonial law has thus changed and, albeit with a certain delay, followed the trends in history and legal history in general. A major new trend of the last two decades in legal history, however, has been visible only slightly. That is the emphasis on comparative and global aspects of the law. Spanish colonial law, a seeming exception to traditional nationalist legal history as it is, has not yet taken up the comparative challenge. This may be slowly changing as well.[21]

Recently, the uniqueness of Spanish colonial law as separate legal order with its own 'spirit' and identity have been questioned. Hespanha denies the whole existence of *derecho indiano*. According to him, Spanish colonial law is a 'historiographical construction which results more from a certain understanding of Spanish colonization of the Americas than from a conception or a "reality" which exists in historical sources.'[22] If *derecho indiano* is essentially casuistic, as Tau Anzoátegui assumes, its systemic nature falls apart. Early modern European legal orders were not systemic, and to present them as such would be falling into a modern anachronism. Early modern legal orders were pluralist, multilayered combinations of local and general normative ingredients, and in these orders the general normative ingredients (*ius commune*), both in theory

20 Víctor Tau Anzoátegui, *Nuevos horizontes en el estudio histórico del derecho indiano* (Buenos Aires: Instituto Internacional de Historia del Derecho Indiano, 1997), 19–20, 57–126.

21 See, for instance *New Horizons of Spanish Colonial Law: Contributions to Transnational Early Modern Legal History*, eds Thomas Duve and Heikki Pihlajamäki (Frankfurt: Max Planck Institute for European Legal History, 2015). The Max Planck Institute for European Legal History at Frankfurt has recently been establishing itself as a leading center in comparative research on *derecho indiano*.

22 Hespanha, 'Direito de Índias,' 43. Translation from the original Portuguese here by Heikki Pihlajamäki.

and in practice, regularly ceded to local norms. Such a casuistic understanding of Spanish colonial law reduces to a minimum its singularity in comparison to European legal systems. At the same time, understood this way, the existence of *derecho indiano* as a coherent entity disappears completely. Instead of having one *derecho indiano* (even if conceived of as a kind of Spanish American local *ius commune*), we would in fact be faced with a multitude of local legal orders – just as was the case in Spain and elsewhere in Europe. Comparisons reveal other similitudes with the European law as well, and we will return to them below. It is sufficient to say now that the similitudes between Spanish colonial law and the European legal orders are perhaps more striking than the differences and peculiarities of *derecho indiano* – which of course exist.

The present stage of research on Spanish colonial law suggests an inevitable conclusion. *Derecho indiano* is not separate legal order, and even less a legal system, but at the most an umbrella term for the law and legal orders of the Spanish colonies in the Americas. The way Castile organized the law and legal administration in the colonies did not radically differ from the way European empires and conglomerate states organized the laws of their different constituent part in the Old Continent. This does not mean that Spanish colonial law was in no way different from other early modern legal orders and other colonial legal orders, but only that future comparative research will need to dig out the differences and similitudes – as comparatists do. It obviously means even less that Spanish colonial law could not constitute a research object of its own.

One field of comparison in which researchers of *derecho indiano*, so far, have engaged themselves only little, are comparisons with other early modern colonial laws.[23] This chapter cannot remedy the lack of research. However, we shall see how Portuguese colonial law differed from its Spanish counterpart.

2.2 *Sources of Spanish Colonial Law*

Spanish colonial law was based on the law of Castile. Until the beginning of the seventeenth century, Castilian law was automatically in force in America as well, unless a local rule existed on the matter. This normative ideology was

---

23 See, however, the articles of Richard Ross and Heikki Pihlajamäki in *New Horizons of Spanish Colonial Law*, eds Thomas Duve and Heikki Pihlajamäki (Frankfurt: Max Planck Institute for European Legal History, 2015); Richard J. Ross, 'Legal Communication and Imperial Governance: British North America and Spanish America Compared' in *The Cambridge History of Law in America, vol. 1, Early America (1580–1815)*, eds Michael Grossberg and Christopher Tomlins (Cambridge: Cambridge University Press, 2008), 104–142; and the various articles of António Manuel Hespanha cited in the notes to this chapter.

not in any way at variance with the contemporary European theory of legal norms. First came the local norms, then the norms of larger political units and at last the European *ius commune*, a form of European 'common law,' based on Roman and canon law. The norms of some large polities, such as the Kingdom of Castile in the case of Spanish America, could also be considered of kind of *iura communia.*[24] In theory, local norms had always precedence over general.

Spanish colonial law consisted of five components: European *ius commune*, Castilian law, legislation specifically issued for or in the Americas, and customary law as developed in Spanish America. In addition to that came Indigenous law, which remained partly in force. The European conquerors did not arrive at a legal vacuum. The preconquest legal cultures, however, were oral which is why our information of them relies mainly on Spanish sources. Some main characteristics of those legal cultures are relatively clear. As archaic legal orders tend to, American Indigenous legal cultures emphasized the family and clan instead of the individual. The laws of the Indigenous people were complexly intertwined with the communities' customary societal and religious practices and beliefs.[25]

As was the case in early modern legal pluralism, Castilian law and *ius commune* were deeply intertwined. The norms of *ius commune* had affected the legal practice in Castile since the beginning of university education in law in the thirteenth century and educated jurists had issued commentaries on it. *Ius commune* also directly affected the contents of Castilian law. The *Siete Partidas*, a collection of laws from the mid-thirteenth century under King Alfonso X, is a good example of intermingling of Castilian law (both written and customary) and *ius commune.*[26] In Castile, as in most regions of Europe, local customs, and laws as *iura particularia* complemented the general Castilian law. In the same way as Castilian customs and laws, colonial laws also complemented the Castilian law and *ius commune*.

When central political power concentrated in the crown in Castile, attempts to restrict the use of Roman law soon followed. The *Ordenanzas Reales de Castilla* (1480), *Leyes de Toro* (1505), and *Nueva Recopilación de Castilla* (1567) are the major examples of collections of Castilian law aiming at exclusivity. Despite the attempt at limiting Roman law, though, it continued widely in use.

However, it would be a modern fallacy to assume that early modern law consisted mainly of grand collections of law. Instead, early modern law was

24 On the difficult concept of common law, see H. Patrick Glenn, *On Common Laws* (Oxford: Oxford University Press, 1992).

25 See chapters 1 and 2 in this volume.

26 See generally, Mirow, *Latin American Law*, 49–54.

a jungle of norms ranging from a wide variety of piecemeal legislation carrying different names (ordinances, decrees, letters, *cédulas*) and privileges. Comparative legal historians group much of this piecemeal legislation under the common term of *policia* (*politia*, '*buen gobierno*,' *Polizey*). In order to govern effectively, early modern rulers commonly used *policia* legislation to regulate the minutest details of social life. Targets of control and regulation included a wide range of phenomenon such as, for example, luxury items and weddings, fire watch, weights and measures, coinage, trade sanitary measures, itinerant clowns and circuses, food supply, and poor relief. Some of the legislation included general provisions intended for everyone, while others responded to special legislative needs arising from individual cases and could be directed to specific authorities in America.

Privileges created and consolidated the positions of the different estates: nobility had its own privileges, while clergy and bourgeoisie had theirs. The great majority of the European population in early modern Europe, the peasants, in most countries, had no privileges. Castilian law remains incomprehensible without taking privileges and piecemeal legislation into account.

From the beginning of the American conquest, the Castilian crown and other organs in the peninsula issued large amounts of piecemeal legislation and privileges to regulate life in the conquered territories. In many cases, Castilian laws were not useful in the different circumstances that the conquerors encountered. Some American authorities, mainly the local *cabildos* and regional *audiencia*, issued normative material and developed customary law.

Law in the Americas thus consisted of several different layers, often difficult to keep track of and to distinguish from each other. As often happens in this kind of situation, at some point compilations of legal materials emerge. Often, the first collection grows out of private initiative, while official collections follow suit later. This was the case in Spanish America as well. The first collections appeared in the early sixteenth century, but few acquired success. The most widespread collections were those of Rodrigo de Aguiar y Acuña and León Pinelo. The most important official collection, *Recopilación de leyes de Indias* (1680), was based on their works. It is telling that León Pinelo, the compiler of the *Recopilación de las leyes de las Indias*, is said to have extracted the 11,000 laws of the compilation from approximately 400,000 royal laws.[27]

In addition to statutory law, legal literature was an important source for practicing lawyers. The most influential works were Juan de Matienzo's *Gobierno*

27 Clarence Haring, *The Spanish Empire in America* (Oxford: Oxford University Press, 1947), 113. See also Mirow, *Latin American Law*, 47–48.

del Perú, Política Indiana of Juan de Solórzano Pereira, and *Curia Philippica* of Juan de Hevia Bolaños. By way of introduction to these important works, a few words on each are merited.

Born in Valladolid in 1520, Juan de Matienzo first made a legal career in the chancery of his hometown. In 1538, he took an appointment as *oidor* (judge) at the Audiencia of Charcas, Vice-Royalty of Peru, and stayed in that position until his death in 1579. In Peru, Matienzo gained a reputation as an able lawyer and became one of the most important counsellors of Viceroy Francisco de Toledo. Matienzo published extensively. From the point of view of colonial law, his most important study was *Gobierno del Perú*. Written in Peru in 1567, the work never achieved print during the colonial period, but circulated in manuscripts. *Gobierno del Perú* appeared in print for the first time in 1910 and even then, based on a partial manuscript. The whole book was printed only 400 years after its completion, in 1967. Although a legal book, Matienzo's work is not a standard legal treatise. The Council of the Indies used *Gobierno del Perú* as a reference work, and it gained further acclaim as Juan de Solórzano Pereira referred to it extensively in his *Política Indiana*. *Gobierno del Perú* was a product of Renaissance humanism, and Tau Anzoátegui has described it as drafted with 'the same freedom as a person recently arrived in the New World felt.'[28] Matienzo used ancient literature, but as a Renaissance humanist scholar, he was less interested in the correct interpretation of sources than in using scholarship to meet the new challenges that Spaniards met in the New World.[29]

Born in Madrid in 1575, Solórzano studied law in Salamanca. He arrived in Peru in 1609 to serve as an *oidor* in the Audiencia of Lima and stayed there until 1627. Upon his return to Madrid, Solórzano was first appointed *fiscal* at the Treasury Council (*Consejo de Hacienda*) in 1628 and then in the following year, a member of the prestigious Council of the Indies (*Consejo de Indias*). In 1640, he was appointed member of the Council of Castile. Solórzano published many important works, some of which were concerned with other themes than Spanish colonial law. His first-hand experiences of colonial judicial administration in both the homeland and overseas led Solórzano to publish *De indiarum iure* (1629) and, ten years later, *De gubernatione* (1639). These two works were written in Latin and thus intended first as academic contributions, while

---

28 Víctor Tau Anzoátegui, *El jurista en el nuevo mundo: pensamiento, doctrina, mentalidad* (Frankfurt am Main: Max Planck Institute for European Legal History, 2016), 49.

29 On Juan de Matienzo and on the *Gobierno del Perú* especially, see Víctor Tau Anzoátegui, 'Gobierno del Perú' in *The Formation and Transmission of Western Legal Culture: 150 Books that Made the Law*, eds Serge Dauchy, Georges Martyn, Anthony Musson, Heikki Pihlajamäki, and Alain Wijffels (Cham: Springer: 2016), 121–123.

Política Indiana (1647) was a Spanish-language version of the two. *De indiarum iure* appeared in two volumes in six parts altogether. The parts had the following themes: the legitimacy and the reasons of the conquest; the relation between the crown and the Catholic Church; the government of the Indies; and the economy. Solórzano vigorously defended the Spanish conquest and possession of the Americas and its treatment of Indigenous people, which he thought should be and had been just.[30]

Juan de Hevia Bolaños, born in 1570 in Oviedo, differs from Matienzo and Solórzano in that he was primarily not an academic but a legal practitioner. He most probably did not have a university training but had learned law in practice. Hevia Bolaños started young, working at ten at a notarial office in Oviedo and at fourteen as a court clerk in Madrid. In 1588 or 1589, he was already in the New World, as a clerk at the Audiencia of Quito. In the beginning of the seventeenth century, Hevia Bolaños apparently worked as an advocate (*procurador*) in Lima, but always without an official position at the *audiencia*. He is known for his *Curia Philippica* (1603), as part of which an earlier work on commercial law was included. *Curia Philippica* was, above all, a procedural treatise. It first describes the royal courts and then explains the different procedures (civil, criminal, and ecclesiastical). The author also discusses the *residencia* procedures and the appeals system. *Curia Philippica* has been described as belonging to the tradition of *mos italicus*, although based mostly on Spanish legislation not Roman law. The book carries a large apparatus of notes with a huge number of scholarly references. Judged by the many editions it went through in the early modern period and even in the nineteenth century (the last edition appeared in 1841), *Curia Philippica* was a useful tool in the hands of practitioners.[31] The judicial structures where Matienzo, Solorzano, and Hevia Bolaños gained some of their legal experience, were matched by significant administrative structures.

2.3 *Administration and Its Controls in Spanish America*

In the early modern world, administrative structures could not be completely separated from judicial structures. The highest organ in charge of the overseas territories was the Council of the Indies with its seat in Seville. The

30 On Juan de Solórzano Pereira and on *De indiarum iure* especially, see M.C. Mirow, 'Juan Solórzano Pereira,' in *Great Christian Jurists*, 240–258; Ditlev Tamm, 'De indianum iure,' in *The Formation*, 182–184.

31 On Juan de Hevia Bolaños and on *Curia Philippica* especially, see Agustín Casagrande, 'Curia Philpppica,' in *The Formation*, 156–158.

Council enjoyed far-reaching legislative, advisory, administrative, and judicial functions.[32]

Two viceroys (in New Spain and Peru) together with several governors, as representatives of the crown, formed the top of the judicial and administrative hierarchy in the early Spanish American colonies. Below them, the *audiencias* were the highest judicial and administrative organs in the New World. They were modelled after the Castilian appeals courts in Valladolid and Granada. Unlike the Castilian courts, the American courts were not only judicial but also administrative organs. They were in charge of both civil and criminal cases emanating from lower instances, and had some first-instance jurisdiction as well. *Audiencias* acted also as *Real acuerdo*, the highest consultative body in service of viceroys and governors, and they were also in charge of issuing local legislation. At the levels of both viceroys and *audiencias*, *fiscales* oversaw the interests of the crown. With time, the *fiscalía* developed into an important consultative organ. Hence the saying '*como dice el Fiscal*' ('let us do as the fiscal says').[33]

This short presentation cannot go into the details of the complex local administration that the Spaniards established over time in America. The administrative structure was not uniform, and the administrative districts did not even cover the whole territory nominally under Spanish rule. The *corregidores* (and *alcaldes mayores*) represented the crown in towns, *Corregidor de Españoles* in Spanish towns, and *Corregidor de Indios* in Indigenous settlements. Besides other functions, the *Corregidor* was also a judge of first instance. By the mid-sixteenth century, *cabildos* (or town councils, following the model of the peninsula) were already in charge of town administration. The *cabildos* consisted of a varying number of *regidores*, or town councilors. The *cabildo* chose every year two *Alcaldes mayores*, municipal judges. This meant that town dwellers had three first-instance judges to choose from, the *Corregidor* or one of the *Alcaldes*.[34]

As Richard Ross has shown, the Spanish crown constructed an impressive network of legal communication to ensure at least a certain measure of legal control over the American colonies. The Council of the Indies exercised a key role here. The Council had the right to issue statutes independently, and it counselled the crown in legislative matters as well as those concerning mercy.

---

32 Horst Pietschmann, *Die staatliche Organisation des kolonialen Iberoamerika* (Stuttgart: Klein-Cotta, 1980), 110–111.

33 Ibid., 116–118. See also, Mirow, *Latin American Law*, 22–25.

34 Pietschmann, *Die staatliche Organisation*, 128–134. See also Mirow, *Latin American Law*, 24–27.

After the viceroys (who exercised no judicial function), the Council formed the top of the administrative hierarchy of America, thus leading the military, financial, judicial, and civil administration. Administering the proprietary rights of the crown vis-à-vis the Catholic Church, the Council also supervised the contact of the local clergy with the papal curia. The supervision of maritime affairs and overseas commerce belonged to the domain of the Board of Trade (*Casa de contratación*) as the first instance, but also here the Council of the Indies had the final word. Finally, yet importantly, the Council was the highest judicial instance in both civil and criminal cases emanating from America. During most of the sixteenth century, the members of Council had legal education. Towards the end of the century, also non-jurists with practical administrative experience from the colonies began to be appointed.[35]

Lawyers, however, remained always important. From early on, the Spaniards established a corps of legal professionals in the American colonies. Of course, jurists were not present in every township and court, but they existed and staffed at least the higher courts, the *audiencias*. The Spanish established universities with law faculties from early on: the University of San Marcos (Lima), for instance, was founded in 1551. Several more were created in other regions throughout the colonial period, becoming as central to daily life as the crown's bureaucracy.

The Spanish not only established an impressive bureaucracy in America. They also tried to ensure the controllability of the administrative and judicial machinery. In this, the procedures of *residencia* and *visita* were instrumental. *Residencia* was a legal innovation of the Spaniards themselves and had been used in Spain since the Middle Ages. In the Americas, however, the institution came to its widest use. At the end of his term in office, every crown official from viceroys to *corregidores* and *alcaldes* went through an audit or *residencia*. In the *residencia*, organized in form of public trial, a specially appointed judge (*juez de residencia*, normally the already chosen next officeholder) went through the accounts and other official documents produced during the term of the official under scrutiny. Those willing could also present accusations. Only after the documentary scrutiny was over and accusations cleared was the official physically free to leave the site. In case of irregularities, the official could be fined or even forbidden ever to hold public offices again.[36]

35 Richard Ross, 'Legal Communications and Imperial Governance: British North America and Spanish America Compared' in *The Cambridge History of Law in America, Vol. 1, Early America (1580–1815)*, eds Michael Grossberg and Christopher Tomlins (Cambridge: Cambridge University Press, 2008), 104–143.

36 See José María Mariluz Urquijo, *Ensayo sobre los juicios de residencia indianos* (Sevilla: Escuela de Estudios Hispano-Americanos, 1952).

The visitation (*visita*) was another significant instrument of control that the crown used to keep its functionaries in check. Visitation had its roots in medieval canon law, from which it had spread to secular administration and gained widespread use. Here too a special judge was appointed for the task. Visitations could be used flexibly for various purposes. Often, suspicions or rumors led to sending a judge on a mission of visitation to inspect whether particular officials or crown organs were performing their duties, as they should. Visitations could be routine or organized to inspect whether courts and administrative officials were following certain laws.

2.4 *Substance of Spanish Colonial Law*

Some of the law in the American colonies hardly differed from peninsular law, while other branches of law distinguished themselves from their peninsular and European counterparts over time. Private law, criminal law, as well as civil and criminal procedure were mostly the same as in Spain. Spanish and Portuguese shared the main features of private, criminal, and procedural law following the early modern *ius commune*, which was slowly but surely developing into local or national versions all over Europe. Unfortunately, we cannot enter into detail here.

In fact, *policia* or '*buen gobierno*' formed the kernel of the specifically colonial legislation and thus *derecho indiano* narrowly defined. Although the technique of legislation – issuing great numbers of statutes controlling and regulating a hugely wide variety of things – did not differ from police law in Europe or North America, its substance often bore a distinctively colonial mark. Some such areas of regulations were public administration, protection of Indigenous peoples, mines, and *haciendas*. Many of the matters covered by police regulations were not essentially characteristic for the colonies, although their details corresponded to American conditions. Examples include norms on judiciary, lawyers, notary, trade tariffs, prison, luxury products, construction, roads, postal service, and tithes.

The other aspect in which the law of the colonies distinguished itself from peninsular (and European) law was that, to a certain extent, the Indigenous laws and customs remained in force even after the conquest. Spaniards tolerated these laws in much the same way as local and religious laws were often tolerated in Europe, insofar as they did not conflict with rules of higher order. Indigenous laws, furthermore, only applied within the certain tribe and its members. The best-known exception of an Indigenous legal institution which survived the conquest and gained extensive application was the *mita*, an Incaic system of forced labor. In the *mita* system, each Indigenous tribe was to provide a certain number of workers for some months each year. The workers were transported to where their labor was needed.

2.5 *Portuguese Colonial Law*

'Without settlement there is no good conquest, and if the land is not conquered, the people will not be converted. Therefore, the maxim of the conqueror must be to settle,' wrote Francisco López de Gómara, a sixteenth-century historian of Spanish America.[37] The quote nicely encapsulates the essence of the Spanish conquest and clarifies its crucial difference to the Portuguese conquest. While the Spanish wanted to conquer and to settle, as they had done in the *Reconquista*, the Portuguese sought to secure their commercial interests by establishing plantations, trade posts, and maritime routes.

In social and political terms, Portugal was in many ways different from Spain. The crown of Portugal played an important part in the economy, while the national bourgeoisie was relatively weak. Revenues from the colonies were a significant source of income for the crown, although, for a long time, Brazil's economic importance remained far less important than India's. The king also enjoyed a strong cultural and religious role. He had wide-reaching powers of patronage and played an important role in the nomination of bishops and priests.

The historiography of Portuguese colonial law is different of that of *derecho indiano*. No Portuguese counterpart to Spanish colonial law as a distinct field of research ever emerged. No '*direito das Indias*' thus has ever existed. The reasons for this would merit a study of its own. The lack of Portuguese colonial law as a distinct field of study undoubtedly has something to do with the fact that no Portuguese equivalent to *hispanoamericanismo*, as a fertile ground to Portuguese colonial law, ever emerged. The self-conception that the Portuguese started developing in the late nineteenth century was worlds apart from the Spanish identities. The key figure in the construction of the Portuguese colonial self-image was the historian Joaquim Pedro de Oliveira Martins (1845–1894). In various works, he developed a theory of the 'genius of the Portuguese,' which consisted of the following characteristics, each one of which was in deep opposition to the characteristics of the Spanish people. The Portuguese was 'vague and fugitive,' not 'bluntly affirmative' like the Spaniard. A 'noblesse' of 'Lusitanian heroism,' unlike the 'fury [of their] neighbors'

37 Francisco López de Gómara, *Historia general de las Indias* (Madrid, 1852), 151; cited in J.H. Elliott, 'The Spanish Conquest and the Settlement of America' in *The Cambridge History of Latin America, Volume 1: Colonial Latin America*, ed. Leslie Bethell (Cambridge: Cambridge University Press, 1984), 149.

characterized the Portuguese. They had a sense of sentimentality and irony, which the Spaniards lacked. The Spanish were described as violent conquistadors, the Portuguese as emotional and sentimental seafarers.[38]

This self-conception affected, according to Hespanha, the way the history of Portuguese colonialism turned out in the writings of historians. Whereas the Spaniards and Latin American authors of *derecho indiano* constructed the image of colony as based on territorial sovereignty and a clear-cut legal system, the Portuguese historians described their colonial laws in vastly different terms. Whereas the Spaniards implanted relatively homogenous institutions in their colonies, the Portuguese chose a more multifaceted array of arrangements, which took into consideration the local conditions and preexisting institutions. The tradition of seeing Portuguese colonial history this way has continued until modern historiography. In 1985, Luís Filipe Tomás in an influential article explained that the Portuguese had invested relatively little in colonial administration and law and more in a communications network beneficial for commerce.[39]

Does the picture of Portuguese colonization of the Americas and other colonies stand the test of empirical historical scholarship? Although the aspects of a 'suave colonization' may have been exaggerated to fit the corresponding self-image, some characteristics nevertheless seem typical for the Portuguese legal take on the colonies and less so for the Spanish conquest. First, the Portuguese had clearly fewer resources to invest in their colonies. This is true for both human and material resources. Therefore, they were forced not even to attempt 'full' territorial conquest but instead to limit their control to the essential trading post and maritime routes.[40] For the same reason, it was a natural choice for the Portuguese to rely on the local, preexisting administrative structures – and laws. It was more economical than trying to implement a homogenous legal and administrative structure to cover all ultramarine possessions, not to speak of replicating the Portuguese system in the colonies. Normative material for the colonies was issued, but it was never compiled into a comprehensive

38 Valentim Alexandre, 'Questão nacional e questão colonial em Oliveira Martins' (1996) 31(1) Analise Social 185.

39 See Luís Filipe Tomás, *Estrutura política e administrativa de Estado da India no século XVI* (Lisboa: Instituto Investigação Científica Tropical, 1985); Hespanha, 'O "direito das Indias,"' 71–72.

40 It may be questioned; however, how 'full' Spanish territorial sovereignty was. The differences between Spanish and Portuguese colonies may better be described as differences in degree. See Lauren Benton, *A Search for Sovereignty: Law and Geography in European Empires, 1400–1900* (Cambridge: Cambridge University Press, 2015).

collection in the same way as was, for instance, the *Recopilación de las Leyes de Indias* for Spanish America.

Unlike the Spanish in their colonies, the Portuguese founded no universities in Brazil, although Jesuits set up their establishments of higher learning. The first law faculties were established only after the independence in 1827 (the law faculties of São Paulo and Olinda). No legal literature on colonial law, comparable to the Spanish works of Matienzo, Solórzano, and Hevia Bolaño, appeared during the early colonial period.

The Portuguese settlement of Brazil was slower than that of the Spaniards on their side of the 370-league line. In the beginning, the colonial interests of the Portuguese were mainly commercial. They were, therefore, less eager to establish permanent administrative structures to gather large tracks of land. It was far more important for them to secure sea routes and trading posts. After unsuccessful attempts to gain control of the North African continent in the fifteenth century, the Portuguese first turned to West African Islands, such as Madeira, Azores, the Canary Islands, and the Cape Verde Islands. The uninhabited Atlantic islands were legally construed as extensions of the Portuguese kingdom. The islands were given as fiefs (*doações*) to Portuguese seigneurs and then settled by immigrants from the mainland. Along Africa's west coast, the Portuguese adopted a different strategy. They adopted a practice of the medieval Italian merchant towns called (in Portuguese) *feitoria*, a fortified trading post.

The *feitoria* played a prominent role until 1534, when Portugal changed its colonial strategy. Instead of the *feitoria* system, the crown now decided to apply the same successful policy to the Atlantic islands. The entire land mass that according to the papal bulls 'belonged' to Portugal, east of the Tordesillas line, was divided with geometrically straight horizontal lines from north to south into fourteen captaincies. These huge tracts of lands were enfeoffed to fourteen lords along the lines of the feudal systems used in Europe. The donations were hereditary and belonged, together with their inhabitants, to the jurisdiction of the lord. As vassal of the Portuguese king, each lord was entitled to taxes from his captaincy, and he appointed the notaries, scribes, judges, and other officials. As in any feudal system, the noble vassal could in turn enfeoff parts of his land to vassals of his own. Even if the new strategy may have looked good on paper, in practice it did not work and most of the captaincies soon proved complete failures. The population of mainland Portugal was simply too small and the pressures to emigrate meagre. The American colonies could not attract enough settlers and Indigenous resistance was often a great obstacle to the settlers' interests.

The Portuguese crown was soon forced to take similar measures as the Spaniards had done on their side of the Tordesillas line: the royal government extended itself to America. In 1549, the first governor, Tomé de Sousa, took office in Brazil. This did not mean the abolition of the captaincies which formally remained until the great reforms of the eighteenth century. One of the governor's tasks was now to assist militarily the captaincies and their heads (captain-generals if appointed by crown and captains if hereditary officeholders). The original hereditary captains were assisted by crown judges (*ouvidores*). In 1588, a High Court of Appeals was set up in Bahia (*Relação de Bahia*), although the court did not begin to function until 1609, only to be suppressed again in 1626 as an economic measure due to the Dutch War. The High Court returned in 1652. The Court was presided by the governor-general and consisted of professional judges. The *ouvidores* of the captaincies were thus judges of first instance, while the High Court remained Brazil's only appeals court until the mid-eighteenth century.[41]

Portugal had organized its central colonial administration already before the conquest of Brazil. Most importantly, following Vasco de Gama's expedition, the *Casa de Índia* was established in 1501. During the sixteenth century, *Casa de Índia* became the most important institution administering all of Portugal's overseas colonies. Its main functions, however, were economic: the *Casa de Índia* was in charge of overseeing the crown's economic interests, crown monopolies, and customs. Most of the central institutions remained after 1580 when Portugal entered into a dual monarchy with Spain until 1640. After 1591, the *Casa* de *Índia* shared authority with the *Conselho de Fazenda* (Treasury Council), the *Casa de Suplicação* (an appeals court), the *Desembargo do Paço* (the supreme court for the kingdom and the colonies), and the *Mesa de Consciência e Ordens* for religious affairs. The most significant change during the dual monarchy was the founding of the Council of India (*Conselho de Índia*) in 1604. It was abolished in 1615 because of internal jurisdictional struggles between the different councils and tribunals.

Compared to the Spanish legal mechanisms described above, the Portuguese never created effective means of ensuring the flow of legal information from the colonies to Lisbon and from Lisbon to the colonies.[42] When it came to the governor-general of Brazil, the institutions of *residencia* and *visita* were in use. From 1621 to 1778, the Portuguese crown produced only 6,574 different

41 See Frédéric Mauro, 'Portugal and Brazil: Political and Economic Structures of Empire, 1580–1750' in *The Cambridge History of Latin America: Vol. 1, Colonial Latin America*, ed. Leslie Bethell (Cambridge: Cambridge University Press, 1984), 447–448.

42 Hespanha, 'O "direito de Índias,"' 79–80.

statutes altogether, and of these 954 were intended for the colonies. Half of all the statutes pertained roughly to the domain of economy and policing. The Portuguese crown thus contributed little in the way of legislation to the colonies, especially when compared to Castile.[43]

3 Conclusion

In J.H. Elliott's words, 'the operations of [Spain's] administrative and judicial bureaucracy were governed by a set of laws, dispositions, and practices that … had been developed in Castile but were subsequently adapted, as the occasion demanded, to the special requirements of the Indies.'[44] As the review of recent scholarship above has shown, describing Spanish colonial law as a well-organized system may be an overstatement. It is probably correct to draw the conclusion that many of these descriptions which in the past have made Spanish colonial law appear extremely well organized, owe much to the nineteenth-century picture of law as an autonomous, hierarchical system of norms. These images owe considerably to the traditional picture of Spain, created in the beginning of the twentieth century through historical, philological, and philosophical scholarship.

Despite these reservations, it seems that Spanish colonial law and its judicial system were nevertheless highly institutionalized, when compared to most other colonial systems. Portugal and Brazil are a case in point. Spain managed to create in and transfer to its American colonies legal institutions that enabled it to oversee, to control, and to steer the legal course of the overseas lands with relative efficiency. Portugal never got that far in the early colonial period. Portugal's starting points were different: its population was too small to yield any large contingents of settlers and, geographically, Brazil was extremely demanding. Portugal's main interests were, therefore, economic; it sought to secure commercial routes and trade posts, while the Portuguese legal infrastructure remained thin. Nonetheless, much more comparative research on early modern colonial laws is needed to say anything close to definitive about this.

---

43 See footnote 28.

44 J.H. Elliott, *Empires of the Atlantic World: Britain and Spain in America, 1492–1830* (New Haven: Yale University Press, 2006), 127.

References

Benton, Lauren. *A Search for Sovereignty: Law and Geography in European Empires, 1400–1900*. Cambridge: Cambridge University Press, 2015.

De la Fuente, Alejandro, and Ariela J. Gross. *Becoming Free, Becoming Black: Race, Freedom and Law in Cuba, Virginia, and Louisiana*. Cambridge: Cambridge University Press, 2020.

Duve, Thomas, and Heikki Pihlajamäki, eds. *New Horizons in Spanish Colonial Law: Contributions to Transnational Early Modern Legal History*. Frankfurt: Max Planck Institute for European Legal History, 2015.

Elliott, J.H., *Empires of the Atlantic World: Britain and Spain in America, 1492–1830*. New Haven: Yale University Press, 2006.

García-Gallo, Alfonso. *Estudios de historia del derecho indiano*. Madrid: Instituto Nacional de Estudios Jurídicos, 1972.

Hespanha, António Manuel, 'Direito comum e direito Colonial.' *Panoptica* 3(1) (2006): 95–117.

Hespanha, António Manuel, 'Uncommon Laws: Law in the Extreme Peripheries of an Early Modern Empire.' *Zeitschrift der Savigny-Stiftung: Germanistische Abteilung* 130 (2013): 180–204.

Hespanha, António Manuel, 'Modalidades e limites do imperialismo jurídico na colonização portuguesa.' *Quaderni fiorentini* 41 (2012): 101–135.

Hart, Jonathan. *Empires and Colonies*. London: Polity, 2008.

Levene, Ricardo. *Introducción al estudio del derecho indiano*. Buenos Aires: Valerio Abeledo, 1924.

Mariluz Urquijo, José María. *Ensayo sobre los juicios de residencia indianos*. Seville: Escuela de Estudios Hispano-Americanos, 1952.

Mirow, M.C. *Latin American Law: A History of Private Law and Institutions in Spanish America*. Austin: University of Texas Press, 2004.

Muldoon, James. *The Americas in the Spanish World Order: The Justification for Conquest in the Seventeenth Century*. Philadelphia: University of Pennsylvania Press, 1994.

Pietschmann, Horst. *Die Staatliche Organisation des kolonialen Iberoamerika*. Stuttgart: Klett-Cotta, 1980.

Ross, Richard. 'Legal Communications and Imperial Governance: British North America and Spanish America Compared.' In *The Cambridge History of Law in America, Vol. 1, Early America (1580–1815)*, edited by Michael Grossberg, Christopher Tomlins, 104–143. Cambridge: Cambridge University Press, 2008.

Seed, Patricia. *Ceremonies of Possession in Europe's Conquest of the New World, 1492–1640*. Cambridge: Cambridge University Press, 1995.

Tau Anzoátegui, Víctor. *Casuismo y sistema: Indagación histórica sobre el espíritu del Derecho Indiano*. Buenos Aires: Instituto de Investigaciones del Derecho Indiano, 1992.

Tau Anzoátegui, Víctor. *Nuevos horizontes en el estudio del derecho indiano*. Buenos Aires: Instituto de Investigaciones del Derecho Indiano, 1997.

The Cambridge History of Latin America: Vol. 1, Colonial Latin America. Edited by Leslie Bethell. Cambridge: Cambridge University Press, 1984.

Zorraquín Becú, Ricardo. 'Las aspiraciones del derecho indiano: Contrapuntos entre Ricardo Levene y Ernesto Quesada.' In *Memoria del X Congreso del Instituto Internacional del Derecho Indiano*, edited by Instituto Internacional del Derecho Indiano, 1767–1804. México: Escuela Libre de Derecho, 1995.

Zorraquín Becú, Ricardo. 'Nuevas consideraciones sobre el Derecho indiano.' *Revista de Historia del Derecho* 25 (1997): 501–524.

CHAPTER 4

From Justice to Law: Late Colonial and Early Republican Eras

Sarah C. Chambers

1 Introduction

The period from roughly 1750 to 1850 in Latin America, as in many parts of the world, was transitional for law, marked by gradual shifts toward the centralization and professionalization of legal practice and the concentration of judicial authority increasingly within state jurisdictions. The period also witnessed the expansion of popular presence in the courts whether as plaintiffs or defendants. By 1825, most of the region also underwent an important shift in political sovereignty from colonial to independent governance and, with the exception of Brazil, from monarchy to republics. This political change affected the legal transformations already underway but did not instigate a rupture in legal practice. Rather, leaders of new nations built upon incremental reforms initiated by Iberian monarchs in the eighteenth century. Until the mid-nineteenth century, the body of civil and criminal law remained largely intact, but the larger legal framework allowed for institutional tinkering and shifts in interpretation. As first the Iberian monarchies and then the emerging nation-states attempted to make state law dominant over existing plural legal fora, initiatives from above often created unanticipated openings for subalterns to press their own claims. This chapter argues that diverse Latin Americans over this period participated in transforming the legal culture – albeit in gradual, uneven, and still incomplete ways – from one that prioritized a flexible ideal of justice to keep society in balance to one more observant of positive law and standardized procedure.[1]

1 For comparative studies of similar shifts, see Lauren A. Benton, *Law and Colonial Cultures: Legal Regimes in World History, 1400–1900* (New York: Cambridge University Press, 2002), and Laura F. Edwards, *The People and Their Peace: Legal Culture and the Transformation of Inequality in the Post-revolutionary South* (Chapel Hill: University of North Carolina Press, 2009). I am grateful for feedback on earlier drafts of this chapter from Bianca Premo, Barbara Welke, Susanna Blumenthal, Kirsten Fischer, Lisa Norling, Katharine Gerbner, and members of the Atlantic Workshop at the University of Minnesota, to Sueann Caulfield for reading suggestions on Brazil, and to the editors Matthew Mirow and Victor Uribe. I do not hold them

 | DOI:10.1163/9789004436091_006

The subtle distinctions between law and justice are expressed linguistically in the terms *ley/derecho* (Spanish) and *lei/direito* (Portuguese). While the former in each dyad is translated quite easily into the English term 'law' and most often refers to written legislation, the latter carries multivalent meanings of both what is right (just) as well as a specific right under the law. As a shorthand, we could say that over this period right as justice shifted more toward rights as written in law. For most of the colonial period, dispute resolution was decentralized in multiple jurisdictions, connected symbolically and sometimes practically by the king's role as the ultimate arbiter of justice. Officials with judicial authority, only some of whom were professional judges, had wide latitude (*arbitrio judicial*) to consult not only multiple legal sources – canon and Roman law as well as local ordinances and royal compilations – but also custom and judicial commentaries in order to arrive at outcomes that they, and ideally litigants, perceived as fair and just.

Equity did not mean equality: judges adapted their sentences to the social status, ethnic identity, and gender of those involved as well as the particular circumstances of the crime or dispute. Often the goal was not a definitive ruling at all, but to reach conciliation among the parties.[2] Iberian monarchs in the eighteenth century began to centralize and to streamline this judicial system, attempting to subordinate the plurality of jurisdictions to new or reformed institutions more directly under their control. In addition, royal officials increased criminal enforcement of moral norms including matters that had previously fallen under the purview of the Catholic Church. For all the political rhetoric by national leaders after independence to distance themselves from colonial rule, they continued and even intensified the legal trends already underway. They completed the shift to an independent judicial branch, except at the very local level, and also expanded policing and criminal prosecution.

These transformations of legal practice were tied into larger trends in the Atlantic world, although with local variations. The philosophies and treatises that are categorized under the umbrella of the Enlightenment influenced both royal and republican reformers to promote uniformity in governance and law. One goal of rationalization was to promote freer circulation of land and labor,

---

responsible for the interpretation I put forward, but they all challenged me to deepen and clarify my ideas.

2 For an introduction to the colonial justice system, see Tamar Herzog, *Upholding Justice: Society, State, and the Penal System in Quito (1650–1750)* (Ann Arbor: University of Michigan Press, 2004) and Charles R. Cutter, 'The Legal Culture of Spanish America on the Eve of Independence' in *Judicial Institutions in Nineteenth-Century Latin America*, ed. Eduardo Zimmerman (London: Institute of Latin American Studies, 1999), 8–24.

but major changes in Latin American economies would not take off until the latter part of the nineteenth century. The ideal of universal legal personhood would also evolve slowly, but some status distinctions began to erode even under the monarchies. Although absolutists embraced philosophies that facilitated centralization of their rule, liberals also invoked new ideas to advocate checks on monarchical, if not state, power. Beginning around 1810, before the movements for independence, liberal parliamentarians in Spain and Portugal drafted constitutions that would institutionalize the separation of powers, set limits on royal absolutism, and extend universal laws throughout the empires. As the empires broke apart, new nation-states built upon these liberal reforms, promulgated their own constitutions, and established national judiciaries. Although constitutions marked an important shift in public law, most Spanish and Portuguese civil and criminal compilations from the colonial period remained in effect until nations issued new codes, in most cases not until several decades after independence. Within this legal pluralism, eighteenth-century monarchs and post-independence statesmen alike shared the goal of bringing greater adherence to state, or as it was called at the time 'national,' law (the term for royal orders and compilations as well as parliamentary legislation) over canon law and custom. Moreover, the wide discretion judges exercised in sentencing allowed them to adapt laws dating from the medieval and early modern eras to contemporary conditions, whether in the late colonial or early national period.

This chapter will trace the relative transition from justice to law in this period, therefore, through gradual shifts in practice and interpretation more so than through lawmaking. Viewed from below, the degree to which these trends were empowering or disempowering varied, depending on the particular context and on one's positionality in terms of ethnicity, socioeconomic status, and gender. Since courts were spaces where official and vernacular legal idioms were put into conversation, institutional reforms promulgated at the top created opportunities for popular engagement. In the eighteenth century, women and the enslaved embraced Enlightenment ideas about universal natural rights and increasingly sought written rulings establishing that they were entitled to protection from abuse. On the other hand, women along with men also found themselves more frequently targeted by police on morals or vagrancy charges. Independence further transformed legal as well as political subjectivity. Men who were mobilized to fight in the wars of independence between 1810 and 1825 subsequently claimed rights as citizen-soldiers and household heads, including the supervision of those defined legally as dependents. Although men of color were less likely to have effective means to claim citizenship, legal distinctions by race were largely removed from written law.

As heterogeneous legal subjects under imperial monarchies were reconfigured by their inclusion in or exclusion from citizenship, popular legal activism and institutional reforms mutually constituted the relative shift from justice to law.

This chapter draws on a robust historiography produced both within and beyond the Iberian world. Our understanding of jurisprudence and legal institutions is particularly indebted to scholars in Europe and Latin America, many of whom trained in law faculties. Historians in both North and South America, influenced by anthropological or sociological methodologies, initially turned to legal records in the archives in search of subaltern lifeways and traces of accommodation or resistance to domination. In recent decades, these approaches have converged to a degree as some legal scholars recognize that law cannot be isolated from society and some historians acknowledge that everyday life is infused with law.[3] Taking key insights from this literature, this chapter traces the gradual standardization and ascendancy of state law as the most distinctive trend in this period. Of course, generalizations will not apply uniformly throughout the region, as the relative timing of shifts and milestones varied, especially for the case of Brazil where the monarchy survived independence and enslaved labor remained widespread. Therefore, the chapter combines thematic and chronological organization. It will begin by examining legal claims and practices during the wars of independence to show that royalists and republicans largely invoked the same legal principles during this contest over sovereignty. Political independence opened new possibilities for legal subjectivity, but its impact on the practice of law would unfold only over several decades. The following sections, therefore, step back to consider trends that began during the late eighteenth century and continued after independence in three areas: reforms to judicial institutions and state law, criminal prosecution, and civil law.

1.1 *Independence: Parallel Applications of Law in Wartime*

The independence wars themselves are rarely studied from the perspective of legal history, but both royalists and separatists invoked the law to defend

3 For an earlier overview of some of these scholarly trends, see Carlos Aguirre and Ricardo Salvatore, 'Introduction: Writing the History of Law, Crime, and Punishment in Latin America' in *Crime and Punishment in Latin America: Law and Society since Late Colonial Times*, eds Ricardo Salvatore, Carlos Aguirre, and Gilbert Joseph (Durham: Duke University Press, 2001), 1–32. As a transnational field, different 'schools' or approaches are not as coherent as in U.S. legal history, but some of the works that have most influenced my thinking draw upon the 'Law as …' approach. Catherine L. Fisk and Robert W. Gordon, '"Law As …": Theory and Method in Legal History' (2011) 1(3) UC Irvine Law Review 519–542.

their own actions and denounce those of their enemies. In general, military commanders on both sides of the conflict justified the use of summary justice in wartime, while their civilian counterparts tried to preserve some degree of regular procedures. In either case, officials interpreted existing sources of law, such as medieval provisions on treason, rather than articulating new legal doctrines. Three arenas of law stand out: international norms governing warfare, special courts to consider charges of treason and collaboration, and the seizure of property from suspected enemies.

By the late eighteenth century many colonial elites who followed political developments around the Atlantic world hoped to loosen metropolitan restrictions on trade and exercise a greater degree of local governance. Some argued that independence was necessary to achieve those goals, but others pinned their hopes on reform rather than revolution. Those at lower levels of the social hierarchy – Indigenous peasants, artisans, the enslaved – also held diverse opinions on whether their interests were better served within or apart from the empire. A crisis at the top opened an opportunity for action in the colonies, but only after years of war and dashed hopes for liberalization within the empires did most Iberian colonies achieve independence.

Napoleon's invasion of first Portugal in 1807 and then Spain in 1808 triggered years of instability throughout those empires. In relative terms, Brazilians experienced less disruption because the Portuguese royal court evacuated to Rio de Janeiro. Brazilian subjects gained the opportunity to present petitions directly to João VI, and he raised the profile of Brazil by making it a co-equal kingdom to Portugal. There were some regional revolts calling for the establishment of republican rule, but none were successful. With the expulsion of the French from Portugal, liberals in parliament began drafting a constitution and recalled the king in 1821. When they also recalled his son the following year, Prince Pedro refused, joining with local elites to declare Brazil's independence and becoming its first emperor.

While the Portuguese royal family had escaped Napoleon, the Spanish monarch was captured in 1808. This power vacuum opened opportunities for colonial subjects, whether they favored reform or independence. Initially, few explicitly called for separation and those that did faced opposition from many of their fellow colonials as well as from resident Spaniards. When Ferdinand VII was restored to his throne in 1814, he launched military campaigns of retribution and attempted to tighten control over the colonies, measures that increasingly pushed local elites toward favoring independence. Although the intensity and timing varied, most regions experienced violent conflict at some point between 1810 and 1825, when the last royal troops were defeated on the continent. In some cases, the same territory changed hands multiple times, adding to polarization and uncertainty about the outcome.

Officers in both the royal army and pro-independence forces claimed to respect international law, yet both sides also frequently violated such norms. They negotiated truces and capitulations and issued amnesties and pardons, but given the shifting fortunes of war, these often held only temporarily or were not observed on the ground. Each side tried to claim the moral high ground, yet each could also be credibly accused of violations: summary executions of prisoners of war, massacres of civilians, sexual assaults on women. A famous proclamation by independence leader Simón Bolívar in 1813, as he fought to reestablish a republic in Venezuela after its defeat by royalists, captures such contradictions and double standards. He denounced the royalists for violating 'the most solemn agreements and treaties as well as basic rights, committing every manner of crime,' and declared that 'Justice demands vengeance.' Out of 'magnanimity,' he offered amnesty to Spaniards who would renounce their allegiance to the king and cooperate with the independence forces, but those who did not accept 'will be considered treacherous enemies and shot by a firing squad without chance of pardon.' On the other hand, those who had been born in the colonies (*americanos*) would be spared regardless of their allegiance: 'Spaniards ... you cannot claim neutrality. Unless you actively espouse the cause of *América*'s liberation, you will die. *Americanos*, you will live, despite any past misdeeds.'[4] Thus Bolívar variously characterized his enemies as combatants in an international conflict or accused them of treason under existing Spanish law.

As control of territory and claims to sovereignty shifted between royalist and pro-independence forces, questions of allegiance and loyalty became fraught. In the wake of battles, determinations of and retributions for infidelity were often made in courts martial with limited options for mounting a defense. Civilians and bureaucrats protested such summary procedures, pointing out that some accused of collaboration with the enemy had simply remained in their posts out of fear and the threat of violence. Throughout Spanish America, therefore, both parties established 'Purification' boards to determine the innocence or degree of culpability along with penalties, especially for administrators who had worked under opposition governments. A study of the board established by royal authorities after the reconquest of Bogotá in 1816 found that about 60 percent of 449 individuals examined were found guilty and

4 From the translation in Sarah C. Chambers and John Chasteen, *Latin American Independence: An Anthology of Sources* (Indianapolis: Hackett Publishing Company, 2010), 118–119.

sentenced to either fines or service in the army.[5] Acts such as desertion and espionage, however, continued to fall under military jurisdiction and could be punished with death, even for civilians. Women as well as men were accused of espionage or collaboration with the enemy if they crossed the battle lines between armies carrying letters or provisions.[6]

Another form of retribution used across Spanish America by both sides against their enemies and alleged collaborators was the seizure of real estate and other assets. Those who tried to establish a republic in Venezuela in 1811 confiscated property from royalists, and with the Spanish reconquest of that territory in 1814 the tables were turned. The commander of the expedition, Pablo Morillo, ordered the confiscation of property belonging to leaders of the rebellion against the crown, whose 'notoriety' meant there was no need for trials 'in order to be declared criminals of high treason.' Others accused of more 'passive' cooperation or of having fled from approaching royal troops also faced seizures but might have property restored or indemnified if they could prove their innocence or were pardoned. Even as the war continued, members of the Council of the Indies in Spain and royal magistrates in Caracas debated the legalities of specific measures, arguing, for example, that wives and children should not be punished for the crimes of husbands and fathers. Over the objections of Morillo, they often restored properties to returning émigrés or their families.[7] When an expedition similarly restored royal authority over Chile in 1814, the property of suspected insurgents was sequestered pending trials in which confiscation could be a penalty for treason. The trials were still unfinished in 1817 when pro-independence forces reclaimed Santiago and seized all assets of anyone who fled. Citing the relevant Castilian laws on punishment for treason, they argued that flight was evidence of allegiance to and collaboration with royal authorities.[8] Nevertheless, the new republican authorities did not conduct trials and frequently sold or awarded the seized property to third parties, setting the stage for ongoing lawsuits in the decades following the war.[9]

During the extended period of military conflict in Spanish America, the adherence to or violation of norms on the conduct of war, the establishment

5 Rebecca A. Earle, *Spain and the Independence of Colombia, 1810–1825* (Exeter: University of Exeter Press, 2000), 75–90.

6 Sarah C. Chambers, *Families in War and Peace: Chile from Colony to Nation* (Durham: Duke University Press, 2015), 75–88.

7 Stephen K. Stoan, *Pablo Morillo and Venezuela, 1815–1820* (Columbus: Ohio State University Press, 1974), 81–86, 123–127, quote on 83.

8 Cristián Guerrero Lira, *La contrarrevolución de la independencia en Chile* (Santiago: Editorial Universitaria y Centro de Investigaciones Diego Barros Arana, 2002), 260–275.

9 Chambers, *Families in War and Peace*, 91–154.

of purification or loyalty tribunals, and the seizure of property were carried out in parallel ways by both royalists and republicans, referencing the same laws and norms. Indeed, many Spanish Americans justified independence not with new doctrines, but medieval principles of governance. Asserting that their ancestors had made a pact directly with the monarch rather than the Spanish nation, they reclaimed popular sovereignty.[10] Rather than mark a rupture, independence was one moment of contestation over law in a period of gradual transformation.[11] The following sections will consider this longer process from the middle of the eighteenth to the middle of the nineteenth centuries. After analyzing the reform of legal institutions to prioritize state law initiated from above, the chapter will explore engagement and contestation from below in the areas of criminal prosecution and civil litigation.

1.2 *Jurisdictions and Judicial Reforms: The Prioritization of Royal and National Law*

First Iberian monarchs and then national governments gradually centralized and strengthened state law over this period, by subordinating rather than eliminating other sources of law and jurisdictions. Although there were calls by some reformers in both the late colonial and early national periods to revise thoroughly and to update the body of law, few new comprehensive civil or criminal codes were issued until the second half of the nineteenth century. Near the end of colonial rule and continuing after independence, constitutions were promulgated that set new parameters for the separation of powers, exercise of due process, and terms of legal personhood, but most litigation continued under existing Spanish or Portuguese law that remained in effect. Continuity in written laws, however, did not necessarily mean continuity in

10 José Carlos Chiaramonte, 'The Principle of Consent in Latin and Anglo-American Independence' (2004) 36 Journal of Latin American Studies 563–586; Chiaramonte, 'The "Ancient Constitution" after Independence (1808–1852)' (2010) 90(3) Hispanic American Historical Review 455–488; Brian Hamnett, 'The Medieval Roots of Spanish Constitutionalism' in Scott Eastman and Natalia Sobrevilla Perea, *The Rise of Constitutional Government in the Iberian Atlantic World: The Impact of the Cádiz Constitution of 1812* (Tuscaloosa: University of Alabama Press, 2015), 19–41.

11 War did disrupt the regular course of non-military litigation; see Sarah C. Chambers, *From Subjects to Citizens: Honor, Gender, and Politics in Arequipa, Peru, 1780–1854* (University Park: Pennsylvania State University Press, 1999), 141–145; Reuben Zahler, 'Liberal Justice: Judicial Reform in Venezuela's Courts, 1786–1850' (2010) 90(3) Hispanic American Historical Review 489–522. For examples in which parties to lawsuits used political arguments or appealed to wartime pardons, see Victor Uribe-Uran, *Fatal Love: Spouse Killers, Law, and Punishment in the Late Colonial Spanish Atlantic* (Stanford: Stanford University Press, 2016), 240–270; Chambers, *Families in War and Peace*, 71–74.

the interpretation of those laws. Spanish and Portuguese judicial systems granted wide discretion to magistrates to consult multiple compilations as well as custom, jurisprudence, and commentaries to arrive at outcomes they deemed appropriate for particular cases, and after independence, constitutional law was added to this legal corpus.[12] Judicial discretion had never meant that sentencing was completely arbitrary: litigants could forum shop among competing jurisdictions or appeal decisions to higher authorities. The expectation that judges would be attentive to the ideas and contexts of their times may even have lessened the urgency for recodification.

Around the middle of the eighteenth century, Spanish and Portuguese monarchs initiated reforms influenced by Enlightenment ideas about rationalizing governance. Known in the Spanish empire as 'Bourbon,' owing to the shift from the Habsburg to Bourbon royal dynasties, and in the Portuguese empire as 'Pombaline,' after the chief minister who oversaw their design and implementation, these reforms affected various areas of administration: fiscal, bureaucratic, military, and legal. Although officials in both kingdoms developed proposals for drafting new comprehensive law codes, a process known as codification, these were never implemented. Instead, legislation accrued in a piecemeal fashion, which jurists then reorganized in new compilations. Meanwhile, legal commentaries and law-school curricula in the eighteenth century drew upon earlier humanist philosophies as well as the rising Enlightenment emphasis on natural law.[13]

Rather than new codes, monarchs issued decrees about the order in which judges should consult various sources of law. Under the administration of the Marquis de Pombal (1750–1777), the Portuguese prioritized royal law (called *direito pátrio* or national law) over canon and Roman law. Judges were ordered to first consult Portuguese statutes, custom, and the findings and interpretations from the high court of appeals; if these sources did not address a specific issue, they could look to Roman law only if it passed the 'litmus test of natural reason.' Jurist Pascoal José de Mello Freire dos Reis introduced this regalist interpretation of law to Coimbra University, where all imperial magistrates, administrators, and lawyers received their training. And his publications, which set out to order the eclectic accumulation of laws, were consulted in the absence of a new code, remaining influential in Brazil well into the nineteenth

12 Liliana Obregón, 'Between Civilisation and Barbarism: Creole Interventions in International Law' (2006) 27(5) Third World Quarterly 815–832, especially 821–822.

13 Hamnet, 'The Medieval Roots of Spanish Constitutionalism'; Bianca Premo, *The Enlightenment on Trial: Ordinary Litigants and Colonialism in the Spanish Empire* (New York: Oxford University Press, 2017).

century. In matters of family law, for example, he described marriage as a civil contract as much as a sacrament and, therefore, subject to secular as well as ecclesiastical jurisdictions.[14]

The Bourbon monarchs similarly ordered that Spanish law be taught in universities throughout the empire and take precedence over Roman and canon law, and they expanded and strengthened secular jurisdictions. The general organization of the judicial system, where officials at various levels held both executive and judicial authority, remained in place: local *alcaldes* and governors retained jurisdiction over first-instance lawsuits and trials, within certain parameters in terms of the value of assets at stake or the seriousness of violent crimes, and the magistrates on the regional royal courts (*audiencias*) also exercised some political authority. Despite this underlying continuity, the crown promoted greater specialization of officials toward either administration or justice. The Council of the Indies, which considered judicial appeals from overseas territories and advised the king on policy matters, was newly divided into two chambers dedicated to justice and governance respectively, and in 1787 a ministerial position was established to oversee matters of justice in the Indies. In the colonies, the crown began appointing regents in 1776 to oversee each *audiencia* and to prioritize the magistrates' judicial duties. In the 1780s, Spain also introduced to most overseas territories an intendancy system, which created a layer of regional officials to implement the broader Bourbon reform program and to oversee provincial governors. The ordinances issued for these new professionals gave them broad powers, including over police and justice, and appointed university-trained legal officers to advise them on such matters. As detailed later in the chapter, increasing numbers of litigants, including women and people of color, chose to bring lawsuits to the new intendancy courts.[15] Although professionalization did not reach the local level, additional lay judges were appointed to arrest delinquents, mediate smaller disputes in

14 Linda Lewin, *Surprise Heirs I: Illegitimacy, Patrimonial Rights, and Legal Nationalism in Luso-Brazilian Inheritance, 1750–1821* (Stanford: Stanford University Press, 2003), 16–17, 117–150; Kenneth Maxwell, *Pombal: Paradox of the Enlightenment* (Cambridge: Cambridge University Press, 1995), 87–108.

15 M.C. Mirow, *Latin American Law: A History of Private Law and Institutions in Spanish America* (Austin: University of Texas Press, 2004), 21–32, 45–48; Bernardino Bravo Lira, *El juez entre el derecho y la ley: Estado de Derecho y Derecho del Estado en el mundo hispánico, siglos XVI a XXI* (Santiago: LexisNexis, 2006); Premo, *The Enlightenment on Trial*, 87–88, 142–148, 170.

oral hearings, and initiate more serious cases that could be raised to the next level for adjudication.[16]

Alongside this royal system of courts and judges, other specific jurisdictions continued to exist, but the Iberian monarchs tried to subordinate these to centralized oversight. Although the Catholic Church retained legal authority over its personnel and sacraments, secular courts took over other matters such as bigamy, extramarital relations, and disputes between parents and children over marriage choice. In 1775 (Portugal) and 1776 (Spain), royal edicts allowed parents to object to marriages by their minor offspring (generally under twenty-five) with partners they deemed social unequals, a shift from custom and canon law that emphasized spiritual free will in betrothals. The Spanish pragmatic allowed children to appeal parental dissent over marriage choice, but in royal rather than ecclesiastical courts.[17] Furthermore, in reviewing the appeal from Lima of a 'divorce' settlement (separation of bed and board but without ending a marriage), the Council of the Indies in 1787 recognized the jurisdiction of ecclesiastical courts to grant or deny divorces, but shifted law-suits over the resulting financial arrangements – such as court costs, dowries, alimony, and child support – to secular courts.[18]

The implications of military jurisdiction were complex and intersected with changes to legal personhood that began to erode some status distinctions in the colonies, albeit in subtle and limited ways. Beginning in 1768, Spanish Bourbons began expanding, professionalizing, and centralizing both the army and militias. Key to recruitment was granting soldiers the prerogative (*fuero*) to defend themselves, and in some cases even sue, within military jurisdiction. Moreover, beneficiaries of this privilege included people of color who could gain upward mobility under the reformed military, which prioritized merit

16 María Victoria Montoya Gómez, '¿Cómo debían ser los jueces?: Una reflexión en torno a los jueces pedáneos de la ciudad de Antioquia (1750–1809)' (julio-diciembre 2014) 32 Signos Históricos 86–121. New research reveals that the Bourbons also began officially appointing Indigenous legal personnel to work with *audiencias*. Alcira Dueñas, 'Indian Colonial Actors in the Lawmaking of the Spanish Empire in Peru' (2018) 65(1) Ethnohistory 51–73.

17 The literature on the Spanish Marriage Pragmatic is vast, but well summarized in Steinar A. Saether, 'Bourbon Absolutism and Marriage Reform in Late Colonial Spanish America' (2003) 59(4) The Americas 475–509; Steiner emphasizes its intent to strengthen royal authority generally rather than over the church specifically. For Portugal and Brazil, see Muriel Nazzari, *Disappearance of the Dowry: Women, Families, and Social Change in São Paulo, Brazil (1600–1900)* (Stanford: Stanford University Press, 1991), 131–132.

18 Bianca Premo, *Children of the Father King: Youth, Authority, and Legal Minority in Colonial Lima* (Chapel Hill: University of North Carolina Press, 2005), 155; Premo, *The Enlightenment on Trial*, 89–91. The decree was subsequently incorporated into the *Novísima recopilación de leyes de España* (Madrid, 1805), 208.

over purity of blood. Municipal justices, generally elite Americans of Spanish descent (creoles), complained that soldiers and militiamen of African descent felt emboldened to commit offenses and to disrespect authority because they would be protected by their military commanders. By upholding and even expanding access to the military *fuero*, the king as the ultimate commander over the armed forces strengthened central authority over that of local officials and city councils.[19] Laws changing the official status of individuals even beyond the military similarly triggered disputes in colonial society. Both the Portuguese king in 1775 and the Spanish monarch in 1794 declared that foundlings (*expósitos*) were royal children who would be considered free, of legitimate birth and, by implication, racially pure. The Spanish Bourbons also expanded access to legal procedures by which persons of mixed race or out-of-wedlock birth could request that the king officially remove those stigmas, allowing them access to higher education and professions.[20]

As Iberian monarchs issued ordinances and decrees aimed at consolidating royal authority, liberals within their realms advocated their own ideas about public law. While King Ferdinand VII was held captive by Napoleon, deputies to the Spanish parliament (*Cortes*) issued a constitution in 1812 that would apply throughout the empire. This charter recognized the monarchy, but limited its powers, dividing the government into separate executive, legislative, and judicial branches.[21] Furthermore, the multiplicity of legal subjectivities was reduced as the constitution widened male suffrage and recognized Indigenous people (although not all people of African descent) as Spanish nationals eligible for citizenship. In the city of Antequera in Mexico

19 For an insightful recent treatment of military jurisdiction (*fuero*), which references earlier scholarship, see Mónica Ricketts, 'The Rise of the Bourbon Military in Peru, 1768–1820' (2012) 21(3) Colonial Latin American Review 413–439.

20 See Lewin, *Surprise Heirs I*, 82; Cynthia E. Milton, *The Many Meanings of Poverty: Colonialism, Social Compacts, and Assistance in Eighteenth-Century Ecuador* (Stanford: Stanford University Press, 2007), 1141–1148; Ann Twinam, *Public Lives, Private Secrets: Gender, Honor, Sexuality, and Illegitimacy in Colonial Spanish America* (Stanford: Stanford University Press, 1999); Ann Twinam, *Purchasing Whiteness: Pardos, Mulattos, and the Quest for Social Mobility in the Spanish Indies* (Stanford: Stanford University Press, 2015).

21 M.C. Mirow, *Latin American Constitutions: The Constitution of Cádiz and Its Legacy in Spanish America* (New York: Cambridge University Press, 2015); Eastman and Sobrevilla Perea, *The Rise of Constitutional Government*. For an English translation of the text, see http://www.cervantesvirtual.com/obra-visor/the-political-constitution-of-the-spanish-monarchy-promulgated-in-cadiz-the-nineteenth-day-of-march--0/html/ffd04084-82b1-11df-acc7-002185ce6064_1.html; M.C. Mirow, *Florida's First Constitution, The Constitution of Cádiz: Introduction, Translation, and Text* (Durham: Carolina Academic Press, 2012).

(today Oaxaca), for example, many people turned out for elections and two non-whites were elected to the city council. Although Spanish liberals aimed to break up corporate bodies and to emphasize individual citizenship, many Indigenous communities were able to use their elected municipal councils to protect their communal lands and identity.[22] The practical application of the Spanish constitution, however, was limited. It was in force only briefly: from 1812 to 1814 (when the king was absent), 1820 to 1823 (when a liberal revolt forced him to briefly reinstate it), and 1836 (after most of the colonies had separated from Spain). It was applied throughout New Spain (Mexico and Central America) and the Andean Viceroyalty of Peru, but not in other colonial territories already in revolt.[23] Nevertheless, it was briefly adopted by Portugal and so applied to Brazil until the new empire adopted its own constitution in 1824, and its influence continued as one model to be consulted as the newly independent countries subsequently drafted their own constitutions.

Over the course of the nineteenth century, Latin Americans would draft and implement more than one hundred constitutions. Peru alone had six between 1823 and 1839.[24] One can legitimately question, therefore, how relevant constitutional law was in the face of such instability. In many countries it was just as common for the force of arms as peaceful elections to bring a new government to power. Nonetheless, military officers turned heads of state cared about legitimating their rule by convoking congresses to draft new constitutions.[25]

---

22 On municipal councils, see Federica Morelli, '"Entre confianza y armas": La justicia local en Ecuador del Antiguo Régimen al liberalismo' (2011) 37 Revista Complutense de Historia de América 27–47. On citizenship in the 1812 Constitution, see also Tamar Herzog, *Defining Nations: Immigrants and Citizens in Early Modern Spain and Spanish America* (New Haven: Yale University Press, 2003), 141–163. On Oaxaca, see Peter Guardino, *The Time of Liberty: Popular Political Culture in Oaxaca, 1750–1850* (Durham: Duke University Press, 2005), 143–147.

23 Victor Uribe-Uran, 'La Constitución de Cádiz en la Nueva Granada, teoría y realidad, 1812–1821' in *La Constitución de 1812 en Hispanoamérica y España*, ed. Heraclio Bonilla (Bogotá: Editorial Universidad Nacional de Colombia-Alcaldía Mayor de Bogotá, 2012), 273–303. Although elections were held under its aegis, there was insufficient time to thoroughly reorganize the judicial system. On magistrates resisting implementation, see Linda Arnold, *Bureaucracy and Bureaucrats in Mexico City, 1742–1835* (Tucson: University of Arizona Press, 1988), 56–66.

24 See Roberto Gargarella, *Latin American Constitutionalism, 1810–2010: The Engine Room of the Constitution* (Oxford: Oxford University Press, 2013). Texts of many Spanish American constitutions can be found at http://www.cervantesvirtual.com/portales/constituciones_hispanoamericanas/.

25 José Carlos Chiaramonte asserts that even the declaration of dictatorships had Roman precedents and could be legitimate if approved by elected legislatures and limited to a particular length of time. Chiaramonte, 'The "Ancient Constitution" after Independence,' 481–486.

Moreover, some revolts were carried out in the name of defending particular constitutions. In 1833, for example, citizens turned out in large numbers for elections in Arequipa, Peru, even defending their right to gather against attacks from the police. When conservative President Agustín de Gamarra refused to recognize the selection of liberal rival José Luís Orbegoso as his successor by the National Convention, Arequipa was at the forefront of a rebellion to defend the constitutional process. In recognition, Orbegoso dubbed it 'The Province of the Law.'[26]

Roberto Gargarella identifies three 'ideal' types from among the many constitutions, acknowledging that in practice many charters contained mixed elements. Conservative models favored centralist governments with strong executives and senates in the interest of maintaining order and stability. Far fewer were those that he calls 'radical' or 'majoritarian' because they subordinated individual rights to the will of the majority; these charters promoted federalism, direct elections, and large representative bodies (including in some cases unicameral legislatures) with greater powers relative to the presidency. Finally, he identifies a 'liberal' model that emphasized individual liberties and tried to balance the alleged tendencies of the other two models toward either tyranny or anarchy. Although liberal constitutions tended to establish strong senates and executives, they also placed limits on presidential power to veto legislation or to invoke emergency powers.[27] Constitutions enacted soon after independence tended to be more liberal and inclusive in terms of defining citizenship and suffrage. There were no formal racial exclusions, and men with at least some financial independence (such as artisans and small farmers) could vote; those defined as dependent, such as women, servants, and the enslaved, however, were excluded from active citizenship. In reaction to the popular mobilization that these charters facilitated, constituent congresses in some countries later replaced the more liberal constitutions promulgated at independence with more centralized and restrictive charters, increasing franchise requirements in terms of property, income, or literacy.[28]

Because Brazil remained a monarchy after independence, its constitution was conservative and, despite some liberalizing reforms in 1834, endured until

26 Chambers, *From Subjects to Citizens*, 224–227.

27 Roberto Gargarella, 'Towards a Typology of Latin American Constitutionalism, 1810–1860' (2004) 39(2) Latin American Research Review 141–153. See also Gargarella, *Latin American Constitutionalism*.

28 Sarah C. Chambers, 'New Nations and New Citizens: Political Culture in Nineteenth-Century Mexico, Peru, and Argentina' in *A Companion to Latin American History*, ed. Thomas H. Holloway (Oxford: Blackwell Publishing, 2008), 215–229.

the establishment of a republic in 1889. Emperor Pedro I convoked a constituent assembly but dissolved it before it issued a constitution and promulgated a charter with elements that strengthened his own authority. He granted himself the prerogative to appoint members to the executive council of state as well as senators; deputies in the lower chamber were to be elected but the emperor could override the legislature under certain conditions. Brazil also was the first Latin American nation to issue a new penal code in 1830. Continuing a trend from the era of Pombal's reforms, it reduced the severity of penalties for many offenses.[29] Remarkably, however, Brazil was one of the last countries in the region to issue a new civil code in 1917. Keila Grinberg attributes the delays and difficulties for potential drafters to the centrality of a labor system that variously treated enslaved people as things but also persons who could themselves enter into contracts to buy and sell property or their own labor. Such contradictions prevented jurists from formulating unitary legal definitions for civil rights. As one drafter exclaimed in exasperation when he resigned from the project, 'liberty is indivisible.'[30]

Leaders throughout Latin America believed that new nations would require new legal codes, but in the meantime could adapt existing sources of law to the contemporary context. Like the eighteenth-century monarchs before them, new governments established an order of precedence by which judges should consult laws. Constitutional articles and laws passed by post-independence legislatures were prioritized, but when these did not cover matters under review, judges could turn to the relevant Iberian sources so long as they did not contradict constitutional principles. Furthermore, since the eighteenth century there had been recommendations and in a few cases requirements that judges apply the laws more strictly and explain their judicial reasoning with reference to them.[31] Nonetheless, most contemporaries agreed that judges should continue

29 Linda Lewin, *Surprise Heirs II: Illegitimacy, Inheritance Rights, and Public Power in the Formation of Imperial Brazil, 1822–1889* (Stanford: Stanford University Press, 2003), 8–33, 88–106. Other criminal codes promulgated in the 1830s include Bolivia, New Granada (later Colombia), and some states within Mexico.

30 Keila Grinberg, 'Slavery, Liberalism, and Civil Law: Definitions of Status and Citizenship in the Elaboration of the Brazilian Civil Code (1855–1916)' in *Honor, Status, and Law in Modern Latin America*, eds Sueann Caulfield, Sarah C. Chambers, and Lara Putnam (Durham: Duke University Press, 2000), 109–127, quote on 112.

31 On laws requiring judges to explain sentencing, see Víctor Brangier, 'Cultura política-judicial: gestión social del modelo del buen juez: Zona central de Chile, 1824–1875' (2019) 46(1) Anuario Colombiano de Historia Social y de la Cultura, 231–254; Linda Arnold, 'Privileged Justice?: The *Fuero Militar* in Early National Mexico' in *Judicial Institutions in Nineteenth-Century Latin America*, 49–64.

to exercise discretion, especially in cases where medieval laws and penalties were inappropriate to the current age. With the exception of summary justice in wartime, a trend away from torture and severe forms of corporal punishment began during the late colonial period before ultimately being formalized in constitutions and reformed penal codes in the nineteenth century.[32]

In the nineteenth century, first the Iberian and then post-independence constitutions delineated a separation of powers and guidelines for due process that moved legal culture further from justice toward law. All constitutions established a separate judicial branch with a clear line of appeal from judges of first instance through appellate courts and ultimately a supreme court.[33] Professionalization of judicial personnel was the goal, but given the political instability, ongoing wars, and fiscal limitations of the early national period, most countries experienced shortages and turnover among judicial personnel at some point.[34] Some form of lay judges – local officials or justices of the peace, variously appointed or elected – survived at the local level, and therefore the same person might exercise both political and judicial (and sometimes even military) authority. In theory, university-trained magistrates would exercise oversight of police and lay judges and offer avenues of appeal to ensure compliance with constitutional protections for suspects and defendants, but practice varied. In Buenos Aires, for example, the shortage of legally trained professionals led to a system in which critical early steps in the judicial process were delegated to police who either skipped steps of due process in oral trials or passed to professional judges written case files that were already tilted toward particular outcomes.[35]

Multiple jurisdictions also persisted but the trend toward narrowing their purview and establishing central oversight continued. Although the Catholic

32 Uribe-Uran, *Fatal Love*, especially 209–270.

33 For an overview, see Mirow, *Latin American Law*, 107–115. The United Provinces of the River Plate did not have a supreme court until 1862 after they unified as Argentina; Osvaldo Barreneche, *Crime and the Administration of Justice in Buenos Aires, 1785–1853* (Lincoln: University of Nebraska Press, 2006), 54. Mexico was distinctive for having both state and federal court systems; Arnold, *Bureaucracy and Bureaucrats in Mexico City*, 76–80.

34 Thomas Flory, *Judge and Jury in Imperial Brazil, 1808–1871: Social Control and Political Stability in the New State* (Austin: University of Texas Press, 1981), 36–40; Victor M. Uribe-Uran, 'Colonial Lawyers, Republican Lawyers and the Administration of Justice in Spanish America' in *Judicial Institutions*, 25–48.

35 Mark D. Szuchman, *Order, Family, and Community in Buenos Aires, 1810–1860* (Stanford: Stanford University Press, 1988), 17–64; Osvaldo Barreneche, 'Criminal Justice and State Formation in Early Nineteenth-Century Buenos Aires' in *Judicial Institutions*, 86–103; and Barreneche, *Crime and the Administration of Justice*, especially 88–102.

Church continued to have its own courts, particularly for matters related to its personnel, the Inquisition was abolished. Other special jurisdictions (such as those for merchants or Indigenous people) came under scrutiny, but were not ended immediately. The military *fuero* generally survived, although some countries established courts made up of both ordinary and military judges to review first-instance decisions. How military courts operated in practice after independence varied and merits further research. For Mexico, Linda Arnold found that they did not show special preference for soldiers being sued by civilians, such as women seeking child support or landlords seeking to enforce rental contracts. James Wood, on the other hand, argues that military commanders in Chile used their jurisdiction over enlisted men to inflict corporal punishment and to prevent them from freely exercising the franchise.[36]

Again, Brazil's reformed judicial system after independence had some important differences from Spanish America. Although its Constitution of 1824 gave ample powers to the emperor, it called for the establishment of a new, independent judiciary that was to include lay judges and a jury system. In practice, jurisdictional conflicts and political wrangling between the liberal and conservative parties generated a series of reforms that moved first toward decentralization before reversing course, another reminder that trends over this period were neither linear nor definitive. In 1827 liberal legislators established annually elected justices of the peace at the local level with the authority to adjudicate a wider range of cases than their colonial predecessors, who had been little more than conciliators. The 1832 Procedural Code added a network of professional district judges, but also increased the powers of the justices of the peace and established a jury system as called for by the constitution setting off multiple jurisdictional skirmishes. When conservatives gained a legislative majority in the 1840s, they re-prioritized professionalization and centralization. They could not eliminate the elected justices of the peace and juries mandated by the constitution, but subjected them to greater oversight by university-trained magistrates who were authorized to appeal jury decisions. They also established a system of appointed police officials alongside the elected justices of the peace and directed sheriffs to review juror eligibility, based upon raised requirements in terms of income and literacy. In the words of Thomas Flory, 'In effect, the Conservatives had replaced this elected local judge with extensive police functions by an appointed local police officer with extensive judicial functions.'[37]

36 Arnold, 'Privileged Justice?'; James A. Wood, 'The Burden of Citizenship: Artisans, Elections, and the Fuero Militar in Santiago de Chile' (2002) 58(3) The Americas 443–469.

37 Flory, *Judge and Jury in Imperial Brazil, 1808–1871*, 173.

Although specific forms of organization varied, the expansion of police forces was another shared trend across the region between 1750 and 1850, beginning in the larger cities. After failed attempts in 1694 and 1750, in the 1780s an effective urban police force was implemented in Mexico City, organized into eight wards, each with a judge and up to twenty police officers, along with a city-wide night force. Between 1780 and 1800 there was a tenfold increase in arrests and prosecution on charges such as vagrancy, illegal gambling, theft, and alcohol-related offenses.[38] In Peru, officials in Lima also established a municipal police force to patrol the city's diverse population during the late colonial period, but the municipal council in the provincial city of Arequipa delayed similar measures for more than a decade awaiting royal approval of their funding proposal. In Brazil, the royal court that fled from Napoleon transferred the Portuguese system of policing to Rio. Other than a brief period after independence, when constitutional due process was enforced, Thomas Holloway argues that the principal role of the police in Brazil was to maintain forcefully the order of the slave society.[39] The establishment of police forces facilitated a rise in criminal prosecution beginning in the late colonial period and continuing after independence that brought greater numbers of people into contact with the state judicial system.

1.3 *Criminal Law: Social Control and Rights Claims*

Having laid out trends over this period toward the prioritization of state law and the increasing professionalization of the justice system, it is equally critical to investigate the practice of law as an arena of conflict and negotiation. Here, we have to rely on local archival research into case law, which reveals regional differences in terms of timing and intensity. In the late eighteenth century, colonial authorities at various levels began to crack down on what they perceived to be the disorderly behavior of the populace.[40] In the wake of often-prolonged wars of independence and fearing that men of the lower

38 Michael C. Scardaville, '(Hapsburg) Law and (Bourbon) Order: State Authority, Popular Unrest, and the Criminal Justice System in Bourbon Mexico City' (1994) 50(4) The Americas 501–525; Michael C. Scardaville, 'Justice by Paperwork: A Day in the Life of a Court Scribe in Bourbon Mexico City' (2003) 36(4) Journal of Social History 979–1007.

39 Thomas H. Holloway, *Policing Rio de Janeiro: Repression and Resistance in a Nineteenth-Century City* (Stanford: Stanford University Press, 1993); Holloway, 'Punishment in Nineteenth-Century Rio de Janeiro: Judicial Action as Police Practice' in *Reconstructing Criminality in Latin America*, eds Carlos A. Aguirre and Robert Buffington (Wilmington: Scholarly Resources, 2000), 85–112.

40 Pamela Voekel, 'Peeing on the Palace: Bodily Resistance to Bourbon Reforms in Mexico City' (1992) 5(2) Journal of Historical Sociology 183–208.

orders might translate their new political liberties into libertinage, national officials continued efforts at social control. Whether under royal or republican rule, responses from below to these measures ranged from evasion to protest. Nonetheless, with the publication of constitutions, particularly after independence, claims to due process were often successful.

In their quest for order Bourbon officials increased policing and criminal prosecution, particularly in larger cities, but also had to contend with varied reactions from the colonial populace. Under the police force and municipal courts established in Mexico City in the 1780s, prosecution of crime increased but most cases were handled expeditiously in oral hearings with penalties, particularly fines and labor on public works, that reflected the Bourbon goals of economic utility. Moreover, Michael Scardaville argues that municipal courts were not only a space for top-down social control. More than one-third of arrests were made after complaints filed by the targets of crime against perpetrators from roughly the same socioeconomic standing. In addition, widespread evasion and opposition limited the success of some measures, most notably repeated campaigns against alcohol consumption. Arrests for public drunkenness were high, but the penalties relatively lenient, and efforts to reduce the number of taverns and to discourage 'idling' in such spaces ran into evasion and resistance, not only by the customers but also by the wealthier proprietors and even municipal officials who relied on the tax revenue.[41] In rural areas, Bourbon officials launched campaigns against moral offenses such as adultery and sexual relations among unmarried partners, regardless of race or ethnicity, though with mixed results. Throughout the province of Antioquia (today in Colombia), newly established lay judges actively targeted extramarital relationships, contributing to an increase in prosecutions from single digits per decade in the 1760s to forty-one and forty-three respectively in the 1780s and 1790s. Nevertheless, governors also complained that many local judges did not themselves set proper examples for their communities, including one who was punished after he bragged that he had sex with almost all the women in his town.[42]

As with policing, criminal prosecution generally intensified first in larger cities before extending to the provinces. Criminal cases heard by the Real

41 Michael C. Scardaville, 'Alcohol Abuse and Tavern Reform in Late Colonial Mexico City' (1980) 60(4) The Hispanic American Historical Review 643–671. For similar responses to regulations against gambling, see Chambers, *From Subjects to Citizens*, 125–160.

42 Montoya Gómez, '¿Cómo debían ser los jueces?,' 86–121. For an argument that Bourbon legal reforms failed at the local level in the region of Quito, see Morelli, 'Entre confianza y armas.'

Audiencia of Lima rose from 1,104 throughout the entire eighteenth century to 1,784 trials during the final two decades of the colonial period (1800 to 1820).[43] In Arequipa, Peru, the increase occurred later, from only 184 criminal trials during the last four decades of the colonial period to 1,021 during the first three decades after independence. Equally striking was a change in prosecutorial procedures as the number of cases in Arequipa pursued directly by the court (*de oficio*) increased to surpass those initiated by the injured party (*de parte*). During the colonial period, for example, even targets of theft were responsible not only for reporting the crime, but also for presenting witnesses and formally accusing the defendant; after independence, judicial personnel usually took over all aspects of the investigation and prosecution. Furthermore, under Spanish laws injuries (*injurias*) could be either verbal insults or physical harm; in the colonial period, both kinds of cases were pursued by plaintiffs but after independence the courts took over most prosecution of assault and battery regardless of whether the injured party wished to press charges.[44]

Although social control from above increased, with material and bodily consequences for the targets of such campaigns, there was space for legal negotiation as well as conflict. The timing of campaigns against crime could make a difference in the response from below. After independence, defendants were aware of constitutional protections and claimed their rights with, and sometimes without, the assistance of legal representatives. Evidence suggests they were often successful. Linda Arnold argues that judges in Mexico City conducted weekly inspections of the jails and diligently followed up on complaints of prisoners, such as delays in bringing them to trial.[45] Reuben Zahler has demonstrated the widespread knowledge in Venezuela about constitutional protections. When Pablo Minalla cited specific articles of the constitution to protest his detention for six days without a warrant, for example, a judge took measures in 1826 to 'ensure that [he] gets full use of his rights.'[46] The people of Arequipa, from various socioeconomic strata, also asserted their rights as citizens. They complained of and fought back against what they perceived as abuses by the police, and as often as not judges took their side. They also appealed to an executive order of 1821 protecting all free (i.e., not enslaved) people from the lash, whether the whip was wielded by authorities

43 Alberto Flores Galindo, *Aristocracia y Plebe: Lima, 1760–1830* (Lima: Mosca Azul Editores, 1984); Premo, *Children of the Father King*, 285n4 for the number of criminal cases.

44 Chambers, *From Subjects to Citizens*, 137–155.

45 Linda Arnold, 'Vulgar and Elegant: Politics and Procedure in Early National Mexico' (1994) 50(4) The Americas 481–500.

46 Zahler, 'Liberal Justice,' 514–515.

or civilians. Accusing another of whipping his nephew, one man called on the judge to prosecute it as a public crime 'because it affects the fatherland and the very society.'[47]

When arrested, especially on charges of vagrancy or suspicious behavior, plebeian men were exonerated only if they could convince judges that they were respectable and hardworking. Although some people of color were released on the testimony of character witnesses, those found guilty tended to be disproportionately of Indigenous or African descent. In Mexico City, political leaders from various parties agreed that vagrancy posed a threat, but in comparison to the late colonial period, conviction rates initially declined in the immediate aftermath of independence when suffrage was broad and politicians courted popular support. As the government became more centralized and suffrage more restricted, however, conviction rates rose and federal police targeted suspected vagrants for conscription into the army.[48] Although women were not arrested in large numbers, the late colonial trend to target them on morals offenses intensified further after independence. Charges or suspicions against women tended to be bad morals – sexual, drinking – not related to vagrancy. As non-citizens ideally relegated to the domestic sphere, moreover, they were less able to mount a character defense based upon the observance of a work ethic, much less military service to the republic.[49]

1.4 *Civil Law: From Custom to Rights*

The expansion of state courts resulted in increased criminal prosecution but also offered a venue for plaintiffs to file their own lawsuits and constitute new forms of legal personhood. Women and people of color could advance rights claims in the universalizing language of the era but risked losing the special protections afforded to vulnerable groups by royal justice. After independence,

47 Chambers, *From Subjects to Citizens*, 180–200, quotes on 183.

48 Richard Warren, 'Mass Mobilization versus Social Control: Vagrancy and Political Order in Early Republican Mexico' in *Reconstructing Criminality in Latin America*, 41–58. See also Ricardo D. Salvatorre, *Wandering Paysanos: State Order and Subaltern Experience in Buenos Aires during the Rosas Era* (Durham and London: Duke University Press, 2003).

49 Chambers, *From Subjects to Citizens*, 200–215; for a similar dynamic in northern Mexico, see Laura M. Shelton, *For Tranquility and Order: Family and Community on Mexico's Northern Frontier, 1800–1850* (Tucson: University of Arizona Press, 2010), 75–95. Nonetheless, rates of prosecution against women for abortion and infanticide remained low from the colonial period through the middle of the nineteenth century. Nora E. Jaffary, *Reproduction and Its Discontents in Mexico: Childbirth and Contraception from 1750 to 1905* (Chapel Hill: University of North Carolina Press, 2016), 77–137.

citizen rights seemed to promise equality before the law but hinged on the terms of inclusion and exclusion.

In a comprehensive study of six rural and urban jurisdictions in Spain, Mexico, and Peru, Bianca Premo identified a dramatic increase in litigation in the colonies across the eighteenth century, particularly during the century's final decades. Strikingly, there was a disproportionate increase in cases bought by subordinates – women, Indigenous commoners, and enslaved people of African descent – against their immediate authority figures – husbands, native authorities, and slaveowners. These groups had long had access to courts in colonial Spanish America, but in earlier periods they generally had appealed to community leaders to intervene on their behalf or filed their petitions in ecclesiastical courts, which had jurisdiction over the marital relations of free and enslaved alike. Therefore, their increasing recourse to secular jurisdictions, including the new intendancy courts, signaled an important shift away from justice-oriented dispute resolution toward formal litigation. Moreover, the language they and their legal representatives used in these lawsuits drew from Enlightenment discourses about natural rights to be free from 'tyranny.'[50]

Significantly, Premo argues that these changes were pushed as much from the bottom up as the top down because arguments put forward by litigants often led to rather than followed from new legal precedents. The example of the royal decree of 1787 assigning jurisdiction over alimony and related court fees to secular rather than ecclesiastical courts was in response to a divorce case appealed from Peru to the Council of the Indies; moreover, rather than an example of ideas moving from the metropole to the periphery, the decree was later extended to courts in Spain. Through litigation, women were able to turn the practice of husbands paying the living expenses (*alimentos*) of wives who were placed in convents or honorable homes during ecclesiastical divorce proceedings into a formal obligation of husbands to continue providing alimony, child support, and legal expenses when women took up new residence after separation. Key to their legal arguments was that they had a natural right to self-preservation, echoing a concept also elaborated by Enlightenment jurists, but applied here to having the means to live free from cruel husbands. As Ana

50 Premo, *The Enlightenment on Trial*, especially 64–116. In the *audiencia* district of Quito, Bourbon rules on exemption from court fees increased the number of impoverished litigants who qualified. Milton, *The Many Meanings of Poverty*, 215–244. For more on the efforts of Indigenous commoners to limit the privileges of the native nobility, see Charles F. Walker, 'Crime in the Time of the Great Fear: Indians and the State in the Peruvian Southern Andes, 1780–1820' in *Crime and Punishment in Latin America*, 35–55, and Guardino, *The Time of Liberty*.

Cárdenas of Trujillo, Peru, put it in her 1790 lawsuit, she had a 'natural right' not to be subjected to 'a life in tyrannical captivity.'[51] Wives earlier in the colonial period more often had used a language of seeking protection and asking authority figures to pressure husbands to act more responsibly. Claiming rights was striking and new.

Even as women successfully elicited recognition of natural rights in royal rather than ecclesiastical courts, they did not uniformly benefit during a shift from (in the shorthand of this chapter) justice to law. As Bourbons increasingly took over the provision of poor relief from the church, for example, they also standardized the criteria of eligibility. Widows of royal administrators throughout the colonial period had petitioned the king directly for financial assistance or pensions based upon their particular circumstances, reinforcing his status as a benevolent father to his vulnerable subjects. When a formal pension system was established in 1765, widows who met the strict and generic criteria benefited, but those who did not could no longer make special pleas by appealing to Christian values of mercy. According to Cynthia Milton, this Bourbon reform 'undercut long-standing webs of obligation, so that royal charity and paternalism were no longer bestowed by the hand of the monarch or his close representatives.'[52]

As ecclesiastical jurisdiction was increasingly restricted, moreover, women without substantial property or assets to litigate often found that their complaints of abusive husbands were not taken seriously by lay judges. Frustrated when civic authorities in Arequipa took no action against her violent husband in 1817, Tomasa Castillo appealed to the vicar's court, but he averred that he had no jurisdiction over lay persons, foiling her attempt at forum shopping. Both secular and ecclesiastical authorities generally ordered married couples to live under the same roof unless one party had obtained an ecclesiastical divorce. Castillo had not pursued such a suit, yet declared, perhaps thinking of natural rights, that '[t]o the company of a man like my husband, no law can compel me.'[53] The introduction of constitutional law further differentiated

51 Premo, *The Enlightenment on Trial*, 121–158, quote on 147.

52 Milton, *The Many Meanings of Poverty*, 99–122, 191–214, quote on 197. When the Chilean government was deluged with applications for pensions from military widows after independence, it took the step of formally changing the rules to expand eligibility. Chambers, *Families in War and Peace*, 155–181.

53 Sarah C. Chambers, '"To the Company of a Man Like My Husband, No Law Can Compel Me": The Limits of Sanctions against Wife Beating in Arequipa, Peru, 1780–1850' (1999) 11(1) Journal of Women's History 31–52, quote on 44. See also Steve J. Stern, *The Secret History of Gender: Women, Men, and Power in Late Colonial Mexico* (Chapel Hill: University of North Carolina Press, 1995).

men and women's legal standing. In her study of lawsuits to which women were parties in Venezuela between 1786 and 1904, Arlene Díaz found that after independence women explicitly referred to themselves as citizens and invoked the concept of equality before the law when suing to administer their own property, to keep their wages, and to choose their own place of residence. Nevertheless, their arguments had little success. In general, judges upheld patriarchal authority over women's bodies and assets, although they also made fathers and husbands fulfill their financial responsibilities to support wives and children.[54]

Success in lawsuits over alimony and child support (*alimentos*) was an area in which trends from the late eighteenth century continued into the early decades after independence. In her sample of cases from 1835 to 1840, Arlene Díaz found twenty support disputes; of these all nine on behalf of children born out of wedlock as well as seven of the eleven cases for wives and legitimate children were either settled or sentenced in favor of plaintiffs.[55] In Chile, lawsuits over *alimentos* began to rise in the 1830s. Male heads of households, citizens of the new republic, protested many of these claims on the grounds either that they did not recognize paternity of children or that adult legitimate offspring should be self-supporting. Nevertheless, judges in Santiago, drawn from the same elite families, repeatedly ordered responsible parties to provide for dependent relatives regardless of age or birth status.[56]

These cases offer an interesting window into the complex and uneven nature of a shift in legal culture from justice as equity to positive law. Chilean judges, who were required after 1837 to justify their rulings with regard to specific laws, cited articles from the medieval *Siete Partidas* on the parental responsibility to provide for their children. But they still exercised discretion in determining paternity and assessing patriarchal duties relative to filial obedience, largely by relying upon the testimony of relatives and neighbors.[57] In the 1850s as legislators began to accuse litigants born out of wedlock of making false allegations in an attempt at social climbing, however, judges began to give greater weight to men's denial of paternity against witness testimony. As a result, the success of support lawsuits began to decline even before the promulgation of

54 Arlene Díaz, *Female Citizens, Patriarchs, and the Law in Venezuela, 1786–1904* (Lincoln: University of Nebraska Press, 2004), 132–170.

55 Ibid., 74–75.

56 Sarah C. Chambers, 'The Paternal Obligation to Provide: Political Familialism in Early Nineteenth-Century Chile' (2012) 117(4) American Historical Review 1123–1148.

57 Chambers, *Families in War and Peace*, 182–212.

a new Civil Code in 1857 that outlawed judicial inquiries into paternity.[58] Thus, even within the existing corpus of law, judges could shift from enforcing what medieval sources defined as fathers' natural obligations to dependents toward upholding the liberty of men as citizens in a republic to manage freely their current assets and future estates.

Linda Lewin traces a similar rise in intergenerational disputes in Brazil, but one resulting in a return to earlier sources of law rather than a new civil code. Liberal legislators after independence initially built upon the Pombaline reforms to secularize family law. Offspring born out of wedlock took advantage of the increased access to local, public courthouses to bring lawsuits over inheritance rights, much to the embarrassment of 'respectable' families. In response, Conservatives passed a law in 1847 that only paternally recognized children were entitled to inheritance and child support, overturning centuries of Luso-Brazilian custom. Along with other reforms that reinforced ecclesiastical oversight of marriage, mid-nineteenth-century Brazilian jurists re-prioritized Roman and canon law so that 'eighteenth-century legal nationalism came to be regarded as a century of deviation from what otherwise had been an overarching civil law tradition.'[59]

As disputes over inheritance imply, property was another key concern over this period from the mid-eighteenth to the mid-nineteenth centuries, but progress toward promoting its circulation in free markets was uneven. In the late eighteenth century, for example, Iberian monarchs tried to make it more difficult for the nobility to establish entailed estates, but only the subsequent national governments successfully abolished such privileges outright.[60] On the other hand, post-independence proposals to subdivide communal lands into private, alienable lots often foundered until later in the nineteenth century. In Andean nations, governments continued to rely on revenue collected from head taxes and Indigenous tributaries resisted payment without access to usufruct rights in communal property.[61] Ongoing lawsuits over assets that had

58 Nara B. Milanich, *The Children of Fate: Childhood, Class, and the State in Chile, 1850–1930* (Durham: Duke University Press, 2009), 46–60.

59 Lewin, *Surprise Heirs II*, 120.

60 As with other reforms, Spanish liberals also abolished entailed estates in 1811 only to have Ferdinand VII reverse the measure when restored to the throne. Jaime E. Rodríguez O., *'We Are Now the True Spaniards': Sovereignty, Revolution, Independence, and the Emergence of the Federal Republic of Mexico, 1808–1824* (Stanford: Stanford University Press, 2012), 39–40; Mirow, *Latin American Law*, 151–153; and Lewin, *Surprise Heirs II*, 16, 22, 60–64, 306.

61 Charles Walker, *Smoldering Ashes: Cuzco and the Creation of Republican Peru, 1780–1840* (Durham: Duke University Press, 1999), especially 199–221; Guardino, *The Time of Liberty*, 246–274.

been seized during the wars of independence also muddied property rights.[62] Post-independence governments went further than their colonial predecessors in promoting freer markets, but only in the second half of the nineteenth century were such principles formalized in new civil codes that facilitated more dramatic rates of economic growth.[63]

Reformers across this period also advocated legal reforms to free up labor, but again change was gradual. Iberian monarchs abolished guild privileges in the eighteenth century but upheld Indigenous forced labor as a subsidy to mine owners even as they increasingly relied on wage labor. After independence, however, in the face of a collapsing mining economy and continued Indigenous resistance, national governments abolished the draft.[64] In regions where agricultural exporters relied on forced labor, African slavery remained legal well into the nineteenth century. Nonetheless, enslaved people, particularly those in or near urban areas, successfully expanded their ability to purchase their freedom over this period. In her analysis of late colonial courts, Premo demonstrates how increased litigation brought by the enslaved changed the interpretation of laws that had existed since the medieval period. One enslaved woman boldly referenced the *audiencia* as the place 'where the Law of the Realm has directed slaves to claim their liberty whenever they want to avail themselves of the help and refuge that the law dispenses.' The *Partidas* explicitly declared only magistrates could require that an owner who severely mistreated a slave sell him or her to another. By the end of the eighteenth century, enslaved persons had invoked natural laws of self-preservation to achieve the right to self-purchase or to seek a new owner under expanded notions of what constituted mistreatment.[65] The increasing number and success of freedom suits generally continued after independence, and historians have credited the activism of enslaved people within the courts for weakening the system of bondage and accelerating abolitionism.[66]

---

62 Chambers, *Families in War and Peace*, 125–154.

63 Here, Brazil also followed a somewhat different trajectory. Coffee production and exports began to expand soon after independence. Although Brazil had no new civil code until 1917, it passed a Commercial Code and major land laws in 1850. Nazzari, *Disappearance of the Dowry*, 91–106.

64 Enrique Tandeter, *Coercion and Market: Silver Mining in Colonial Potosí, 1692–1826* (Albuquerque: University of New Mexico Press, 1993).

65 Premo, *The Enlightenment on Trial*, 191–223, quote on 203. In her study of lawsuits involving women in Caracas between 1786 and 1790, Arlene Díaz found that eleven of fourteen cases filed by social inferiors against superiors, were enslaved women claiming freedom. Díaz, *Female Citizens, Patriarchs, and the Law in Venezuela*, 63.

66 Christine Hünefeldt, *Paying the Price of Freedom: Family and Labor among Lima's Slaves, 1800–1854* (Berkeley: University of California Press, 1994); Camillia Cowling, *Conceiving*

Nevertheless, employers also turned to the courts in their efforts to hold onto laborers, relying increasingly on the enforcement of debt obligations and vagrancy laws in regions where Indigenous drafts and African slavery had been abolished. Laura Shelton shows that in Sonora, Mexico, late colonial judges presiding over custody disputes favored guardians who had raised children in their household as servants over the claims of biological parents. The power of employers grew further after independence. Under Mexico's federalist system, authorities in Sonora enforced both national laws on vagrancy and enacted state laws that limited the ability of servants to leave households while they were indebted to their employers. Strikingly, owners of agricultural enterprises and mines were authorized to administer local justice for petty crimes and detain suspected vagrants. Under such jurisdiction, investigations into the deaths of servants resulting from authorized corporal punishment rarely led to murder charges.[67]

2 Conclusion: From Justice to Law

Over the period from roughly 1750 to 1850, the corpus of civil and criminal law changed little, but Bourbon and Pombaline officials initiated institutional reforms that post-independence governments extended. Regalists curtailed the jurisdiction of ecclesiastical courts, created new royal tribunals such as the intendancy courts, and appointed legal advisers to counsel administrative officials with judicial powers. Within these overarching trends, constitutional declarations of equality before the law and separation of powers – first articulated in Spanish and Portuguese constitutions but only fully implemented after independence – were major milestones. Although fiscal pressures and shortages of trained judges placed some limits on expanding the court system in the new Latin American nations, the works examined in this chapter show that in many regions there was a functioning, if not perfect, independent judiciary. Except for wartime disruptions, criminal and civil litigation remained steady or increased from colonial levels. Moreover, personnel took their duties

Freedom: Women of Color, Gender, and the Abolition of Slavery in Havana and Rio de Janeiro (Chapel Hill: University of North Carolina Press, 2013).

67 Shelton, *For Tranquility and Order*. For custody lawsuits and circulation of child labor in Chile, see Milanich, *Children of Fate*; Chambers, *Families in War and Peace*, 197–210. On channeling youth who were on the street or charged with crimes into apprenticeships and other forms of labor, see also Milton, *The Many Meanings of Poverty*, 136–141; Premo, *Children of the Father King*, 109–136.

seriously, whether inspecting jails in Mexico City, upholding due process in Caracas, or calling up juries in Brazil.

Judges and other legal personnel used this growing capacity in part to increase social control from above, at different paces in different regions. Police forces expanded and arrests increased. Further research could investigate whether a shift toward the prosecution of criminal cases directly by the state rather than at the initiative of the affected parties was more widespread.[68] Reforms from the top also engaged activism from below. Subalterns filed lawsuits against both public and private authority figures and turned to courts to mediate disputes with their peers. Criminal defendants, on their own or with the assistance of legal representatives, insisted on due process, especially under constitutional regimes. Whether or not subalterns viewed state law as legitimate, by filing lawsuits or mounting defenses they participated with elites, lawyers, and jurists in transforming legal cultures.[69] In the sixteenth and seventeenth centuries, they had appealed as vulnerable vassals to the representatives of monarchs who presented themselves as the font of justice. In the late colonial period, women and enslaved persons increasingly made claims against husbands and owners by referencing Enlightenment discourse around natural rights. Plaintiffs and defendants after independence could invoke their constitutional protections and rights, but the latter might be limited to those who qualified as citizens, men with at least some independence of means.

Increasingly litigants took their disputes to state courts, but the transition from an early modern legal culture oriented more toward justice to one oriented more toward positive law was gradual and uneven. Some who went to court continued to invoke ideals of social harmony and conciliation, and others still pursued dispute resolution in local communities that left few written traces. But there was a trend, when litigants had the means and access, toward appealing to professional judges when not satisfied with the results of other forms of resolution. Although more research needs to be done on

68 For an analysis of public and private law on the books, see Victor M. Uribe-Uran, 'The Great Transformation of Law and Legal Culture: "The Public" and "the Private" in the Transition from Empire to Nation in Mexico, Colombia, and Brazil, 1750–1850,' in *Empire to Nation: Historical Perspectives on the Making of the Modern World*, eds Joseph W. Esherick, Hasan Kayali, and Eric Van Young (Oxford: Rowman & Littlefield, 2006), 68–105.

69 Charles Walker and Ricardo Salvatore argue that judicial systems in Peru and Argentina during this period were not hegemonic: Walker, 'Crime in the Time of the Great Fear'; Salvatorre, *Wandering Paysanos*. For scholars who see greater hegemony of law, see Scardaville, '(Hapsburg) Law and (Bourbon) Order'; Chambers, *From Subjects to Citizens*; Guardino, *Time of Liberty*; Milton, *The Many Meanings of Poverty*.

judicial sentencing, there are some indications that professional magistrates also began to explain their sentences through greater reliance on national law.

Although subalterns pursued their interests within the state justice system, changing definitions of legal personhood affected their odds of success. In this area, post-independence changes carried particular weight. In the colonial period, there was no equality before the law. Women, the enslaved, and Indigenous people had less standing than white men, but could appeal to special protections and invoke natural rights. Legal definitions of citizenship after independence, which eliminated official racial exclusions and did not yet impose high property requirements, provided grounds for many men to claim constitutional rights. Those who did not qualify for the active exercise of citizenship, because they were considered dependent upon others, could still go to court; although technically they were entitled to due process protections, they were not equal before the law. On balance, women and children born out of wedlock saw their possibilities for demanding financial support and even physical safety decrease by the middle of the nineteenth century, a trend subsequently formalized by civil codes that lessened married women's property rights and outlawed judicial investigations into paternity. As dependents, domestic servants and indebted laborers often found themselves subject to the legal authority of their employers. Some free men of African descent may have qualified for citizenship, but police on the streets of Rio likely wielded a whip before investigating the status of suspects of color. For those who could not claim citizenship, particularly as the independence-era constitutions were replaced by conservative charters that increasingly raised the criteria of eligibility, the law may have seemed ever farther from their hopes for justice.

References

Aguirre, Carlos A. and Robert Buffington, eds. *Reconstructing Criminality in Latin America.* Wilmington: Scholarly Resources, 2000.

Arnold, Linda. 'Vulgar and Elegant: Politics and Procedure in Early National Mexico.' *The Americas* 50(4) (1994): 481–500.

Barreneche, Osvaldo. *Crime and the Administration of Justice in Buenos Aires, 1785–1853.* Lincoln: University of Nebraska Press, 2006.

Caulfield, Sueann, Sarah C. Chambers, and Lara Putnam, eds. *Honor, Status, and Law in Modern Latin America.* Durham: Duke University Press, 2005.

Chambers, Sarah C. *Families in War and Peace: Chile from Colony to Nation.* Durham: Duke University Press, 2015.

Chambers, Sarah C. *From Subjects to Citizens: Honor, Gender, and Politics in Arequipa, Peru, 1780–1854*. University Park: Pennsylvania State University Press, 1999.

Chambers, Sarah C. 'The Paternal Obligation to Provide: Political Familialism in Early Nineteenth-Century Chile.' American Historical Review 117(4) (2012): 1123–1148.

Chiaramonte, José Carlos. 'The "Ancient Constitution" after Independence (1808–1852).' *Hispanic American Historical Review* 90(3) (2010): 455–488.

Díaz, Arlene. *Female Citizens, Patriarchs, and the Law in Venezuela, 1786–1904*. Lincoln: University of Nebraska Press, 2004.

Dueñas, Alcira. 'Indian Colonial Actors in the Lawmaking of the Spanish Empire in Peru.' *Ethnohistory* 65(1) (2018): 51–73.

Eastman, Scott, and Natalia Sobrevilla Perea, eds. *The Rise of Constitutional Government in the Iberian Atlantic World: The Impact of the Cadiz Constitution of 1812*. Tuscaloosa: University of Alabama Press, 2015.

Flory, Thomas. *Judge and Jury in Imperial Brazil, 1808–1871: Social Control and Political Stability in the New State*. Austin: University of Texas Press, 1981.

Gargarella, Roberto. 'Towards a Typology of Latin American Constitutionalism, 1810–1860.' *Latin American Research Review* 39(2) (2004): 141–153.

Gargarella, Roberto. *Latin American Constitutionalism, 1810–2010: The Engine Room of the Constitution*. Oxford: Oxford University Press, 2013.

Holloway, Thomas H. *Policing Rio de Janeiro: Repression and Resistance in a Nineteenth-Century City*. Stanford: Stanford University Press, 1993.

Lewin, Linda. *Surprise Heirs*, 2 vols. Stanford: Stanford University Press, 2003.

Milanich, Nara B. *The Children of Fate: Childhood, Class, and the State in Chile, 1850–1930*. Durham: Duke University Press, 2009.

Milton, Cynthia E. *The Many Meanings of Poverty: Colonialism, Social Compacts, and Assistance in Eighteenth-Century Ecuador*. Stanford: Stanford University Press, 2007.

Mirow, M.C. *Latin American Constitutions: The Constitution of Cádiz and Its Legacy in Spanish America*. Cambridge: Cambridge University Press, 2015.

Mirow, M.C. *Latin American Law: A History of Private Law and Institutions in Spanish America*. Austin: University of Texas Press, 2004.

Nazzari, Muriel. *Disappearance of the Dowry: Women, Families, and Social Change in São Paulo, Brazil (1600–1900)*. Stanford: Stanford University Press, 1991.

Premo, Bianca. *Children of the Father King: Youth, Authority, and Legal Minority in Colonial Lima*. Chapel Hill: University of North Carolina Press, 2005.

Premo, Bianca. *The Enlightenment on Trial: Ordinary Litigants and Colonialism in the Spanish Empire*. New York: Oxford University Press, 2017.

Saether, Steinar A. 'Bourbon Absolutism and Marriage Reform in Late Colonial Spanish America.' *The Americas* 59(4) (2003): 475–509.

Salvatore, Ricardo, Carlos Aguirre and Gilbert Joseph, eds. *Crime and Punishment in Latin America: Law and Society since Late Colonial Times*. Durham: Duke University Press, 2001.

Scardaville, Michael C. 'Alcohol Abuse and Tavern Reform in Late Colonial Mexico City.' *Hispanic American Historical Review* 60(4) (1980): 643–671.

Scardaville, Michael C. '(Hapsburg) Law and (Bourbon) Order: State Authority, Popular Unrest, and the Criminal Justice System in Bourbon Mexico City.' *The Americas* 50(4) (1994): 501–525.

Sellers-García, Sylvia. The Woman on the Windowsill: A Tale of Mystery in Several Parts. New Haven: Yale University Press, 2020.

Shelton, Laura M. *For Tranquility and Order: Family and Community on Mexico's Northern Frontier, 1800–1850*. Tucson: University of Arizona Press, 2010.

Stern, Steve J. *The Secret History of Gender: Women, Men, and Power in Late Colonial Mexico*. Chapel Hill: University of North Carolina Press, 1995.

Twinam, Ann. *Public Lives, Private Secrets: Gender, Honor, Sexuality, and Illegitimacy in Colonial Spanish America*. Stanford: Stanford University Press, 1999.

Twinam, Ann. *Purchasing Whiteness: Pardos, Mulattos, and the Quest for Social Mobility in the Spanish Indies*. Stanford: Stanford University Press, 2015.

Uribe-Uran, Victor. *Fatal Love: Spouse Killers, Law, and Punishment in the Late Colonial Spanish Atlantic*. Stanford: Stanford University Press, 2016.

Uribe-Uran, Victor. *Honorable Lives: Lawyers, Family, and Politics in Colombia, 1780–1850*. Pittsburgh: University of Pittsburgh Press, 2000.

Uribe-Uran, Victor, 'La Constitución de Cádiz en la Nueva Granada, teoría y realidad, 1812–1821.' In *La Constitución de 1812 en Hispanoamérica y España*, edited by Heraclio Bonilla, 273–303. Bogotá: Editorial Universidad Nacional de Colombia-Alcaldía Mayor de Bogotá, 2012.

von Germeten, Nicole. *The Enlightened Patrolman: Early Law Enforcement in Mexico City*. Lincoln: University of Nebraska Press, 2022.

Zahler, Reuben. 'Liberal Justice: Judicial Reform in Venezuela's Courts, 1786–1850.' *Hispanic American Historical Review* 90(3) (2010), 489–522.

Zimmermann, Eduardo, ed. *Judicial Institutions in Nineteenth-Century Latin America*. London: Institute of Latin American Studies, 1999.

CHAPTER 5

Liberalism

Timo H. Schaefer

By 1830, the countries of Latin America were close to existing in their current territorial shape. Embattled Uruguay had finally established itself as an independent state in 1828. Colombia, Venezuela, and Ecuador were well on their way to emerging as the successor states of the failed union of (what historians would later call) Gran Colombia. The Central American nations would remain federated for about another decade, and warfare would change the boundaries of some Latin American countries, and even create the new state of Panama, during the next century or so. Still, with certain exceptions, the political divisions of the region were recognizably as they remain today.

Also, by 1830 Latin America's new nation-states had decisively rejected the political legacy of the colonial era and acquired the constitutional foundations of liberal republics. Even Brazil, alone among Latin American countries in its choice of a monarchical form of government, had passed a constitution that extended to all citizens the equal protection of the law. Building up the new countries' legal systems became a major ambition – perhaps *the* major ambition – of Latin America's postcolonial nation-builders because it combined the tasks of external and internal consolidation. Extending the power of the law over all parts of the new countries' territory would create compact nations with distinct, well-defined boundaries. Ideally, the concepts of legality and nationhood would come to coincide.

Andrés Bello – poet, linguist, and author of the most influential of Latin America's nineteenth-century civil law codes (the Chilean of 1855) – expressed the romantic, almost religious attitude towards the law shared by many of the era's statesmen when he described the law as man's only possible homeland. One of a handful of Latin American statesmen who made their careers in countries different from those of their birth (he was born in the Captaincy General of Venezuela), Bello wrote that

> our true homeland is that rule of conduct indicated by the rights, obligations, and functions that we have and that we owe each other; it is that rule which establishes public and private order, which strengthens, secures, and imparts all their vigor to the relationships that unite us, and forms that body of association of rational beings in which we find the

 | DOI:10.1163/9789004436091_007

> only good, the only desirable things in our country. Therefore that rule is our true homeland, and that rule is the law, without which everything disappears.[1]

For Bello, the rule of law was more than a necessary component of statehood. It was the link between citizens and a secular kind of transcendence, the defining essence of the nation.

Compared to the intense attention that nineteenth-century statesmen devoted to matters of law, scholarly interest in Latin America's postcolonial legal history was until recently notably scant. Or rather, scholars showed only a certain kind of interest in legal history, treating the law in nineteenth-century Latin America as something that existed apart from society – as either floating above society or acting upon it in a hostile, ill-fitting manner.[2] They assumed that the law – with its foreign influences and formal procedures – had little to do with how Latin Americans lived or how their societies were constituted. The actual relationship between the law and Latin American societies was underexplored because historians did not regard nineteenth-century Latin American states as proper 'nations,' with citizenries that interacted in a reciprocal manner with state institutions.

A new interest in the social history of the law in nineteenth-century Latin America – in the history of the law not only as a body of written rules but as a structuring principle of social reality – has come from the discovery that ordinary Latin Americans were often deeply invested in ideas of nationhood and legality. When Bello called the law his true homeland, he was expressing (and, perhaps, exaggerating) a sentiment shared by Latin Americans from widely different walks of life. Postcolonial Latin America was a region where peasants started rebellions in the name of the law: 'our liberty lies in law,' a peasant manifesto from southern Mexico declared in a phrase that Bello might have enjoyed. Indigenous Peruvians in the province of Huantla frequently rose up in 'defense of the law.' And Latin Americans from the humblest of backgrounds sought the law's help in their personal affairs, litigating over issues as petty as unreturned small loans and as momentous as freedom from slavery.[3]

1 Iván Jaksić, *Andrés Bello: Scholarship and Nation-Building in Nineteenth-Century Latin America* (Cambridge: Cambridge University Press, 2001), 177–178.

2 Jorge Esquirol, 'The Fictions of Latin American Law (Part I)' (1997) Utah Law Review 425–470, and 'Continuing Fictions of Latin American Law' (2003) 55 Florida Law Review 41–114.

3 The Mexican peasant rebels are cited in Peter Guardino, 'Barbarism or Republican Law? Guerrero's Peasants and National Politics, 1820–1846' (1995) 75(2) Hispanic American Historical Review 186 and the Peruvian ones in Cecilia Méndez, 'Tradiciones liberales en

In this chapter I attempt to take stock of what we know about the social history of the law in postcolonial Latin America. I describe substantive legal changes in areas such as property, family, and housing law – first from 1830 to approximately 1880 and then from approximately 1880 to 1930, when new ideas about social improvement began to influence countries' legislative agendas. I also explore the geographical distribution of the tribunals and public-security forces that mediated between the law and Latin American citizens, and I discuss the procedural innovations by which governments intended to move from a colonial to a republican culture of law. While I try to be attentive to the diversity of legal institutions in postcolonial Latin America, my emphasis is on finding common patterns and defining dominant trends.

1 Legal Change, 1830–1880

The legislative agenda of Latin America's postcolonial republics was dominated by the fight against legal privilege. Lawmakers began by abolishing titles of nobility and opening careers to talent. An 1825 law in Gran Colombia, for example, for the first time allowed 'illegitimate sons' to obtain a university education. Striking exclusionary provisions from republican lawbooks was the easy part of the egalitarian agenda. Legislators soon found, however, that the fight against inequality opened up some thorny philosophical problems. To achieve true legal equality, it was desirable to put an end to Indigenous village corporations and to the institution of slavery, yet both of those objectives came into tension with the protection liberals felt they owed to the institution of property.[4]

In colonial Latin America, Indigenous towns and villages were in important (though by no means in all) respects self-governing corporations with their own peculiar legal cultures and governing structures. At the basis of their relative autonomy was the corporations' control over village- and townlands, some of which were held in common and some distributed in private parcels among village and town folk. Replacing the exclusionary structures of these corporations with racially inclusive municipal governments became a crucial aim of liberal nation-builders in Latin America. This was easy to do in places where Indigenous people were, for all effects and purposes, the only population.

los Andes: militares y campesinos en la formación del estado peruano' (2004) 15(1) Estudios Interdisciplinarios de América Latina 51.

4 On the 1825 law, see Victor Uribe-Uran, *Honorable Lives: Lawyers, Family, and Politics in Colombia, 1780–1850* (Pittsburgh: University of Pittsburgh Press, 2000), 77.

In such places – in many parts of the Andes, for example, and some parts of southern Mexico – Indigenous governments could simply adopt republican municipal forms without losing any of their previous powers. Things were more difficult in areas with mixed populations.

A central function of colonial Indigenous governments had been to govern the distribution of village lands. But turning that task over to inclusive municipal governments risked violating the property rights of the individuals who had composed the Indigenous village corporation, since non-Indigenous residents might now lay claim to land parcels that previously had been the collective property of Indigenous residents. One effect of the dismantling of a system of law that had segregated Latin Americans by race was thus the transfer of Indigenous property into non-Indigenous hands. More commonly, however, liberal assumptions about the sanctity of property rights stood in the way of such blatant acts of robbery. Mixed-race municipalities that historians have examined in depth – for example Diriomo in Nicaragua or Huixquilucan in Mexico – came to be dominated by economically powerful, non-Indigenous minorities soon after independence. But corporate land in these municipalities remained under the control of formally disbanded Indigenous governments, which carried on a kind of shadow existence long after Mexican and Nicaraguan independence.[5] Aspects of Indigenous corporate governance continued to function in practice even as they were abolished on paper.

The abolition of the colonial Indigenous corporation, then, was impeded by the existence of collective land rights. Only when collective lands had been privatized would it also be possible to do away with Indigenous corporate structures. In the second half of the nineteenth century, liberal governments across Latin America therefore decreed the privatization of corporate landholding. By ordering collectively held property distributed between the members of the extinguished village corporation, they hoped to turn collective property into individual property. This made the property freely alienable and therefore consistent, as collective property had not been, with the value of personal freedom without violating the property rights corporate villages had conferred on their individual members. The outcome of the liberal privatization programs hinged on a number of factors, including the previous uses and the desirability of the land to be privatized. Titling land that had previously been held in individual

5 David McCreey, *Rural Guatemala, 1760–1940* (Stanford: Stanford University Press, 1994), 55–57. Elizabeth Dore, *Myths of Modernity: Peonage and Patriarchy in Nicaragua* (Durham: Duke University Press, 2006); Daniela Marino, *Huixquilucan: Ley y justicia en la modernización del espacio rural mexiquense, 1856–1910* (Madrid: Consejo Superior de Investigaciones Científicas, 2016).

usufruct was easier than dividing terrains that had been used collectively – for the extraction of firewood or the pasture of animals, for example – or that had been rented out, at a profit, by corporate governments or religious brotherhoods. Furthermore, quickly rising land values (usually in areas growing commodities for export) increased the likelihood of fraud during the privatization process.

The municipality of Papantla in southeastern Mexico offers an example of what could happen when liberal privatization laws were applied in an area that lacked a clearly established land-use pattern and suddenly found itself at the center of a commodity boom. As demand for native vanilla soared on the world market, Indigenous elites and mestizo merchants joined forces to privatize Totonac Indigenous lands. But because the Totonacs had been practicing a form of slash-and-burn agriculture – clearing new patches of forest every few years to give the land time to recuperate – no strong individual claims to particular patches of land existed. That context, together with skyrocketing land values, led to a frenzied and irregular privatization process, generating resistance and, eventually, descending into violence. The army came in, the militia was mobilized, and resisters were hunted down and murdered. When the smoke cleared, Totonac elites and some of their merchant allies were left in possession of large tracts of the best-located land, while some of the poorer Totonac farmers had been entirely defrauded of their right to a parcel. This was not, however, the norm. In many Indigenous towns privatization did leave behind an ample class of agricultural smallholders, and in some Mexican regions, Indigenous towns even managed to hold on to their collective property by constituting themselves as shareholding companies – a highly innovative solution that married liberal contract law to an ancient form of corporate social organization.[6]

6 On privatization in Papantla, see Emilio Kourí, *A Pueblo Divided: Business, Property, and Community in Papantla, Mexico* (Stanford: Stanford University Press, 2004). On smallholding beneficiaries of land privatization see e.g., Mark Thurner, *From Two Republics to One Divided: Contradictions of Postcolonial Nationmaking in Andean Peru* (Durham: Duke University Press, 1997), 48–52 and Edgar Mendoza García, *Los bienes de comunidad y la defensa de las tierras en la Mixteca oaxaqueña: Cohesión y autonomía del municipio de Santo Domingo Tepenene, 1856–1912* (México: Senado de la República, 2004). On Indigenous shareholding companies in Mexico, see e.g., Antonio Escobar Ohmstede, 'Los condueñazgos Indígenas en las Huastecas Hidalguense y Veracruzana: ¿Defensa del espacio comunal?' in *Indio, nación, y comunidad en el México del siglo XIX*, ed. Antonio Escobar Ohmstede (México: Centro de Estudios Mexicanos y Centroamericanos, 1993), 171–188 and Benjamin Smith, *The Roots of Conservatism in Mexico: Catholicism, Society, and Politics in the Mixteca Baja, 1750–1962* (Albuquerque: University of New Mexico Press, 2012), 169–175, 308–313.

If individual freedom was the central value of nineteenth-century liberal thought, the most urgent task of liberal nation-builders in Latin America, more urgent even than the extinction of corporate landholdings, was the abolition of slavery. But in the matter of slavery, too, the principle of freedom conflicted with established property rights. Under slavery, human beings were held in property and valued in hard money. To abolish slavery, then, someone would have to pay to release slaves from their shackles. It is a measure of the influence that slaveholders continued to hold over policy in the independent nations – and of the fragility of liberal values in the face of that influence – that those paying were often the slaves and rarely the slaveowners.

Latin American countries where slavery had become marginal to the economy, such as Chile, Mexico, and the Central American republics, decreed the end of slavery in the 1820s, very soon after independence. While the abolition of slavery was also an item on the political agenda of other postcolonial republics, slave-owner opposition in countries with significant slave populations (organized politically in the region's conservative parties) meant that abolition typically turned into a gradual process with various stages: the prohibition of the slave trade, the freeing at birth of the children of slaves, and finally the emancipation of any remaining slaves (always with government compensation for slaveowners). This last step often did not happen until various decades after independence: in 1852 in Colombia, for example, in 1854 in Venezuela, and in 1855 in Peru. In those countries, long before the abolition of slavery was complete, many slaves had already achieved their freedom through self-purchase or by running away.[7]

Imperial Brazil, home to the largest slave population in the Americas, lagged behind the Spanish-American republics both in the timing of abolition and in the rights it afforded to freed slaves. The former Portuguese colony only outlawed the slave trade in 1830, and that in a law that for various decades would be rarely enforced. It freed newborn children of slaves in 1871 and finally abolished the institution of slavery in 1888. Before that date, furthermore, even freed Afro-Brazilians were treated as a class of citizens apart. In direct contradiction to Brazil's relatively liberal Constitution of 1824, the country's

7 Manuel Moreno Fraginals, 'La abolición de la esclavitud' in *Historia general de América Latina: La construcción de las nuevas naciones latinoamericanas*, eds Manuel Miño Grijalva and Josefina Zoraida Vázquez, vol. 6 (Madrid: Editorial Trotta, 2004); Russell Lohse, 'Reconciling Freedom with the Rights of Property: Slave Emancipation in Colombia, 1821–1852, with Special Reference to La Plata' (2001) 86(3) Journal of Negro History 203–227; Jason McGraw, 'Spectacles of Freedom: Public Manumissions, Political Rhetoric, and Citizen Mobilization in Mid-Nineteenth-Century Colombia' (2011) 32(2) Slavery & Abolition 269–288.

lawmakers introduced explicit limitations on the civil rights of freed Africans in 1832 in its code of criminal procedure, requiring African freemen to carry a passport for any travel within Brazilian territory. Black Brazilian citizens were often treated as runaway slaves unless they could provide positive proof of their freedom.[8]

The gradual destruction of legal privilege and legal handicaps, while never perfect, expanded the realm of freedom to previously excluded social groups and is a dominant motive in the legislative history of Latin America between 1830 and about 1880. This motive was subtly repeated in other, less eye-catching measures designed to advance the cause of liberalism. For example, the abolition of *mayorazgos* (entailed estates that could not be divided through sale or inheritance) freed landed property from a major hindrance to its unimpeded circulation. The social impact of this abolition was sometimes enormous, leading, for example, to a rapid shrinking of average landholding size in the Brazilian province of Rio Grande do Sul.[9] Innovations in contract law, too, were designed to keep up with changing social and economic circumstances and to facilitate commerce and productive investment. Until close to the end of the nineteenth century, in any case, the development of substantive law after Latin American independence appeared to move slowly but steadily in the direction of greater freedom, autonomy, and protection for adult, male individuals.

2 The Geography of Legal Rule

Not only the substance of Latin American law changed in the decades following the region's independence. So did the geography of the law's infrastructural presence. The basic building block of the new legal systems in most of Latin America's postcolonial republics was the municipality, seat of the local judges – the magistrates and justices of the peace – who, for a vast majority of Latin Americans, became the faces of republican justice. While the responsibilities of municipal judges were similar to what they had been under the colonial period, after independence those responsibilities were no longer shared with other officials, such as crown-appointed *corregidores* and *alcaldes*

8 Sidney Chalhoub, 'The Precariousness of Freedom in a Slave Society (Brazil in the Nineteenth Century)' (2011) 56 International Review of Social History 405–439; Adriana Chira, 'Affective Debts: Manumission by Grace and the Making of Gradual Emancipation Laws in Cuba, 1817–68' (2018) 36(1) Law and History Review 1–33.

9 John Charles Chasteen, 'Background to Civil War: The Process of Land Tenure in Brazil's Southern Borderland, 1801–1893' (1991) 71(4) Hispanic American Historical Review 737–760.

mayores or (after the Bourbon reforms) *subdelegados* and *intendentes*. Latin America's republican governments had no tolerance for the ambiguity and rivalry that had characterized colonial jurisdictions. Under liberal governments judges were also selected in a new way: by election rather than appointment. Conservative-leaning governments, however, held on to (or reintroduced) the practice of judicial appointment, and the question of whether justice was better served by elected or appointed officials became a major point of contention in the politics of postcolonial Latin America.

The most significant difference between colonial and republican judges is also the most easily overlooked. It is the sheer number of them. Municipalities in Latin America had multiplied during the independence period – from fifty-two to 680 in Peru, for example, and from 200 to 1205 in Mexico – and local judges had multiplied with them. More research about the scale of this multiplication remains to be done. Many of the new municipalities took the place of colonial Indigenous governments, whose *gobernadores* (governors or mayors) had also carried out judicial functions. But not all new Indigenous municipalities had previously been self-governed. And new municipalities were also formed in areas where Indigenous towns were few. The Mexican state of Guanajuato had nine municipalities in 1804, but twenty-three by the early 1820s. The presence of judges, as a result, was no longer restricted to a few urban centers. This multiplication of judges and tribunals was not an incidental byproduct of the creation of new municipalities. It was a deliberate policy pursued by Latin America's postcolonial governments. Thus, even in the La Plata region, where local justice was uncoupled from the functions of municipal governments, provincial governments rapidly increased the number of justices of the peace in the countryside.[10]

In practical terms, the increase in municipalities and local judges after independence signified an enormous territorial expansion of the legal state: populations that had been weakly linked to the judicial apparatus of colonial governments now counted with local courts. The judges staffing those courts performed similar tasks across Latin America. They were responsible for

10 On the number of municipalities in Peru and Mexico, see Antonio Annino, 'Imperio, Constitución y diversidad en la América hispana' (2008) 70(2) Ayer 47–48. On the number of municipalities in Guanajuato, see José Antonio Serrano Ortega, *Jerarquía territorial y transición política: Guanajuato, 1790–1836* (Zamora: El Colegio de Michoacán, México: Instituto Mora, 2001), 147. On the administration of justice in Buenos Aires, see Juan Carlos Garavaglia, 'Paz, orden y trabajo en la campaña: la justicia rural y los juzgados de paz en Buenos Aires, 1830–1852' (1997) 146 Desarrollo Económico 241–262 and Oreste Cansanello, *De súbditos a ciudadanos: Ensayo sobre las libertades en los orígenes republicanos: Buenos Aires, 1810–1852* (Buenos Aires: Ediciones Imago Mundi, 2003).

judging small civil lawsuits (or, where possible, reconciling the contending parties), carrying out the first steps in criminal investigations, and in general preventing or breaking up any disturbances to the local peace. In concrete terms, this meant that judges spent much of their time hearing complaints from battered wives, slandered neighbors, and defaulted creditors. Considered minor by the law, such matters in fact constituted the bulk of the region's legal business. Under an 1837 Mexican law, for example, justices of the peace had to deal with all property disputes valued under 100 pesos and hence, in effect, with most litigation connected to local industry, commerce, and agriculture.[11]

A key feature of the republican legal culture that spread through the Latin American countryside after independence was its participatory nature. The rule of law thrived to the extent that citizens were willing to make it so. Thus, the office of magistrate or justice of the peace – as, indeed, almost all municipal offices – in most places was honorary. Whether elected or appointed, until late in the nineteenth century local judges were not as a rule paid for their services. Nor were members of the guards, militias, constabularies, and neighborhood watches who assumed the bulk of the police work in the postcolonial republics. Made up of adult, male citizens who rotated guard duties between themselves, these non-professional forces patrolled the streets, arrested troublemakers, and in general assisted local authorities in their efforts to protect lives and property. In places where professional police forces did exist – for example, big cities or the Buenos Aires countryside – militias or neighborhood watches were still often called on to stand by in case their assistance was needed. It should be added that these civic police forces have not been much studied. With certain exceptions, their diligence and effectiveness remain a matter of conjecture.[12]

---

11 'Arreglo provisional de la administracion de justicia en los juzgados y tribunales de fuero comun' 23 May 1837, article 113, in *Legislación Mexicana, ó, Colección completa de las disposiciones legislativas expedidas desde la independencia de la República*, eds Manuel Dublán and José María Lozano (México: Imprenta del Comercio, 1876), vol. 3, 403.

12 Roberto Hernández Ponce, 'La Guardia Nacional de Chile: Apuntes sobre su origen y organización, 1808–1848' (1984) 19 Historia 53–114. Oreste Cansanello, 'Las milicias rurales bonaerenses entre 1820 y 1830' (1998) 19 Cuadernos de Historia Regional 7–51 and Cansanello, *De súbditos a ciudadanos*; Osvaldo Barreneche, *Crime and the Administration of Justice in Buenos Aires, 1785–1852* (Lincoln: University of Nebraska Press, 2006), 62; Eduardo Martins, *A invenção da vadiagem: Os termos do bem vivir e a sociedade disciplinar no Império do Brasil* (Curitiba: Editora CRV, 2011), 58–61; Timo H. Schaefer, *Liberalism as Utopia* (Cambridge: Cambridge University Press, 2017), 79–89; Thomas Flory, *Judge and Jury in Imperial Brazil 1808–1871: Social Control and Political Stability in the New State* (Austin: University of Texas Press, 1981).

Expanding the reach of the legal state in postcolonial Latin America was a project that was especially pushed forward by liberal political forces. Conservative politicians often impeded the extension of the republics' judicial infrastructure. Those politicians typically argued that the creation of courts in too many places would lower the quality of justice. They held that many settlements lacked the literate, financially independent men necessary to administer justice competently and fairly. Semiliterate judges without steady income, they reasoned, were too easily manipulated or corrupted to be entrusted with the sacred task of representing the law. As a result, conservative governments often withdrew municipal status from small or poor settlements, making inhabitants of those settlements dependent on the tribunals of distant bigger or wealthier towns. Justice became less accessible, and the activities made possible by an accessible justice system, less common. Settlements lacking municipal status, for example, were usually prohibited from holding markets, which stimulated local economies but were also known to attract disorder.[13]

In areas of Latin America with many *haciendas* – agricultural estates – the expansion of a republican justice system met social as well as political obstacles. *Haciendas*, though privately owned, often contained substantial settlements of tenants, workers, and sharecroppers. They were enterprises that also functioned as public spaces, just like other settlements with hundreds and sometimes thousands of inhabitants. Given *haciendas*'s status as private property, however, it was difficult to bring them under the authority of the law. In the geography of Latin American state formation, agricultural estates emerged as blank spaces into which the authority of the state was barely able to reach – even during the reign of liberal governments. In Mexico, the conversion of *haciendas* into municipalities (with due compensation of the owners) became a project for some peasant rebels and, toward the middle of the century, for a group of political reformers: the so-called social liberals, who argued that wherever *haciendas* dominated the countryside, any talk of the rule of law was mere delusion. But only on a handful of Mexican *haciendas* was such a conversion achieved in practice.[14]

The absence of legal institutions on agricultural estates need not mean that landowners were usurping the power of the state. In the early years of the postcolonial era, most Latin American economies were in a slump, with *hacienda*

13 Méndez, 'Tradiciones liberales en los Andes,' 35–63. Dore, *Myths of Modernity*, 62; Martins, *A invenção da vadiagem*, 58–61; Schaefer, *Liberalism as Utopia*, 43–47, 102–103.

14 Schaefer, *Liberalism as Utopia*, 97–128; Juan Carlos Sánchez Montiel, 'De poblados de hacienda a municipios en el altiplano de San Luis Potosí' (2006) 31 Estudios de Historia Moderna y Contemporánea de México, 57–81.

owners as much affected as anyone else. Controlling the people who lived on their land was, for many, a low priority. For peasants and rural workers, *haciendas* could therefore emerge as spaces of freedom of sorts: territories where they could work, drink, trade, and quarrel far from the disapproving eyes of the judge or the greedy purse of the tax collector. In the La Plata region, where an expansive frontier of cattle ranches relied on a floating population of rural laborers, governments in the 1820s introduced passbooks as a means of labor control. But to little effect. For decades longer, the region's nomadic cowhands, or *gauchos*, continued to cheat landlords out of wage advances, changing employers whenever they pleased.[15] However, landowners did exercise quasi-judicial functions, in support of often coercive labor regimes, in areas where society was strongly structured by racial hierarchies. In Bolivia and Ecuador, Indigenous laborers were bound to landed estates to whose owners they owed various kinds of labor service. In Brazil, plantation owners continued to lock black tenants up in private stocks or prisons until well after the abolition of slavery.[16]

The power and prevalence of *haciendas* in postcolonial Latin America increased over time. In the late nineteenth and early twentieth centuries, during a period of strong, export-led economic growth, privately owned territories took up increasing amounts of social space. *Haciendas* became larger and, in the most economically dynamic areas of countries such as Ecuador, Peru, Bolivia, and Mexico, began swallowing up surrounding peasant towns. *Hacienda* owners, furthermore, demanded the right to discipline workers with growing stridency. On Mexican henequen or Nicaraguan coffee plantations, agricultural capitalists kept their laborers in conditions of quasi-slavery. They applied the whip at will and, sometimes, locked laborers up overnight to prevent their escape. And it was not only agricultural enterprises that were responsible for a shrinking of the territorial reach of the law. Company towns in mining regions became private fiefdoms in which capitalists often completely captured the legal authority of the state by owners staffing local governments, tribunals, and police forces. When faced with the power of big capital, in short,

15 *La ley es tela de araña: Ley, justicia y sociedad rural en Buenos Aires, 1780–1830*, ed. Raúl Fradkin (Buenos Aires: Prometeo Libros, 2009); Ricardo Salvatore, *Wandering Paysanos: State Order and Subaltern Experience in Buenos Aires during the Rosas Era* (Durham: Duke University Press, 2003).

16 Brooke Larson, *Trials of Nation Making: Liberalism, Race, and Ethnicity in the Andes, 1810–1910* (New York: Cambridge University Press, 2004), 103–140, 202–245; Fraga, *Crossroads of Freedom*, 98–101.

the expansion of the legal state in Latin America, so prominent a trait of the first half-century after independence, found its limits.[17]

3 The End of Discretion

By expanding the infrastructure of legal rule, Latin American nation-builders aimed to make the law both binding and accessible to people who had previously lived at the margins of the formal rules of society. But to bind and to protect people truly, the law also had to be made transparent. Only if people understood their rights and obligations would they be able to approach the law serenely. Only if they knew what to expect from the law would they be able to make it their lives' compass. The rule of law as liberals understood it thus required an end to judicial discretion. It required the existence of clear laws, competent judges, and uniform legal procedures. After independence, legislators worked hard to bring this about. They prohibited the use of torture as a means of collecting evidence and the confiscation of goods as a form of punishment. They defined the conditions under which the state was allowed to deprive people of their liberty, typically mandating that charges were to be laid against detainees and detainees apprised of those charges within a short period of their arrest. As the nineteenth century wore on, most Latin American countries further strengthened the protection of individual rights. Mexico, for example, included a catalogue of rights in its Constitution of 1857 and established a judicial mechanism, the writ of *amparo*, that allowed citizens to seek (and often to find) judicial protection against unconstitutional exercises of state power such as arbitrary imprisonment or impressment into the army.[18]

---

17 John Kenneth Turner, *Barbarous Mexico* (Austin: University of Texas Press, 1969); Rodney Anderson, *Outcasts in Their Own Land: Mexican Industrial Workers, 1906–1911* (DeKalb: Northern Illinois University Press, 1976); Gabriel Salazar, *Labradores, peones y proletarios: Formación y crisis de la sociedad popular chilena del siglo XIX* (Santiago: Ediciones Sur, 1985), 204–221; Jeffrey Gould, *To Die in This Way: Nicaraguan Indians and the Myth of Mestizaje, 1880–1965* (Durham: Duke University Press, 1998), 53; Dore, *Myths of Modernity*, 115–117; Larson, *Trials of Nation Making*; Schaefer, *Liberalism as Utopia*, 189–197; Alan Knight, 'Mexican Peonage: What Was It and Why Was It?' (1986) 18(1) Journal of Latin American Studies 41–74.

18 Jaime Hernández Díaz, *Orden y Desorden Social en Michoacán: El Derecho Penal en la República Federal 1824–1835* (Morelia: Universidad Michoacana de San Nicolás de Hidalgo/Instituto de Investigaciones Históricas/Escuela de Historia/Morevallado Editores, 1999); Graciela Flores Flores, *La justicia criminal ordinaria en tiempos de transición: La construcción de un nuevo orden judicial (Ciudad de México, 1824–1871)* (México: Universidad Nacional Autónoma de México, Instituto de Investigaciones Sociales, 2019); Timothy

Latin America's post-independence lawmakers also cut down on judges' margin of discretion during a trial. Judicial discretion had been a common and accepted feature of the legal culture of the colonial period. The old regime had acknowledged the imperfect nature of written law and recognized the value of considering factors or circumstances not foreseen by the lawmaker. This legal culture had come under attack late in the colonial period – during the so-called Bourbon reforms – and, by the time independence was achieved, was largely associated with the corrupt and arbitrary nature of colonial rule. Post-independence lawmakers thus insisted on clear and precisely regulated procedural steps that would produce as impartial and objectively correct a judgment as possible. For minor matters of civil law, however, lawmakers made an exception. Such matters were to be treated in quick oral hearings. The thorough and fastidious procedural rules of republican law were relaxed, even sacrificed, for the relief of a speedy decision – itself a kind of protection against the major interruption of business or personal affairs that trials could signify.[19]

A major consequence of lawmakers' crackdown on judicial discretion was that considerations of the social status of litigants tended to cede to impartial considerations of the quality of evidence and the meaning of legal rules. This was a significant change in Latin American legal culture. During the colonial period, considerations of a person's status and honor had done much to influence their treatment in court. In Buenos Aires, for example, black defendants (whether free or enslaved) had been the most likely to suffer torture (in order to extract confessions) in criminal processes or to suffer corporal punishments such as lashes in case they were convicted. Commercial law had differentiated between people based on their guild membership, itself a function of their social condition. After independence, on the other hand, the procedural steps of prosecuting a black artisan and a creole merchant were exactly the same – as were the laws applied and the punishment given.[20]

James, *Mexico's Supreme Court: Between Liberal Individual and Revolutionary Social Rights, 1867–1934* (Albuquerque: University of New Mexico Press, 2013), 1–26; Sarah Chambers, *From Subjects to Citizens: Honor, Gender, and Politics in Arequipa, Peru 1780–1854* (University Park: Pennsylvania State University Press, 1999).

19 Chambers, *From Subjects to Citizens*; M.C. Mirow, *Latin American Law: A History of Private Law and Institutions in Spanish America* (Austin: University of Texas Press, 2004), 107–115; Reuben Zahler, *Ambitious Rebels: Remaking Honor, Law, and Liberalism in Venezuela, 1780–1850* (Tucson: University of Arizona Press, 2013); Águeda Venegas de la Torre, *Los avatares de la administración de justicia en Zacatecas, 1812–1835* (México: Instituto de Investigaciones Dr. José María Luis Mora, 2016).

20 Jeremy Adelman, *Republic of Capital: Buenos Aires and the Legal Transformation of the Atlantic World* (Stanford: Stanford University Press, 1999); Barreneche, *Crime and the Administration of Justice*; Reuben Zahler, *Ambitious Rebels*.

While Latin America's post-independent legal systems offered citizens new remedies against legal abuses, the quality of local justice remained influenced by social and political factors. In every country there were areas where colonial-era elite networks, through their control of municipal politics, remained in control of the local apparatus of justice. In those areas, the republican principle of legal equality was for large parts of the population no more than a promise. In Chile, to give an extreme example, throughout the nineteenth century most justices of the peace were closely linked to regional power networks. Judges active in Chile's higher tribunals almost always belonged to families with illustrious colonial backgrounds, making 'justice' (and especially justice in social conflicts that pitted popular against elite sectors of society) a kind of class imposition. In northeastern Brazil, in the decades preceding the abolition of slavery, slaves alleging abuses from their owners (there were laws regulating the treatment and punishments owners were allowed to inflict on their slaves) knew that they had to present themselves before judges in the city of Salvador – rather than the smaller, rural towns closest to most plantations – if they wanted to receive a fair hearing. Indigenous Latin Americans could also face hurdles in their encounters with the law. In towns dominated by non-Indigenous minorities, they often suffered the loss of their own magistrates – and, with that, the loss of their chance to receive a fair hearing when they had quarrels with their mestizo betters.[21]

To shrink the margin of discretion in judicial proceedings, nineteenth-century governments in Latin America also aimed to professionalize their countries' justice apparatus and to create comprehensive legal codes that would leave no room for interpretive ambiguity. The social effects of these judicial-reform projects are understudied and difficult to assess, in part because they took so long to implement. For decades Latin America's postcolonial republics relied on untrained, lay judges to staff local tribunals because legal professionals were scarce and their services expensive. The multiplication of local tribunals (discussed in the previous section) was possible because the office of magistrate or justice of the peace was almost always honorary. Whether lay

21 Walter Fraga, *Crossroads of Freedom: Slaves and Freed People in Bahia, Brazil 1870–1910* trans; Mary Ann Mahony (Durham: Duke University Press, 2016), 23, 67–68; Maria Rosaria Stabili, 'Jueces y justicia en el Chile liberal' in *Constitucionalismo y orden liberal: América Latina, 1850–1920*, ed. Marcello Carmagnani (Torino: Otto Editore, 2000); Dore, *Myths of Modernity*, 62; Daniela Marino, 'La fuerza de la ley. Leyes, justicias y resistencias en la imposición de la propiedad privada en México, segunda mitad del siglo XIX' in *Sangre de ley*, 203–234; Chalhoub, 'Precariousness of Freedom'; Yuko Miki, *Frontiers of Citizenship: A Black and Indigenous History of Postcolonial Brazil* (New York: Cambridge University Press, 2018).

justices did more to improve the accessibility of republican law or to render it unpredictable and inefficient (as their critics charged) is a question historians are still debating. The evidence is not easy to read, as citizen complaints of judicial misconduct (of which there were many) could be signs both of a miscarriage of justice and of the vigor by which citizens held judges accountable. What seems at least clear is that lay judges, no matter how challenged in the daily exercise of their duty, were kept busy by the varied conflicts and affairs of their jurisdictions. They arrested thieves, locked up violent husbands, and guaranteed the circulation of credit. If they were all too fallible, they were also clearly needed. As the decades passed and state finances improved, Latin American nations generally tried to replace lay with professional judges – a process that at the beginning of the twentieth century remained incomplete.[22]

The creation of comprehensive legal codes in nineteenth-century Latin America had a similar aim as the professionalization of justice. It was meant to eliminate the role of custom and judicial discretion in the administration of justice. Many lawmakers, furthermore, considered the rejection of the colonial corpuses of laws, and their replacement with modern, national legal codes, an urgent necessity for the true independence of their nations. 'The lack of codes that regulate the duties and rights of man,' wrote the Guatemalan politician Agustín Gutiérrez Lizaurzábal in 1834, 'forces us to be ruled by laws gleaned from other nations, which, because of their antiquity, the spirit of the government by which they were made, and their confusion are absolutely inadequate.' Chile's House of Representatives in 1831 called the law as it then existed 'a bottomless and immense chaos … without unity nor a relationship to the enlightened principles [*luces*], the customs, and the nature of our government.'[23]

---

22 Victor M. Uribe-Uran, 'Colonial Lawyers, Republican Lawyers and the Administration of Justice in Spanish America,' in *Judicial Institutions in Nineteenth-Century Latin America*, ed. Eduardo Zimmermann (London: Institute of Latin American Studies, 1999), 44–46. Juan Manuel Palacio, 'Judges, Lawyers, and Farmers: Uses of Justice and the Circulation of Law in Rural Buenos Aires, 1900–1940' in *Crime and Punishment in Latin America: Law and Society since Late Colonial Times*, eds Ricardo Salvatore, Carlos Aguirre, and Gilbert Joseph (Durham: Duke University Press, 2001), and *La paz del trigo: Cultural legal y sociedad local en el desarrollo agropecuario pampeano, 1890–1945* (Buenos Aires: Edhasa, 2004); Marino, 'La fuerza de la ley'; Andrés Botero Bernal, 'La tensión entre la justicia legal y la justicia letrada durante la primera mitad del siglo XIX: el caso de Antioquía (Nueva Granada)' (2010) 7 Iuhistoria 65–88; Venegas de la Torre, *Los avatares de la administración de justicia*.

23 Quotations in Alejandro Guzmán Brito, 'La influencia del código civil francés en las codificaciones americanas' (2004) 9 Cuadernos de Extensión Jurídica (Universidad de los Andes) 21. See also Victor Tau Anzoátegui, *La codificación en la Argentina, 1810–1870: Mentalidad social e ideas jurídicas* (Buenos Aires: Imprenta de la Universidad, 1977), 119–123. On the early process of codification see Victor M. Uribe-Uran, 'The Great Transformation of Law and Legal Culture: "The Public" and "The Private" in the Transition from Empire to Nation

In reality, colonial legislation had never been quite as chaotic as nineteenth-century politicians made it out to be. Major colonial laws had eventually been collected in comprehensive compilations (most notably in the 1680 *Compilation of the Laws of the Kingdoms of the Indies*), and a system of precedence had established which sources of law should prevail in cases where different bodies of law were in conflict. After independence, legislators updated this system of precedence, now placing the new laws passed by the republican legislatures (sometimes referred to as the *ley patria*) in first place. This mode of proceeding allowed lawmakers to supersede colonial laws that went against the grain of their liberal principles. And it gave them time to develop the expertise, and wait for the political stability, that were necessary for a more thorough overhaul of their nations' written sources of law.[24]

Still, Latin American lawmakers held on to their vision of a new beginning in the matter of law. The radical political break of the independence revolutions encouraged such a remaking. Furthermore, France's Napoleonic Code of civil law (also assembled in the aftermath of a major revolution) provided not only an example to follow but also a model to copy and modify. Thus, the first civil codes in Latin America – Haiti's code of 1825, Bolivia's of 1830, Peru's of 1836, and Costa Rica's of 1842 – were close imitations of the Napoleonic example. Only in the second half of the nineteenth century did Latin American jurists create their own civil codes, combining Napoleonic elements with Hispanic legal traditions, especially in the matters of family and inheritance law. Of those, Chile's 1855 civil code, drafted by Andrés Bello, was the most influential, being widely adopted in other Latin American countries.[25] Most Latin American governments over the course of the nineteenth century also passed criminal, procedural, and commercial codes, so that the break with the legal order of the old regime was total.

As to the effects of codification – its actual impact on legal cultures and processes – the historiography is divided into opposed interpretations. One position sees codification as the culmination of exactly those procedural innovations that since independence had tended to make the administration of

in Mexico, Colombia, and Brazil, 1750–1850,' in *Empire to Nation: Historical Perspectives on the Making of the Modern World*, eds Joseph W. Esherick, Hasan Kayali, and Eric Van Young (New York: Rowman & Littlefield, 2005), 68–105.

24 Alejandro Guzmán Brito, *Historia de la codificación civil en Iberoamérica* (Madrid: Fundación Histórico Tavera, 2000), 100–101, 122–124, 164–167; M.C. Mirow, 'Borrowing Private Law in Latin America: Andrés Bello's use of the *Code Napoléon* in Drafting the Chilean Civil Code' (2001) 61 Louisiana Law Review 291–329; Mirow, *Latin American Law*, 126–135.

25 Guzmán Brito, 'La influencia del código civil francés.'

justice transparent and fair. In Argentina, for example, the nation-wide adoption of a commercial code occurred in the same year (1862) as the abolition of a Commercial Tribunal with close ties to an established merchant elite. Codified commercial law became the province of independent district tribunals and commissary judges, rather than of the exclusive successor organization to a colonial-era guild. In Mexico, a gradual process of criminal-justice reform, which found its final expression in the 1871 criminal code of the Federal District and Baja California (also the principal model for the codes Mexico's other states would adopt), led to much greater regularity in criminal sentencing.[26]

There is also evidence that newly codified laws could become part of the framework in which non-elites conducted their lives and their business. Such popular usages were not always foreseen by lawmakers. In the booming coffee town of Tapachula, Mexico, for example, people soon began using the rules and language of an 1871 civil code to formalize commercial transactions that were technically too insignificant to fall under the code's compass. While lawmakers had not intended the new rules for the sphere of petty trade, the new laws' rapid adoption by small and medium entrepreneurs nevertheless suggests that they were filling a popular need. A few decades later, during the Mexican Revolution, the civil code had become influential enough – even among poor and illiterate folk – to be the preferred frame of reference for inheritance disputes taking place in territory controlled by the Zapatista revolutionary faction.[27]

The rival historiographical position instead focuses on instances in which the growing dominion of written sources of law separated the administration of justice from the cultural and material reality of the lives of popular sectors of society. According to this view, codification was the culmination of a larger process of eliminating local custom as a valid source of law. While this elimination may have made the law more predictable for people with the means to afford lawyers, the argument goes, for most people it simply made the law more inaccessible.[28] For example, in 1850 Brazil's land law, which required all possessions in land to be measured and formally registered, made it difficult

26 Adelman, *Republic of Capital*; Flores Flores, *La justicia criminal ordinaria*.

27 Casey Lurtz, 'Codifying Credit: Everyday Contracting and the Spread of the Civil Code in Nineteenth-Century Mexico' (2021) 39/1 Law and History Review 97–133; Helga Baitenmann, 'Zapata's Justice: Land and Water Conflict Resolution in Revolutionary Mexico (1914–16)' (2019) Journal of Latin American Studies 1–28.

28 For an influential general statement of this position on codification, see Paolo Grossi, *Mitología jurídica de la modernidad*, trans. Manuel Martínez Neira (Madrid: Editorial Torra, 2003).

for poor farmers to hold on to their possessions. The law also opened the door to fraudulent land takeovers by those with the means to game the system. In nineteenth-century Colombia, too, peasant farmers who performed the hard labor of opening up fields on the country's agricultural frontier were frequently displaced, or turned into renters, by agrarian entrepreneurs who obtained title through their mastery of the legal process.[29]

The impact of codification on the social history of the law is still an under-explored topic in the historiography on nineteenth-century Latin America. Helping to make justice more uniform and predictable, codification could also make it more remote from the social contexts of many of those most in need of the attention of courts and magistrates. On balance, codification probably helped the advance of procedural justice but hindered, or at least complicated, the accessibility of the law. It increased citizens' formal rights and protections but made claiming those rights and protections that much more difficult.

4 Legal Changes, 1880–1930

If the tendency of legal change in the first four to six decades after independence was towards the liberalization of Latin American societies – towards the creation of more rights and freedoms for more people – laws passed in the next half-century pursued more diverse political and ideological imperatives. The liberal agenda was by no means spent: Latin American women, for instance, between 1880 and 1930 would be gradually freed from the tutelage of husbands and fathers. But this liberal agenda now had to compete with rival legislative projects – with laws aimed first at disciplining workers and other lower-class citizens, and then, in one major country, at producing radical social change.

Women, like Indigenous and Afro-descended Latin Americans, entered the postcolonial era with distinct legal handicaps. While adult women had the rights to start litigation and to own and manage property, they held those rights only as long as they were free from the patriarchal authority (the *patria potestad*) of both husband and father. In practice, this meant women were fully capacitated in a legal sense only if they were widowed or, if unmarried, if their fathers had died. Within marriages, husbands not only controlled

29 James Holston, *Insurgent Citizenship: Disjunctions of Democracy and Modernity in Brazil* (Princeton: Princeton University Press, 2008), 131–139; Catherine LeGrand, *Frontier Expansion and Peasant Protest in Colombia, 1850–1936* (Albuquerque: University of New Mexico Press, 1986); Hermes Tovar Pinzón, *Que nos tengan en cuenta: colonos, empresarios y aldeas: Colombia 1800–1900* (Bogotá: Tercer Mundo, 1995).

women's rights to litigate and to sign contracts but also administered women's property. Women, however, did retain formal ownership of the property they brought into marriage, and were allowed to sue husbands who squandered that property away – a situation that favored them over their counterparts in most European and North American countries. In Brazil, all property became pooled in marriage, but husbands needed their wives' permission to sell or mortgage real estate.

While women's relative incapacity in the legal realm stemmed from the pervasiveness of the (male) interests it satisfied, it was also an expression of the fiscal and institutional precarity of postcolonial legal structures in Latin America. Those structures depended on patriarchal gender relations as a critical extralegal source of normativity: men who disciplined women, children, and even unmarried adult sons and daughters played a vital part in the maintenance of order and stability, relieving the work of magistrates and tribunals. Accordingly, laws regulating gender relations began changing, slowly and gradually, only toward the end of the century, when states had achieved an increased measure of confidence and fiscal capacity. Perhaps most importantly, laws passed in the second half of the century freed adult women from the *patria potestad* of their fathers, making it possible for women to stay single, and grow into full legal competency, absent the death of their progenitors. Only very late – first, in 1887 in Costa Rica, then, in the early twentieth century in Mexico and the other Central American countries, and even later in South America – were married women given the power to manage their property without interference from their husbands.[30]

Even as lawmakers continued giving new rights and freedoms to many Latin American citizens, however, they stripped away the rights of others. Most notoriously, a number of Latin American republics in the late nineteenth century expanded or introduced various forms of labor coercion. In countries with high numbers of Indigenous citizens, such as Ecuador, Peru, Bolivia, Guatemala, and Nicaragua, labor coercion often picked up on colonial precedents. After independence, colonial-era coercive labor schemes had often been abolished

30 Silvia Arrom, 'Changes in Mexican Family Law in the Nineteenth Century: The Civil Codes of 1870 and 1884' (1985) 10(3) Journal of Family History 305–317; Elizabeth Dore, 'One Step Forward, Two Steps Back: Gender and the State in the Long Nineteenth Century' in *Hidden Histories of Gender and the State in Latin America*, eds Elizabeth Dore and Maxine Molyneux (Durham: Duke University Press, 2000); Carmen Diana Deere and Magdalena León, 'Liberalism and Married Women's Property Rights in Nineteenth-Century Latin America' (2005) 85(4) Hispanic American Historical Review 627–678; Arlene Díaz, *Female Citizens, Patriarchs, and the Law in Venezuela, 1786–1904* (Lincoln: University of Nebraska Press, 2004).

or allowed to fall into desuetude. In the second half of the nineteenth century, however, the dynamism of Latin America's agricultural sectors led to an acute labor shortage. Meanwhile, the new ideology of positivism stressed the need to impose discipline on the laboring classes. Forced work was once more justified as a civilizing measure. And while the laws instituting such coercion were usually couched in a universal language, they were nevertheless executed (and there can be little doubt that lawmakers had expected them to be executed) in a racially discriminatory way, specifically targeting Indigenous people.[31]

Forced-labor laws came in various kinds. Some mandated Indigenous towns or communities to provide a number of laborers for public-work projects such as road-building. Others mandated the delivery of laborers to capitalist enterprises. Still others regulated the practice of debt peonage – of advancing money to rural laborers and forcing them to keep working for their employer until the debt was paid off. All such laws were designed to invest capitalists with extraordinary disciplinary power over their laborers. For example, in 1862 a Nicaraguan law stipulated that 'A peon contracted … for any enterprise that requires uninterrupted labor cannot leave the *hacienda* until the harvest is completed, whether or not he received a cash advance [*adelanto*], unless he, his wife, children, or parents are gravely ill, or unless he finds a substitute to replace him.' In Brazil, anti-vagrancy laws were used to force former slaves to keep working in the plantation economy after abolition.[32]

Illegitimate children were another group who in the second half of the nineteenth century lost important rights. Under colonial law, these children and their mothers had been able to claim a right to paternal support (alimony). After the fathers' death, they had had a right to a portion of the inheritance. Fathers unwilling to publicly own their paternity could still be made to do so if they had given signs of acknowledging their paternity in private, for instance by showing their children special affection. In 1857 Chile's civil code, however, widely adopted by other countries in the region, made any rights to alimony and inheritance subject to a father's formal and voluntary acknowledgment of his paternity. In effect, it was now entirely up to the father whether or not he wanted to support his illegitimate children. Other laws facilitated the reintegration of fatherless children into middle- and upper-class families as unpaid servants. In one documented case from northeastern Brazil (where orphaned

31 Kim Clark, 'Indians, the State and Law: Public Works and the Struggle to Control Labor in Liberal Ecuador' (1994) 7(1) Journal of Historical Sociology 49–72; Larson, *Trials of Nation Making*, 117, 176, 207; Dore, *Myths of Modernity*, 44; McCreery, *Rural Guatemala*.

32 Knight, 'Mexican Peonage'; McCreery, *Rural Guatemala*, 187–193, 220–228; Fraga, *Crossroads of Freedom*, 101–102, 213. The quote is from Dore, *Myths of Modernity*, 114.

children were in high demand due to a labor scarcity), the biological father of a twelve-year-old orphan accepted the boy into his family, not as his child but as a ward to whom, he said, he would teach 'the habit of work.' Wards were subjected to their guardians' disciplinary authority but had no inheritance rights. In some places they were passed between families in what amounted to an informal market in child bondage.[33]

Laws to bind laborers to estates or children to guardians strengthened the disciplinary power of private interests and diminished the capacity of lower-class citizens to appeal to the legal authority of the state. Other laws weakened the ability of citizens to seek legal protection against the actions of the state itself. In big cities, new housing and sanitary regulations imposed impossible construction standards on all dwellings, in effect declaring large sections of the existing building stock – and of the people dwelling in those buildings – illegal. In Rio de Janeiro, for example, up to a quarter of the city's population lived in large, shared buildings that in the early twentieth century did not meet the standards laid out in building and sanitary codes. While city officials often turned a blind eye, a large section of the city's population was, in effect, living illegally and on public sufferance. Anybody living in such a dwelling now depended on the tolerance of public authorities for their basic shelter. States similarly regulated prostitution in a way that effectively invested authorities with enormous amounts of arbitrary power in their dealing with brothels and prostitutes. In many Brazilian cities, lawmakers also prohibited the exercise of cultural practices associated with black Brazilians, such as *batuque*, *samba*, and *capoeira*. All of these laws were ultimately designed to give authorities the power to police and to disrupt the lives of specific groups (Afro-descendants, prostitutes, the urban poor) at their discretion.[34]

---

33 Nara Milanich, *Children of Fate: Childhood, Class, and the State in Chile, 1850–1930* (Durham: Duke University Press, 2009); Joan Meznar, 'Orphans and the Transition from Slave to Free Labor in Northeast Brazil: The Case of Campina Grande, 1850–1888' (1994) 27(3) Journal of Social History 499–515; Ann Blum, *Domestic Economies: Family, Work and Welfare in Mexico City, 1884–1943* (Lincoln: University of Nebraska Press, 2009).

34 Donna Guy, *Sex and Danger in Buenos Aires: Prostitution, Family, and Nation in Argentina* (Lincoln: University of Nebraska Press, 1991); Katherine Bliss, *Compromised Positions: Prostitution, Public Health, and Gender Politics in Revolutionary Mexico City* (University Park: Pennsylvania State University Press, 2001); Dain Borges, 'Healing and Mischief: Witchcraft in Brazilian Law and Literature, 1890–1922' in *Crime and Punishment in Latin America*, eds Ricardo Salvatore, Carlos Aguirre, and Gilbert M. Joseph (Durham: Duke University Press, 2001); Brodwyn Fischer, *A Poverty of Rights: Citizenship and Inequality in Twentieth-Century Rio de Janeiro* (Stanford: Stanford University Press, 2008), 19–49; Fraga, *Crossroads of Freedom*, 242.

Laws that regulated prostitution or controlled urban housing increased the state's disciplinary power over impoverished citizens. But as the twentieth century wore on, Latin American countries would increasingly also deal with economic immiseration in a different way. They would pass laws that conferred a new set of social rights on marginalized groups of citizens. In most of the region, such initiatives did not get off the ground until shortly after the period dealt with in this chapter. In Mexico, however, the revolution of 1910–1920 put radical social policies at the top of the legislative agenda, providing an early glimpse at the challenges involved in administering a wide new field of rights and claim-making.

What Mexican jurists found out in the 1920s was that social rights were effective only if peasants and workers were able to claim them without incurring the costs or dealing with the delays and complications that were involved in ordinary legal proceedings. The rights to land or to state protection against unfair dismissal from employment needed to be organized so they could be claimed through swift, uncomplicated administrative channels. These rights therefore came to be handled by labor boards and agrarian commissions that were dependent on the executive rather than the judicial branch of government. To assert these new rights, citizens would need to rely on the goodwill of, or else to put pressure on, whatever administration held the levers of power. Social rights, in other words, were on the way to becoming the realm not of courts or lawyers but of mass politics – to be claimed through organizing, to be disbursed as political patronage.[35]

5 Conclusion

To synthesize the history of legal culture in Latin America between 1830 and 1930 is a tall order. It requires the use of a capacious but imprecise analytical language – of words like 'trend,' 'direction,' and 'tendency.' The dominant trend in the first half century after Latin American independence was for the law to become increasingly egalitarian. Lawmakers eliminated old-regime legal distinctions. They abolished corporations and (agonizingly slowly) turned slaves into rights-bearing citizens. This liberalizing trend in lawmaking was accompanied by less visible but no less significant changes in judicial culture and in the geographical distribution of the legal state. Those changes included the formalization of legal procedures that aimed to ensure the equal treatment of

35 James, *Mexico's Supreme Court*, 51–100.

all citizens in the courtroom. They included the creation of due-process guarantees protecting citizens against unconstitutional exercises of state power. And they included the creation of an increasingly dense web of legal institutions, often staffed by lay judges, that covered more and more of the new nations' territories.

In the second half of the period under study, roughly between 1880 and 1930, the liberalizing trend in Latin America's legal history came to an end. Legislators passed more and more laws that removed certain groups from the legal protection of the state and instead placed them under the disciplinary power of private interests. Other laws removed the due-process guarantees that had protected citizens not just from private adversaries but from the reach of arbitrary state power. The late nineteenth and early twentieth centuries thus saw a sustained attack on the liberties of lower-class citizens in Latin America. Part of this attack resulted from contradictions within nineteenth-century liberalism. Thus, the codification of law was meant to make the administration of justice transparent and fair – but, perhaps involuntarily, also made justice more complex and removed from local contexts. The protection of property rights was a key liberal tenet that nevertheless ended up, during the export boom of the late nineteenth century, taking privately owned territories (*haciendas*, plantations, company towns) out of the effective orbit of the law. Not all of these changes were unintentional, however. The ideology of positivism also gave rise to deliberate legislation that removed legal protections from vulnerable population groups, now deemed in need of a strong disciplinary hand.

There was no definitive moment when a liberalizing gave way to an illiberal legal culture between 1830 and 1930. On the one hand, Latin America's postcolonial legal culture contained illiberal elements, and resistance against the ascendancy of liberal tendencies, from the very beginning. For example, in some countries slavery remained on the books and was vigorously defended by conservative parties for decades after independence. And in the economically dynamic La Plata region, passbook laws designed to bind workers to estates were already passed in the 1820s. On the other hand, the liberalizing tendencies in Latin American law never simply disappeared. Thus, in late nineteenth-century Mexico, at a time when landowners earned themselves increasingly absolute powers over tenants and laborers, there were other places (such as the coffee town of Tapachula in Chiapas) where a properly constituted republican judiciary was finally wresting power from the personalist authority of local strongmen. Instead of a clear succession we should therefore think of an ongoing struggle between liberalizing and illiberal tendencies in the legal culture of postcolonial Latin America: a struggle in which at first the liberalizing and then the illiberal tendency was ascendant but neither tendency at any time completely eclipsed the other.

References

Arrom, Silvia. 'Changes in Mexican Family Law in the Nineteenth Century: The Civil Codes of 1870 and 1884.' *Journal of Family History* 10(3) (1985): 305–317.

Botero Bernal, Andrés. 'La tensión entre la justicia lega y la justicia letrada durante la primera mitad del siglo XIX: el caso de Antioquia (Nueva Granada).' *Iuhistoria* 7 (2010): 65–88.

Cansanello, Oreste. *De súbditos a ciudadanos: Ensayo sobre las libertades en los orígenes republicanos; Buenos Aires: 1810–1852*. Buenos Aires: Ediciones Imago Mundi, 2003.

Chalhoub, Sidney. 'The Precariousness of Freedom in a Slave Society (Brazil in the Nineteenth Century).' *International Review of Social History* 56 (2011): 405–439.

Chambers, Sarah. *From Subjects to Citizens: Honor, Gender, and Politics in Arequipa, Peru 1780–1854*. University Park: Pennsylvania State University Press, 1999.

Díaz, Arlene. *Female Citizens, Patriarchs, and the Law in Venezuela, 1786–1904*. Lincoln: University of Nebraska Press, 2004.

Dore, Elizabeth. *Myths of Modernity: Peonage and Patriarchy in Nicaragua*. Durham: Duke University Press, 2006.

Flores Flores, Graciela. *La justicia criminal ordinaria en tiempos de transición: La construcción de un nuevo orden judicial (Ciudad de México, 1824–1871)*. México: Universidad Nacional Autónoma de México, 2019.

Guzmán Brito, Alejandro. 'La influencia del código civil francés en las codificaciones americanas.' *Cuadernos de Extensión Jurídica (Universidad de los Andes)* 9 (2004): 17–50.

Irurozqui, Marta, and Mirian Galante, eds. *Sangre de ley: Justicia y violencia en la institucionalización del Estado en América Latina, siglo XIX*. Madrid: Ediciones Polifemo, 2011.

Larson, Brooke. *Trials of Nation Making: Liberalism, Race, and Ethnicity in the Andes, 1810–1910*. New York: Cambridge University Press, 2004.

LeGrand, Catherine. *Frontier Expansion and Peasant Protest in Colombia*. Albuquerque: University of New Mexico Press, 1986.

Lurtz, Casey. *From the Grounds up: Building an Export Economy in Southern Mexico*. Palo Alto: Stanford University Press, 2019.

Marino, Daniela. *Huixquilucan: Ley y justicia en la modernización del espacio rural mexiquense, 1856–1910*. Madrid: Consejo Superior de Investigaciones Científicas, 2016.

Martins, Eduardo. *A invenção da vadiagem: Os termos do bem vivir e a sociedade disciplinar no Império do Brasil*. Curitiba: Editora CRV, 2011.

Milanich, Nara. *Children of Fate: Childhood, Class, and the State in Chile, 1850–1930*. Durham: Duke University Press, 2009.

Mirow, M.C. 'Borrowing Private Law in Latin America: Andrés Bello's Use of the Code Napoléon in Drafting the Chilean Civil Code.' *Louisiana Law Review* 61 (2001): 291–329.

Salvatore, Ricardo, Carlos Aguirre, and Gilbert Joseph, eds. *Crime and Punishment in Latin America: Law and Society since Late Colonial Times*. Durham: Duke University Press, 2001.

Salvatore, Ricardo. *Wandering Paysanos: State Order and Subaltern Experience in Buenos Aires during the Rosas Era*. Durham: Duke University Press, 2003.

Schaefer, Timo. *Liberalism as Utopia: The Rise and Fall of Legal Rule in Post-Colonial Mexico, 1820–1900*. New York: Cambridge University Press, 2017.

Tau Anzoátegui, Victor. *La codificación en la Argentina, 1810–1870: mentalidad social e ideas jurídicas*. 2nd ed. Buenos Aires: Librería Histórica Emilio J. Perrot, 2008.

Zahler, Reuben. *Ambitious Rebels: Remaking Honor, Law, and Liberalism in Venezuela, 1780–1850*. Tucson: University of Arizona Press, 2013.

CHAPTER 6

Enacting Legal Reforms, Reshaping Modern Societies: The Transformation of Latin American Law from 1930 to the Present

Cristián Villalonga

1 Introduction

The early twentieth century was a turning point for the social, economic, and political development of Latin America, bringing about the crisis of its previous model of liberal modernization. Migration to cities and centers committed to the exploitation of raw materials, persistent poverty, lack of housing and health services – the so-called, social question – mobilized urban workers, peasants and the emerging middle class to varying degrees, and undermined the institutional system crafted by the elites that ruled the young republics.[1] Between 1910, the outset of the Mexican Revolution, and the aftermath of the Great Depression of 1929 virtually all Latin American countries began to search for a new socioeconomic order. Such an aim would persist in the *longue durée*. If we could synthesize the period from the aristocratic regimes' collapse until the end of the twentieth century, we could roughly identify at least three successive waves of institutional transformation: (a) the emergence of populist governments organized toward charismatic leaders, inter-class alliances, and state-corporatist bargaining, which attempted to cope with the main challenges of the social question; (b) different answers to the failures of the early populist regimes, operating in the context of Cold War politics such as socialist and bureaucratic authoritarian dictatorships; and (c) the liberalization of economy and politics initiated in the 1980s.[2]

These streams of institutional transformation represented alternative attempts to 'modernize' Latin American societies through top-down processes

1 Jeremy Adelman and Miguel A. Centeno, 'Between Liberalism and Neoliberalism: Law's Dilemmas in Latin America' in *Global Prescriptions: The Production, Exportation, and Importation of a New Legal Orthodoxy*, eds Yves Dezalay and Bryant G. Garth (Ann Arbor: University of Michigan Press, 2002), 148–151.

2 Thomas E. Skidmore and Peter H. Smith, *Modern Latin America* (New York: Oxford University Press, 2005), 51–61.

 | DOI:10.1163/9789004436091_008

oriented by the state. According to the opinion of public intellectuals of the period, the gap between Latin America and the rest of the Western world mirrored defective social structures and poor governance of the former, with considerable consequences in aspects like the institutional capacity of the state, economic production, and political participation.[3] Looking back in history, the different waves of modernization tried to amend these flawed institutional arrangements, resembling a contest to break the path dependence that prompted 'underdevelopment.'

This chapter explains how law played a major role in such streams of institutional change and provided the scaffolding and tools in efforts to restructure society. Even when these processes cannot be reduced to only their legal aspects, it is relevant to note that each carried out a set of policy preferences in the form of legal reforms. Like liberal constitutions and civil codes envisioned to foster stability and commerce in the nineteenth century, the new regimes employed a broad repertoire of legal strategies to achieve goals such as property redistribution or democratic consolidation. Although without matching a well-established model of the rule of law, and in a very faulty style, populist leaders, iron fisted dictatorships, and free-market advocates rested on a legalist culture that assumed that social relations were shaped by comprehensive legal regulations and employed at least a veneer of legal rationality in the name of the polity.

Nonetheless, this significant place of law in the modernization of twentieth-century Latin America should be problematized with two caveats. I do not deny here that numerous pockets of lawlessness marked by informality, violence, and arbitrariness characterized the period under examination.[4] Neither do I rebut that social change, such as urbanization, has had a considerable impact on the diagnosis that inspires public policy and the everyday functioning of the legal system. Simply, I emphasize that the big picture of Latin American law during this period can be better explained as an embodiment of various attempts of modernization driven by state politics. A final caveat is that, like any work of synthesis and historical interpretation, this chapter is a selective account.

---

3 Tulio Halpering Donghi, 'Two Centuries of South American Reflections on the Development Gap between the United States and Latin America' in *Falling Behind: Explaining the Development Gap between Latin America and the United States*, ed. Francis Fukuyama (New York: Oxford University Press, 2008), 11–47.

4 For a survey in the literature see, Lisa Hilbink and Janice Gallagher, 'State and Law in Latin America: A Critical Assessment' in *Routledge Handbook of Law and Society in Latin America*, eds Rachel Sieder, Karina Ansolabehere, and Tatiana Alfonso (New York: Routledge, 2019).

2 Populist Regimes, Corporatist States, and the Socialization of Law (from the Late 1920s to the 1950s)

Latin America underwent profound political changes since about 1920, initiating a new process of modernization that promised to replace political and economic liberalism reigning until those years. Since the turn of the century, aristocratic elites enacted statutes to tackle the most urgent issues related to labor and urban poverty but seemed mild considering the gravity of the social question. As an answer to their apparent unresponsiveness, the region went through transitions to populist regimes characterized by charismatic leaders in charge of strong executive branches and who led inter-class alliances. These governments were expected to promote social regeneration by a state-oriented action. As early as 1910, they came out violently in Mexico, where a real political revolution promised to bring social justice. They also emerged gradually in countries like Argentina, Uruguay, Chile, and Brazil, reaching its zenith between the Great Depression and the early 1950s. By those decades, the Institutional Revolutionary Party in Mexico, Perón in Argentina, or Vargas's *Estado Nôvo* in Brazil echoed the political transition throughout the region. With authoritarian or more democratic variants, National Populism became the standard Latin American regime.[5]

The institutional reforms carried out by National Populist governments materialized a deep dissatisfaction against the previous economic and political order. Nevertheless, populist leaders' pragmatism should not be misunderstood as a mere anti-liberal reaction. They also represent different ideological commitments to which they ascribed in a very loose way: Indigenism (Mexico, Peru, and Bolivia), Catholic natural corporatism (Brazil and Argentina), and allusions to soft versions of liberalism and socialism (Colombia, Cuba, Uruguay), among others. This ideological mixture served to conduct state-sponsored bargaining aiming to establish a non-conflictive and well-regulated society.[6]

Law professors who backed these regimes became sharp critics of liberal legal institutions. Some of these faultfinding analyses against free will, absolute private property, and the language of individual rights were already present in the legal culture of the continent during the first two decades of the century with Alejandro Álvarez as an example. The dissemination of these complaints came out particularly notorious after the French jurist Léon Duguit delivered

5 Adelman and Centeno, 'Between Liberalism,' 149–150.

6 Howard J. Wiarda, 'Law and Political Development in Latin America: Toward a Framework for Analysis' (1971) 19(3) American Journal of Comparative Law 448.

several conferences at the University of Buenos Aires on reorganizing the legal system toward the concept of solidarity and the division of social labor. These lectures were critical in spreading the idea of the social function of property in the continent afterward.[7] Since 1930, the popularity among Latin American lawyers of European jurists like Georges Ripert reflected this deep skepticism vis-à-vis liberal legal institutions, an attitude which consolidated itself over time.[8]

As populist regimes advanced, some Latin American lawyers took the lead as protagonists in debates on institutional design. A complete cadre of jurists engaged intellectually with specific reforms to liberal-individualist law, like Mario de la Cueva (Mexico) and Pedro Lira (Chile).[9] Some of them participated in a legal defense of the new populist regimes as a whole. This is the case of the Argentinian Arturo Enrique Sampay, who wrote works that condensed the outcries against the former individualist order and that served as his platform to become the mastermind of Perón's Constitution in 1949. In his well-known oeuvre *The Crisis of the Liberal-Bourgeoise State*, Sampay described how mass democracy seemed incompatible with the liberal rule of law and its former constitutional structure, leading to a rebuttal of both fascism and communism with Sampay's simultaneous appreciation for the corporatist system of Portugal.[10] Something similar can be said about the Brazilian jurist Francisco Campos, author of Getúlio Vargas's Constitution of 1937 and his Minister of Justice. Perhaps, Campos reflected as any other legal mind the support to the charismatic leadership upon mass society, assuring that 'there [was] no one people without asking for a Cesar.'[11]

2.1 *Social Constitutionalism and Its Projection towards State Politics*

Violent turmoil or a coup d'état triggered the emergence of populist regimes. As part of the political break, leaders often advanced deep constitutional

---

7 M.C. Mirow, 'Origins of the Social Function of Property in Chile' (2011) 80 Fordham Law Review 1183–1217; M.C. Mirow, 'Léon Duguit and the Social Function of Property in Argentina' in *Léon Duguit and the Social Obligation Norm of Property: A Translation and Global Exploration*, eds Paul Babie and Jessica Viven-Wilksch (Cham: Springer 2019), 267–285.

8 Pedro Lira, *El código civil y el nuevo derecho* (Santiago: Nascimento, 1944).

9 Ibid.; Mario De la Cueva, *Derecho del Trabajo Mexicano* (México: Porrúa, 1949).

10 Arturo Enrique Sampay, *La crisis del Estado liberal burgués* (Buenos Aires: Losada, 1942). On Sampay see Susan Ramella, 'Arturo Enrique Sampay' in *Law and Christianity in Latin America: The Work of Great Jurists*, eds M.C. Mirow and Rafael Domingo (London: Routledge, 2021), 470–482.

11 Josef Kunz, *La filosofía del derecho latinoamericana en el siglo XX* (Buenos Aires: Losada, 1951), 47.

reforms or directly enacted new constitutions to rearrange political structures.[12] Table 6.1 illustrates there were several constitutional reorganizations in the region between 1917 and 1955 from the year of the Mexican constitution to the end of the Peron's first rule, respectively. They range from some enshrining presidentialism and social rights, as found in Mexico and Venezuela, to constitutions that squarely purposed corporatist aims, such as Brazil's. These texts maintained the most relevant contributions of nineteenth-century constitutionalism, such as the republican system, separation of powers, and fundamental civil rights. Over this structure, they placed new provisions to correct the prior liberal spirit, intending to target social-question issues and, in many cases, to prevent the advent of socialism.[13] From a theoretical point of view, these constitutions had two main groups of sources. On the one hand, both the Constitution of Mexico (1917) and the German Constitution of Weimar (1919) served as models for the earlier and most moderate populist regimes. On the other hand, the Polish (1935) and Portuguese Constitutions (1933) inspired corporatist attempts.[14]

National populism established presidential regimes in almost all the constitutions passed during the period, whether to overcome former aristocratic rules identified with Congress or as a way to assure policy preferences through expedited decision making. The executive branch took control over the lawmaking process, assuming the power to set the debates and timeline, and to fund the most relevant legislative projects related to the structures of the state, such as the establishment of administrative agencies. At the same time, these arrangements formally or informally gave the executive space to issue governmental regulations to fix pricing, to bestow social benefits, and to protect national industry. As a result, the executive branch led to the growth of bureaucratic offices and the unsystematic regulations of the administrative state.[15] Some countries, such as Brazil, Mexico, and Argentina, possessed federal systems that geographically decentralized some decision making but these

12 Adelman and Centeno, 'Between Liberalism,' 149–150.

13 For an alternative typology of the constitutional regimes between 1930 and 1980, see Roberto Gargarella, *Latin American Constitutionalism 1810–2010* (New York: Oxford University Press, 2013), 105–131.

14 M.C. Mirow, *Latin American Constitutions: The Constitution of Cádiz and Its Legacy in Spanish America* (New York: Cambridge University Press, 2015), 212; José Guillermo Guerra, *La Constitución de 1925* (Santiago: Balcells, 1929); Tulio Enrique Tascón, *Historia del Derecho Constitucional Colombiano* (Bogotá: Universidad Externado de Colombia, 2005), 269; Arturo Enrique Sampay, *La crisis del Estado liberal burgués*; Gargarella *Latin American Constitutionalism*, 115–121.

15 Mirow, *Latin American Constitutions*, 230–231.

TABLE 6.1 New constitutional texts (1917–1955) (selection)

Country	Year	Strong executive	Literacy	Protection to family	Social rights	Protection to Labor	Social function of Property	Corporatist Structures
Mexico	1917	■			■	■		■
Chile	1925	■	■		■	■	■	
Peru	1933		■	■	■	■	■	
Uruguay	1934[(a)]			■	■	■		■
Brazil	1937[(a)]	■	■	■	■	■		■
Bolivia	1938[(a)]	■	■	■	■	■	■	■
Cuba	1940			■	■	■		
Paraguay	1940	■			■	■	■	■
Guatemala	1945	■	■	■	■	■		
Venezuela	1947[(a)]	■		■	■	■	■	
Costa Rica	1949	■		■	■	■	■	
Argentina	1949	■		■	■	■	■	

Notes: Shaded sections indicate inclusion within the constitutional text. Literacy means a literacy requirement for electoral rights.
(a) Countries with more than one constitution in the period. I have selected the most representative one.

structures reproduced populist dynamics in the regions and did not mitigate the power of the federal executive enough to eclipse its political dominion.[16] Exceptionally, there were also constitutions recognizing formats of parliamentarism in Peru, Uruguay, and Cuba, although strong leaders prevailed, thereby imposing de facto presidential regimes.

Concerning courts, these constitutions kept most of the hierarchical structures and procedures established at the end of the nineteenth century. Nonetheless, they simultaneously granted the executive some significant leverage on the process of appointments, budgetary assignments, and political impeachment of justices. Populist regimes employed these last powers gradually to curb judicial independence. Although some judiciaries previously had exerted significant control of the executive branch and new constitutions recognized judicial review and other jurisdictional means to control administration, political attacks from new regimes targeted courts. More than a few populist leaders purged judiciaries or employed appointments and patronage to fill the courts with compliant judges. As a result, the entire judicial system of several countries, or some sections of them, such as labor courts, were submitted to government control at least once in, for example, Mexico, Brazil, Argentina, and Colombia. In other cases, such as Chile, political attacks at the early stage of populist regimes encouraged judicial deference.[17] Something similar happened with administrative controllers established in some countries of the Andean region such as Colombia, Chile, Ecuador, Bolivia, and Peru following the Kemmerer report in the 1920s. Those offices frequently operated as actual administrative tribunals suffering similar constraints experienced by ordinary judges. Overall, courts and controllers were less consequential in overseeing the executive branch and administrative agencies and exerted weak authority over the political process.[18]

---

16 Laurence Whitehead, 'State Organization in Latin America since 1930' in *Latin America: Economy and Society since 1930*, ed. Leslie Bethell (New York: Cambridge University Press, 1998), 390–393, 396–408.

17 For some examples: Pilar Domingo, 'Judicial Independence: The Politics of the Supreme Court in Mexico' (2000) 32(3) Journal of Latin American Studies 705–735; Lisa Hilbink, *Judges beyond Politics in Democracy and Dictatorship: Lessons from Chile* (New York: Cambridge University Press, 2007), 55–63; Lêda Boechat Rodrigues, *História do Supremo Tribunal Federal IV* (Rio de Janeiro: Civilização Brasileira, 2002), vol. 1, 31–33; Ezequiel Abásolo, 'La dimensión política de la Corte Suprema durante el régimen peronista (1947–1955)' (2014) 13(2) Estudios Interdisciplinarios de América Latina y el Caribe; Anibal Pérez-Liñán and Andrea Castagnola: 'Presidential Control of High Courts in Latin America: A Long-Term View (1904–2006),' Journal of Politics in Latin America, 1, 2, 87–114.

18 For the Brazilian, Mexican, and Argentinian cases on judicial control of political power such as acts of authority and the political question doctrines see Kenneth L. Rosen and

Populist regimes used to broaden citizenship as a prerequisite of mass mobilization. Answering to their growing relevance in cultural and economic life, new constitutional texts and electoral statutes extended citizenship gradually to women who became active supporters of national populism. In about thirty years, all the countries of the continent advanced to bestow suffrage to women, beginning with Ecuador in 1929. In parallel, women began slowly to hold offices in cabinets, Congress, and the judiciary during the 1940s. By the same token, new political constitutions eliminated the literacy requirement for suffrage during the same decades, favoring the urban poor, peasants, and Indigenous people. By the late 1970s, neither women nor illiterate people were excluded legally from electoral participation.[19]

Despite expanding citizenship, national populism limited electoral competition and banned radical versions of Marxism and anarchism. By the 1930s, most Latin American countries had already adopted legislation barring organizations affiliated with these ideologies, although such prohibitions were not regularly enforced with rigor. The Uruguayan Constitution (1934), for instance, prohibited 'any social and political organization that tend[ed] to destroy the fundamental grounds of the nationality by violent means' (art. 70), and Vargas's *Estado Novo* established a National Security Court for political crimes. At the outset of the Cold War in the late 1940s, these regimes passed statutes to outlaw communist parties as part of a hemispheric strategy prompted by the United States to stop Soviet influence.[20] Populism took advantage of that context to close the circle against dissidents and compromised itself to uphold democratic values. Even Peron's rule, highly committed to authoritarianism, could express in his Constitution of 1949: 'The state does not recognize the freedom to attack freedom' (art. 15).

The social rights comprised a significative aspect of those constitutions. All the new constitutions introduced different state duties to provide access to health, workers' housing, and social security. At the end of the period, ambitious programs of state action appeared within this realm, such as the famous Chapter Three of the Argentinian Constitution of 1949 that enumerated a long

---

Keith Karst, *Law and Development in Latin America: A Casebook* (Los Angeles: University of California Los Angeles Latin American Center, 1975), 103–255. See also for Chile, Julio Faundez, *Democratization, Development, and Legality Chile, 1831–1973* (London: Palgrave MacMillan, 2007), 138–148. For Kemmerer see Mirow, *Latin American Law*, 168, 212.

19 Skidmore and Smith, *Modern Latin America*, 62–64; Jonathan Hartlyn and Arturo Valenzuela, 'Democracy in Latin America after 1930' in *Latin America: Politics and Society since 1930*, ed. Leslie Bethell (New York: Cambridge University Press, 1998), 33–39.

20 Alan Angell, 'The Left in Latin America since 1920' in *Latin America: Politics and Society since 1930*, 103–105.

list of social rights to protect workers, elders, and the youth.[21] In the same light, several constitutions set special sections to shelter marriage and family and supported related access to education, housing, and economic compensations, for example in 1937 in Brazil.[22] Others, like the Constitution of Mexico, had significant provisions to regulate work and social security. Apart from the constitutional protection of labor, the state economic capacity limited most social rights, which were not expected to be enforced by judicial means. Instead, they served as a programmatic orientation for lawmakers. As a corollary, populist rules established ministries of labor, health, and housing, which gradually advanced from the coordination of charities to the direct provision of services by public agencies.

Property deserves a special mention within these constitutional reforms. Under different wording, most constitutions asserted explicitly that ownership performed a critical social role and that private domain must be harmonized with social interest orientated by state action. The response against the *laissez-faire* political economy and Léon Duguit's ideas had a determinant influence on drafting those provisions.[23] In the long term, the constitutional guidelines upon social property laid the ground for further economic reorganization. First, they served as support for the increasing regulation on markets. Many constitutions set some rules on public economic order, like the banning of monopolies or mandatory national shareholders in banking. Additionally, statutes and administrative norms materialized the social character of property in areas like price-fixing, antitrust practices, industrial subsidies, and taxes levied upon importations and economic gains.[24]

Second, constitutional provisions on ownership usually recognized the state power to conduct redistributive policies, which were particularly relevant for land reform in the following decades.[25] For instance, Article 27 of the Mexican Constitution of 1917 did not assert straightly social function of the property but structured the nation's original property rights over lands and waters

21 Gargarella, *Latin American Constitutionalism*, 111–120.

22 Isabel Jaramillo, 'The Social Approach to Family Law: Conclusions from the Canonical Family Law Treatises of Latin America' (2010) 58(4) American Journal of Comparative Law 859.

23 M.C. Mirow, *Latin American Law*, 221–222; Agustín Parise, 'Property' in this volume.

24 Gerardo Caffera, 'The Economic Conditions of Contract in South American Law: An Historical Approach' in *The Future of Contract Law in Latin America*, eds Rodrigo Momberg and Stefan Vogenauer (Oxford: Hart, 2017), 118–119. For antitrust policies, see for example: Mexican Antitrust Law (1934), Colombian Law N°155 (1959), Chilean Law N° 13305 (1959).

25 M.C. Mirow, *Latin American Law*, 219–227.

carefully. The government employed those rules to break large estates and to exclude foreigners and the Catholic Church from land ownership, advancing an extensive policy of land redistribution and communal organization of peasants (*ejidos*) in the 1920s and 1930s. In the context of the Cold War between the late 1940s and the early 1970s, Venezuela, Bolivia, Chile, Peru, and Central American countries implemented processes of agrarian reforms.[26] In all of them, constitutional provisions on the social function of ownership were critical to recognize state redistributive power and to diminish due compensation.

Third, that broad understanding of the social function of property also served to advance the nationalization of natural resources and the establishment of national industries. Although the foresaid constitutions asserted the state's domain on minerals, land, and waters, mining and other extractive industries were usually in the hands of American or British corporations. Under the argument of the sovereignty over natural resources, several Latin American countries advanced processes of nationalization that, unlike expropriations, offered very limited or no compensation: Mexican oil (1938), Bolivian silver and tin (1952), and Brazilian oil (1953). Exceptionally, populist regimes also took into the public sector some non-extractive industries, such as Peron's nationalization of the British railroad in 1948.[27] As part of a general strategy of industrialization by substituting importations, these regimes developed an extensive policy of establishing new state-owned industries in areas such as electricity, public works, steel mills, banking, and aircraft.[28]

Finally, populist regimes promoted social participation and built corporatist structures that engaged with the emerging administrative state. Charismatic leaders acted as spokesperson of the nation and the downtrodden, but the state wove a complex network of social interests that, under different configurations, included middle-class sectors, urban workers, peasants, and national industrialists. Those multiclass alliances, supported by legal means, constituted an actual corporatist game arbitrated by the executive branch.[29]

States actively promoted a wide-ranging array of associations. In some cases, that promotion of partnerships obeyed a constitutional mandate, such as in the Bolivian Constitution of 1938, which prescribed that 'the state shall encourage

26 See for instance, Law N° 200 in Colombia (1936) and Decree 03464 in Bolivia (1953); Joseph R. Thome, 'The Process of Land Reform in Latin America' (1968) 1968 Wisconsin Law Review 9–22; Rosen and Karst, *Law and Development in Latin America*, 286–305.

27 Amy Chua, 'The Privatization-Nationalization Cycle: The Link between Markets and Ethnicity in Developing Countries' (1995) 95(2) Columbia Law Review 227–243.

28 Whitehead, 'State Organization in Latin America,' 408–437.

29 Wiarda, 'Law and Political Development,' 448–460.

the creation of any kind of cooperatives by legislative means' (art. 123), and it 'shall recognize and guarantee the existence of Indigenous communities' (art. 165). In most countries, however, new rules for unionization were incorporated into labor codes and other statutes. As a result, the number of unions, professional associations, and other guilds grew exponentially since the 1930s. Populist regimes frequently intervened in their creation, like the Mexican Workers Federation or the Coffee Producers Federation of Colombia. Those unions held a quasi-public nature and negotiated labor and trade regulations directly with governments. In the same vein, professional guilds became highly dependent on the financial support and their status as gatekeepers granted by the state. These associations were usually incorporated into the administrative apparatus and held some public functions. Nevertheless, there were some rare examples of unions that remained with high levels of autonomy, such as the mining workers unions in Bolivia after the 1952 revolution.[30]

The process of state-corporatist bargaining was critical for economic planning, particularly concerning industrial subsidies and price-fixing. As a venue to materialize such negotiation, populist regimes used panels for economic decision making that looked to shape state policy and to support presidential arbitration. For instance, the Brazilian Constitution of 1937 asserted that state intervention in the economic domain is legitimate 'to coordinate the factors of production to avoid or resolve their conflicts, introducing into the game of individual competitions the interests of the nation' (art. 135). Accordingly, the same text created a National Economic Council, integrated by representatives of the different areas of production, professional associations, and workers' unions, whose attributes ranged from trade and labor regulation to 'promoting the corporative organization of the national economy' (art. 57).

The boundaries of such a state-corporatist game were not uniform. There were corporations and groups that, depending upon the national political context, did not participate. Except for Vargas's rule and the first Perón term, which vested some benefits in the Catholic Church, most populist regimes did not actively engage with religious associations, and instead promoted the separation of secular and religious orders on constitutional grounds. In some cases, populist governments even imposed severe limitations on religious

30 For a general view on state and labor and peasants' organizations, see Ruth Berins Collier and David Collier, *Shaping the Political Arena: Critical Junctures, the Labor Movement, and Regime Dynamics in Latin America* (Princeton: Princeton University Press, 1991), 51–52, 167–201. For industrial associations see Ben Schneider Ross, *Business Politics and the State in Twentieth-Century Latin America* (New York: Cambridge University Press, 2004), 59–208.

autonomy, such as Mexico in the 1920s and 1930s, and Perón after 1949. The state frequently did not take Indigenous and peasant groups into account before the late 1950s. Nonetheless, Mexico and Bolivia developed extensive policies to provide land and social services to these groups. Other groups that initially enjoyed less capacity to exert political pressure, such as shantytown dwellers and unemployed people, were also excluded.[31]

2.2 *Adapting Private Law to New Social Values*

Although civil and commercial codes in force during this period dated back to the nineteenth or early twentieth century, private law was far from stagnant in the following decades. Bearing in mind the social question, populist regimes revisited those codes, usually by means of new statutes or legislative reforms. In so doing, they reformulated significant legal aspects like owners' rights and theories of will in contracts. Such a reformulation intended to substitute the former prevalence of individualism by a corrective social justice thus privileging the state function of maintaining a well-regulated commonwealth. These legal changes were not only an answer to new technological and socioeconomic conditions but also an attempt to shape institutional structures according to new social values.

The most significant piece that mirrored that transformation is the Mexican Civil Code for the Federal District (1928). Its drafting commission provided a critical appraisal of the previous legal order, indicating that the former code 'had turned unable to govern the new necessities ... that emerged from the great industry and the progressive triumphs of the principle of solidarity.'[32] The commission's motivation, therefore, claimed for a social law that extended its scope from 'the rich to the poor, from the owner to the worker, ... and from the man to the woman, ... harmonizing individual and collective interests.'[33] The new code incorporated several provisions embracing that underlying approach, such as the equal legal capacity between men and women (art. 2), the voidability of covenants in which one side got excessive profits by taking advantage of the inexperience or miserable condition of the other (art. 17), and the judicial discretion for excusing certain violations to statutes committed by intellectually disabled and destitute people (art. 21). Following similar premises, Guatemala (1933), Peru (1936), and Venezuela (1942) enacted new civil

31 Wiarda, 'Law and Political Development,' 448–460. See also, William Suárez-Potts, 'Peasants and Workers' in this volume.

32 Thorsten Keiser, 'Social Conceptions of Property and Labour-Private Law in the Aftermath of the Mexican Revolution and European Legal Science' (2012) 20 Rechtsgeschichte 260.

33 Ibid., 261.

codes. They modernized some provisions according to new legal doctrines. These modifications included family law, viewed as a social reality featured by interdependence and solidarity, whose regulation was closely connected to social welfare.[34] The Venezuelan code, for instance, facilitated the proofs to establish paternity of illegitimate offspring, bestowed some patrimonial rights for non-marital partners (*concubinato*), and recognized state's duties concerning orphaned children.[35]

Several Latin American countries such as Argentina in 1929 and 1954, created drafting commissions for partial organic amendments, looking for comprehensive updating of civil codes. In the 1940s and 1950s, deep reforms to specific aspects of civil legislation renewed critical sections of the code in the region. Their most relevant topics were related both to family and urban life: married women's legal capacity, adoption, neighborhood relations, horizontal property, and dwellings' tenancy.

The Colombian Supreme Court in the late 1930s stands out as the best illustration of how, exceptionally, those changes came from the judicial arena. Justices employed innovative methods of interpretation to adapt the private law to new social demands, issuing creative decisions regarding strict liability for risky activities, mistake in law, flexible approaches to the binding effects of contracts, and the formalization of land tenure, among other topics. Such a doctrinal transformation carried out by 'the golden court' constituted a milestone in Colombian legal culture, but it was not consolidated through statutory reform. The government called for the incorporation of such criteria into the code at the end of the decade. Nevertheless, this initiative failed due to the new anti-leftist sentiment of the 1940s and the distrust of judicial creativity.[36]

Besides the reforms described above, the abundant normative production of the state indirectly challenged the place of the civil and commercial codes. A myriad of specific statutes aimed to protect personal or national interest, like the Chilean D.L N° 520 on securing livelihood (1932) and the Brazilian Water Code (1934), affected the liberal spirit of the prior private legislation. Public administration gradually imposed public encumbrances on property to face urgent social needs and the increasing requirements of the state such as

34 Jaramillo, 'The Social Approach to Family Law,' 859–869.

35 Eugenio Hernández-Bretón and Claudia Madrid Martínez, 'Codification in Venezuela' in *The Scope and Structure of Civil Codes*, ed. Julio César Rivera (New York: Springer, 2013), 457.

36 Diego López Medina, *Teoría Impura del Derecho: La transformación de la cultura jurídica latinoamericana* (Bogotá: Legis, 2004), 326–340.

regulations on residential rents, and the expropriation of underused agricultural lands to establish agricultural colonies.[37]

There were some efforts to revise commercial codes, particularly regarding corporations and new partnership models known as cooperatives, of which Colombian legislation of 1929 and Venezuelan legislation of 1938 serve as examples. Nonetheless, pervasive administrative regulations in areas like the state's price-fixing powers, insurance, and banking, kept businesses within sophisticated state-corporatist bargaining rather than in market competition. The centrality displayed by public regulation in economic life perhaps explains the underdevelopment of some areas like antitrust and corporate law.[38]

The emergence of labor law, a field removed from private matters oriented by freedom of contract, deserves a particular examination. As early as the first decade of the century, all Latin American countries began to pass statutes on the utmost pressing labor issues, including protection against accidents and the banning of children's work. In the 1920s, some lawmakers also introduced bills for more wide-ranging codification on this subject, which, however, failed to be approved. Only the consolidation of a new political context after the Great Depression allowed the appearance of more systematic labor codes.[39]

Post-revolutionary Mexico offers the earliest and most prominent example of a labor code in the making. Although the Constitution of 1917 did not declare the social nature of labor, its Article 123 comprised rather detailed rules on its protection, such as restrictions for pregnant workers, minimum wages, and mandatory clauses for contracts. The federal judiciary employed these rules to support administrative structures for decision making on labor questions and to develop issues such as the right to strike.[40] By the late 1920s, the government reached a compromise with unions and industrial sectors to entrust labor relations to the federal government under a comprehensive bill.[41]

The Mexican *Ley Federal del Trabajo* (1931) kicked off a trend of more than sixteen labor codes that disseminated across the continent between 1931 and 1963 (See Table 6.2). Therefore, a complete movement of jurists and lawmakers advocated for the advancement of labor legislation, which includes doctrinal

37 Lira, *El Código Civil*, 175–192.

38 Mirow, *Latin American Law*, 212; Phanor J. Eder, 'Company Law in Latin America' (1951) 27(1) Notre Dame Lawyer 31–32.

39 Humberto Villasmil Prieto, 'Pasado y Presente del Derecho Laboral Latinoamericano y las vicisitudes de la relación de trabajo' (primera parte) (2015) 21 Revista Latinoamericana de Derecho Social 203–228.

40 William J. Suarez-Potts, *Making of Law: The Supreme Court and Labor Legislation in Mexico, 1875–1931* (Palo Alto: Stanford University Press, 2012), 161–219.

41 Ibid., 233–255.

TABLE 6.2 Consolidation of labor law (1931–1963)

Country	Year	Country	Year
Mexico	1931	Guatemala	1947
Chile	1931	Panama	1947
Venezuela	1936	Colombia	1948
Ecuador	1938	Dominican Rep.	1951
Bolivia	1939	Honduras	1959
Brazil	1943	Haiti	1961
Costa Rica	1943	Paraguay	1961
Nicaragua	1945	El Salvador	1963

Note: Ibid., 299.

authors such as the Mexican Mario de la Cueva. Meanwhile, social constitutionalism reconceptualized labor as a subject whose significance exceeded private interest, thereby needing public protection. Latin American countries incorporated the different agreements of the International Labour Organization (est. 1919), providing legitimacy for that new regulation of labor.[42]

Labor law and policy were closely linked to state-corporatist bargaining.[43] The Mexican constitution, for instance, created boards of conciliation and arbitration composed of workers, employers, and governmental representatives, bestowing a defining role to determine industrial relations to the latter (art. 123).[44] Something similar happened regarding the tripartite boards that set minimum wages in other countries. In specific cases like Argentina, Uruguay, and Peru, however, populist governments preferred to eschew comprehensive labor codes until the 1970s. In this way, they circumvented the most controversial issues and maintained permanent leverage in political negotiation with workers.[45]

42 Humberto Villasmil Prieto, 'Pasado y Presente del Derecho Laboral Latinoamericano y las vicisitudes de la relación de trabajo' (segunda parte) (2016) 22 Revista Latinoamericana de Derecho Social 293–325.

43 For a general view on the origins of labor law, see: *Labor Justice across the Americas*, eds Juan Manuel Palacio and Leon Fink (Chicago, University of Illinois Press, 2017).

44 Suárez-Potts, *Making of Law*, 161–219.

45 In the case of Peru and Argentina, this relation produced a direct relation of populist regimes and labor movements. Collier and Collier, *Shaping the Political Arena*, 314–315.

3 The Cold War Heyday: Law in Times of Radical Politics (from the 1960s to the Early 1980s)

By the late 1950s, Latin America began to experience mounting anxiety regarding socioeconomic 'underdevelopment.' Despite the welfare policies established by populist regimes in the prior decades, economic stagnation and the persistence of poverty showed that such an institutional model presented signs of deterioration. As the Cold War reached its zenith, after the Cuban Revolution of 1959, the region entered into a period of extreme political polarization characterized by a contest between capitalism and socialism. Although most policies described in the previous section continued to be in place, Cold War politics partially recast them and disrupted earlier populist approaches to modernization.[46]

Analysis coming from social scientists partially swayed the frustration concerning the socioeconomic situation and suggested structural changes to reach a more enduring development. The U.N. Economic Commission for Latin America projected deepening industrialization through import substitution and land reform of the agrarian sector. The American Alliance for Progress, launched by Kennedy in the early 1960s, openly supported such proposals. Meanwhile, Marxist academics went further towards the theory of dependency and explained underdevelopment as a part of an unequal organization of the international markets that could only be overcome by a greater state control of national economies.[47] Likewise, Argentinian sociologist Gino Germani began to address an asynchrony in recent Latin American history in which premodern economic and legal institutions obtruded dynamic democratic politics.[48]

These accounts of underdevelopment persuaded many elite lawyers and law professors across the region. Even though they held different political views, almost all of them possessed a profound dissatisfaction regarding the situation of the legal system vis-á-vis socioeconomic reality. This perception included a gap between social practices and delayed statutes, a defective lawmaking process, and lack of access to justice. In Brazil and Chile, there was an awareness that sociologists and economists displaced lawyers from the

---

46 Skidmore and Smith, *Modern Latin America*, 56–61.

47 Joseph L. Love, 'Economic Ideas and Ideologies in Latin America since 1930' in *Latin America, Economy and Society since 1930*, 391–460.

48 Gino Germani, *Política y sociedad en una época en transición: De la sociedad tradicional a la sociedad de masas* (Buenos Aires: Paidós, 1962).

main settings of social and political power.[49] In growing urban sprawls, such as Caracas and Rio de Janeiro, lawyers were also surprised by the appearance of informal popular justice among shantytowns squatters.[50] These insights into the shortcomings of the law were particularly acute among those who ascribed to the socioeconomic reforms. For instance, a former legal officer at the Inter-American Development Bank explained: 'many initiatives meant to advance economic and social changes have not translated into reality since we lack adequate juridical tools, or because we have confusing and archaic statutory provisions.'[51]

The legal profession got involved in different initiatives to tackle these drawbacks. Latin American law schools organized several conferences on reforming legal education according to a pragmatic and realistic approach that included sociological materials for example in Mexico in 1959 and Lima in 1961. Similarly, the Ford Foundation carried out different projects to export American legal methodologies into the region, instilling law and development approach among young scholars of Costa Rica, Brazil, Chile, Peru, and Colombia. All those initiatives produced some early achievements but were frustrated by both political conditions and the limitations of their flawed instrumentalist grasp.[52]

As in the past decades, the fate of law continued to be intertwined with the state. Due to civil war or political violence, elites reached agreements in Costa Rica and Colombia, assuring democratic stability by constitutional amendments. Something similar happened in Venezuela, where the Constitution of 1961 introduced sophisticated provisions aimed to reinforce political covenants, such as the Judicial Council and a high legislative quorum to pass some critical bills. Uruguay established a collegiate executive intending to moderate populist leadership, but it failed after a decade.[53] Meanwhile, Mexico's longstanding one-party government deployed several authoritarian measures

---

49 Yves Dezalay and Bryant Garth, *The Internationalization of the Palace Wars: Lawyers, Economists, and the Contest to Transform Latin American States* (Chicago: University of Chicago Press, 2002), 21.

50 Kenneth L. Karst, Murray L. Schwartz, and Audrey James Schwartz, *The Evolution of Law in the Barrios of Caracas* (Los Angeles: University of California Los Angeles Latin American Center, 1973); Boaventura De Sousa Santos, 'The Law of the Oppressed: The Construction and Reproduction of Legality in Pasargada' (1977) 12(1) Law & Society Review 5–126.

51 Luciano Tomassini, 'Derecho y cambio social en América Latina' (1972) 37–38 Revista de Derecho Económico 30.

52 Gardner, *Legal Imperialism*, 57–60, 257; Mirow, *Latin American Law*, 188–190.

53 Russell H. Fitzgibbon, 'Adoption of a Collegiate Executive in Uruguay' (1952) 14(4) Journal of Politics 616–642.

to guarantee its prevalence. Other countries conducted structural reforms in the more confrontational style of the Cold War. For example, Frei's revolution in liberty in Chile proposed a complete program of socioeconomic change attuned with the United States Alliance for Progress (1964–1970), and Velasco Alvarado's military rule in Peru did so laying bridges to the socialist world (1968–1975).[54] Overall, several Latin American nations went deeper with populist policies, such as passing legislation to empower farmers and shantytown dwellers. Some of them advanced land reforms and nationalized critical economic sectors, such as Peruvian mining, and Venezuelan oil.[55] Nevertheless, socialist and the bureaucratic-authoritarian projects became the most paradigmatic institutional models of these decades.

3.1 *Socialist Revolutions and Their Legal Strategies*

After the victory of the Cuban Revolution in 1959, the socialist cadres that reached power pledged to keep their original promises of reestablishing the Constitution of 1940 and instituting land reform, issuing legislation with that purpose during their first months in power. As Cuba was within the Soviet orbit, its leaders engaged in the production of a socialist polity. Accordingly, the new regime began a profound social and economic restructuring guided by the state and advocated for a dictatorship of the proletariat as a vehicle for building socialism.

Although some elements of the former Constitution of 1940 survived, they operated as a façade for socialist authoritarianism organized around the Cuban Communist Party and Fidel Castro himself. Modifications of the previous constitution in 1959 reorganized the executive branch to strengthen its power and replaced Congress by a Council of Ministers appointed by the Executive in charge of lawmaking. Castro employed such an institutional design to rearrange the civil service and armed forces. The design linked grassroots groups to the state apparatus to establish a one-party government.[56] Revolutionary tribunals headed by guerrilla members extended to the rest of the country for more than a decade, judging former military, dissidents, and saboteurs even by applying summary death sentences.[57]

---

54 Mirow, *Latin American Constitutions*, 226–230.

55 Rosen and Karst, *Law and Development in Latin America*, 286–305; Chua 'The Privatization-Nationalization Cycle,' 232–243.

56 Gargarella, *Latin American Constitutionalism*, 125.

57 Jesse Berman, 'The Cuban Popular Tribunals' (1969) 69(8) Columbia Law Review 1317–1354.

During the first years in power, the new regime carried out a radical economic reorganization. For example, it nationalized oil refineries, sugar mills, and banks, and developed extensive land redistribution by establishing collective agrarian cooperatives. At the same time, it advanced different legal reforms to assure the state-run provision of education and health and severely limited private ownership. Specific statutes passed by the Council of Ministers materialized these reforms, preserving the old Spanish civil, commercial, and procedural codes in all that did not hinder the new revolutionary orientations.[58]

Despite the instrumental role of the law in this process, the first years after the revolution harbored a profound distrust of the former legal system and of legal expertise itself. Traditional legal education decreased dramatically, being overpassed by night law school organized along party lines. Likewise, lay judges adjudicated labor disputes and other claims as a means of political pedagogy. Castro himself would sarcastically clarify the role of the legal profession in the revolution: 'Lawyers, what for?'[59]

Under the direction of the leader Blas Roca Calderio and the Commission of Legal Studies of the Cuban Communist Party, the regime conducted a thoughtful revision of its legal organization in the 1970s. In 1976, a referendum approved a new political constitution heavily influenced by the Soviet Constitution of 1936. In its preamble, this declared that Cuba was a socialist state of workers that adhered to the teachings of Marx, Engels, Lenin, and Martí. The text regulated planning, the guiding role of the Communist Party, and established a new legislative body: the National Assembly of the Popular Power.[60] The regime also enacted abundant legislation like the Law of Criminal Procedure (1973), the Family Code (1974), the New Law of the Organization of the Judicial System (1977), and the Criminal Code (1979). These all institutionalized the new order and indoctrinated socialist discipline among the population.[61]

Besides the Cuban model to reach power, which was mimicked by more than a dozen guerrilla movements, the Chilean way to socialism came out as an alternative path. In 1970, a coalition led by the Socialist and Communist parties elected Salvador Allende, who won the presidential race with 36 percent of the votes. Insofar as he needed to be confirmed by a congressional majority that distrusted his coalition democratic credentials, Allende was ratified only after a constitutional amendment that enhanced political rights. During its almost three years in power, Allende's rule asserted to be laying the

58 Marjorie Zatz, *Producing Legality: Law and Socialism in Cuba* (New York: Routledge, 1994).

59 Ibid., 99–103.

60 Gargarella, *Latin American Constitutionalism*, 126.

61 Zatz, *Producing Legality*, 54–55, 64–94.

foundations of a genuine socialist state. He achieved Congress's unanimous agreement to modify the constitution, nationalizing copper mining in 1971 and advancing land reform by employing prior legal provisions. At the same time, he introduced legislation on neighborhood courts, state education, and a single-chamber Congress, which was not passed because he lacked the necessary votes in Congress.[62]

Allende's Popular Unity coalition attempted to take substantial economic sectors, principally industries and banks under state control. Because it could not count on Congress's support, to achieve these purposes, under the guidance of progressive jurist Eduardo Novoa Monreal, it employed several legal loopholes. Resorting to a decree of 1932 on livelihood regulation, for instance, the executive addressed shortages and work-stoppages, carried out through supporters' strikes, to confiscate, intervene, and expropriate industries. Similarly, the government employed its planning agency's buying powers to acquire stocks of banks and other business corporations that, at the same time, its officials threatened to nationalize without compensation. Such a legal strategy accomplished initially its political goal, to nationalize de facto a substantial segment of the Chilean economy.[63]

In a context of increasing polarization and an acute economic crisis, courts and the Comptroller began to render adverse decisions against such actions after late 1971, arguing that they sought to bypass legislative approval of expropriations. Allende disregarded those judicial decisions and refused to enforce them. In the meantime, Congress passed a constitutional amendment organizing three economic areas to limit state control, but the government failed to enact it. Left-leaning workers exerted pressure to continue with expropriations and to create a popular power outside legal structures, and Allende entered into a direct conflict with the Supreme Court, the Comptroller, and Congress. Given political violence, the armed forces staged a coup ending the Chilean socialist experience in 1973.[64]

3.2 *Modernization through an Iron Fist: The Bureaucratic-Authoritarian Model*

Since the mid-1960s, a new model of military dictatorship proliferated in the southern cone, in Brazil (1964), Argentina (1966 and 1976), Chile (1973), and Uruguay (1976). This kind of regime, called bureaucratic-authoritarianism by

62 Faundez, 'Democratization through Law,' 176–178.

63 Villalonga, Cristián, *Revolución y Ley: La teoría crítica del derecho en Eduardo Novoa Monreal* (Santiago: Centro de Estudios Bicentenario, 2018).

64 Ibid.; Faundez, 'Democratization through Law,' 201–227.

political scientist Guillermo O'Donnell, differs from other forms of dictatorships usually associated with traditional pretorian leadership or populist experiences. Despite some differences among countries, this form of dictatorship presented several distinctive features: a) it attempted a political demobilization by setting limits to democratic deliberation and popular groups' participation; b) state decision making was framed as a technical process led by persons trained in complex organizations such as the military and business corporations; and, c) it reduced redistributive shares deferring economic welfare to further economic growth, and by measures of economic stabilization aimed to favor foreign investment. In the context of the Cold War politics, bureaucratic-authoritarianism offered a model of modernization to answer economic deadlock, political hyper-mobilization, and the socialist threat. Inspired by national security doctrines disseminated by the military as a contention to Marxism, this sort of regime envisioned a reorganization of the state and, from that setting, a rearrangement of the economy for reincorporation into global markets.[65] Like any process of state-led modernization, bureaucratic-authoritarianism attempted to cope with some drawbacks coming from the previous political cycle and engaged extensively with legal means.

As the control of the state was its most immediate priority, this sort of regime first tackled reforms to constitutional law. After they reached power, military dictatorships suspended some sections of the constitutions in force, which remained applicable as long as the new authorities did not revoke their provisions. By this means, they assumed constituent powers. These authoritarian governments passed general decrees with supra-constitutional nature at their outset to dismiss former civil officers and disband political parties.[66] Still, there were significant variations. For example, Brazil initially kept Congress as a channel of restricted bi-partisan competition, being led by successive presidents backed by the armed forces. Various military juntas commanded the Argentinian dictatorships that resorted to very loose legality. The Army Chief Commander Augusto Pinochet headed the Chilean dictatorship, but within a

65 Guillermo O'Donnell, 'Reflexiones sobre las tendencias de cambio del Estado burocrático-autoritario' (1977) 39(1) Revista Mexicana de Sociología 9–59. For a comparison to other authoritarian experiences in the region, see Brian Loveman, *The Constitution of Tyranny: Regimes of Exception in Spanish America* (Pittsburgh: University of Pittsburgh Press, 1993).

66 Diego Valadez, *La Dictadura Constitucional en Latinoamérica* (México: Universidad Nacional Autónoma de México, 1974).

military junta that assumed all lawmaking powers and followed a law-abiding style in its internal relations.[67]

The Brazilian and Chilean authoritarian rulers appointed drafting commission for new constitutions. In 1967, Brazil issued a new constitution that strengthened presidential authority, established a Council of National Security as a political organ, and laid the foundations of a market economy. In 1969, an amendment toughened its political line, closed Congress, bestowed lawmaking powers to the executive branch, and pointed to an all-out war against opposition by hardening restrictions on political rights.[68] In mid-1970s Chile, a drafting commission published gradually partial acts to modify the former constitution. After a revision of its draft and a referendum with less than minimal political guarantees, the junta enacted the Constitution of 1980. Although this also gave an essential place to political restrictions associated with national security issues, it went further than its Brazilian counterpart in terms of endorsing private property, freedom of enterprise, and writs to protect some constitutional rights. Bearing in mind an itinerary for a forthcoming democratic transition, a substantial part of its constitutional design addressed political entrenchment through non-elected senators and high supra-majoritarian legislative quorums.[69]

Besides the constitutional arena, bureaucratic-authoritarianism conducted measures of economic stabilization as the central leitmotiv for its legal reforms, addressing the chronic problems of the Latin American economy: fiscal deficits and the lack of capital. They controlled monetary inflation by reducing social expenditure and ended some barriers to free trade to encourage foreign investment. All of them pledged to protect property rights, deregulated mining and water law, and severely limited labor unions and the right to strike. In specific cases, like Chile, these governments privatized health services and social security systems for retirement, to reduce public expenditure and to facilitate the accumulation of capital. Thus, these regimes attempted to reinforce their comparative advantages in global markets to reactivate economic growth.[70]

67 Robert Barros, *Constitutionalism and Dictatorship: Pinochet, the Junta, and the 1980 Constitution* (New York: Cambridge University Press, 2002).

68 Leonardo Andrade Barbosa, *História Constitucional Brasileira: Mudança constitucional, autoritarismo e democracia no Brasil pós-1964* (Brasilia: Câmara dos Diputados, 2013), 49–141.

69 Barros, *Constitutionalism and Dictatorship*, 167–215.

70 Alejandro Foxley, *Experimentos Neoliberales en América Latina* (México: Fondo de Cultura Económica, 1988), 25–34, 93–108.

The repression of dissidents constitutes one of the most controversial aspects of bureaucratic-authoritarianism. These regimes resorted both to former legality on national security and to new broad decrees to prosecute guerillas, left-leaning cadres, and oppositional unionist leaders. These statutes authorized prison, banishment, and exile as penalties against members of banned organizations and for violations of weapons control laws, among other activities. Their security apparatuses, organized by the mean of specialized intelligence agencies of their armed forces and the police, also carried out brutal repression by lethal violence: 364 deaths and disappearances in Brazil, more than 3,000 in Chile, and about 30,000 in Argentina (1976–1983). Although illegal, torture became a widespread practice.[71]

Depending on the particular context of each country, the relation between political repression and law followed different patterns. As part of a tradition of collaboration, courts integrated by military and civil judges and a prosecution directed by a civilian characterized repression in Brazil. Habeas corpus was recognized partially, and public political trials were appealed before the ordinary judiciary. Meanwhile, Chilean courts alleged an apolitical nature to skirt a climate of wartime legality and state violence. The dictatorship regularly organized repression through undisclosed trials before first-instance military courts and ordinary tribunals did not enforce habeas corpus rights. By contrast, the 1976 Argentinian dictatorship relied broadly on extra-institutional means in response to a significant threat comprised by armed actions from *Montoneros* and the Revolutionary People's Army since the late 1960s. There, the ratio of those tried in military courts to those killed extrajudicially was of one out of seventy-one individuals.[72]

Human rights advocacy rose to answer political repression. In the 1970s in Brazil, defense attorneys counted on courts that were open to hearing them, and the *Ordem dos Advogados* committed itself to protect its prerogative to litigate. They achieved some victories such as the strategic use of acquittals and the relaxation of censorship in some academic settings. Under different conditions, counterparts such as the Catholic Vicariate for Solidarity in Chile or the Center for Legal and Social Studies in Argentina were less successful in the judicial arena. Amnesties laws in Chile (1978), Brazil (1979), and Argentina (1983) preempted further criminal prosecution of state violence until the late

71 Anthony W. Pereira, *Political (In)Justice: Authoritarianism and the Rule of Law in Brazil, Chile and Argentina* (Pittsburgh: University of Pittsburgh Press, 2005), 21.

72 Pereira, *Political (In)Justice*, 19–32; Mark J. Osiel, 'Dialogue with Dictators: Judicial Resistance in Argentina and Brazil' (1995) 20(2) Law & Social Inquiry 481–560.

1990s, when courts began to qualify these actions as crimes against humanity.[73] By then neoliberalism was in full swing.

4 Neoliberal Modernization: From the Rule of Law Revival to the Politics of Rights (after the Mid-1980s)

After 1980, both old-style populism and bureaucratic-authoritarian regimes entered a period of decline. The economic crisis of the decade impacted emerging Latin American economies, indebted to foreign banks, stirring social unrest. And although guerrilla and left-leaning terrorism thrived in countries like Nicaragua, Peru, and Colombia, the political transformation initiated in the Soviet bloc after 1985 turned Marxism into a less formidable menace. Towards 1990, the end of the Cold War, the preeminence of liberal democracy, and the market-based economy drove some to think that Washington consensus would spread throughout the entire Western world. As part of this critical juncture, most Latin American countries began transitions to democracy and deepened the implementation of free-market policies. Some of them such as Mexico, Brazil, and Chile continued trends initiated at the end of populist or authoritarian regimes; others such as Peru, Argentina, Uruguay, and Guatemala began these processes abruptly after authoritarianism's downfall. Still others did so in specific troubled contexts, such as Colombia in the middle of the war on drugs. By and large, we can refer to the mid-1980s as the opening of a new political cycle in the region characterized by attempts at political and economic liberalization.[74]

The elite that led this process, comprised by mass parties' politicians and technocrats trained in public policy and economy, was closely linked to the foreign influence of western Europe and the United States (for example Menem in Argentina, Salinas in Mexico, and Cardoso in Brazil). For them, electoral democracy was tied to open markets and a monetarist understanding of the economy, the core of the so-called neoliberal thought.[75] This stream of modernization conceived of individuals as rational agents acting in political and economic life and the state as an organization aimed at fostering liberal rights to play openly within those settings.[76] Privatization of utilities and other industrial sectors brought the presence of business corporations, while significant

73 Pereira, *Political (In)Justice*, 63–158.
74 Skidmore and Smith, *Modern Latin America*, 58–61.
75 Dezalay and Garth, *The Internationalization of the Palace Wars*, 163–196.
76 Whitehead, 'State Organization in Latin America,' 438.

segments of the population still lacked formal services. This transformation also included gradually the fight against corruption, the organization of public-private cooperation, and the recognition some social rights. Bolstering fledgling democracies and advancing the institutional predictability and efficiency of markets, these administrations participated in what Thomas Carothers calls the Rule of Law Revival. Accordingly, they promoted reforms to significant sections of the legal system.[77]

Neoclassical economists constituted a critical part of the new reigning technocracy at the beginning of this transformation. Nevertheless, elite legal professionals steadily joined them as part of transnational governmental and academic networks, habitually featured by importing expertise and normative prescriptions. Selected Latin American attorneys with experience in big law firms drafted free-trade agreements and regulatory norms, particularly in Mexico and Brazil. Legal scholars embedded in the law and development movement or legal theory participated actively in policy reform as well. For instance, Carlos Santiago Nino, a noted Argentinian legal philosopher who taught periodically at Yale, led the Council for the Consolidation of Democracy and died while advising on Bolivian constitutional reforms. Nino is a good illustration of this archetype, but indeed not the only one.[78] Although most of these actors imported expertise, some entrepreneurs advocated for legal reforms from within the region. For example, Alberto Binder and other experts sought to restructure criminal procedure.[79] Those policies counted on the financial and technical support of state-backed foreign aid agencies such as USAID, the Inter-American Development Bank, and the Spanish International Development Cooperation Agency.[80]

As a projection of post-1980s institutional change, this wave of modernization yielded a more contested scenario after 2000. New actors became agenda-setters in gender, environmental, and social justice issues, taking advantage of the opportunities opened by democratization. A myriad of think-tanks and advocacy groups, such as *De Justicia* in Colombia and *Fundar* in Mexico, contributed to legal reform by the mean of policy reports and public interest litigation. Moreover, justices of Latin American high courts such as Carlos Gaviria and Luis Roberto Barroso, began to render decisions with a direct impact on

77 Thomas Carothers, 'The Rule of Law Revival' (1998) 77(2) Foreign Affairs 95–106.

78 Dezalay and Garth, *The Internationalization of the Palace Wars*, 214–216, 220–245.

79 Maximo Langer, 'Revolution in Latin American Criminal Procedure: Diffusion of Legal Ideas from the Periphery' (2007) 55 American Journal of Comparative Law 642–646.

80 Pilar Domingo and Rachel Sieder, eds, *Rule of Law in Latin America: The International Promotion of Judicial Reform* (London: Institute of Latin American Studies, 2001).

public policy, primarily through judicial review. Something similar happened with the Inter-American Court of Human Rights. All these latecomers have tended to reframe a more inclusive concept of the rule of law that goes beyond procedural justice, replacing older Kelsenian theories of law as state action by local adaptations of Dworkin, Alexy, and Rawls's concepts of individual rights and adjudication. For some of these actors, the direct application of fundamental rights through judicial channels has engendered a fresh conceptualization of law, now identified under the label of new constitutionalism.[81]

4.1 *Democratization and the New Constitutional Regime*

The constitutional change of the period was closely associated with democratization, and most countries of the region experienced constitutional reform at the end of authoritarianism. Although constitutional transformation occurred in non-authoritarian contexts, those exceptional cases also were informed by similar concerns of restraining political power and violence. Besides reasserting electoral competition, new constitutions prompted a nuanced idea of polity that included diffusion of power and accountability through legal means, prerequisites of both democracy and free markets. Accordingly, they introduced provisions regarding constitutional jurisdiction, a more robust view of rights, and territorial decentralization, among other matters.[82]

The constitutional renovation of the period enshrined central elements of the mid-twentieth-century regimes, such as presidential preeminence and social rights, but these texts went farther than their mere reestablishment. In agreement on limiting political power, they also began to speak about a new legal paradigm they called the constitutional and democratic rule of law. For institutional design, these texts looked principally at the constitutions of Italy (1948), Germany (1949), France (1958), and Spain (1978). Drafters employed these models selectively by way of legitimating their emphasis on constitutional principles, rights, and state organization.

Despite their commonalities, constitutional changes have followed different patterns determined by national political contexts (see shaded sections of Table 6.3 that highlight the main milestones in political liberalization). Peru, Ecuador, Brazil, Guatemala, and Paraguay enacted new constitutions in the years immediately after the authoritarian downfall. Similarly, Argentina and

81 Javier Couso, 'The Transformation of Constitutional Discourse and the Judicialization of Politics in Latin America' in *Cultures of Legality Judicialization and Political Activism in Latin America*, eds Javier Couso, Alexandra Huneeus, and Rachel Sieder (New York: Cambridge University Press, 2012).

82 Faundez, 'Democratization through Law.'

TABLE 6.3 Constitutional transformation: 1980–2010 (selection)

Country	Constitution	Constitutional reforms	Judicial review	Judicial council	IACHR	HR. Off.
Argentina	1857	1994	SC	1994	1984	1994
Bolivia[a]	1967, 2009	1994, 2004	CT	1994	1979	1994
Brazil	1988	1993	CT	1977, 1988	1992	1994
Chile	1980	1989, 2005	SC-CT		1990	2009
Colombia	1991		CT	1979 (1981), 1991	1973	1991
Costa Rica	1949	1989	CT	1993, 1997	1970	1993
Dominican R.	1994		SC	1994	1993	2004
Guatemala	1986		CT	1999	1978	2001
Mexico	1917	1994, 2008, 2011	SC	1994	1981	1992
Paraguay	1992		SC	1992	1989	1995
Peru[b]	1979, 1993	2001	CT	1971, 1979, 1993	1978	1993
Uruguay	1967	1989, 2004	SC	1981 (1985)	1985	2008
Venezuela[c]	1961, 1999	1973, 1983	SC	1961, 1988	1977	1999

a Populist Regression after 2009
b Competitive Authoritarianism 1993–2000
c Authoritarian Regression after 1999. Judicial Council abolition in parentheses. *Abbreviations*: SC: Supreme Court; CT: Constitutional Tribunal; IACHR: Inter-American Convention on Human Rights Ratification; HR. Off.: Autonomous Human Rights Office. Shaded fields indicate main milestones in political liberalization.

Uruguay abolished dictatorships' decrees, reestablished their previous political constitutions, and gradually advanced constitutional amendments. Chile and Panama's dictatorships passed new constitutional texts containing authoritarian transitions designed to preserve their policy choices, which were however modified steadily along with their democratic transitions. Meanwhile, the Colombian Constitution of 1991, and the Dominican Republic and Mexico's amendments in 1994, were triggered by different state's failures such as lack of control on political violence and corruption.[83] Except for Venezuela, Ecuador,

83 Rodrigo Uprimny, 'The Recent Transformation of Constitutional Law in Latin America: Trends and Challenges' (2011) 89 Texas Law Review 587.

and Bolivia in the 2000s, these processes of liberalization have been deepened over time through new constitutional amendments or complementary statutes.

Legal scholars criticized ample powers in the executive branch, and new constitutions set aside presidentialism. There were some restrictions to hyperpresidential spirit through more refined rules on impeachment, electoral courts, and presidential succession, which have been employed frequently.[84] Nevertheless, those reforms did not alter substantively political practices, since the executive kept its supremacy over the legislative process, budgetary determinations, and the control on the cabinets, eclipsing congressional authority in most countries of the region.[85] By and large, new constitutional texts chose other paths to check executive and political power in general, implementing a more stringent control on state bureaucracy, territorial decentralization, judicial independence, and a broader institutional apparatus for the protection of fundamental rights.

Administrative agencies have continued their exponential growth after 1990, but the complete control of the executive branch over them has diminished. Throughout the region, newfangled constitutions have underscored the legality of the state action, and complementary statutes have regulated carefully civil servants' responsibilities and administrative procedures as part of the modernization of the state.[86] Furthermore, some agencies have emerged as autonomous managerial bodies directed by independent boards in areas such as education, labor, and public finance. In this way, lawmakers have isolated some areas of decision making from the most intense political pressures.

The new constitutional regimes also intended to decentralize political power territorially. Brazil, Mexico, and Argentina have consolidated their federal structures, reproducing separation of powers and public organization at the state level. And even in non-federal nations, elected officials have replaced presidential delegates as heads of subnational entities. Meanwhile, municipalities and regional states have become relevant providers of services, investing a substantial portion of the social expenditure. Beyond legal reforms, however,

---

84 Aníbal Pérez Liñán, 'A Two-Level Theory of Presidential Instability' (2014) 56(1) Latin American Politics and Society 34–54.

85 John M. Carey, Matthew S. Shugart, and Octávio Amorin Neto, 'Appendix: Outlines of Constitutional Powers in Latin America' in *Presidentialism and Democracy in Latin America*, eds Scott Mainwaring and Matthew Soberg Shugart (New York: Cambridge University Press, 2011), 440–460; Gargarella, *Latin American Constitutionalism*, 149–150.

86 Cristina Zurbriggen, 'Governance: A Latin America Perspective' (2014) 33 Policy and Society 345–360.

presidential patronage that characterized old-style populism still remains in place.[87] The judiciary, in contrast, experienced major changes.

Considering that courts have suffered substantial constraints in the past, the strengthening of the judicial branch was a critical part of revival of the rule of law.[88] New constitutions vested judicial review either to supreme courts or specialized constitutional tribunals, and, under different terms, maintained or created concrete injunctive legal actions to vindicate fundamental rights, such as *amparo*, *mandado de segurança*, *tutela*, and *recurso de protección*.[89] Inspired by the Italian and Spanish examples, new constitutions also safeguarded judicial independence. Almost all of them established judicial councils in charge of appointments and accountability and usually allowed courts' financial self-rule.[90] Additionally, constitutional regulations on judicial governance were complemented by policies like judicial schools for training and higher salaries for judges. After 2000, judicial independence has leveraged courts as consequential actors in the public realm, and courts have begun to intervene directly in policy-making or have served as a watchdog over political power, as in the *Lava Jato* case in Brazil 2014.

International instruments and the structures of support to protect human rights have become a significant part of the new regimes. Most Latin American constitutions have recognized some legal status for guarantees conferred by international treaties, thereby introducing international human rights law into domestic adjudication.[91] And all the countries of the region have ratified the Inter-American Convention of Human Rights, recognizing the Inter-American Court's jurisdiction, a relevant judicial forum at the regional level.[92]

They have also established independent national agencies for human rights surveillance, ranging from an updated version of the Ombudsman (*Defensor del Pueblo*) to autonomous councils. These entities conduct studies and public

87 Tulia G. Falleti, *Decentralization and Subnational Politics in Latin America* (New York: Cambridge University Press, 2010).

88 Mirow, *Latin American Law*, 174.

89 Allan R. Brewer-Carías, *Constitutional Protection of Human Rights in Latin America: A Comparative Study of Amparo Proceedings* (New York: Cambridge University Press, 2008).

90 Mark Ungar, *Elusive Reform: Democracy and the Rule of law in Latin America* (London: Lynne Rienner, 2002), 169–186.

91 Fernando Basch and Jorge Contesse, 'International law and Domestic Adjudication' in *The Latin American Casebook: Courts, Constitutions, and Rights*, eds Juan F. Gonzalez-Bertomeu and Roberto Gargarella (New York: Routledge, 2016), 248–264.

92 Diego García-Sayán, 'The Inter-American Court and Constitutionalism in Latin America' (2011) 89(7) Texas Law Review 1835–1862.

interest litigation, focusing their attention mainly on minority groups such as Indigenous peoples, LGBT population, and the urban poor.[93]

As part of the constitutional streamlining, the new texts recognize basic principles and broaden the repertoire of rights. In their preambles or at beginning of their running texts, they assert the respect for human dignity, the elimination of poverty, and the legality of state action. In some cases, they also claim an explicit model of polity, such as their adherence to the social or the democratic rule of law as in Brazil and Colombia. These general provisions have served as interpretive guidelines for courts and policymakers. Regarding fundamental guarantees, the new constitutions maintain a reshuffled version of prior liberal and social rights but innovating within this realm as well. Thus, they usually incorporate a long list of entitlements as a way of bolstering welfare and personal autonomy. The Colombian Constitution of 1991, for instance, adopts robust conceptions of economic, social, and cultural guarantees such as the free development of the personality, or the state's duty to protect the peace, secure food production, and safeguard the environment. It promotes access to culture, sports activities, and social security. Something similar happens with the constitutional amendment in Argentina in 1994, which included the citizens' initiative to propose legislation, environmental and consumer protection, access to personal information, and Indigenous peoples' cultural identity.[94]

Such a catalog of rights has been extended progressively, both by international treaties and public interest litigation. For example, Convention 169 of the International Labor Organization on Indigenous and Tribal Peoples (1989) has had a considerable impact on the region, determining the participation of native communities in natural resources management, providing for access to bilingual education, and acknowledging their spiritual beliefs. Meanwhile, domestic and international courts have rendered decisions broadening the understanding of constitutional or conventional rights, creating new ones beyond their textual wording, through an implied or unenumerated rights doctrine.[95] For example, the Colombian Constitutional Court decriminalized the consumption of low doses of drugs as part of the right of free development of personality (1994); Brazilian federal courts have consistently ruled in favor of a comprehensive access to the newest generation of HIV medication beyond

93 Ungar, *Elusive Reform*, 38.

94 Uprimny, 'The Recent Transformation of Constitutional Law,' 1587–1594.

95 Héctor Gros, 'Los derechos humanos no enunciados o no enumerados en el constitucionalismo americano y en el artículo 29.c) de la Convención Americana sobre Derechos Humanos' (2000) 4 Anuario Iberoamericano de Justicia Constitucional 145–173.

state plans; and the Mexican Supreme Court has recognized same-sex marriage against the constitutional provisions on family (2010), among many other illustrations.[96] In a similar vein, the Inter-American Court of Human Rights has issued decisions establishing new guarantees, such as a right to know the truth regarding human rights violations (*Almonacid v. Chile*, 2006), and the recognition of Indigenous communal property with a different extension than ordinary civil ownership (*Comunidad Mayagna v. Nicaragua*, 2001).[97]

4.2 *Restraining Power by Legal Means: Free Markets, Citizenship, and Accountability*

Post-1980 liberal regimes have devoted significant efforts to organize free markets and to extend a model of citizenship that goes beyond mere electoral participation. At different times and with different depths, they have gradually advanced measures to restrain the power of the state, businesses, interest groups, to make them accountable to society and responsive to individual rights. This goal has exceeded constitutional provisions and the general administrative rationalization mentioned above, and has materialized through statutes that address private property, higher levels of transparency in decision making, and the reorganization of the state's institutional capacity. Table 6.4 shows a snapshot of some of legal adjustments that have restructured the economy and society. With the expansions of constitutional rights, these reforms have changed the legal culture of the region, replacing bureaucratic decision making and political bargaining with more litigious and adversarial approaches.

Between the 1980s and the 2000s, most countries of the region committed to the free market economy. Considering numerous cases of expropriation in the prior decades, constitutional provisions looked to restrain the state's dominion and confiscatory power. Besides conserving references to the social function of property, constitutions of the period strengthened private ownership and freedom of enterprise as fundamental guarantees, thereby providing security to investors. Other constitutional amendments embraced similar purposes. For instance, Cardoso promoted some modifications to the constitution to advance the privatization of state companies and natural resources in Brazil; Mexico amended Article 27 of its constitution to limit the redistribution

96 For recent trends on constitutional rights evolution see Gonzalez-Bertomeu and Gargarella, *The Latin American Casebook*.

97 Gonzalo Candia, 'Derechos implícitos y Corte Interamericana de Derechos Humanos: una reflexión a la luz de la noción de estado de derecho' (2015) 42(3) Revista Chilena de Derecho 873–902.

TABLE 6.4 Main legal reforms 1980–2016 (selection)

Country	Main trade agreements[a]	Antitrust law	Consumer protection	Environmental law	Transparency law	Judicial reforms
Argentina	MERCOSUR	1980, 1999	1993, 1997	1993, 2002	2016	military, criminal
Bolivia		1994	2009	1992		criminal, civil
Brazil	MERCOSUR	1994, 2000	1990, 1997	1981, 2003	2011	
Chile	APEC	1973, 2004	1997	1994	2008	criminal, family, labor
Colombia		1992	1982, 1992	1994	2014	criminal
Costa Rica		1994	1995	1996	2014	criminal, civil
Dominican Republic		2008	2005	1990, 2000	2004	criminal
Guatemala			2003	1986, 1997		criminal
Mexico	NAFTA, APEC	1993, 2006	1992	1988	2002	criminal
Paraguay	MERCOSUR		1998	2000		criminal
Peru	APEC	1991, 1992	1991, 1995	1990, 2005	2003	criminal, labor
Uruguay	MERCOSUR	2007	2000	1990, 2000	2008	civil
Venezuela		1992	1995	1976, 2006		criminal

a Main Trade Agreements signed after 1990. *Abbreviations*: MERCOSUR: Southern Common Market (full-members), APEC: Asian-Pacific Economic Cooperation Forum, NAFTA: Northern America Free Trade Agreement.

SOURCE: DATASET ELABORATED BY THE AUTHOR

of land; and Menem's Argentina passed a constitutional reform to assure the value of money.[98] With different degrees of autonomy, several constitutions of the period regulated central banks as a means to promote monetary stability.[99]

Under a similar rationale, more than a few legal reforms complemented the constitutional foundations of free markets at the international and domestic statutory levels.[100] During the 1990s, the region transited from restricted economic treaties with a protectionist spirit signed in the 1960s and 1970s, such as the Central American and the Andean Common Markets, to bilateral, regional, or global free-trade agreements. These aimed to broaden the circulation of goods and services and to adhere to non-state rules and mechanisms of arbitration in commercial dispute resolution, such as those NAFTA, MERCOSUR, and the World Trade Organization provided for.[101] As a corollary to their incorporation into open markets, most Latin American countries reorganized their economic structures to focus on activities in which they enjoyed competitive advantages. A significant number of them privatized state-run industries and utilities or at least allowed the participation of private stockholders, even through participation of small investors and citizens, a case in point being the Bolivian Capitalization Law of 1994. By the same token, they extended the protection to intellectual and industrial property licenses, eschewed barriers to financial flows, and loosened up mid-twentieth-century mining, water, and labor statutes as a way to attract investment and to stimulate economic growth.[102]

Some countries enacted new commercial codes (e.g., Colombia 1977, Mexico 2011), or civil codes (e.g., Peru, 1984, Brazil 2002, Argentina 2015), fostering innovative forms of partnerships and diminishing transaction costs in contracts. Scholars also have made important efforts to harmonize regional contract law at the academic level.[103] Nevertheless, such changes seem marginal in the context of Latin American economic liberalization, failing to match the critical role that codification performed in the nineteenth century.

---

98 Gargarella, *Latin American Constitutionalism*, 152.

99 Luis Jácome, 'Central Banking in Latin America: From the Gold Standard to the Golden Years' (2015) International Monetary Fund Working Paper 33–45.

100 For an analysis of the Colombian case, see: Jairo Estrada Álvarez, 'Orden neoliberal y reformas estructurales en la década de 1990: Un balance desde la experiencia colombiana' (2006) 1 Ciencia Política 141–178.

101 José Antonio Moreno Rodríguez, 'Contracts and Non-State Law in Latin America' (2011) 16 Uniform Law Review 877–889.

102 Mirow, *Latin American Law*, 210–212, 230–232.

103 Rodrigo Momberg, 'The Principles of Latin American Contract Law: Nature, Purposes and Projections' (2018) 2 Latin American Legal Studies 209–223.

To counterbalance the mounting power of businesses, almost all Latin American countries have set reforms in regulatory areas like antitrust, consumer protection, and environmental law (see Table 6.4). Antitrust legislation has addressed mergers and acquisitions to sustain free markets, replacing former competition law designed through state bargaining.[104] Consumer protection has left behind old production quotas and state price-fixing to be adapted to the capitalist economy, incorporating regulations on defective products and contracts of adhesion.[105] Meanwhile, environmental legislation has answered slowly to the damages produced by rising industrialization and has occasionally been complemented by court decisions such as judicially managed cleaning plan for the *Riachuelo Matanza* Basin in Buenos Aires in 2006.[106] Unlike Europe and the United States, where the regulation in these areas was promoted by litigation and advocacy groups, this transformation was carried out initially by technocratic elites to provide legitimacy to pro-market policies. After the 2000s, however, the new adversarial legal culture has boosted the incorporation of more sophisticated rules in these fields, such as class actions and punitive damages.

To fight political and business corruption, the new liberal regimes have advanced measures to assure integrity and to prevent interest groups and illegal associations' capturing of the state. Thus, they passed various statutes to penalize money laundering and to regulate lobbying and the financial sources for electoral campaigns. At the same time, quite a few of them also have enacted transparency laws to reveal sensitive information for decision making and to make state officials accountable to society (see Table 6.4). After some initial resistance by civil servants, these instruments have become a vital part of democratic life, as long as they have empowered average citizens to scrutinize political and economic power.

But the logic of individual rights and the pursuit of restraining power has also touched more traditional legal areas. For example, a higher level of autonomy has been incorporated into family relations. Far behind Mexico that legalized divorce in 1917, civil reforms have done so more recently in countries like

104 Julián Peña, 'Promoting Competition Policies from the Private Sector in Latin America' in *Competition Law and Policy in Latin America*, eds Eleanor Fox and Daniel Sokol (Oxford: Hart, 2009), 469–470.

105 Robert G. Vaughn, 'Consumer Protection Laws in South America' (1994) 17(2) Hastings International and Comparative Law Review 275–322.

106 Felipe Paez, 'Environmental Framework Laws in Latin America' (1996) 13 Pace Environmental Law Review 625–684.

Brazil (1977), Argentina (1987), Colombia (1992), and Chile (2004).[107] Although still in a controversial sphere, several countries have decriminalized adultery, homosexual intercourse, and some types of abortion. Some of them have also conferred a legal status for cohabitation and same-sex marriage.[108] Part of the public opinion has understood such reforms both as an expansion of personal autonomy and a recognition of the limits of the state's lawmaking function.

In a similar vein, the rule of law revival has renovated judicial procedure. For instance, as a way to moderate the application of criminal law as the most extreme manifestation of state power, Latin American countries abolished inquisitorial systems in which judges prosecuted and adjudicate. As a substitute, they set an adversarial procedure in which the responsibility of investigation and indictment lie in an autonomous office (*Ministerio Público*), and courts try individuals adequately represented in an oral trial. In this way, the scholars who designed criminal process reforms incorporated procedural fairness and higher human rights standards through due process and a rigorous assessment of the evidence.[109] Besides the expansion of alternative dispute resolution in businesses and some minor changes to facilitate debt collection, this deep restructuring has become the most relevant procedural innovation in the region, far ahead of other areas like the civil and labor processes. Such a prevalence mirrors the centrality of restraining public power within this new backdrop.

5 *Quo Vadis* Latin American Law?

The transformation of Latin American law is an unfinished process in which legal rules and institutions resemble a multilayered patchwork. Its evolution not only includes Indigenous, colonial, and nineteenth-century legacies that traditionally have stimulated scholars' academic inquiries. Far from staying static, more recent and contended processes of modernization have reframed law within the region during the last one hundred years or so. This recent process has been composed of different streams of institutional reform in which the state has employed law extensively to reshape social structures. As explained above, under the rules and institutions of the period, we can find

107 *El divorcio en el Derecho Iberoamericano*, eds Ángel Acedo and Leonardo Pérez (Madrid: Reus, 2009).

108 For diverse works in that direction, see: *Gender and Sexuality in Latin America: Cases and Decisions*, eds Cristina Motta, and Macarena Sáez (New York: Springer, 2013).

109 Langer, 'Revolution in Latin American Criminal Procedure.'

the traces of different programs for socioeconomic development that provide the clues to comprehend legal evolution after 1930. Indeed, there have been several legal areas that this chapter has not covered. This analysis has not appropriately addressed relevant matters like criminal law, civil procedure, the regulation of the legal profession, or international dispute resolution, to name only a few. It is likely, however, that the transformation of those matters can be explained, at least partially, under the same streams of modernization described throughout this chapter.

But the beginning of the twenty-first century does not mean the end of history. Since about 2000, some countries have openly diverged from the process of liberalization kicked off by the Washington consensus and revisited both the republican system and some elements of the private law. For instance, the Venezuelan Constitution of 1999 has adhered to models of competitive authoritarianism that mixed socialism, plebiscitary devices, and an extreme concentration of power in the hands of the executive branch. The Ecuadorean Constitution of 2008, and the Bolivian Constitution of 2009 have incorporated elements of a pluri-national state with a significant role for Indigenous peoples. Meanwhile, the Cuban Constitution of 2019 shows that democracy is still far away there.[110] The details and variations of these recent developments exceed the scope of this chapter. Nevertheless, they show that not only common patterns but also deep divergences are a critical element to comprehend present Latin American law.

The naïve constructivist spirit that relied upon a top-down process guided by the state to transform society will likely not be determinative as an explanatory outline to understand the legal evolution of the region for the years to come. The persistence of profound social inequality, corruption, and pockets of violence have fueled social turmoil and political polarization, calling into question the capacity of plain legal reform to bring progress. Likewise, the devices for checks and balances aimed at the oversight of power have overloaded the political system, putting state action at risk of paralysis. And as an unintended consequence of liberalization and higher standards of human dignity, the discourse of rights and judicialization have also brought a more adversarial and individualistic legal culture that shapes a society increasingly harder to govern than in the past.[111] The subsequent transformation of Latin American law will face both the opportunities and uncertainty of a new stage

110 Gargarella, *Latin American Constitutionalism*, 172–179.

111 Javier Couso, 'Los desafíos de la democracia constitucional en América Latina: entre la tentación populista y la utopía neoconstitucional' (2010) 6 Anuario de Derechos Humanos 33–47.

in modernization. Perhaps, the legal historians of the future will need interpretive frameworks other than state action to explain them.

References

Adelman, Jeremy, and Miguel Angel Centeno. 'Between Liberalism and Neoliberalism: Law's Dilemmas in Latin America.' In *Global Prescriptions: The Production, Exportation, and Importation of a New Legal Orthodoxy*, edited by Yves Dezalay and Bryant G. Garth, 139–160. Ann Arbor: The University of Michigan Press, 2002.

Caffera, Gerardo. 'The Economic Conditions of Contract in South American Law: An Historical Approach.' In *The Future of Contract Law in Latin America*, edited by Rodrigo Momberg and Stefan Vogenauer, 97–123. Oxford: Hart, 2017.

Couso, Javier. 'The Transformation of Constitutional Discourse and the Judicialization of Politics in Latin America.' In *Cultures of Legality Judicialization and Political Activism in Latin America*, edited by Javier Couso, Alexandra Huneeus, and Rachel Sieder, 141–160. New York: Cambridge University Press, 2012.

Dezalay, Yves, and Bryant G. Garth. *The Internationalization of the Palace Wars: Lawyers, Economists, and the Contest to Transform Latin American States*. Chicago: Chicago University Press, 2002.

Domingo, Pilar, and Rachel Sieder, eds. *Rule of Law in Latin America: The International Promotion of Judicial Reform*. London: Institute of Latin American Studies, 2001.

Faundez, Julio. 'Democratization through Law: Perspectives from Latin America.' *Democratization* 12(5) (2005): 749–765.

García-Sayán, Diego. 'The Inter-American Court and Constitutionalism in Latin America.' *Texas Law Review* 89(7) (2011): 1835–1862.

Gardner, James A. *Legal Imperialism: American Lawyers and Foreign Aid in Latin America*. Madison: University of Wisconsin Press, 1980.

Gargarella, Roberto. *Latin American Constitutionalism, 1810–2010*. New York: Oxford University Press, 2013.

Hilbink, Lisa, and Janice Gallagher 'State and Law in Latin America: A Critical Assessment.' In *Routledge Handbook of Law and Society in Latin America*, edited by Rachel Sieder, Karina Ansolabehere, and Tatiana Alfonso, 37–50. New York: Routledge, 2019.

Jaramillo, Isabel. 'The Social Approach to Family Law: Conclusions from the Canonical Family Law Treatises of Latin America.' *American Journal of Comparative Law*, 58(4) (2010): 843–872.

Keiser, Thorsten. 'Social Conceptions of Property and Labour – Private Law in the Aftermath of the Mexican Revolution and European Legal Science.' *Rechtsgeschichte* 20 (2012): 258–273.

Langer, Maximo. 'Revolution in Latin American Criminal Procedure: Diffusion of Legal Ideas from the Periphery.' *American Journal of Comparative Law* 55 (2007): 617–677.

Loveman, Brian. *The Constitution of Tyranny: Regimes of Exception in Spanish America*. Pittsburgh: University of Pittsburgh Press, 1993.

Mirow, M.C. *Latin American Law: A History of Private Law and Institutions in Spanish America*. Austin: University of Texas Press, 2004.

Mirow, M.C. *Latin American Constitutions: The Constitution of Cádiz and Its Legacy in Spanish America*. Cambridge: Cambridge University Press. 2015.

Palacio, Juan Manuel and Leon Fink, eds. *Labor Justice Across the Americas*. Chicago: University of Illinois Press, 2017.

Pereira, Anthony W. *Political (In)Justice: Authoritarianism and the Rule of Law in Brazil, Chile and Argentina*. Pittsburgh: University of Pittsburgh Press, 2005.

Rosen, Kenneth L., and Keith Karst. *Law and Development in Latin America: A Casebook*. Los Angeles: University of California Los Angles Latin American Center, 1976.

Thome, Joseph R. 'The Process of Land Reform in Latin America.' *Wisconsin Law Review* 1 (1968): 9–22.

Ungar, Mark. *Elusive Reform: Democracy and the Rule of law in Latin America*. London: Lynne Rienner, 2002.

Uprimny, Rodrigo. 'The Recent Transformation of Constitutional Law in Latin America: Trends and Challenges.' *Texas Law Review* 89 (2011):1587–1609.

Whitehead, Laurence. 'State Organization in Latin America since 1930.' In *Latin America: Economy and Society since 1930*, edited by Leslie Bethell, 381–440. New York: Cambridge University Press, 1998.

Wiarda, Howard J. 'Law and Political Development in Latin America: Toward a Framework for Analysis.' *American Journal of Comparative Law* 19(3) (1971): 434–463.

PART 2

Historical Actors

CHAPTER 7

Legal Education and the Legal Profession

Rogelio Pérez-Perdomo

1 The Iberian Period

1.1 *Legal Education in Spanish America*

There were not any universities in Brazil under Portuguese rule. Brazilians who wanted a university legal education and the formal title of lawyers (*advogados*) went to Portugal and studied at the University of Coimbra. Spain had a different colonial policy and established universities and legal studies from the earliest days of colonization. Consequently, this section refers only to Spanish America.

In the sixteenth century, when the conquest and colonization of America started, legal education was well established in Spanish universities. Salamanca was created in 1215 and was the leading university, but other important universities were in Valladolid, Alcalá de Henares, and Barcelona. In the sixteenth century, Salamanca was an active center of legal and theological scholarship and was among the most important European universities.[1] Professors Francisco de Vitoria, Domingo de Soto, and other leading theologians-jurists constituted the so-called Salamanca School. From the sixteenth century onwards, a university legal education was required to become a lawyer. In Portugal, the University of Coimbra was also created in the thirteenth century, Luis de Molina and Francisco Suárez taught there in the sixteenth and seventeenth centuries respectively.

Legal studies concentrated on Roman and canon law. The royal (*patrio*) law was not taught in the universities, even if the royal decrees ordered that in practice this legislation had priority over any other form of law. The preference for Roman law was not only a result of inertia: it was the core of the European *ius commune*. It was considered the true law and provided the language and concepts of the law. In practice, it was also applied by the judges.[2]

1 Maria Lourdes Martínez de Moretin Llamas, 'La contribución de la Escuela de Salamanca al desarrollo de la ciencia jurídica' (2017) 14 Glossae: European Journal of Legal History 399.

2 Mariano Peset Reig, 'Derecho romano y derecho real en las universidades del siglo XVIII' (1975) 45 Anuario de Historia del Derecho Español 273.

 | DOI:10.1163/9789004436091_009

Legal education in Spanish America followed the model of Salamanca. By 1551 universities with legal studies were created in Santo Domingo, Mexico City, and Lima. By the end of the sixteenth century there were universities in Quito, Bogotá, and Cuzco. In the seventeenth and eighteenth centuries they were established in Chuquisaca (Sucre, Bolivia), Guatemala, Caracas, Havana, Santiago de Chile, Córdoba, and Guadalajara. All the universities taught Roman law, canon law, and theology, in addition to the basic subjects (or *estudios menores* of Latin, grammar, logic, and rhetoric). The universities conferred the titles of bachelor, *licenciado*, and doctor after several years of studies and examination in one of the two laws: Roman law or canon law. It was also possible to take the examination in both laws (*utriusque juris*).

University studies were reserved for the social elite, which meant a particular sector of the white population. A certificate of 'pure blood old Christian' was required. People from Moorish, Jewish, or African descent were not accepted. Native Americans ('*indios*' or '*hijos de la tierra*') were not formally excluded, but it was not expected that they would pursue a university education.

Not all whites had an interest in or the social capacity to pursue university studies. Recent immigrants from Spain were white free people, but they did not have high social status. They were '*blancos de orilla*,' white people who lived in the outskirts of the city. It was not easy for them to obtain the pure blood certificate, and many did not have the means or leisure to study at the university. In fact, the social status of *blancos de orilla* was close to that of the *pardos* (free people of color). Both groups shared residence on the city outskirts and engaged in small commerce or manual work, *oficios viles*. All these regulations were formal. In practice, there were nuances and exceptions. A number of *conversos* (recently converted Catholics mostly of Jewish origin) and mixed-race people pursued successful university careers.

Uribe Uran documented cases of *pardos* who in late colonial times gained a legal education in New Granada (today Colombia).[3] In Venezuela, the best documented case is Juan Germán Roscio (1763–1821), grandson of an Indian (native) and son of a Milanese at the service of the Spanish crown (a '*blanco de orilla*'). The protection of the Count of San Javier's daughter allowed him to study law. He was a specially gifted student and became professor of civil (Roman) law in 1798 in Caracas.[4] He later became one of the leading intellectuals of Venezuelan independence.

3 Víctor M. Uribe-Uran, *Honorable Lives: Lawyers, Family, and Politics in Colombia 1780–1850* (Pittsburgh: University of Pittsburgh Press, 2000).

4 Luis Ugalde, *El pensamiento teológico-político de Juan Germán Roscio* (Caracas: Bid and Co. 2007); Rogelio Pérez-Perdomo, 'Juan Germán Roscio: Equality and Freedom in Early

The basic lawbook was Justinian's *Corpus Juris Civilis*, just as it had been in medieval universities. Similarly, teaching followed the medieval method of commented reading (*lectio*) and structured discussion of legal issues (*questio*), adapted in the Spanish tradition as '*disputas*.' In the eighteenth century the reading of the *Digest* lost centrality, and the *Institutes*, the best organized book of the *Corpus*, gained in importance. The most commonly used edition of the *Institutes* was by Vinnius (later additionally annotated by Heineccius). Vinnius incorporated much of modern natural law in his commentaries, converting the *Institutes* into a kind of rationalist book.[5] Heineccius completed Vinnius's job. The teaching style of the time also allowed the incorporation of the Spanish legislation (mostly the *Siete Partidas*) in the *disputas*. The teaching of *patrio* ('national') legislation and at the same time the reconstruction of law as a rational system were dominant ideas in the eighteenth century, favored by the Spanish monarchy. Under the appearance of continuity with the medieval tradition, law teaching accepted the influx of seventeenth- and eighteenth-century rationalist and 'nationalist' legal thought.

Not all the law graduates had an interest in becoming '*abogados*.' A legal education was important for priests climbing the church hierarchy or bureaucracy, but priests could not appear in courts as lawyers, except in cases of their own or involving their family members. For this reason, priests had an interest in studying law but not in going further to obtain the degree of lawyers. A legal education was a sign of intellectual and social distinction by itself. For men with a noble title, the additional title of lawyer thus did not make much sense, particularly because it did not add anything to one's honor and also because of implied obligations that it was probably better to avoid such as paying fees or serving Indigenous and poor people for free.[6] It was reasonable to study law without any interest in becoming a lawyer. Thus, the number of law graduates was much higher than the number of lawyers. For example, in Venezuela, 272 people graduated in law between 1750 and 1800, but in 1800 there were fewer than 100 lawyers.[7]

Nineteenth Century Venezuela' in *Law and Christianity in Latin America: The Work of Great Jurists*, eds M.C. Mirow and Rafael Domingo (London: Routledge, 2019).

5 Laura Beck Varela, *Literatura jurídica y censura: Fortuna de Vinnius en España* (Sevilla: Universidad de Sevilla, 2013).

6 Rogelio Pérez-Perdomo, *Latin American Lawyers: A Historical Introduction* (Stanford: Stanford University Press, 2006).

7 Rogelio Pérez-Perdomo, *Los abogados en Venezuela: Una elite intelectual y política 1780–1980* (Caracas: Monte Ávila, 1981), 64 and 72.

1.2 *Lawyers*

The accreditation as lawyer (*abogado*) was given by the *audiencia*, the highest law court of the jurisdiction. Above the audience, there was only the Consejo de Indias in Madrid. From the sixteenth century onwards the university degree of bachelor or *licenciado* in law was required for obtaining the title of '*abogado*.' A number of years of practice and an examination were also required. The length of these requirements changed over time, but the university title and the practice were always required. The title of lawyer was an additional social distinction, relatively equivalent to a noble title. The title was '*abogado de la Audiencia de Santo Domingo*' or Mexico, or Caracas. This title made the lawyer a royal functionary, except without pay. It was a source of honor because of its implied service to the King and its relation to state power.[8] Members of the profession came from 'good families' and the title of lawyer increased their high social status.

The number of lawyers was low in early colonial times: a handful of them in the most important cities. A modest growth occurred in the eighteenth century. By the mid-eighteenth century there were enough lawyers in most important cities for the creation of *colegios de abogados*, important public bodies during the Hispanic period. Functionally, *Colegios de abogados* were generally similar to a present-day bar association but the differences between them reveal the different role and social status of lawyers at that time. Membership in the *Colegio* was a requirement for lawyers. The *Colegio* was in charge of monitoring lawyers' appropriate behavior. As a case in point, the *Colegio* had to authorize the wedding of a lawyer, to avoid a 'bad' marriage, for example, with a woman of lower status. A bad marriage could affect the honor of the entire bar. Most lawyers were accepted into the *Colegio* when they were about twenty-five years of age and married when they were thirty, at least in Mexico.[9] Another example is the sanction placed on lawyer José Domingo Gil in 1791. His grave sin was to play cards with *mulatos* (mixed race people with some African blood), something the *Colegio* considered offensive to the quality of his birth and the noble occupation of a lawyer. His behavior 'darkened the splendor of the *abogacía*.'[10]

For admission to the *Colegio*, the candidate had to solicit the title from the *audiencia* and establish a new proof of 'clean' blood. Again, the case of

8 Uribe-Urán, *Honorable lives*; José Antonio Maravall, *Poder, honor y elites en el siglo XVII* (Madrid: Siglo XXI, 1977).

9 Alejandro Mayagoitia, 'Las últimas generaciones de abogados virreinales. Un ensayo' in *Los abogados y la formación del estado mexicano*, eds Óscar Cruz Barney, Hector Fix-Fierro, and Elisa Speckman Guerra (México: UNAM, 2013).

10 Pérez-Perdomo, *Los abogados en Venezuela*, 97.

Juan Germán Roscio is significant. When he tried to register in the *Colegio de Abogados de Caracas*, the *Colegio*'s board first delayed taking action. In 1798 he decided to press the issue. Supposing that the delay arose from an objection to his mother's race, he argued that Native Americans were free vassals of the Spanish crown and therefore they were equal to white Europeans. He invoked *derecho indiano*, but he also used theological and historical arguments. He went even further and argued for the equality of men. His challenge escalated into an angry dispute, and the *Colegio*'s board accused Roscio of subversion before the *audiencia*. The Fiscal of the Audiencia did not accept the *Colegio*'s accusation. In the end, Roscio produced new documents and a new board accepted him into the *Colegio* in 1805.[11]

An important issue was the remuneration of lawyers' work and the economic dimension of legal practice. A lawyer was not required for representation in court. Still more, in some jurisdictions, such as in commercial tribunals or the *Consulado*, representation by lawyers was forbidden. A petition written in lawyerly style could be refused.

In addition to lawyers there were *procuradores*. They did not have university legal training nor the title of lawyers but were accepted by courts for the bureaucratic management of cases. In a way, they competed with lawyers, but their social status was lower. *Escribanos* (functionally equivalent to notaries who wrote and registered documents) and *tinterillos* or *pica-pleitos* also performed minor legal functions. They were not law graduates but had some kind of practical training for operating within the legal system. The *tinterillos* were usually lower-class men who were perceived as more connected to the general population. The lawyers' high social standing was an obstacle to this connection. Given all these obstacles and the traditional and rural type of society, there was not much business for lawyers. This does not mean that lawyers were poor. In fact, many of them were wealthy, but the source of their income was familial. They were members of wealthy families or, as a result of their high social status, were able to marry wealthy women.[12]

An important source for lawyers' employment was the colonial bureaucracy.[13] They had two limitations in this respect: the colonial bureaucracy was

---

11 Rogelio Pérez-Perdomo, 'Roscio y el Colegio de Abogados de Caracas. Un caso para entender el cambio de mentalidad en el temprano siglo XIX' (2019) 39 Revista Mexicana de História del Derecho 77–93.

12 Alejandro Mayagoitia, 'Las últimas generaciones de abogados virreinales'; Pérez-Perdomo, *Latin American Lawyers*, 35.

13 John Kicza, 'The Legal Community of Late Colonial Mexico: Social Composition and Career Patterns' in *Five Centuries of Law and Politics in Central Mexico*, eds Ronald Spores

TABLE 7.1 Lawyers in Spanish America in the late colonial period

Country and year	Number of lawyers	Lawyers per 100k population
Cuba 1792	85	17
Chile 1797	77 (33)	11 (4)
New Spain (Mexico) 1802	432 (243)	7 (4)
Venezuela 1805	105	10
New Granada (Colombia) 1806	140	7
Peru 1813	177	14

(FIGURES IN PARENTHESES ARE PRACTICING LAWYERS). TABLE REPRODUCED FROM PÉREZ-PERDOMO, *LATIN AMERICAN LAWYERS*, 33

reduced and in the eighteenth century, most important positions, like *oidores* in the *audiencias*, were almost forbidden to those born in the territory (*hijos del país*). In practice, most *oidores* and other high colonial functionaries were peninsular Spaniards.[14] These limitations on employment opportunities can explain the perception that there was an excess (a *multitud*) of lawyers by 1800, even if they were very few by today's standards.[15] Table 7.1 gives the approximate numbers by the end of the Spanish period.

Perhaps there were fewer than one thousand lawyers in Spanish America. Lawyers were a rather small, educated elite but with great difficulties to find a remunerative occupation or to exercise political power. The number of practicing lawyers was still lower, as Table 7.1 shows. The concern of the Spanish crown about the excess of lawyers was justified because there was no occupation for this intellectual elite. When the Spanish monarchy entered into crisis

---

and Ross Hassig (Nashville: Vanderbilt University, 1984); Renán Silva, *Universidad y sociedad en el Nuevo Reino de Granada* (Bogotá: Banco de la República, 1992).

14 Mark Burkholder and Dewitt S. Chandler, *From Impotence to Authority: The Spanish Crown and the American Audiencias 1687–1808* (Columbia: University of Missouri Press, 1980).

15 Jaime del Arenal Fenochio, 'Los abogados en México y una polémica centenaria, 1784–1847' (1980) Revista de Investigaciones Jurídicas 39–47; Pérez-Perdomo, *Latin American Lawyers*, 33; Victor M. Uribe-Uran, 'Colonial Lawyers, Republican Lawyers and the Administration of Justice in Spanish America,' in *Judicial Institutions in Nineteenth-Century Latin America*, ed. Eduardo Zimmermann (London: Institute of Latin American Studies, 1999), 25–48.

early in the nineteenth century and Brazil had to declare independence with the leadership of the Crown Prince, lawyers became central to the independence process and the construction of the new nations.[16]

2 Nineteenth and Early Twentieth Centuries

The independence of Latin American countries was not only a process of separation from Spain or Portugal but also an effort to create national states along the model of liberal republics or constitutional monarchies. Until 1808, Spain and Portugal were absolute Catholic monarchies.[17] The Napoleonic invasion shook the foundations of both empires. The failing of Spanish kings when submitting to Napoleon's pressures was a powerful argument for independence. Spain and Portugal's erratic policies in relation to their American populations made the independence of American territories almost inevitable. Twenty years later the political map had changed radically and was much closer to present-day Latin America. It had not been an easy transition; and it was more difficult in Spanish America than in Brazil which was able to preserve the monarchical legitimacy until the end of the nineteenth century. The discussion on the political and social role of the Catholic Church divided the elites as conservatives and liberals. The liberals' triumph clashed with the political practices and highly stratified social structures of the past.[18] The political turmoil led to the primacy of *caudillos* and dictators in several regions. Still, liberal ideas and practical needs had a complex impact on legal education and practice.

2.1 *Legal Education*

At the beginning of national independence, law schools became the institutions for educating the new political elite, the *huestes de estado*.[19] Of course,

16 *Los abogados y la formación del estado mexicano*, eds Óscar Cruz Barney, Hector Fix-Fierro, and Elisa Speckman Guerra (México: UNAM, 2013); *Juristas de la independencia*, eds José M. Pérez Collados, and Samuel Rodríguez Barbosa (Madrid: Marcial Pons, 2012); Pérez-Perdomo, *Latin American Lawyers*.

17 *Inventando la nación. Iberoamérica siglo XIX*, eds Antonio Annino, and Françoise-Xavier Guerra (México: Fondo de Cultura Económica, 2003).

18 *Liberalismo y poder: Latinoamérica en el siglo XIX*, eds Iván Jaksic and Eduardo Posada Carbó (México: Fondo de Cultura Económica, 2011).

19 Julio Gaitán Bohórquez, *Huestes de estado, la formación universitaria de los juristas al comienzo del estado colombiano* (Bogotá. Centro Editorial Universidad del Rosario, 2002); Joachim Falcão, *A Criação dos cursos jurídicos no Brasil* (Rio de Janeiro: Câmara

legal education had to be reformed to adapt to this new and important role. The best documented discussion happened in Brazil where the first congress tackled this job almost simultaneously with drafting the constitution of the new nation.[20] The desire for modernity was moderated by the dangerous subversive character of some subjects and books. Otherwise, the discussion was rather general in most other Latin American countries. It was not an easy task to determine what subjects to teach. The most difficult challenge was to adapt a particular region's law and politics to the new doctrines mostly developed in Protestant rationalist Europe while, at the same time, maintaining Catholic orthodoxy. In any case, depending on the country, in the decade after independence or sometime thereafter, Latin American countries produced new curricula for their law schools. As an example, Table 7.2 shows the new law curricula in five countries.

These curricula could be organized yearly or biannually; the list only indicates the general order prescribed in the study's plan. The analysis of curricula reveals the persistence of tradition: Roman and canon law continued to be taught, except in a few instances where canon law was replaced by the history of the Catholic Church. The only exception was Brazil, which suppressed Roman law in 1827 but brought it back in 1854.[21] The new offerings are striking: natural law, constitutional law, political economy, and international law. These are the signs of the new times and show the purpose of educating the political elite. In some cases, the title itself reveals the reference to an author. Principles of universal legislation is clearly a reference to the book *Tratado de legislación civil y penal* (Paris, 1823, in its Spanish version) by Jeremy Bentham, an author revered by liberals in the first part of the nineteenth century and demonized by conservatives.[22]

One hundred years later the legal curriculum looks completely different: canon law had disappeared in most schools, and courses in 'positive' national law's national codes or legislation, now formed the core of legal

dos Deputados, Centro de Documentação e Informação, publicado em convênio com Fundação Rui Barbosa, 1977).

20 Joachim Falcão, *A Criação dos cursos*; Joachim Falcão, *Os cursos jurídicos e as elites políticas brasileiras*, ed. Aurelio W. Bastos (Brasília: Câmara dos Deputados, 1978).

21 João Paulo Allain Teixeira, Gustavo Ferreira Santos, and Marcelo Labanca Corrêa Araújo, 'La enseñanza del Derecho en Brasil como actividad política: impactos en la configuración del Derecho y en la práctica de los juristas' in *La educación legal como política pública en América Latina*, ed. Gorki González Mantilla (Lima: Palestra, 2018), 22.

22 *Tratado de legislación civil y penal*, Paris 1823, in its Spanish version see Theodora McKennan, 'Jeremy Bentham and the Colombian liberators' (1978) 34 The Americas 460–475.

TABLE 7.2 Law curriculum in five Latin American countries in the early nineteenth century

Colombia 1826	Brazil 1827	Venezuela 1827	Mexico 1834	Chile 1844
Universal legislation	Natural law 1	Justinian's *Institutes*	Natural law	Natural law
International law	International law 1	Religion & church history	Public law	Universal legislation
Administrative science & institutions	Natural law 2	Natural law	Principles of legislation	Political economy
Roman & national civil law 1	International law 2	Church history	Roman law	International law
Church public law	National civil law 1	Constitution & administrative science	Civil law 1	Roman law
Roman & national civil law 2	National criminal law	International law	Criminal law 1	National & constitutional law
Political economy & Col. Statistics 1	National civil law 2	International law	Canon law 1	Canon law
International law 1	Church public law	Principles of universal legislation	Civil law 2	
Political economy & Col. Statistics 2	Public law	Civil and criminal practice	Criminal law 2	
International law 2	Imperial constitution 1	Political economy	Canon law 2	
	Imperial constitution 2	Legal medicine	Academia	
	Commercial law			
	Procedural theory & practice			

TABLE TAKEN FROM PÉREZ-PERDOMO, *LATIN AMERICAN LAWYERS*, 71

studies. The education of the political elite, still a function of the law school, is no longer highlighted. The study of positive law aimed at preparing students for the professional practice of law.[23] Legal education became more 'technical,' 'professional,' or specialized. In the process of this transformation, the political liberal values that were at the roots of the creation of the new nations were forgotten.

During the nineteenth century there was also an important change in teaching methodology. The reading of materials and the *disputas* (discussions) were replaced by professors' explanations or lectures (*clases magistrales*). In addition, graduates had practical training that was not provided by the schools but by the students' practice of working as clerks in the courts or in lawyers' offices, usually involving a modest payment. The small number of law students and their family connection with established lawyers facilitated this type of training. In the nineteenth century reading became more common, especially among the reduced urban elite. There were alarmed voices that reading had become an epidemic (*epidemia lectora*) and that by the end of the nineteenth century this epidemic had spread even to women. Higher levels of literacy made students interested in literary and political discussions. During the nineteenth and early twentieth centuries, lawyers were *letrados*, people informed on literature, politics, and history. Frequently they became journalists or writers.

Dominant ideas in legal education also changed. In early independent times, new states adapted European, modern, liberal constitutional and legal thinking to their new circumstances. This adaptation was not exempt of originality, like the work on international law by Andrés Bello or Manuel Calvo. Late in the nineteenth or early twentieth century the more 'scientific' positivist or evolutionist authors became critical of liberalism and paid more attention to the historical roots and social structures of the new countries. Pragmatic law professors did not care about these theories and authors; they considered their job explaining and commenting on the codes.

The quality and number of law students also changed during this period. The universities stopped requiring 'pure blood' for admission, but in fact only those from upper- or middle-class backgrounds successfully aspired to study law. In Brazil, the São Paulo law school was expected to receive the coffee planters' sons, while the Olinda (later Recife) law school was mostly for the sugar cane planters' sons.[24] Chile still required the law students to come from

---

23 Pérez-Perdomo, *Latin American Lawyers*.

24 Eliane B. Junqueira, 'Brazil: The Road of Conflict Bound to Total Justice' in *Legal Culture in the Age of Globalization: Latin America and Latin Europe*, eds Lawrence Friedman and Rogelio Pérez-Perdomo (Stanford: Stanford University Press, 2003).

TABLE 7.3 Number of lawyers in five Latin American countries ca. 1850 and 1950

Country / year	Lawyers' absolute number	Lawyers per 100k population
Brazil / 1850–1950	1,383–15,660	19–30
Chile / 1854–1945	282–943	19–17
Colombia / 1849–1951	520–5,813	24–50
Mexico / 1869–1950	667–6,258	7–22
Venezuela / 1840–1941	120–957	12–25

SOURCE: PÉREZ-PERDOMO, *LATIN AMERICAN LAWYERS*, 86

'good families,' but without defining who was excluded. This informal social selection ensured only a moderate growth in the number admitted to the bar.

2.2 *Lawyers*

In the nineteenth and early twentieth centuries most law graduates became lawyers and the absolute number of lawyers increased dramatically. Nonetheless, if we relate these numbers to the increase in population, the perceived growth was more modest. Table 7.3 shows the numbers for five Latin American countries.

During this period the state was the main employer of lawyers, but with two important changes. First, at the beginning of the period, lawyers mainly occupied only the highest positions in the state, like cabinet ministers or members of Parliament. By the mid-1900s, they also occupied middle level positions and this trend extended even to lower ranks of the administration in the second half of the twentieth century.

Second, there was an increase in the number of lawyers who supported themselves by offering legal services to the general public. This change generally occurred in the first half of the twentieth century or in some countries a few decades earlier. The image of lawyers in this period was of a man in a dark suit and tie, and with an office in the city center, not far from the courts. During this period the lawyers who practiced the profession were usually organized as solo practitioners or as small firms often made up of lawyers with family ties with one another. Women generally served as secretarial assistance, answering the phone and typing documents. By the mid-twentieth century a small number of women became lawyers.

The degree of economic development is related to this transformation: when the economy developed, such as when a significant commercial sector developed or foreign investment started to flow, the provision of legal services became a source of income for many lawyers.

As the demands for legal services were not too intense, lawyers continued their interest in politics, history, and literature. Lawyers were members of the intellectual elite. Many of them dabbled in journalism, which at that time was mostly opinion journalism. Many lawyers were also poets, writers, or even musicians. They wrote opinion articles on politics or historical essays. In general, lawyers were multifunctional: they were journalists, politicians, public functionaries, in addition to running legal practices, mostly when political positions were not open to them.

The trends in education and occupation implied important tensions. Legal education was impregnated with political liberalism, at least in some subjects like constitutional and administrative law. Lawyers could boast about being defenders of freedom and legality, but in practice many of them were state employees or collaborated with *caudillos* and dictators.[25] The cognitive dissonance between the values they were trained to uphold, and the realities of their work probably was more acute among lawyers in high political positions who were in close collaboration with dictators or other personalist or authoritarian rulers. Describing and explaining how distinguished legal authors dealt with this dissonance remains to be done, but the diffusion of a positivist and a more 'neutral,' technical or instrumental vision of law probably helped in managing the dissonance.[26]

3 From National Development to Globalization

The second half of the twentieth century was a time of industrialization and rapid urbanization in most Latin American countries. The idea that economic and social development could be attained through correct public policies based on state regulation had an important role in the process of development. The nation was the framework for development and the national economy had to be protected from international competition. The law played an important role in the expression and implementation of these policies. National

25 Joachim Falcão, 'Lawyers in Brazil: Ideas and Praxis' (1979) 7 International Journal of the Sociology of Law 355–375.

26 Rogelio Pérez-Perdomo, *Los juristas académicos de Venezuela: Historia institucional y biografía colectiva* (Caracas: Universidad Metropolitana, 2014).

development, strengthening the state, control of the economy, and the center stage for the administrative law were the different aspects of these national development policies. But the traditional private law, limiting the power of the state and protecting property rights and the sanctity of contracts, could be an obstacle for development.[27]

By the end of the twentieth century, policies of national development might have reached their limits and economic growth had slowed dramatically. Most countries were deep in debt and corruption was widespread, two features associated with state interventionism. As international relations became more extensive, the law had to adapt to this new era of increased international exchanges and economic opening to international competition. National governments needed to be mindful of constitutional limits, human rights, international treaties, contracts, and property rights. This was the era of globalization. At the same time, anti-globalization voices pointed to the people left out of economic prosperity and the increased inequality within and between nations.

3.1 *Legal Education*

These changes in the conditions and in political and economic ideologies affected legal education in many ways. For example, urbanization implied some social democratization: more people had access to primary and secondary education. As a consequence, access to law schools became easier too. The number of law students and lawyers steadily increased. At the same time, there was growing uneasiness with legal education. Some believed that the law school was completely out of synch with the new times[28] or even that law was an obstacle to development.[29] This democratization also meant that a number of law students entered law school with a weaker academic preparation than earlier. The opening of enrollment to a wider public generated the perception that the quality of students and law schools declined. The need for law school reform became a kind of mantra.[30]

At the beginning of this period, there were a small number of private universities, most of which were created by the Catholic Church to answer to

27 Eduardo Novoa Monreal, *El derecho como obstáculo al cambio social* (México: Siglo Veintiuno Editores, 1975).

28 Francisco Clementino de San Tiago Dantas, 'A Educação Jurídica e a Crise Brasileira' (1955) 159 Revista Forense 449–459.

29 Novoa Monreal, *El derecho como obstáculo al cambio social.*

30 Gorki González Mantilla, *Reforma de la educación jurídica o los molinos de viento* (Lima: Pontificia Universidad Católica del Perú, 2008); Lorenzo Zolezzi Ibárcena, *La enseñanza del derecho* (Lima: Pontificia Universidad Católica del Perú, 2017); Pérez-Perdomo, *Latin American Lawyers.*

the successes of laicism and liberal ideas. There also were some universities or law schools created by liberal-minded people in answer to the conservative trends in education. In the second half of the twentieth century the creation of private and public universities with distinctive purposes and missions became common. Many law schools are in fact 'manufacturers of illusions' (*fábricas de ilusões*) where students learned very little but received a university degree.[31] Most Latin American countries (Brazil is one of the exceptions) do not require bar examinations and law school graduates can practice law after mere bureaucratic registration. Their status as lawyers thus depends on the perceived quality of their school. In contrast, other schools adopted new trends in legal education or insisted on high-quality traditional instruction. In the early twenty-first century, it is fair to say that there are few common features among law schools of the region. The prestige of one's law school has become an important predictor of success in the profession.

Another trend in legal studies during this period was internationalization. In the past, only a few individuals studied law in a jurisdiction other than where they planned to practice. In the second part of the twentieth century, studies abroad after studies in the home country became more common. In the beginning, young Latin American graduates preferred to go to Europe for further studies, but from the 1970s onwards an increasing number of Latin American lawyers went to the United States to undertake master's, and in exceptional cases, doctoral programs. These further studies were generally related to changes in the legal profession. Law firms, with a degree of specialization among the lawyers who formed them, started appreciating knowledge of foreign languages and foreign legal cultures. This was a boost for master's or specialization degrees outside of one's native country. A number of universities in Latin America also established specializations, master's, and doctoral programs.

Law schools changed in important ways during this period. In the 1960s most law professors were lawyers or judges who dedicated a few hours each week to lecturing at the universities. Most of them did not have experience of foreign legal education, and they did not publish much, if at all. In the last part of the twentieth century a number of universities started hiring full-time law professors and requiring higher degrees and publications. Law journals multiplied. Centers and institutes for legal research were created. Many law schools,

31 Eliane B. Junqueira, *Faculdades de direito, ou, fábricas de ilusões?* (Rio de Janeiro: IDES and Letra Capital, 1999).

TABLE 7.4 Number of lawyers in five Latin American countries ca. 1970 and 2015

Country / year	Lawyers' absolute number	Lawyers per 100k population
Brazil / 1970–2014	37,710–839,758	41–408
Chile / 1970–2015	4,306–40,000	44–225
Colombia / 1968–2013	13,000–225,000	65–478
Mexico / 1970–2014	14,669–321,000	30–258
Venezuela / 1971–2017	8,102–257,060	70–757

SOURCES: PÉREZ-PERDOMO (*LATIN AMERICAN LAWYERS*, 114) FOR 1970. GÓMEZ AND PÉREZ-PERDOMO ('CORPORATE LAWYERS AND MULTINATIONAL CORPORATIONS IN LATIN AMERICA AND SPAIN 1990–2015') FOR 2015. LYNCH (*LEGAL ROLES IN COLOMBIA*) FOR COLOMBIA 1968. GÓMEZ AND PÉREZ-PERDOMO ('A DISPATCH FROM THE ABYSS') FOR VENEZUELA

but by no means all of them, became more scholarly places. At the same time, there was an increased concern about better preparing students.

3.2 *Legal Profession*

National development policies led to the creation of many decentralized state agencies and public corporations. Serving the legal needs of the many resultant entities required an army of lawyers. Private business also grew, and foreign investments became very important. These events increased the demand for lawyers. In this period of globalization, many public corporations were privatized, and municipalities and provinces obtained greater autonomy. Private and international business thrived. These trends explain the rapid growth in the number of lawyers, much faster than population growth as a whole, as shown in Table 7.4.

The legal profession not only grew in size. As in many other professions there was also a strong tendency to specialize by areas of law and activity. Organizationally, lawyers grouped themselves into firms, or they became in-house counsel for large business. In some cases, the in-house counsel adopted the form of a law firm. For example, the *consultoría jurídica* of the Venezuelan oil business in 2000 had 144 lawyers: it was larger than the largest Venezuelan law firm at the time. Late in the twentieth century, teaching and research on law became a special branch of the profession. The production of legal literature increased substantially with the professionalization of the legal academy.

TABLE 7.5 Average size of ten largest law firms in seven Latin American countries

Country	1999	2015	% Growth
Argentina	85.4	114.6	134
Brazil	87.3	372.8	427
Chile	29.5	87.9	298
Colombia	25.4	67.5	266
Mexico	56.1	97.7	174
Peru	26.2	98.6	376
Venezuela	41.5	40.4	-1

SOURCE: GÓMEZ AND PÉREZ-PERDOMO, 'CORPORATE LAWYERS AND MULTINATIONAL CORPORATIONS IN LATIN AMERICA AND SPAIN 1990–2015,' 16

The surge of law firms in Latin America is a relatively recent phenomenon. In 1999 only twenty-three law firms in Latin America had more than fifty lawyers and only in Brazil, Argentina, and Mexico was the average size of the ten biggest firms more than fifty lawyers. By 2015 the average size of the ten largest law firms increased substantially. Table 7.5 shows this growth.

In general, the growth of law firms is associated with economic growth and the level of investments. In the period analyzed in Table 7.5, growth and investments were moderate in Argentina and intensive in Brazil, Peru, Chile, Colombia and Mexico, the countries with more economic growth and the greatest expansion of law firms. In contrast, Venezuela as part of its Chavist revolution placed obstacles to investments and placed a significant part of the economy under state control. The shrinking of law firms accelerated when the crisis became more acute in Venezuela: in 2018 the average size of the ten largest firms was twenty-seven lawyers, a decrease of one third when compared to 1999.[32]

Law firms mean specialization and hierarchization. Law firm partners generally occupy the top stratum of the legal profession, a place where they are in the company of the heads of boutique firms and the most prestigious litigants. Their income and their connections to money and power are part of their status, but also frequently their distinction is related to substantial knowledge and experience. Professional academic lawyers also attain an important place

32 latinlawyer.com/edition/1000801/latin-lawyers-250-2018.

in the hierarchy of the stratified profession, mostly based on their knowledge, intellectual production, and prestige.

Other new groups within the profession are the 'cause' lawyers. Very frequently they work in NGOs. Human rights' lawyers are probably the best known and both most influential and internationally connected.[33] There are also other causes, such as the protection of the environment, consumers, and workers, that attract a number of lawyers. Still, lawyers working in the public administration and, in general, the public sector, are the most numerous. Solo practitioners or lawyers who work in small associations to share expenses, the most traditional form of law practice, are still numerous. Technology has greatly facilitated the work of lawyers of all types, including those with traditional practices.

In the early twentieth century some lawyers from Europe and the United States came to Latin America and opened legal practices or established law firms, frequently in association with local lawyers. Nevertheless, they were not numerous. In the second half of the twentieth century this trend became more accentuated. In 1955, Baker and McKenzie was the first international law firm that established an office in Latin America (in Caracas). Now, this law firm has offices in Argentina, Brazil, Chile, Colombia, Mexico, and Peru. Many other international law firms have followed. At the same time some Latin American law firms have become international: Philippi, Prietocarrizosa, Ferrero, DU and Uría, for instance, has a presence in Chile, Colombia, Peru, and Spain.[34] Several Central American law firms have been established, some of them comprising more than one hundred lawyers each.[35]

Most lawyers in law firms, including multinational law firms, are local. They have been trained in the jurisdiction where the law firm, or branch of the law

33 Kathryn Sikkink, 'The Transnational Dimension of the Judicialization of Politics in Latin America' in *The Judicialization of Politics in Latin America*, eds Rachel Sieder, Line Schjolden, and Alan Angell (London: Palgrave Macmillan, 2005); Stephen Meili, 'Latin American Cause Lawyering Networks' in *Cause Lawyering and the State in a Global Era*, eds Austin Sarat and Stuart A. Scheingold (New York: Oxford University Press, 2001); Manuel A. Gómez, 'Political Activism and the Practice of Law in Venezuela' in *Cultures of Legality: Judicialization and Political Activism in Latin America*, eds Javier Couso, Alexandra Huneeus, and Rachel Sieder (Cambridge: Cambridge University Press, 2010).

34 Manuel A. Gómez and Rogelio Pérez-Perdomo, 'Corporate Lawyers and Multinational Corporations in Latin America and Spain 1990–2015' in *Big law in Latin America and Spain*, eds Manuel Gómez and Rogelio Pérez-Perdomo (London: Palgrave Macmillan, 2018).

35 Carlos Taboada and Manuel Gómez, 'Big Law in Central America, Panama and the Dominican Republic: Growth Strategies in Small Economies' in *Big Law in Latin America and Spain*, eds Manuel A. Gómez and Rogelio Pérez-Perdomo (New York: Springer International Publishing, 2018).

firm, is located. However, increasingly these lawyers are cosmopolitan: they speak at least one foreign language (generally English), and they are familiar with foreign legal cultures or specific aspects of a foreign law. To the degree that businesses become international, or that businesspeople seek advice in matters of investments or taxes, law-firm expertise in some aspects of foreign law and frequently foreign practice becomes relevant. Another form of globalization is represented by the expatriate lawyer practicing in a jurisdiction other than the country of original training. In the past, this has occurred as part of colonization: lawyers from England and other colonial powers went to colonies or former colonies or to jurisdictions where the legal profession was not developed enough to respond to the legal needs of new investors and business.[36] Legal scholars moved between European countries or to the United States, Australia, and Latin America as a consequence of European political troubles and war.[37]

Particularly, a number of law professors from Spain and other European countries sought refuge in Latin America in the 1930s and 1940s. There were also lawyers in search for new business opportunities. This was the case with Venezuela in times of great prosperity, when lawyers from United States, Spain, Italy, and other Latin American countries established a presence there.[38] In the twentieth century these practices expanded. Lawyers became more cosmopolitan. If they have been educated in a law school that emphasizes comparative law, or they have done master's degrees in a foreign country, or they have joined international law firms or law firms with strong international ties, emigration for these lawyers is an alternative in case of difficulties or when the opportunities for work are better in another country. Venezuelan lawyers are a case in point. More than 10 percent of the Venezuelan population has emigrated in the last few years, and among this group there are probably thousands of lawyers.[39] Of one cohort of about 450 graduates from one private

36 Richard Abel, 'The Underdevelopment of Legal Professions: A Review Article on Third World Lawyers' (1982) 7 American Bar Foundation Research Journal, 871; Arm Tungnirum, *Practicing on the Moon: Globalization and Practice of Foreign Corporate Lawyers in Myanmar* (2018) SJD dissertation, Stanford Law School.

37 *Jurists Uprooted: German-Speaking Émigré Lawyers in Twenty-Century Britain*, eds Jack Beatson and R. Zimmerman (Oxford: Oxford University Press 2004).

38 Rogelio Pérez-Perdomo, 'Abogados golondrinas o la internacionalización de la profesión jurídica: el caso de Venezuela' (2020) 1 Revista Latinoamericana de Sociología Jurídica 134–155.

39 Manuel Gómez, Gilberto Guerrero, and Rogelio Pérez-Perdomo, work in progress.

Venezuelan university, more than half work outside the country and most of them have obtained law-related jobs.[40]

The internationalization of the legal profession and the mobility of lawyers indicate that law is now less territorial and national than it was in the past. This tells us something about how to think about legal education and the profession in our time.

4 Conclusion

In 1800, there were lawyers in each Latin American country, as there are lawyers today. In both periods, lawyers were educated at the universities. The law professors had control of entrance to the legal profession. But are they the same class of beings? Lawyers in 1800 were all men; now the majority are women. Lawyers in 1800 had a very high social status; now we speak of a stratified profession. Lawyers in 1800 were about a thousand in all Latin America; today they are more than a million. Their knowledge and training were different, and what they did before and now is different too. Universities and law schools have also changed widely. A description like the one done by Merryman in 1975 for the law schools of the civil law tradition no longer describes the law schools of Latin America.[41] Even the purposes and methodologies of law teaching have changed. Heraclitus was right: it is never the same water, but the question is if the river itself has changed to the point we cannot recognize it anymore.

The test we propose is whether the people who were called lawyers in 1800 and today would recognize themselves as members of the same class or the same craft. If they spoke, would they understand each other? They would speak in Spanish or Portuguese, and many legal terms would be recognizable. Our colleague of 1800 would perhaps use more terms and expressions in Latin, but the basic language would be the same. The distant colleagues probably would refer more to justice and natural law, while the present lawyers would talk preferably about the rule of law (*estado de derecho*) and human rights. Still, after some necessary explications, probably they would recognize they are talking about the same ideas, and they would share similar values. This basic identity has made possible this chapter on the history of legal education

40 Victoria Capriles and Rogelio Pérez-Perdomo, 'Los abogados graduados en la Universidad Metropolitana 2006–2016. Estudio de una cohorte profesional en tiempos de revolución' (2019) 6(1) Revista Pedagogía Universitaria y Didáctica del Derecho 23–42.

41 John H. Merryman, 'Legal Education There and Here: A Comparison' (1975) 27 Stanford Law Review 859.

and lawyers of Latin America. We have focused on changes, many of them substantial, but certainly an identity of sorts continues to exist.

References

Abel, Richard. 'The Underdevelopment of Legal Professions: A Review Article on Third World Lawyers.' *American Bar Foundation Research Journal* 7 (1982): 871.

Annino, Antonio, and François-Xavier Guerra. *Inventando la nación: Iberoamérica. Siglo XIX*. México: Fondo de Cultura Económica, 2003.

Araujo, Marcelo L.C., Gustavo F. Santos, and João P.A. Teixeira. 'La enseñanza del derecho en Brasil como actividad política: impactos en la configuración del derecho y en la práctica de los juristas.' In *La educación legal como política pública en América Latina*, edited by Gorki González Mantilla, Lima: Palestra, 2018.

Arenal Fenochio, Jaime del. 'Los abogados en México y una polémica centenaria, 1784–1847.' In *Revista de Investigaciones Jurídicas*. México: Escuela Libre de Derecho, 1980.

Bastos, Aurelio W. *Criação dos cursos jurídicos no Brasil*. Brasília, Câmara dos Deputado. Rio de Janeiro: Fundação Rui Barbosa, 1977.

Bastos, Aurelio W. *Os cursos jurídicos e as elites políticas brasileiras*. Brasília: Câmara dos Deputados, 1978.

Beatson, Jack, and Reinhard Zimmerman. *Jurists Uprooted: German-Speaking Émigré Lawyers in Twentieth-Century Britain*. Oxford: Oxford University Press, 2004.

Beck Varela, Laura. *Literatura jurídica y censura: Fortuna de Vinnius en España*. Valencia: Tirant lo Blanch, 2013.

Burkholder, Mark, and Dewitt S. Chandler. *From Impotence to Authority: The Spanish Crown and the American Audiencias 1687–1808*. Columbia: University of Missouri Press, 1980.

Capriles, Victoria, and Rogelio Pérez-Perdomo. 'Los abogados graduados en la Universidad Metropolitana de Caracas 2006–2016. Estudio de una cohorte profesional en tiempos de revolución.' Submitted to *Pedagogía Universitaria y Didáctica del Derecho*, 2019.

Cruz Barney, Óscar, Hector Fix-Fierro, and Elisa Speckman Guerra, eds. *Los abogados y la formación del estado mexicano*. México: UNAM, 2013.

Dantas, Francisco Clementino de San Tiago. 'A educação jurídica e a crise brasileira.' *Revista Forense* 159 (1955): 449–459.

Falcão, Joachim. 'Os cursos jurídicos e a formação do estado nacional.' In *Criação dos cursos jurídicos no Brasil*, edited by Aurelio W. Bastos. Brasília: Câmara dos Deputado. Rio de Janeiro: Fundação Rui Barbosa, 1978.

Falcão, Joachim. 'Lawyers in Brazil: Ideas and Praxis.' *International Journal of the Sociology of Law* 7 (1979).

Gaitán Bohórquez, Julio. *Huestes de estado, la formación universitaria de los juristas al comienzo del estado colombiano*. Bogotá: Centro Editorial Universidad del Rosario, 2002.

Gómez, Manuel A. 'Political Activism and the Practice of Law in Venezuela.' In *Cultures of Legality: Judicialization and Political Activism in Latin America*, edited by Javier Couso, Alexandra Huneeus, and Rachel Sieder, Cambridge: Cambridge University Press, 2010.

Gómez, Manuel A., and Rogelio Pérez-Perdomo. 'Corporate Lawyers and Multinational Corporations in Latin America and Spain 1990–2015.' In *Big Law in Latin America and Spain*, edited by Manuel Gómez and Rogelio Pérez-Perdomo. London: Palgrave Macmillan, 2018.

Gómez, Manuel A., and R. Pérez-Perdomo. 'A Dispatch from the Abyss: Venezuelan Lawyers (1988–2018).' In *Lawyers in the Twenty-First Century*, edited by Richard Abel, Ole Hammerslev, Ulrike Schultz, and Hilary Sommerlad. Oxford: Hart Publishing, 2020.

González Mantilla, Gorki. *Reforma de la educación jurídica o los molinos de viento*. Lima: Palestra and Pontificia Universidad Católica del Perú, 2008.

Icaza Dufour, Francisco de. *La abogacía en el Reino de la Nueva España*. México: Porrúa, 1998.

Jaksic, Iván, and Eduardo Posada Carbó, eds. *Liberalismo y poder. Latinoamérica en el siglo XIX*. México: Fondo de Cultura Económica, 2011.

Junqueira, Eliane B. 'Brazil: The Road of Conflict Bound to Total Justice.' In *Legal Culture in the Age of Globalization: Latin America and Latin Europe*, edited by Lawrence Friedman and Rogelio Pérez-Perdomo. Stanford: Stanford University Press, 2003.

Junqueira, Eliane B. *Faculdades de direito ou fábricas de ilusões?* Rio de Janeiro: IDES and Letra Capital, 1999.

Kicza, John. 'The Legal Community of Late Colonial Mexico: Social Composition and Career Patterns.' In *Five Centuries of Law and Politics in Central Mexico*, edited by Ronald Spores and Ross Hassing. Nashville: Vanderbilt University, 1984.

Lynch, Dennis O. *Legal Roles in Colombia*. Uppsala: Scandinavian Institute of African Studies, 1980.

Maravall, José Antonio. *Poder, honor y elites en el siglo XVII*. Madrid: Siglo XXI, 1977.

Mayagoitia, Alejandro. 'Las últimas generaciones de abogados virreinales. Un ensayo.' In *Los abogados y la formación del estado mexicano*, edited by Óscar Cruz Barney, Héctor Fix-Fierro, Elisa Speckman Guerra. México: UNAM, 2013.

Martínez de Moretin Llamas, Maria Lourdes. 'La contribución de la Escuela de Salamanca al desarrollo de la ciencia jurídica.' *Glossae: European Journal of Legal History* 14 (2017): 399.

Mckennan, Theodora. 'Jeremy Bentham and the Colombian liberators.' *The Americas* 34 (1978).

Meili, Stephen. 'Latin American Cause Lawyering Networks.' In *Cause Lawyering and the State in a Global Era*, edited by Austin Sarat and Stuart Scheingold. New York: Oxford University Press, 2001.

Merryman, John H. 'Legal Education There and Here. A Comparison.' *Stanford Law Review* 27 (1975): 859.

Merryman, John H., and Rogelio Pérez-Perdomo. *The Civil Law Tradition*. 4th ed. Stanford: Stanford University Press, 2019.

Muñoz Machado, Santiago, ed. *Historia de la abogacía española*, 2 vols. Madrid: Aranzadi, 2015.

Novoa Monreal, Eduardo. *El derecho como obstáculo al cambio social*. México: Siglo Veintiuno, 1975.

Pérez Collados, José M., and Samuel Rodríguez Barbosa, eds. *Juristas de la independencia*. Madrid: Marcial Pons, 2012.

Pérez-Perdomo, Rogelio. *Los abogados en Venezuela: Una elite intelectual y política 1780–1980*. Caracas: Monte Ávila, 1981.

Pérez-Perdomo, Rogelio. *Latin American Lawyers: A Historical Introduction*. Stanford: Stanford University Press, 2006.

Pérez-Perdomo, Rogelio. *Los juristas académicos de Venezuela: Historia institucional y biografía colectiva*. Caracas: Universidad Metropolitana, 2014.

Pérez-Perdomo, Rogelio. 'La reforma de la educación jurídica ¿tarea para Sísifo?' In *Revista de Pedagogía Universitaria y Didáctica del Derecho* 1(3) (2016).

Pérez-Perdomo, Rogelio. 'Roscio y el Colegio de Abogados de Caracas. Un caso para entender el cambio de mentalidad en el temprano siglo XIX.' In *Revista Mexicana de Historia del Derecho*. Mexico: Unam, 2019.

Pérez-Perdomo, Rogelio. 'Juan Germán Roscio. Equality and Freedom in Early Nineteenth Century Venezuela.' In *Law and Christianity in Latin America: The Work of Great Jurists*, edited by M.C. Mirow and Rafael Domingo. London: Routledge, 2021.

Peset Reig, Mariano, and José Luis Peset. *La universidad española (siglos XVIII y XIX): despotismo ilustrado y revolución liberal*. Madrid: Taurus, 1974.

Peset Reig, Mariano. 'Derecho romano y derecho real en las universidades del siglo XVIII.' *Anuario de Historia del Derecho Español* 45 (1975): 273.

Sikkink, Kathryn. 'The Transnational Dimension of the Judicialization of Politics in Latin America.' In *The Judicialization of Politics in Latin America*, edited by Rachel Sieder, Line Schjolden, and Alan Angell. London: Palgrave Macmillan, 2005.

Silva, Renán. *Universidad y sociedad en el Nuevo Reino de Granada*. Bogotá: Banco de la República, 1992.

Tungnirum, Arm. *Practicing on the Moon: Globalization and Practice of Foreign Corporate Lawyers in Myanmar*. SJD dissertation. Stanford: Stanford Law School, 2018.

Ugalde, Luis. *El pensamiento teológico-político de Juan Germán Roscio*. Caracas: Bid and Co., 2007.

Uribe-Uran, Víctor M. *Honorable Lives: Lawyers, Family, and Politics in Colombia 1780–1850*. Pittsburgh: University of Pittsburgh Press, 2000.

Zolezzi Ibárcena, Lorenzo. *La enseñanza del derecho*. Lima: Pontificia Universidad Católica del Perú, 2017.

CHAPTER 8

The Panorama of Indigenous Legal History

Brian P. Owensby

This chapter is divided into three sections. I begin with an extended account of historical processes and their rough periodization. My goal is to show that law, legality, and justice, far from the 'ordered irrelevancy' they were long thought to be in Latin American history, have shaped and been shaped by the lives and possibilities of Indigenous people from the earliest moment of their encounter with Europeans.[1] Section two discusses broad methodological and historiographical issues that have conditioned scholarly approaches. A third section considers recent directions in the global Indigenous movement, a transnational development to which law and legal process have been central and to which collaborative scholarship has contributed importantly. Given the diversity of the 'Indigenous experience' in Latin America, I have emphasized the shared contextual, institutional, and experiential background relative to the experiences of broad groups of Indigenous people.

1 Historical Processes

On the eve of European arrival to the fourth continent, what many contemporary Indigenous communities refer to as Abya Yala, ideas regarding social norms and their adherence varied dramatically among Native peoples. In the Caribbean, as many as two million Arawak-speaking Taínos, who had migrated from the Orinoco region of South America to the Antilles beginning around 200 CE, lived on the islands that came to be known as Hispaniola, Cuba, and Jamaica. These kinship societies were organized into competing chieftainships that traded with and fought one another. Thousands of miles south, Tupí-Guaraní migrants from the Amazon basin had settled around the Paraná River ca. 1300–1400 CE. Agriculturalists as well as hunter-gatherers, they were organized into kinship groups ranging from a few hundred to a few thousand, led by chiefs whose authority or prestige, in the case of the Tupí, was rooted

1 William Taylor, 'Between Global Processes and Local Knowledge: An Inquiry into Early Latin American Social History, 1500–1800' in *Reliving the Past: The Worlds of Social History*, eds William Taylor and Olivier Zunz (Chapel Hill: University of North Carolina Press, 1979), 162.

 | DOI:10.1163/9789004436091_010

in martial prowess, and in the case of the Guaraní, in reciprocal generosity and oratorical quality. While evidence of law-giving and law-keeping is limited for such groups, it appears that chiefs helped maintain norms by embodying broadly accepted virtues and modeling proper conduct. Ordinary folk were expected to correct behavior that deviated from accepted mores. Persistent failure to do so might result in punishment by physical coercion, or exile from the community, either outcome likely representing a rough community consensus.[2] Among such people, legality as a distinct sphere of social experience may have been something of a novelty when it was introduced by Spaniards. Nevertheless, they understood that the violation of social norms could threaten collective life and they agreed that breaches might imply retributive or restorative actions.

In Mesoamerica and the Andes, where extensive agriculture met the needs of large populations (perhaps 20 million in what is now central Mexico and Yucatan; 10–12 million for Andean Tawantinsuyu),[3] social hierarchies rested on norms and customs that governed relations between individuals and enveloping political systems. Among the Nahua of Mesoamerica, customary law offered robust precepts regarding morals, family life, manners, various kinds of property, collective as well as individual, commercial exchange, and relations between individuals and governing structures. Elected neighborhood judges heard minor disputes. Guild-like groups of merchants and craftsmen exercised jurisdiction over their members. Judges meeting in *tecalli* (community courts) dealt with ordinary civil and criminal matters in the first instance. According to post-conquest reports, these judges were 'very skilled at arguing' and were known for their probity, making no distinction between 'important or common, rich or poor.'[4] Their rulings could be appealed to panels of higher judges (*tlacxitlan*), especially when nobles were involved. Above them, the *tlatoani* (*speaker* in Nahuatl, ruler of his *altepetl* or city state), sat in judgment every twelve days to decide sensitive or important matters. Inca legal process was similar, less formalized than among the Nahua perhaps, though no less rigorous in moral and behavioral demands or in prizing good order among citizens.

2 E. Adamson Hoebel, *The Law of Primitive Man: A Study in Comparative Legal Dynamics* (Cambridge: Harvard University Press, 1954), 18–28.

3 Alexander Koch, Chris Brierley, Mark M. Maslin, and Simon L. Lewis, 'Earth System Impacts of the European Arrival and the Great Dying in the Americas after 1492' (2019) 207 Quaternary Science Review 15–16.

4 Jerome Offner, *Law and Politics in Aztec Texcoco* (Cambridge: Cambridge University Press, 1983), 223–224; Jerome Offner, Chapter 1 of this volume; Alonso de Pomar y Zurita, *Relación de Texcoco: Breve relación de los señores de la Nueva España; Varias relaciones antiguas* (México: Imprenta de Francisco Díaz de León, 1891); Ramírez, Chapter 2 of this volume.

Local officials judged civil and criminal cases according to established customs and expectations. Their decisions could be referred up a bureaucratic chain culminating in the royal court, where the Inca emperor might or might not hear a plea. In matters touching on larger imperial concerns, inspectors answering directly to the Inca could act independently of local administrator-judges.[5] In sum, in Nahua Mesoamerica and the Inca Andes, it is clear that Indigenous people were broadly familiar with the idea of a legal regime and attendant processes of giving evidence, making arguments, and hearing judgments, long before Europeans arrived.

As was true of Indigenous social life generally, the early sixteenth-century Great Encounter with Europeans threw established legal norms and practices into disarray. Scaffolded legal-administrative systems, such as those of the Nahua and the Inca, disarticulated. Less formal norm-based regimes faced unprecedented pressures. European invaders relied on Native nobles to administer Indigenous populations, subject to Spanish administrators and judges. This relationship introduced novel ideas and incentives that upended established concepts of governance, authority, hierarchy, labor, property, tribute, and collective life. The resulting tensions led Nahua and Inca nobles, *caciques* and *kuracas*, to take up Spanish law against Spaniards and against each other. By the 1530s, barely a decade after the fall of Tenochtitlan in central Mexico, Indigenous claimants pursued lawsuits before Spanish *corregidores*, or took grievances directly to the *audiencia* (court) in Mexico City. By mid-century, in the words of a contemporary Spanish observer, *caciques* had become 'avid litigators' over labor, tribute, and land. Indigenous nobles noted that 'the Indians had given themselves over to lawsuits because [Spaniards] had forced them to.' In New Spain, it was said, such claims were paid for by the 'sweat of Indian commoners, whose belongings are sold in order to litigate.' A similar pattern appears to have held in the Andes. Native nobles began to bring suit in newly instituted courts less than a decade after Atahualpa's execution at Cajamarca. By the mid-1540s, they had sparked an 'explosion of litigation,' hiring advocates to represent their interests in Lima.[6] There, as in New Spain, it was chiefly

5 See Susan Kellogg, *Law and the Transformation of Aztec Culture, 1500–1700* (Norman: Oklahoma University Press, 1995), XXVII–XXVIII; Terence N. D'Altroy, *The Incas* (New York: Wiley Blackwell, 2014), 235–236.

6 Brian P. Owensby, *Empire of Law and Indian Justice in Colonial Mexico* (Stanford: Stanford University Press, 2008), 43; José Carlos de la Puente Luna, 'That Which Belongs to All: Khipus, Community, and Indigenous Legal Activism in the Early Colonial Andes' (2015) 72(1) The Americas 19–21 [19–54].

kuracas (local chiefs and nobles), who brought these suits, sometimes to benefit their communities, other times to pursue private interests.

Meanwhile, the legal fate of Indigenous people writ large remained uncertain. Father Montesinos's cry from Hispaniola in 1511 regarding justice for the *indios* (Indians) was only an opening statement to the decades-long debate over the humanity and political status of the New World's Native peoples within the Spanish empire. Francisco de Vitoria argued in the 1530s that Indigenous territory belonged to the natives of these lands and concluded that the Spanish monarch could not deprive the 'indios' of their 'dominion' over it.[7] Simultaneously, a growing clamor from missionaries in the New World prompted royal edicts condemning the mistreatment of Indigenous laborers and Indians generally. In 1542, the crown passed the New Laws, holding that *indios* were free by nature, like any other human being, and not subject to enslavement. By conferring the legal personality of *indio*, the law enabled Indigenous people to litigate, but at the cost of blurring manifold local identities. The New Laws were not well received among Spaniards. In Lima, angry *encomenderos* killed the viceroy who tried to implement them. Perhaps prudently, the viceroy in Mexico City chose not to enforce the edict.

Contention over the legal status of Indigenous people culminated in the famed debate of 1550–1551 between Father Bartolomé de las Casas, ex-*encomendero* and Dominican 'defender of the Indians,' and Juan Ginés de Sepúlveda, court theologian. Extending Vitoria's arguments and pointing to the depravities of Spaniards in their treatment of the New World's inhabitants, Las Casas argued that the king should declare once and for all that the 'Indians' were his vassals, entitled to the same liberties as his other subjects. Sepúlveda, drawing on Aristotelian notions of 'natural slavery,' argued that Native people lacked the rational capacity to govern themselves, and so should be ruled by Spaniards for their own good. (While this argument did not demand the Indians' physical servitude, it almost certainly would have made it easier to enslave them outright.) King Carlos I (Holy Roman Emperor Carlos V) did not decide this dispute on the merits, though by the 1560s a steady stream of royal pronouncements favoring the 'liberty' of 'los indios' (the Indians) and ordering their 'good treatment' as vassals made clear that Las Casas's position had been substantially adopted as the legal baseline for the treatment of Native peoples

7 Francisco de Vitoria, 'On the American Indians (*De Indis*)' in *Political Writings*, eds Anthony Pagden and Jeremy Lawrance (Cambridge: Cambridge University Press, 1991), 231–292.

in the Spanish empire.[8] There were political and theological reasons for this, but the 'Great Dying' of Indigenous people in the New World – Amerindian population collapsed by as much as 90 percent between 1520 and 1620 – may have been the king's chief motivation; without 'Indians' there would be few vassals and no workers left in the New World.[9] The destruction of the Taíno in Hispaniola by the 1550s, through war, enslavement, overwork, and disease, had become an object lesson for Spanish officials.[10]

During the balance of the sixteenth century, Indigenous claimants leveraged this recognition by bringing suits over labor, land, tribute, title, and privileges. Nobles, *caciques*, and *kuracas* frequently initiated lawsuits to redress wrongs – land seizures, denials of liberty, miserable work relations – or to defend their communities. They might also litigate in order to tighten control over local labor, sell land to Spaniards, or pursue titles or status. One of the ironies of these decades is that the Native nobility, initially tapped by the crown to govern at the local level, gradually lost prerogative as war, forced labor, and epidemic disease shattered preexisting social and political structures. So, while Spanish law recognized Indigenous nobles as having greater privilege, authority, and status than Indigenous commoners, universal Indian vassalage and bureaucratic realities exerted a subtle leveling effect enabling *macehuales* (Indian commoners) to pursue individual or collective agendas that could be at odds with those of local power holders, whether Indigenous *caciques* or European grandees.

Would-be litigants were aided by the doctrine of *miserables* (the wretched). Medieval Spanish law had recognized that the 'humble' were entitled to be protected against 'arrogant' superiors, because it was a ruler's duty to defend his most vulnerable subjects, who were the object of his 'love.' Originally this idea had embraced people without a protector – orphans, widows, or, broadly, all who 'suffer wrong or violence from others more powerful than they.'[11] The doctrine also had roots in Roman law, where the poor were to be afforded legal assistance in civil disputes. In the context of the New World, '*personas*

8 Lewis Hanke, *All Mankind Is One: A Study of the Disputation between Bartolomé de Las Casas and Juan Ginés de Sepúlveda in 1550 on the Intellectual and Religious Capacity of the American Indian* (Carbondale: Northern Illinois University Press, 1994).

9 Koch, Brierley, Maslin, and Lewis 'Earth System Impacts,' 20–22.

10 Charles C. Mann, *1493: Uncovering the New World Columbus Created* (New York: Knopf, 2011), 11–12.

11 *Las Siete Partidas*, ed. Robert Burns (University of Pennsylvania Press, 2001), vol. 3, 710 (3.18.41); António Manuel Hespanha, 'Las Categorías de lo Político y de lo Jurídico en la Época Moderna' (1994) 3–4 Ius Fugit Revista Interdisciplinar de Estudios Histórico-Jurídicos 66–67.

miserables' broadened to comprise all 'Indians,' but especially those most rawly exposed to abuse. 'Defenders' or 'Protectors' of the Indians, advocates charged with enforcing the king's law, gave Indigenous claimants an acknowledged, albeit unreliable, ally in seeking justice.[12] The privilege of 'wretchedness' – that is, recognition of vulnerability to the powerful – did not take shape all at once. But by the end of the sixteenth century, King Felipe II had ordered that his Indian vassals 'be more protected as people who are more miserable and of less defense' than his Spanish vassals in the New World.[13] This doctrinal expansion of *miserables* coincided with a growing realization within Spanish officialdom that law and legal process, despite the energy and expense Indigenous petitioners were putting into them, was not curbing the overreach of local Spaniards. As one Indigenous observer complained late in the century, Native peoples had become so litigious 'because you do not understand us, nor do we understand you or know what you want. You have taken away our good order and form of government. And the one you have put in its place we do not understand, and so all is confused, without order, or concert.' The Indians 'never reach what they want,' he continued, 'because you [Spaniards] are the law and the judges and the parties, and you cut into us wherever you want, and whenever and however you like.'[14]

Fearing the utter failure of law if Indigenous vassals were unable to reach the king's justice, the monarchy approved reforms late in the sixteenth century to ensure Indigenous access to legal process. In 1590–1591, the viceroy in Mexico City established the *Juzgado General de Indios* (General Court of the Indians) as a tribunal of first instance for Indian claimants, regardless of geographic location or status. The idea underlying the Juzgado was that society could be rigorously cleaved into a Republic of Spaniards and a parallel Republic of Indians, separate jurisdictions converging at the king's throne. In this understanding, Spanish settlers and Indians were entitled and obliged to *what properly pertained to them according to their station*, a principle that could be sustained only if legal process was available to all, so that imbalances might be corrected. As soon as it began to operate, the Juzgado gave rise to a wave of claims by Indigenous petitioners. These litigants were motivated, in part, by the availability of the writ of *amparo* (protection), a non-adversarial legal

12 Caroline Cunhill, *Los defensores de indios de Yucatán y el acceso de los Mayas a la justicia colonial, 1540–1600* (México: UNAM, 2012); Mauricio Novoa, *The Protectors of the Indians in the Royal Audience of Lima: History and Legal Culture, 1575–1775* (Boston: Brill, 2016).

13 *Colección de documentos para la historia de la formación social de Hispanoamérica, 1493–1810*, ed. Richard Konetske, vol. 1 (Madrid: CSIC, 1953), 528.

14 Pomar y Zurita, *Relación de Texcoco*, 110.

remedy that froze a situation on the ground until a court could hear a matter on the merits, thereby creating a rebuttable presumption in favor of a given status quo. Since Indigenous petitioners generally sought to stop 'powerful hands' from appropriating land, enclosing people, or adjusting tribute levels, the *amparo* proved useful against Spaniards and Indian elites. Of course, an *amparo* could not block a persistent opponent, only force him to court. But that alone enabled thousands who would otherwise not have been heard to express their grievances before a judge.

In Peru, the effects of legal change were mixed. Earlier Toledan reforms (1570s) had sought to streamline tribute collection and secure a labor force for the silver mine at Potosí, the world's richest at the time. Elite Spaniards had relied on their wealth and power to appropriate land and labor, with profound consequences for Indigenous communities. These changes disrupted Andean social and political life, long anchored in the relative autonomy of distinct populational enclaves separated by rough terrain. These two facts may explain why a special Indian court was not established in Peru. Nevertheless, the same legal principles applied in Peru as in Mexico. As a judge in Lima noted in 1602, 'the poor and *personas miserables*, in litigation with a powerful person' were entitled to special consideration.[15] So while reforms in Peru appear not to have had the same effect as in Mexico, they did notably strengthen Indigenous petitioners' capacity to engage the legal system.

Recent scholarship indicates that from the late sixteenth century to the eighteenth, Indigenous men and women in Mexico and Peru, and elsewhere, incorporated legal process and notions of justice into their collective lives. Communities sued Spaniards to keep land, appealing to *time immemorial* in justifying their claims. They might start a dispute at the local level, knowing they could dispatch representatives to Mexico City and Lima to defend villages, reinforce customary rights, insist on the liberty of place, face down corruption, readjust tribute payments, limit labor demands, and insist on local autonomy. Communally and individually, legal activists articulated a quasi-political language in the context of a system that did not acknowledge politics as distinct from the pursuit of justice. Women learned to use legal process to insulate themselves somewhat from gendered violence, often by accusing men of crimes. Petitioners learned to navigate parallel jurisdictions, bringing their grievances before more than one judge at a time. In civil and criminal actions, litigants charged others with wrongdoing, Spaniards but also other Indians. Seeking 'justicia,' they learned to live with the fact that they might

15 Juan de Hevio Bolaños, *Curia philippica* (Valladolid: Lex Nova, 1989), vol. 1, 50, 57.

lose. Well-financed claimants might travel to lay their cases before the throne in Madrid, understanding that law was never a purely local affair, because the king's justice implicated the entire empire – an early 'cosmopolitan' legality.[16]

Through their actions Indigenous petitioners changed the context of their complaints, though it was rarely their intention to do so. By appealing to law, they acknowledged Spanish authority and accepted the rules structuring legal encounters. They demanded liberty by asserting their status as vassals, defended land but began to think in terms of property, affirmed community autonomy by paying tribute. The possibility of bringing suit opened new avenues for asserting community identities, but also reshuffled notions of hierarchy, aggravating tensions over the use of common resources, at times warping local particularities and maiming inclusion. In the process, Native actors became their own legal advocates looking to law, and the moral arguments and normative codes undergirding it, to advance claims. Adversaries of those who abused position, they could also be bedfellows of convenience with Spaniards who might help secure a benefit. Their relationship to legality was always mediated, by linguistic and cultural difference, by interests, by gradients of power and hierarchy, and by the act of writing itself. Through it all, they may have become

16 This paragraph and the next draw on the following sources: R. Jovita Baber, 'Law, Land, and Legal Rhetoric in Colonial New Spain: A Look at the Changing Rhetoric of Indigenous Americans in the Sixteenth Century' in *Native Claims: Indigenous Law against Empire, 1500–1920*, ed. S. Belmessous (Oxford: Oxford University Press, 2011); Woodrow Borah, *Justice by Insurance: The General Court of the Indians of Colonial Mexico and the Legal Aides of the Half-Real* (Berkeley: University of California Press, 1983); Nancy E. van Deusen, *Global Indios: The Indigenous Struggle for Justice in Sixteenth-Century Spain* (Durham: Duke University Press, 2015); Alcira Dueñas, *Indians and Mestizos in the 'Lettered City': Reshaping Justice, Social Hierarchy, and Political Culture in Colonial Peru* (Boulder: University of Colorado Press, 2010); Karen Graubert, 'Shifting Landscapes: Heterogeneous Conceptions of Land Use and Tenure in the Lima Valley' (2017) 26(1) Colonial Latin American Review 62–84; Tamar Herzog, *Upholding Justice: Society, State, and the Penal System in Quito (1650–1750)* (Ann Arbor: University of Michigan Press, 2004); Tamar Herzog, 'Colonial Law and "Native Custom": Indigenous Land Rights in Colonial Spanish America' (2013) 69(3) The Americas 303–321; José Carlos de la Puente Luna, *Andean Cosmopolitans: Seeking Justice and Reward at the Spanish Royal Court* (Austin: University of Texas Press, 2018); Owensby, *Empire*; Steve Stern, *The Secret History of Gender: Women, Men, and Power in Late Colonial Mexico* (Chapel Hill: University of North Carolina Press, 1995); Yanna Yannakakis, 'Witnesses, Spatial Practices, and a Land Dispute in Colonial Oaxaca' (2008) 65(2) The Americas 161–192; Yanna Yannakakis, 'Beyond Jurisdictions: Native Agency in the Making of Colonial Legal Cultures: A Review Essay' (2015) 57(4) Comparative Studies in Society and History 1070–1082; Yanna Yannakakis, 'Making Law Intelligible: Networks of Translation in Mid-Colonial Oaxaca' in *Indigenous Intellectuals: Knowledge, Power, and Colonial Culture in Mexico and the Andes*, eds Gabriela Ramos and Yanna Yannakakis (Durham: Duke University Press, 2014), 79–105.

the crown's most reliable allies in upholding the spirit of royal law regarding Indigenous people, coming to think of themselves as entitled to the king's justice. When they felt they were being shut out, they might rebel.

Law varied dramatically across the New World's vast geographical and cultural expanse. In northern New Spain, at the margins of empire, practice might be truncated and applied more loosely, though the same precepts applied as in Mexico City and Lima.[17] In these remote areas, law appears to have been an erratic resource, at best. Petitioners might enjoy some semblance of legal process, but with more limited success. In Paraguay, Indigenous social arrangements rooted in extended kinship and chieftainship, and the circuits of reciprocity and alliance crucial to maintaining them, were pulverized under the pressures of war, work, and disease during the sixteenth and early seventeenth centuries. Communities were reduced to the smallest scale consistent with bare survival. In such circumstances, and absent an effective royal bureaucracy at Asunción, litigation seems to have been an unreliable strategy for Indigenous groups, though this did not stop many from trying.[18]

In legal terms, Portuguese Brazil represented a realm unto itself. Law there appears to have had far less impact on Indigenous people than in Spanish America. The Portuguese king had proclaimed the liberty of the Indians in 1570, but nevertheless allowed them to continue to be taken in 'just wars.' And though the two kingdoms were unified between 1580 and 1640, and therefore bound by the same royal pronouncements, Brazil was always a case apart. Indigenous people lacked ready access to processes taken for granted in much of Spanish America by the early seventeenth century. Settlers and local power holders held sway, enabling them to flout royal commands. In fact, through the seventeenth century, settlers continued to enslave Indigenous people.[19] The Portuguese crown, less concerned to rein in local power than Madrid was, did not press the issue. This left Native people in Brazil, mostly widely scattered Amazonians, with few possibilities to act as their own legal advocates. Religious groups, especially the Jesuits, tried to fill this gap, establishing missions in an attempt to separate Indians from settlers, but in most places, this only involved a minority of Indigenous people, leaving the remainder to fend

17 Charles Cutter, *The Legal Culture of Northern New Spain, 1700–1810* (Albuquerque: University of New Mexico Press, 1995).

18 Brian Owensby, *New World of Gain: Europeans, Guaraní, and the Global Origins of Modern Economy* (Stanford University Press, 2021), Chapters 2, 3.

19 Yanna Yannakakis, *Go-Betweens and the Colonization of Brazil, 1500–1600* (Austin: University of Texas Press, 2005), 181–182, 191–192.

for themselves, without the leverage of law.[20] Future archival research may alter or clarify this still fuzzy picture.

The high-water mark of Spanish-American imperial legality came in 1681, with the publication of the *Recopilación de leyes de los reynos de las Indias*. A compendium of royal decrees, ordinances, and principles reflecting a century and half of legal experience in the New World, the *Recopilación* became the touchstone for legal culture and practice until the end of Spanish empire in the early nineteenth century. Book VI of this compilation specifically addressed laws regarding Indians.[21] Through long experience, Indigenous people, even commoners, learned to cite chapter and verse of the collection, as did two Oaxacan day laborers in 1799 who refused to pay a Spanish tithe collector. The *Recopilación* bore the stamp of Hapsburg theories of governance, stressing equilibrium and harmony among the various elements of a hierarchical society. The law's role was to assure each part of a shared social order its due, according to social position.[22] To this end, the king and his officers were charged with settling disputes and restoring the balance that would secure the common good and so ensure justice and social peace. In theory, this principle obliged all members of society, a responsibility in sharp tension with the pursuit of private interests at the expense of the king's most vulnerable vassals – a predicament Indigenous litigants mobilized to resist.

Dynastic change from Hapsburgs to Bourbons after the succession crisis of 1701–1714 gradually undermined Indians' legal status during the eighteenth century. Bourbon monarchs, who saw Spain as losing ground and prestige to France, Holland, and Britain, sought to shore up royal power, increase revenues, and regain political control from local power holders in America. Earlier willingness to allow Indigenous communities to govern themselves, so long as they promptly paid tribute, weakened as the crown sought to make Indians more 'useful' to commerce and the royal treasury.[23] Meanwhile, *criollos* (American-born Spaniards), intent on securing land and labor for themselves, pressed Indigenous people at every turn. Even Indian elites might seek to leverage hereditary rights for their own gain. Across Spanish-America,

20 Rainer Grote, 'The Status and Rights of Indigenous People in Latin America' 502–503. http://www.zaoerv.de © 1999, Max-Planck-Institut für ausländisches öffentliches Recht und Völkerrecht, accessed 8 April 2020.

21 *Recopilación de leyes de los reynos de las Indias* (Madrid: Ivlian Paredes, 1681).

22 Hespanha, 'Las Categorías de lo Político.'

23 Brian Owensby, 'Justice and Economics: "Indians" and Reformism in Eighteenth-Century Spanish Imperial Thought' in *Legal Pluralism and Empires, 1500–1800*, eds Lauren Benton and Richard Ross (New York University Press, 2013), 143–172.

Indigenous litigants responded to these challenges by filing lawsuits to defend land and affirm rights of autonomy. Trained in the heat of legal conflict during the seventeenth century, these litigants followed 'the outlines of prescribed procedure' with 'striking' uniformity.[24] Royal and local officials reacted by condemning the law as empowering litigants to undercut new royal priorities. Increasingly, Spanish officials saw Indigenous litigation as a 'political infirmity' that had made the Indians 'useless.'[25] Andean thinkers pushed back against such criticism in the mid-eighteenth century, proposing a parallel jurisdiction for Indians, an idea rooted in Andean and Hapsburg notions of balance, harmony, and the common good, now at odds with emergent Bourbon reasons of state and economic priorities.[26] Taken together, the spike in lawsuits in Mexico and the claims coming out of Peru suggest that Indigenous understandings of law now clashed with an imperial agenda focused on economic productivity and a reinvigorated royal authority.

By 1800, Indigenous people had entered a new phase of uncertainty regarding their relationship to law. The *Recopilación*, still a monument to imperial legality, now stood on unstable ground. Fresh theories of sovereignty and authority, as well as new economic concerns, were undermining claims to social justice that had anchored Indigenous legality since the sixteenth century. Custom, long an accepted basis for claims-making among Indigenous petitioners, began to lose legitimacy in legal disputes across Spanish realms.[27] For two and a half centuries, legal process had enabled Indigenous people, speaking from their own circumstances, to lead power to act on their behalf in many instances. Through their actions, they had breathed life into the letter and spirit of the law, often in stark contrast to well-off Spaniards who, as one royal official had noted in the mid-seventeenth century, were 'less attentive' to the king's commands.[28] Without Indigenous participation, it is unlikely that royal laws regarding the treatment of Indians would have retained much force. And yet, while recourse to law afforded them a measure of influence over the terms of conquest and somewhat insulated them from imperial overreach and

24 Bianca Premo, *The Enlightenment on Trial: Ordinary Litigants and Colonialism in the Spanish Empire* (Oxford: Oxford University Press, 2017), 63.

25 Hipólito Villaroel, *Enfermedades políticas que padece la capital de esta Nueva España* (México: CONACULTA, 1994), 94–95.

26 Dueñas, *Indians and Mestizos*, 182–183; Owensby, 'Between Justice and Economics,' 157–160.

27 Bianca Premo, 'Custom Today: Temporality, Customary Law, and Indigenous Enlightenment' (2014) 94(3) Hispanic American Historical Review 355–379.

28 Juan Solórzano y Pereira, *Política indiana* (Madrid: Biblioteca Castro, 1996), vol. 2, 1177.

more importantly the locally powerful, it also helped give permanence to their subjection.

Napoleon's occupation of the Iberian Peninsula in 1808 shattered Indigenous peoples' relationship to law. Under pressure from invading French troops, the *Cortes* (parliament) adopted Spain's first written constitution. The idea was to garner the support of the overseas territories against the French by rebalancing the relationship to allow for American representation. According to the 1812 Constitution of Cádiz, *indios* were to be recognized as citizens, bearers of civil and political rights through their membership in Indigenous municipalities. This limited franchise recognized that Indians' status as vassals in the old regime entitled them to citizenship in a new social and political pact.[29] The experiment was short lived. When Ferdinand VII resumed the throne in 1814, he revoked the Constitution. The crisis of legitimacy that followed led to independence movements across the American hemisphere.

'Revolutions' in America ushered to power a group of *criollo* elites and, with them, novel political arrangements that denied any specific role for Indians in a still-emerging regime. In the process, Latin America's legal landscape was reordered. The notion of separate republics for Indians and Spaniards, a legal reality long after it had ceased to be a social one, fell by the wayside. So too did the concept of *miserables*, which had explicitly recognized power differentials between Spaniards and Indians. The *Recopilación* and its acknowledgment of Indigenous custom, local autonomy, and collective identity was nullified.

For three hundred years, Indigenous claimants had sought to align themselves with royal law, as they understood it, to challenge mistreatment by local elites. The founding documents of new nations now insisted that Indians were equal citizens alongside these very elites, in principle no different from other (white, male European) citizens.[30] This Enlightenment notion, fundamentally opposed to differentially applied royal authority, clashed with Indigenous legal sensibilities that conceived of the king's power as a defense of those

29 See Bartolomé Clavero, *Freedom's Law and Indigenous Rights: From Europe's Oeconomy to the Constitutionalism of the Americas* (Berkeley: University of California Press, 2005); Mónica Quijada, 'La caja de Pandora. El sujeto político indígena en la construcción del orden liberal' (2006) 33 Historia Contemporánea 605–637; Brian Owensby, 'Comunidades indígenas y gobernanza en la época de la independencia—antecedentes virreinales, transformaciones decimonónicas' in *Declaraciones de independencia: Los textos fundamentales de las independencias americanas*, eds Alfredo Ávila, Erika Pani, and Jordana Dym (México: El Colegio de México, 2013), 81–108.

30 *Las declaraciones de independencia: Los textos fundamentales de las independencias americanas*, eds Alfredo Ávila, Jordana Dym, and Erika Pani (México: Colegio de México/UNAM, 2013).

who remained vulnerable to the depredations of propertied, well-connected, and often unchecked power holders. Indian communities worried that new, supposedly egalitarian arrangements would expose them to abuse without recourse. Thus, when national governments initially abolished tribute, many communities asked that it be re-imposed, fearing they would be unable to claim the reciprocal protection royal law had provided. When tribute was reintroduced on harsher terms and forced labor allowed to persist, Indigenous complainants had nowhere to turn other than to the very governments that had passed such measures. The state's undifferentiated jurisdiction over all its citizens could not compass a reality in which some citizens wielded lasting prerogative over others (a reprise of imperial hierarchies, without acknowledgment of power differences). In Brazil, which did not undergo a war of independence, Indigenous people who had been 'freed' (after more than two centuries) by the Law of Liberties in 1755 remained largely without legal protections throughout the nineteenth century. In other countries, notably Mexico, Native communities faced a decades-long effort by local and national elites to abolish communal landholding in favor of private property.

Indigenous people sought to adapt to this turbulent reality. Some refused to identify with emergent nation-states based on arbitrarily drawn borders that had not existed during the vice-regal period. Others acknowledged citizenship in new nations, so long as communal rights to land and to cultural autonomy were recognized.[31] Denied juridical personality *as Indians*, many Indigenous communities strained to combine liberal categories with a sense of justice developed during the legal struggles of the seventeenth century.[32] Would-be Indigenous claimants were in a bind. To the extent they engaged new legal regimes, they legitimized political and social understandings that had little place for them. If early national constitutions had, at least nominally, considered Indigenous people to be citizens, by the late nineteenth century 'Indians' had been consigned to an inferior status in the grand confrontation between 'civilization and barbarism.'[33] Scientific racism concluded that Indigenous people were incapable of progress, fit only for history's midden. By century's end, Native people had found no consistently effective means other than episodic rebellion to defend themselves, their lands, their communities,

31 See Peter Guardino, *The Time of Liberty: Popular Political Culture in Oaxaca, 1750–1850* (Durham: Duke University Press, 2005); Grote, 'The Status,' 503–505.

32 Jennie Purnell, 'With All Due Respect: Popular Resistance to the Privatization of Communal Lands in Nineteenth-Century Michoacán' (1999) 34(1) Latin American Research Review 8; Quijada, 'La caja de Pandora.'

33 Quijada, 'La caja de Pandora,' 635.

and their cultures. As one scholar has observed, 'Indigenous people were the big losers in the process of eradicating a jurisdiction-centered justice system with provisions for limited autonomy.'[34] In Mexico, the lack of other options led communities to join revolutionary struggles between 1910 and 1920, a fight that enshrined the *ejido* (communal landholding) in the Constitution of 1917. Through all of this, Indigenous groups never completely abandoned efforts to find their voice in relation to liberal notions of law which, if nothing else, allowed them to argue from a position of citizenship denied.

Yet law and litigation offered limited opportunities for Indigenous claims-making in the twentieth century. Just as the U.S. government was completing its enclosure, removal, and genocide of American Indians, national governments in Latin American countries with robust Indigenous cultures and large mestizo populations recognized the presence of Indigenous peoples, at least rhetorically and historically, while pushing a policy of integration that sought homogenization through *mestizaje* (racial and cultural mixing). In effect, Indigenous people could be full, equal citizens of the nation – as promised in early nineteenth-century declarations and constitutions – *if* they relinquished their identities and claims as Indigenous people, to become *campesinos* (peasants) or *mestizos* (mixed-race people). Such 'indigenist' projects took various forms across Latin America, spanning the gamut from tutelary status to malign neglect.[35] Broadly, Indigenous people found themselves in the conceptual gap between 'rational' citizens and ethnically distinct peoples. Lacking the legal tools to defend lands or communities, they remained vulnerable to appropriations, exploitation, and marginalization within modernizing economies.[36] Some, emboldened by the rhetoric of *indigenismo* (Indianism), found ways to fight for land and to assert identities.[37] Nevertheless, through the 1950s, the 'Indian question' remained unresolved across Latin America, relegating Indigenous people to precarity at the edges of national societies.

---

34 Thomas Duvé, 'Indigenous Rights in Latin America: A Legal Historical Perspective' (2017) 4 Max Planck Institute for European Legal History Research Paper 1–20.

35 Rebecca Earle, *The Return of the Native: Indians and Myth-Making in Spanish America, 1810–1930* (Durham: Duke University Press, 2007).

36 Grote, 'The Status,' 505–506.

37 Brett Troyan, 'Re-Imagining the "Indian" and the State: *Indigenismo* in Colombia, 1926–1947' (2008) 33(65) Canadian Journal of Latin American and Caribbean Studies/Revue Canadienne des études latino-américaines et caraïbes (Special issue on Human Security/Numéro special sur la sécurité humaine, 2008), 81–106; Laura Gotkowitz, *A Revolution for Our Rights: Indigenous Struggle for Land and Justice in Bolivia, 1880–1952* (Durham: Duke University Press, 2007).

Beginning in the 1940s, Indian groups began to experiment with novel alignments and confederations, at first within nations and later between them. Some forged alliances with other Indigenous groups and even poor mestizos. Others rejected the choice between being Indians and being citizens, choosing instead to find ways to live at the boundary between the two. In Bolivia, for instance, Indigenous communities adopted the language of citizenship to advance claims for communal land and collective identity in the face of a liberal property-rights regime. Much as they had done during the imperial period, they delegated representatives to appear in court as needed. They adopted flexible strategies, pursuing legal battles in the city, often with the support of unionized workers, while undertaking rural protests.[38] Similar movements emerged in other Andean and Mesoamerican countries, a development that set the stage for a wider reconsideration of Indigenous rights as human rights from the late twentieth century forward.

From the 1960s, Native groups began to expand legal and political spaces from which to speak. Actions by Indigenous people during the 1970s and 1980s led to reforms conceding the distinctness of Indigenous cultures across the region, in particular their spatial organization, rootedness in place, social formations, linguistic heritage, and ways of knowing and living.[39] By the 1990s, most Latin American countries had recognized, at least on paper, that Indigenous peoples were entitled to certain status, benefits, and rights. Backpedaling from earlier calls to 'incorporate' Indians as indistinguishable citizens of the nation, some countries began to accept the ethnic specificity of Indigenous peoples, recognize their right to live in ancestral lands, and explicitly acknowledge the pluricultural and multiethnic character of the nation – a novel and unsettling idea for republics premised on liberal notions of individual personhood.[40] At the same time, Indigenous groups relied on legal discourse to speak to broader conditions within and across national societies. As of roughly 2000, Native groups intensified efforts to coordinate beyond the borders of nation-states, while continuing to honor local laws and customs in everyday life.[41] In 2007, their decades-long efforts bore fruit with the passage of the UN Declaration on the Rights of Indigenous People, which affirmed 'the right of all peoples to be different, to consider themselves different, and to be respected as such.'

38 Gotkowitz, *A Revolution for Our Rights*.

39 Rodolfo Stavenhagen, 'Las organizaciones Indígenas: actores emergentes en América Latina' (1997) 62 Revista de la CEPAL 63.

40 Grote, 'The Status,' 508.

41 S. James Anaya, *International Human Rights and Indigenous Peoples* (New York: Aspen Publishers, 2009).

This does not mean that Indigenous groups have finally gained solid legal footing in the post-imperial world, though arguably they now have more to work with than at any time since 1830. By referring to notions of justice traceable to the seventeenth century alongside liberal precepts of legal equality denied in the nineteenth century, they have learned to advance claims amid epistemological uncertainty and unstable understandings of law. By reaching across borders and pursuing a strategy of 'hybridization' that blends custom with national and international norms, Indigenous groups have articulated a profound challenge to the foundations of the modern nation-state predicated on the uninflected individual citizen as the fundamental political unit of human community. At the same time, by asserting a *right to difference*, they have stretched the idea of human rights beyond a narrow liberal frame.[42]

In the face of such challenges, dominant political and legal arrangements have often failed to deter assaults on Indigenous lands, prevent or punish assassinations of Indigenous activists, or address the economic precarity of Indigenous communities. To this extent, and despite the transformations they have seen over five centuries of engagement with law, legality, and justice, Indigenous people in Latin America find themselves in a situation no less difficult for being so familiar.

2 Methodological and Historiographical Issues

In the early twentieth century, Argentine historian and jurist Ricardo Levene named a phenomenon that had been largely forgotten or ignored by scholars since the wars of independence – *derecho indiano*, or the Law of the Indies. In two works written in 1918 and 1924, Levene drew attention to the vast corpus of royal decrees, compilations, treatises, council deliberations, viceregal proclamations, and orders that had scaffolded imperial legality. The letter of the law did not suffice to describe legal reality, Levene insisted, for beneath it moved a living law animated by the encounter between unfamiliar circumstances, opposed interests, and imperfectly aligned ideas.[43] For Rafael Altamira this implied that law was not only an intellectual matter, but as well a 'form of knowledge available to all men … even the most unlettered.'[44] Despite

42 Duvé, 'Indigenous Rights,' 1.

43 Ricardo Levene, *Notas para el estudio del derecho indiano* (Buenos Aires: Coni, 1918), 6; Ricardo Levene, *Introducción a la historia del derecho indiano* (Buenos Aires: Valerio Abelardo, 1924).

44 Rafael Altamira, *Manual de investigación de la historia del derecho indiano* (México: Ed. Stylo, 1948), 51.

this methodological opening to ordinary folk, there was little sense that the insight might apply to Indigenous people. Through the first two-thirds of the twentieth century, scholars commonly read the Spanish monarchy's many orders regarding the 'good treatment of the Indians' as little more than a hypocritical counterpoint to the so-called *Black Legend* (the view that Spain had been uniquely brutal in its treatment of Indigenous people). A steady stream of royal edicts aiming to protect the Indians contrasted sharply with images of murderous conquistadors, described by Las Casas and other chroniclers, and etched in the popular European imagination by Dutch engraver Theodore De Bry. Subsequent scholarship through the 1960s made the obvious point that such sources could not be given the final word on Spain's Indian policy. Royal commands, oft-repeated and as often ignored, said the revisionists, had amounted to little more than an arid formalism in relation to the Indians. In consequence, law had been 'irrelevant' to Indigenous people, utterly 'alien, therefore without moral force,' completely 'divorced' from their daily lives.[45]

In the early 1980s, Woodrow Borah proposed a new approach to thinking about *derecho indiano* that brought Indigenous people into the frame of legal analysis. In one way, nothing could have been clearer: to understand law's role in the lives of those it affected, historians should look to the enormous body of case records in Latin America's legal-administrative archives. Focusing on New Spain, Borah examined the proceedings of the General Indian Court to argue that ordinary people, Indians, mestizos, and Spaniards alike, had availed themselves of legal process throughout the imperial period.[46] Though he laid out a roadmap for future research, it was another couple of decades before historians began to take his approach to heart.

Two reasons explain this delay. For those who saw the law chiefly as a 'mask for colonial power,' the point was to show how legality had served Spain's broader hegemonic agenda by locking Indigenous people into an institutional arrangement from which there was no escape.[47] From this perspective, there was little occasion to think about the inner workings of law or Indigenous people's relationship to it; attention should be on resistance to and rebellion against oppression. A second, deeper reason scholars did not sooner take up

45 Charles Gibson, *Spain in America* (New York: Harper & Row, 1966), 109; Stanley Stein and Barbara Stein, *The Colonial Heritage of Latin America: Essays on Economic Dependence in Perspective* (Oxford University Press, 1970), 81; Howard Wiarda, *The Soul of Latin America: The Cultural and Political Tradition* (New Haven: Yale University Press, 2001), 29.

46 Borah, *Justice by Insurance*.

47 *Crime and Punishment in Latin America*, eds Ricardo Salvatore, Carlos Aguirre, and Gilbert Joseph (Durham: Duke University Press, 2001), 7.

Borah's challenge may have been a methodological impasse. Whatever 'legal history' might have meant in the context of viceregal Latin America, it bore little resemblance to 'modern' conceptions of law rooted in constitutions and legal codes. Indeed, early national Latin American elites had pointedly turned their backs on centuries of law and experience. As a result, unlike Anglo-American legal history, which has always presumed historical continuity with colonial law and before that English law, Latin American 'legal history' has tended to operate on opposite sides of a historical and historiographical rupture, as though there were nothing 'modern' law might learn from its 'colonial' past. There was, therefore, no historiographical position from which to study imperial legality, much less its effects on Indigenous people.

An answer to this riddle came with the publication of Víctor Tau Anzoátegui's *Casuismo y sistema* in 1992. Although Tau was in close conversation with the Levene/Altamira strain of thought, his central point was that imperial law could only be understood on the basis of its own epistemological underpinnings.[48] Modern, 'rationalist' conceptions of law, he argued, could make no sense of the openness, flexibility, and constructive ambiguity of *derecho indiano* (the law of the Indies). That law, said Tau, had been rooted in a 'casuistic' approach that privileged the particularities of each specific 'case.'[49] This was no abstract proposition for Tau. He pointed out that writers and jurists of the late sixteenth and early seventeenth centuries recognized that the world was so multiple and diverse as to defy general propositions, especially in the New World, where the very presence of Indigenous people made it utterly unlike Spain itself.[50] On this view, the law could proceed only by attending closely to the facts of each case. According to Tau, this imperative gradually gave way to more 'systematic' legal thinking after the mid-seventeenth century, at least among jurists. Nevertheless, concluded Tau, the casuistic approach remained crucial to understanding the actions of Indigenous claimants, since it gave

48 Joaquín García-Huidobro and Diego Pérez Lasserre, 'De Altamira y Levene a Tau Anzoátegui (pasando por García-Gallo). Tres aproximaciones al derecho indiano' (2017) 39 Revista de Estudios Histórico-jurídicos 195–212.

49 Víctor Tau Anzoátegui, *Casuísmo y sistema: indagación histórica sobre el espíritu del derecho indiano* (Buenos Aires: IIHD, 1992).

50 Francisco Bermúdez de Pedraza, *Arte legal para estudiar la jurisprudencia* (Salamanca: Emprenta de Antonia Ramirez, 1612), 135; Sebastián de Covarrubias, *Tesoro de la lengua castellana o española* (Barcelona: Horta, 1943 [1611]), 316; Solórzano y Pereira, *Política Indiana*, 3:3092 (5.11.5).

space and legitimacy to Native usages and practices, which might vary dramatically from one place to another.[51]

'The case,' thus, opened up the world of Indigenous litigation to scholarly attention, just as Borah had envisioned. Indians did not write legal treatises, but they did bring lawsuits, frequently and in abundance. In the process, they became 'entangled' with the practices, procedures, and principles of legality at every level, and with the people who produced the thick sediment of paper that settled in the archive.[52] Voluminous records of litigation represent a distributed corpus for Indigenous ideas regarding land, autonomy, liberty, self-governance, crime, and justice, worked out in numberless quotidian legal dramas. Read carefully in light of the decrees, ordinances, and treatises of Spanish jurisprudence, these records show that Indian litigants spoke, and wrote, alongside many other actors – notaries, protectors, advocates, judges, administrators, *caciques*, figuratively, the king himself – revealing imperial law to have been a collective and highly contested project (as all law is) that could tolerate imprecise outcomes reached in the face of imperfect and contested 'legal intelligibility.'[53]

Through it all, Indigenous litigants navigated a legal terrain that lay unevenly over the 'diverse geographical and human realities' of the New World.[54] The cases uncovered by recent scholarship strongly suggest that Indigenous litigants emphasized the specificities of local contexts, customs, and norms in ways that flout 'modernist' assumptions regarding uniformity in the application of legal principles. Rather than a *common law* that looked to distill general rules from shared usages, recent research points to a *differential law* that adapted broad principles to localized situations in light of justice. Indigenous

---

51 Víctor Tau Anzoátegui, *El Poder de la costumbre. Estudios sobre el Derecho Consuetudinario en América hispana hasta la Emancipación* (Buenos Aires: IIHD, 2001), 134–143.

52 Graubert, 'Shifting Landscapes,' 63.

53 Dueñas, *Indians and Mestizos*; Rolena Adorno, *Guaman Poma: Writing and Resistance in Colonial Peru* (Austin: University of Texas Press, 1986); Kathryn Burns, *Into the Archive: Writing and Power in Colonial Peru* (Durham: Duke University Press, 2010); *Justice in a New World: Negotiating Legal Intelligibility in British, Iberian, and Indigenous America*, eds Brian P. Owensby and Richard J. Ross (New York: New York University Press, 2018); Yanna Yannakakis, 'Making Law Intelligible: Networks of Translation in Mid-Colonial Oaxaca' in *Indigenous Intellectuals: Knowledge, Power, and Colonial Culture in Mexico and the Andes*, eds Gabriela Ramos and Yanna Yannakakis (Duke University Press, 2014), 79–103.

54 Víctor Tau Anzoátegui, 'Provincial and Local Law of the Indies: A Research Program' in *New Horizons in Spanish Colonial Law: Contributions to Transnational Early Modern Legal History*, eds Thomas Duvé and Heikki Pihlajamäki (Frankfurt am Main: Max Planck Institute for European Legal History, 2015), 237.

claimants appealed to custom in defending autonomy and difference, an outcome Hapsburg authorities had been willing to abide so long as doing so did not threaten social balance and peace.

By the mid-eighteenth century, the casuistic fluidity of Hapsburg law that had animated this outlook among Indigenous people began to rigidify. Bourbon emphasis on command and sovereignty and the primacy of royal will over royal justice eroded local usages and norms. Indigenous litigants responded by doubling down on what they had come to know from two centuries of legal experience – that their rights lay as much in the assertion of custom as in written legislation, particularly if a law on the books had not stood the test of time and if its sense of justice could not be readily discerned. This is not to say they treated custom as a static concept impervious to change, or that they refused to engage emergent ideas of eighteenth-century European 'rationality.'[55] To the contrary, as historians have begun to show, they acted so as to avoid a false choice between a sterile 'formalism' that would take the letter of the law as the bedrock of legality and a 'realism' that would set hard limits to their capacity to act.[56]

Against this background, scholars have begun to grapple with the complexities of the transition from the colonial to the national period. While there is much yet to understand, research suggests that Indigenous litigants neither abandoned centuries of experience with *derecho indiano*, nor outright rejected legal systems rooted in liberal assumptions of private property, strictly individual legal personality, and aspirational notions of equality (often denied in fact). Despite losing the 'privileges' of imperial legality – a legally recognized ethnic identity *cum* 'legal personality,' acknowledgment of their vulnerability to powerful people, and a right to litigate collectively over land and community – Indigenous people have sought to adapt their actions to emergent circumstances.[57] For instance, during the independence period, Indigenous communities in southwest Colombia proclaimed themselves *royalists* and appealed to laws dating to the seventeenth century to protect their communities, rather than join with *criollo* insurgents seeking to break with the Spanish monarchy.[58] The challenge was then and remains now an epistemological

55 Herzog, 'Colonial Law'; Premo, 'Custom Today'; Premo, *The Enlightenment*.

56 Herzog, 'Colonial Law,' 320.

57 Clavero, *Freedom's Law*; Karen Caplan, 'The Legal Revolution in Town Politics: Oaxaca and Yucatán, 1812–1825' (2002) 83(2) Hispanic American Historical Review 255–293.

58 Marcela Echeverri, *Indian and Slave Royalists in the Age of Revolution: Reform, Revolution, and Royalism in the Northern Andes, 1780–1825* (Cambridge: Cambridge University Press, 2016).

one: How to mediate between distinct understandings of law – on one hand, the difference, diversity, heterogeneity, autonomy, and protection against local power holders that grounded Indigenous encounters with law from the sixteenth to the early nineteenth centuries and, on the other hand, the homogenizing, systematizing, rationalizing, individualizing, universalizing, and power-blind thrust of 'modern' legality? As often as not, liberal notions of law have been traps for Indigenous communities with respect to political representation, retention of land, and defense of autonomy. Against the underlying assumption of 'modern' rule of law, the problem for Indigenous people in Latin America through most of the imperial period was not monarchical overreach – royal absolutism – but the power of local grandees, on whom royal law had been a check. When imperial law ended during independence, law no longer shielded Indigenous litigants from the arbitrariness of local power as it once had. As one legal scholar has noted, Indigenous people have long known 'that common citizenship in the singular ... does not mean equal rights.'[59] While this is broadly acknowledged, its implications for contemporary Indigenous legality remain unclear. Nothing within 'modern' law tells Native claimants (or scholars) how to judge – or engage with – legal regimes that have treated Indigenous people as less-equal-than in the context of national life.

Anthropology has offered a vital perspective on the problem among contemporary Indigenous groups.[60] Under many national legal regimes, Indigenous people must assert the status of 'Indian/*indio*' (as they did during the imperial period), in order to affirm identity or claim rights vis-à-vis the state. Such claims generally have to be documented to be cognizable by courts that privilege written texts. While Indigenous litigants do ground their claims in documentary evidence, it is clear that they also appeal to collective *memory* – a kind of proxy for *custom* and an opening to reimagining. Memory is inherently malleable in ways that may contradict available documentation. This situation can produce sharp tensions between the very specific claims of particular groups and 'egalitarian' notions of individual citizenship.

Much of the debate in contemporary cases involving Indigenous litigants has to do with bridging these two positions. For historians wed to the written word, the divide represents a methodological riddle, for Indigenous claims can seem 'antihistorical' to the extent memory and documentation diverge.[61]

59 Clavero, *Freedom's Law*, 139.

60 See, e.g., *Indigenous Law and the State*, eds Bradford W. Morse and Gordon R. Woodman (Providence: Foris Publications, 1988).

61 Joanne Rappaport, *Cumbe Reborn: An Andean Ethnography of History* (Chicago: University of Chicago Press, 1994), 176.

Ethnographic method, by emphasizing orality and local knowledge, can help create archives of memory inaccessible to scholars working strictly through printed material. Of course, the point of such research cannot be to supplant written documents with oral testimony. It must instead seek to create a new, more inclusive, constantly evolving archive built up from both, rejecting any sharp distinction between emic and etic approaches. This is the crucial contribution of what might be called legal ethnohistory, a relatively recent development not limited to Latin America.[62] By considering how internal processes have overlapped with wider legal regimes, ethnohistorians may be able to understand how Indigenous people have invoked Western legal norms without limiting themselves to the accepted meanings of those norms.[63] In doing so, they may also help explain that this implies neither inconsistency nor a lack of rationality on the part of Indigenous claimants, or of those rediscovering their 'Indianness.' It reveals, rather, the extent to which Indigenous legal actors, and their insistence on speaking from a position of indigeneity, have put basic Western legal principles into question, including foundational concepts such as identity, rights, evidence, and reason, even as they continue to rely on these ideas in their struggles.

3 Recent Directions

The scholarly challenge with respect to contemporary Indigenous movements is to embrace this conundrum as Amerindian people advance claims in a world of law that is always simultaneously global, regional, national, tribal, and local – a 'cosmopolitan' legality potentially involving hundreds of millions of Indigenous people across the globe who insist that questions of justice are not limited to nationality or national borders.[64] With the establishment of the UN's Permanent Forum on Indigenous Issues in 2002, the passage of the UN Declaration on the Rights of Indigenous Peoples in 2007, and the Organization of American States' approval of the American Declaration on the Rights of

62 Christian McMillen, *Making Indian Law: The Hualapai Case and the Birth of Ethnohistory* (New Haven: Yale University Press, 2007); Katrina Jagodinsky, *Legal Codes & Talking Trees: Indigenous Women's Sovereignty in the Sonoran and Puget Sound Borderlands, 1854–1946* (New Haven: Yale University Press, 2016).

63 Duvé, 'Indigenous Rights,' 12–14.

64 Boaventura de Sousa Santos and César A. Rodríguez-Garavito, 'Law, Politics, and the Subaltern in Counter-Hegemonic Globalization' in *Law and Globalization from Below: Towards a Cosmopolitan Legality*, eds Boaventura de Sousa Santos and César A. Rodríguez-Garavito (Cambridge: Cambridge University Press, 2005), 13.

Indigenous Peoples in 2016, recognition has grown that Indigenous peoples in the western hemisphere and across the globe, bring a unique perspective to historical processes that have spanned European expansion, the rise of nation-states, and the triumph of capitalism on the global stage since the sixteenth century.[65]

As I have argued here, recent scholarship has shown how robust, expansive, and generative the study of law in relation to Indigenous people can be, particularly if we take the long view. It is no accident that the global Indigenous movement of recent decades, mediated by national and international law, has been so deeply connected to the original peoples of the Americas: they have had the most enduring and intimate experience with Europeans since the sixteenth century and have lived longest with the impacts of 'globalization.' If Latin America's Indigenous people have found ways to speak from the 'tribal village' to the 'global village,' it is due to long centuries of legal struggle.[66] Contemporary accounts of Indigenous efforts can only be understood against this deep historical background. Yet the goal of historical thinking cannot be to liquidate this past to make way for the future. Instead, it must seek to demonstrate how, through law, Indigenous peoples have continually asserted their ways of being in the face of pressures that would negate them, revealing that historical time cannot be neatly segmented into past, present, and future.

While Indigenous people remain the primary agents of such projects, scholars can contribute to their advancement, much as legal interlocutors and go-betweens did in the past. These collaborations are inherently interdisciplinary and intercultural, bringing together anthropologists, economists, historians, legal scholars, linguists, philosophers, political scientists, and sociologists, with Indigenous knowledge-makers and knowledge-keepers. Such work begins from the recognition that epistemological and ontological tensions are at the core of inquiry. Indeed, one of the central paradoxes of the 'juridical idiom' for Indigenous people, from the imperial period to the present, has been their instrumental acceptance of the legal status of 'Indian' (*indio*), with its threat to erase prior or self-claimed identities. In effect, 'the European construction of the other, as it is interpreted in law, is basic to an Indigenous definition of self,' at least in relation to law.[67] From this position, Indigenous legal actors have employed the identity of *indio* while rejecting its one-size-fits-all imperative,

65 Walter R. Echo-Hawk, *In the Light of Justice: The Rise of Human Rights in Native America and the UN Declaration on the Rights of Indigenous Peoples* (Golden: Fulcrum, 2013).

66 Alison Brysk, *From Tribal Village to Global Village: Indian Rights and International Relations in Latin America* (Stanford: Stanford University Press, 2000).

67 Rappaport, *Cumbe Reborn*, 26.

arguing that it is possible both to critique and to deploy, to question and to engage conventional legal understandings, by bringing local customs, usages, and histories to bear on purportedly rational and universal legal precepts. Scholars have helped crystallize the incongruities and possibilities of this stance for others to see and have made clear that the point is not merely to criticize the limitations of past and present legal frameworks. Rather, the goal must be to find ways for claimants to speak from a position of difference and diversity – and perhaps a 'bias for hope' – so as to promote the ongoing 'renaissance of Indigenous people for/towards the law.'[68]

In this regard, it is worth pointing out that there is a need for much more scholarly work on contemporary Indigenous women's relationship to the law. While women have been entangled with the law since the sixteenth century, recognition of women's rights is still contested, even among Indigenous groups themselves. The Zapatista movement promulgated the *Women's Revolutionary Law*, alongside other revolutionary laws, in 1994. The result of a consensus achieved over several years, the law spoke not only to the women of Chiapas, but in seven of its ten provisions addressed women in wider Mexican and even global society. More recently, the OAS published a report recognizing the structural inequalities women face and how they might be taken account of in national and international law. Reflecting the efforts of Indigenous women and men, Western scholars, and international civil servants, the report acknowledged that Indigenous women face obstacles of patriarchy, violence, and limited voice in relation to 'Indigenous justice systems,' and hurdles of racism and inaccessibility in relation to 'state-operated justice systems.' The report insisted that Indigenous people have a right to their own justice systems and customary law and called upon Indigenous leaders and states to take urgent action to face women's concerns.[69]

It is, perhaps, an 'ironic twist' that 'one of the most intellectually and ethically powerful challenges to the hegemony of Western categories has come from the Indigenous people whose localized, premodern existence was supposed to have crumbled under the pressures of modernity—colonialism, capitalism,

68 Brysk, *From Tribal Village*, x; Carlos Federico Marés, *O Renascer dos Povos Indígenas Para o Direito* (Curitiba: Juruá Editôra, 2000); Jonathan Lear, *Radical Hope: Ethics in the Face of Cultural Devastation* (Cambridge: Harvard University Press, 2006). A useful mapping resource for assessing legal status at a local and global scale may be found at www.landmarkmap.org.

69 Inter-American Commission on Human Rights, OAS, 'Indigenous Women and Their Human Rights in the Americas' (2017); Symposium 'Indigenous Geographies and Caribbean Feminisms: Common Struggles against Global Capitalism' St. Augustine University, Trinidad and Tobago, March 31, 2017.

and the "development project."'[70] Certainly, the mid-sixteenth century, when Aztec and Andean peoples first learned to use the law brought by the conquerors, can seem distant. In fact, given what America's Indigenous people have faced since then, it might astonish the casual observer that they have persisted in looking to law as an instrument for action and to justice as a moral resource. And yet, from the paradox of their legal personality as *others* to European *selves*, first as vassals, then as citizens, and now as bearers of transnational rights, Latin America's Indigenous people have affirmed their understandings of how to live, insisting on dignity, self-determination, collective rights, a right to difference – a politics of agonistic inclusion through law. Through a thick veil of misunderstanding, scholarship has helped bring this accomplishment to broader attention, offering a panorama of Latin American (and global) Indigenous legal history stretching half a millennium from the sixteenth to the twenty-first centuries, one that has only begun to be sketched out.[71]

References

Anaya, S. James. *International Human Rights and Indigenous Peoples*. New York: Aspen Publishers, 2009.

Brysk, Alison. *From Tribal Village to Global Village: Indian Rights and International Relations in Latin America*. Stanford: Stanford University Press, 2000.

Clavero, Bartolomé. *Freedom's Law and Indigenous Rights: From Europe's Oeconomy to the Constitutionalism of the Americas*. Berkeley: University of California Press, 2005.

Cunhill, Caroline. *Los defensores de indios de Yucatán y el acceso de los Mayas a la justicia colonial, 1540–1600*. México: UNAM, 2012.

Cutter, Charles. *The Legal Culture of Northern New Spain, 1700–1810*. Albuquerque: University of New Mexico Press, 1995.

Van Deusen, Nancy E. *Global Indios: The Indigenous Struggle for Justice in Sixteenth-Century Spain*. Durham: Duke University Press, 2015.

Dueñas, Alcira. *Indians and Mestizos in the 'Lettered City' Reshaping Justice, Social Hierarchy, and Political Culture in Colonial Peru*. Boulder: University of Colorado Press, 2010.

70 César A. Rodríguez-Garavito and Luis Carlos Arenas, 'Indigenous Rights, Transnational Activism, and Legal Mobilization: The Struggle of the U'Wa People in Colombia' in *Law and Globalization from Below: Towards a Cosmopolitan Legality*, 241.

71 American Historical Association, Session 142, 'Toward a Global Indigenous Legal History: Agency, Intelligibility, and the Ethics of Representation' New York, January 4, 2020.

Echeverri, Marcela. *Indians and Slave Royalists in the Age of Revolution: Reform, Revolution, and Royalism in the Northern Andes, 1780–1825*. Cambridge University Press, 2016.

Gotkowitz, Laura. *A Revolution for Our Rights: Indigenous Struggle for Land and Justice in Bolivia, 1880–1952*. Durham: Duke University Press, 2007.

Hanke, Lewis. *All Mankind Is One: A Study of the Disputation between Bartolomé de Las Casas and Juan Ginés de Sepúlveda in 1550 on the Intellectual and Religious Capacity of the American Indian*. Carbondale: Northern Illinois University Press, 1994.

Herzog, Tamar. *Upholding Justice: Society, State, and the Penal System in Quito (1650–1750)*. Ann Arbor: University of Michigan Press, 2004.

Hespanha, António Manuel. 'Las Categorías de lo Político y de lo Jurídico en la Época Moderna.' *Ius Fugit Revista Interdisciplinar de Estudios Histórico-Jurídicos* (1994): 3–4.

Novoa, Mauricio. *The Protectors of the Indians in the Royal Audience of Lima: History and Legal Culture, 1575–1775*. Boston: Brill, 2016.

Owensby, Brian. *Empire of Law and Indian Justice in Colonial Mexico*. Stanford: Stanford University Press, 2008.

Solórzano y Pereira, Juan. *Política indiana*. Madrid: Biblioteca Castro, 1996 [originally published 1647].

Premo, Bianca. *The Enlightenment on Trial: Ordinary Litigants and Colonialism in the Spanish Empire*. Oxford: Oxford University Press, 2017.

de la Puente Luna, José Carlos. *Andean Cosmopolitans: Seeking Justice and Reward at the Spanish Royal Court.* Austin: University of Texas Press, 2018.

Recopilación de leyes de los reynos de las Indias. Madrid: Ivlian Paredes, 1681 (Book VI).

Stern, Steve. *The Secret History of Gender: Women, Men, and Power in Late Colonial Mexico*. Chapel Hill: University of North Carolina Press, 1995.

Tau Anzoátegui, Víctor. *El Poder de la costumbre: Estudios sobre el Derecho Consuetudinario en América hispana hasta la Emancipación*. Buenos Aires: IIHD, 2001.

Yannakakis, Yanna. *The Art of Being In-between*. Durham: Duke University Press, 2008.

CHAPTER 9

Africans and Afro-Americans

Robert J. Cottrol

The experience of Africans and Afro-Americans in Latin America began, of course, with chattel slavery in the region. The extent to which the law actually affected living conditions, punishment, the ability of slaves to marry and have families, and the possibilities for manumission and citizenship is regularly debated by historians. Some argue the importance of the legal codes found in colonial Latin America, others argue that demographic and economic circumstances, not written law, determined the life experiences of most slaves.

The debate over the importance of law in Latin American slavery is further complicated by the vastness of the topic. Slavery in Spanish colonies and Brazil took place over an immense geographic territory extending from Argentina to what is now northern California in the United States. Slavery in Latin America would begin with the first Spanish and Portuguese arrivals at the end of the fifteenth century and last through the 1880s with the final abolition of the institution in Cuba in 1886 and Brazil in 1888.

The legal history of Africans and their descendants in Latin America thus resists easy generalization. There has been, at least since the 1946 publication of Frank Tannenbaum's *Slave and Citizen: The Negro in the Americas*, a robust debate among students of Latin American history concerning the importance of law in the lives of the millions of slaves who lived, toiled, and died in the Spanish Empire and Brazil before emancipation. The law sanctioned slavery and, at least in theory, played a clear role in defining racial categories. Yet, it also provided legal protection for the lives, dignity, and access to freedom for enslaved persons in the Spanish and Portuguese Empires. These formal legal protections were often part of slave systems that otherwise encompassed great physical cruelty and harsh conditions for enslaved persons. Emancipation would bring about not only the end of slavery, but also a formal recognition of the equality before the law of persons of all races. This formal recognition of citizenship and equality was proclaimed in the constitutions of the nations emerging in the region after independence. Yet the principles of equality proclaimed in the constitutions and statutes of the independent nations of Latin America often served to mask strong racial discrimination and profound racial inequality buttressed by the laws and governmental policies of the different nations. The modern effort to overcome the legacies of slavery and strong

 | DOI:10.1163/9789004436091_011

patterns of racial discrimination and inequality in the region are now recognized as key parts of the effort to achieve democratic governance and the rule of law throughout Latin America.[1]

1 The Iberian Heritage

The legal history of peoples of African descent in Latin America has to begin with a discussion of the law of slavery as it developed on the Iberian Peninsula before the Columbian voyages to the Americas. The formal adoption of Roman law by Castilian King Alfonso the Wise in the thirteenth century would form the basis for the law of slavery in both Spain and its New World colonies. This codification of Roman, feudal and canon law, *Las Siete Partidas*, provided, at least in theory, relatively strong protections for a certain minimum of rights for slaves. It placed limits on the amount and severity of punishment that a master could mete out. The code also provided for prosecution for masters who murdered their slaves. Slaves who were the victims of severe mistreatment had the right to petition the courts for forced sale to a more benevolent master.

Under *Las Siete Partidas* slaves had the right to marry. The Spanish law also provided extensive protection for the manumission of slaves. Portuguese law, influenced by *Las Siete Partidas* and the Justinian Code, had many of the same features. To be sure, both Spain and Portugal had also developed local disciplinary codes that specified curfews for slaves and prohibited them from selling goods, carrying weapons, or engaging in other behavior deemed inappropriate to their status, irrespective of race.

Slavery on the Iberian Peninsula had existed since ancient times and had originally not been linked to race. By the fifteenth century that started to change. Black Africans had begun to appear in noticeable numbers in the region and also on the sugar plantations of the Azores and the Canary Islands.

1 Sociologist Frank Tannenbaum played a critical role in focusing scholarly attention on the role of law in constructing patterns of slavery and race relations in Latin America. See, Frank Tannenbaum, *Slave and Citizen: The Negro in the Americas* (New York: Vintage Books, Random House, 1946). The debate over Tannenbaum's work has remained important for students of race and slavery well into modern times. See e.g., Alejandro de la Fuente, 'Slave Law and Claims-Making in Cuba: The Tannenbaum Debate Revisited' (2004) 22(2) Law and History Review 339–369.

In some locations ordinances were enacted that specified restrictions for blacks that went beyond the disciplinary codes meant for slaves generally.[2]

As was the case in most slave societies, Spanish and Portuguese law had to contend with the slave's dual status. Slaves were items of commerce governed by commercial codes including codified provisions protecting slave purchasers from fraud and ensuring fair prices. The law also recognized the slave as a human being and one whose behavior the law was especially anxious to control. Spain's late eighteenth-century *Código Negro*, a revision of the law written to govern slaves and free people of African descent in the Spanish Empire, acknowledged that slaves charged with serious offenses should be allowed trials like other defendants. But the code also recognized the subordinate status of people of African descent and often prescribed harsh physical punishments. Blacks and mulattoes who failed to show proper respect for whites were subject to flogging. People of African descent who raised a hand to whites could be subject to 100 lashes, mutilation, or even death.[3]

Spanish and Portuguese law also theoretically specified certain protections for slaves and included slaves in the broader community protected by the church and the crown. Spain's *Código Negro* required that slaves be baptized and instructed in the Catholic faith. It also prohibited slaveowners from having their slaves work on Sundays and religious holidays. The code also specified fines for masters who had sexual relations with their slaves. The *Código Negro*, like the early codification *Las Siete Partidas*, also recognized the right of slaves to marry.[4]

The strength of these and other protective provisions are a matter of considerable dispute. On the one hand, they clearly reflected the influence of the Catholic Church and the Church's desire that slaves be brought within the Catholic faith and that marriage and the slave's ability to have a family be protected. On the other hand, protective laws in the Spanish and Portuguese Empires seemed to have been evaded frequently and, in any event, often did relatively little to mitigate the often harsh conditions that existed in the sugar plantations and mines in the New World where slaves toiled and regularly perished in large numbers.

---

2 See generally, Alan Watson, *Slave Law in the Americas* (Athens: University of Georgia Press, 1989); Frédéric Mauro, *Le Portugal, le Brésil et l'Atlantique au XVIIe siècle: Étude économique* (Paris: Fondation Calouste Gulbenkian, 1983), 167–171.

3 Manuel Lucena Salmoral, 'El Texto del Segundo Código Negro Español, También Llamado Carolino, Existente en el Archivo de Indias' (1995) 12 Estudios de historia social y económica de América 275, 299, 313–315.

4 Ibid., 270–273, 304–305.

1.1 *The Law of Castes and Slavery*

The law was especially concerned with the problem of maintaining European dominance in Brazil and the Spanish colonies where whites were a distinct minority overshadowed by much larger Indigenous and African populations. Portugal and Spain, prodded by the Catholic Church, outlawed the formal enslavement of Indians in the sixteenth century, even though these restrictions were sometimes evaded and Indians were often required to render mandatory labor service. The law did not protect Africans and their descendants from slave status. Still, Spanish civil and ecclesiastical authorities were generally concerned with keeping the black and Indigenous populations separate in part to prevent them from making common cause against the Spanish and in part because the Church feared that exposure to Indian and African religions would interfere with the conversion of both groups to Catholicism.[5]

One legal device that was employed to keep the subject peoples of the Spanish and Portuguese Empires divided was a meticulous system of racial or color classifications. Spanish authorities were particularly artful at codifying every conceivable degree of racial mixture. Racial categories that had originated in Spain were adapted and modified in the Americas. Mexican anthropologist Gonzalo Aguirre Beltrán reported on codes employed in colonial Mexico to delineate various categories reflecting racial mixture: the offspring of a

1. Spaniard with an Indian (woman) (is a) Mestizo.
2. Mestizo (woman) with a Spaniard (is a) Castizo.
3. Castizo (man) with a Spanish woman (is a) Spaniard.
4. Spaniard (man) with a Black (woman) (is a) Mulatto.
5. Mulatto (woman) with a Spaniard (is a) Morisco.
6. Morisco (man) with a Spanish woman (is a) Chino.
7. Chino (man) with an Indian (woman) (is a) Step Backward.
8. A Step Backward (man) with a Mulatto woman (is a) Wolf.
9. A Wolf (man) with a Chino (woman) (is a) Gibaro.
10. A Gibaro (man) with a Mulatto (woman) (is a) Leper.
11. A Leper (man) with a Black (woman) (is a) Cambujo (very dark).
12. A Cambujo (man) with an Indian (woman) (is a) Zambaigo.
13. A Zambaigo (man) with a Wolf (woman) (is a) Calpa Mulatto.
14. A Calpa Mulatto (man) with a Cambujo (woman) (is a) Stay in the Air.

5 Robert J. Cottrol, *The Long, Lingering Shadow: Slavery, Race and Law in the American Hemisphere* (Athens: University of Georgia Press, 2013), 35–37.

15. A Stay in the Air (man) with a Mulatto (woman) (is an) I Don't Understand Thee.
16. An I Don't Understand Thee (man) with an Indian (woman) (is a) Step Backwards.

Similar classifications schemes could be found throughout colonial Latin America.[6]

This legal attempt to make fine racial distinctions seems to have had an ironic consequence. Far from strengthening the boundaries between the different subordinate groups, the multiplicity of racial classifications actually contributed to something of a culture of racial mobility. Not only did individuals try to informally improve their racial classifications, it was possible to legally improve one's racial standing as well. Baptismal records, which provided official documentation of an individual's racial classification, were known to be of dubious accuracy. A free person of African or Indigenous descent if sufficiently accomplished – and sufficiently wealthy, could purchase a document, the *gracias al sacar*, that provided proof of their white status despite their ancestry and often their phenotype as well.[7] Slaves could use other legal mechanisms in their favor.

An important aspect of slavery in both colonial Brazil and in the Spanish colonies was the ability of slaves to make legally enforceable contracts for their freedom. Slaves could contract with their owners to purchase themselves for a specified sum and could enforce such agreements in courts. The law in the Spanish Empire was particularly comfortable with manumission and the elevation of free people of color to the status of citizen. Spanish law, starting with *Las Siete Partidas*, was probably the most favorable to manumission of any body of slave law in the Americas. In Spanish colonies slaves had the legal right to take their owners to court, have the court declare a fixed price for their self-purchase, and then have the court enforce the manumission agreement between master and slave. Research by historians Michelle A. McKinley and Alejandro de la Fuente, among others, shows that a number of slaves in certain settings were often successful in using the courts of the Spanish Empire to vindicate claims of freedom under Spanish law.[8]

6 Gonzalo Aguirre Beltrán, *La población negra de México, 1519–1810: Estudio etnohistórico.* (México: Fondo de Cultura Económica, 1946), 176–177.

7 See generally, Ann Twinam, *Purchasing Whiteness: Pardos, Mulattos and the Quest for Social Mobility in the Spanish Indies* (Stanford: Stanford University Press, 2015); R. Douglas Cope, *The Limits of Racial Domination: Plebian Society in Mexico City, 1660–1720* (Madison: University of Wisconsin Press, 1999), 49–57.

8 Michelle A. McKinley, *Fractional Freedoms: Slavery, Intimacy, and Legal Mobilization in Colonial Lima, 1600–1700* (New York: Cambridge University Press, 2016). Alejandro de la

The law in the Spanish Empire, at least in those cases where the question was engaged, maintained the view that the slave, despite a servile status, held a position as a member of the community whose life and even honor and dignity were entitled to the law's protection. Perhaps nowhere is this better illustrated than in the late eighteenth-century petition for freedom brought in Guayaquil in what is now Ecuador by María Chiquinquirá Diaz. Her petition was based on the claim that she was born free because her putative master had abandoned her mother before her birth. Her mother, according to the claim should be deemed to have been abandoned because she had leprosy and was forced to turn to prostitution to survive. Chiquinquirá was able to base her petition in part on the doctrine, found in *Las Siete Partidas*, that a master who dishonored a slave or forced a female slave into prostitution would lose the right to the slave and that the slave would be set free. The case, as related is instructive from several points of view. Spanish authorities had procedures to hear such cases. Chiquinquirá was able to rely on a procurador or government attorney to present her case to the court. The honor of Chiquinquirá's mother was the key issue in the case and although mulatas and negras were assumed to have less honor and sexual chastity than white women, the law would nonetheless punish the master who forced a slave into prostitution, even an infirm black slave.[9]

Cases like Chiquinquirá's or those of slaves who successfully sued their owners to enforce manumission contracts represented one aspect of the law of slavery in the Spanish Empire, but we should be cautious about taking such cases as representative. Slavery in the Spanish Empire could be brutal especially in venues where large profits could be made in the use of slave labor in mines and on large plantations. Slaves in such venues while theoretically under the law's protection were often, as a practical matter, beyond the law's reach in terms of any real protection. Often in remote areas where few officials were willing to venture, particularly to extend the law's protection to slaves, slaves lived and died under often miserable conditions. The law on occasions was able to extend a measure of protection to the lives, freedoms, and dignity of some fortunate slaves who got to plead their cases before the courts of the empire. In such instances some jurists were able to fulfill the law's nobler aspirations of preserving a body of legal doctrine that protected the slave. But we

---

Fuente, 'Slaves and the Creation of Legal Rights in Cuba: Coartación and Papel' (2007) 87(4) Hispanic American Historical Review 659–692.

9 See generally Maria Eugenia Chaves, *Honor y libertad: Discursos y recursos en la estrategia de libertad de una mujer esclava (Guayaquil a fines del período colonial)* (Göteborg: Instituto Iberoamericano de la Universidad de Göteborg, 2001).

should exercise due caution before taking such cases as representative of the treatment of slaves as a whole in the Spanish Empire.

2 Independence and Emancipation

The nineteenth century wars for independence would spell the beginning of the end for slavery in the former colonies of Spain. Spurred on in part by the liberal ideology that informed Latin America's wars for independence and also by the large-scale participation of slaves and free men of color in the armies that fought for independence, the new nations formed out of the Spanish Empire put antislavery provisions into their new constitutions or abolished slavery by statutory means. The legal mechanisms for abolition varied in different nations. In 1824 Guatemala, El Salvador, Honduras, Nicaragua, and Costa Rica – which at the time were united in the Central American Federation – abolished slavery by an act of the National Constituent Assembly. The abolitionist statute also called for indemnification of slaveholders. In 1822 Mexico formally abolished the colonial caste system by legislation. Seven years later Mexico abolished slavery in an 1829 statute. Chile's Constitution of 1825 contained a Declaration of Emancipation.

Some nations took a longer route to emancipation. Colombia and Venezuela, part of independence leader Simón Bolívar's Gran Colombia, passed gradual emancipation legislation in 1821 and faced decades of subsequent extralegal resistance to emancipation on the part of slaveowners. In 1813 Argentina passed a 'Law of the Free Womb' statute declaring free all children born after January of that year. The statute actually granted the children only a fairly conditional freedom. Their status was that of 'libertos' and the law required that they had to live in the homes of their mothers' owners as servants, females until the age of sixteen, males until twenty. Libertos could be bought and sold like slaves. Slave importation continued into Argentina well into the 1830s. The Argentine Constitution finally outlawed slavery in 1853. Slavery continued in Buenos Aires until the province was reunited with the Argentine Confederation in 1861.

Peruvian emancipation also began with 'free womb' legislation enacted in 1821. The path toward ultimate abolition proved particularly difficult in Peru. That nation's gradual emancipation legislation specified that male libertos would be obligated to work for their patrons until the age of twenty-four, females until twenty. A subsequent decree proclaimed by Simón Bolívar granted libertos and slaves the right to change owners in order to secure better conditions, particularly better possibilities for manumission. Beginning in the 1830s pro-slavery forces made strenuous efforts to reverse the antislavery gains of the 1820s. Pro-slavery forces got legislation enacted that declared libertos to be slaves until they were twenty-one. They also pushed through legislation prohibiting slaves and libertos from changing bosses and declaring that libertos had to remain under the patronage of their bosses until age fifty. By the end of the 1830s slavery was in fact being strengthened rather than weakened. Throughout the 1840s and 50s slaves, libertos, and their antislavery supporters fought to fortify or reestablish the emancipationist legislation of the 1820s. The Civil Code of 1851 represented a vindication of these efforts. That code, among other things, stipulated that once a price had been agreed upon for a slave's self-purchase, the owner could not raise the price. The legislation also prohibited the sale of slaves to other regions without their consent and restored the rights of slaves to change owners in order to find owners more amenable to self-purchase arrangements. Peruvian slavery would finally be totally abolished by decree in 1854 as rival factions in that nation's civil war sought to enlist slaves to their cause.[10]

3 Final Abolition: Cuba and Brazil

While the first half of the nineteenth century saw both rough and smooth transitions from slave to free societies in many of the former Spanish colonies, slavery would continue well into the latter half of the nineteenth century in the surviving Spanish colonies of Puerto Rico and Cuba. The law of slavery in nineteenth-century Cuba reflected the tensions between the liberalizing influences of the Enlightenment that were posing problems for slavery throughout the Atlantic world, and the economic demands of Cuba's robust sugar economy. The late eighteenth-century *Código Negro* restated and strengthened some of the rights and protections for slaves. The new code included new limitations on punishment and granted slaves additional free time on holidays. While the code was often ignored by Cuban slaveholders, it did reflect the Enlightenment's influence on Spanish law. Spain also had to adjust to growing opposition, led by Britain, to the Atlantic slave trade. In 1820 Spain signed a treaty prohibiting the trade. Africans nonetheless continued to be imported into Cuba well into the 1860s reflecting the demand for slave labor driven by sugar plantations on the island. This increase in slaves, particularly slaves born in Africa, in the first decades of the nineteenth century brought about renewed

10 Carlos Aguirre, *Breve historia de la esclavitud en el Perú: Una herida que no deja de sangrar* (Lima: Fondo Editorial del Congreso del Perú, 2005), 159–171, 245.

concerns with security and control of the slave population. This was reflected in a code promulgated in 1842 that included new restrictions designed to prevent runaway slaves. The code also provided for new restrictions on free Afro-Cubans. The process of abolition in Cuba would begin with the passage of 'free womb' legislation in 1870. The legislation also freed slaves over sixty and those who had performed military service for Spain. A royal decree formally ended slavery throughout the empire in 1886.[11]

The most important slave society in nineteenth-century Latin America and the one with the most complex legal history was Brazil. Brazil achieved its independence from Portugal in 1822. The new nation was an empire with a thriving slave economy. As both a colony and an independent empire, Brazil received more Africans from the Atlantic slave trade than any other American society – nearly five million or better than 45 percent of the more than ten million estimated to have come to the Americas. The Brazilian slave economy was expanding in the nineteenth century particularly with the development of slave-based coffee cultivation in São Paulo. The African slave trade would continue well into the 1850s when it was finally halted under considerable pressure from Britain.[12]

Although often physically harsh, Brazilian slavery was not at all hostile to manumission or the prospect of citizenship for free Afro-Brazilians. Indeed, the Constitution of 1824 recognized the legal equality and citizenship of all free Brazilians. The law of the newly independent Brazilian Empire would continue the Portuguese legal tradition of facilitating manumissions although slaveowners often tried to resist such. Roman law scholar Alan Watson's research indicates that Brazilian law preserved the Roman doctrine that the children of masters and slave women were to be freed at birth, although a number of masters disregarded this rule.[13]

The standard form for the manumission of slaves in Brazil was the Alforria. Portuguese and later Brazilian law recognized two kinds of Alforria. The perfect Alforria was granted after self-purchase and with it came an unconditional freedom. The other Alforria, the imperfect one, was seen as an act of charity, the gift of freedom from a benevolent master. The imperfect Alforria was often accompanied by conditions that created manumissions that could be revoked by former masters. Individuals conditionally manumitted were known as

---

11 Rebecca J. Scott, *Slave Emancipation in Cuba: The Transition to Free Labor, 1860–1899* (Pittsburgh: University of Pittsburgh Press, 1985), 45–83, 127–181.

12 Herbert S. Klein, *The Atlantic Slave Trade* (New York: Cambridge University Press, 2010), 216–217.

13 Alan Watson, *Slave Law in the Americas*, 99.

libertos. Children of libertos were legally free. Brazil's Constitution of 1824 specifically stated that libertos were citizens.[14]

As the nineteenth century unfolded Brazil came under increasing international pressure to end slavery, particularly after the U.S. Civil War ended the institution in North America. In 1871 Brazil passed its own 'law of the free womb legislation' declaring children born of slave mothers to be free. As was the case with other 'free womb' legislation in the hemisphere, children freed by the law would have to serve as indentured servants until reaching the age of twenty-one. Brazil would be the last nation in the Western Hemisphere to completely abolish slavery. The institution would finally be abolished by a statute enacted by the Brazilian Parliament in 1888 putting an end to legal slavery in the Americas.

4 Post-emancipation

The end of slavery in Latin America, unlike abolition in the United States, was generally accomplished with relatively little in the way of newly enacted civil rights legislation and constitutional provisions specifying the legal status or rights of the newly freed Afro-American populations. This lack of new legal measures reflected the fact that, unlike the United States, in Latin America free peoples of color were generally regarded as citizens during the late slave era, that is prior to the enactment of political constitutions. Indeed, although there was both legal and unofficial racial discrimination throughout Latin America during the slave regimes, there were also free people of color, like Afro-Brazilian legal scholar and politician Antonio Pereira Rebouças, who were at the top of their society's social pyramids. With citizenship established before general emancipation, abolition was generally a matter of enacting legal measures to end slavery and little more.[15]

If emancipation brought little in the way of what might be termed civil rights legislation, the post-emancipation era also brought little in the way of formal legal discrimination against domestic populations of African descent in Latin America. This was somewhat remarkable given that the latter half of the nineteenth century and the early decades of the twentieth century were an era of a

14 Cottrol, *The Long, Lingering Shadow*, 60–61.

15 For a biography of Rebouças, a free Afro-Brazilian lawyer who reached the heights of the legal profession in nineteenth-century Brazil see: Keila Grinberg, *O Fiador dos Brasileiros: Cidadania, escravidão e direito civil no tempo de Antonio Pereira Rebouças* (Rio de Janeiro: Civilização Brasileira, 2002).

renewed racialist ideology in much of Latin America. The intellectual currents that brought scientific racism and Social Darwinism to much of the Western world had a strong impact on the thinking of elites in Latin America. They feared that the large populations of Indigenous and African descent found in their countries were a permanent impediment to progress, one that would bar their nations from ever becoming modern progressive societies. Latin American intellectuals like Peru's Eugenio Larrabure y Unánue, Argentina's Domingo Faustino Sarmiento, and Brazil's Raimundo Nina Rodrigues all saw their nation's populations of African and Indigenous dissent as social liabilities that had to be addressed through law and public policies. Rodrigues, a resident of Brazil's overwhelmingly Afro-Brazilian state of Bahia and himself a person with some African ancestry, even went so far as to advocate a regime of legal apartheid with segregation of Afro-Brazilians from others and separate criminal codes for Afro-Brazilians.[16]

Rodrigues's suggestions did not become the law in Brazil or elsewhere in Latin America. But the equation of African descent with racial inferiority and barbarism would have an influence on the application of criminal law in a number of countries. Fear of African culture, particularly its outward manifestations in African religious practices and folk medicine would bring about the use of criminal law to suppress these practices. Cuba and Brazil in the early twentieth century were examples of societies with strong persistence of African religious practices and the use of criminal codes by authorities to suppress them. The law said little about race as such, but authorities made it clear that if the law formally declared all persons born within the nation to be citizens who enjoyed equal rights, the law regarded European culture with favor and African culture with disfavor and would use the criminal law to punish those who were too visible in their keeping of African traditions.[17]

Latin American national legislatures did not enact formal segregation laws calling for the separation of people of different races. But in parts of Latin America visible patterns of separation where people of visible African descent were informally barred from using some public facilities did emerge. This occurred with some frequency in the more fashionable restaurants and hotels in cities throughout the continent. In some venues the discrimination even occurred in publicly owned municipal facilities. In the city of Campinas in the Brazilian state of São Paulo, municipal parks and park benches were

16 Dain Borges, '"Puffy, Ugly, Slothful and Inert": Degeneration in Brazilian Social Thought, 1880–1940' (1993) 25(2) Journal of Latin American Studies 240–241.

17 See Alejandra Bronfman, *Measures of Equality: Social Science Citizenship, and Race in Cuba, 1902–1940* (Chapel Hill: University of North Carolina Press, 2004), 67–117.

frequently closed to Afro-Brazilians even though there was no legislation supporting racial segregation. The fact that offenders who used these municipal facilities were subject to arrest and prosecution usually on charges of vagrancy or disturbing the peace gave these informal prohibitions the force of customary law even though statutory and constitutional provisions proclaimed the equality of all before the law.[18]

If the law in twentieth-century Latin America formally recognized the equality of all citizens regardless of race, the law in the region showed a marked preference for which outsiders could enter the nations of the hemisphere through immigration. Responding to the racial ideology of the era that dictated that the nations of the regions could only make progress through the whitening of their populations, the nations of Latin America would, in the late nineteenth century begin policies of whitening, called *blanqueamiento* in Spanish and *branqueamento* in Portuguese, through policies designed to attract European immigrants and frequently to exclude immigrants of African descent.

Brazil began the process of enlisting immigration law in the effort to whiten the nation immediately after emancipation. Two years after national emancipation, in 1890, Brazilian President Manuel Deodoro da Fonseca issued a decree prohibiting the immigration of peoples descended from the Indigenous populations of Africa and Asia. The ban would later be relaxed in 1892 to allow Japanese immigration. Later legislation in Brazil tightened the restrictions on people of African descent extending the immigration bans not only to Africans, but to people of African descent from the Western Hemisphere as well.[19]

Brazil's disdain for people of African descent and its desire to enter the ranks of white nations were reflected in the South American nation's immigration laws. It was also reflected in administrative policies that might not have risen to the level of formal law but were nonetheless formal governmental policies dictated and enforced by government officials. Early in the twentieth century, for example, the government of Brazil's state of São Paulo had a strict policy of restricting employment in the state's police force to white men.[20]

It should be noted that restrictive immigration policies and unstated but nonetheless real and often strictly enforced racial barriers tell only part of

18 Petrônio Domingues, *Uma História nâo contada: Negro, racism e branqueamento em São pôs-aboliçâo* (São Paulo: Editora Senac, 2004), 157–162.

19 Eunice Aparecida de Jesus Prudente, *Preconceito racial e igualdade jurídica no Brasil.* (Campinas: Julex Livros, 1989), 129–131, 151–153.

20 Petrônio Domingues, *Uma história nâo contada*, 83–132; George Reid Andrews, *Blacks and Whites in São Paulo, Brasil, 1888–1988* (Madison: University of Wisconsin Press, 1991), 68–69.

the story. Paradoxically Brazil, as was the case with a number of other Latin American nations, had a history of some men of African descent rising to the senior ranks of governmental service despite the racism represented by immigration laws and customary barriers. Two Afro-Brazilian jurists, Pedro Lessa and Hermenegildo de Barros, gained appointment to Brazil's Supreme Court, the Supreme Federal Tribunal, in the first three decades of the twentieth century. They like many others who were appointed or elected to high office in Latin America were of mixed racial descent, but nonetheless known to have some African ancestry. The absence of explicitly stated racial barriers codified into law and the presence of high-ranking governmental officials of African descent in Latin America helped contribute to the view that the nations of the region could be characterized as racial democracies free from the kind of formally codified racism found in a number of other societies – the Nuremberg laws of Nazi Germany, the Jim Crow statutes of the southern United States, and Apartheid legislation in South Africa – in the mid-twentieth century.

If the legal framework in the region did not support formal separation and discrimination, the nations of Latin America would, like Brazil, take active legal measures to discourage and indeed prohibit immigration by people of African descent. Legislation prohibiting such was commonplace in the region. Costa Rica enacted legislation barring immigration by people of African descent as early as 1862. Venezuela authorities put a similar ban in its Constitution of 1906. The Panamanian Constitution of 1941 prohibited the immigration of non-Spanish-speaking blacks, a reflection of the tensions between Panama's earlier Spanish-speaking population and the English-speaking black Caribbean minority that had been brought to the Central American nation in the early twentieth century to help build the Panama Canal.

The existence of this racially restrictive legislation certainly reflected the aspirations of Latin American political leaders to transform their nations into societies with white populations and their distaste for the possibility of large or increased numbers of people of African descent joining their nations. The effort at restricting or preventing the immigration of people of African descent also would become another occasion for what many students of law in Latin America have observed, the often significant gap between the law as it is formally stated in the region and the law as it is actually applied. The restrictive legislation was duly enacted and yet in a number of nations the need for labor and pressure from foreign business interests would lead to lax enforcement of or informal policies that evaded the restrictive legislation. Despite restrictive immigration laws, pressure from agricultural and railroad interests to bring in Afro-Caribbean laborers led to the immigration of thousands of people of African descent. They were the subject of discriminatory legislation. Children of Afro-Caribbean immigrants, even if born in Costa Rica, could not obtain citizenship without naturalization. Legislation prevented the Afro-Caribbean population from obtaining many of the more desirable jobs available. Formal legal discrimination against the Afro-Caribbean population would continue until Costa Rica's revolution in 1948. Under the nation's Party of National Liberation, a new Constitution was enacted. It eliminated the legal disabilities of the Afro-Caribbean population.[21]

The new constitution in Costa Rica was part of a series of legal reforms formally rejecting racial discrimination that were enacted in a number of Latin America nations in the 1940s. There had been prior efforts in the region to use the law to express official disapproval of racial discrimination. The Brazilian Constitution of 1934 had a weak provision outlawing racial discrimination but provided no penalties for discriminatory behavior. It was nonetheless an important normative statement. The provision was left out of Brazil's next constitution drafted by the authoritarian government of Getúlio Vargas in 1937. The Cuban Constitution of 1940 had a provision explicitly prohibiting discrimination on the basis of race and color, as well as sex and class. That Constitution also prohibited race-based political parties, in part a reaction to Afro-Cuban political parties that had formed earlier in the twentieth century.[22]

The defeat of Nazi Germany and the resulting discrediting of racist ideology would accelerate the trend of using the law to express condemnation of racial discrimination. Some of these reforms came about because of embarrassing high-profile incidents involving racial discrimination that became international news. In 1945, Venezuela enacted local and national legislation prohibiting racial discrimination after Todd Duncan, a black singer from the United States, was denied entrance to several hotels. The discrimination against Duncan was portrayed in *Time* magazine. Similar discrimination against Katherine Dunham, a black dancer from the United States, led to the enactment in 1951 of Brazil's first statute outlawing racial discrimination, *Lei Afonso Arinos.* The statute would in many ways establish a pattern for anti-discrimination legislation in Latin America. The *Lei Afonso Arinos* prohibited discrimination in public accommodations and employment. It also prohibited

21 Diana Senior Angulo, 'La incoporación social en Costa Rica de la población afrocostarricense durante el siglo XX, 1927–1963' Master's thesis (San José: Universidad de Costa Rica, 2007).

22 Robert Whitney, 'The Architect of the Cuban State: Fulgencio Batista and Populism in Cuba, 1937–1940' (2000) 32(2) Journal of Latin American Studies 435–459.

racism and expressions of racist sentiment. The statute also made racism and racial discrimination crimes.[23]

The *Lei Afonso Arinos* would in many ways set the pattern for anti-discrimination legislation in the region. Civil Rights legislation was enacted providing a strong normative statement against racism and racial discrimination. The law as a normative statement against racial discrimination was made still stronger because the anti-racist legislation treated acts of racism and racial discrimination as crimes. This approach was often advocated by Afro-American civil rights activists in their region who argued that it was important for the law to make a strong statement against racism. Critics have noted that this approach often produces a body of laws that make strong normative statements against racism and discrimination but that often fall short in terms of providing effective remedies against discrimination.[24]

Focus on the law as a tool for combatting racial discrimination in the region would begin to get renewed attention in the last two decades of the twentieth century. The end of Apartheid in South Africa, the successes of the Civil Rights movement in the United States, and the move toward more populist and democratic government in Latin America generally helped spur new activism among people of African descent in the region. These events combined with the development of newer modes of communication, particularly the internet, made racial justice activists more aware of progress being made in other nations and also more aware of the profound often racially linked inequalities in their own. The demand for legal reform to combat racial inequality grew.

An early target of these legal reform efforts were the national constitutions. Restoration of democratic governance could be the occasion for such constitutional reform. Brazil would emerge from twenty years of military government in 1985. The new Constitution adopted in 1988, unlike its predecessors, contained specific provisions designed to address the problem of the unequal treatment of Afro-Brazilians. It declared racism and racial discrimination to be crimes. It also provided constitutional protections for quilombos, Afro-Brazilian communities descended from maroon or runaway slave communities that have maintained a certain degree of cultural distinctiveness. Colombia's Constitution of 1991 contains similar provisions and also provides for a certain minimum representation in the National Congress for certain historically self-governing Afro-Colombian communities. Ecuador, like a number

23 Winthrop R. Wright, 'The Todd Duncan Affair: Acción Democrática and the Myth of Racial Democracy in Venezuela' (1998) 44(4) The Americas 441–459.

24 Wilfredo Ardito Vega, *Las ordenanzas contra la discriminación* (Lima: Pontifica Universidad Católica del Peru, 2009), 5, 12–13.

of other nations in the region, put a provision in its 1998 constitution providing for recognition of communal rights to lands historically occupied by the nation's Afro-American population. Similar provisions were also enacted as part of recent constitutions in Guatemala, Honduras, and Nicaragua. Such provisions applied to people of African descent are modeled on longstanding policies applied to Indigenous populations where there has been a traditional recognition of cultural distinctiveness and semi-autonomous governance. These new constitutional provisions in and of themselves do not address the issues of discrimination and inequality for people of African descent living in the general society.

The existence of egalitarian statutory and constitutional provisions in Latin America has traditionally had little effect on deep patterns of racial inequality in such areas as employment, income, education, and treatment by the criminal justice system. The twenty-first century would bring renewed calls on the part of Afro-American activists for increased measures to combat traditional patterns of discrimination and exclusion. Earlier in the twentieth century, census officials in a number of nations had made administrative decisions to help the project of national whitening by eliminating racial categories that might show significant populations of African descent. By the early decades of the twenty-first century, Afro-American activists were calling for new legislation or administrative rulings to require the census to list the population of African descent. This was part of a broader effort to combat a traditional narrative in many nations in the region that was quite willing to recognize whites and mestizos as part of the nation, but that often overlooked people of African descent. Part of that effort was the struggle to include in national constitutions language that recognized that the nations of the region were multiracial and multicultural and to include specific language protecting the rights of Afro-American populations. As mentioned above, since the 1980s, language specifically recognizing Afro-American populations as part of the nation or providing for certain communal rights for some Afro-American communities has been included in the Constitutions of Colombia, Ecuador, Guatemala, Honduras, Nicaragua, and Brazil.

Beginning in 2001, Brazil developed affirmative action policies designed to redress issues of inequality in education and employment. These new policies began with legislation in the State of Rio de Janeiro mandating quotas for Afro-Brazilian and Indigenous students in the state universities. The public universities, state and federal, are the elite schools of the Brazilian system of higher education. Students who had received their secondary educations in public schools were often at a disadvantage in gaining admission to these universities because they had been poorly prepared for the vestibular, Brazil's rigorous university entrance exams. The Rio model of quotas for students of African descent would, in the decade that followed, be adopted by public universities throughout the nation. Brazil's affirmative action policies became national policy when Brazil's Supreme Federal Tribunal in 2012 rejected challenges to the affirmative action policies at the University of Brasilia and the Federal University of Rio Grande do Sul. Both challenges argued that the affirmative action policies in the two public universities violated the equality principle in the Constitution of 1988. The Brazilian high court rejected both claims noting that efforts to remedy past and continuing discrimination through affirmative action were consistent with the equality principle. Later in 2012, the Brazilian Congress enacted legislation mandating affirmative action in public universities and civil service employment.[25]

Other nations in the region have also developed policies legally mandating affirmative action programs in universities and civil service employment. Ecuador's Constitution of 2008 has language authorizing affirmative action to promote equality. Such policies have also been authorized in Colombia and Costa Rica among other nations in the region.

In the last two decades most of the nations of Latin America have followed the path of trying to improve their anti-discrimination legal regimes with the adoption of new constitutional provisions, civil rights legislation, and affirmative action measures. These new measures have to a large extent been spurred on by a new political militancy among peoples of African descent in Latin America who have insisted that the previously underplayed issues of racism, racial inequality, and racial discrimination be addressed and remedied.

This movement has been somewhat underdeveloped in Cuba. The revolution that brought Fidel Castro to power in 1959 went a considerable way toward addressing traditional problems of racial discrimination and racial inequality in Cuban life. The emphasis of the Marxist government on addressing racial discrimination coupled with the migration of large numbers of mostly white middle class Cubans to the United States brought new opportunities for many Afro-Cubans in employment and education.[26]

Racial reform under the revolutionary government was less a matter of developing legal mechanisms to combat discrimination and more a matter of

25 Supremo Tribunal Federal do Brasil, *Arguição de Descumprimento de Preceito Fundamental 186*, April 26, 2012.

26 Alejandro de La Fuente, *A Nation for All: Race, Inequality and Politics in Twentieth-Century Cuba* (Chapel Hill: University of North Carolina Press, 2001), 260–285; Sarah A. Blue, 'The Erosion of Racial Equality in the Context of Cuba's Dual Economy' (2007) 49(3) Latin American Politics and Society 35–68.

using the command mechanisms of an authoritarian state to break down racial barriers. While these mechanisms managed to lessen racial inequalities for the first three decades after Castro's assumption of power, they have proven to be problematic as vehicles for continued racial reform. With the fall of the Soviet Union in 1991 and the loss of the significant Soviet subsidy to the Cuban government and economy, the Cuban government turned to hotels, restaurants, casinos, and other aspects of the tourist trade in an effort to secure foreign currency. There are widespread reports of discrimination against Afro-Cubans in such establishments. Unlike what has been the case in other countries in the hemisphere, the persistence or reappearance of racial discrimination in Cuba has not led to a strong Afro-Cuban movement for the strengthening of legal measures against discrimination. A grassroots movement to do this has been inhibited by the authoritarian nature of the regime.[27]

The legal regimes governing peoples of African descent and questions of racial discrimination in Latin America had traditionally been issues of the domestic law in the nations of the region. Increasingly in the twenty-first century, those issues have also been viewed through the prism of international human rights law. Racial discrimination runs counter to international law and international human rights norms including the Inter-American Convention on Human Rights. Strong prejudice and discrimination against Haitians and Dominicans of Haitian descent in the Dominican Republic have tested the efficacy of the Inter-American judicial system as a vehicle to enforce international norms against racial discrimination. In 2005 the Dominican government deported some 2000 individuals on the grounds that they 'looked Haitian,' meaning that they were visibly black. In 2011 the Supreme Court of the Dominican Republic upheld an administrative regulation depriving Dominicans of Haitian descent of Dominican citizenship thus making way for their expulsion. The administrative ruling stripped some individuals of Dominican citizenship whose families had been in the nation and recognized as Dominican citizens for as long as three generations.[28]

Victims of the Dominican government's policy appealed to the Inter-American Commission on Human Rights and the Inter-American Court of Human Rights. The Inter-American Commission ruled in favor of the petitioners in 2012. They later received a favorable decision from the Inter-American Court in 2014. Both bodies found that the Dominican government had violated the rights of the petitioners including the right to non-discrimination.

---

27 de la Fuente, *A Nation for All*, 318–334; Blue, 'The Erosion of Racial Equality,' 35–68.

28 *República Dominicana, Suprema Corte de Justicia, Sentencia No. 460.*

The Inter-American Court's decision called for, among other measures, the restoration of the citizenship of the petitioners and the Dominican Republic's recognition of the citizenship of all persons born in the nation regardless of ancestry. The Dominican government as of this writing (May 8, 2020) has so far refused to comply with the orders.[29]

The experience of the Haitian-Dominicans with the Inter-American Court in some ways might be considered illustrative of the broader problem that people of both African and Indigenous descent often find in the effort to use law as a tool to challenge deeply seated prejudices and patterns of social exclusion. In the last two decades of the twentieth century and now in the first two decades of the twenty-first, the constitutions and statutes of the nations of Latin America have gone a long way toward embracing racial inclusion and anti-discrimination as legal norms. But these norms can and often do run into stubborn headwinds. Undoubtedly the first of these is deeply entrenched structural inequality, partially linked to race, partially linked to class. But another headwind has to do with the rule of law itself. These newer more egalitarian legal norms have to be implemented in a region long noted for the problematic nature of the rule of law. The struggle against these headwinds will shape the future of Latin Americans of African descent, as indeed it will shape the futures of others in the region.

References

Aguirre, Carlos. *Agentes de Su Propia Libertad: Los Esclavos de Lima y la Desintegración de la Esclavitud, 1821–1854*. Lima: Pontifica Universidad Católica del Perú, 1993.

Aguirre Beltrán, Gonzalo. *La Población Negra de México, 1519–1810: Estudio Etnohistórico*. México: Fondo de Cultura Económica, 1972.

Andrews, George Reid. *Afro-Latin America, 1800–2000*. New York: Oxford University Press, 2004.

Ardito Vega, Wilfredo. *Las Ordenanzas Contra la Discriminación*. Lima: Pontifica Universidad Católica del Perú, 2009.

Bronfman, Alejandra. *Measures of Equality: Social Science, Citizenship and Race in Cuba, 1902–1940*. Chapel Hill: University of North Carolina Press, 2004.

Cottrol, Robert J. *The Long, Lingering Shadow: Slavery, Race and Law in the American Hemisphere*. Athens: University of Georgia Press, 2013.

29 *Caso de Personas Dominicanas y Haitianas Expulsadas vs. República Dominicana,* Corte Interamericana de Derechos Humanos, Sentencia de 28 de Agosto de 2014 (Excepciones Preliminares, Fonda, Reparaciones y Costas; International Justice Resource Center).

Fuente, Alejandro de la. *A Nation for All: Race, Inequality and Politics in Twentieth-Century Cuba*. Chapel Hill: University of North Carolina Press, 2001.

Fuente, Alejandro de la. 'Slaves and the Creation of Legal Rights in Cuba: Coartación and Papel.' *Hispanic American Historical Review* 87(4) (2007): 659–692.

Grinberg, Keila. *O fiador dos brasileiros: Cídadania, Escravidao e Direito Civil nos Tempo de Antonio Pereira Rebouças*. Rio de Janeiro: Civilização Brasileira, 2002.

Knight, Franklin W. *Slave Society in Cuba during the Nineteenth Century*. Madison: University of Wisconsin Press, 1970.

Mauro, Frederi. *Le Portugal, Le Bresil et L'Atlantique au XVII Siecle (1570–1670: Étude économique)*. Paris: Foundation Calouste Gulbenkian, 1983.

McKinley, Michelle A. *Fractional Freedoms: Slavery, Intimacy and Legal Mobilization in Colonial Lima, 1600–1700*. New York: Cambridge University Press, 2016.

Rout, Leslie B. Jr. *The African Experience in Spanish America.* New York: Cambridge University Press, 1976.

Tannenbaum, Frank. *Slave and Citizen: The Negro in the Americas*. New York: Vintage/ Random House, 1946.

Watson, Alan. *Slave Law in the Americas*. Athens: University of Georgia Press, 1989.

CHAPTER 10

Enslaved Humans

Mariana Dias Paes

The legal status of enslaved humans was a controversial legal issue in Latin America throughout the centuries. At a first glance, it might seem simple to identify a person who appears in the documents as a slave or as a free person. However, recent scholarship shows that this is not a straightforward issue. Latin American societies were not structured in the binary opposition between slavery and freedom. In between these two extremes, there was a wide range of legal categories whose meanings historical actors constantly disputed. It was not clear for historical actors themselves if some of these legal categories were in the framework of 'slavery' or of 'freedom.' Their contours were the object of intense judicial debates from the beginning of colonization until the end of the nineteenth century, when slavery was abolished in Cuba (1886) and Brazil (1888). Who were the enslaved humans? How did someone become enslaved? These questions are at the core of recent academic debates on law and slavery.

Traditionally, Latin American legal history relied on the so-called 'Tannenbaum thesis' in order to analyze the relations between law and slavery in the region. According to this framework, due to an entanglement between Roman law and Catholicism, the law of slavery in Iberian societies granted more chances of manumission and recognized broader legal personality to slaves than other colonial legal systems. In the last decades, historians intensely criticized this thesis. On the one hand, scholars argue that manumission in Latin American was mostly paid by slaves either with money or with services. On the other hand, they claim that it was not necessarily 'the law' that granted slaves some level of legal personality, some recognition of rights, and broader chances of manumission. It was actually enslaved persons themselves who were able to push forward interpretations of norms and legal categories more favorable to them.[1]

Moreover, a considerable number of people did not live in a state of complete autonomy after acquiring manumission and were always under the

1 Alejandro de la Fuente, 'Slave Law and Claims-Making in Cuba: The Tannenbaum Debate Revisited' (2004) 22(2) Law and History Review 304–369; Alejandro de la Fuente and Ariela Gross, 'Comparative Studies of Law, Slavery, and Race in the Americas' (2010) 6 Annual Review of Law and Social Sciences 469–485.

 | DOI:10.1163/9789004436091_012

threat of re-enslavement. Usually, these people did not have complete control over their labor, bodies, and time. Also, manumission did not necessarily completely break the ties of dependency that bound them to their former masters or even to their deceased masters' families. Thus, in Latin America societies, contingent liberty, not complete autonomy, was the rule for people of color, whether they were former slaves or not.[2] Linked to these states of 'quasi freedom,' was the constant threat of re-enslavement both by legal means, such as revocation of manumission, and illegal ones, such as kidnapping, fraudulent sales, and forged baptismal certificates.[3]

Contingent freedom and risk of re-enslavement in the context of a 'suing culture'[4] pushed forward enslaved and freed people to courts.[5] Slaves, free people of color, and many other groups of persons that lived in between slavery and freedom were a constant in Latin America secular and ecclesiastical courts. The paperwork this intense litigation generated is at the core of recent

2 McKinley uses the term 'fractional freedom' to address this issue. Michelle McKinley, *Fractional Freedoms: Slavery, Intimacy, and Legal Mobilization in Colonial Lima, 1600–1700* (Cambridge: Cambridge University Press, 2018). See also Pedro Cantisano and Mariana Dias Paes 'Legal Reasoning in a Slave Society (Brazil, 1860–88)' (2018) 36(3) Law and History Review 471–510; Sidney Chalhoub, 'The Politics of Ambiguity: Conditional Manumission, Labor Contracts, and Slave Emancipation in Brazil (1850s-1888)' (2015) 60 International Review of Social History 161–191; Fernanda Domingos Pinheiro, *Em defesa da liberdade: Libertos, Coartados e Livres de cor nos Tribunais do Antigo Regime Português (Mariana e Lisboa, 1720–1819)* (Belo Horizonte: Fino Traço, 2018); Rebecca Scott, 'Paper Thin: Freedom and Re-enslavement in the Diaspora of the Haitian Revolution' (2011) 29(4) Law and History Review 1061–1087.

3 Sidney Chalhoub, 'The Precariousness of Freedom in a Slave Society (Brazil in the Nineteenth Century)' (2011) 56 International Review of Social History 405–439; Judy Bieber Freitas, 'Slavery and Social Life: Attempts to Reduce Free People to Slavery in the Sertão Mineiro, Brazil (1850–1871)' (1994) 26(3) Journal of Latin America Studies 597–619; Keila Grinberg, 'Re-enslavement, Rights and Justice in Nineteenth-Century Brazil' (2013) 1 Translating the Americas 141–159; Keila Grinberg, 'Illegal Enslavement, International Relations, and International Law on the Southern Border of Brazil' (2016) 35(1) Law and History Review 31–52; Keila Grinberg and Beatriz Mamigonian, 'Le crime de réduction à l'esclavage d'une personne libre (Brésil, XIXe siècle)' (2017) 11 Brésil(s): sciences humaines et sociales; Henrique Espada Lima, 'Sob o domínio da precariedade: escravidão e os significados da liberdade de trabalho no século XIX' (2005) 6(11) Topoi 289–326.

4 Bianca Premo, *The Enlightenment on Trial: Ordinary Litigants and Colonialism in the Spanish Empire* (Oxford: Oxford University Press, 2017), 28.

5 For transcriptions of court cases involving enslaved persons, see Carolina González Undurraga, *Esclavos y Esclavas Demandando Justicia, Chile, 1740–1823: Documentación Judicial por Carta de Libertad y Papel de Venta* (Santiago de Chile: Universitaria, 2014); María de los Ángeles, Meriño Fuentes, and Aisnara Perera Díaz, *Estrategias de Libertad: un Acercamiento a las Acciones Legales de los Esclavos en Cuba (1762–1872)* (La Habana: Editorial de Ciencias Sociales, 2015).

scholarship on law and slavery. Court cases are a privileged kind of source to study issues related to the legal aspects of slavery and freedom because they make evident the role enslaved and freed persons had in framing Latin America law. In some cases, petitions were directly written by slaves and freed people themselves. But even in the cases they were not, their active engagement in judicial disputes, pushing forward their own understandings of norms and legal categories, is evident. Legal knowledge was disseminated among slaves and freed people through daily conversations, gossip, and social interaction inside households and in public spaces, such as markets and squares.[6]

In the following sections, I will draw on recent scholarship on law and slavery in Latin America to highlight the most contested issues concerning the legal contours of slavery and freedom in the region from the fifteenth to the nineteenth centuries.

1 Litigating Slavery and Freedom

Amid the centuries that slavery was a legal institution in Latin America, the definition of someone as a 'slave' was not at all an undisputed issue. On both sides of the Atlantic, in Africa and in the Americas, the main legal principle that legitimized the enslavement of Indigenous and African populations was the 'just war.' Nevertheless, vassalage treaties signed between Indigenous and African authorities and the Portuguese crown granted vassal status to people that lived under the jurisdiction of these treaties which would theoretically preclude their enslavement.[7]

In practice, however, illegal techniques of enslavement were disseminated on both sides of the Atlantic, ranging from kidnapping of adults and children, trickery, falsification of documents, and fraudulent sales. In this context, resorting to colonial courts could be a way to avoid illegal enslavement. In these so-called 'freedom suits,' enslaved persons were not only fighting for their freedom, they were also discussing the concrete meanings of the legal category

6 Camillia Cowling, *Conceiving Freedom: Women of Color, Gender, and the Abolition of Slavery in Havana and Rio de Janeiro* (Chapel Hill: University of North Carolina Press, 2013), 145–148; Premo, *The Enlightenment on Trial*, 31–63.

7 Fernanda Aires Bombardi and Luma Ribeiro Prado, 'Ações de liberdade de índias e índios escravizados no Estado do Maranhão e Grão-Pará, primeira metade do século XVIII' (2016) 5(1) Brasiliana: Journal for Brazilian Studies 174–199; Mariana Candido, 'African Freedom Suits and Portuguese Vassal Status: Legal Mechanisms for Fighting Enslavement in Benguela, Angola, 1800–1830' (2011) 32(3) Slavery & Abolition 447–459.

of 'slavery' and what were the legal possibilities of enslavement. Relatively common in Portuguese jurisdictions was, for example, the principle of original freedom, that is the idea that people living under Portuguese colonial authorities, or under local authorities who had signed vassalage treaties, had a natural freedom status that could not be endangered.[8]

Due to recurrent practices of illegal enslavement triggered by the transatlantic slave trade, colonial authorities in West Central Africa – the geographical origin of the great majority of African slaves trafficked to Latin America – built up a complex judicial system in charge of hearing cases pertaining to slavery and freedom. This scheme was marked by the entanglement of multiple jurisdictions and normative frameworks. For example, by the second half of the eighteenth century, different institutions were operating in West Central Africa to hear cases of enslavement: the interrogator of freedom (*inquisidor da liberdade*), *mucanos* courts, and regular secular judges. The interrogator of freedom, an office sometimes occupied by priests, was in charge of examining if enslaved people coming from the interior and embarking to the Americas were legally slaves. The *mucanos* court was originally an African institution in charge of hearing a great variety of cases. However, by the eighteenth century it was merged with the Portuguese judicial system; it became a court in charge of hearing enslavement cases. By this time, Portuguese and African authorities acted as judges in this institution.[9] Therefore, when enslaved Africans arrived in the Americas, they were already familiar with the possibility of judicially discussing slave and freedom statuses.

As in Africa, in the Americas there were various institutions in charge of hearing enslavement cases. These cases were not only filed by Africans, but also by Indigenous people. Legislation outlawing the enslavement of certain Indigenous groups was issued by both the Spanish crown in the sixteenth century and by the Portuguese crown in the eighteenth century. Nevertheless, prohibition of Indigenous slavery did not meant abolition of all forms of

8 Bombardi and Prado, 'Ações de liberdade de índias'; Candido, 'African Freedom Suits'; José Curto, 'The Story of Nbena, 1817–1820: Unlawful Enslavement and the Concept of "Original Freedom" in Angola' in *Trans-Atlantic Dimensions of Ethnicity in the African Diaspora*, eds Paul Lovejoy and David Trotman (London: Continuum, 2003), 43–64.

9 Candido, 'African Freedom Suits'; Mariana Dias Paes, 'Shared Atlantic Legal Culture: the Case of a Freedom Suit in Benguela' (2020) 17(3) Atlantic Studies 419–440; Catarina Madeira-Santos, 'Esclavage africain et traite atlantique confrontés: transactions langagières et juridiques (à propos du tribunal de mucamos dans l'Angola des XVIIe et XVIIIe siècles)' (2012) 1 Brésil(s): sciences humaines et sociales; Roquinaldo Ferreira, *Cross-Cultural Exchange in the Atlantic World: Angola and Brazil during the Era of the Slave Trade* (Cambridge: Cambridge University Press, 2012), 88–125.

compulsory labor, and nor did it effectively protect them against practices of illegal enslavement.[10]

Different institutions were in charge of hearing cases of Indigenous enslavement throughout colonial Latin America. In Portuguese jurisdictions, the *Junta das Missões* – an ecclesiastical institution – heard various cases of illegal Indigenous enslavement. In Mexico, the General Indian Court was in charge of these cases.[11] Also in Mexico, Asian slaves – *chinos* – resorted to courts in order to restrain illegal enslavement. In the majority of these cases, they put forward the claim of original free status and consequent illegal enslavement. In order to argue the illegal enslavement, they usually stated that they were enslaved by pirates, not in just wars; that they belonged to groups that could not be enslaved; and, in some cases, that they were 'Indians.'[12]

Therefore, a judicial system operated in colonial jurisdictions to hear cases pertaining to slavery and freedom. This system was characterized by the entanglement between multiple normative systems and was recognized by the enslaved population as a way to curtail illegal enslavement or to discuss the contours of slavery. The historiography on law and slavery in Latin America makes evident that enslaved and freed people throughout the continent made use of a similar set of arguments in these judicial disputes. This indicates that there was a shared legal culture in the region and that slaves and freed people were active participants constantly pushing forward legal arguments that would refute enslavement or allow them to have greater margins of autonomy.

10 Neil Whitehead, 'Indigenous Slavery in South America, 1492–1820' in *The Cambridge World History of Slavery*, eds David Eltis and Stanley Engerman (Cambridge: Cambridge University Press, 2011), vol. 3, 248–272.

11 Bombardi and Prado, 'Ações de liberdade de índias e índios escravizados'; Woodrow Borah, *Justice by Insurance: The General Indian Court of Colonial Mexico and the Legal Aides of the Half-Real* (Berkeley: University of California Press, 1983); Brian Owensby, *Empire of Law and Indian Justice in Colonial Mexico* (Stanford: Stanford University Press, 2008), 130–166; Marcia Souza e Mello, 'Desvendando outras Franciscas: mulheres cativas e as ações de liberdade na Amazônia colonial portuguesa' (2005) 13(1) Portuguese Studies Review 1–16; Nancy Van Deusen, *Global Indios: The Indigenous Struggle for Justice in Sixteenth-Century Spain* (Durham: Duke University Press, 2015), 125–168.

12 Chino slavery was prohibited in the 1670s. Tatiana Seijas, *Asian Slaves in Colonial Mexico: From Chinos to Indians* (Cambridge: Cambridge University Press, 2014), 221–227.

2 Becoming an Enslaved Person: The Role of Possession

The documents generated by litigation over slavery and freedom highlight many aspects of enslavement practices and how legal status was determined in Latin America. In this sense, recent scholarship has pointed out the central role that possession had in determining if someone was an enslaved person or not.

In Iberian jurisdictions, both canon law and more broadly the *ius commune* aimed at guaranteeing the continuance of status quo.[13] Therefore, the legal system tended to work by favoring restoration and protection of situations as they were before the 'disruption' caused by conflict and litigation even if that meant a judicial decision contrary to the letter of the law. During the early modern period, the letter of the law had no value *per se* – as in current liberal legal systems – but could be dismissed for the sake of maintaining social stability.

Possession was one of the main legal institutions of this maintenance of status quo mechanism. If someone exercised possession over something for a given period of time and without contestation, the person would acquire rights (usually *dominium*) over that thing. In Iberian legal systems, status was a 'thing' and therefore could be acquired by the exercise of possession. To exercise possession over a freedom-related status was to live 'as a free person' or 'as an enslaved person.' The Spanish *Siete Partidas* established that a servant would acquire freedom by living as a free person in good faith for ten years in the region where his master lived or for twenty years in another region.[14] The Portuguese *Ordenações Filipinas*, in turn, did not explicitly refer to the possibility of acquiring freedom by living as a free person, through prescription. Nevertheless, doctrinal texts and judicial decisions systematically enforced this norm in both colonial and metropolitan jurisdictions.[15]

13 *The ius commune* was a legal system mainly grounded on doctrinal texts that operated in secular jurisdictions roughly between the eleventh and the nineteenth centuries. Tamar Herzog, *A Short History of European Law: The Last Two and a Half Millennia* (Cambridge: Harvard University Press, 2019).

14 *Las Siete Partidas del Rey Don Alfonso el Sabio* (Madrid: Imprenta Real, 1807), 2, 744–745; *Las Siete Partidas*, 3, 124. On the possibility of acquiring freedom by living as a free person in early modern Valencia, see Debra Blumenthal, *Enemies and Familiars: Slavery and Mastery in Fifteenth-Century Valencia* (Ithaca: Cornell University Press, 2009), 239–265. On Louisiana, see Vernon Palmer, *Through the Codes Darkly: Slave Law and Civil Law in Louisiana* (Clark: Lawbook Exchange, 2012), 135–149.

15 Mariana Dias Paes, 'Sobre origens, continuidades e criações: a posse da liberdade nos decisionistas portugueses (sécs. XVI–XVIII) e no direito da escravidão (séc. XIX)' in *Actas del XIX Congreso del Instituto Internacional de História del Derecho Indiano*, ed. Thomas Duve (Madrid: Editorial Dykinson, 2017), vol. 2, 1379–1406.

What was perceived as 'to live as a free person' or 'to live as a slave' varied in time and according to geographical spaces, but it was usually related to control over one's labor, the way one dressed, and the place one occupied in a household. To determine the way someone lived, community recognition was fundamental. In Latin America colonial societies and even into the nineteenth century, titles did not necessarily play an important role in judicial litigation. In court cases, it was usually more important to have favorable witnesses' testimonies than to be able to prove a root of title. Therefore, the way the community perceived someone could define the adjudication of status.[16]

Racialized perceptions played a central role in community recognition of someone as free or slave. For example, in eighteenth-century São Paulo, the grounds of some freedom suits were the Indigenous ancestry of litigants. The plaintiffs claimed that they were held 'as if they were slaves' despite the fact that their ancestors were Indigenous and therefore naturally free. Witnesses were summoned to declare if the plaintiffs were slaves or free persons, that is if they were Indigenous or not. Some of these witnesses referred to the type of hair of the plaintiffs in order to assert if they were Indigenous or not.[17]

Theoretically, freedom could be acquired through prescription, but a person could not be enslaved through this process. In practice, however, court cases show that many people in Latin America became slaves by their continued treatment as slaves. Since the way someone lived and was perceived by the community was determinant in status adjudication, if a putative master was able to hold someone 'as a slave' for some time, he had greater chances of success in a lawsuit. This scenario was relatively common with children. If a newborn was baptized as a slave and held as such for many years, freedom was difficult to establish before a judge. Proof of legitimate ownership was not necessary to baptize someone as a slave. The declaration of the putative master was sufficient.[18]

---

16 Mariana Dias Paes, *Esclavos y tierras entre posesión y títulos: la construcción social del derecho de propiedad en Brasil (siglo XIX)* (Frankfurt am Main: Max Planck Institute for Legal History and Legal Theory, 2021); Pinheiro, *Em defesa da liberdade*; Rebecca Scott, 'Social Facts, Legal Fictions, and the Attribution of Slave Status: The Puzzle of Prescription' (2017) 35(1) Law and History Review.

17 Felipe Garcia Oliveira, *Cultura jurídica da liberdade: autos cíveis e petições envolvendo escravos e forros na cidade de São Paulo, século XVIII*, Master's thesis (São Paulo: Universidade Federal de São Paulo, 2020), 96–106. On race issues in litigation involving enslaved persons, see Hebe Mattos, *Das cores do silêncio: os significados da liberdade no sudeste escravista, Brasil, século XIX* (Rio de Janeiro: Nova Fronteira, 1998).

18 Dias Paes, *Esclavos y tierras entre posesión y títulos*.

The case of Cuba in the context of the Haitian diaspora was paradigmatic for how practices of registration and administration could formalize illegal enslavement. Slavery was abolished in Saint-Domingue in 1794. Due to conflicts related to the Haitian Revolution, many people fled to Cuba during the end of the eighteenth century and the beginning of the nineteenth century. Since slavery was totally abolished in Saint-Domingue in 1794, all people that fled the country after this date were legally free. Slavery however was a highly consolidated institution in Cuba at this time. When refugees arrived at the island, passenger lists showed that some people were enrolled within very ambiguous categories, such as *domestique* and *criado*. Their classification in ambiguous categories in tandem with their treatment as 'living as slave' ended up turning them into 'slaves' to Spanish authorities.[19]

Thus, both in colonial and in post-independence jurisdictions, possession and community recognition were at the core of judicial litigation over slave and free status. This scenario was rendered even more complex for statuses that ranged between slavery and freedom.

3 Between Slavery and Freedom

Over the last decades, research on manumission practices throughout Latin America shows that freedom was often achieved through self purchase or under conditional provisions.[20] Either situation put the manumitted in a legal grey area concerning their status. Self purchase was often made in installments. While the full value was not yet paid, it was not legally clear if the person was enslaved or freed. In Brazil, for example, some jurists referred to persons who had part of their freedom as 'half-slaves' or 'half-freed.'[21] Also, some slaves

---

19 Scott, 'Paper Thin.'

20 Christine Hünefeldt, *Paying the Price of Freedom: Family and Labor among Lima's Slaves, 1800–1854* (Berkeley: University of California Press, 1994); Lyman Johnson, 'Manumission in Colonial Buenos Aires, 1776–1810' (1979) 59(2) Hispanic American Historical Review 258–279; Frank Proctor III, 'Gender and the Manumission of Slaves in New Spain' (2006) 86(2) Hispanic American Historical Review 309–336; Robert Slenes, *The Demography and Economics of Brazilian Slavery (1850–1888)*, PhD thesis (Stanford: Stanford University, 1976); Carlos Eduardo Valencia Villa, *Produzindo alforrias no Rio de Janeiro no século XIX*, Master's thesis (Rio de Janeiro: Universidade Federal do Rio de Janeiro, 2008); Sarah Washbrook, 'Independence for Those without Freedom: Slavery and Manumission in Mérida, Venezuela, 1810–1854' (2018) Slavery & Abolition 708–730.

21 Cantisano and Dias Paes, 'Legal Reasoning in a Slave Society.'

borrowed money to pay for their manumission and signed contracts agreeing to work without payment to the lender for a certain period of time.[22]

In Cuba, *coartación* and *papel de venta* were widespread practices. *Coartación* was the establishment of the manumission price, which the slave would pay in installments. Once fixed, the master could not alter this value. *Papel de venta* was the permit the slave received to find another master. It was usually issued in cases of maltreatment and abuse. *Coartados* expected to have control over their labor and time once they had started to pay the installments for their freedom. Therefore, they often did not consider themselves as 'proper slaves.' Some jurists also did not consider the *coartados* as slaves in a strict sense and even defended that they had the right to have *papel de venta* even without the agreement of their masters. The masters on the other hand tried to assert the enslaved condition of *coartados* and fought against the recognition of any rights to them, including the issuance of *papel de venta* without consent.[23] In colonial Portuguese America, *coartados* were constantly under the risk of re-enslavement and discussions of their legal status were often the object of judicial litigation.[24]

Another group of persons whose legal status was in between slavery and freedom were the *statu-liberi*, that is conditionally manumitted slaves. In Brazil, for instance, passionate legal debates over the legal status of children from conditionally manumitted mothers arose during the nineteenth century. Were children born while their mothers were still in a state of conditional freedom slaves, free, or also conditionally manumitted? In case the children were also *statu-liberi*, what would be the terms of conditions imposed on them? These and other related legal questions were discussed among Brazilian jurists and addressed by *statu-liberi* themselves in court cases, without ever achieving consensus. As *coartados*, *statu-liberi* in Brazil considered themselves more autonomous than 'regular' slaves, while masters fought to keep them under dependency and absolute control.[25]

---

22 Marília Ariza, *O ofício da liberdade: trabalhadores libertandos em São Paulo e Campinas (1830–1888)* (São Paulo: Alameda, 2014); Henrique Espada Lima, 'Freedom, Precariousness, and the Law: Freed Persons Contracting out their Labour in Nineteenth-Century Brazil' (2009) 54 International Review of Social History 391–416.

23 Alejandro de la Fuente, 'Slaves and the Creation of Legal Rights in Cuba: Coartación and Papel' (2007) 87 Hispanic American Historical Review 659–692.

24 Pinheiro, *Em defesa da liberdade*.

25 Mariana Dias Paes, *Escravidão e direito: o estatuto jurídico dos escravos no Brasil oitocentista, 1860–1888* (São Paulo: Alameda, 2019), 283–306; Eduardo Spiller Pena, *Pajens da casa imperial: jurisconsultos, escravidão e a Lei de 1871* (Campinas: Editora da Unicamp, 2001).

It is noteworthy that conditional manumissions generated expectations in slaves. Archives throughout Latin America are filled with court cases initiated because either masters or their heirs did not fulfill conditionally manumitted slaves' expectations of freedom and autonomy. It is true that conditional manumissions – commonly issued in testaments – were a mechanism of social control: as long as the slave had the promise that someday he would be freed, it was expected that he attended his master's expectations for his behavior, obedience, and labor. However, slaves themselves also had their own understandings of what these promises meant and what their legal consequences were. It was not uncommon that conditionally manumitted slaves considered themselves with a status not properly as enslaved persons and acted in accordance with this assumption. These two sets of expectations concerning the social and legal effects of a conditional manumission very often collided. Slaves expected that once they fulfilled the condition, masters or their heirs would keep their promise. However, court cases show that the revocation or disregard of manumission agreements was not uncommon.[26]

A common argument put forward in court cases by conditionally manumitted slaves or by slaves that had received testamentary manumissions was that freedom was their master's will and therefore should be enforced by courts. The master's will was one of the grounds of Latin American legal systems. During the early modern period, both Iberian canon law and the *ius commune* assumed that society should be composed of households led by the *pater familias*, the head of the household, who would govern women, children, slaves, and free dependents with severity but also 'benevolence.' According to this ideological perspective, the head of the household had the last say in issues pertaining to people under his control and therefore his will should not be disregarded, not even by judicial authority.[27] During the nineteenth century, constitutional national states did not break with this ideology. With the rise of liberal discourses among jurists, the will of the 'subject of rights' acquired centrality in Latin American legal systems. Since in most cases the full subject

26 Adriana Chira, 'Affective Debts: Manumission by Grace and the Making of Gradual Emancipation Laws in Cuba 1817–68' (2018) 36(1) Law and History Review 1–33; Michelle McKinley, 'Till Death Do Us Part: Testamentary Manumission in Seventeenth-Century Lima, Peru' (2012) 33(3) Slavery & Abolition 381–401; Edgardo Pérez Morales, 'Manumission on the Land: Slaves, Masters, and Magistrates in Eighteenth-Century Mompox (Colombia)' (2017) 35(2) Law and History Review 511–543.

27 Romina Zamora, *Casa poblada y buen gobierno: oeconomia católica y servicio personal en San Miguel de Tucumán (siglo XVIII)* (Buenos Aires: Prometeo Libros, 2017).

of rights was also master of slaves, civil law doctrine and civil codes built a legal framework that would protect this will as fiercely as possible.[28]

In daily life, slaves and free dependents developed strategies to navigate this world where masters assumed their wills were absolute and should not be disrespected.[29] But even when they were successful in diverging from the master's will, when it came to judicial matters the most secure strategy was actually to reaffirm this ideology and legal principle. In order to have adjudication of free status, enslaved persons claimed in court that they had always acted according to their master's will, fulfilled the conditions the masters established, and therefore should be rewarded with freedom.[30]

4 Litigating the Contours of Slavery: Family and Masters' Mistreatment

Enslaved persons did not go to court exclusively to claim freedom but also to discuss other legal issues, especially the ones related to family and masters' maltreatment. From a legal point of view, it was possible for enslaved persons to resort to courts due to their condition of 'miserable persons,' that is, vulnerable persons who due to this condition were entitled to petition directly to the king. Throughout the centuries, both the Spanish and the Portuguese crowns created a series of offices in charge of representing these persons in courts such as the *abogado de pobres*, *sindico procurador*, *curador*, and *defensores de pobres*.[31] Nevertheless, there were also cases where enslaved persons resorted to courts by themselves. Discussions of legal matters other than freedom could take place in both secular and ecclesiastical jurisdictions.[32]

28 Dias Paes, *Escravidão e direito*, 239–263.

29 Sidney Chalhoub, *Machado de Assis, historiador* (São Paulo: Companhia das Letras, 2003).

30 Dias Paes, *Escravidão e direito*, 239–263.

31 Carlos Aguirre, *Agentes de su propia libertad: los esclavos de Lima y la desintegración de la esclavitud, 1821–1854* (Lima: Fondo Editorial de la Pontificia Universidad Católica del Perú, 1993), 181–242; Dias Paes, *Escravidão e direito*, 69–78; Magdalena Díaz Hernández, 'Esclavos y la imagen de la justicia paternalista del rey y del virrey en el Veracruz colonial' (2015) Nuevo Mundo Mundos Nuevos; Fernanda Domingos Pinheiro, 'Transformações de uma prática contenciosa: as ações de liberdade produzidas em Mariana (1750–69 e 1850–69)' 17(1) (2011) Locus: revista de história 253–271; Lucas Rebagliati, *Pobreza, caridad y justicia en Buenos Aires: los defensores de pobres (1776–1821)*, PhD thesis (Buenos Aires: Universidad de Buenos Aires, 2015).

32 Brian Owensby, 'How Juan and Leonor Won Their Freedom: Litigation and Liberty in Seventeenth-Century Mexico' 85(1) (2005) Hispanic American Historical Review 39–79.

Family issues were commonly heard by ecclesiastical courts. Despite the violence of slavery, enslaved persons formed families.[33] These slave families, however, were always under the threat of future sales that could separate loved ones. As slave marriages were allowed under canon law and enslaved couples acquired marital rights, they sometimes argued before ecclesiastical courts that sales could not separate them.[34]

Courts also heard separation and divorce cases involving enslaved persons. Early modern canon law allowed separation and even divorce in some circumstances, as, for example, the husband's maltreatment and abuse. In these cases, racial and gender discourses profoundly shaped parties' arguments. In order to get a favorable decision, it was paramount for women to show that they were honorable and behaved according to female patterns of Catholic behavior. However, many enslaved women did not live a reclusive home life, but were active economic agents in markets, plazas, and other public spaces. Moreover, racial discourses considered black women 'naturally' immoral. Thus, enslaved women who filed lawsuits for separation needed to overcome racial and gender discourses to convince judges that they were honorable women and therefore did not 'deserve' the violent treatment of their husbands.[35]

As women resorted to courts against their husbands' mistreatment, enslaved persons filed suits against their masters on the basis of violence and abuse. Latin American legal systems determined that masters should guarantee essential food, clothing, and health care for their slaves. The extent to which masters complied with these obligations varied greatly. Slaves' expectations of masters' obligations towards them were also very diversified. For example, in some cases, slaves expected that they would receive the means to perform dutifully religious ceremonies.[36] Also, land usage rights, days free of work, and the possibility to save some money (*pecúlio*) were relatively common slaves' expectations.[37]

---

33 Robert Slenes Wayne, *Na senzala, uma flor: esperanças e recordações na formação da família escrava (Brasil, Sudeste, século XIX)* (Campinas: Editora da Unicamp, 2011); Cowling, *Conceiving Freedom*.

34 Dias Paes, *Escravidão e direito*, 133–148; McKinley, *Fractional Freedoms*, 74–100; Alexander Wisnoski III, 'No es justo que la ley de matrimonio se quebrante por la ley de servidumbre: esclavos casados y sus amos en Lima, siglos XVI-XVII' (2014) 27 Historia y Cultura 23–28.

35 Juliana Barreto Farias, 'Diz a preta mina: cores e categorias sociais nos processos de divórcio abertos por africanas ocidentais, Rio de Janeiro, século XIX' (2018) 44(3) Estudos Ibero-Americanos 470–483.

36 Pérez Morales, 'Manumission on the Land.'

37 Maria Helena Machado, 'Em torno da autonomia escrava: uma nova direção para a história social da escravidão' (1988) 8(16) Revista Brasileira de História 143–160.

Sometimes, slaves sought the intervention of courts or other government officials to restrain abuses of their masters or to force their masters to comply with legal obligations. These cases shed light on slaves' own perceptions of what slavery should be, of what was legally sanctioned, and of what was not in a slave–master relationship.[38] If sometimes slaves were successful in getting judges and government officials to restrain masters' maltreatment, in other cases the abuse and violence they suffered were so massive, that slaves resorted to drastic violence, such as infanticide and murder. In some other cases, the goal was not necessarily to achieve freedom, but to advance better working and living conditions under enslavement.[39]

At times, government authorities issued regulation that sought to curtail masters' abuse. A paradigmatic example is the 1789 *Real Cédula* on the treatment of slaves. In addition to reinforcing that masters should provide their slaves with reasonable food and clothing, it determined that excessive punishment could result in the forcible sale of the slave and criminal prosecution. More importantly, this legislation shifted the initiative to contest judicially masters' abuse from slaves themselves to government officials, such as the *síndicos*. Masters perceived this as an intrusion of government into domestic matters and tried to overthrow this regulation, but without much success.[40]

The tension between what masters considered as their governance prerogatives and government interference in master–slave relations gained new contours during the nineteenth century.

5 Enslaved Persons, Abolitionism, and the Making of National States

Latin American independence reshaped jurisdictional spaces inside the region. Also, different rising national states conducted gradual emancipation policies that greatly differed in their timing and scope spawning legal debates and judicial litigation across Latin American borders. Brazil and Cuba did

38 Alejandro de la Fuente, 'Su único derecho: los esclavos y la ley' (2004) 4 Revista Debate y Perspectivas 7–21.

39 Marcela Echeverri, 'Enraged to the Limit of Despair: Infanticide and Slave Judicial Strategies in Barbacoas, 1788–98' (2009) 30(3) Slavery & Abolition 403–426; Ricardo Pirola, 'Escravos e rebeldes na justiça imperial: dois casos de assassinatos senhoriais em Capos dos Goytacazes (RJ), 1873' (2015) 51 Afro-Ásia 41–80. For the impact of these issues on the realm of criminal law, see Silvia Hunold Lara, *Campos da violência: escravos e senhores na Capitania do Rio de Janeiro, 1750–1808* (Rio de Janeiro: Paz e Terra, 1988).

40 De la Fuente, 'Slaves and the Creation of Legal Rights'; Echeverri, 'Enraged to the Limit of Despair.'

not abolish slavery until the end of the nineteenth century. On the contrary, regions of these jurisdictions experienced the expansion of slave labor propelled by a boom of plantation economies. This economic boom took place alongside the enactment of various pieces of legislation prohibiting the transatlantic slave trade and posing a series of questions concerning the endurance of slave labor.[41] Independent Latin American republics, on the other hand, had an ambiguous relation with the use of antislavery discourses in their nation-building processes and the actual legal policies they conducted towards abolishing slave labor.[42] The entanglement between the making of new national states, the promulgation of gradual emancipation legislation, the rise of abolitionist discourses, and the expansion of slavery in certain regions created a set of new legal issues and judicial disputes.

Enslaved people actively engaged in various processes of independence that erupted in Latin America. In addition to participation in armed conflicts, in groups for or against independence or republicanism, enslaved persons also formulated their own political and legal ideas concerning the shape and outcomes of independence.[43] Nevertheless, the strong freedom rhetoric and even the use of the idea of slavery to characterize the colonial relationship within independence movements did not result in immediate abolition policies but mostly in programs of gradual emancipation.[44]

In recent years, scholarship on the Argentinian Free Womb Law (1813) has shed light on the legal issues posed by this legislation concerning legal status and also highlighted the gendered dimension of these questions. This law declared that after January 31 all children born from enslaved mothers were free. However, legal debates and judicial litigation around the Free Womb Law consolidated a more restrictive legal interpretation that considered these children as 'freed' (*liberto*) rather than 'free.' This was not merely a change in

41 Rafael de Bivar Marquese and Dale Tomich, 'O Vale do Paraíba escravista e a formação do mercado mundial do café no século XIX' in *O Vale do Paraíba e o Império do Brasil nos quadros da Segunda Escravidão*, eds Mariana Muaze and Ricardo Salles (Rio de Janeiro: 7 Letras, 2015), 21–56.

42 Maribel Arrelucea Barrantes and Jesús Cosamalón Aguilar, *La presencia afrodescendiente en el Perú, siglos XVI-XX* (Lima: Ministerio de Cultura, 2015), 79–149; Magdalena Candioti, 'Free Womb Law, Legal Asynchronies, and Migrations: Suing for an Enslaved Woman's Child in Nineteenth-Century Río de la Plata' (2020) 77(1) The Americas 73–99; Erika Edwards, *Hiding in Plain Sight: Black Women, the Law, and the Making of a White Argentine Republic* (Tuscaloosa: University of Alabama Press, 2020), 97–117.

43 Marcela Echeverri, *Indian and Slaves Royalists in the Age of Revolution: Reform, Revolution, and Royalism in the Northern Andes, 1780–1825* (Cambridge: Cambridge University Press, 2016).

44 Candioti, 'Free Womb Law.'

wording, but a change of legal status that put enslaved mothers' children under the patronage of their masters.[45] Since colonial times, freed and free persons did not have the same legal status. There was, for example, a widespread idea that freed persons would still maintain dependency ties with former masters. This idea had important legal effects. In Brazil, for example, freed persons' manumission could be revoked if they were 'ungrateful' towards their former masters or their heirs.[46] Therefore, in this scenario, the shift in the original category of the Argentinian Free Womb Law represented a regression in relation to slaves' former conquests towards freedom, broader autonomy, and control over their body and labor.

Categories of people in between slavery and freedom were not only created through Free Womb Laws but also by legislation that prohibited the slave trade. The first decades of the nineteenth century saw the rise of discourses against the transatlantic slave trade, and Latin American governments suffered considerable pressure from the British government to enact legislation that prohibited this commerce.[47] For example, in 1817, Spain and Britain signed a treaty that prohibited Spanish subjects from trafficking slaves along the African coast north of the equator. The treaty also established that Spanish and British authorities had the right to search vessels, and bilateral courts of mixed commission had the right to judge and condemn those who illegally transported slaves. Illegally transported enslaved Africans would be put under 'apprenticeship' and be considered as liberated Africans (*emancipados*). Liberated Africans however were not legally free. Under the regime of apprenticeship, they were obliged to work and did not enjoy the same level of autonomy as free people.[48]

Throughout the first half of the nineteenth century, Brazilian and British authorities also clashed over the issue of the transatlantic slave trade. After a series of treaties between Portugal and Britain in the first decades of the

45 Candioti, 'Free Womb Law.' On the legal category of *liberto*, see also Paola Revilla Orías, 'No tengo derecho a dejarme anclar: libertos en la representación social de su libertad (La Plata, Charcas 1540–1630)' in *Historia Cultural hoy: trece entradas desde América Latina*, eds María Elisa Fernández and Víctor Brangier (Rosario: Prohistoria, 2018), 249–270.

46 Grinberg, 'Re-enslavement, Rights and Justice.'

47 David Brion Davis, *The Problem of Slavery in the Age of Revolution* (Oxford: Oxford University Press, 1999).

48 Inés Roldán de Montaud, 'The Misfortune of Liberated Africans in Colonial Cuba, 1824–76' in *Liberated Africans and the Abolition of the Slave Trade, 1807–1896*, eds Richard Anderson and Henry Lovejoy (Rochester: University of Rochester Press, 2020), 153–173; Randy Sparks, 'Gavino of the Lucumi Nation: David Turnbull and the Liberated Africans of Havana' in *Liberated Africans*, 198–209.

nineteenth century that established mixed commissions and created the legal category of liberated Africans (*africanos livres*), in 1831, the independent Brazilian government issued a law providing that all slaves that entered Brazil from then on were free. Brazilian authorities ended up making restrictive interpretations of this legislation's wording and considering these people not necessarily as 'free,' but as 'liberated Africans.' Liberated Africans were put under a system of tutelage and had to perform compulsory labor for fourteen years. They could either be assigned to private individuals into whose households they performed labor in conditions similar to that of slaves or they were sent to public works where labor conditions were no better.[49] By the mid-nineteenth century, liberated Africans were also sent to the Amazon region to work, for example, on the opening of roads.[50]

Many liberated Africans, both in Brazil and Cuba, were illegally enslaved or ended up performing compulsory labor for many more years than they were due under apprenticeship and tutelage systems. The subsequent enslavement process that liberated Africans underwent often followed the 'live as slave' pattern.[51] Moreover, legislation that prohibited the importation of slaves to these territories did not efficiently suppress the transatlantic slave trade.[52] Neither did it prevent free people of color living in Latin American republics being illegally enslaved within slavery jurisdictions such as Cuba and Brazil.

The case of the Brazilian southern border is paradigmatic. Uruguay abolished slavery in the 1840s in the context of a civil war. In order to gain freedom, some Brazilian slaves crossed the border to Uruguay generating many diplomatic issues between the two nations. Moreover, there were many estates and ranches in this region and slaves owned by Brazilians were constantly crossing the border back and forth with cattle. According to the law of 1831, once they stepped out of Brazil, they could not re-enter the country as slaves. Some slaves became aware of this norm and resorted to courts to claim their freedom. In addition, there were frequent cases of kidnapping of free people of color in 'free' jurisdictions in order to take and sell them as slaves in Brazil.[53]

---

49 Beatriz Mamigonian, *Africanos livres: a abolição do tráfico de escravos no Brasil* (São Paulo: Companhia das Letras, 2017).

50 Patrícia Sampaio, 'Nos confins do Império: diversidade e etnicidade no mundo do trabalho na Amazônia do século XIX' in *Histórias da escravidão e do pós-abolição para escolas*, ed. Giovana Xavier (Belo Horizonte: Fino Traço, 2015), 179–194.

51 Mamigonian, *Africanos livres*; Sparks, 'Gavino of the Lucumi Nation.'

52 For data on the transatlantic slave trade during the nineteenth century, see https://www.slavevoyages.org/.

53 Rachel da Silveira Caé and Keila Grinberg 'Escravidão, fronteira e relações diplomáticas Brasil-Uruguai (1840–1860)' (2010) 14 Africana Studia 275–285; Keila Grinberg, 'Illegal

Illegal enslavement was often legitimized by courts.[54] Furthermore, in Brazil, the mandatory registration of slaves established by the Free Womb Law also worked in this direction. The Free Womb Law of 1871 determined that masters should register their slaves, otherwise they would be declared free. To register a slave, however, one did not need to prove ownership. Self-declaration could be the only basis for a slave registration. In addition to false declaration, some masters also lied about the age of their slaves to hide the fact that they were imported after the prohibition of the transatlantic slave trade in 1831. In the 1880s, however, Brazilian courts saw a steady flow of cases denouncing these practices. Many cases using false registration as proof of illegal slave trade were put forward by abolitionist lawyers.[55]

The intense legal debates and judicial disputes that arose in the context of gradual emancipation legislation and prohibition of the slave trade throughout Latin America show that the making of national states in the region was deeply entangled with slavery and its legacy.[56] The consolidation of Latin American national states happened in a framework of constant negotiation between masters and politicians pressured by slaves' demands and litigation. On the one hand, gradual emancipation legislation was greatly an outcome of decades-long litigation of enslaved people.[57] On the other hand, recent scholarship shows that after their enactment, these laws often underwent a process of restrictive interpretation that actually restrained slaves' initial gains. Moreover, government and judicial officials could not avoid – and often

Enslavement, International Relations, and International Law on the Southern Border of Brazil' (2016) 35(1) Law and History Review 31–52.

54 Dias Paes, *Esclavos y tierras entre posesión y títulos*; Ariana Espíndola, *Papéis da escravidão: a matrícula especial de escravos (1871)*, PhD dissertation (Santa Catarina: Universidade Federal de Santa Catarina, 2016); Scott, 'Social Facts, Legal Fictions.'

55 Beatriz Mamigonian, 'O direito de ser africano livre: os escravos e as interpretações da Lei de 1831' in *Direitos e justiças no Brasil: ensaios de história social*, eds Silvia Hunold Lara and Joseli Maria Nunes Mendonça (Campinas: Editora da Unicamp, 2006), 129–160; Beatriz Mamigonian, 'O Estado nacional e a instabilidade da propriedade escrava: a Lei de 1831 e a matrícula dos escravos de 1872' (2011) 2 Almanack 20–37.

56 Márcia Berbel, Rafael Marquese and Tâmis Parron, *Slavery and Politics: Brazil and Cuba, 1790–1850* (Albuquerque: University of New Mexico Press, 2016); Tâmis Parron, *A política da escravidão no Império do Brasil (1826–1865)* (Rio de Janeiro: Civilização Brasileira, 2011).

57 Elciene Azevedo, *O direito dos escravos: lutas jurídicas e abolicionismo na província de São Paulo* (Campinas: Editora da Unicamp, 2010); Chalhoub, *Visões da liberdade*; Chira, 'Affective Debts'; Keila Grinberg, *A Black Jurist in a Slave Society: Antonio Pereira Rebouças and the Trials of Brazilian Citizenship* (Chapel Hill: University of North Carolina Press, 2019); Joseli Maria Nunes Mendonça, *Entre a mão e os anéis: a lei de 1885 e os caminhos da abolição no Brasil* (Campinas: Editora da Unicamp, 2008); Pena, *Pajens da casa imperial.*

contributed to – the enslavement of these people or their subjection to life conditions analogous to slavery.[58]

6 Gendered Dimensions of Slavery and Freedom

It is noteworthy how long it took for gender perspectives to make their way into the study of law and slavery, especially considering the long-known link between gender and manumission rates in Latin America.[59] Recent years, however, have seen a boom of research on law and slavery that takes seriously the gendered dimensions of slavery and freedom.

Since colonial times, intimacy and affection played a central role in framing enslaved women's possibilities of manumission, their life conditions under slavery, and the extent of their freedom and autonomy after manumission. Care work was commonly performed by enslaved women and strongly shaped their possibilities of acquiring freedom. Testaments with provisions that freed those slaves who took care of their masters during their last years were common.[60] Moreover, domestic slavery created an 'emotional economy' that allowed the endurance of dependency ties even after manumission, building the grounds for situations of precariousness and contingency of freedom.[61] The role of care work in Latin American slave societies and the complex relations between enslaved women, their female owners, and household children created by this care work have been recently receiving more attention from scholars.[62]

---

58 Paulina Alberto, '*Liberta* by Trade: Negotiating the Terms of Unfree Labor in Gradual Abolition Buenos Aires (1820s-30s)' (2019) 52 Journal of Social History 1–33; Candioti, 'Free Womb Law'; Grinberg and Mamigonian, 'Le crime de réduction à l'esclavage'; Mamigonian, *Africanos livres*; Paola Revilla Orías, '¡Morir antes que esclavos vivir!: República libertaria y esclavitud en Bolivia decimonónica' in *Mitos Expuestos: Falsas leyendas de Bolivia*, eds Nicholas Robins and Rosario Barahona (Cochabamba: Kipus, 2014), 219–245.

59 McKinley, *Fractional Freedoms*, 8–13.

60 McKinley, 'Till Death Do Us Part.'

61 McKinley, *Fractional Freedoms*, 244–246.

62 Camillia Cowling, 'Gendered Geographies: Motherhood, Slavery, Law, and Space in Mid-Nineteenth-Century Cuba' (2018) 27(6) Women's History Review 939–953; Camillia Cowling, Maria Helena Machado, Diana Paton, and Emily West, 'Mothering Slaves: Comparative Perspectives on Motherhood, Childlessness, and the Care of Children in Atlantic Slave Societies' (2017) 38(2) Slavery & Abolition 223–231; Mariana Dias Paes, 'Gabriela, Nineteenth-Century Rio Grande do Sul (Brazil)' in *As If She Were Free: A Collective Biography of Women and Emancipation in the Americas*, eds Erica Ball, Tatiana Seijas, and Terri Snyder (Cambridge: Cambridge University Press, 2020), 331–343; Michelle McKinley, 'Juana de Godinez, Seventeenth-Century Lima (Peru)' in *As If She Were Free*, 110–128.

Scholarship on manumission practices, especially on testamentary and baptismal manumission, has shown that sometimes masters freed the children they had with their slaves. More often than not, however, masters sold the enslaved children they had with their female slaves. Moreover, rape and sexual abuse of enslaved women were naturalized practices among Latin American slaveowners. In Brazil for example rape or sexual abuse of enslaved women was not a criminalized practice.[63] The complicity of the criminal justice system with this kind of sexual violence is evidence that enslaved women's relationship with the law was a bodily relationship.[64]

The law of slavery was intrinsically linked to the control over enslaved women's bodies. The legal principle that enabled the reproduction of slavery in the Americas, even after the abolition of the transatlantic slave trade, was *partus sequitur ventrem*, that is the legal status of children was the same as that of their mothers. On one side, masters claimed absolute control over enslaved women's bodies as a productive and reproductive tool. On the other side, enslaved women employed different strategies to regain total or partial control over their own bodies and pushed forward legal interpretations that would broaden these possibilities either for themselves or for their children. Enslaved women knew that having greater control of their bodies meant not only guaranteeing freedom for future progeny but also the ability to move and perform certain kinds of work that would enable them to pay for their freedom or for their loved one's manumission.[65] To have control over one's body was also associated with the legal notion of possession, central to curtailing attempts of enslavement or re-enslavement.

The various Free Womb Laws enacted throughout Latin America during the nineteenth century were not able to secure the emancipation of enslaved women's children. In Argentina, for example, the Free Womb Law of 1813 declared that children born from slave women would be 'free.' However, a subsequent regulation referred to these children as 'freed' (*liberto*), tying them to their mothers' masters and enforcing the continuation of dependency ties and even coerced labor.[66] In Brazil, the Free Womb Law of 1871 spawned judicial controversies over the legal 'condition of the womb.' These debates got even more intricate when it came to conditional manumissions, cases implicating

63 Sidney Chalhoub, 'Posfácio' in *Fantina: cenas da escravidão*, ed. F.C. Duarte Badaró (São Paulo: Chão Editora, 2019), 119–175.

64 Erica Ball, Tatiana Seijas, and Terri Snyder, 'Introduction' in *As If She Were Free*, 1–24.

65 Ball, Seijas, and Snyder, *As If She Were Free*.

66 Alberto, 'Liberta by Trade'; Candioti, 'Free Womb Law.'

controversy concerning the legal status in between slavery and freedom of *statu-liberi*.[67]

These studies point out that gender played a central role in the framing of the law of slavery in Latin America. Care work, intimacy, and affection were determinants in framing the legal status of enslaved and freed women. They were also determinant in enforcing structural precariousness and contingent freedom in Latin America. The enslaved women's body was also central to many legal issues that arose in slave jurisdictions. Latin American archives abound with court cases filed by enslaved and freed women.[68] The growing engagement of scholars with these sources and the centrality that gender perspectives are acquiring in the field of law and slavery will surely produce insightful and fresh scholarship over the coming years.

7 Final Remarks

The concrete meanings of the legal category of 'slave,' who could and who could not be legally enslaved, and what it meant to be a 'slave' or a 'free person' were issues always under dispute in Latin America. Legal categories that regulated slavery and freedom were not abstract entities created by Roman law and the *ius commune* and transplanted to Latin America. They were the result of disputes and negotiations among various actors, including enslaved people themselves. This process of normative production involving enslaved and freed people significantly took place in courts. Nonetheless, enslaved people's understandings of law and justice took shape long before they resorted to courts. In the daily life of Latin American cities people formed and shared their legal understandings at plazas, markets, monasteries, churches, and inside

67 Margarita Rosa, 'Filial Freedoms, Ambiguous Wombs: *Partus Sequitur Ventrem* and the 1871 Brazilian Free Womb Law' (2020) 41(2) Slavery & Abolition 2019.

68 *Demando mi libertad: Mujeres negras y sus estrategias de resistencia en la Nueva Granada, Venezuela y Cuba, 1700–1800*, eds Carmen Luz Cosme Puntiel and Aurora Vergara Figueroa (Cali: Universidad ICESI, 2018); Carolina González Undurraga, 'En busca de la libertad: la petición judicial como estrategia política: el caso de las esclavas negras (175–1823)' in *Justicia, Poder y Sociedad en Chile: Recorridos históricos*, eds Carolina González Undurraga and Tomás Cornejo (Santiago: Ediciones Universidad Diego Portales, 2007), 57–83; Henrique Espada Lima and Fabiane Popinigis, 'Maids, Clerks, and the Shifting Landscape of Labor Relations in Rio de Janeiro, 1830s–1880s' (2017) 62 International Review of Social History 1–29; Ludmila de Souza Maia and Fernanda Domingos Pinheiro, 'Cativas do corpo, libertas pelo trabalho: casos de mulheres de cor nas fronteiras entre escravidão e liberdade (Mariana, séculos XVIII e XIX)' (2017) Cadernos Pagu 50.

households.[69] In some cases, enslaved people acquired knowledge about colonial norms and judicial systems even before they were trafficked to Latin America. Still, the impact of this Atlantic experience in the legal strategies and litigation of enslaved people in Latin America requires further study.

Enslaved people's active role in normative production happened in a context of contingent manumission and precariousness of freedom within which intimacy and gender relations were decisive. This scenario had a great impact on the strategies they adopted and on the arguments they put forward when suing for freedom or for greater levels of autonomy. Moreover, it shaped enslaved and freed people's expectations concerning the acquisition of rights and life conditions under slavery or freedom. It also played a central role in enslaved people's strategies. For example, the norm that 'to live as a free person' could grant or enforce a non-slavery situation was highly diffused in some jurisdictions and people tried to live accordingly as much as possible. Also, enslaved couples knew that marital ties could grant them some prerogatives before ecclesiastical courts. Enslaved women in turn were well aware that gender roles, intimacy, and affection pervaded legal disputes over separation and also over freedom.

In the nineteenth century, Latin American independence did not directly lead to the complete abolition of slavery. Different governments adopted diverse gradual emancipation strategies. Often these regulations created categories of people in between slavery and freedom who had their statuses subsequently constrained by legal interpretations. Moreover, the formation of Latin America nation-states sometimes happened in tandem with negotiations that safeguarded slaveholders' prerogatives and, in the case of Brazil, enabled massive illegal enslavement.

In conclusion, legal issues pertaining to enslaved humans show that law was not an abstract set of categories and institutions transported to Latin American territories by European vessels. Latin American legal systems were a result of the daily practice and routine habits of both jurists and non-jurists. Also, a grey zone of legal status in between slavery and freedom opened up possibilities to dispute the legal contours of slavery and freedom more generally. Litigation by slaves and freed people therefore played a central role in lawmaking.

---

69 See for example Bianca Premo and Yanna Yannakakis, 'A Court of Sticks and Branches: Indian Jurisdiction in Colonial Mexico and Beyond' (2019) 124 American Historical Review 28–55.

References

Aguirre, Carlos. *Agentes de su propia libertad: los esclavos de Lima y la desintegración de la esclavitud, 1821–1854*. Lima: Fondo Editorial de la Pontificia Universidad Católica del Perú, 1993.

Ball, Erica, Tatiana Seijas, and Terri Snyder. *As If She Were Free: A Collective Biography of Women and Emancipation in the Americas*. Cambridge: Cambridge University Press, 2020.

Bombardi, Fernanda Aires, and Luma Ribeiro Prado. 'Ações de liberdade de índias e índios escravizados no Estado do Maranhão e Grão-Pará, primeira metade do século XVIII.' *Brasiliana: Journal for Brazilian Studies* 5(1) (2016): 174–199.

Candioti, Magdalena. 'Free Womb Law, Legal Asynchronies, and Migrations: Suing for an Enslaved Woman's Child in Nineteenth-Century Río de la Plata.' *The Americas* 77(1) (2020): 73–99.

Chalhoub, Sidney. *Visões da liberdade: uma história das últimas décadas da escravidão na corte*. São Paulo: Companhia das Letras, 1990.

Chira, Adriana. 'Affective Debts: Manumission by Grace and the Making of Gradual Emancipation Laws in Cuba, 1817–68.' *Law and History Review* 36(1) (2018): 1–33.

Cosme Puntiel, Carmen Luz, and Aurora Vergara Figueroa, eds. *Demando mi libertad: Mujeres negras y sus estrategias de resistencia en la Nueva Granada, Venezuela y Cuba, 1700–1800*. Cali: Universidad Icesi, 2018.

Cowling, Camillia. *Conceiving Freedom: Women of Color, Gender, and the Abolition of Slavery in Havana and Rio de Janeiro*. Chapel Hill: University of North Carolina Press, 2013.

de la Fuente, Alejandro. 'Slaves and the Creation of Legal Rights in Cuba: Coartación and Papel.' *Hispanic American Historical Review* 87(4) (2007): 659–692.

Dias Paes, Mariana Armond. *Escravidão e direito: o estatuto jurídico dos escravos no Brasil oitocentista (1860–1888)*. São Paulo: Alameda, 2019.

Echeverri, Marcela. *Indian and Slave Royalists in the Age of Revolution Reform, Revolution, and Royalism in the Northern Andes, 1780–1825*. Cambridge: Cambridge University Press, 2016.

Edwards, Erika. *Hiding in Plain Sight: Black Women, the Law, and the Making of a White Argentine Republic*. Tuscaloosa: University of Alabama Press, 2020.

Farias, Juliana Barreto. 'Diz a preta mina: cores e categorias sociais nos processos de divórcio abertos por africanas ocidentais, Rio de Janeiro, século XIX.' *Estudos Ibero-Americanos* 44 (2018): 470–483.

González Undurraga, Carolina. *Esclavos y esclavas demandando justicia (Chile, 1740–1823): documentación judicial por carta de libertad y papel de venta*. Santiago de Chile: Universitaria, 2014.

Grinberg, Keila. *A Black Jurist in a Slave Society Antonio Pereira Rebouças and the Trials of Brazilian Citizenship*. Chapel Hill: University of North Carolina Press, 2019.

Lara, Silvia Hunold. *Campos da violência: escravos e senhores na Capitania do Rio de Janeiro, 1750–1808*. Rio de Janeiro: Paz e Terra, 1988.

Mamigonian, Beatriz. *Africanos livres: a abolição do tráfico de escravos no Brasil*. São Paulo: Companhia das Letras, 2017.

McKinley, Michelle. *Fractional Freedoms: Slavery, Intimacy, and Legal Mobilization in Colonial Lima, 1600–1700*. Cambridge: Cambridge University Press, 2016.

Owensby, Brian. *Empire of Law and Indian Justice in Colonial Mexico*. Stanford: Stanford University Press, 2008.

Perera Díaz, Aisnara, and María de los Ángeles Meriño Fuentes. *Estrategias de libertad: un acercamiento a las acciones legales de los esclavos en Cuba (1762–1872)*. La Habana: Editorial de Ciencias Sociales, 2015.

Pérez Morales, Edgardo. 'Manumission on the Land: Slaves, Masters, and Magistrates in Eighteenth-Century Mompox (Colombia).' *Law and History Review* 35(2) (2017): 511–543.

Pinheiro, Fernanda Domingos. *Em defesa da liberdade: libertos, coartados e livres de cor nos tribunais do Antigo Regime português (Mariana e Lisboa, 1720–1819)*. Belo Horizonte: Fino Traço Editora, 2018.

Revilla Orías, Paola. 'No tengo derecho a dejarme anclar: libertos en la representación social de su libertad (La Plata, Charcas 1540–1630).' In *Historia Cultural hoy: trece entradas desde América Latina*, edited by María Elisa Fernández and Víctor Brangier, 249–270. Rosario: Prohistoria, 2018.

Scott, Rebecca. 'Paper Thin: Freedom and Re-enslavement in the Diaspora of the Haitian Revolution.' *Law and History Review* 29(4) (2011): 1061–1087.

Seijas, Tatiana. *Asian Slaves in Colonial Mexico: from Chinos to Indians*. Cambridge: Cambridge University Press, 2014.

CHAPTER 11

Women

Alex Wisnoski

1 Introduction

This chapter seeks to provide a meaningful guide to important works and debates in legal history of Latin America pertaining to women, a tall task given the region's long and complex past, and the expansive scholarship produced by historians.[1] The extent of that scholarship is dictated by how one conceives of and defines legal history. This chapter looks through a wide lens and includes women's legal status and their legal activism with considerable emphasis on the latter. Important shifts in the legal system are essential to the region's historical process. Through these legal shifts the scholarship has investigated how the law viewed women, how they engaged with the law, how they avoided it, and how their actions and activism shaped the law.

The early modern and modern legal systems contained their own complexities and contradictions. Even separating modern and colonial legal histories is not a perfect distinction, as continuities certainly crossed the chronological divide from Spanish Empire to independent states and change could be at once regressive and progressive. The organization and application of the law, however, was in many ways fundamentally altered with the birth of the nation. In tracking through both eras, this chapter will give attention to important legal changes and to themes that have most occupied legal historians' attention. Before a more nuanced discussion of scholarship, this chapter opens with a brief overview of the general chronology and the structures at work.

In the earliest years after 1492, legal regimes of Indigenous communities were fracturing and weakening, though often not disappearing altogether. The

1 For comparative or cumulative works, see Kathryn Sloan, 'Women, Law and Crime' in *Women's Roles in Latin America and the Caribbean* (Santa Barbara: ABC-CLIO, 2011); M.C. Mirow, *Latin American Law: A History of Private Law and Institutions in Latin America* (Austin: University of Texas Press, 2004); Alcira Dueñas and Renzo Honores, 'Colonial Legal History of Peru' in *Oxford Bibliographies* (Oxford: Oxford University Press, online 2019); Elizabeth Quay Hutchison, 'Women in Modern Latin American History' in *Oxford Bibliographies* (Oxford: Oxford University Press, 2017); Nara Milanich, 'Women, Gender, and the Family in Latin America, 1820–2000' in *A Companion to Latin American History*, ed. Thomas Holloway (Oxford: Blackwell Publishing, 2008).

 | DOI:10.1163/9789004436091_013

gendered collision of Indigenous and Iberian cultures would be manifest in the legal changes enacted by colonialism. From the moment of encounter and conquest, the legal regime of the Spanish and Portuguese Empires affected women differently from men and affected women differently from each other. The law categorized women, noting those that were Spanish, Indigenous, African, or mixed-race; those that were elite, honorable; free or enslaved; adult or child; religious or lay; married, single, or widowed.

In the aftermath of encounter and conquest, as both civil and ecclesiastical officials were appointed and courts convened, the colonial labyrinth took more formal shape. This formation was particularly the case in the waning years of the sixteenth century. The mere fact that there were distinct legal regimes of the church and state ensured that no single 'law' dominated the region. The ecclesiastical tribunal and the *audiencia*, both its civil and criminal divisions, overlapped significantly leading to both jurisdictional shopping and territorialism among jurists. Adding to the complexity was the overall decentralized nature of the Spanish American legal system that permitted and even encouraged appeals to decisions and challenges to laws. In both venues, litigation was permitted to be initiated by the court's prosecutor or by litigating parties; policing came from both the community and the court. The Inquisitional courts, which only adjudicated *de oficio*, provided yet another legal realm that affected the lives of colonial residents.

Broadly speaking, patriarchal laws dominated Spanish jurisprudence in the early colonial period. The same could be said for the ecclesiastical jurisprudence, and yet this arena gave women legal agency on a scale not seen in the secular courts. The ecclesiastical system provided more protections for women and made more space for them to litigate. Scholars have pointed consistently to the ways that the ecclesiastical courts served their interests and valued their legal personhood in ways that early modern secular legal courts did not. Part of the reason for the clear distinction was the theological underpinnings at work in these Catholic courts, and their concern with the souls of women and men alike. The secular courts, whose focus was the order of the kingdom and the ambitions of the monarchs, did not envision many shared legal spaces for men and women. Given this contrasting logic within the systems, scholars of women and the law have dedicated significant attention to the ecclesiastical legal realm.

Much of the scholarship sees more continuity than change in the legal status and activity of women in the early and middle colonial periods. Within these studies, many scholars demonstrated that women moved within and outside of these systems to advocate for their interests in spite of the prejudices inherent in the institutions and wider society. Women asserted their rights in marriage choice and attempts at marriage separation, as well as utilizing inheritance laws and norms. Scholars have also concluded that legal agency and subjecthood was not limited to elite women, and that marginalized women of lower racial statuses adeptly navigated these legal regimes. For instance, enslaved women, married or divorced, fought for reunification with their families. Indigenous women, in turn, fought for traditional rights and negotiated within the Spanish legal system.

Modest changes in colonial legal regimes occurred during the first two centuries, but most scholarship points to the mid-eighteenth century, coinciding with the Bourbon and Pombaline reforms and adoption of Enlightenment ideology in the legal realm, as the point of starkest change. Just as the monarchs were seeking to retake power and resources from local authorities, the power of familial patriarchs was growing, demonstrated most clearly in the increasing emphasis on parental consent for marriage.

If the eighteenth-century reforms brought legal changes for women, then the independence movements and nation-building processes of the nineteenth century intensified changes, though not always in ways beneficial to women. The instability of legal regimes in the wars and immediate aftermath had consequences for women, as did the evolution of liberal republics, with their dedication to private property and individualism. Family law, property law, and the norms concerning citizenship underwent changes, and women across all statuses continued to negotiate within legal systems in whose construction they had little direct say.

Scholars were skeptical of the way that progressive independent states actually served to benefit women. Historians have shown that 'liberal' changes brought by nineteenth-century politics did not always result in legal empowerment for women. As claims to citizenship and voting rights remained out of their reach, their legal status within their own homes in some ways decreased. Patriarchal claims over women, in some instances, became more pervasive. The decline in influence and direct power of the church and Indigenous communities, relatedly, had a decidedly negative impact on the place of women before the law. Whereas during the colonial era ecclesiastical and native legal prescription and policing oversaw domestic spaces, the home in the early national period fell under the purvey of household patriarchs. That changed by the late nineteenth century, when 'mediation of kinship conflict had moved from the priest's quarters and ecclesiastical tribunal to the courthouse and police station.'[2]

2 Sueann Caulfield, Sarah Chambers, and Lara Putnam, eds, *Honor, Status and the Law in Modern Latin America* (Durham: Duke University Press, 2005), 11.

As secular law gradually replaced the pluralism that defined the colonial period, women fought for changes to the legal regime. Many of these changes were rooted in undermining the patriarchal norms that seemed to dictate much of law's displacement of women. That was a multifaceted fight, and chronologies did not always align across the region. Legal historians have traced changes to citizenship and voting rights, property law, labor law, and family law vis-à-vis women. As they have done so, they have considered the role women had in manifesting these changes and the extent to which genuine progress accompanied the more 'modern' or 'progressive' era.

2 Colonial Period

2.1 *Gender and New World Marriages*

The colonial era has been viewed as a gendered collision in which cultural ideas about women, and thus their treatment by and acceptable engagement with the law, varied between Indigenous communities, Iberians, and Africans.[3] Indigenous views of gender parallelism and gender complementarity were able to endure throughout the colonial period even as European hegemony set in.[4] Marriage was a foundational legal tactic in enforcing colonial control and reproducing Iberian norms in the New World territories. Forced non-marital sexual unions between conquistadors and Indigenous women were common in the earliest years of conquest (though not eliminated altogether afterward), but as church officials became more common and influential, they insisted on legal unions. For Indigenous women in certain areas of the Americas polygamous marriage was the norm. As the Spanish became more populous and asserted their authority, they rejected such unions, sought to whittle down the polygamous family to a single husband and wife, and commit them to a legal Catholic marital pact.[5] Legal Catholic marriage joined not only Spanish spouses but included Indigenous-Iberian marriages, and later marriages that included free and enslaved Africans and mixed-race *castas*. Marriages between Iberians predating New World voyages suffered as a result of the mobility of conquest, as men continued looking for their next payday and not returning to their families. Wives, left behind in Iberia or in more established colonial

3 Karen Viera Powers, 'Andeans and Spaniards in the Contact Zone: A Gendered Collision' American Indian Quarterly 24(4) (2000): 511–536.

4 See, for example, Irene Silverblatt, *Moon Sun, and Witches: Gender Ideology and Class in Inca and Colonial Peru* (Princeton: Princeton University Press, 1987).

5 Mirow, *Latin American Law*, 57.

outposts, submitted petitions with varying success to the court to wrangle these runaway husbands, or at the very least receive some financial compensation for their absence.

This moment happened to coincide with wider Catholic discussion on the logistics and practice of marriage, spurred in whole or in part by the Counter Reformation. The key legal treatises and gatherings speaking directly to marriage, the *Siete Partidas* (thirteenth century), the *Council of Trent* (sixteenth century), and the *Leyes de Toro* (sixteenth century), provoked colonial debates on the extent of the need for a priest, witnesses, and consent of parents and party. These interpretations were not incidental, and they had grave implications for the extent to which women held power in their own marriage decisions.

Marriage was a key legal tactic for Indigenous women to assert themselves, and such marriages were made legal in 1514.[6] Marriage to a Spaniard might provide physical protection and status elevation. Scholars have even pointed to the ways that early Indigenous-Spanish marriages could serve to raise the status of these women, and more importantly, often label their children as Spaniards. Nonetheless, using marriage as a tactic could also draw on hierarchies inherent in Indigenous communities. In the Andes, Capac women maintained much of the status and political influence from Inca reign. Initially, endogamy among Capac lineage sought to maintain a coherent noble group and claims to past legitimacy and perhaps even sovereignty. As the Spanish observed the nobility of these Indigenous women, Capac women marrying Spanish men created a cross-cultural noble group that claimed legitimacy in both camps. According to Guengerich, women were active agents in creating legal marriages and, at other times, mimicking them, constantly aware of the stakes at hand.[7]

Not all unions were legal marriages, and these relationships would also bring women's lives into the courtroom. Women who had been promised marriage could litigate to compel men to follow through on their promises, especially if they had been 'deflowered.' When children were had entirely out of wedlock, women also used the courts to identify the fathers to ensure certain racial classifications beneficial to the child and to require absent fathers to provide financial support.

6 Ibid.

7 Sara Vicuña Guengerich, 'Capac Women and the Politics of Marriage in Early Colonial Peru' (2015) 24(2) Colonial Latin American Review 147–167.

2.2 *Inquisition*

The Inquisition was active in the New World in 1522, but this legal apparatus cannot be neatly categorized along the divide between church and state. It was most certainly aimed at religious ends, but the monarch's control of the institution gave the state significant influence. These cases were known for their ability to marshal communal surveillance, with many cases hinging on neighbors' testimonies. At its core, the Inquisition sought to root out heresy in all in its forms, and women frequently found themselves subject to its litigation. Not all women, however, were subject to the Holy Office, with Indigenous peoples exempted from the court beginning in 1571.[8]

What became known as witchcraft was highly gendered in the Spanish Inquisition, and women's use of special medicines, rites, and other practices drew the ire of inquisitors. In the midst of this targeting, some colonial women used such associations to assert their legal and social agency. Martha Few's *Women Who Live Evil Lives* provides a glimpse at women's assertion of political and cultural authority, the pervasiveness of patriarchy, and the Inquisition's role in policing violations of patriarchal and religious norms. Few's analysis of Inquisition records focuses on women who were sorcerers, healers, midwives, and religious leaders – all positions that established a cultural authority for these women and invited attention from the Holy Inquisition. These cases tried in inquisitorial courts sought to curb heterodoxy – the essential function of the Holy Office – but also found ways to strip away female authority established in everyday life.[9]

Seemingly devout religious women also found themselves threatened by inquisitors. Those women who were dedicated to Catholicism, but whose dedication took the form of mystics, did not conform to legal or orthodox (in this context, the two terms become synonymous) manifestations of religious fidelity. Labeled as mystics, these women often found themselves subject to inquisitorial inquiry. In the late colonial period, enlightened ideals began to invade inquisitorial litigation. Nora Jaffary describes how physicians became influential in these cases, especially in the ways that they reframed heretical behavior by women as 'hysterical.' Where these new medical professionals testified to

8 Jacqueline Holler, 'Holy Office of the Inquisition and Women' in *Religion and Society in Latin America: Interpretive Essays from Conquest to the Present*, eds Lee M. Penyak and Walter Petry (Maryknoll: Orbis, 2009).

9 Martha Few, *Women Who Live Evil Lives: Gender, Religion and the Politics of Power in Colonial Guatemala* (Austin: University of Texas Press, 2002).

mental illness, judges continued to insist on deviancy and faked miraculous encounters.[10]

Inquisitors also invested significant resources in policing bigamy. That marital separations were deliberated on by the ecclesiastical tribunal and bigamies tried by the Inquisition provide a clear example of the intersection of jurisdictions in colonial Latin America. Richard Boyer has shown how men were far more likely to be bigamists, leaving women undersupported and at times completely abandoned. While communal reporting at times brought this heterodoxy to the attention of the court, abandoned wives played a vital role in identifying their husband's deviant acts.[11]

2.3 *Law and Enslaved Women*

Enslaved women suffered multiple layers of subjugation in colonial society. By their gender, racial classification, and enslaved status, they were constrained on all sides by legal systems. Even as they bore children, the law of the womb, itself drawn from ancient Roman legal principle *partus sequitur ventrem*, ensured their offspring would likewise be enslaved.[12] Many scholarly inquiries have addressed enslaved women's abilities to navigate the institutional structures to avoid and to limit the harm of those legal precepts and assert their own agency over their lives and the lives of their family. Some historians have suggested that enslaved women were more likely to use legal rather than extralegal means to assert their agency than enslaved men.[13]

The legal parameters of testamentary manumission and *coartación* have been important subjects of scholarly concern, as the chapter on enslavement makes clear.[14] Testamentary manumission permitted owners to include in their last will and testament a directive to free their enslaved people upon the owner's death. *Coartación* allowed enslaved people to purchase their own freedom based on an agreed upon price and timeline with their owners.[15] Such

10 Nora Jaffary, *False Mystics: Deviant Orthodoxy in Colonial Mexico* (Lincoln: University of Nebraska Press, 2004).

11 Richard Boyer, 'Women, La Mala Vida, and the Politics of Marriage' in *Sexuality and Marriage in Colonial Latin America*, ed. Asunción Lavrin (Lincoln: University of Nebraska Press, 1989).

12 This was also emphasized in the *Siete Partidas*. Camilla Cowling, *Conceiving Freedom: Women of Color, Gender, and the Abolition of Slavery in Havana and Rio de Janeiro* (Chapel Hill: University of North Carolina Press, 2013).

13 Ibid., 51.

14 See, Dias Paes, 'Enslaved Humans' in this volume.

15 Later in the century, the *patronato* system became the primary process through which enslaved Cubans were gradually permitted freedom. Rebecca Scott, *Slave Emancipation*

an arrangement became a right for slaves in Cuba in 1842. In Cuba, before and after the slave code of 1842, women were more likely to pursue *coartado* status than men and more likely to be successful in such arrangements.[16] For women, testamentary manumission was a more common path to freedom, and research has begun to probe the ways that affective ties played a significant role in the choice to free an enslaved person. Whether as a wet-nurse who served in a de facto mothering role or an enslaved woman who seemed like a sister to a female owner who inherited her, these life experiences shaped uses of the law in freeing practices.[17]

Testamentary manumissions did not always occur without incident, and when freedom was called into question women used their knowledge of the law to ensure their liberty. In many cases, disputes following a death of an owner questioned whether a manumission grant was actually made in a written will or only verbally, and whether circumstances allowed for contesting such provisions. Michelle McKinley demonstrates the important ways enslaved women would litigate for the manumission they had been promised. Such legal conflicts could take many years, nine in one example cited, and would be costly for the enslaved litigant. This proved particularly tricky as during this moment the legal classification of party was in question. The formerly enslaved woman occupied a liminal space, not fully free but neither fully enslaved.[18]

Enslaved women's litigation was a somewhat common part of the colonial regime, and perhaps exceptional considering the legal agency of enslaved women in other locales. Work on marriage has shown enslaved women's ability and initiative to enter into legal Catholic marriages, at times marrying free persons. Enslaved women who were married also struggled against masters' disregard of such legal unions. Even when masters could not prevent enslaved women from getting married, they would attempt to separate spouses based on labor needs and other factors. Enslaved women demonstrated understandings of the legal logic and intricacies of the overlapping systems, and initiated court proceedings to demand reunification of the family. They at times succeeded,

---

in Cuba: The Transition to Free Labor 1860–1899 (Pittsburgh: University of Pittsburgh Press, 1985), esp. Chapter 6.

16 Cowling, *Conceiving Freedom*, 51–53.

17 Michelle A. McKinley, *Fractional Freedoms: Slavery, Intimacy, and Legal Mobilization in Colonial Lima, 1600–1700* (Cambridge, Cambridge University Press, 2016); Bianca Premo, '"As if She Were My Own": Love and Law in the Slave Society of Eighteenth-Century Peru' in *Sexuality and Slavery: Reclaiming Intimate Histories in the Americas*, eds Diana Ramey Berry and Leslie M. Harris (Athens: University of Georgia Press, 2018).

18 Michelle McKinley, 'Till Death Do Us Part: Testamentary Manumission in Seventeenth-Century Lima, Peru' (2012) 33(3) Slavery & Abolition 381–401.

but perhaps as important, showed an adeptness at navigating the legal system, working with legal professionals, and rallying witnesses to their aid. Much of this litigation took place in ecclesiastical tribunals that gave greater legal agency to enslaved men and women than did the secular courts.[19]

Trey Proctor investigates an important aspect of enslaved litigation, one in which women consider the question of gender as it relates to colonial law and practice. In *sevicia* cases from eighteenth-century Peru, Proctor finds that enslaved women protested treatment by their masters by citing that such treatment was 'alien to their sex.' Yet, the large bodies of law outlining appropriate conduct for masters and the bounds of punishment did not comment on distinctions based on sex or gender. It was not until the short-lived codes of 1789 that the Spanish Empire gave gender-specific guidelines on the treatment of slaves. Women of Lima had been making gendered claims about their treatment more than half a century earlier. Claims often centered on a labor site deemed masculine – namely the *panadería* and the *hacienda* – or that they were forced into domestic work *and* additional labor – a double burden. These gendered petitions did not often result in guilty verdicts against masters, but judges began echoing the sentiment that enslaved women should be treated appropriately according to their sex.[20]

But even in the era of abolition, women experienced the shift in ways fundamentally different from men. The Laws of the Womb meant that enslavement passed through mothers. In the early eighteenth century, several Latin American states passed a Free Womb Law that would liberate all offspring of enslaved women. Iterations of these laws in Brazil and Cuba later in the century proved particularly important legal shifts. Children would be nominally free, but the mother would remain enslaved. These free children still remained subject to some supervision by their mother's owners, placing them in an in-between space of liberation. In the aftermath of these laws, women's legal activity increased dramatically, in large part because of mothers' position as advocates for their free children. Camilla Cowling has argued that women in Brazil and Cuba used both legal and social conceptions of motherhood in claims-making for the freedom of their offspring.[21] From the first enslaved

19 Alexander Wisnoski, '"It Is Unjust for the Law of Marriage to be Broken by the Law of Slavery": Married Slaves and Their Masters in Early Colonial Lima' (2013) 25(2) Slavery & Abolition 234–252.

20 Frank Trey Proctor, '"Alien to My Sex": Enslaved Women and Their Gendered Notions of Abuse in Eighteenth-Century Lima, Peru' (2019) 31(2) Journal of Women's History 57–79.

21 Cowling, *Conceiving Freedom*.

women through the abolition period, women made use of the law despite their diminished status before it.

2.4 *Property and Commerce*

Historians have seen the dynamic of women's position before the law in colonial Latin America as contradictory. On the one hand, male domination and female subordination underpinned much of the legal structure in Spain and Spanish America, and yet the decentralization of Spanish legal tradition meant that spaces for women's legal agency could shine through, at times surpassing that of other early modern locales.

In the case of property ownership, inheritance laws mark an important legal precept. Medieval and early modern Spanish Empire dictated partible inheritance, in which all offspring received a significant share. As originally outlined in medieval *fueros*, four-fifths of the parent's property had to be distributed evenly among offspring, while the remaining one-fifth could be dealt strategically. This meant that daughters were not disenfranchised in the Iberian and Latin American world, in the same way they were in early modern European households. In light of this policy, Spanish law on inheritance has been described as both 'specific and flexible'; the terms were laid out in great detail, but the last will and testament still served to provide a counterpoint to these precepts. As Karen Graubart put it, 'Early colonial wills ... demonstrate a savviness about the legal system and a real tension between the practices of changing rural communities and new urban centers.' Indigenous women in particular made use of wills and testaments as part of what Graubart describes as a creolization, or a transculturation in which Indigenous agency in the apparatus of colonialism creates a new society inflected from all sides. Though such testamentary authorship was not altogether unique to women, their uses of it within the patriarchal structures of Latin American legal regimes stands out.[22]

Women's ability to own property and legally engage in commerce has received significant attention. How that legal activity has been conceived by historians has varied. In colonial Quito, women were active bakers, traders, and market owners, even if married women's work was fronted by her husband. In these instances, wives ran the family business and husbands represented the family in legal circumstances, as necessary. Legal parameters that

22 Karen Graubart, *With Our Labor and Sweat: Indigenous Women and the Formation of Colonial Society in Peru, 1550–1700* (Stanford: Stanford University Press, 2007), 96.

dictated men as the legal agent did not prevent women from acting as primary owners and managers.[23]

Some scholars have argued that such legal space reveals the absence of patriarchy within the Iberian legal tradition. Kimberly Gauderman, in her study on seventeenth-century Quito, highlights how this legal regime provided more space for women than the 'European model,' asserting colonial Latin America as non-patriarchal. In fact, Gauderman argues that Ecuadorian law of the late twentieth century that permitted wives to litigate against husbands 'was not an example of a society overcoming its colonial past; instead, it returns to women rights they held several hundred years earlier.'[24] While scholars continue to agree on the specific legal attributes of the judicial system, most remain unconvinced these laws and women's assertion of their own agency signify an absence of patriarchy and male domination.[25]

2.5 *Women in an Era of Reform*

Along with taxation policies and other elements of the Bourbon and Pombaline reforms, family laws changed as part of a broader shift in governing policies that some have viewed as a decentralization project. Who had a say in how marriages were made, and how this changed during the Bourbon era gained attention first with Patricia Seed's *To Love, Honor, and Obey*. In her study of marriage consent laws, and the cases that such laws produced, Seed argues that marriages in early colonial Mexico were mostly free of parental persuasion and instead created by the free will of the spouses. By the mid-eighteenth century, emphasis on free will was removed and parental oversight and approval were made necessary for marital unions. For Seed, this change illustrated an increase in patriarchal power embodied in codes and legal activity during an era of Enlightenment and nascent capitalism.

At this same moment, Enlightenment ideals were circulating within the Atlantic and supposedly setting the stage for independence rebellions to come in later decades. Bianca Premo challenges conceptions that top-down changes occurred in the intellectual and philosophical realm of the independence movements. Whereas most scholars have attributed the changes in legal regimes to the intellectual elites of the Enlightenment and the (mostly) elite

23 Jane Mangan, *Trading Roles: Gender, Ethnicity, and the Urban Economy in Colonial Potosí* (Durham: Duke University Press, 2005).

24 Kimberly Gauderman, *Women's Lives in Colonial Quito: Gender Law and the Economy in Spanish America* (Austin: University of Texas Press, 2003), XII.

25 See most recently Allyson Poska, 'The Case for Agentic Gender Norms for Women in Early Modern Europe' (2018) 30(2) Gender & History 354–365.

rebel leaders of the wars for independence, Premo sees a shift happening on the ground, so to speak. In her comparative study of Mexico, Peru, and Spain, she demonstrates that so-called Enlightenment changes occurred within the courtroom and notary office. In several core case studies, she sees women's petitions as embodying and perhaps setting on track what would become cornerstone ideals of the *ilustrados* and others seeking 'modern' conceptions of justice.[26]

Uribe-Uran also examined changing conceptions and applications of the law in the Spanish Empire during the Atlantic Enlightenment in his comparative study of spousal homicide cases in New Spain, New Granada, and Spain. His study importantly draws the legal and social distinction between homicides writ large and spousal homicides. The examination contextualizes the continued importance of ancient, medieval, and early modern legal sources, providing a useful roadmap to any scholar seeking to study the law in late colonial and early modern Iberian Atlantic. The extant cases reveal continued legal discrimination against subalterns and women, while marginalized people simultaneously made use of the juridical apparatus. While a modernizing did occur in these spaces, Uribe-Uran points to the ways revised interpretations of traditional legal sources drove this change, rather than a nascent Enlightenment shift as Michel Foucault argued for France.[27]

3 National Period

3.1 *Changes, Continuity, and Honor*

From a bird's eye view, there had been the assumption that the modernization and liberalization that formed and came alongside the nation-state proved beneficial for women's legal status and activity. Yet scholars at least since the 1980s have questioned the validity of such a simple change-over-time narrative. Seed's work mentioned above actually saw women's place before the law decrease with the increase in individualism found in the marriage consent laws of the eighteenth century. For the nineteenth century, Dore's argument that 'changes in state policy increased more than decreased gender inequalities'

26 Bianca Premo, *Enlightenment on Trial: Ordinary Litigants and Colonialism in the Spanish Empire* (New York: Oxford University Press, 2017).

27 Victor Uribe-Uran, *Fatal Love: Spousal Killers, Law, and Punishment in the Late Colonial Spanish Atlantic* (Stanford: Stanford University Press, 2015).

continues this skepticism of clear chronological progress.[28] Parsing where the nation's laws benefitted or inhibited women's expression and power becomes a foundational focus of much of the scholarship on Latin American women in the middle period, from 1780 to 1900.

The first moments of nationhood did not seem particularly liberating for women. New constitutions conceived of citizenship as a male domain. The Colombian constitution made this eminently clear: 'No one can be a good citizen who is not a good father, good son, good brother, good friend, and good husband.'[29] In the absence of citizenship, the law had other ways of conceiving of women's participation in the state, and women fought for other ways to make the law work for them.

The shift to the new nation-state brought about a potent and aggressive police force, but it also ushered in a new discourse that 'decried tyranny and lauded constitutional rights.'[30] These could and would be competing ambitions. Colonial historians have pointed to the ways that the ecclesiastical legal structure made more room for women, similarly for Indigenous norms and legal autonomy. Thus, when the nineteenth century privileged the secular state at the expense of the other legal regimes, women's place before the law was certain to change.

Despite claims for significant breaks with the colonial past, historians of the nineteenth century, and beyond, have pointed to the ways that colonial remnants continued to inform the legal system. In particular, conceptions of honor remained important for social expectations and the assertion and adjudication of legal rights. Scholars of women and the law have also sought to reconcile the extent of change or continuity of the pervasiveness of role of law in defining and enforcing conceptions of honor. In particular, women's honor as tied to their sexual experience or reputation and patriarchs' honor as tied to their wives and daughters' sexual honor were not removed from the legal arena of new nation-states. According to the editors of *Honor, Status, and Law*, 'Liberal law uniformly accepted as natural the gender relations of the family as well as the notion that family honor depended on women's sexual fidelity and priority.'[31]

---

28 Elizabeth Dore, 'One Step Forward, Two Steps Back: Gender and the State in the Long Nineteenth Century' in *Hidden Histories of Gender and the State in Latin America*, eds Elizabeth Dore and Maxine Molyeux (Durham: Duke University Press, 2000), 5.

29 As cited in Nara Milanich, 'Women, Gender, and Family,' 462.

30 Sarah Chambers, *From Subjects to Citizens: Honor, Gender, and Politics in Arequipa, Peru, 1780–1854* (State College: Penn State University Press, 1999), 189.

31 Caulfield, Chambers, and Putnam, *Honor, Status and the Law*, 10.

One question faced by the legal regimes of these new states was what constituted a space where new legal codes should apply. Households that included a patriarch were deemed parts of the private sphere, and thus outside the purview of the courts. Similar households without a paternal figure, or those in which the paternal figure elicited skepticism, were defined as public and required the action of the court.[32] Because national secular courts intentionally neglected to pursue crimes within the 'private' realm, more often the purview of ecclesiastical courts during the colonial period, women seeking to protect their honor against verbal insults or deflowering initiated litigation themselves. At times the arguments brought by women were mostly ignored by jurists; however, scholars have also shown how women's legal arguments, even those not rooted in previously accepted legal logic, shaped jurisprudence and altered the priorities of judges.[33] The new legal regimes began to try *rapto* cases, and convictions (about 50 percent in Arequipa, Peru) demonstrate the republican legal system's desire to uphold the sexual mores and honor envisioned by the nascent state. While the courts did not view spousal abuse or incest as public crimes, rape was public and therefore a state affair. This designation of public tended to hinge upon the patriarchal authority under which the victim resided. If the crime was committed 'within' the patriarchal umbrella, the court was more likely to view the behavior, regardless of its morality, as private conduct.[34]

In challenging the potential overreach or abuse by new judicial systems, plebeians leaned on conceptions of honor framed as virtue. In Arequipa, subaltern men used conceptions of honor, most often rooted in a work-ethic and military service, as the basis for their claims to rights. They invoked these claims in asserting their innocence in criminal trials or in appealing for light sentences when guilt was no longer disputed. Legal discourse around women left no such space for claims making. Women's attempts to invoke 'republican motherhood' seldom produced legal victories, and when it succeeded, it was mostly women of the elite classes. Even attempts by women to draw on the language of labor as a republican value likewise found little judicial merit. Further complicating their status before the new juridical regime, women also bore the brunt of the new state's attempts at asserting a moral standard.[35]

---

32 See Donna Guy, 'Parents before the Tribunals: The Legal Constructions of Patriarch in Argentina' in *Hidden Histories of Gender and the State in Latin America*, eds Elizabeth Dore and Maxine Molyeux (Durham: Duke University Press, 2000).

33 See, for example, Part 2 of *Honor, Status and the Law in Modern Latin America*, 131–248.

34 Sarah Chambers, 'Private Crimes, Public Order: Honor, Gender, and the Law in Early Republican Peru' in *Honor, Status and the Law*.

35 Chambers, *From Subjects to Citizens*.

3.2 *New Rights and New Powers*

How nineteenth-century Latin Americans understood the legal changes for women and how historians view them have been at odds in certain instances. Arrom discusses how nineteenth-century Mexicans trumpeted the gender progress brought about by republican laws. The text of the legal codes themselves, however, often copied the ideas from colonial codes, at times repeating the text verbatim. Arrom's discussion of nineteenth-century Mexico provides an important example of post-independence legal developments. Colonial private law continued until the first national civil code in 1870; however, national discussions on the need for modernization of the law had been brewing since independence. In the Mexican example, these changes ended up bridging conservative and liberal political lines. The culmination of this consensus produced several concrete changes. The age of majority was lowered from twenty-five to twenty-one, meaning children became individuals earlier and were no longer subject to a father's *patria potestad*. For Arrom and others, these changes in majority age reveal a weakening of patriarchal logic within national laws. While the age of majority laws applied to both men and women, continued perceptions of the fragility of women compelled jurists to institute an accompanying law that required single daughters to receive parental permission before moving out of their parents' house. While still perceived as the fairer sex, women's abilities to manage property, take on employment, sign contracts, and marry without parental permission mark important changes in women's place before national laws.[36]

As women gained 'independence' in these and other ways, laws were also granting them new legal claims to authority in the form of *patria potestad*. Whereas colonial society gave parental control firmly to fathers and other men, even in the event of divorce or death of a father, new national laws began to permit mothers guardianship and *patria potestad*. While this reversed colonial policy, restrictions on a mother's practice reinforced the limits of gendered changes in national legal policies. The contradiction was produced by a competition between individualism and patriarchalism, and modern nations sought to make them as compatible as possible.[37]

In the late nineteenth century, most Latin American states removed the ecclesiastical control over marriage, placing the responsibility of creating marriages and adjudicating legal disputes around them in the hands of state jurists. Mexico shifted to civil marriage in 1859, part of a broader legal shift

36 See especially Silvia Arrom, 'Changes in Mexican Family Law in the Nineteenth Century: The Civil Codes of 1870 and 1884' (1985) 10(3) Journal of Family History, 87–102.

37 Arrom, 'Changes in Mexican Family Law,' 90–93.

in national law. Most other nations required state-approved marriages by the 1880s, although Bolivia retained ecclesiastical marriages until 1911. Civil divorce in most cases followed closely behind, though the justifications and the parameters of the divorce varied.[38]

The success of the nation and the equality of women seemed incompatible in early national laws. Arrom explains this as a perceived dissonance: 'equality of husbands and wives was incompatible with corporate notions of social control.'[39] For jurists, a clear (gendered) hierarchy in the family was essential to the flourishing of the state. Newer studies have argued that nineteenth-century codes actually improved the position of wives before the law.[40] Deere and León conducted a study of early civil codes from fourteen countries and found that wives saw significant progress before the law across most of Latin America. For their study, the changes in legal treatment of women came not from influences originating in Spain and France, as had been previously argued. Instead, they tracked shifts in Latin American policy to the imitation and adaptations of laws originating in the United States and England. While they acknowledge these codes contained influences from the Napoleonic Code, a recurring assertion in the literature, the property rights concerning married women were drawn more from common law sources.

Despite the significant changes in the law, including those that reduced women's status, women did not disengage from the legal system. In the midst of these changes, the legal apparatus was expanding significantly. Women took advantage of a robust judicial system and were frequent litigants in domestic disputes. Milanich considers the possible explanations for this activity: 'Their frequent recourse to law may reflect the fact that they simply had myriad grievances to air. But it could also indicate that they found the courts to be a useful tool for negotiating, even tempering, patriarchal power.'[41]

3.3 *Suffrage*

In Latin America, the fight for women's suffrage came to the fore in the early part of the twentieth century. In most countries, the momentum for legal voting rights arose from concessions of universal male suffrage in these nations. In assessing the advocating for legal changes to voting rights, scholars have

38 See Uribe-Uran, 'Family, Divorce, Domestic Violence' in this volume.

39 Arrom, 'Changes in Mexican Family Law,' 310.

40 Carmen Diana Deere and Magdalena León, 'Liberalism and Married Women's Property Rights in Nineteenth-Century Latin America' (2005) 85(4) Hispanic American Historical Review 627–678.

41 Milanich, *Women, Gender, and Family*, 463.

noted the decentralized organizing, in which many groups pursued suffrage marshalling different evidence for the same end. Within these various organizations, women from all classes pursued changes in voting laws. These organizations likewise cut across national lines, as Pan-Latin American and International groups often led the way in agitating for reform. These women and their organizations were not singularly interested in suffrage. Often, their agendas focused on many other legal reforms such as equal pay and the establishment of juvenile courts. As the latter example makes clear, their demands for legal reform were not focused solely on 'women's rights.'[42] For scholars such as Asunción Lavrin, an emerging 'self-consciousness' as members of the body politic spurred such activism.

Passage of these laws took circuitous routes. Early legal arguments contended that the Uruguayan constitution of 1917 gave women voting rights. Pushback to these interpretations prevented women's voting until a new constitution was passed in 1934. Miller has argued that this final breakthrough had less to do with liberating women, and more to do with empowering native-born Uruguayan women as a way to shut out immigrant representation in the diversifying state.[43] In Argentina, important bills had initial success as early as 1930s but would not become law until Peron's presidency in the late 1940s. In Chile, suffrage came in piecemeal form. After women's groups continuous lobbying, women's suffrage was permitted in 1934, but only to literate women over twenty-one and only in municipal elections. Elections the following year illustrated women's use of their new rights, as tens of thousands voted and twenty-five women were elected to office. Chile did not make universal women's suffrage law until 1948. Uruguay was more of a pacesetter for Latin American suffrage.[44]

3.4 *Sex Work and the Law*

Before national debates around suffrage began, Latin American nations grappled with women's roles as workers in the new state. In Argentina, skepticism of women's labor bled into conversations of sex work. In 1875, prostitution was legalized but confined to licensed brothels. The purported reason for this change had to do with moral and physical health. A flood of unmarried men in

42 Francesca Miller, 'The Suffrage Movement in Latin America' in *Confronting Change, Challenging Tradition: Women in Latin American History*, ed. Gertrude Matyoka Yeager (Wilmington: Scholarly Resources, 1994).

43 Miller, 'The Suffrage Movement in Latin America,' 170.

44 Asunción Lavrin, *Women, Feminism, and Social Change in Argentina, Chile, and Uruguay, 1890–1940* (Lincoln: University of Nebraska Press, 1998).

cities like Buenos Aires, according to municipal leaders, led to a rise in prostitution. With that came a rise in the spread of venereal diseases, which gained the attention of public health experts whose social significance was increasing. The law was passed under the guise of limiting the spread of diseases and protecting the urban population, but in practice it served to place more police scrutiny over women's sex work and made their working conditions at times jail-like, complete with curfews and mandatory hospital visits. As evidence of the law's distinction between men and women's bodies, men were not required to register or submit to compulsory exams until 1936. This continued the trend of national laws ensuring the surveillance of women and women's work.[45]

In Mexico, Bliss traced the history women's sex work from the Porfiriato to post-revolution. She opens her book with a legal petition submitted by prostitutes in which they demand legal protections embodied in the spirit of the Mexican Revolution. It turns out that Mexico was less willing to see how revolutionary values might apply to those sex workers. The nation's attention was focused on how the law should define, locate, and surveil women sex workers, while less legal attention was paid to the men who would patronize prostitutes either in brothels or less sanctioned spaces. Bliss also points to the ways that increases in attention to the science of medicine influenced laws regarding prostitution, most overtly when registered prostitutes were forced to submit to weekly or monthly hospital visits to check for sexually transmitted diseases. Across the studies of law and prostitution in Latin America (and beyond), we begin to see an increase in the way the medical community, and specific public health officials, held significant weight in what went into the law. Their development of institutions and treatment plans served, primarily or additionally, to surveil the urban populace, with particular attention to women.

3.5 *Reproduction, Women's Health, and Abortion*

Legal scholars of modern Latin America have recently dedicated attention to the histories of childbirth, abortion, and infanticide, though most often treating them separately. Some early trends in scholarship moved more towards social and medical histories, but the consideration of law and its effect on cultural perception and medical advancements has become more commonplace. Recent interventions have demonstrated the benefits of interdisciplinary conversations, particularly for historians of gender and historians of science and medicine.

45 Donna Guy, 'White Slavery, Public Health, and the Socialist Position on Legalized Prostitution in Argentina, 1913–1936' (1988) 23(3) Latin American Research Review 60–80.

In Spanish America, the development of nation-states served as one key moment of change, as the legal oversight of women's bodies moved from mostly the purview of the ecclesiastical courts to the secular (national) courts. More generally, the rise of republicanism throughout Latin America brought women's bodies even further under the purview of the nation-state. For Nora Jaffary, the legal apparatus of nineteenth-century Mexico did not instantly become an attribute of the intrusive modern state. Jaffary treats the Spanish Penal Code of 1870 as an important moment of change, particularly the elements of the code that lightened the penalties for infanticide. Many other Latin American states passed similar legislation near the end of the nineteenth century. In Mexico after 1870, social denunciation rather than legal incursion was the method of policing of reproductive practices. Jaffary explains the increase in litigation regarding infanticide in the late nineteenth century was the result of these milder penalties; not because of some legal initiative in the court system but because neighbors, friends, and other community members were more willing to report suspicious behavior and investigate possible infanticide with what they presumably saw as more reasonable or just penalties.[46] In this instance, changes in the law affected public perception, which, in turn, had an impact on the prevalence of prosecution, bringing more legal oversight.

In Brazil, both the onset of republican forms of governance *and* the late abolition of slavery (1888) resulted in changes regarding the surveillance and policing of childbirth, abortion, and infanticide around the same time. Cassia Roth investigates this legal and medical transition in Brazil, arguing that this shift in attention to women's reproductive practices was part of a larger state transformation. For Roth, this increased attention to all aspects of women's reproductive lives – from pregnancy and childbirth to abortion and infanticide – was tied to the perception that 'women reproduced the country that the elites were intent on shaping.' These legal changes brought the law and public health into an uneven partnership. The result was the increased criminalization of women's reproductive decisions buoyed, in the capital city of Rio de Janeiro in particular, by the expansion and consolidation of the police force and criminal justice system. Yet, governmental and philanthropic efforts were unable to match this expanded legal apparatus with a sufficient increase in access to reproductive health services. A poor woman's miscarriage was dealt with in the police precinct as an unlawful act, a possible abortion, rather than in a public hospital as a medical event. A shift in legal oversight occurred in

46 Nora E. Jaffary, *Reproduction and Its Discontents in Mexico: Childbirth and Contraception from 1750 to 1905* (Chapel Hill: University of North Carolina Press, 2016).

Brazil with the ascension of the Vargas government and the progression to the Estado Novo in the late 1930s. As Vargas expanded medical access throughout the decade, physicians became the enforcers of policies on reproduction, taking the place of police and judges. Policing abortion proved to be a foundational element of legal changes seemingly meant to protect women's health.[47]

3.6 *Violence against Women*

Throughout the national period, litigation of violence against women was a moving target in part because conceptions of gender and conceptions of the crimes themselves were continually contested and negotiated. As with abortion and infanticide, medical professionals became increasingly important actors in the legal arena from the late nineteenth and early twentieth centuries. Their medical expertise informed decisions, and especially sentencing. And while courts became more willing to intervene in domestic issues, 'reasonable' gender violence rooted in maintaining control of one's household could still be legally acceptable. The court's intervention was often limited to curbing the most extreme manifestations of gender violence.[48]

Most recently, the later part of the twentieth century was marked by the rampant increase in and focus on domestic violence and feminicide. Research and surveys by scholars, national committees, and international organizations show the extent of violence against women across Latin American nations. In addition to the creation of governmental committees and non-profits to support women and curb domestic violence, Latin American governments including Mexico, Nicaragua, Colombia, and others passed new laws and constitutional amendments altering the way assault and rape against women was adjudicated.[49] The feminicide epidemic was prevalent in many Latin American states and elicited responses from women's organizations calling for legislative and social action. The willingness of states to craft new laws to address the issue varied. In 2008, eleven countries had classified feminicide as a crime. By 2019, that number was eighteen. In some instances, the provision was a standalone law, and in other nations it was outlined in a more comprehensive homicide provision. Despite these laws, no significant decrease has occurred. This

47 Cassia Roth, *Miscarriage of Justice: Women's Reproductive Lives and the Law in Twentieth-Century Brazil* (Stanford: Stanford University Press, 2020), 5.

48 Astrid Cubano-Iguina, 'Legal Constructions of Gender and Violence against Women in Puerto Rico under Spanish Rule, 1860–1895' (2004) 22(3) Law and History Review 531–564.

49 Victor Uribe, 'Physical Violence against Wives and the Law in the Spanish American World, 1820s-2000s,' in *Murder and Violence in Modern Latin America*, eds Ricardo Salvatore, Pieter Spierenburg, and Eric Johnson (London: Blackwell-Wiley, 2013), 49–80.

lack of change is due in larger part to women's limited access to legal recourse and gender bias in policing and legal procedures. To date much of this research has been done by Pan-American non-profit and governmental organizations, sociologists, criminologists, and journalists. However, as this grave trend persists, it is increasingly being addressed by historians.[50]

4 Reflection

This scholarship across both periods has provided us with the attention scholars have paid to women as objects of the law (and the various ways that legal regimes have conceived of who women are and what rights they have) and as subjects (agents of legal activity and legal change). In the colonial period, patriarchal structures placed clear limits on women's legal status. Still, women made full use of the legal regimes of the colonial period, claiming their law-given rights as well as asserting agency, influence, and demanding resources even when such things were not outlined in legal provisions. Women certainly gained their legal victories but also found legal activity as a way to gain victories outside the courts.

The national period did not usher in a moment of equality in status before the law. Colonial vestiges and modern patriarchal values continued women's subjected place before the law. But even as legal structures and norms changed, women found spaces to use the law to their advantage. More than in the colonial period, they also created ways to advocate for large-scale legal changes, from voting rights to feminicide laws.

Whether the sixteenth or the twenty-first century, women's experiences were not dictated solely by laws created from above. Their legal activity shaped their lives, the law, and the society around them.

References

Arrom, Silvia. 'Changes in Mexican Family Law in the Nineteenth Century: The Civil Codes of 1870 and 1884.' *Journal of Family History* 10(3) (1985).

50 Alicia Deus and Diana Gonzalez, 'Analysis of Femicide/ Feminicide Legislation in Latin America and the Caribbean and a Proposal for a Model Law' (2018) UN Women; 'Inter-American Model Law on the Prevention, Punishment and Eradication of the Gender-Related Killing of Women and Girls (Femicide/Feminicide)' (2019) OAS.

Caulfield, Sueann, Sarah Chambers, and Lara Putnam, eds. *Honor, Status and the Law in Modern Latin America*. Durham: Duke University Press, 2005.

Chambers, Sarah. *From Subjects to Citizens: Honor, Gender, and Politics in Arequipa, Peru, 1780–1854*. State College: Penn State University Press, 1999.

Cook, Alexandra Parma, and N. David Cook. *Good Faith and Truthful Ignorance: A Case of Transatlantic Bigamy*. Durham: Duke University Press, 1991.

Cowling, Camillia. *Conceiving Freedom: Women of Color, Gender, and the Abolition of Slavery in Havana and Rio de Janeiro*. Chapel Hill: University of North Carolina Press, 2013.

Cubano-Iguina, Astrid. 'Legal Constructions of Gender and Violence against Women in Puerto Rico under Spanish Rule, 1860–1895.' *Law and History Review* 22(3) (2004): 531–564.

Deere, Carmen Diana, and Magdalena León. 'Liberalism and Married Women's Property Rights in Nineteenth-Century Latin America.' *Hispanic American Historical Review* 85(4) (2005): 627–678.

Diaz, Arlene. *Female Citizens, Patriarchs, and the Law in Caracas, Venezuela, 1786–1904*. Lincoln: University of Nebraska Press, 2004.

Dore, Elizabeth, and Maxine Molyeux, eds. *Hidden Histories of Gender and the State in Latin America*. Durham: Duke University Press, 2000.

Few, Martha. *Women Who Live Evil Lives: Gender, Religion and the Politics of Power in Colonial Guatemala*. Austin: University of Texas Press, 2002.

Gauderman, Kimberly. *Women's Lives in Colonial Quito: Gender Law and the Economy in Spanish America*. Austin: University of Texas Press, 2003.

Guy, Donna. 'White Slavery, Public Health, and the Socialist Position on Legalized Prostitution in Argentina, 1913–1936.' *Latin American Research Review* 23(3) (1988): 60–80.

Jaffary, Nora. *Reproduction and Its Discontents in Mexico: Childbirth and Contraception from 1750 to 1905*. Chapel Hill: University of North Carolina Press, 2016.

Lavrin, Asunción. *Women, Feminism, and Social Change in Argentina, Chile, and Uruguay, 1890–1940*. Lincoln: University of Nebraska Press, 1998.

Mannarelli, María Emma. *Private Passions and Public Sins: Men and Women in Seventeenth-Century Lima*. Albuquerque: University of New Mexico Press, 2007.

McKinley, Michelle. *Fractional Freedoms: Slavery, Intimacy, and Legal Mobilization in Colonial Lima, 1600–1700*. Cambridge: Cambridge University Press, 2016.

Nazzari, Muriel. *Disappearance of the Dowry: Women, Families, and Social Change in São Paulo, Brazil (1600–1900)*. Stanford: Stanford University Press, 1991.

Premo, Bianca. '"As if She Were My Own": Love and Law in the Slave Society of Eighteenth-Century Peru.' In *Sexuality and Slavery: Reclaiming Intimate Histories in the Americas*, edited by Diana Ramey Berry and Leslie M. Harris. Athens: University of Georgia Press, 2018.

Premo, Bianca. *Enlightenment on Trial: Ordinary Litigants and Colonialism in the Spanish Empire*. New York: Oxford University Press, 2017.

Proctor, Frank Trey. '"Alien to My Sex": Enslaved Women and Their Gendered Notions of Abuse in Eighteenth-Century Lima, Peru.' *Journal of Women's History* 31(2) (2019): 57–79.

Roth, Cassia. *Miscarriage of Justice: Women's Reproductive Lives and the Law in Twentieth-Century Brazil*. Stanford: Stanford University Press, 2020.

Sloan, Kathryn A. *Runaway Daughters: Seduction, Elopement, and Honor in Nineteenth-Century Mexico*. Albuquerque: University of New Mexico Press, 2008.

Stoner, K. Lynn. *From the House to the Streets: The Cuban Woman's Movement for Legal Reform, 1898–1940*. Durham: Duke University Press, 1991.

CHAPTER 12

Immigrants and Outsiders

Diego Acosta

The categorization of immigrants and outsiders in Latin America, from the colonial period to the present, represents an extremely complex endeavor. The legal construction and regulation of not only the foreigner but also the national and the citizen have been and are surrounded by numerous edges and apparent contradictions. Debates on who belongs to the polity, under which conditions, and with which rights, have been ongoing since before the independence of the Latin American states in the early nineteenth century. Race, class and regional affinities, a sort of Hispano-Americanism, were central components in the process of building new states and nations in the territories that emerged as independent from the demise of the Spanish and Portuguese empires.

Latin America has always had an organic juxtaposition between openness and closure towards foreigners. This peculiarity is already visible during the colonial era but becomes accentuated with independence. Yet, Latin Americans have often constructed narratives and portrayed themselves as open territories to make claims of exceptionalism when compared with the United States and Europe. As some authors have explained, thinkers such as Manuel Ugarte 'went so far as to claim that no one in South America was capable of hating blacks, Indians, or Jews. Yet his underlying political goal was clear: race becomes a tool to attack the evils of U.S. imperialism and to galvanize "Latin peoples" around myths of tolerance, inclusion, and harmony.'[1] With this background in mind, this chapter offers an overview of the legal construction of the national, the citizen, the regional migrant, and the foreigner. It does so across four different historical periods, namely pre-independence, the nineteenth century, the twentieth century, and the period from the 1990s to today.

1 Eduardo Elena, 'Nation, Race and Latin Americanism in Argentina: The Life and Times of Manuel Ugarte 1900–1960s' in *Making Citizens in Argentina*, eds Benjamin Bryce and David M.K. Sheinin (Pittsburgh: University of Pittsburgh Press, 2017), 71.

 DOI:10.1163/9789004436091_014

1 Before Independence

During the colonial period there were three central elements that left an indelible mark on Latin America. At first foreigners were not allowed to emigrate to or even trade with the Spanish possessions in the Americas.[2] Their only option was to either obtain a royal license or to naturalize themselves as Spanish.[3] Similarly, in the case of Brazil, it was only in 1808 that Portugal, through the *Carta Régia* of November 25, first accepted the immigration of foreigners to its colony and grants of lands to them. Previously, immigration by foreigners was, as in the case of the Spanish colonies, forbidden,[4] although there had been some, notably Portuguese, in places like colonial Potosi or colonial Lima.[5] The first colony of foreigners in Brazil, Nova Friburgo, composed of Swiss, was created in 1819, three years before independence in 1822.

This had important repercussions for the way in which the Americas understood their relationship with the metropolis. Centralism barred the possibility to liberalize economic trade and excluded those not born in the Iberian Peninsula, begrudged by Latin American elites, from the highest administrative positions. Furthermore, colonial administrators were unwilling or unable to populate large territories, often presented as vacant. These developments heightening the search for independence.

Another important aspect had to do with the composition of the populations in the Americas. Generally speaking, although with logical differences between the various territories, the body of the people was composed of *criollos*, or European descendants, and by Indigenous and African-descended people, who were largely excluded. In the case of the latter, their particular position in society had been rendered more complex by the waves of fear aroused by the Saint-Domingue black slaves' revolution and Haiti's subsequent declaration of independence in 1804, especially in Brazil, Venezuela, and Cuba that largely depended on slave labor. Let us not forget that, for instance, five

2 See for an in-depth analysis T. Herzog, *Defining Nations: Immigrants and Citizens in Early Modern Spain and Spanish America* (New Haven: Yale University Press, 2003).

3 Diego Acosta, *The National versus the Foreigner in South America: 200 Years of Migration and Citizenship Law* (Cambridge: Cambridge University Press, 2018), 43.

4 Sacchetta Ramos Mendes, José Aurivaldo, *Laços de Sangue: Privilégios e Intolerância à Imigração Portuguesa no Brasil (1822/1945)* (São Paulo: EDUSP/FAPESP, 2011).

5 Nelson E. Pereyra Chávez, 'Extranjeros integrados. Portugueses en la Lima virreinal, 1570–1680 por Gleydi Sullón Barreto' (2018) 23(1) Fronteras de la Historia.

million African slaves were forcefully transported to Brazil in three centuries (ten times more than to the United States).[6]

2 After Independence: The Nineteenth Century

In the early nineteenth century, twelve new states emerged – ten in South America, Mexico, and the Federal Republic of Central America – in a very short period from territories that had been part of the Spanish and Portuguese empires for more than three centuries. As a first task, these countries needed to build statehood through demarcating their territories, establishing their forms of government and, most importantly for our purposes, deciding on who would be part of their legitimate populations. This last element though had implications that went far beyond state-building to the invention of the nation itself. Indeed, in a post-French Revolution historical context, where sovereignty had to, in theory, reside in the nation rather than the monarch, the legal definition of who was going to be a national and, by opposition, who was going to be a foreigner, was the central element in any attempt to construct nations. It was San Martín, liberator of Peru, who most clearly verbalized this in his famous Decree of 1821: 'in the future the aborigines shall not be called Indians or natives; they are children and citizens of Peru, and they shall be known as Peruvians.'[7]

In fact, all early Latin American constitutions define the nation inclusively by automatically granting nationality to all those freemen born in their territories (*ius soli*) without any distinction as to race or social class but excluding slaves. This was different in the United States where neither Indigenous nor African-descent populations obtained citizenship, a status available only to free white men. This was an ingenious, liberal, and inclusive attempt to create nationals out of populations divided by class, race, and gender. Even in Latin American countries, a distinction was early made between nationality and citizenship. This divide meant that even if the nation was inclusively defined, the body politic remained the domain of a few. Indeed, citizenship carried political rights and was only offered to those men who, in addition to being nationals, had also capital or property. The qualities of the citizen were described in

6 Yuko Miki, *Frontiers of Citizenship: A Black and Indigenous History of Postcolonial Brazil* (Cambridge: Cambridge University Press, 2018), 10.

7 Peru, Decree of August 27, 1821, cited in Benedict Anderson, *Imagined Communities: Reflections on the Origin and Spread of Nationalism* (London: Verso, 1983), 49–50.

'racialized and gendered terms.'[8] The holder of political rights had to be male, literate, married and individually autonomous either through property, trade, capital or an independent profession. This meant an unsatisfactory distribution of rights that, in practice, resulted in a 'servile citizenship'[9] for many, notably Afro-descendants and Indigenous populations. As Miki aptly depicts in the Brazilian case, 'other "nations" outside propertied white citizens were not considered to be part of the good society.'[10]

The erection of racialized hierarchies in the new societies became even clearer through a third central mechanism of nation-building, open borders for foreigners. Beginning with the short-lived Venezuelan Constitution of 1811, laws all over Latin America introduced open border provisions and clauses announcing admittance for all foreigners from any nation with freedom to reside, security, and equal rights for themselves and their properties. Whilst these announcements were, on paper, directed to any foreigner – for example, Asians arriving to Peru – the true addressees were Europeans. It cannot be ignored that when Alberdi claimed in Argentina that to govern was to populate, he saw such settlement as a means of civilization, to be performed by those he considered to be civilized, that is, Europeans.[11] Not every single European was desirable though. Indeed, governments in Argentina had, since the 1850s, 'advocated increased immigration from northern European countries because they believed that such an infusion would bring "healthy" traits to the population and thereby rid Argentina from its inferior Latin, Indian and African racial character.'[12]

In fact, the opening of borders represented a project based on notions of civilization and racial and demographic factors, but not a humanistic one. It was understood that Europeans would bring the civilization to the continent through arts, sciences, industry, and capital, thus facilitating development and the incorporation of the new states into global markets. Likewise, it was assumed that immigration by white Europeans would contribute to

8 Nancy P. Appelbaum, Anne S. Macpherson, and Karin Alejandra Rosemblatt, 'Introduction. Racial Nations' in *Race and Nation in Modern Latin America*, eds Nancy P. Appelbaum, Anne S. Macpherson, and Karin Alejandra Rosemblatt (Chapel Hill: University of North Carolina Press, 2003), 4.

9 I borrow the term from Miki, *Frontiers of Citizenship*, 241.

10 Ibid., 102.

11 Juan Bautista Alberdi, *Bases y Puntos de Partida para la Organización Política de la República Argentina derivados de la Ley que Preside al Desarrollo de la Civilización en América del Sud* (Buenos Aires: Imprenta Argentina, 1852).

12 Julia Rodriguez, *Civilizing Argentina: Science, Medicine, and the Modern State* (Chapel Hill: University of North Carolina Press, 2006), 4.

the whitening of local populations. The arrival of white European migrants was welcomed as a step forward towards 'racial improvement' in national censuses because 'mestizaje was presumed to reduce the relative influence of Indianness or Africanness on the nation, while enhancing the influence of Europeanness or native "whiteness" – never the reverse.'[13] Finally, through the expansion of the frontier, native groups were either exterminated or forcefully assimilated in countries like Argentina, Brazil, and Chile, their lands declared as empty or unoccupied and thus made available for colonization by European immigrants. Thus, the creole elites also used migration and citizenship policies as tools to define nationhood and the contours of the body politic.

In order to have a complete overview of the legal construction of the foreigner and the national or citizen, two further aspects must be briefly highlighted. First, foreigners, whilst encouraged to naturalize after very short periods of residence, were never granted the same rights as nationals by birth when it came to full access to all the highest offices in the three branches of government: executive, legislative, and judicial. Rather, they were always referred to as *extranjeros naturalizados*, their continuous foreignness further accentuated by the order of the words in the Spanish language, with 'foreigner' coming first and 'naturalized' only second. The *extranjero naturalizado* has always been a different legal figure with inferior rights. In the Mexican case, Hoyo has explained this as being prompted by a 'defensive nationalism' resulting from concerns about foreign intervention in the new states.[14] Whilst this could be more understandable in the nineteenth-century context, all countries in Latin America still today prohibit access to certain of the highest offices in the country to those not nationals by birth. They also limit the rights of foreigners in other ways. For example, naturalized citizens can be more easily deprived of their nationality in some cases than nationals by birth.[15]

Second, another legal figure emerged after independence: the Hispano-American, who was a former Spaniard from the Americas, Brazilians thus being excluded. Hispano-Americans, arguably those who could be identified as creoles, represented a different type of membership, and this partly explains the difficulties in building nations in territories where the gap 'between white, black and Indian within countries was always greater than the differences

---

13 Mara Loveman, *National Colors: Racial Classification and the State in Latin America* (Oxford: Oxford University Press, 2014), 154.

14 Henio Hoyo, 'Report on Citizenship Law: Mexico' (Florence: EUDO Citizenship, EUI, 2015).

15 Diego Acosta, 'Regional Report on Citizenship. The South American and Mexican Cases' (Florence: EUDO Citizenship, EUI, 2016).

between any of these groups across borders.'[16] According to Centeno, creoles did not see themselves as 'separate from their creole neighbours' and indeed 'identified themselves as Americans – as opposed to Spaniards – but not as a specific subnationality.'[17] Being Hispano-American carried tangible entitlements when moving across the region. They enjoyed access to the rights available to foreigners in general and often more rights. They also had privileged and faster routes to naturalization and more political rights. Both before and after naturalization, they were categorically closer to national citizens than to other foreigners, either from Europe or elsewhere.[18] This construction subsided only in the twentieth century but has re-emerged in the twenty-first century with debates about a South American citizenship, discussed below.

3 Excluding the Foreigner: The Twentieth Century

Despite their efforts, Latin American countries did not receive large numbers of foreigners during the nineteenth century. The dispatching of specialized recruiting agents to Europe, tax exemptions, free passage, and free land did not serve to lure the desired Europeans. Everywhere, parliaments discussed the root causes of such a collective failure. Some countries, mainly Peru after enslaved humans had been freed in the first half of the nineteenth century, relied on more than 100,000 Chinese indentured laborers.[19]

This changed around the 1870s as a result of five global revolutions that took place simultaneously and that transformed Latin America until the 1930s – mostly South America but also Cuba – into the second largest recipients of migrants at a global level, only after the United States. In fact, Argentina itself was the second country in the world to receive more migrants in this period and, if one accounts for the number of migrants per national, it received more than the United States on this basis. For example, 'in 1910, 46% of the 1.2 million residents of the city of Buenos Aires were foreign nationals, and in 1914,

16 Miguel A. Centeno, *Blood and Debt: War and the Nation-State in Latin America* (University Park: Penn State University Press, 2002), 175.

17 Ibid., 172.

18 Acosta, *The National*, 60–85.

19 Isabelle Lausent-Herrera, 'Tusans (tusheng) and the Changing Chinese Community in Peru' in *The Chinese in Latin America and the Caribbean*, eds W. Look Lai and T. Chee-Beng (Leiden: Brill, 2010), 143–184.

30% of the country's 7.9 million residents were foreigners.'[20] This large immigration to Latin America was composed not only of western Europeans but also of those coming from the Russian Empire, including Jews, and others from far East Asia and the Ottoman Empire, mainly Arab Christians from what is now Lebanon and Syria.[21]

Moya has masterfully argued how the Industrial Revolution led to demographic change in Europe with internal migrations taking place from the countryside to the city. This increased urban population demanded agricultural products that were more easily produced in the Americas and transported faster to Europe. Trains and steamships not only enhance trade but also movement of people. Finally, the liberal revolution meant that the Americas were open to the arrival of foreigners, and Europe finally accepted the emigration of certain of its subjects. These five revolutions combined made Latin America – mainly Argentina, Brazil, Cuba, and Uruguay, in that order – the recipient of a vast number of migrants, and incorporated the region into the world capitalist system.[22]

By the turn of the century, Latin American elites became increasingly concerned about the nature of European immigration. These were not 'the yeoman farmers from Protestant Europe' they had hoped to attract but instead uneducated commoners,[23] who often brought notions about rights and equality considered subversive. Coupled with these concerns were racist prohibitions targeting Asians, mostly Chinese, Roma, Africans, Jews,[24] and many others considered unapt due to their political views, physical or mental disabilities, age, gender, or class.[25] In brief, since the late nineteenth century until the

20 Benjamin Bryce and David M.K. Sheinin, 'Introduction: Citizenship in Twentieth-Century Argentina' in *Making Citizens in Argentina*, eds Benjamin Bryce and David M.K. Sheinin (Pittsburgh: University of Pittsburgh Press, 2017), 3.

21 *Arab and Jewish Immigrants in Latin America: Images and Realities*, eds Ignacio Klich and Jeffrey Lesser (Abingdon: Routledge, 1998); Mariusz Kalczewiak, *Polacos in Argentina* (Tuscaloosa: University of Alabama Press, 2019); Jeffrey Lesser, *Immigration, Ethnicity, and National Identity in Brazil, 1808 to the Present* (*New Approaches to the Americas*) (Cambridge: Cambridge University Press, 2013); *The Chinese in Latin America and the Caribbean*, eds Walton Look Lai and Chee-Beng Tang (Leiden: Brill, 2010); Daniel M. Masterson with Sayaka Funada-Classen, *The Japanese in Latin America* (Champaign: University of Illinois Press, 2004).

22 José Moya, *Cousins and Strangers: Spanish Immigrants in Buenos Aires, 1850–1930* (Berkeley: University of California Press, 1998), 45–59.

23 David FitzGerald and David Cook-Martin, *Culling the Masses: The Democratic Origins of Racist Immigration Policy in the Americas* (Cambridge, MA: Harvard University Press, 2014), 312.

24 Ibid.

25 Acosta, *The National*, 86–111.

1980s, Latin American states increasingly constructed the foreigner, whether European or not, as a potential threat. This process found its maximum expression in the immigration and nationality laws adopted in many South American states in the 1960s and 1970s, within a Cold War, post-Cuban Revolution context when the United States backed up heinous military regimes that abused and disregarded the rights of nationals and foreigners.

The enormous popularity of restrictions and migration controls during the twentieth century, as well as their adoption, even by countries that received little immigration, has been explained by McKeown as resulting from perceptions 'of how a civilized country should define its social and political borders' since this appeared as a requirement 'for international recognition as a modern nation state.'[26] The proliferation of undemocratic regimes all over the continent also had as a side effect the final demise of the large European migrations to Latin America, the last groups of mostly Spanish, Portuguese, and Italian emigrants arriving primarily to Venezuela in the 1960s and 1970s.[27]

4 Developments since the 1990s

With the general return to democracy in Latin America in the late 1980s, three important aspects affected the legal construction of immigrants and outsiders, as well as the rights of nationals. These are the salience of international human rights law, the emigration of Latin American nationals and, finally, regional integration processes.

4.1 *The Salience of International Human Rights Law*

The return to democracy, as well as the end of the Cold War, facilitated the emergence of so-called new Latin American Constitutionalism. This would be defined by the inclusion of more actors into discussions about constitutional development and by the incorporation of extensive catalogues of rights protecting vulnerable groups – such as women, Afro-descendants, Indigenous populations, and migrants.[28] At the same time, this new Latin

26 Adam M. McKeown, *Melancholy Order: Asian Migration and the Globalization of Borders* (New York: Columbia University Press, 2008), 320–321.

27 Adela Pellegrino, *Historia de la Inmigración en Venezuela Siglos XIX y XX* (Caracas: Academia Nacional de Ciencias Económicas, 1989).

28 *Transformative Constitutionalism in Latin America: The Emergence of a New Ius Commune*, eds Armin von Bogdandy, Eduardo Ferrer Mac-Gregor, Mariela Morales Antoniazzi, Flávia Piovesan, and X. Soley (Oxford: Oxford University Press, 2017).

American Constitutionalism is also affected and enhanced by a more relevant role for International Human Rights law in the region, with the ratification of numerous international instruments, including a renewed role for the Inter-American Commission and Court through their interpretation and implementation of the American Convention of Human Rights. The hurried ratification of human rights treaties by Latin American countries during the democratic transition period can be also explained as an 'antidote against authoritarian regressions.'[29]

Since the 1980s, Latin America has not only ratified international human rights law but has also created new legal instruments better suited to their own reality. Paramount among these is the Cartagena Declaration that extended the scope of who could be considered a refugee to also include those 'who have fled their country because their lives, safety or freedom have been threatened by generalized violence, foreign aggression, internal conflicts, massive violation of human rights or other circumstances which have seriously disturbed public order.'[30] The Declaration, which followed the model established by the Organization of the African Union, was adopted during a period of tremendous violence in Central America in the 1980s, which led to thousands fleeing their homes.[31] Although the Declaration has been incorporated into the legislation of fifteen states in the Americas,[32] its application in practice remains a challenge as seen with the example of the Venezuelans below.

4.2 *The Emigration of Latin American Nationals*

Although Mexicans, and to a lesser extent Central Americans, had emigrated in the past, that was not the case, by and large, for South Americans. Indeed, states in South America were always immigration countries until the 1960s. This changed with the establishment of military dictatorships which led to the

---

29 Victor Abramovich, 'Autonomía y Subsidiariedad: El Sistema Interamericano de Derechos Humanos Frente a los Sistemas de Justicia Nacionales' in *El Derecho en América Latina: Un Mapa para el Pensamiento Jurídico del Siglo XXI*, ed. César Rodríguez Garavito (Buenos Aires: Siglo Veintiuno, 2011), 217.

30 Cartagena Declaration on Refugees, Colloquium on the International Protection of Refugees in Central America, Mexico, and Panama. Adopted by the Colloquium on the International Protection of Refugees in Central America, Mexico, and Panama, held at Cartagena, Colombia, November 19–22, 1984.

31 Eduardo Arboleda, 'The Cartagena Declaration of 1984 and its Similarities to the 1969 OAU Convention – A Comparative Perspective' (1995) 7 International Journal on Refugee Law 87–101.

32 Argentina, Belize, Bolivia, Brazil, Chile, Colombia, Ecuador, El Salvador, Guatemala, Honduras, Mexico, Nicaragua, Paraguay, Peru, and Uruguay.

exile and emigration of thousands, and as later accentuated by economic crisis with the results that millions of Latin Americans now live outside the region, mostly in the United States and in Europe. With such important emigration, the figure of the emigrant was reevaluated. Historically considered as traitors, emigrants came to be seen in a different light. During the 1990s, 'emigrant communities came to be viewed as economic footholds in developed economies … [they] were reconceived as a kind of natural resource.'[33] Remittances became a major source of income, whilst emigrants also reduced unemployment rates at home.

It is within this context that we can understand reforms in Latin America to facilitate dual citizenship for emigrants, voting rights in national elections, and other services allocated to those residing in the national territory.[34] This creates new patterns of belonging to different territories and new understandings about entitlements to participate in political decisions even for those not residing in the home state. This also, in turn, affects the rights of immigrants in Latin America since many times the new acceptance of dual citizenship also means that immigrants can keep their nationality of origin upon naturalizing in a particular Latin American state.

4.3 *Regional Integration Processes*

Since the turn of the twenty-first century, numerous regional integration organizations have deepened free movement of people through various international agreements. Paramount among these new frameworks are the two MERCOSUR Residence Agreements. They provide that nationals of MERCOSUR Member States – a group that expanded to include Bolivia and Venezuela, currently suspended – and Associate Member States Chile, Colombia, Ecuador, Guyana, Peru, and Suriname, may reside and work for a period of two years in another Member State if they can prove citizenship and a clean criminal record. Guyana, Suriname, and Venezuela still need to incorporate the Residence Agreement into national legislation before it can take effect. The treaty also provides a number of rights to these migrants, including the right to equal working conditions, family reunification, and access to education for children. After two years, the permit may be transformed into permanent residency.[35]

---

33 Peter J. Spiro, *At Home in Two Countries: The Past and Future of Dual Citizenship* (New York: New York University Press, 2016), 89.

34 Luicy Pedroza, Pau Palop, and Bert Hoffmann, *Emigrant Policies in Latin America and the Caribbean* (Santiago de Chile: FLASCO Chile, 2016).

35 Acosta, *The National*, 173–198.

Beyond MERCOSUR, other Regional Organizations such as the Andean Community, CARICOM, or the *Sistema de Integración Centroamericana* (SICA), also have free movement regimes with different degrees of development. This has shifted the meaning of nationality and alienage. Regional migrants cannot be considered as normal foreigners any longer, but rather as regional semi-citizens exercising their rights of residence and who are entitled to equal treatment in a number of areas. Whist deeper discussions about a possible South American citizenship have now been, perhaps momentarily, left aside, developments on freedom of movement and residence in the region cannot be ignored as attested by the 2.6 million residence permits that have been granted under the MERCOSUR Residence Agreement between 2009 and 2016.[36]

5 Key Challenges Moving Forward

Since 2000, numerous Latin American countries adopted more progressive migration and asylum laws. This is so for many countries in South America, including Argentina (2004), Uruguay (2008), Bolivia (2013), Brazil, Ecuador, Peru (2017), Chile (2021), and Paraguay (2022) and Central America, including Nicaragua (2011), Guatemala (2016), and Mexico (2011). These laws were usually adopted within contexts where emigration was the norm and where the number of immigrants was usually very low and mostly coming from neighboring countries.

There are signification migration flows occurring within the region that would deserve further attention such as Nicaraguans to Costa Rica or Cubans, Dominicans, and Haitians towards South America. Nonetheless, two major developments have captured everyone's attention in the region: the emigration of more than seven million Venezuelans to countries in the region since 2015, and the migrant caravans from the Northern Triangle of Central America (Guatemala, Honduras, and El Salvador) to the United States and to Mexico.

Regarding the former, Venezuelans have mostly arrived to Colombia (approximately 2.5 million), Peru (1.3 million), Chile (more than a 450 thousand) Ecuador (approximately 500 thousand), and then Brazil, Argentina, Panama and Dominican Republic. Whilst the displacement of Venezuelans could certainly fall under the larger definition of refugees from the Cartagena Declaration (e.g., 'internal conflicts, massive violation of human rights or other

36 International Organization for Migration (IOM), *Evaluación del Acuerdo de Residencia del MERCOSUR y su incidencia en el acceso a derechos de los migrantes* (Buenos Aires: Organización Internacional para las Migraciones, 2018).

circumstances which have seriously disturbed public order'), no country in the region, with the exception of Brazil – which has granted ca. 50,000 permits to Venezuelans – and some cases of Mexico, is offering Venezuelans refugee status. Rather, countries have created a panoply of ad hoc, discretionary, and temporary residence permits, which allow Venezuelans some access to residence, employment, and other basic rights. Numerous Venezuelans in the region, however, remain irregular due to the various bureaucratic obstacles to obtain residence permits. The introduction of visa requirements by countries such as Peru or Ecuador, following steps that had already been taken by others such as Panama, might indeed lead to a further aggravation of the number of those who find themselves undocumented and thus subject to possible exploitation and deprivation of rights.[37]

In turn, the flight of families and individuals from El Salvador, Guatemala, and Honduras, which rank among the world's most violent countries, is putting pressure on Mexico's characteristic discourse of human rights protection for migrants. This discourse is grounded in Mexico's critique of the United States and the rights of Mexicans there. Mexico now becomes the destination of many of those who do not manage to reach the United States or who are expelled, a true challenge. Needless to say, Central Americans coming from these three countries could also fall under the Cartagena Declaration as refugees, but Mexico has so far used temporary visas coupled with a further militarization of the southern frontier.[38]

6 Conclusion

Discussions on immigrants and outsiders, and their categorization, have been ongoing in Latin America since the colonial period. Any debate on these issues has been historically intertwined with other debates about political rights, race, class, and gender, and about the legal status of foreigners who stayed in the region even after they were naturalized. Latin America has a long history of openness towards foreigners, but it also has an equally long history of closure. This leads to what I have labelled as an organic juxtaposition between openness and closure in the regulation of the rights of immigrants in the region.

37 Diego Acosta, Feline Freier, and Cécile Blouin, 'La Emigración Venezolana: Respuestas Latinoamericanas,' Fundación Carolina, Madrid, Documentos de Trabajo 3/2019.

38 Rodrigo Dominguez-Villegas 'Protection and Reintegration: Mexico Reforms Migration Agenda in an Increasingly Complex Era,' Migration Policy Institute, Feature, March 7, 2019.

The current challenges of Venezuelans and Central Americans arriving to South America and Mexico, respectively, are perfect examples of this organic juxtaposition. On the one hand, governments in the region attempt to accommodate these new arrivals by creating special, ad hoc, temporary permits that provide the individual with a right to work and other basic rights such as health care. At the same time, considering such individuals as refugees, as clearly defined under the Cartagena Declaration, and thus offering them a more permanent status with greater legal certainty is hardly discussed. This is coupled with bureaucratic obstacles, challenges to the rule of law, and a prevalent position by executives in the regulation of these issues. Nonetheless, there are numerous advances, most notably exemplified by the MERCOSUR Residence Agreements. Numerous legal, political, and social aspects have to be taken into consideration when discussing membership and belonging in Latin America, a region still affected by ongoing discrimination against nationals themselves based on race or class. At the same time, the region and its legal thinkers are capable of leading central debates on immigration and refugee law at the global level.

References

Acosta, Diego. *The National versus the Foreigner in South America: 200 Years of Migration and Citizenship Law*. Cambridge: Cambridge University Press, 2018.

Acosta, Diego and Freier, Luisa Feline. 'Turning the Immigration Policy Paradox Up-Side Down? Populist Liberalism and Discursive Gaps in South America.' International Migration Review 49 (2015): 659–697.

Appelbaum, Nancy P., Anne S. Macpherson, and Karin Alejandra Rosemblatt, eds. *Race and Nation in Modern Latin America*. Chapel Hill: University of North Carolina Press, 2003.

Centeno, Miguel A., and Agustín E. Ferraro, eds. *State and Nation Making in Latin America and Spain: Republics of the Possible*. Cambridge: Cambridge University Press, 2013.

Devoto, Fernado J. *Historia de la Inmigración en la Argentina*. Buenos Aires: Editorial Sudamericana, 2003.

Domenech, Eduardo. '"Las Migraciones son como el Agua": Hacia la Instauración de Políticas de "Control con Rostro Humano". La Gobernabilidad Migratoria en Argentina.' *Polis Revista Latinoamericana* 35 (2013): 1–20.

FitzGerald, David Scott, and David Cook-Martin. 2014. *Culling the Masses: The Democratic Origins of Racist Immigration Policy in the Americas*. Cambridge: Harvard University Press.

Góngora-Mera, Manuel, Gioconda Herrera, and Conrad Müller. 'The Frontiers of Universal Citizenship. Transnational Social Spaces and the Legal Status of Migrants in Ecuador.' desiguALdades.net Working Paper Series 71 (2014).

Herzog, Tamar. *Defining Nations: Immigrants and Citizens in Early Modern Spain and Spanish America*. New Haven: Yale University Press, 2003.

Klich, Ignacio, and Jeffrey Lesser, eds. *Arab and Jewish Immigrants in Latin America: Images and Realities*. Abingdon: Routledge, 1998.

Lesser, Jeffrey. *Immigration, Ethnicity, and National Identity in Brazil, 1808 to the Present* (*New Approaches to the Americas*). Cambridge: Cambridge University Press, 2013.

Look Lai, Walton, and Tan Chee-Beng, eds. *The Chinese in Latin America and the Caribbean*. Leiden: Brill, 2010.

Loveman, Mara. *National Colors: Racial Classification and the State in Latin America*. Oxford: Oxford University Press, 2014.

Mateos, Pablo, ed. *Ciudadanía Múltiple y Migración: Perspectivas Latinoamericanas*. México: CIDE, 2015.

Miki, Yuko. *Frontiers of Citizenship: A Black and Indigenous History of Postcolonial Brazil*. Cambridge: Cambridge University Press, 2018.

Mirow, Matthew C. *Latin American Constitutions: The Constitution of Cádiz and Its Legacy in Spanish America*. Cambridge: Cambridge University Press, 2015.

Moya, José. *Cousins and Strangers: Spanish Immigrants in Buenos Aires, 1850–1930*. Berkeley: University of California Press, 1998.

Pedroza, Luicy, Pau Palop, and Bert Hoffmann. *Emigrant Policies in Latin America and the Caribbean*. Santiago de Chile: FLASCO Chile, 2016.

Ramírez, Jacques, ed. *Ciudad-Estado, Inmigrantes y Políticas: Ecuador, 1890–1950*. Quito: Editorial IAEN, 2012.

Sacchetta Ramos Mendes, José Aurivaldo. *Laços de Sangue: Privilégios e Intolerância à Imigração Portuguesa no Brasil* (*1822/1945*). São Paulo: EDUSP/FAPESP, 2011.

Von Vacano, Diego. *The Color of Citizenship: Race, Modernity and Latin American/Hispanic Political Thought*. Oxford: Oxford University Press, 2012.

CHAPTER 13

Peasants and Workers

William Suárez-Potts

1 Introduction

A historical survey of the law relevant to peasants and workers spanning several hundred years, from the 1500s to 2000s, may note that the categories of 'peasant' and 'worker' are legally as well as socially and historically formulated. Most definitions of peasant and worker are largely modern, from the twentieth century, and, indeed, predominantly social scientific or ideological classifications. Each term is associated with social classes long evolving, especially since the nineteenth and twentieth centuries. Approximately at the same time, the laws and legal orders that denoted these classes or contributed to their construction as social categories underwent extensive change, both in relation to them and in connection with other political and economic developments.

It is therefore helpful to consider a few lines to demarcate the subjects of discussion in this chapter. Peasants have been defined as subaltern laborers in rural zones who control their means of production, which remains close to subsistence levels. Typically they must convey a surplus of their production to an outsider, whether the external agent is a state official or landlord, and whether the surplus is tribute, tax, rent, or personal service.[1] Peasants are

1 Economic historian John Coatsworth briefly defined 'peasant' as follows: 'Usually the term refers to rural producers who possess (but do not necessarily own) the means of producing their own subsistence and a marketable surplus – that is, smallholders, squatters, members of corporate Indian villages, service tenants, cash renters, sharecroppers and the like. In this sense, the term excludes slaves, permanent resident workers on large estates (including debt peons), cowboys … migrants and other wage laborers and supervisory personnel.' John Coatsworth, 'Patterns of Rural Rebellion in Latin America' in *Riot, Rebellion, and Revolution: Rural Social Conflict in Mexico*, ed. Friedrich Katz (Princeton: Princeton University Press, 1988), 22. Coatsworth cited to then recent debates about the conceptualization of peasant and peasant movements, ibid., n. 2. Anthropologists have distinguished different types of Latin American peasantry, in accord with their organization and relationship with other social elements. Peasants historically controlled their land collectively, in corporate form, predominated in highland areas, and formed the base of Spanish colonialism. In lower altitudes, over time societies of peasant farmers developed and were more closely tied to markets. Differing legal regimes applied to each type. Eric R. Wolf, 'Types of Latin American Peasantry: A Preliminary Discussion' (1955) 57 American Anthropologist 452–471.

 | DOI:10.1163/9789004436091_015

normally distinguished from slaves and farmers, but not always altogether from seasonal laborers, employees residing on large estates, or sharecroppers. Workers might be conceived merely as industrial, urban laborers, but a broader definition simply contrasts free labor from enslaved. Over time, rural estate residents, mineworkers, artisans, shop workers, and, later, factory and transport workers, were all deemed covered by the same category. The common notion is that of an individual who must furnish his or her service or potential to labor to another, for bargained compensation, but without altogether formally surrendering personal freedom.

Along with successive notions of peasant and worker, and the rules and doctrines regulating or governing them, there have been major shifts in the legal orders of Latin America related to those occurring throughout the Atlantic world. Scholars have noted the transformation of law since the early modern period.[2] In Latin America, one discerns a colonial legal regime characterized by the organization of society into corporate forms and which recognized Iberian sovereigns as ultimate authority. Subjects of the crown, however, including peasants or laborers, vied with other social and ethnic groups, frequently in forums that asserted jurisdiction competitively, over issues concerning their land, labor, and political status. By 1810, the formally rigid hierarchies were breaking apart. A new era had begun, and while rarely exclusively predominant in the following decades, with independence from Spain and Portugal, liberal legal principles became pervasive. Toward the end of the nineteenth century, a liberal legal regime, characterized by political constitutions in the now delimited public sphere, and civil and commercial codes in the private, reigned fully. During the liberal era of the 1800s, corporate Indigenous communities' hold over lands was undermined, as collectively owned property was privatized. Free labor was affirmed as a liberal principle in constitutions and civil codes, even if in actuality labor practices remained dependent or sometimes coercive. By the end of the nineteenth century, however, the liberal regime faced new challenges. Incipient industrialization began to generate a new working class. The social problems associated with the new class, often encompassed in the euphemistic phrase, 'the social question,' led to a reformist reevaluation

2 See, e.g., *New Horizons in Spanish Colonial Law: Contributions to Transnational Early Modern Legal History*, eds Thomas Duve and Heikki Pihlajamäki (Frankfurt am Main: Max Planck Institute for European Legal History, 2015); Duncan Kennedy, 'Three Globalizations of Law and Legal Thought: 1850–2000' in *The New Law and Economic Development: A Critical Appraisal*, eds David M. Trubek and Alvaro Santos (Cambridge: Cambridge University Press, 2006).

of the doctrinal premises of liberal law and was followed by the enactment of social legislation throughout Latin America. Constitutional reform as well as new statutes and codes became law from country to country through the 1950s. Then, beginning in the 1970s and gaining momentum in the late 1980s and through the 1990s, there occurred a turn away from the statist approach to the extensive regulation of economic and social relations. Into the new millennium, there has been a partial reversal of this trend. In conclusion, one discerns that the law affecting peasants and workers is in flux, seemingly as much a political function as a legal one.

This chapter accordingly outlines briefly the legal history of people as they have become peasants and workers, alternating between the two subjects in chronological order, yet centering on developments since the turn of the twentieth century, when the laboring classes were more clearly identified and self-identified as peasantry or proletariat in relation to their respective aims while still subject to the concerns of more powerful interests. As already suggested, the relevant law implicates much of the entire legal system at a given moment; nevertheless, this chapter limits the topics treated, and notes only in passing further areas for discussion, some of which are addressed in other chapters of this companion.

1.1 *The Colonial Era (1500s to 1810)*

The Spaniards and Portuguese who conquered Indigenous people in the Americas did so primarily to appropriate wealth – either wealth that already existed and could be seized, such as war booty, or wealth produced by subjugated people. Along with the desire of enrichment through the labor of others, Iberians sought to evangelize the Indigenous population and justify their conquests and colonization in religious and legal terms. In the first decades of encounters between Iberians and Indigenous peoples, the enslavement of Indians was frequent, even while Africans were brought to the Americas as slaves. The native sedentary societies that Spaniards took over were already stratified, and to a large extent the labor and tributary demands placed on them built on previously existing systems, now refashioned and articulated in a Spanish legal vocabulary. Spaniards initially aimed to ensure that the native populations would be available to support them as lords and later moved to consolidate landed estates. The religious orders tasked with evangelizing Indigenous people pressed the monarchy to curb the worst abuse of them. In response, the crown issued protective laws, but also passed legislation to regularize landed property toward the end of the sixteenth century and in the early seventeenth century.[3]

Spanish legislation repeatedly prohibited the enslavement of Native Americans, most definitively with the New Laws of 1542. The monarchy in the sixteenth century, however, allowed for the exploitation of Indigenous labor just short of slavery. The two principal institutions that Spaniards refashioned to obtain and apportion labor amongst themselves were the *encomienda* and *repartimiento*. Indigenous communities assigned to Spanish *encomenderos* were required to supply laborers for nominally finite periods of time or to furnish tribute. In actuality, the *encomienda* too frequently amounted to brutal and deadly exploitation. As the Spanish monarchy moved to derogate the *encomienda*, as of 1542, and confronted fierce resistance to its reforms from *encomenderos*, the *repartimiento* was instituted to allocate limited, rotating labor drafts of Indians among Spanish mine owners and some landholders. Spanish state officials administered the *repartimiento*, and normally collaborated with mine owners and others demanding Indigenous labor. The system was subject to abuse in practice, too, which led to its suppression, around 1630. It was sustained, however, until the end of the colonial period for mine operations in the Andes.[4] Both the *encomienda* and *repartimiento* had Iberian legal and institutional antecedents, and through the sixteenth century were the subject of legal disputations among Spanish jurists, theologians, and crown officials. Native Americans also struggled against the demands placed on them by the conquerors and their successors. Although the legal literature then did not refer to them as peasants, nor fully acknowledge pre-Hispanic antecedents, Indigenous claims and petitions raised issues common among peasants, related to labor exactions, the appropriation of surplus production, as well as control over land and maintenance of local autonomy.[5]

3 An earlier historiography touched on the legal aspects of the exploitation and protection of the Indian during the first century of conquest, as it debated the extent of the black legend of Spanish cruelty and, alternatively, Spanish justice. See Benjamin Keen, 'The Black Legend Revisited: Assumptions and Realities' (1969) 49(4) Hispanic American Historical Review 703–719. See also, for a contemporaneous account of labor exploitation written by one of the first Spanish judges toward the end of the sixteenth century, Alonso Zorita, *Life and Labor in Ancient Mexico: The Brief and Summary Relation of the Lords of Spain*, trans. and with an introduction by B. Keen (New Brunswick: Rutgers University Press, 1963).

4 See Enrique Tandeter, *Coercion and Market: Silver Mining in Colonial Potosí, 1692–1826* (Albuquerque: University of New Mexico, 1993).

5 In comparison, in colonial Brazil, as historian Stuart Schwartz has commented, '[p]easantry ... came from no precolonial heritage. It was, instead, a "reconstituted" peasantry, a direct result of the colonial economy and slavery that emerged at the edges of the slave economy and then grew in importance alongside it. ... this free rural population of small farmers,

Indigenous, peasant-like legal claims in New Spain concerned land issues, as Spaniards turned to consolidating their ownership of estates and the monarchy aimed to concentrate Indian populations in administrative units of villages or pueblos and to mediate or to adjudicate conflicts between Spaniards and the native population. In the early 1590s, the monarchy established a special tribunal to protect Indigenous interests, and Indians readily turned to it and others to defend their lands, and, soon thereafter, as the *repartimiento* was derogated in the early seventeenth century, labor rights. In colonial tribunals, Indigenous litigants, often collectively, conceded and affirmed their subordinate status to the crown as tributaries, but insisted that as tributaries they could not be exploited by Spanish private interests, or corrupted public officials, and deprived of their freedom. More research has been undertaken of Indigenous litigation in New Spain through the end of the colonial period, but Andean Indians actively litigated and defended their interests as well.[6]

In a rural world, peasant exploitation was extensive, as was peasant resistance in the legal arena. Similarly, the exploitation of labor in Spanish America's important silver mining industry, as well as in sectors of commercialized production – sugarcane cultivation, cochineal dye extraction, and domestic, textile manufacturing – was not negligible. Large landholders, moreover, shifted to the use of contracted, formally voluntary labor while the *repartimiento* faltered. Even though each of these economic sectors had specific characteristics and labor needs none developed a fully articulated labor market of free workers. Slaves of African descent were used with variations over time in both Mexican and Andean mines, as were, more regularly, Indigenous laborers supplied through the *repartimiento* or *mita*, as the labor draft was called in the Andes due to its pre-Hispanic antecedent. In Cuba, slaves worked in copper mines, eventually becoming property of the king in the late seventeenth century upon the royal expropriation of the private mines. There is evidence that, along with free people of color, these royal slaves litigated intensely against

tenants, and dependents remained … even unnamed. The word "peasant" (*campones*) was rarely used to refer to them and was replaced instead by a variety of terms describing variations in tenure, dependence, or rusticity (*matuto, caipira*, etc.).' Stuart B. Schwartz, *Slaves, Peasants, and Rebels: Reconsidering Brazilian Slavery* (Urbana: University of Illinois Press, 1992), 66.

6 For New Spain (Mexico) see especially Brian Owensby, *Empire of Law and Indian Justice in Colonial Mexico* (Stanford: Stanford University Press, 2008), on which this paragraph is based; for the Andean region, see e.g., Sergio Serulnikov, *Subverting Colonial Authority: Challenges to Spanish Rule in Eighteenth Century Southern Andes* (Durham: Duke University Press, 2003).

the crown over land, property, inheritance, and labor conditions.[7] Free workers were predominant especially in Mexico, and some were compensated with the right to keep part of what they mined. The complexity of mining and smelting operations was reflected in a division of labor involving laborers with different statuses. Production in *obrajes* (textile manufactories) was also carried out by laborers with distinct legal statuses such as convicts, vagabonds, and debtors.[8]

In general, operations and labor requirements were regulated by law and legally recognized custom, but research has not yet ascertained if workers litigated claims like Indigenous peasants. Silvio Zavala's scholarship, for both New Spain and Peru, is a starting point for future study.[9] Complicating any analysis of non-peasant labor relations was the social status of many free workers, who, as *castas* (i.e., people of mixed heritage), were legally constrained from certain activities, such as artisanal professions; and, indeed, skilled artisanal occupations were regulated through formally constituted guilds.[10] Constraint of a different kind existed in agriculture – as did free labor.

The degree to which rural laborers employed by large estates were constrained and the prevalence of peonage are issues historians have debated.[11] No consensus exists, in part because it has become apparent that there was variation in employment relations across regions and time periods. Evidence of contracting with advanced payments of workers, and of indebtedness, probably indicates peonage sometimes, but at other times suggests that workers needed to be enticed with persuasive offers to accept employment or remain employed. From a legal perspective, it is apparent that rudimentary contracts

---

7 María Elena Diaz, *The Virgin, the King and the Royal Slaves of El Cobre: Negotiating Freedom in Colonial Cuba 1670–1870* (Stanford: Stanford University Press, 2000).

8 Enrique Florescano, Isabel González Sánchez and Jorge González Angulo, *De la colonia al imperio*, vol. 1 of *La clase obrera en la historia de México*, ed. Pablo González Casanova (México: Siglo Veintiuno, 1990).

9 Silvio Zavala, *El servicio personal de los indios en la Nueva España* (México: Colegio de México, 1984–1995), 7 vols.; Silvio Zavala, *El servicio personal de los indios en Perú: extractos del siglo xvi* (México: El Colegio de México, 1978–1980), 3 vols.

10 Manuel Carrera Stampa, *Los gremios mexicanos: la organización gremial en Nueva España, 1521–1861* (México: Edición y Distribución Iberoamericana de Publicaciones, 1954).

11 Florescano et al., *De la colonia al imperio*. For a wide-ranging historiographical discussion encompassing all of Spanish America as well as the colonial, nineteenth, and twentieth centuries see Arnold Bauer, 'Rural Workers in Spanish America: Problems of Peonage and Oppression' (1979) 59(1) Hispanic American Historical Review 34–63. Bauer's argument was criticized. Brian Loveman, 'Critique of Arnold J. Bauer's "Rural Workers in Spanish America: Problems of Peonage and Oppression"' (1979) 59(3) Hispanic American Historical Review 478–485; see also Bauer's reply: Arnold Bauer, 'Reply' (1979) 59(3) Hispanic American Historical Review 486–489.

of employment existed along with the notion of free labor. From a social-economic perspective, through the end of the colonial era labor markets failed to mature.

1.2 *Independence*

Between approximately 1808 and 1825, most Latin Americans established their formal independence from Spain or Portugal. In Spanish America, a majority of the newly drafted constitutions adopted liberal principles but in the first post-independence decades much of the legal tradition of the *ancien régime* persisted, especially in the ordering of economic and social relations including those affecting peasant communities. Throughout much of the nineteenth century, the contest between liberal principles and more traditional ones was grounded in the colonial past implicating political status and the tenurial and property relations of Indigenous people.[12] Indeed, the Constitution of 1812, drafted in Cádiz in the face of the French occupation of the Iberian Peninsula, and meant to apply across the Spanish world, already contemplated the abolition of the special, subordinate status of the Indian.[13] Legislation to privatize the collectively held lands of Indigenous-peasant communities followed in the newly constituted republics, although such laws were only sporadically enforced through the first half of the century.[14] Still, they portended the coming transformation in property. Thus, in April 1824, before Simón Bolívar's forces had defeated Spanish royalists, he issued decrees in Trujillo recognizing the full rights in property of the Indigenous and allowing the sale of community lands for their division among the peasants occupying them. Peru's Law of the Constituent Congress of March 31, 1828, recognized Indians and mestizos as holding absolute ownership of their lands, provided they were occupied and partitioned.[15]

Recent historiography has reviewed the constitutional processes surrounding independence as well as the legal nature of the transition to

12 See Andrés Lira, *Comunidades indígenas frente a la Ciudad de México: Tenochtitlán y Tlatelolco, sus pueblos y barrios, 1812–1919* (México: El Colegio de México, 1995).

13 M.C. Mirow, *Latin American Constitutions: The Constitution of Cádiz and Its Legacy in Spanish America* (Cambridge: Cambridge University Press, 2015), 91–95.

14 Daniela Marino, 'Nuestros hijos recibirán como legado esta cuestión … Los Indígenas y el derecho en el siglo XIX (Estado de México)' (2004) 46 TRACE: Travaux et Recherches dans les Amériques du Centre 45 (focusing on Mexico and discussing the Decree of January 4, 1813).

15 See Carlos Ferdinand Cuadros Villena, *Derechos Reales* (Lima: Empresa Editora Latina, 1995), vol. 2.

republican social orders.[16] The conflicts over the property relations and statuses of Indigenous communities, moreover, have received specific attention from scholars; these struggles reflected complex situations that can no longer be reduced to simple accounts concerning the expropriation of the peasantry's land and the creation of large estates.[17] It has been argued, at least for Mexico, that two distinct but overlapping moments affected the Indigenous peasantry after independence. Initially, the proclamations of political and civil equality encompassing the Indigenous (such as those in the Cádiz Constitution of 1812 and comparable legislation) contributed to their losing control over their communities, which in turn corroded their hold over land. Then, later legal reforms directly affected communal property ownership.[18]

In the second half of the nineteenth century, in Mexico, a process that lasted decades resulted in the breakup of corporately owned Indigenous, peasant lands – a privatization of property, pursuant to the Ley Lerdo of June 1856, and the liberal Constitution of 1857. Again, the process was complex and is presently the subject of ongoing historical research. What is apparent now is that Indigenous peasant communities were hardly constituted on an egalitarian basis by the end of the colonial period. As corporate lands were fragmented toward the end of the nineteenth century, in some places members of the communities themselves participated in the process and sometimes benefited, even as many others lost their property interests and were reduced

16 See e.g., *Inventando la nación. Iberoamérica. Siglo XIX*, eds Antonio Annino and François-Xavier Guerra (México: Fondo de Cultura Económica, 2003); Carlos Garriga, 'La recusación judicial: del derecho indiano al derecho mexicano' in Cuadernos del Instituto de Investigaciones Jurídicas, *La supervivencia del derecho español en Hispanoamérica durante la época independiente* (México: UNAM, 1998), 203–239; and Marta Lorente Sariñena, 'Las resistencias a la ley en el primer constitucionalismo mexicano' in ibid., 299–327. Compare Timo Schaefer, *Liberalism as Utopia: The Rise and Fall of Legal Rule in Post-Colonial Mexico, 1820–1900* (Cambridge: Cambridge University Press, 2017).

17 A starting point, however, which contends that the liberal laws of the nineteenth century facilitated the consolidating of large haciendas at the expense of Indigenous communities in the highlands of Peru, is the work of legal historian Fernando de Trazegnies Granda, *La idea de derecho en el Perú republicano del siglo XIX*, 2nd ed. (Lima: Pontificia Universidad Católica del Perú, Fondo Editorial, 1992).

18 Daniela Marino, 'Indios, pueblos y la construcción de la Nación. La modernización del espacio rural en el centro de México, 1812–1900' in *Nación, Constitución y Reforma, 1821–1908*, ed. Erika Pani (México: Fondo de Cultura Económica, 2010), citing, among others, Bernardo García Martínez, 'Jurisdicción y propiedad: una distinción fundamental en la historia de los pueblos de indios del México colonial' (1992) 53 European Review of Latin American and Caribbean Studies 47–60.

to a proletarian status.[19] Peasants individually – and collectively – litigated extensively against the privatization of communal property, but courts typically upheld liberal constitutional principles and attendant legislation against them. In 1882, Mexico's supreme court ruled definitively that the corporate communities lacked legal personality, while allowing individual peasants to continue litigating.[20]

The late nineteenth century was the apogee of the liberal regime, an order formally centered on the individual and his rights in relation to other individual's rights or the state's authority. It was not only a nation's constitution, such as the Mexican Constitution of 1857 or the Argentine Constitution of 1853, which embodied individualist principles, but also the civil codes promulgated across Latin America in the course of the 1800s, that affirmed absolute property rights and stipulated the applicable law of contracts (or obligations). In his discussion of nineteenth-century Peru, for instance, Fernando de Trazegnies contends that the nation's civil code of 1852 was as important as any constitution for the consolidation of private property and militated against peasant interests.[21]

If the individualist, liberal legal framework of the late nineteenth century impinged on the collective interests of peasants, its impact on workers was barely more salubrious.[22] Latin America remained largely rural long after independence. There were artisan and small working-class populations in the cities, and some of these populations reacted against liberalizing tariff policies that opened up textile markets to European imports.[23] Generally, it appears that corporatist guild regulations fell into desuetude (although more research

---

19 Emilio Kourí, 'Sobre la propiedad comunal de los pueblos. De la Reforma a la Revolución' (2017) 66(4) Historia Mexicana 1923–1960, 1939 and citations therein discussing recent historiography; Helga Baitenmann, 'Ejerciendo la justicia fuera de los tribunales: de las reivindicaciones decimonónicas a las restituciones de la reforma agraria' (2017) 66(4) Historia Mexicana 2013–2072.

20 Pablo Mijangos y González, *El nuevo pasado jurídico mexicano: Una revisión de la historiografía jurídica mexicana durante los últimos 20 años* (Madrid: Universidad Carlos III de Madrid, 2011), 80. In the case of Peru, Trazegnies Granda contends that peasants continued to use tribunals to resist encroachments on their property in the post-independence period. Trazegnies Granda, *La idea de derecho*, 184.

21 See generally Trazegnies Granda, *La idea de derecho*.

22 But compare Schaefer, *Liberalism as Utopia*.

23 For Colombia, see Enrique Gaviria Liévano, *El liberalismo y la insurrección de los artesanos contra el librecambio* (Bogotá: Universidad de Bogotá Jorge Tadeo Lozano, 2002), cited in Víctor M. Uribe-Uran with Germán Palacio, 'Origins of Labor Rights and Justice in Colombia, 1850–1950' in *Labor Justice across the Americas*, eds Leon Fink and Juan Manuel Palacio (Urbana: University of Illinois Press, 2018).

on the laws concerning nineteenth-century workers and their practical effect could be undertaken); there is historical evidence for Mexico indicating that workers or artisans cited or utilized articles of the civil code.[24] This nation's constitution explicitly guaranteed the principle of free labor, which the federal judiciary regularly applied in favor of agricultural workers and against coerced labor. This actually suggests the existence of peonage in certain parts of the country, as well as a liberal legal stance against it.[25] In other Latin American and Caribbean countries civil law, too, framed labor relations, which frequently varied from ideal, liberal principles of voluntary labor. However, the historiography about workers through the middle of the nineteenth century, particularly the law relevant to their employment relationship, is sparse.[26]

1.3 *Toward Social Legislation*

By the last decade of the nineteenth century, the process of Latin America's integration with the economies of western Europe and the United States, apace in a few regions with industrialization and the commercialization of agriculture, led to the emergence of larger working classes and, in some rural areas, the further proletarianization of labor. Strikes, incipient labor organizing, and radical working-class ideologies seemed to challenge the established social and political order. As in western Europe and the United States, the demands and revolutionary language of the new working classes were deemed 'the social question.' Progressive legal reformers across the Western world advocated for legislation to address myriad issues, and reorient the liberal, individualist regime of nominally free contracts between workers and employers toward a social order that recognized the reality of relations in which the contractual parties obviously had unequal bargaining power. Informed by the new legal orientation, in the first decades of the twentieth century, Latin American policymakers also began to adopt laws to counter revolutionary agitation and ameliorate social and working conditions. Workers and their representatives participated in these developments, sometimes ambivalently, at other times more cooperatively, still, however, based on the capital–labor relationship.

---

24 See Carlos Illades, *Hacia la república del trabajo: La organización artesanal en la ciudad de México, 1853–1876* (México City: El Colegio de México y Universidad Autónoma Metropolitana-Iztapalapa, 1996).

25 See William Suárez-Potts, *The Making of Law: The Supreme Court and Labor Legislation in Mexico, 1875–1931* (Stanford: Stanford University Press, 2012), 25–6, and 41–66; and, on the issue of actual peonage, Bauer, 'Rural Workers in Spanish America.'

26 James P. Brennan, 'Latin American Labor History' in *The Oxford Handbook of Latin American History*, ed. José C. Moya (Oxford: Oxford University Press, 2010).

Scholars have recounted the intellectual and doctrinal transition in Latin America from a liberal-legal regime to a socially oriented one in the first half of the twentieth century.[27] The actual implementation of social legislation, was, of course, chiefly a political process, albeit one informed by legal considerations. Land reform impacting peasants was also undertaken, although its approximate timeline typically differed from that of labor legislation, except in Mexico and later Bolivia and Cuba, or, to a lesser extent where it was aborted in Ecuador (1929–1937), Guatemala (1952–1954), Venezuela (1945–1948), and Chile (1970–1973).[28] The legal underpinnings of agrarian reform, namely, that property was a social function and that tenurial relations in the countryside in the form of latifundia were inequitable and economically regressive, had their origins in the intellectual and legal currents that also influenced labor legislation. Nonetheless, outside of Mexico, agrarian reform did not proceed very far, until the Bolivian Revolution of 1952 and the Cuban Revolution of 1959.[29] There, revolutionaries began a process of collectivizing property. In reaction to the Cuban Revolution, in the early 1960s, the United States promoted agrarian reform through the Alliance for Progress. Programs to redistribute land ensued, with mixed success, thereafter, in Venezuela, which had already undertaken land colonization, Colombia, the Dominican Republic, Chile, and Peru; and, in the 1970s and 1980s, in Nicaragua and El Salvador. Peasants or agricultural workers benefited the most in Mexico, Bolivia, and Cuba. Peasants or rural workers frequently were active participants in the implementation of land redistribution programs. But agrarian reform and the law that it spawned, *derecho agrario*, was dominated by lawyers and policymakers. The originating impetus, moreover, as in the case of the labor legislation, was political (if not revolutionary).[30]

---

27 See e.g., Kennedy, 'Three Globalizations of Law'; Juan Manuel Palacio, 'From Social Legislation to Labor Justice: The Common Background in the Americas' in *Labor Justice Across the Americas*, and citations therein.

28 See generally, Cristóbal Kay, 'Latin America's Agrarian Reform: Lights and Shadows' (1998) 2 Land Reform 8–31; Ruth B. Collier and David Collier, *Shaping the Political Arena: Critical Junctures, the Labor Movement, and Regime Dynamics in Latin America* (Princeton: Princeton University Press, 1991), 200–201 and 424–425 (on Venezuela); 568–570 (on Chile).

29 On Bolivia's extensive agrarian reform, see Guillermo de la Peña's succinct account, 'Rural Mobilizations in Latin America since c. 1920' in *The Cambridge History of Latin America*, ed. Leslie Bethell, vol. 6 (Cambridge: Cambridge University Press, 1995), 379–482, 426.

30 For an overview of agrarian reform in Latin America, see Kay, 'Latin America's Agrarian Reform.' Much of this paragraph draws from his essay.

In Mexico, for instance, revolutionary civil wars between 1910 and 1920, resulted in a revised constitution in 1917, which incorporated distinct articles mandating land reform and labor legislation (Articles 27 and 123, respectively). The raising to constitutional status of these social provisions was partly due to the mobilization of peasants and workers. In particular, peasants in the Plan of Ayala (1911) had called for the restitution of lands expropriated pursuant to the liberal reform initiated in 1856–1857, among other things. Meanwhile, union leaders and other working-class advocates had made demands adopted in Article 123 since the early 1900s. At the same time, the intellectual framework of Article 123 owed much to the mentioned social-legal doctrines circulating in the Atlantic world.[31] Article 27, in part, also reflected these currents, but its provisions for agrarian reform were more particularly influenced by its drafters' reinterpretation of the *ejido*. Traditionally the term had denoted lands such as woods or pastures held by peasant villages, for common use by residents, in contrast to other village holdings, such as those assigned to resident families for cultivation. As land redistribution was carried out pursuant to Article 27, the *ejido* came to designate a new institution: the peasant community and all the land it was granted by the state, which had to be held collectively.[32]

Peasant demands, insofar as they encompassed land redistribution, appeared to pose a more radical threat to existent property relations, especially where large landowners predominated.[33] Mexico was not exceptional. Determined political will was necessary, such as in Peru under the nationalist, military dictatorship of 1968–1975, which finally implemented agrarian reform in the Andean highlands where the Indigenous peasantry was concentrated.

In contrast, in Chile the reconceptualization of property as a social function, adopted by that nation's constitution in 1925, was primarily influenced by the social legal thought of León Duguit, who visited Buenos Aires in 1911.[34] In Argentina, the reorientation of individualist, liberal law toward social legislation had begun by then, in answer to the 'social question.'[35] But this turn

---

31 See generally Suárez-Potts, *The Making of Law*.

32 See Emilio Kourí, 'La invención del ejido' Nexos (January 2015) for a more detailed account of this legal and institutional reconceptualization, and of the nature of agrarian reform, which actually was contrary to what peasants like the Zapatistas had demanded in the Plan of Ayala. On the drafting history of both Articles 27 and 123, see Pastor Rouaix, *Génesis de los artículos 27 y 123 de la Constitución Política de 1917*, 2nd ed. (México: INEHRM, 1959).

33 See e.g., Collier and Collier, *Shaping the Political Arena*, 196.

34 M.C. Mirow persuasively argues this point in 'Origins of the Social Function of Property in Chile' (2011) 80 Fordham Law Review 1183–1217.

35 Eduardo Zimmermann, 'Un espíritu nuevo: La cuestión social y el Derecho en la Argentina (1890–1930)' (2013) 73(257) Revista de Indias 81–106.

toward social law did not lead immediately in either country to land reform (indeed, Argentina hardly had a peasantry). Rather, it was focused on labor legislation and was responsive to the evolving labor movements.

Government policy toward workers' demands and labor mobilizations throughout most of Latin America in the early twentieth century normally had been repressive. As labor historian Michael Hall quipped, in connection with the emergence of a militant working class in São Paulo and Rio de Janeiro, 'the social question remained in a famous phrase of the period, "one for the police."'[36] Yet repression became intermittently more selective and was accompanied by piecemeal legislation. Then, toward the middle of the century (1930s to the early 1950s), more comprehensive laws, even systematic codes, were enacted. Scholars, from different perspectives, have concurred in identifying this pattern. For example, political scientists Ruth and David Collier in their major work, *Shaping the Political Arena*, argue that incorporation (presumably into society or polity) of labor movements by governments was a crucial development of state authority in twentieth-century Latin America, resulted in the structuring and channeling of labor organizations – and was accomplished in large part through labor legislation. Such legislation normally recognized the collective entity of the union, even privileging its operation and the status of its leadership, but also conditioning the union's lawful operations on acceptance of the state and the business enterprise. Collier and Collier thus identify a first phase of 'conservative modernizers,' followed by 'a second phase during which state initiatives generally assumed a more vigorous form.'[37] Similarly, but more centered on the laws approved, labor historian Juan Manuel Palacio identifies a 'first wave' occurring in the first thirty years of the twentieth century during which liberal-conservative governments accepted specific statutes on such issues as workers' compensation, or protective standards for female and child labor, parallel with the organization of labor departments; and 'a second wave' prompted by the economic crisis of the 1930s.[38]

The second period of extensive social legislation, including social constitutions, varied from country to country, dependent mostly on specific political conditions.[39] Uruguay under the two administrations of José Batlle y

36 Michael M. Hall, 'Labor and the Law in Brazil' in *The Rise and Development of Collective Labour Law*, eds Marcel van der Linden and Richard Price (Bern: Peter Lang, 2000), 80.

37 See Collier and Collier, *Shaping the Political Arena*, 6–7, for a more precise articulation of their historical argument, and 162, for the quotation.

38 Palacio, 'From Social Legislation to Labor Justice.'

39 On the phenomenon of social constitutions, see the contemporary account by Moisés Poblete Troncoso, 'The Social Content of Latin American Constitutions' (1942–1943) 21(1) Social Forces 100–106.

Ordóñez was the first nation in Latin America to establish essentially a welfare state, from approximately 1903 to 1907, and pivotally between 1911 and 1915. Similarly, the Colliers demarcate the onset of the reform period in Colombia as of 1930, and lasting until 1945, and in Peru lasting into the 1940s; Venezuela's reformist years are complicated by military coup and encompass 1945–1948. In Argentina, with its relatively large working class, the turn toward social legislation began earlier, but initiatives under the Radical government of 1916–1922 were stalled until the rise to power of Juan Perón in the mid-1940s, and his alliance with sectors of the leadership of organized labor through the department and then secretariat of labor. Then, a series of presidential decrees and laws were issued, which established, according to the historian Jeremy Adelman, a contractualist labor relations system in which the state played an important role supporting what became the dominant labor organizations (due in large part to this state support).[40]

In Mexico, Chile, and Brazil, comprehensive labor legislation was enacted, along (if not coincident) with constitutional changes. Thus, after more than a decade of states passing statutes, Mexico promulgated the equivalent of a national labor code (Ley Federal del Trabajo) in 1931. In the same year, so did Chile. Mexico's law paradigmatically outlined the regulation of the individual employment contract, protectively qualifying contractual terms and conditions in favor of workers, which included limits on maximum work hours for women and men. It required workers compensation, profit sharing, and the fixing of minimum wages. Furthermore, it stipulated the rights to organize and to strike, and ratified an extensive, tripartite, administrative system of boards to resolve both collective and individual labor disputes. Chile's labor code likewise was the result of a political process evolving since the early 1920s. In neither instance was the legislation the outcome of a triumphant workers' movement that had assumed state power. Indeed, Chile's code was directly influenced by the principles set out in Part XIII of the Treaty of Versailles and adopted by the International Labour Organization, as publicized by its intermediaries, including the renowned lawyer Moisés Poblete Troncoso.[41]

The Brazilian state soon after the 'Revolution of 1930' undertook through law and presidential decree to regulate the labor movement. Importantly, Decree 19770 (issued March 9, 1931) provided rules for official union recognition and

40 See generally Jeremy Adelman, 'Labour Law in Twentieth Century Argentina' in *The Rise and Development of Collective Labour Law*.

41 Moisés Poblete Troncoso, 'Influencia de la legislación en las ramas tradicionales del derecho; tendencias a la codificación de la legislación social en América Latina' (1941) 3(3) Revista Mexicana de Sociología 53–62.

the privileging of a single union in a particular economic sector and region. Tripartite labor tribunals were announced in 1932, and the Constitutions of 1934 and 1937 included labor provisions. Finally, the Consolidated Labor Laws (Consolidação das Leis do Trabalho), an elaborate statute, was passed in 1943 to codify the nation's industrial relations system and its relevant laws. Historians debate the extent to which this system replicated Italy's fascist, corporatist industrial order or was merely inspired by it, as well as other sources, while practically diverging from it.[42]

Implementation of comprehensive labor legislation signifies for the Colliers the establishment of corporatism: 'Corporatism in Latin America thus involved the legalization and institutionalization of an organized labor movement, but one that was shaped and controlled by the state.'[43] The issue of corporatism or the extent to which legally articulated systems of industrial relations became corporatist is still subject to discussion by scholars.[44] What is evident is that despite government projects to subordinate labor pursuant to the enactment of comprehensive legislation, among other strategies, workers and labor leaders, sometimes by utilizing the labor laws and institutions implemented by the state, continued to pursue their interests with or without official sanction.[45]

2 Conclusion: The Neoliberal Turn

Beginning in the 1970s, then gaining momentum toward the end of the 1980s and during the 1990s, most Latin American national governments substantially amended their labor laws.[46] In approximately the same period, agrarian

42 Compare, e.g., Hall, 'Labor and the Law in Brazil,' 88–90 (finding close similarities with the fascist model) with Angela de Castro Gomes and Fernando Teixeira da Silva, 'Bringing Justice to the Workplace: Labor Courts and Labor Laws in Brazil, 1930s-1980s' in *Labor Justice across the Americas*, 212, 220–222 (disputing Brazil's system is a fascist copy while describing it corporatist).

43 Collier and Collier, *Shaping the Political Arena*, 7.

44 See e.g., Leon Fink, 'Conclusion: The Rise and Consolidation of the Mediatory State' in *Labor Justice across the Americas*, and chapters therein on Brazil, Argentina, and Mexico. For further reflection on the nature of labor law in Brazil, compare John D. French, *Drowning in Laws: Labor Law in Brazilian Political Culture* (Chapel Hill: University of North Carolina Press, 2004).

45 The historiography on labor movements in twentieth-century Latin America (some of it touching on relevant laws) is voluminous. Compendium chapters, with their bibliographies, provide a starting point. See, e.g., Brennan, 'Latin American Labor History.'

46 See Maria Lorena Cook, *The Politics of Labor Reform in Latin America: Between Flexibility and Rights* (University Park: Penn State University Press, 2007), Chapter 2, 29–58.

reform, at least as a project to expropriate and to redistribute land, effectively ended. The changes in policy were political determinations, but at the same time were informed by economic theories and legal doctrines. The apparent exhaustion of the project of import substitution industrialization, underscored by high rates of inflation in the 1970s, and worse economic crises during the 1980s, provided the scenario for adopting new market-oriented policies termed neoliberal. Moreover, international organizations, including the World Bank and the International Monetary Fund, frequently conditioned financial and technical assistance on labor law reform. Unions resisted, and the process, as a social and political one, varied through the end of the twentieth century and has continued to the present, as governments have shifted ideologically and politically. The general outcome has resulted in laws affording greater discretion to employers to set the terms of employment with workers, summed up in the word 'flexibilization.' Likewise, governments as of the 1990s have tried to curb the power of labor organizations, even weakening the relationship between unions and the state. Parallel to this trend in the reorientation of labor law, national governments undertook to liberalize land regimes where agrarian reform had been carried out and collective forms of property had been organized. As national governments could rarely dictate policy change seamlessly, the practical effects of reforms implicating workers and peasants differed not only from country to country but also within one nation or another. Relevant scholarship, some of it reviewed in Maria Lorena Cook's monograph on neoliberal reform, has disputed the effectiveness or extent of this transformation, but as to both peasants and workers, the current social world in Latin America contrasts from the one legally inflected with the social language of earlier decades.[47] The social and corporatist legal regime has given way to a neoliberal one.

Mexico exemplifies these points. Actions to curb the power of union leaders, or to amend the nation's comprehensive labor legislation, were undertaken intermittently by distinct political parties as of the late 1980s. At times, independent labor organizations challenged employers, government supported

47 Ibid., 54–58, regarding the range in scholarship on Cook's position: 'In short, the dominant pattern in the region during the market reform period has been the weakening of employment protections traditionally present in the law, and at the same time failure to address deficits in the protection of collective labor rights. This assessment is somewhat at odds with other recent evaluations of labor reforms during the 1980s and 1990s.' On the turn away from 'the social' see Kennedy, 'Three Globalizations of Law and Social Thought' and, in general, other essays collected in the same book, *The New Law and Economic Development*.

union leaderships, and the state. Finally, in late 2012, the federal government promulgated a broad set of legal changes to the employment relationship, largely benefitting employers.[48] Then, in 2017, Article 123 was amended, ostensibly to enhance union democracy, but also evidently with the aim of dismantling the corporatist labor regime. One significant provision directed the eventual transfer of labor cases to the judicial branch along with the derogation of the administrative system long recognized to favor unrepresentative (if not corrupt) union leaders and employers. Under a new president avowedly opposed to his neoliberal predecessors, implementing regulations followed with amendments to the federal labor law in 2019.[49] Whether or not a radical transformation of industrial relations will ensue is still an open question.[50]

In the early 1990s, it had proved politically more feasible for Mexico to amend the Constitution's Article 27, so as to allow for the sale and privatization of collectively owned *ejido* lands, than to alter the industrial relations system formally. The impact of the constitutional amendment and implementing legislation is still ongoing and requires more analysis. Fifteen years after promulgation of the 1991 constitutional reform much of Mexico's ejidal land had not been fully privatized, contrary to many scholars' assumptions.[51] Studies have noted the persistence of ejidal holdings amidst complex evolving circumstances (such as expanding urbanization encroaching on ejidal land).[52]

48 Maria Lorena Cook, *The Politics of Labor Reform*, Chapter 5, 161–173 and 182–192.

49 See Graciela Bensusán, and Kevin J. Middlebrook, 'Democratic Labor Reform in Mexico' (2020) Wilson Center, Mexican Institute (the authors contend the constitutional amendment of 2017 resulted from the pressures of negotiating the Trans-Pacific Partnership and the United States-Mexico-Canada Agreements, while the implementing legislation was favored by the advent of a more socially oriented presidential administration in Dec. 2018).

50 Bensusán and Middlebrook note positive developments in their paper and are cautiously optimistic, see ibid.

51 See, e.g., Richard Velásquez Perales, 'Mexico's Ejido Experiment. Post-Revolutionary Agrarian Politics through Capitalist Restructuring' (2022) Spectre Journal (online publication, https://spectrejournal.com/mexicos-ejido-experiment/) (citing to literature assuming the demise of the *ejido* but then pointing out the contrary); and Melissa Schumacher, et al., 'Evolution and Collapse of *Ejidos* in Mexico – To What Extent Is Communal Land Used for Urban Development?' (2019) 8(10) Land (online publication, https://www.mdpi.com/2073-445X/8/10/146) (analyzing two specific cases of ejidal losses in the context of urbanization, but simply assuming that 'The *ejido* system, based on communal land in Mexico, was transformed to private ownership due to neoliberal trends in the 1990s').

52 See, e.g., Joel Cervantes Herrera, et al., 'Promoción legal de la gran propiedad agraria para modernizar el campo: una equivocación probada' (2017) 96 Alegatos 399–418, 410 (arguing that data contravene predictions of the privatization of ejidal property, and asserting, inter alia, that between 1992 and 2007 ejidal land actually expanded by 7 million hectares or 23.39 per cent, i.e., from 30,032,643 hectares in 1991 to 37,057,776 hectares in 2007; this

Across Latin America, the resistance of labor organizations certainly has slowed the process of transforming collective labor law, even as reform of the individual employment contract proceeded, in accord with neoliberal concepts of creating more flexible working arrangements that presumably enhanced productivity as labor markets were strengthened.[53] Argentina and Brazil present examples of this process. Initially, at least, Argentine unions held off attempts to undermine their organizational interests, such as control over social welfare funds, or the decentralization of collective bargaining, while accepting Law 24,013, passed in 1991, which permitted the operation of a range of temporary individual employment contracts.[54] In Brazil, the drafting of the Constitution of 1988 involved negotiations over labor provisions and resulted, according to Cook, in 'an ambiguous and hybrid document where labor relations were concerned.'[55] The same industrial relations specialist recounts the progression of neoliberal reforms into the 1990s, only to be stymied because of the economic, social, and political turmoil of 2001–2002. In Chile, where an authoritarian government remained in power from 1973 through 1990, the state was able to undertake more extensive neoliberal reform in both the agricultural and industrial sectors, ultimately due to its recourse to military force.

To conclude, the mixed, economic results of the neoliberal turn across the region, along with actual political and social struggles and changes in governments, overshadow any final dictum about the state of the law as it concerns peasants and workers, whose conceptualization as social classes is, moreover, in play. More peasants engage in wage work, as agricultural laborers, a trend evident for decades; and farms operating as market-driven businesses are more extensive, as some peasants have become farmers (again, not an altogether novel development).[56] Labor unions persist, but their bargaining power with employers and relationship with the state are evolving. The legal rights

---

study's analysis is drawn from INEGI, Mexico's national institute on geographical and statistical information). See also, Eric P. Perramond, 'The Rise, Fall, and Reconfiguration of the Mexican Ejido' (2008) 98(3) The Geographical Review 356–371. It may be noted that since 1992 not all ejidal land has to be used collectively: the constitutional amendment to Art. 27 legalized a range of tenurial relations.

53 This paragraph's brief summary is based on Cook, *The Politics of Labor Reform*. An alternative explanation of the relative success or failure of labor reforms, based on the nature of labor markets, is presented by Matthew E. Carnes, *Continuity Despite Change: The Politics of Labor Regulation in Latin America* (Stanford: Stanford University Press, 2014).

54 See Cook, *The Politics of Labor Reform*, 40, 74–76.

55 Ibid., 70 (citations omitted).

56 See Kay, 'Latin America's Agrarian Reform' writing in 1998, on which these points are based. He adds: 'Thus future State interventions in the land tenure system are likely to be confined to a land policy that focuses not on expropriation but on progressive land tax,

of individual workers are extensive but not always readily enforceable, while women's presence in labor markets has become more pronounced. In brief, the history of the law as to peasants and workers indicates both this law's plasticity and its intimate connection with the political, economic, and social relations of these subjects. As workers and peasants undergo significant economic and social transformations, they continue to contribute to the shaping of the laws that affect them. But they largely remain in asymmetrical relations of power and hold weaker positions vis-á-vis other historical subjects who also determine the nature of labor and agrarian law.

References

Adelman, Jeremy. 'Labour Law in Twentieth Century Argentina.' In *The Rise and Development of Collective Labour Law*, edited by Marcel van der Linden and Richard Price, 19–42. Bern: Peter Lang, 2000.

Annino, Antonio, and François-Xavier Guerra, eds. *Inventando la nación: Iberoamérica; Siglo XIX*. México: Fondo de Cultura Económica, 2003.

Baitenmann, Helga. 'Ejerciendo la justicia fuera de los tribunales: de las reivindicaciones decimonónicas a las restituciones de la reforma agraria.' *Historia Mexicana* 66(4) (2017): 2013–2072.

Bauer, Arnold. 'Rural Workers in Spanish America: Problems of Peonage and Oppression.' *The Hispanic American Historical Review* 59(1) (Feb. 1979): 34–63.

Bauer, Arnold. 'Reply.' *The Hispanic American Historical Review* 59(3) (Aug. 1979): 486–489.

Bensusán, Graciela, and Kevin J. Middlebrook. 'Democratic Labor Reform in Mexico.' Wilson Center, Mexican Institute (2020) (https://www.wilsoncenter.org/publication/democratic-labor-reform-mexico) (accessed July 13, 2023).

Brennan, James P. 'Latin American Labor History.' In *The Oxford Handbook of Latin American History*, edited by José C. Moya. Oxford: Oxford University Press, 2010.

Carnes, Matthew E. *Continuity Despite Change: The Politics of Labor Regulation in Latin America*. Stanford: Stanford University Press, 2014.

Carrera Stampa, Manuel. *Los gremios mexicanos: la organización gremial en Nueva España, 1521–1861*. México: Edición y Distribución Iberoamericana de Publicaciones, 1954.

---

land settlement, colonization, land transfer and financing mechanisms, land markets, registration, titling and secure property rights.' Ibid., 28.

Castro Gomes, Angela de, and Fernando Teixeira da Silva. 'Bringing Justice to the Workplace: Labor Courts and Labor Laws in Brazil, 1930s-1980s.' In *Labor Justice across the Americas*, edited by Leon Fink and Juan Manuel Palacio, 211–234. Urbana: University of Illinois Press, 2018.

Cervantes Herrera, Joel, José Alfredo Castellanos Suárez, and Artemio Cruz León. 'Promoción legal de la gran propiedad agraria para modernizar el campo: una equivocación probada.' *Alegatos* 96 (2017): 399–418.

Coatsworth, John. 'Patterns of Rural Rebellion in Latin America.' In *Riot, Rebellion, and Revolution: Rural Social Conflict in Mexico*, edited by Friedrich Katz, 21–62. Princeton: Princeton University Press, 1988.

Collier, Ruth B., and David Collier. *Shaping the Political Arena: Critical Junctures, the Labor Movement, and Regime Dynamics in Latin America*. Princeton: Princeton University Press, 1991.

Cook, Maria Lorena. *The Politics of Labor Reform in Latin America: Between Flexibility and Rights*. University Park: Penn State University Press, 2007.

Cuadros Villena, Carlos. *Derechos Reales*, vol. 2. Lima: Empresa Editora Latina, 1995.

De la Peña, Guillermo. 'Rural Mobilizations in Latin America since c. 1920.' In T*he Cambridge History of Latin America*, edited by Leslie Bethell, vol. 6, 379–482. Cambridge: Cambridge University Press, 1995.

Diaz, María Elena. *The Virgin, the King and the Royal Slaves of El Cobre: Negotiating Freedom in Colonial Cuba, 1670–1870*. Stanford: Stanford University Press, 2000.

Duve, Thomas, and Heikki Pihlajamäki, eds. *New Horizons in Spanish Colonial Law: Contributions to Transnational Early Modern Legal History*. Frankfurt am Main: Max Planck Institute for European Legal History, 2015.

Fink, Leon. 'Conclusion: The Rise and Consolidation of the Mediatory State.' In *Labor Justice Across the Americas*, edited by Leon Fink and Juan Manuel Palacio, 259–266. Urbana: University of Illinois Press, 2018.

Florescano, Enrique, Isabel González Sánchez, and Jorge González Angulo. *De la colonia al imperio*, vol. 1 of *La clase obrera en la historia de México*, edited by Pablo González Casanova. México: Siglo Veintiuno, 1990.

French, John D. *Drowning in Laws: Labor Law in Brazilian Political Culture*. Chapel Hill: University of North Carolina Press, 2004.

García Martínez, Bernardo. 'Jurisdicción y propiedad: una distinción fundamental en la historia de los pueblos de indios del México colonial.' *European Review of Latin American and Caribbean Studies* 53 (1992): 47–60.

Garriga, Carlos. 'La recusación judicial: del derecho indiano al derecho mexicano.' In Cuadernos del Instituto de Investigaciones Jurídicas, *La supervivencia del derecho español en Hispanoamérica durante la época independiente*, 203–239. México: UNAM, 1998.

Gaviria Liévano, Enrique. *El liberalismo y la insurrección de los artesanos contra el librecambio*. Bogotá: Universidad de Bogotá Jorge Tadeo Lozano, 2002.

Hall, Michael M. 'Labor and the Law in Brazil.' In *The Rise and Development of Collective Labour Law*, edited by Marcel van der Linden and Richard Price, 79–95. Bern: Peter Lang, 2000.

Illades, Carlos. *Hacia la república del trabajo: La organización artesanal en la ciudad de México, 1853–1876*. México City: El Colegio de México y Universidad Autónoma Metropolitana-Iztapalapa, 1996.

Kay, Cristóbal. 'Latin America's Agrarian Reform: Lights and Shadows.' *Land Reform* 2 (1998): 8–31.

Keen, Benjamin. 'The Black Legend Revisited: Assumptions and Realities.' *Hispanic American Historical Review* 49(4) (1969): 703–719.

Kennedy, Duncan. 'Three Globalizations of Law and Legal Thought: 1850–2000.' In *The New Law and Economic Development: A Critical Appraisal*, edited by David M. Trubek and Alvaro Santos. Cambridge: Cambridge University Press, 2006.

Kourí, Emilio. 'La invención del ejido.' *Nexos*, January 2015 (https://www.nexos.com.mx/?p=23778) (accessed April 23, 2021).

Kourí, Emilio. 'Sobre la propiedad comunal de los pueblos. De la Reforma a la Revolución.' *Historia Mexicana* 66(4) (2017): 1923–1960.

Lira, Andrés. *Comunidades indígenas frente a la Ciudad de México: Tenochtitlán y Tlatelolco, sus pueblos y barrios, 1812–1919*. México City: El Colegio de México, 1995.

Lorente Sariñena, Marta. 'Las resistencias a la ley en el primer constitucionalismo mexicano.' In Cuadernos del Instituto de Investigaciones Jurídicas, *La supervivencia del derecho español en Hispanoamérica durante la época independiente*, 299–327. México: UNAM, 1998.

Loveman, Brian. 'Critique of Arnold J. Bauer's "Rural Workers in Spanish America: Problems of Peonage and Oppression."' *The Hispanic American Historical Review* 59(3): 478–485.

Marino, Daniela. 'Indios, pueblos y la construcción de la Nación. La modernización del espacio rural en el centro de México, 1812–1900.' In *Nación, Constitución y Reforma, 1821–1908*, edited by Erika Pani, 163–204. México: Fondo de Cultura Económica, 2010.

Marino, Daniela. 'Nuestros hijos recibirán como legado esta cuestión … Los Indígenas y el derecho en el siglo XIX (Estado de México).' *TRACE: Travaux et Recherches dans les Amériques du Centre* 46 (2004): 42–58.

Mijangos y González, Pablo. *El nuevo pasado jurídico mexicano: Una revision de la historiografía jurídica mexicana durante los últimos 20 años*. Madrid: Universidad Carlos III de Madrid, 2011.

Mirow, M.C. *Latin American Constitutions: The Constitution of Cádiz and Its Legacy in Spanish America*. Cambridge: Cambridge University Press, 2015.

Mirow, M.C. 'Origins of the Social Function of Property in Chile.' *Fordham Law Review* 80 (2011): 1183–1217.

Owensby, Brian. *Empire of Law and Indian Justice in Colonial Mexico*. Stanford: Stanford University Press, 2008.

Palacio, Juan Manuel. 'From Social Legislation to Labor Justice: The Common Background in the Americas.' In *Labor Justice across the Americas*, edited by Leon Fink and Juan Manuel Palacio, 16–43. Urbana: University of Illinois Press, 2018.

Perramond, Eric P. 'The Rise, Fall, and Reconfiguration of the Mexican Ejido.' *The Geographical Review* 98(3) (2008): 356–371.

Poblete Troncoso, Moisés. 'Influencia de la legislación en las ramas tradicionales del derecho; tendencias a la codificación de la legislación social en América Latina.' *Revista Mexicana de Sociología* 3(3) (1941): 53–62.

Poblete Troncoso, Moisés. 'The Social Content of Latin American Constitutions.' *Social Forces* 21(1) (1942–1943): 100–106.

Rouaix, Pastor. *Génesis de los artículos 27 y 123 de la Constitución Política de 1917*, 2nd ed. México: INEHRM, 1959.

Schaefer, Timo. *Liberalism as Utopia: The Rise and Fall of Legal Rule in Post-Colonial Mexico, 1820–1900.* Cambridge: Cambridge University Press, 2017.

Schumacher, Melissa, Pamela Durán-Díaz, Anne Kristiina Kurjenoja, Eduardo Gutiérrez-Juárez, and David A. González-Rivas. 'Evolution and Collapse of *Ejidos* in Mexico – To What Extent Is Communal Land Used for Urban Development?' *Land* 8(10) (2019): 146 (https://www.mdpi.com/2073-445X/8/10/146).

Schwartz, Stuart B. *Slaves, Peasants, and Rebels: Reconsidering Brazilian Slavery.* Urbana: University of Illinois Press, 1992.

Serulnikov, Sergio. *Subverting Colonial Authority: Challenges to Spanish Rule in Eighteenth Century Southern Andes*. Durham: Duke University Press, 2003.

Suárez-Potts, William. *The Making of Law: The Supreme Court and Labor Legislation in Mexico, 1875–1931*. Stanford: Stanford University Press, 2012.

Tandeter, Enrique. *Coercion and Market: Silver Mining in Colonial Potosí, 1692–1826.* Albuquerque: University of New Mexico, 1993.

Trazegnies Granda, Fernando de. *La idea de derecho en el Perú republicano del siglo XIX*, 2nd ed. Lima: Pontificia Universidad Católica del Perú, Fondo Editorial, 1992.

Uribe-Uran, Víctor M., with Germán Palacio. 'Origins of Labor Rights and Justice in Colombia, 1850–1950.' In *Labor Justice across the Americas*, edited by Leon Fink and Juan Manuel Palacio, 142–163. Urbana: University of Illinois Press, 2018.

Velásquez Perales, Richard. 'Mexico's Ejido Experiment. Post-Revolutionary Agrarian Politics Through Capitalist Restructuring.' *Spectre Journal* (2022) (https://spectrejournal.com/mexicos-ejido-experiment/).

Wolf, Eric R. 'Types of Latin American Peasantry: A Preliminary Discussion.' *American Anthropologist* 57 (1955): 452–471.

Zavala, Silvio. *El servicio personal de los indios en la Nueva España*, 7 vols. México: El Colegio de México, 1984–1995.

Zavala, Silvio. *El servicio personal de los indios en Perú: extractos del siglo xvi*, 3 vols. México: El Colegio de México, 1978–1980.

Zimmermann, Eduardo. 'Un espíritu nuevo: La cuestión social y el Derecho en la Argentina (1890–1930).' *Revista de Indias* 73(257) (2013): 81–106.

Zorita, Alonso. *Life and Labor in Ancient Mexico: The Brief and Summary Relation of the Lords of Spain*, trans. and with an introduction by Benjamin Keen. New Brunswick: Rutgers University Press, 1963.

PART 3

Selected Topics

CHAPTER 14

Land and Other Property

Agustín Parise

1 Introduction

This chapter examines land and other property relations in Latin America, starting in the sixteenth century and extending until the final decades of the twentieth century. The essay aims to provide an inventory of the main motivations that accompanied and help explain the changes in the history of land and other property in Latin America.[1] That exercise should expose the dual character of property law: homogeneity and heterogeneity.[2]

The inventory in this chapter will follow the evolution of ownership paradigms as experienced in Latin American jurisdictions. The legal literature previously referred to paradigms of ownership,[3] yet no leading definition seems to have been proposed. In this chapter, ownership paradigms consist of the abstract understanding of what constitutes the right of ownership and what this right comprises. That abstract understanding finds consensus amongst jurists, provides model problems and solutions, and changes according to time and place. Ownership paradigms should be considered tools to assess the conditions of the right of ownership, and the way actors perceive societies and trigger law's change and application.

The study is divided into three parts, addressing the different ownership paradigms that were experienced in Latin American jurisdictions. The Allocation paradigm was the first link in an uninterrupted chain of ownership paradigms

1 The idea of an 'inventory' was borrowed from Paolo Grossi, who used it in 1976 when presenting a seminal collection of articles dealing with property law during the nineteenth and twentieth centuries. Paolo Grossi, 'Pagina Introduttiva' (1976–1977) 5–6 Quaderni Fiorentini per la storia del pensiero giuridico moderno 3. The content of this chapter was extracted from the PhD dissertation of the author: Agustín Parise, *Ownership Paradigms in American Civil Law Jurisdictions: Manifestations of the Shifts in the Legislation of Louisiana, Chile, and Argentina (16th-20th Centuries)* (Leiden: Brill, 2017).

2 Jean-Louis Bergel alerted us to this duality. Jean-Louis Bergel, *La Propriété* (Paris: Dalloz, 1994), 2.

3 See, amongst the copious literature, the references in Antonio Gambaro, 'Property Rights in Comparative Perspective: Why Property Is So Ancient and Durable' (2011) 26 Tulane European and Civil Law Forum 26.

 | DOI:10.1163/9789004436091_016

in Latin American jurisdictions. That link extends mainly during the early modern period. The second link comprised the Liberal[4] paradigm, which developed mainly during the nineteenth century, together with the legislation that emanated from the new republics and states. The third link comprised the Social Function paradigm, which started to develop at the turn of the century and took force during the first decades of the twentieth century. Finally, this chapter offers concluding remarks and provides a list of references.

2 Allocation Paradigm

An Allocation paradigm of ownership was shaped during the pre-independence period and started with the arrival of Europeans to the Americas in 1492. That paradigm extended for more than 300 years, until the different new American republics and states dictated their own legislation that dealt with property, mainly during the nineteenth century. Property was allocated to different actors within that early period, reacting to their various interests at different times. These jurisdictions, however, shared a common legal grounding during the entire period.[5] That common ground grew from the constant enactment of common norms, from the exchange of officers amongst regions, and from the internal migration of actors, ultimately resulting in a common perception of legal identity.[6]

2.1 *Native American Land Relations*

Native American groups had, in the words of Alfonso García-Gallo, a 'mosaic of different legal systems [*derechos*].'[7] Those legal systems had reached various

4 This paradigm is also referred to in the literature as liberal-individualistic, Napoleonic-Pandectist, or Bourgeois Property. Abelardo Levaggi, 'El proceso desamortizador y desvinculador de los bienes de manos muertas desde la óptica jurídica' in *Cuadernos de Historia Lationamericana 7: El Proceso Desvinculador y Desamortizador de Bienes Eclesiásticos y Comunales en la América Española. Siglos XVIII y XIX*, eds Hans-Jürgen Prien and Rosa María Martínez de Codes (The Netherlands: Asociación de Historiadores Latinoamericanistas Europeos, 1999), 60.

5 Ricardo D. Rabinovich-Berkman, *Principios generales del derecho latinoamericano* (Buenos Aires: Astrea, 2006), 241.

6 Ibid.

7 Alfonso García-Gallo, 'El pluralismo jurídico en la América española' in *Los orígenes Españoles de las Instituciones Americanas: Estudios de Derecho Indiano*, ed. Alfonso García-Gallo (Madrid: Real Academia de Jurisprudencia y Legislación, 1987), 300. See also Abelardo Levaggi, 'La réception du système juridique espagnol par les systèmes indigènes

degrees of development, depending on the different groups.[8] Land relations of Native American groups were marked by communal and individual control over property. The natives had property rights that aimed to fulfil their needs, while not sharing the European understanding of ownership.[9] Native American land relations included the union with nature and the connection of the community with the territory.[10] Early accounts by new settlers attested to the existence of communitarian holdings of land amongst specific native groups, mainly when dealing with crops and pastures.[11] The trend towards holdings in common was related to the conception those groups had regarding land, marked with spiritual connotations linked to their religious beliefs.[12] Yet not all land was held in common, because some groups recognized some rights in land, enabling, inter alia, transfers of land and inheritance.[13] In some American regions, such as Mesoamerica and the Andes, land use and production indicated the coexistence of communal and individual holdings.[14]

Land relations of Native American groups were indeed marked by communal and individual holdings. The arrival of Iberian settlers did not bring to an end the communal and individual control over property. Some Native American laws and customs prevailed, as long as they did not contradict the Catholic faith, natural law, and the crown's jurisdiction,[15] such as the *cacicazgo*.[16]

---

en Amérique' in *La Réception des Systèmes juridiques: implantations et destins*, eds Michel Doucet and Jacques Vanderlinden (Brussels: Etablissements Emile Bruylant, 1994), 334.

8 Katherine A. Hermes, 'The Law of Native Americans, to 1815' in *The Cambridge History of Law in America*, eds Michael Grossberg and Christopher L. Tomlins (Cambridge: Cambridge University Press, 2008), vol. 1, 38.

9 Kenneth H. Bobroff, 'Retelling Allotment: Indian Property Rights and the Myth of Common Ownership' (2001) 54 Vanderbilt Law Review 1573; Bradley Bryan, 'Property as Ontology: On Aboriginal and English Understandings of Ownership' (2000) 13 Canadian Journal of Law and Jurisprudence 17. See also, Jerome A. Offner, 'Law before European Contact: Mesoamerica' in this volume.

10 Bryan, 'Property as Ontology,' 26.

11 Rafael Altamira y Crevea, *Historia de la Propiedad Comunal* (Madrid: J. López Camacho, 1890), 301.

12 Alterini, Corna, and Vásquez, *Propiedad Indígena*, 41.

13 Bobroff, 'Retelling Allotment,' 1571.

14 Federico Brito Figueroa, *El Cuadro Histórico de la Propiedad Territorial en las Colonias Hispanoamericanas* (Caracas: Universidad Santa María, 1982), 16–17. See Offner, 'Law before European Contact: Mesoamerica' in this volume.

15 Abelardo Levaggi, *Manual de Historia del Derecho Argentino (Castellano-Indiano/Nacional)*, 2nd ed. (Buenos Aires: Depalma, 1996), vol. 1, 170.

16 Law 3, Title 7, Book 6 of the *Recopilación de Leyes de Indias* of 1680 instructed the preservation of the way in which the chief of a group (*cacique*) was to be succeeded. *Recopilacion de Leyes de los Reynos de las Indias* (Madrid: Ivlian de Paredes, 1681), vol. 2, f. 219v. See also Levaggi, *Manual de Historia del Derecho Argentino*, vol. 1, 170.

The land relations of Native American groups changed during the centuries that followed the arrival of Europeans. For example, mainly during the nineteenth century, the emergence of a Liberal paradigm of ownership motivated the elimination of many of the holdings in common, aiming to enhance the individualistic character of ownership.[17] Even later, starting during the last decades of the twentieth century, long after the Social Function paradigm had gained ground, other changes emerged. National and international efforts were undertaken to recognize Native American rights in land. Several national constitutions enacted at the time dealt with Native American property relations.[18] In addition, the Inter-American Commission on Human Rights alerted that when Native American property was not recognized, the cultural and spiritual development of the groups was affected.[19] In similar lines, the Inter-American Court of Human Rights ruled that the protection of property as stated in the American Convention on Human Rights (1969) included the rights of Native American groups within the framework of communal property.[20] Another important change was provided by the incorporation of the Indigenous and Tribal Peoples Convention (1989) of the International Labour Organization into the framework of several Latin American jurisdictions.[21] These changes pointed also towards the constitutionalization of private law.

2.2 *European Access to Lands in the Americas*

The early expansionist movements of the Castilian and Portuguese crowns may be defined as foundational[22] or, within the scope of this chapter, as a means to allocate the recently discovered territories. The early movements aimed to

17 Abelardo Levaggi, 'Tratamiento legal y jurisprudencial del aborigen en la Argentina durante el siglo XIX' in *El aborigen y el derecho en el pasado y el presente*, ed. Abelardo Levaggi (Buenos Aires: Universidad del Museo Social Argentino, 1990), 260.

18 Pablo María Corna and Carlos Alberto Fossaceca, 'La propiedad indígena comunitaria: un análisis crítico del articulado del Proyecto de Código Civil y Comercial Unificado' (2012) 249 El Derecho 789.

19 Irene Pujol de Zizzias, 'La propiedad indígena en el Proyecto de reforma del Código Civil y Comercial' (2012-IV) Jurisprudencia Argentina 11 (online).

20 Ibid.; Inter-American Commission on Human Rights, *Derechos de los pueblos indígenas y tribales sobre sus tierras ancestrales y recursos naturales: normas y jurisprudencia del sistema interamericano de derechos humanos* (OEA/Ser.L/V/II. Doc. 56/09); Juan Manuel Salgado, 'La exclusión de las normas sobre pueblos indígenas del Proyecto de Código Civil y Comercial de la Nación, aprobado por el Senado' *Jurisprudencia Argentina 2014-III*, 2014, 1 [online].

21 Inter-American Commission on Human Rights, *Derechos de los pueblos indígenas*, 6.

22 Bernardino Bravo Lira, *Derecho Común y Derecho Propio en el Nuevo Mundo* (Santiago: Editorial Jurídica de Chile, 1989), 193.

the settlement and creation of new societies, with their own cultures, being different from that of European and Native American groups yet building on the preexisting conditions on both sides of the Atlantic Ocean.[23]

In Spanish America, all discovered territories were a royal holding (*regalía*) of the crown of Castile. The monarchs did not own those territories, only having dominium and jurisdiction over them, something similar to the eminent domain of which Hugo Grotius would later speak in the early seventeenth century.[24] The *Recopilación de Leyes de Indias* of 1680, the authoritative compilation of *derecho indiano* stated in Law 1, Title 1, Book 3 that the 'Occidental Indies shall always be united to the crown of Castile and may not be alienated.'[25] Furthermore, Law 14, Title 12, Book 4 of the same text stated that monarchs held all territories, while that royal holding extended to the surface and underground.[26] These were part of the crown of Castile, and were not owned individually by the monarchs, hence explaining the royal interest in exploiting the land.[27] Accordingly, any possible rights of others on the land had to be granted by the monarch, by means of a grace (*gracia*).[28]

The royal holding by the Castilian crown found support in at least three points. First, in the Capitulations (*Capitulaciones*) of Santa Fe, by which Christopher Columbus agreed with the monarchs on April 17, 1492, the extent of his expeditionary rights.[29] Second, in a series of papal

---

23 Bravo Lira, *Derecho Común y Derecho Propio*, 193.

24 Antonio Dougnac Rodríguez, *Manual de Historia del Derecho Indiano* (México: Universidad Nacional Autónoma de México, 1994), 400.

25 *Recopilacion de Leyes de los Reynos de las Indias*, vol. 2, f. 1.

26 Ibid., f. 103v. It should be noted that the law was interpreted by some scholars as not meaning necessarily the nationalization of all land. See José María Mariluz Urquijo, 'La propiedad en el derecho indiano' (1970) 6 Revista Chilena de Historia del Derecho 155; José María Mariluz Urquijo, *El Régimen de la Tierra en el Derecho Indiano*, 2nd ed. (Buenos Aires: Editorial Perrot, 1978), 22. See also María Victoria Daract, 'La historia de la propiedad' in *Poder, propiedad y propiedades en Argentina: Informe final de investigación (SECyT UNCuyo 06/F184)*, ed. Susana T. Ramella (Mendoza: Universidad Nacional de Cuyo, Facultad de Ciencias Políticas y Sociales, 2005–2007), 25 http://bdigital.uncu.edu.ar/1509.

27 Adolfo Omar Cueto, *Historia del Proceso de Enajenación de la Tierra Fiscal en Mendoza (siglos XVI–XIX): Estudio sobre la aplicación de la Legislación Indiana en la época colonial; Su vigencia y proyección durante el siglo XIX en Mendoza* (Mendoza: Universidad Nacional de Cuyo, Facultad de Filosofía y Letras, 1999), 85.

28 José María Ots Capdequí, *El régimen de la tierra en la América española durante el periodo colonial: Cursillo dictado en la Universidad de Santo Domingo del 27 de noviembre al 13 de diciembre de 1944* (Ciudad Trujillo: Universidad de Santo Domingo, 1946), 41.

29 See the text of the Capitulations in the version preserved in the Archives of the Crown of Aragon, available at 'Santa Fe Capitulations.' Memory of the World, UNESCO. http://www.unesco.org/new/en/communication-and-information/flagship-project-activities/memory-of-the-world/register/full-list-of-registered-heritage/registered

bulls.[30] These official papal communications with lead seals (*bullas*) affixed to them allocated different geographical areas for the commercial and evangelization activities of the Castilian and Portuguese crowns.[31] Three bulls were dated May 3 and 4, 1493,[32] and aimed to bring to similar standing the pretensions of the Castilian crown with those of the Portuguese crown.[33] The *Inter caetera* of May 3 established sovereignty in lands not previously occupied by other Christian monarchs;[34] while the *Eximiae devotionis* stated that evangelization was the reason for permitting that sovereignty, and it granted no lesser rights than those previously established for the Portuguese crown.[35] The second *Inter caetera* of May 4, set out the geographical scope of the rights and duties of the Castilian crown.[36] Third, the royal holding found support in the

-heritage-page-8/santa-fe-capitulations/. See also the text in Francisco Morales Padrón, *Teoría y leyes de la conquista* (Madrid: Ediciones Cultura Hispánica del Centro Iberoamericano de Cooperación, 1979), 54–55.

30 This chapter addresses only three bulls (i.e., first and second *Inter caetera* and the *Eximiae devotionis*). There were, however, other bulls that preceded them (mainly referring to Portugal), and other bulls that aimed to further explain the three previously mentioned. Amongst those other bulls, it is possible to mention *Dudum siquidem* (1493), *Piis fidelium* (1493), *Mius falciti* (1505), and *Universalis ecclesiae* (1508). See Óscar Cruz Barney, *Historia del Derecho Indiano* (Valencia: Tirant lo Blanch, 2012), 71; Ismael Sánchez Bella, Alberto de la Hera, and Carlos Dīaz Rementería, *Historia del Derecho Indiano* (Madrid: Editorial MAPFRE, 1992), 119. For a comprehensive study of the bulls of Pope Alexander VI, see Alfonso García-Gallo, 'Las Bulas de Alejandro VI y el ordenamiento jurídico de la expansión portuguesa y castellana en África e Indias' in Alfonso García-Gallo, *Los orígenes Españoles de las Instituciones Americanas: Estudios de Derecho Indiano*, 313. See also, Hekki Pihlajamäki, Chapter 3 in this volume.

31 Ron Seckinger, *The Brazilian Monarchy and the South American Republics, 1822–1831: Diplomacy and State Building* (Baton Rouge: Louisiana State University Press, 1984), 56; and Levaggi, 'La réception du système,' 337.

32 There is debate on the date of the different bulls. See Sánchez Bella, de la Hera, and Díaz Rementería, *Historia del Derecho Indiano*, 117.

33 On the parallels between the three Castilian bulls and the three Portuguese bulls, see Alfonso García-Gallo, *Manual de Historia del Derecho Español*, 7th ed. (Madrid: s.n., 1977), vol. 1, § 1191.

34 The texts in Latin and Spanish of the bulls *Inter caetera* of May 3 and 4 are available at García-Gallo, 'Las Bulas de Alejandro VI,' 623–633. See also Cruz Barney, *Historia del Derecho Indiano*, 70.

35 The text in Latin and Spanish of the bull *Eximiae devotionis* is available at García-Gallo, 'Las Bulas de Alejandro VI,' 633–636. See Sánchez Bella, de la Hera, and Díaz Rementería, *Historia del Derecho Indiano*, 117; and Cruz Barney, *Historia del Derecho Indiano*, 70.

36 García-Gallo, 'Las Bulas de Alejandro VI,' 627; Sánchez Bella, de la Hera, and Díaz Rementería, *Historia del Derecho Indiano*, 117.

right to conquest and just war.[37] The prevailing *ius commune* in Europe stated that conquering monarchs should have *potestas* over the discovered territories and inhabitants.[38] Scholars such as Francisco de Vitoria, Alberico Gentili, and Grotius advocated for this understanding, providing support to the claims of sovereignty and taking by the different monarchs.[39]

2.3 *Allocating Multiple Interests*

In the new territories multiple actors had, and defended, multiple interests, some of which overlapped and were concurrent. Many aimed to the allocation of ownership, hence shaping a unique and new paradigm. The Pope had universal ownership, the crown had primordial ownership, and Native Americans and European settlers could have private ownership within the different territories.[40] That private ownership, however, was limited if compared with the one that prevailed during the period of the Liberal paradigm. When property was allocated, it aimed to the common good, being therefore subject to termination if the requirements made at the time of granting the right were not fulfilled.[41] Finally, it should be noted that the allocation was individual or communal, and sought to fulfil the different interests of the actors.

The crown was an important actor. It had multiple interests in the allocation of ownership, in particular the effective settlement of population (political interest), the transformation of land into a means of economic production (economic interest), and the inclusion of local populations as subjects of taxation (tax interests).[42] Two other interests of the crown were related to the

---

37 Daract, 'La historia de la propiedad,' 25; Sánchez Bella, de la Hera, and Díaz Rementería, *Historia del Derecho Indiano*, 345; Levaggi, 'La réception du système,' 337; and Cueto, *Historia del Proceso de Enajenación*, 85.

38 Cueto, *Historia del Proceso de Enajenación*, 109; and Bravo Lira, *Derecho Común y Derecho Propio*, 195.

39 Michael Burger and Paul Frymer, 'Property Law and American Empire' (2012) 34 University of Hawaii Law Review 471–523.

40 It should be noted that, amongst others, Francisco de Vitoria refuted the claim that the Pope had universal ownership. Accordingly, the Pope lacked temporal authority, and thus, the Pope could not give something over which he had no control, possession, or dominium. See Agustín Parise, 'The Valladolid Controversy Revisited: Looking back at the Sixteenth-Century Debate on Native Americans While Facing the Current Status of Human Embryos' (2008) 1 Journal of Civil Law Studies 123; Robert A. Williams, Jr., 'The Medieval and Renaissance Origins of the Status of the American Indian in Western Legal Thought' (1983) 57 Southern California Law Review 75. See also Dougnac Rodríguez, *Manual de Historia del Derecho Indiano*, 402.

41 Dougnac Rodríguez, *Manual de Historia del Derecho Indiano*, 402.

42 Abelardo Levaggi, *Manual de Historia del Derecho Argentino (Castellano-Indiano/Nacional)* (Buenos Aires: Depalma, 1987), vol. 2, 210.

allocation of ownership, at least tangentially: monarchs were interested in protecting Native Americans, as indicated by the inclusion of a specific reference by Isabella I in her testament; and they were likewise interested in the propagation of the Catholic faith, as indicated by the inclusion of representatives of the church in discovery expeditions.[43]

The church was likewise an important actor, and its interests were present in the Americas. Monarchs had the exclusive duty to evangelize the new territories, a paramount interest naturally shared with the church.[44] All other interests were subordinated to evangelization: *Salus animarum suprema lex esto*.[45] As early as 1501, the crown devoted efforts that persisted during the sixteenth and seventeenth centuries to avoid the settling of, amongst others, heretics, Jews, and Muslims in the Americas, while welcoming Europeans who had received the sacrament of baptism.[46] Accordingly, the first book of the *Recopilación* (1680) dealt with the Catholic faith throughout twenty-four titles.[47]

Native Americans were actors that likewise had an interest in the allocation of ownership. As they had done before the arrival of European settlers, the natives generally held and exploited lands in common.[48] With time, settlers started to seek some of these lands due to their good location and quality.[49] Peninsular and creole settlers found it difficult to accept the idea of hunting grounds being held by nomadic groups, and this motivated the acknowledgment of ownership only in cases of sedentary groups.[50] Even when Native Americans had some privileges at the time of disposing of property and had an officer that acted as their protector (*protector de naturales*), they were subject to many abuses and usurpations due to their lack of legal knowledge and of royal supervision.[51]

43 Dougnac Rodríguez, *Manual de Historia del Derecho Indiano*, 18–19; and Ots Capdequí, *El régimen de la tierra*, 14.

44 Bravo Lira, *Derecho Común y Derecho Propio*, 196; Dougnac Rodríguez, *Manual de Historia del Derecho Indiano*, 277.

45 Bravo Lira, *Derecho Común y Derecho Propio*, 196.

46 Sánchez Bella, de la Hera, and Díaz Rementería, *Historia del Derecho Indiano*, 308.

47 See generally *Recopilacion de Leyes de los Reynos de las Indias* (Madrid: Ivlian de Paredes, 1681), vol. 1.

48 Levaggi, *Manual de Historia del Derecho Argentino*, vol. 2, 210.

49 Ibid.

50 Ibid., 211; and Sánchez Bella, de la Hera, and Díaz Rementería, *Historia del Derecho Indiano*, 347.

51 Native Americans had, for example, the right to retract (*retracto*) and sales had to be publicly announced (*pregones*). Dougnac Rodríguez, *Manual de Historia del Derecho Indiano*, 324; Levaggi, *Manual de Historia del Derecho Argentino*, vol. 2, 211.

2.3.1 Individual

The crown allotted individual ownership to settlers starting with the first expeditions, in accordance with the main interests of the crown, both secular and spiritual. The crown found in the settlers a partner to comply with the allocation of the new territories. Several efforts were devoted to allotting ownership, and they were effectuated by different means, starting with the previously mentioned capitulations. For example, allotment of individual ownership could be effectively achieved through public auction of tracts of land since 1591, or it could be pursued by means of the *encomienda*.[52]

The primary means to allot individual ownership, however, was the emission of royal land grants, *mercedes*. The *Recopilación* addressed different aspects of ownership mainly in Titles 1 and 12 of Book 4. For example, all of Title 12 dealt with the emission of royal land grants (*mercedes reales de tierras*). The individual allocation of ownership responded to the different concurring interests of the various actors. The allocation through royal land grants, with origins in the Iberian Peninsula, was applied in the Americas, being the dominant means to allot individual ownership. *Mercedes* were indeed implemented in a ritualistic manner through petition, survey, drafting of title, entering into possession, and registration in notarial act. This system enabled settlers to become partners of the crown in the American efforts. The implementation of *mercedes* showed that there was a joint effort between the monarchs who granted those documents and the different settlers who aimed to secure the different tracts of land.

2.3.2 Communal

The Allocation paradigm was shaped both by individual and communal control over property. The crown allotted communal ownership, again, starting already with the first expeditions and responding to its main secular and spiritual interests. Communitarian holding continuously influenced the settlement endeavors of the crown.[53] Communal allocation, therefore, coexisted with

52 Cueto, *Historia del Proceso de Enajenación*, 91–93, 229–238; Ots Capdequí, *El régimen de la tierra*, 55–58; Solon L. Barraclough, ed., *Agrarian Structure in Latin America: A Resume of the CIDA Land Tenure Studies of: Argentina, Brazil, Chile, Colombia, Ecuador, Guatemala, Peru* (Lexington: Lexington Books, 1973), 4. See generally Silvio Zavala, *La Encomienda Indiana*, 3rd ed. (México: Porrúa, 1992).

53 José María Ots Capdequí, *Estudios de historia del derecho español en las Indias. (El derecho de propiedad. El municipio colonial. El derecho de sucesión. Condición jurídica del extranjero. Aportaciones para la historia de la iglesia. La expansión del derecho español en los territorios indianos)* (Bogotá: Editorial Minerva, 1940), 80; José María Ots Capdequí, *Manual de historia de derecho español en las Indias y del derecho propiamente indiano* (Buenos Aires: Editorial Losada, 1945), 451.

individual allocation, and found its origins, as other legal transplants, in the Iberian Peninsula.[54] For more than 300 years, and on both sides of the Atlantic Ocean, the crown allotted communal ownership through different means and to different actors. Communal allocation responded to the needs to secure life and offer protection.[55] In America, for example, water sources and pastures were of paramount importance for the raising of livestock, while woodlands were fundamental sources for timber.[56] Accordingly, at that time some property could be held in common (*comunales*) by all neighbors of a settlement (such as, city or village) and by all members of a Native American group. Property held in common belonged to and was exploited jointly by all those actors, and it extended over woodlands (*montes*), pastures (*pastos*), and water sources (*aguadas*).[57] Those actors comprised a universality of holders. Only members of that universality could benefit from the ownership, and as clearly advocated by José Berní y Catalá, in his *Instituta Civil y Real* (1745), 'those foreign to the neighborhood could not use [the property] unless they had a permit from the universality.'[58] Furthermore, property could be held commonly directly by settlements (*propios*), when local administrations secured on behalf of all settlers the exploitation of property, aiming to generate income for the settlement.[59] Allotting communal holdings, both in *comunales* and in *propios* aimed to achieve one of the paramount interests of the crown, to secure effective settlement by establishing a nucleus of population.[60] Communal allocation could indeed assist in achieving that objective.

Ejidos were a specific type of *comunales* that merit special attention, since they spread across all three ownership paradigms in Latin America.[61] This type

54 For more information on the evolution of communal holdings in the Iberian Peninsula (together with some primary documents), see Alejandro Nieto, *Bienes comunales* (Madrid: Editorial Revista de Derecho Privado, 1964), 101–132.

55 Joaquín de Camps y Arboix, *La propiedad de la tierra y su función social* (Barcelona: Bosch, 1953), 95.

56 Carlos Mario Storni, *Investigaciones sobre la historia del derecho rural argentino: Españoles, criollos, indios y gauderios en la llanura pampeana* (Buenos Aires: Instituto de Investigaciones de Historia del Derecho, 1997), 20.

57 Levaggi, *Manual de Historia del Derecho Argentino*, vol. 2, 212.

58 Joseph Berní y Catalá, *Instituta civil, y real, en donde con la mayor brevedad se explican los §§. de Justiniano, y en su seguida los casos practicos, segun Leyes Reales de España, muy util, y provechoso à los que desean el bien comun* (Valencia: Benito Monfort, 1760), 55–56.

59 María Belén Clemente Campos, 'Notas sobre la subasta de bienes de propios a principios del siglo XIX' (1994–1995) 12–13 Anuario de la Facultad de Derecho 441.

60 Ots Capdequí, *El régimen de la tierra*, 27.

61 See, for example, note 204 below, and accompanying text. For more information on the *ejido*, stretching beyond the first half of the twentieth century, see generally Emilio Duhau, 'A Case Study on the Implementation and Outcomes of the 1992 Reforms on the Mexican

of communal allocation was located close to dwelling areas, and was used for grazing livestock and crop cultivation; while the *dehesa*, which was located farther away from dwelling areas, was used also in common.[62] *Ejidos* took their name from the Latin word *exitus* and were intended for the benefit of all neighbors, rich and poor.[63] Official documents in the Americas occasionally referred without distinction to *ejidos*, *dehesas*, or even *propios*; yet the predominant term was indeed *ejido*.[64] *Ejidos*, for example, found a place in the *Ordenanzas* of Philip II of 1573. The latter provision instructed that *ejidos* should be developed foreseeing population growth and always assure that neighbors could recreate and livestock graze without causing damage.[65] Another example is found in documents of the *cabildo* of Santiago (in the present-day territory of Chile) that indicated that the *ejido* would welcome the horses of the poorest neighbors, while in the *dehesa* all other neighbors could keep their horses.[66] Towns of Native Americans could likewise hold *comunales* and *propios*. The 1680 *Recopilación* included references to communal holdings, as presented in Law 8, Title 3, Book 6, establishing the need of *ejidos* for Native Americans.[67] For example, the *Ordenanzas* of Francisco de Alfaro of 1611 and 1612 – for parts of the present-day territory of Argentina – referred to the need of *ejidos* for Native American groups.[68] It should be noted that in the Americas, the *ejidos* could find parallels with the *mapu* of the Mapuche, the *calpulli* of the Aztec, and the *ayllu* of the Inca.[69]

Agrarian Property Institutions: An *ejido* in the Frontier of the Urbanisation Process' in *Legalising Land Rights: Local Practices, State Responses and Tenure Security in Africa, Asia and Latin America*, ed. Janine M. Ubink (Leiden: Leiden University Press, 2009), 388.

62 Akio Sato, *Legal Aspects of Landownership in Colonial Spanish America* (Tokyo: Institute of Developing Economies, 1976), 9.

63 Michel J. Godreau and Juan A. Giusti, 'Las concesiones de la corona y la propiedad de la tierra en Puerto Rico, siglos XVI–XX: Un estudio jurídico' (1993) 62 Revista Jurídica Universidad de Puerto Rico 431.

64 Carlos Luque Colombres, 'Los ejidos de Córdoba y la enfiteusis' (1958) 9 Revista del Instituto de Historia del Derecho 98.

65 See chapter 129 of the *Ordenanzas* in Morales Padrón, *Teoría y leyes*, 513.

See also Zelia Nuttall, 'Royal Ordinances Concerning the Laying out of New Towns' (1921) 4(4) Hispanic American Historical Review 748; Ots Capdequí, *Manual de historia de derecho español en las Indias*, 451; Mariluz Urquijo, *El Régimen de la Tierra*, 64.

The provision of chapter 129 was then included as Law 13, Title 7, Book 4 of the 1680 *Recopilación*. See also Abelardo Levaggi, 'Marco jurídico de la propiedad comunal civil en hispanoamérica hasta el siglo XIX' (2010) 22 Revista Chilena de Historia del Derecho 943.

66 Mario Góngora, *El estado en el derecho indiano: época de fundación (1492–1570)* (Santiago: Editorial Universidad de Chile, 1951), 141.

67 See also Dougnac Rodríguez, *Manual de Historia del Derecho Indiano*, 328.

68 Mariluz Urquijo, *El Régimen de la Tierra*, 117.

69 Godreau and Giusti; 'Las concesiones de la corona,' 431.

3 Liberal Paradigm

Latin American jurisdictions gradually shifted to the new Liberal paradigm that was consequently adopted in local nineteenth-century civil codes.[70] That century has been deemed 'the codification century of civil law'[71] and all private law tended to revolve around the new codes. No full grasp of land and other property relations can be attained without a full understanding of the codification phenomenon. That scenario helps explain why tracing changes mainly in codes help explain the shifts in ownership paradigms. These new texts embraced the liberal ideal of an absolute, unique, and perpetual real right of ownership, subject to the will of a single owner, but limited by some legal conditions related to public responsibilities.[72]

Ownership was traditionally governed by provisions found originally within European civil codes. Latin American jurisdictions found the French model the most appealing.[73] Accordingly, the new American jurisdictions turned towards the model provided by the *Code Napoléon*, especially in the area of property, which was a symbol of modernity and liberalism.[74] Property law occupied, indeed, a central place in the French code.[75] Article 544 of the *Code Napoléon* was present, verbatim or by substantive adaptation, in many of the resulting civil codes on both sides of the Atlantic Ocean. That article read in an English translation: 'ownership is the right to enjoy and dispose of things in the most absolute manner, provided they are not used in a way prohibited by law or by regulations.'[76] That text provided the paramount example of the new paradigm; and it assisted in the distinction between ownership and usufruct, and in the eradication of any potential feudal remnants.[77]

---

70 Abelardo Levaggi, 'El proceso de transformación del régimen de la propiedad según la codificación iberoamericana del siglo XIX' in *Actas do XII Congresso Internacional de AHILA*, ed. Eugénio dos Santos (Porto: Faculdade de Letras da Universidade do Porto, 2001), vol. 5, 413.

71 Julio César Rivera, 'The Scope and Structure of Civil Codes: Relations with Commercial Law, Family Law, Consumer Law and Private International Law. A Comparative Approach' in *The Scope and Structure of Civil Codes*, ed. Julio César Rivera (Dordrecht: Springer, 2013), 7.

72 Levaggi, 'El proceso de transformación del régimen de la propiedad,' 419.

73 Kenneth L. Karst and Keith S. Rosenn, *Law and Development in Latin America: A Case Book* (Berkeley: University of California Press, 1975), 45.

74 Jean-Louis Halpérin, *Histoire du droit des biens* (Paris: Économica, DL, 2008), 266.

75 Jean-Louis Halpérin, *The Civil Code*, trans. by David W. Gruning and Alain A. Levasseur (Baton Rouge: Center of Civil Law Studies, 2000), 37.

76 *Code civil des français. Édition originale et seule officielle* (Paris: De l'Imprimerie de la République, an XII, 1804), 100.

77 Gambaro, 'Property Rights,' 237; Halpérin, *The Civil Code*, 38.

3.1 *Codification*

Codification, as understood today, finds its origins in Europe, where it experienced a significant development during the eighteenth and nineteenth centuries.[78] Endeavors on codification spread throughout the Western Hemisphere and reached the Americas, building on European sources, though on occasion pollinated by American texts. Latin American jurisdictions were thus not immune to comprehensive codification movements and adopted civil codes[79] to regulate their private law needs after independence from European control.[80] There was interest in the region for grasping the panorama of civil law legislation in a succinct and comprehensive way. There was also a demand for examination of the ideas in place in other civilized states that had reached codification.[81] By replicating European events, many American jurisdictions started to replace their versions of Europe's *ius commune* with codified systems of national laws.[82]

The new codes were consistent with liberalism and with the gradual abolishment of the Iberian past.[83] Accordingly, the idea of the free circulation of property spread across the continent, while the idea of entailments started to be rejected.[84] Eighteenth-century ideas such as those of Gaspar Melchor de

---

78 See generally Agustín Parise, 'Libraries of Civil Codes as Mirrors of Normative Transfers from Europe to the Americas: The Experiences of Lorimier in Quebec (1871–1890) and Varela in Argentina (1873–1875)' in *Entanglements in Legal History: Conceptual Approaches, Global Perspectives on Legal History*, ed. Thomas Duve (Frankfurt am Main: Max Planck Institute for European Legal History 2014) 318–319, http://dx.doi.org/10.12946/gplh1; Alain A. Levasseur 'On the Structure of a Civil Code' (1970) 44 Tulane Law Review 693; and Jean-Louis Bergel, 'Principal Features and Methods of Codification' (1988) 48 Louisiana Law Review 1073.

79 The list of Latin American jurisdictions and the years of effect of their first civil codes reads as follows: Haiti, 1826; Bolivia, 1831; Peru, 1836; Costa Rica, 1841; Dominican Republic, 1844; Chile, 1857; El Salvador, 1860; Panama, 1860; Ecuador, 1861; Venezuela, 1862; Uruguay, 1868; Argentina, 1871; Mexico, 1871; Nicaragua, 1871; Colombia, 1873; Guatemala, 1877; Paraguay, 1877; Honduras, 1880; Cuba, 1889; Puerto Rico, 1889; and Brazil, 1917. There were many failed attempts. M.C. Mirow, 'The Power of Codification in Latin America: Simón Bolívar and the *Code Napoléon*' (2000) 8 Tulane Journal of International and Comparative Law 83–116.

80 Agustín Parise, 'The Place of the Louisiana Civil Code in the Hispanic Civil Codifications: Inclusion in the Comments to the Spanish Civil Code Project of 1851' (2008) 68 Louisiana Law Review 831.

81 Ferdinand Stone, 'A Primer on Codification' (1955) 29 Tulane Law Review 307; cited also in John W. Cairns, *Codification, Transplants and History: Law Reform in Louisiana (1808) and Quebec (1866)* (Clark: Talbot Publishing, 2015), 17.

82 Bravo Lira, *Derecho Común y Derecho Propio*, 54.

83 Mirow, *Latin American Law*, 133.

84 Levaggi, 'El proceso desamortizador,' 52.

Jovellanos in Spain, limiting entailments, started to percolate in society, and were in harmony with nineteenth-century products such as the French *Code Napoléon*.[85] In Latin American jurisdictions, however, the new paradigm did not fully eliminate the public responsibility of owners, departing therefore from the traditional liberal economy doctrine.[86]

3.2 *Encapsulation*

Latin American jurisdictions encapsulated the Liberal paradigm in constitutional texts and in civil codes. The new paradigm was well established across the continent before the start of the twentieth century, and a number of civil codes were instrumental in achieving that paradigm shift.

The civil code of Chile (1855) provided a paramount example of how the liberal ideas were encapsulated in the Americas.[87] It can be considered as a legal corpus with a continental projection, becoming a blueprint for many codification projects across Latin America.[88] An examination of its content and impact helps explain changes in the history of land and other property in Latin America. After all, the *Código Civil de la República de Chile*, work of Andrés Bello, could be deemed the most influential code in the Americas.[89] Bello's code was grounded in the old law but restated it according to modern codification techniques. While following the Roman and Spanish provisions, it included provisions of the juridical liberalism of that time.[90] The Chilean Code, for instance, inclined in a moderate way towards the new paradigm of ownership.[91] Bello welcomed the liberal doctrine of the *Code Napoléon*, believing it provided a strong element for progress.[92] He aimed towards a free ownership, and not bound to archaic and demanding ties.[93] Bello defended the

---

85 Pedro Lira Urquieta, *El Código Civil y el Nuevo Derecho* (Santiago: Imprenta Nascimento, 1944), 167.

86 Levaggi, 'El proceso de transformación del régimen de la propiedad,' 419.

87 See generally Alejandro Guzmán Brito, *La codificación civil en Iberoamérica: Siglos XIX y XX* (Santiago: Editorial Jurídica de Chile, 2000), 374–425.

88 Alejandro Guzmán Brito, *Vida y Obra de Andrés Bello especialmente considerado como Jurista* (Cizur Menor: Thomson-Aranzadi, 2008), 100; Bernardino Bravo Lira, 'La difusión del código civil de Bello en los países de derecho castellano y portugués' (1982) 7 Revista de Estudios Histórico-Jurídicos 93–94.

89 Mirow, *Latin American Law*, 137.

90 Guzmán Brito, *La codificación civil*, 373.

91 Levaggi, 'El proceso de transformación del régimen de la propiedad,' 414.

92 Pedro Lira Urquieta, 'Introducción al Código Civil de Andrés Bello' in *Obras Completas de Andrés Bello*, ed. Rafael Caldera, 2nd ed. (Caracas: Fundación La Casa de Bello, 1981), vol. 14, XXXI.

93 Ibid.

free circulation of things, not in the hands of a few, but as a way to promote economic progress for society.[94] Another example of the moderate adoption of the principles of juridical liberalism concerned not only ownership but also real rights, and contracts, yet it was not adopted in the area of successions.[95]

The Chilean Code's Article 582 read in its first paragraph: 'ownership (also called property) is the real right in a corporeal thing to enjoy and dispose thereof as the owner wishes, provided that it is not contrary to the law or the rights of a third party.'[96] That article endorsed the Liberal paradigm, and reflected the subjective right to enjoy and dispose arbitrarily of a thing as stated in Article 544 of the *Code Napoléon*.[97] Together with six other articles, which are still in effect in Chile, Article 582 provided basic tenets for the understanding of ownership.[98] Those provisions, however, preserved traditional property expectations that were part of the local society and family structure.[99] The Chilean Code was in reality a blend of liberal and conservative principles: property tended to be liberal, while family and dispositions of family property were more traditional, in line with pre-independence society.[100]

3.3 *Pollination*

The Liberal paradigm of ownership spread across the continent as a result of pollination of codes previously adopted by other jurisdictions, which were handy tools and provided models to follow. Existing codes, such as the ones of Argentina (1871) and Chile, contributed to that transfer of provisions by acting as examples of successful codification. In addition, codifiers turned to drafts of

94 Alejandro Guzmán Brito, *Andrés Bello codificador: Historia de la fijación y codificación del derecho civil en Chile* (Santiago: Ediciones de la Universidad de Chile, 1982), vol. 1, 455.

95 Guzmán Brito, *Vida y Obra de Andrés Bello*, 99.

96 *Código Civil de la República de Chile* (Santiago: Imprenta Nacional, 1856), 147.
Readers should note that even the drafter of the Chilean Code acknowledged the interchangeability of terms, and he referred in his seminal provision to ownership and property as synonyms. See Arturo Alessandri Rodríguez, Manuel Somarriva, and Antonio Vodanovic, *Tratado de los Derechos Reales*, 6th ed. (Santiago: Editorial Jurídica de Chile, 2001), vol. 1, 35.

97 Guzmán Brito, *Andrés Bello codificador*, 455.

98 *Código Civil de la República de Chile*, 147–149.

99 M.C. Mirow, 'Borrowing Private Law in Latin America: Andrés Bello's use of the *Code Napoléon* in Drafting the Chilean Civil Code' (2001) 61 Louisiana Law Review 292.

100 Ibid., 302. See the recent study on the social relations of class and family in Chile, in Nara Milanich, *Children of Fate: Childhood, Class, and the State in Chile, 1850–1930* (Duke University Press, 2009).

codes, such as the works by Augusto Teixeira de Freitas for Brazil or by David Dudley Field for New York.[101]

Some jurisdictions adopted the Liberal paradigm by following closer than others nineteenth-century wordings. For example, the *Code Napoléon* was a source of inspiration in the Americas. The codes of Haiti (1826), Bolivia (1831), Peru (1836), Costa Rica (1841), and Dominican Republic (1844) benefited by borrowing the wording originated in France.[102] The civil code of Spain (1889) also served as an important model, offering a wording that was followed in the codes of Cuba (1889) and Puerto Rico (1889).[103] Portions of the code of Mexico (1871)[104] found an antecedent in, amongst others, the text provided by Article 391 of the 1851 Spanish project of a civil code led by Florencio García Goyena.[105]

The Chilean Code, as already mentioned, offered a paramount example of pollination. The text of Article 582 was replicated throughout the continent when several jurisdictions adopted its wording. For example, the civil codes of El Salvador (1860),[106] Panama (1860),[107] Ecuador (1861),[108] Venezuela (1862),[109] Nicaragua (1871),[110] Colombia (1873),[111] and Honduras

101 Article 1680 of the Argentine Code is a translation of Article 1324 of the project of a civil code of the state of New York. The Argentine note referred exclusively to the North American draft. See 'Ley 340 – Código Civil' in *Anales de Legislación Argentina, Volumen 1852–1880* (Buenos Aires: La Ley, 1954), 666.

102 Guzmán Brito, *La codificación civil*, 605.

103 Article 348 of the Spanish civil code. See *Código Civil–Edición Oficial Reformada* (Madrid: Imprenta del Ministerio de Gracia y Justicia, 1889), 70. The Spanish civil code of 1889 took effect in the Philippines, Cuba, and Puerto Rico by means of a *Real Decreto* on July 24, 1889. See *Código Civil de Puerto Rico Comentado* (Oxford: Equity Publishing, 1984), 9.

104 Article 827 of Mexico. See *Código Civil del Distrito Federal y Territorio de la Baja-California, mandado observar en el Estado de Hidalgo* (México: Imprenta de E. Ancona y M. Peniche, 1871), 280.

105 Rodolfo Batiza, *Las fuentes del código civil de 1928: Introducción, notas y textos de sus fuentes originales no reveladas* (México: Editorial Porrúa, 1979), 95.

106 Article 608 of El Salvador. See *Código Civil de la República del Salvador*, 2nd ed. (San Salvador: Imprenta del Comercio, 1880), 71.

107 Article 732 of Panama. See *Código Civil del Estado de Panamá* (New York: Imprenta de Esteban Hallet, 1861), 87.

108 Article 571 of Ecuador. See *Código Civil y Código de Enjuiciamientos en Materia Civil de la República del Ecuador* (New York: Imprenta de Hallet y Breen, 1871), 110.

109 Article 1, Law 1, Title 2, Book 2 of Venezuela. See *Código Civil. Edición Oficial* (Caracas: Imprenta de El Independiente, 1862), 77.

110 Article 582 of Nicaragua. See *Código Civil de la República de Nicaragua* (Managua: Imprenta de 'El Centro-Americano, 1871), 76.

111 Article 669 of Colombia. See *Código civil colombiano expedido por el congreso de 1873 y adoptado por la ley 57 de 1887: con un suplemento de las leyes que lo adicionan y reforman, desde 1887 hasta 1892. Edición Oficial* (Bogotá: Imprenta Nacional, 1895), 108.

(1880)[112] all adopted an almost verbatim version of the Chilean text. The Chilean code was likewise influential in the drafting of the civil codes of Uruguay and Argentina. In Uruguay, a report drafted in 1867 by a Codifying Commission mentioned as its sources, amongst others, the 'codes of Europe, those of America, and specially the correctly praised code of Chile.'[113] The Chilean influence in Argentina is likewise sensed. In 1865, Dalmacio Vélez Sarsfield stated that when drafting the first book of his code he had 'considered all the codes published in Europe and America … I have used mainly the Spanish Project of Mr. Goyena, [and] the Code of Chile, that much surpasses the European codes.'[114]

As a corollary, it can be claimed that there was a Pan-American understanding of ownership during the nineteenth century. That understanding can be traced to European codes and to American elaborations. Accordingly, ownership cannot be regarded as merely a European construct because local developments played a role in its shaping. When drafting civil codes in the Americas, jurists also looked at vernacular sources.

4 Social Function Paradigm

The twentieth century experienced a change in the ownership paradigm in many Latin American jurisdictions. The Liberal paradigm of ownership was gradually replaced by the social function of property. Jurisdictions in Latin America abandoned the Liberal paradigm and incorporated the tenets of the Social Function paradigm within their legal frameworks.

4.1 *Gestation*

Private law experienced a socialization process in the period 1890–1930,[115] since the Liberal paradigm had offered few limitations to the right of ownership. Gradual changes started to occur in society regarding the extent of that right, and the Social Function paradigm eventually developed across the

112 Article 661 of Honduras. See *Código Civil de la República de Honduras 1880* (Tegucigalpa: Tipografía Nacional, 1880), 158.

113 Parise, 'The Place of the Louisiana Civil Code, 850–851; Orestes Araújo, Oscar Arias Barbe, Saúl D. Cestau and Manuel O. López, *Código Civil Anotado* (Montevideo: Facultad de derecho y ciencias sociales. (Montevideo: Universidad de Montevideo, 1949), vol. 1, XXIII.

114 Parise, 'The Place of the Louisiana Civil Code,' 848–849; Abelardo Levaggi, *Dalmacio Vélez Sarsfield, Jurisconsulto* (Córdoba: Ciencia, Derecho y Sociedad, 2005), 310.

115 Jean-Louis Halpérin, *Histoire du droit privé français depuis 1804* (Paris: Presses Universitaires de France, 1996), 186.

Western Hemisphere. That approach entailed a less 'egoistic' understanding of ownership.[116] Changes had occurred in the social and economic structures of different jurisdictions, with massive migrations into cities and the effects of the Industrial Revolution.[117] Accordingly, the crude individualistic paradigm started to be challenged as a reaction to the social problems surfacing in Western societies.[118] The change was sensed early with the revolutionary events of 1848 and with the writings of, amongst others, Pierre-Joseph Proudhon, Karl Heinrich Marx, and Auguste Comte.[119] In 1851, Comte had already stated that ownership had a social function that aimed to shape and administer the goods for subsequent generations.[120] Changes in the understanding of ownership therefore started to develop in academic circles, where theorists pointed to what they deemed existing conditions. Changes were then followed by decisions by courts and by the implementation of alterations in the positive laws, both in Europe and in the Americas.

Advocates for a change in paradigm soon emerged throughout continental Europe, not limited to socialist scholars and writings.[121] The need for change was also present in English-speaking jurisdictions, though not necessarily along the same lines or to the same extent as in continental Europe.[122] The new

---

116 Beatriz Areán, *Curso de Derechos Reales: Privilegios y Derecho de Retención*, 3rd ed. (Buenos Aires: Abeledo-Perrot, 1994), 188.

117 Eduardo Cordero Quinzacara, 'De la propiedad a las propiedades. La evolución de la concepción liberal de la propiedad' (2008) 31 Revista de Derecho de la Pontificia Universidad Católica de Valparaíso, 503.

118 Gumersindo de Azcárate, *Ensayo sobre la historia del derecho de propiedad y su estado actual en Europa* (Madrid: Imprenta de la Revista de Legislación, 1883), vol. 3, 357–453.

119 Ibid., 359; Manuel I. Adrogué, *El Derecho de Propiedad en la Actualidad: Introducción a sus Nuevas Expresiones* (Buenos Aires: Abeledo-Perrot, 1991), 32–34; Thomas T. Ankersent and Thomas Ruppert, 'Tierra y Libertad: The Social Function Doctrine and Land Reform in Latin America' (2006) 19 Tulane Environmental Law Journal 98; Bergel, *La Propriété*, 18; and Mariano Peset, 'Fundamento ideológico de la propiedad' in *Historia de la Propiedad en España siglos XV–XX: Encuentro Interdisciplinar; Salamanca, 3–6 de junio de 1998*, eds Salustiano de Dios, Ricardo Robledo Hernández, Eugenia Torijano Pérez, and Javier Infante Miguel-Mota (Madrid: Centro de Estudios Registrales, 1999), 443, 449.

120 Auguste Comte, *Système de politique positive, ou traité de sociologie, Instituant la Religion de l'humanité* (Paris: Librairie Scientifique Industrielle de L. Mathias, 1851), vol. 1, 156. See also de Camps y Arboix, *La propiedad de la tierra*, 200.

121 See, for example, the works by Heinrich Ahrens, Gumersindo de Azcárate, Otto von Gierke, Henri Hayem, Anton Menger, and José María de Semprún y Gurrea. See also José Castán Tobeñas, *La propiedad y sus problemas actuales*, 2nd ed. (Madrid: Reus, 1963), 63; and Vera Bolgár, 'The Magic of Property and Public Welfare' (1960) 2 Inter-American Law Review 288.

122 See, for example, the works by James Barr Ames, Benjamin Nathan Cardozo, Richard Theodore Ely, Oliver Wendell Holmes, Jr., and Frederic Pollock.

paradigm was present likewise in the writings of the Roman Catholic Church, which upheld the existence of both a social and an individual character for ownership.[123] A social doctrine of the Church was developed, and aimed to humanize property, a natural right burdened with a *social hypoteque*.[124]

Léon Duguit was the paladin of the Social Function paradigm,[125] claiming early that the Liberal paradigm was becoming extinct.[126] This French jurist and publicist popularized the term 'social function' (*fonction sociale*) in 1905;[127] and a few years later, in August and September 1911, he delivered a series of six lectures at the University of Buenos Aires (Argentina), where he advocated for the social function in private law.[128] In the sixth lecture, dealing with the social function of property, he indicated that ownership was subject to socialization, implying two things: 'that individual ownership [was] no longer an individual right, and was transform[ed] into a social function; and second, that there [was]

123 See, for example, the encyclicals *Rerum novarum* (1891) of Pope Leo XIII, *Quadragesimo anno* (1931) of Pope Pius XI, *Mater et magistra* (1961) of Pope Saint John XXIII, and *Populorum progressio* (1967) of Pope Paul VI. Adrogué, *El Derecho de Propiedad*, 34. See, for example, the statement of Pope Pius XI in the encyclical *Quadragesimo anno*. 'Quadragesimo anno.' The Holy See, § 45. http://w2.vatican.va/content/pius-xi/en/encyclicals/documents/hf_p-xi_enc_19310515_quadragesimo-anno.html. See also, M.C. Mirow, '*Rerum Novarum*: New Things and Recent Paradigms of Property Law' (2016) 47 University of the Pacific Law Review 183–197.

124 Expression coined by Pope Saint John Paul II. See Adrogué, *El Derecho de Propiedad*, 34.

125 On the life and work of Léon Duguit, see generally the commemorative volume in Fabrice Melleray, ed., *Autour de Léon Duguit: Colloque commémoratif du 150e anniversaire de la naissance du doyen Léon Duguit; Bordeaux, 29–30 mai 2009* (Brussels: Bruylant, 2011); José Calvo González and José Luis Monereo Pérez, 'Léon Duguit (1859–1928): jurista de una sociedad en transformación' (2005) 4 Revista de Derecho Constitucional Europeo 483; M.C. Mirow, 'Léon Duguit' in *Great Christian Jurists in French History*, eds Olivier Descamps and Rafael Domingo (Cambridge: Cambridge University Press, 2019), 358–371. On the general tenets of Léon Duguit, see Luis Claro Solar, *Explicaciones de Derecho Civil Chileno y Comparado* (Santiago: Editorial Jurídica de Chile, 1979), vol. 3:VI: I (De los bienes), 409–412; Marc Réglade, 'Théorie générale du droit dans l'œuvre de L. Duguit' (1932) 1–2 Archives de Philosophie du droit et de Sociologie juridique 21.

126 Léon Duguit, *Les transformations générales du droit privé depuis le Code Napoléon* (Paris: Félix Alcan, 1912), 155.

127 Halpérin, *Histoire du droit privé français depuis 1804*, 197.

128 On the content of the six lectures, see Duguit, *Les transformations générales* M.C. Mirow, 'The Social-Obligation Norm of Property: Duguit, Hayem, and Others' (2010) 22 Florida Journal of International Law 198, 203–209. For a study on the impact of the postulates of Léon Duguit on private law, see generally Gaston Morin, 'L'œuvre de Duguit et le droit privé' (1932) 1–2 Archives de Philosophie du droit et de Sociologie juridique 153. For a recent English translation of the sixth lecture and analytical essays see *Léon Duguit and the Social Obligation Norm of Property: A Translation and Global Exploration*, eds Paul Babie and Jessica Viven-Wilksch (Cham: Springer, 2019).

an increase in the number of cases of wealth allocated to collectivities, that [should] be subject to juridical protection.'[129] Duguit also stated that owners could use things as long as they fulfilled a social function. They had to undertake three duties:[130] (i) to enjoy things when satisfying individual or collective needs; (ii) not to leave things without use or exploitation; and (iii) to allow the use of things when aiming to fulfil social interests.[131] The author addressed the existence of subjective rights, and defended that 'ownership [was] therefore not the subjective right of the owner, it [was] the social function of the holder of the wealth.'[132] The ideas and writings of Duguit triggered debate and further studies.[133] The postulates of Duguit were welcomed in Latin American jurisdictions, after his Buenos Aires Lectures.[134]

The reception of the Social Function paradigm was not limited to the first decades of the twentieth century or to the European legal discourse.[135] A series of social and ideological twentieth-century shifts related to the Mexican and Russian Revolutions, WWI, and WWII, also had an impact on the reshaping of ownership.[136] The paradigm was welcomed in legislation and scholarly writings throughout the entire century, entering even into the twenty-first century. A diversity of legal provisions reflected a departure from the Liberal paradigm. For example, at the American level, the American Convention on Human Rights addressed a social interest for property.[137] A diversity of authors,

129 Duguit, *Les transformations générales*, 148–149.

130 Ibid., 165–166, cited also by Alessandri Rodríguez, Somarriva, and Vodanovic, *Tratado de los Derechos Reales*, 41–42. See also Raymundo M. Salvat, *Tratado de Derecho Civil Argentino: Derechos Reales*, 5th ed. (Buenos Aires: Tipográfica Ed. Argentina, 1962), vol. 2, 17.

131 Duguit, *Les transformations générales*, 165–169.

132 Ibid., 158. English text extracted from Mirow, 'The Social-Obligation Norm,' 207.

133 On the different degrees of acceptance and rejection of the ideas of Léon Duguit, see Nader Hakim, 'Duguit et les privatistes' in *Autour de Léon Duguit: Colloque commémoratif du 150e anniversaire de la naissance du doyen Léon Duguit; Bordeaux, 29–30 mai 2009*, ed. Fabrice Melleray (Brussels: Bruylant, 2011), 81.

134 Daniel Bonilla, 'Liberalism and Property in Colombia: Property as a Right and Property as a Social Function' (2011) 80 Fordham Law Review 1135–1170; Thorsten Keiser, 'Social conceptions of Property and Labour – Private Law in the aftermath of the Mexican Revolution and European Legal Science' (2012) 20 Rechtsgeschichte 269; M.C. Mirow, 'Léon Duguit and the Social Function of Property in Argentina' in *Léon Duguit and the Social Obligation Norm*, 267–285.

135 See also Mirow, 'The Social-Obligation Norm,' 196.

136 Susana T. Ramella, 'Propiedad en función social en la Constitución de 1949: Una "mentalidad" del Antiguo Régimen representada en el constitucionalismo social de la época' (2007) 35 Revista de Historia del Derecho, 320.

137 See Article 21 of the *American Convention on Human Rights* in 'American Convention on Human Rights "Pact of San Jose, Costa Rica" (B-32),' Department of International

likewise, made manifest a departure from the traditional Liberal paradigm. Latin American jurisdictions, as already mentioned, experienced the reception of the new paradigm. That reception took place mainly in the first decades of the twentieth century, and some recent texts continue to incorporate the idea of a social function.[138]

4.2 *Reception*

The Social Function paradigm spread across Latin America, and motivated corresponding changes in the wording of constitutions and civil codes. It also induced changes in the interpretation by courts and in the development of special legislation that advocated for the new approach to land and other property relations.

4.2.1 *Social Constitutionalism*

The Social Function paradigm was encapsulated early within the constitutions of different jurisdictions. These ideas were first welcomed in the Mexican Constitution of 1917 and in the social ideas included in the Weimar Constitution of 1919. These constitutions included references to the responsibility that derived from the ownership and control of property. The reception of the paradigm was ignited by those two constitutions; and the idea was soon welcomed by other constitutions of Europe and of Latin America.[139] The reception of the new paradigm within the text of constitutions increased during the interwar period,[140] yet it continued throughout the entire century. The new paradigm ultimately represented a mentality and ideal that soon predominated throughout the Western Hemisphere.[141]

Law, Organization of American States, Washington D.C. http://www.oas.org/dil/treaties_B-32_American_Convention_on_Human_Rights.htm. See also Areán, *Curso de Derechos Reales*, 189.

138 For example, Article 56, Paragraph 1 of the 2009 Political Constitution of Bolivia referred to the social function of property. See 'República del Bolivia, Republic of Bolivia, Constitución de 2009. Constitution of 2009,' Political Database of the Americas. http://pdba.georgetown.edu/Constitutions/Bolivia/bolivia09.html.

139 Ankersent and Ruppert, '*Tierra y Libertad*,' 96. The effective extent to which the Mexican Constitution helped in disseminating the new paradigm in Latin America has been challenged by some authors. See M.C. Mirow, 'Origins of the Social Function of Property in Chile' (2011) 80 Fordham Law Review 1215.

140 Joaquín Ruíz-Giménez, *La Propiedad: Sus Problemas y su Función Social* (Salamanca: Ediciones Anaya, 1961), vol. 1, 118.

141 Ramella, 'Propiedad en función social,' 319.

Mexico provided the first social constitution.[142] Changes in property law were mainly included in Article 27 of the Constitution, which resembled a codified text by providing solutions for single practical problems.[143] The new wording converted private property into a privilege instead of a right.[144] The third paragraph of that article read in part:

> The Nation shall have at all times the right to impose on private property the modalities that the public interest may demand, as well as the right to the use of natural elements subject to appropriation, to undertake an equitable distribution of public wealth and to secure their conservation. According to that objective, the necessary measures will be dictated for the fragmentation of the *latifundios* … and [to] avoid the destruction of natural elements and damages that property may suffer in detriment of society.[145]

Germany provided another early and influential constitutional text that welcomed the new paradigm of ownership. The Constitution of 1919 of the Weimar Republic introduced the social function dimension, defending that owners should fulfil certain obligations and accept a number of limitations to their rights.[146] Accordingly, individual ownership was preserved, yet it lost its absolute character, welcoming a more social conception of law.[147] The tenets of this new paradigm were present mainly in two articles: on the one hand, in Paragraph 3 of Article 153, which in an overt form stated that 'property obliges,' and then declared that property should also be used for the common good.[148] Paragraph 1 of Article 155, added in part that the 'distribution and use of land [is] controlled by the Nation in a manner that prevents abuse and secures healthy housing for all German families.'[149] Paragraph 3 of the same

142 Ankersent and Ruppert, '*Tierra y Libertad*,' 96.

143 Keiser, 'Social Conceptions of Property and Labour,' 265.

144 Stephen Haber, Herbert S. Klein, Noel Maurer, and Kevin J. Middlebrook, *Mexico since 1980* (New York: Cambridge University Press, 2008), 13–14.

145 'Constitución política de los Estados Unidos Mexicanos que reforma la de 5 de febrero del 1857' in *Diario Oficial: Órgano del Gobierno Provisional de la República Mexicana; Tomo V. 4ª Época. Número 30. Lunes 5 de febrero de 1917*, 150. See also the translation by David S. Browning, 'Historic Basis of Mexican Mining Law' (1965) 7 Inter-American Law Review 3.

146 Halpérin, *Histoire du droit des biens*, 325.

147 Salvat, *Tratado de Derecho Civil Argentino*, 19.

148 'Die Verfassung des Deutschen Reichs vom 11. August 1919' (1919) 152 Reichsgesetzblatt 1412.

149 Ibid., 1413.

article reads that the 'exploitation and use of the land [is] an obligation of the landowner with the community.'[150] The German text indeed characterized the social content of ownership.[151]

Several European jurisdictions adopted the new paradigm in their constitutions.[152] In the interwar period, for example, Estonia (1919), Poland (1921), Danzig (1922), and Lithuania (1928) imposed limitations on individual property in their fundamental laws.[153] Spain also received influences from the Weimar text.[154] The new paradigm was likewise adopted in common law jurisdictions when the Republic of Ireland adopted a constitution in 1937.[155] Other European jurisdictions incorporated the new paradigm into their post-WWII texts, when the social function of property was revamped in different constitutions.[156] Examples of these last texts are found in the Italian Constitution (1947) and in the Basic Law for the Federal Republic of Germany (1949); subsequent examples are found in the constitutions of Yugoslavia (1953) and Portugal (1953).[157]

Latin American jurisdictions were not immune to the reception of the new paradigm within the texts of their constitutions. Most constitutions there incorporated explicitly the Social Function paradigm[158] during the first half of the twentieth century. Drafters in the Americas found grounding in the writings of Duguit for the changes in their constitutions,[159] and they benefited from the texts that had been drafted in other parts of the Western Hemisphere. A 'contagion'[160] of constitutions developed in the region and increased during the post-WWII period. Examples of constitutions that resulted from that

150 Ibid.

151 Ankersent and Ruppert, '*Tierra y Libertad*,' 98.

152 See, for example, Fernando Legón, *Tratado de los Derechos Reales en el Código y en la Reforma* (Buenos Aires: Valerio Abeledo, 1942), vol. 6, 264.

153 Ramella, 'Propiedad en función social,' 318.

154 Ruíz-Giménez, *La Propiedad*, 118.

155 See generally Rachael Walsh, 'Private Property Rights in the Drafting of the Irish Constitution: A Communitarian Compromise' (2011) 33 Dublin University Law Journal 86.

156 Castán Tobeñas, *La propiedad*, 64; and Cordero Quinzacara, 'De la propiedad a las propiedades,' 511.

157 See also Alessandri Rodríguez, Somarriva, and Vodanovic, *Tratado de los Derechos Reales*, 44; Santiago Carretero Sánchez, *La Propiedad: Bases sociológicas del concepto en la sociedad postindustrial* (unpublished Ph.D. thesis, Madrid: Universidad Complutense de Madrid, 1994), 120; Cordero Quinzacara, 'De la propiedad a las propiedades,' 512; Halpérin, *Histoire du droit des biens*, 325; and Ramella, 'Propiedad en función social,' 319.

158 Ankersent and Ruppert, '*Tierra y Libertad*,' 99.

159 Mirow, 'The Social-Obligation Norm,' 195.

160 This term is borrowed, *mutatis mutandis*, from Linda Colley, 'Empires of Writing: Britain, America and Constitutions, 1776–1848' (2014) 32(2) Law and History Review 237.

'contagion' and that incorporated the Social Function paradigm are found in the texts of Chile (1925, according to reforms of 1963 and 1967), Brazil (1934), Bolivia (1938 and 1947), Colombia (1936 and 1945), Nicaragua (1939), Paraguay (1940), Guatemala (1946), Ecuador (1946), Panama (1941 and 1946), Peru (1947), Venezuela (1947), El Salvador (1950), and Honduras (1957).[161]

The Argentine Constitution of 1949 provides an illustration of social constitutionalism in the Americas.[162] In 1949, during the presidency of Juan Domingo Perón, a short-lived[163] reform to the constitutional text was implemented, incorporating tenets of the Social Function paradigm that had developed during the first half of that century.[164] The 'contagion' of social constitutions therefore reached Argentina, and the social doctrine of the Church, together with the ideas of authors such as Duguit, prevailed in the constitutional text adopted at the national level in 1949.[165] Protection of private property, together with its limitations, were addressed in the Constitution.[166] To introduce fully the new paradigm, the new charter dedicated an entire fourth chapter to the social function of property.[167] Article 38, part of that chapter, read: 'Private property has a social function and therefore is subject to the obligations towards common good established by law.'[168] Even though the current Argentine Constitution no longer refers to the social function of property,

161 Guillermo L. Allende; *Panorama de Derechos Reales* (Buenos Aires: La Ley, 1967), 377; Ankersent and Ruppert, *'Tierra y Libertad,'* 96, 99; Castán Tobeñas, *La propiedad*, 102; Gustavo Ferreira Santos, 'La constitucionalización de los derechos sociales: puentes entre Brasil y México' (2016) 10(38) Revista IUS (México) 2; Legón, *Tratado de los Derechos Reales*, 264; Ramella, 'Propiedad en función social,' 318.

162 Mirow, 'Léon Duguit and the Social Function of Property in Argentina.'

163 See 'Proclama del 27 de abril de 1956' in *Anales de Legislación Argentina* (Buenos Aires: La Ley, 1956), vol. 16-A, 2; Benjamín Burgos, *Curso de derecho constitucional* (Salta: Virtudes Editorial Universitaria, 2001), 72. That reform was overruled in 1956. In 1957, however, a constitutional reform incorporated Article 14bis, which still today encapsulates the main tenets of social rights. See the text of Article 14bis of the Argentine Constitution in an English translation, at 'República de Argentina, Argentine Republic, Constitución de 1994, 1994 Constitution.' Political Database of the Americas. http://pdba.georgetown.edu/Constitutions/Argentina/argen94_e.html.

164 Burgos, *Curso de derecho constitucional*, 72.

165 Ramella, 'Propiedad en función social,' 320.

166 Tonya Caprarola Giannoni, *The Evolution of Property Rights in Argentina, 1853–1949* (unpublished Ph.D. thesis, Washington, DC: The George Washington University, 2010), 284–288.

167 The chapter comprised Articles 38–40.

168 *Constitución de la Nación Argentina: La reforma de la carta magna; Aprobada y Jurada por la Convención Nacional Constituyente (16 de marzo 1949)* (Buenos Aires: Editores Ciordia & Rodríguez, 1951), 15–16.

some Argentine provinces, following the example from 1949, adopted constitutions that explicitly refer to the social function of property. Examples are found in the provincial constitutions of Chubut (1957), La Pampa (1960), and Santa Fe (1962).[169]

4.2.2 *Doctrine of Abuse of Rights*

Civil codes also welcomed the new paradigm. Changes that had started in the constitutional arena soon found their way into the provisions of civil codes that welcomed the new paradigm. Societies had changed and new ideas on property law developed and were placed within new or reformed codes.[170] The Social Function paradigm entered the new text of codes through the development and reception of the doctrine of abuse of rights. This doctrine succinctly stated that 'whoever abuses his [or her] legal rights should be held liable for the consequences of such abuse.'[171] This conception thus holds that rights are not absolute rights, and their enjoyment should be exercised according to the spirit of the law itself.[172] The new wording in civil codes did not welcome abuses and did not refer to the absolute character of property. Rather than an absolute or rigid principle property was subject to limitations.[173]

Abuse of rights opened the door for the new paradigm. Scholars in France towards the end of the nineteenth century explored this idea, though its origins could be traced back to Roman law.[174] The theory redeveloped together with the social movements and legal innovations that followed in the nineteenth and twentieth centuries, and scholarly writing in France allowed its crystallization and eventual integration into French law.[175] Louis Josserand, perhaps the doctrine's best exponent, indicated that when analyzing the abuse of rights doctrine within property law, a 'desire to harm others is in essence antisocial;

169 Marina Mariani de Vidal, *Derechos Reales*, 7th ed. (Buenos Aires: Zavalía, 2004), vol. 1, 308.

170 Mirow, *Latin American Law*, 196.

171 Vera Bolgár, 'Abuse of Rights in France, Germany, and Switzerland: A Survey of a Recent Chapter in Legal Doctrine' (1975) 35 Louisiana Law Review 1015.

172 Luis Moisset de Espanés, 'Introducción al abuso del derecho' (Córdoba: Academia Nacional de Derecho y Ciencias Sociales de Córdoba, 2001), 1–2. http://www.derecho.unc.edu.ar/acaderc/doctrina/articulos/introduccion-al-abuso-del-derecho.

173 Salvat, *Tratado de Derecho Civil Argentino*, 16–17.

174 Pascal Ancel and Claude Didry, 'L'abus de droit: une notion sans histoire? L'apparition de la notion d'abus de droit en droit français au début du XXe siècle' in *L'abus de droit: Comparaisons franco-suisses*, eds Pascal Ancel, Gabriel Aubert, and Christine Chappuis (Saint-Étienne: Publications de l'Université de Saint-Étienne, 2001), 52–65; A.N. Yiannopoulos, 'Predial Servitudes,' 4th ed., in *Louisiana Civil Law Treatise* (St. Paul: West, 2004–2012), vol. 4, § 3:17.

175 Ancel and Didry, 'L'abus de droit,' 52–65.

it never may represent the purpose of any legal concept.'[176] This doctrine, not defended by all scholars, and challenged by, for example, renowned French legal scholar Marcel Planiol, germinated within American universities and eventually reached lawmakers.[177] Further, it should be noted that abuse of rights was not restricted to property law.

The doctrine of abuse of rights was welcomed by civil codes in Europe and in the Americas, which referred to the social or economic purposes of the law.[178] In Europe, abuse of rights was present in, for example, the *Bürgerliches Gesetzbuch* (1900) and in the civil codes of Switzerland (1912), Italy (1942), Greece (1946), and Portugal (1967).[179] Codes in the Americas also welcomed the doctrine; occasionally, without defining it and before it had gained popularity. For example, references to the objection to the abuse of rights were included in the civil codes of Uruguay, Guatemala (1966), and Peru (1984).[180] Further, the civil code of Mexico (1932) incorporated ideas of social progress and social solidarity, tending to eliminate the differences between rich and poor, employee and employer, and men and women.[181] That text further described property as a social function, and followed the important changes implemented by the Constitution of 1917.[182]

There is harmony between the doctrine of abuse of rights and the Social Function paradigm,[183] and the Argentine codification experience serves as an illustration. Several major and comprehensive revision efforts were undertaken in Argentina to alter the text of the 1871 civil code. As per some scholars, a third major and comprehensive revision effort, completed in 1968, resulted in a *new civil code*.[184] The drafting of the new texts was led by Guillermo Antonio Borda,

176 Louis Josserand, *De l'abus des droits* (Paris: Arthur Rousseau, 1905), 19.

177 Moisset de Espanés, 'Introducción al abuso del derecho,' 1; Luis de Gasperi, 'El Futuro de la Codificación' (1955) 29 Tulane Law Review 229.

178 Moisset de Espanés, 'Introducción al abuso del derecho,' 9.

179 Alessandri Rodríguez, Somarriva, and Vodanovic, *Tratado de los Derechos Reales*, 75–76; Salvat, *Tratado de Derecho Civil Argentino*, 16 (n. 23); Legón, *Tratado de los Derechos Reales*, 115.

180 Atilio Aníbal Alterini and Roberto M. López Cabana, 'El abuso del derecho. Estudio de Derecho Comparado' (1990) 1990-B Revista Jurídica Argentina La Ley 1102.

181 Olivier Moréteau and Agustín Parise, 'Recodification in Louisiana and Latin America' (2009) 83 Tulane Law Review 1138.

182 Alessandri Rodríguez, Somarriva, and Vodanovic, *Tratado de los Derechos Reales*, 75–76; Ankersent and Ruppert, '*Tierra y Libertad*,' 101; Mirow, *Latin American Law*, 196.

183 Adrogué, *El Derecho de Propiedad*, 123.

184 See generally Guillermo A. Borda, *Tratado de Derecho Civil: Parte General*, 9th ed. (Buenos Aires: Editorial Perrot, 1987), vol. 1, 143; Julieta Marotta and Agustín Parise, 'On Codes, Marriage, and Access to Justice: Recent Developments in the Law of Argentina' (2014) 7 Journal of Civil Law Studies 245–250; Graciela Medina, 'Argentina on the Eve of a New

and the revision work introduced principles of social solidarity in a code that had been known as individualistic.[185] The revision of 1968 introduced the doctrine of abuse of rights, mainly in Articles 1071, 2513, and 2514 of the code.[186] Article 1071 introduced the doctrine. In its previous wording it had defended that the exercise of one's rights could not turn any act illegal.[187] The new text, in radically different lines, rephrased the original wording and added a second paragraph indicating that 'the law does not protect the abusive exercise of rights. It will be deemed abusive an exercise that contradicts the aims that the law had when recognizing them or an exercise that exceeds the limits imposed by good faith, morals and good customs.'[188] Borda reaffirmed his opposition to the Liberal paradigm in other writings. For example, he also stated in his widely read treatise that in 'Argentina, being inserted in the Christian civilization, ownership is the most complete and full right on a thing, yet it is not absolute.'[189] Moreover, he claimed that the change in philosophy was found in the alterations made to Articles 2513 and 2514, which simply wiped out the absolute character of ownership.[190] According to the new text of Article 2513, owners should exercise their right in a regular way, and no longer be conferred the right to destroy the thing.[191] According to the new text of Article 2514, that exercise should not be limited as long as it was not abusive.[192] Finally, Borda defended that exercising the right of ownership against the social function would be abusive.[193]

Civil and Commercial Code' in *The Scope and Structure of Civil Codes*, ed Julio César Rivera (Dordrecht,: Springer, 2013), 51.

185 Levaggi, *Manual de Historia del Derecho Argentino*, vol. 2, 271.

186 Adrogué, *El Derecho de Propiedad*, 119.

187 See Article 1071, 'Ley 340 Código Civil,' 614–615.

188 See the new wording of Article 1071, in 'Código Civil de la Nación,' Infoleg, Ministerio de Economía y Finanzas Públicas, http://www.infoleg.gov.ar/infolegInternet/anexos/105000-109999/109481/texact.htm.

189 Guillermo A. Borda, *Tratado de Derecho Civil: Derechos Reales*, 5th ed. (Buenos Aires: La Ley, 2008), 217.

190 Adrogué, *El Derecho de Propiedad*, 123; and Borda, *Tratado de Derecho: Civil Derechos Reales*, 219.

191 See Article 2513, 'Código Civil de la Nación.' See also Borda, *Tratado de Derecho Civil: Derechos Reales*, 220, 222.

192 See Article 2514, 'Código Civil de la Nación.' See also Borda, *Tratado de Derecho Civil: Derechos Reales*, 220.

193 Borda, *Tratado de Derecho Civil: Derechos Reales*, 220.

4.2.3 *Land Reform*

It should be noted that civil codes had started to lose their paramount place within private law during the first decades of the twentieth century. The central stage was now shared with special legislation. Special legislation contributed to creating a new status quo or social dimension.[194] It introduced deep-rooted reforms to property law, transforming ownership into a right limited by the common well-being.[195] Latin American jurisdictions incorporated the Social Function paradigm within such special legislation and new *satellite* codes. A seminal example of special legislation is found in the land reform enactments that spread across the region.

Land-reform legislative enactments paved the way for the reception of the new paradigm in Latin America. Land reform commonly referred to as agrarian reform, has been described in different ways, and has no single meaning.[196] These reforms may be seen as historical processes that developed from hardly foreseeable internal and external political impulses.[197] The processes can be narrowly defined as means to provide land to inhabitants that possess none, followed by a redistribution of land, tending to benefit small farmers and agricultural laborers.[198] A set of conditions are necessary to trigger these reforms. The land tenure structure must be inadequate, characterized by *latifundistas* and by laborers with very limited (or no) access to land. In addition, there must be notorious poverty in rural areas where small farmers have no access to the benefits of agricultural and industrial developments. Finally, political instability must accompany this scenario.[199]

Efforts towards achieving land reform spread across the world and experienced a significant development during the second half of the

194 Cordero Quinzacara, 'De la propiedad a las propiedades,' 504.

195 Juan Francisco Delgado de Miguel, ed., *Instituciones de Derecho Privado: Reales* (Madrid: Civitas, 2002), vol. 2, 62.

196 Ankersent and Ruppert, '*Tierra y Libertad*,' 71; and Mirow, *Latin American Law*, 219.

197 Plinio Sampaio, *La Reforma Agraria en America Latina.* RLAC/93/10 – DERU-46 (Santiago: Organización de las Naciones Unidad para la Agricultura y la Alimentación, Oficina Regional de la FAO para América Latina y el Caribe, 1993), 45.

198 Barraclough, *Agrarian Structure in Latin America*, 33. See also Hung-chao Tai, *Land Reform and Politics: A Comparative Analysis* (Berkeley: University of California Press, 1974), 11; Doreen Warriner, *Land Reform in Principle and Practice* (Oxford: Clarendon Press, 1969), xiv, cited also by Karst and Rosenn, *Law and Development in Latin America*, 241.

199 Solon Barraclough, '¿Qué es una reforma agraria?' in *Reformas Agrarias en la América Latina: Procesos y Perspectivas*, ed. Óscar Delgado (México: Fondo de Cultura Económica, 1965), 145.

twentieth century.[200] Early precedents in the Americas had followed the Mexican Revolution, while in Europe several jurisdictions had implemented land reforms after WWI, for example Spain in the 1930s.[201] Land-reform legislative enactments were present in Latin America and developed with different degrees of success in Europe, Africa, Asia, and later in Australia.[202] This worldwide trend towards land reform ultimately resulted in the first United Nations World Conference on Agrarian Reform and Rural Development, held in Rome in 1979.[203]

Land reform ultimately would become an important component of property law in many American jurisdictions, a group considered a leader in the unequal distribution of land, where 90 percent of the land was owned by 10 percent of the population during the 1960s.[204] This traditional land tenure pattern shaped the existing social system where peasants tended to lack formal education, proper medical care, and suitable housing.[205] Land reform took place across Latin American jurisdictions. The first experience occurred in Mexico, starting in 1915, soon after the Revolution, since that jurisdiction adopted an

200 The purpose of land redistribution can nevertheless be traced back to the ancient Greeks. Ankersent and Ruppert, '*Tierra y Libertad*,' 72.

201 Florencio Durán Bernales, *Población, Alimentos y Reforma Agraria* (Santiago: Editorial Universitaria, 1966), 172–174; Ricardo Robledo and Luis Enrique Espinoza, 'La Reforma Agraria en la II República: El Proceso de Asentamiento de Comunidades de Campesinos en la Provincia de Salamanca' in *Historia de la Propiedad*, 406.

202 Henri A.L. Dekker, *The Invisible Line: Land Reform, Land Tenure Security, and Land Registration* (Aldershot: Ashgate, 2003), 78, 88–102; Halpérin, *Histoire du droit des biens*, 312–319. See also Bertus de Villiers, *Land Reform: Issues and Challenges; A Comparative Overview of Experiences in Zimbabwe, Namibia, South Africa and Australia* (Johannesburg: Konrad-Adenauer-Stiftung, 2003), 89–129; Tai, *Land Reform and Politics*; Eduardo Conesa, 'El impuesto a la tierra libre de mejoras, recursos naturales, hidrocarburos y el federalismo en la Argentina' (Portal Académico. Facultad de Derecho, Universidad de Buenos Aires, 2012), 5. http://portalacademico.derecho.uba.ar/catedras/archivos/catedras/19/el_impuesto_tierra_libre_de_mejoras_y_a_los_recursos_naturales_en_general_en_el_regimen_federal_argentino_copia.pdf.

203 Rogelio Parra Silva, 'Conferencia internacional sobre reforma agraria y desarrollo rural' (2006) 31 Estudios Agrarios 239–240.

204 Ankersent and Ruppert, '*Tierra y Libertad*,' 70; Karst and Rosenn, *Law and Development in Latin America*, 242; Nancy D. Lapp, *Landing Votes: Representation and Land Reform in Latin America* (New York: Palgrave Macmillan, 2004), 2; Mirow, *Latin American Law*, 227.

205 Robert J. Alexander, *Agrarian Reform in Latin America* (New York: Macmillan, 1974), 101; Barraclough, *Agrarian Structure in Latin America*, 40. For a sociological analysis of agrarian reform in Latin America, see the seminal works of Antonio García. Antonio García, *Sociología de la reforma agraria en América latina* (Buenos Aires: Amorrortu editores, 1973).

array of legislation that was relevant for achieving reform.[206] The Constitution of 1917 welcomed elements of land reform, mainly in Article 27.[207] Further steps towards reform were taken in 1934, through de-codification, when the Agrarian Code was enacted in Mexico.[208] That Code stimulated the creation of the *ejido* through which land could be cultivated collectively or distributed amongst holders.[209] Several jurisdictions followed Mexico on the path towards land reform during the next half-century, though some jurisdictions such as Argentina and Uruguay seem not to have demanded reform.[210] A 'contagion' of land reform legislative enactments took place in the region. Examples of the first land-reform legislative enactments[211] are found in Colombia (1936), Venezuela (1940), Puerto Rico (1941), Guatemala (1952), Bolivia (1953), Cuba (1959), Dominican Republic (1961), Chile (1962), Costa Rica (1962), Honduras (1962), Panama (1962), Paraguay (1963), Peru (1963), Ecuador (1964), Nicaragua (1979), and El Salvador (1980).[212] Land reform experienced a peak in the 1960s

206 Willem Assies and Emilio Duhau, 'Land Tenure and Tenure Regimes in Mexico: An Overview' in *Legalising Land Rights: Local Practices, State Responses and Tenure Security in Africa, Asia and Latin America*, eds Janine M. Ubink, André J. Hoekema and Willem J. Assies (Leiden: Leiden University Press, 2009), 359–360; Halpérin, *Histoire du droit des biens*, 313–314; Pedro Hernández Gaona, 'Evolución y proyección de la legislación agraria mexicana' (1991) 3–1991 Anuario Mexicano de Historia del Derecho, 93; Mirow, *Latin American Law*, 219–222.

207 Alexander, *Agrarian Reform*, 25; Halpérin, *Histoire du droit des biens*, 313–314; Mirow, *Latin American Law*, 206.

208 Hernández Gaona, 'Evolución y proyección,' 88; Jean Meyer, 'Mexico: Revolution and Reconstruction in the 1920s' in *The Cambridge History of Latin America*, ed. Leslie Bethell (Cambridge: Cambridge University Press, 1998), vol. 5, 187.

209 Alexander, *Agrarian Reform*, 26.

210 Lapp, *Landing Votes*, 14. See generally Alexander, *Agrarian Reform*.

211 Some jurisdictions enacted multiple laws on land reform. For example, Colombia enacted land reform laws in 1936, 1961, and 1980. Sampaio, *La Reforma Agraria*, 10.

212 Ibid.; Alexander, *Agrarian Reform*, 40; Jacques Chonchot, 'Razones económicas, sociales y políticas de la reforma agraria' in *Reformas Agrarias*, 100; Alain de Janvry, Gustavo Gordillo, Elisabeth Sadoulet, and Jean Philippe Platteau 'The Changing Role of the State in Latin American Land Reforms' in *Access to Land, Rural Poverty and Public Action* (Oxford: Oxford University Press, 2001), 279; Halpérin, *Histoire du droit des biens*, 314–315; Lapp, *Landing Votes*, 13; Keith S. Rosenn, 'Puerto Rican Land Reform: The History of an Instructive Experiment' (1963) 73 Yale Law Journal 335; James W. Wilkie, *Measuring Land Reform: Supplement to the Statistical Abstract of Latin America with a Special Map and Graph Series on Land Reform by Richard W. Wilkie and John Marti* (Los Angeles: UCLA Latin American Center, 1974), 1; Annelies Zoomers and Gamma van der Haar, 'Introduction: Regulating Land Tenure under Neo-liberalism' in *Current Land Policy in Latin America: Regulating Land Tenure under Neo-liberalism*, eds Annelies Zoomers and Gemma van der Haar (Amsterdam: Royal Tropical Institute, 2000), 19.

and slowed down in the 1980s.[213] It has even been claimed that changes in the agrarian structures of those jurisdictions were greater during the period from 1930 to 1980 than they were during the prior 400 years.[214]

Reforms varied significantly to the extent they restructured land tenure and production.[215] The measures required, amongst other things, the setting of limitations on privately held ownership and the expropriation of large tracts of land.[216] The programs varied in scope: some granted practically all land individually to be cultivated as family farms; others opted for mixed systems, welcoming cooperative agriculture and private landholding; while several more opted for the socialization of land.[217] The enactment of law reform legislation, however, did not necessarily mean that land reform took place.[218] Even though it can certainly be claimed that land reform enactments ultimately did not alter substantially the agrarian structure of the region, or were in some jurisdictions *no more than a gesture*, they assisted in welcoming the reception of the new paradigm.[219]

The Chilean experience of land reform provides an illustration of how the Social Function paradigm was welcomed within special legislation. Land-reform legislative enactments in Chile had, compared with other jurisdictions, the highest degree of impact on the modernization of agriculture.[220] The land tenure structure in Chile had been inherited from the Spanish period and continued during the first decades of the republican periods.[221] Changes were ignited during the presidency of Arturo Fortunato Alessandri Palma in 1920 when the political power of landowners started to be eroded.[222] During that century, industrialization and capitalism percolated into the rural sector, weakening the landowning elite.[223] The main reforms were undertaken in

---

213 Antonio García, *Modelos operacionales de reforma agraria y desarrollo rural en América Latina* (San José: Instituto Interamericano de Cooperación para la Agricultura, 1985), 120; Tai, *Land Reform and Politics*, 15.

214 Norman Long and Bryan Roberts, 'The Agrarian Structures of Latin America, 1930–1990' in *The Cambridge History of Latin America*, ed. Leslie Bethell (Cambridge: Cambridge University Press, 1994), vol. 6, 325.

215 Ibid., 362.

216 Zoomers and van der Haar, 'Introduction: Regulating Land,' 19.

217 Alexander, *Agrarian Reform*, 58.

218 Karst and Rosenn, *Law and Development in Latin America*, 274.

219 Alexander, *Agrarian Reform*, 40; Sampaio, *La Reforma Agraria*, 15.

220 Sampaio, *La Reforma Agraria*, 20.

221 Joseph R. Thome, 'Expropriation in Chile under the Frei Agrarian Reform' (1971) 19 American Journal of Comparative Law, 491.

222 Ibid., 494.

223 Lapp, *Landing Votes*, 54.

the 1960s and consolidated in the 1970s, during the presidencies of Eduardo Nicanor Frei Montalva, Jorge Alessandri Rodríguez, and Salvador Guillermo Allende Gossens. The rural areas of Chile before these significant reforms were characterized by large estate owners, who preserved an almost feudal relationship with tenants, where 80 percent of agricultural land was divided amongst 3 percent of rural families.[224] There was a clear dichotomy between large landholders on *haciendas* and small farmers owning lands that hardly sufficed for subsistence.[225] Even when *haciendas* seemed to be multifamily properties, they remained uniform economic units and the *latifundio* was the dominant economic and social unit.[226] In Chile, during the era of revolution (1960–1980), some groups aimed to depart from capitalism and adopt socialism.[227]

The social function paradigm was welcomed with different intensity across Latin America. It percolated into new constitutional texts, into civil code revision efforts, and into the enactments of special legislation. Accordingly, the degree of departure from the liberal paradigm differed by jurisdiction, some being more conservative than others. Jurisdictions welcomed the new paradigm in their enactments, some even referring to the term *social function*. Embracers of the new paradigm weakened the absolute character of ownership by adopting doctrines and principles that had an indirect impact on that fundamental pillar of property law.

5 Closing Remarks

Land and other property relations experienced changes in Latin America since the sixteenth century. This chapter offered an inventory of some of the main motivations that accompanied and help explain those changes. The inventory followed the evolution of ownership paradigms as experienced in Latin

224 Solon L. Barraclough, *Land Reform in Developing Countries: The Role of the State and Other Actors; Discussion Paper No. 101, June 1999* (Geneva: United Nations Research Institute for Social Development, 1999), 20–21; Enrique Brahm García, 'Algunos aspectos del proceso de socialización del derecho de propiedad en Chile durante el gobierno del general Carlos Ibañez del Campo (1927–1931)' (2012) 20 Rechtsgeschichte, 254.

225 Barraclough, *Agrarian Structure in Latin America*, 133–134; Dekker, *The Invisible Line*, 7.

226 James Becket, 'Problemas de la reforma agraria' in *Reformas Agrarias*, 561; James Petras and Maurice Zeitlin, 'Agrarian Radicalism in Chile' in *Agrarian Problems and Peasant Movements in Latin America*, ed. Rodolfo Stavenhagen (Garden City: Anchor Books, 1970), 507.

227 Antonio Bellisario, 'The Chilean Agrarian Transformation: The Pre-agrarian Reform Period (1955–1965)' (2006) 6(2) Journal of Agrarian Change 169.

American jurisdictions. With their own nuances, jurisdictions shifted paradigms during different periods.

The Allocation paradigm was the first to emerge in Latin American jurisdictions. This chapter first addressed the different land relations of Native American groups, stretching even to the final decades of the twentieth century. These groups comprised a 'mosaic of different legal systems,' and their land relations were marked by communal and individual control over property. The chapter further focused on the access by European settlers to the new American territories. The main grounds for the holding of those territories were the capitulations, the papal bulls, and the right to conquest and just war. The different concurring interests that different actors had in ownership followed. The interests were interconnected amongst actors, resulting ultimately in the allocation of ownership. Accordingly, settlement in the Americas was undertaken both by private and public intervention. Furthermore, allocation was individual (royal land grants) or communal (*comunales* and *propios*) and aimed to fulfil the different interests of actors. The efforts to allot were so clear that there was no perpetual allocation. If property was neglected by actors, the reason for allocation would motivate a change in the beneficiary. It should be noted, in addition, that allocation prevailed beyond the disappearance of the Iberian administration and extended until a new Liberal paradigm was established.

The Liberal was the second paradigm to emerge in Latin American jurisdictions. The nineteenth century was deemed the century of codification, and civil codes occupied a paramount, exclusive, and exhaustive place in private law. Scholars venerated the letter of the codes, and the encapsulations of ownership in those texts were deemed authoritative. For example, the wordings in different code articles, such as Article 544 of the *Code Napoléon* and Article 582 of the Chilean code, illustrated that paramount place for individual actors. The pollination of civil code provisions assisted in sharing the Liberal paradigm across Latin America. As indicated in this chapter, ownership as incorporated in civil codes was an absolute right that followed the tenets of the Liberal paradigm. Civil codes provided the center for private law provisions and encapsulated the most seminal of institutions of property law. Codification developed within social and legal contexts that were replicated throughout different parts of the Americas. Codification took place within a Pan-American context that sought the adoption of codes. The Chilean Civil Code was clearly a blueprint for the Americas, enabling jurisdictions to share a similar understanding of ownership. There was a circulation of legal ideas and a flow of paradigms that linked jurisdictions within the continent. Nonetheless different political and social backgrounds provided different scenarios for codification. There are common legal bases and temporal parallels amongst jurisdictions, yet each jurisdiction merits its own study.[228] The study of the pollination helped demonstrate that interest was not limited to Europe, and that when drafting in the Americas jurists also looked at vernacular sources. Codification, therefore, was not limited to normative transfers in the Americas. It also extended to intellectual challenges regarding creation and adaptation.[229]

The Social Function paradigm was the third paradigm to emerge in Latin American jurisdictions. The chapter demonstrated that the adoption of a new paradigm took time, starting during the second half of the nineteenth century, and experiencing a peak in the period from 1890 to 1930. It also showed that the new paradigm developed both in Europe and in the Americas, and found reception that was not limited to English, French, German, and Spanish legal literature, and even found expression in the writings of the Church. Special attention was devoted to the writings of Duguit, who may be considered the paladin of the new paradigm, and to the reception of his ideas on both sides of the Atlantic Ocean. Changes in paradigm reflected in civil codes, in constitutions, and in special legislation. Civil codes were no longer the main source of private law, and other enactments took the stage, on occasion leading to reaffirming the paradigm shifts, such as the enactments on land reform. Civil codes welcomed at that time the doctrine of abuse of rights, showing a paradigm shift. The doctrine of abuse of rights served as a channel for the reception of the new paradigm as found in the civil codes of many Latin American jurisdictions. A pollination of that doctrine was contemporaneously experienced in the Old World and in the New World. Furthermore, changes were reflected in constitutions, when several amendments were introduced to the existing texts, triggered after the Mexican and Weimar constitutions, to provide a path towards the adoption of the new paradigm. The transatlantic 'contagion' of constitutions and the global development of land-reform legislative enactments indeed helped in achieving a paradigm shift: moving towards the Social Function paradigm that was shared across jurisdictions. Society demanded a departure from the established Liberal paradigm of the nineteenth century, and legislatures were open to the reception of a new understanding of ownership. Those enactments succeeded in reaching a paradigm shift, even in jurisdictions where constitutional texts or civil codes were not subject to substantive changes.

228 Víctor Tau Anzoátegui, *La Codificación en la Argentina (1810–1870): Mentalidad Social e Ideas Jurídicas*, 2nd ed. (Buenos Aires: Perrot, 2008), 16.

229 See generally Parise, 'Libraries of Civil Codes,' 353–354.

A look into Latin American jurisdictions demonstrated that land and other property relations are remote from consideration as being dormant areas of law. The interplay of actors and things motivated paradigm shifts, since social conditions affected local cultures and those impacts triggered changes in property law.[230] A comparative legal historical approach makes manifest that current understandings are not uncontested dogmas.[231]

References

Alexander, Robert J. *Agrarian Reform in Latin America*. New York: Macmillan, 1974.

Alterini, Atilio Aníbal, and Roberto M. López Cabana. 'El abuso del derecho. Estudio de Derecho Comparado.' *Revista Jurídica Argentina La Ley* 1990-B (1990): 1101–1117.

Ankersent, Thomas T., and Thomas Ruppert. '*Tierra y Libertad*: The Social Function Doctrine and Land Reform in Latin America.' *Tulane Environmental Law Journal* 19 (2006): 69–120.

Babie, Paul, and Jessica Viven-Wilksch, eds. *Léon Duguit and the Social Norm of Property: A Translation and Global Exploration*. Cham: Springer, 2019.

Barraclough, Solon, ed. *Agrarian Structure in Latin America: A Resume of the CIDA Land Tenure Studies of: Argentina, Brazil, Chile, Colombia, Ecuador, Guatemala, Peru*. Lexington: Lexington Books, 1973.

Bravo Lira, Bernardino. *Derecho Común y Derecho Propio en el Nuevo Mundo*. Santiago: Editorial Jurídica de Chile, 1989.

Cordero Quinzacara, Eduardo. 'De la propiedad a las propiedades. La evolución de la concepción liberal de la propiedad.' *Revista de Derecho de la Pontificia Universidad Católica de Valparaíso* 31 (2008): 493–525.

Delgado, Óscar, ed. *Reformas Agrarias en la América Latina: Procesos y Perspectivas*. México and Buenos Aires: Fondo de Cultura Económica, 1965.

Dougnac Rodríguez, Antonio. *Manual de Historia del Derecho Indiano*. México: Universidad Nacional Autónoma de México, 1994.

Duguit, Léon. *Les transformations générales du droit privé depuis le Code Napoléon*. Paris: Félix Alcan, 1912.

García, Antonio. *Sociología de la reforma agraria en América latina*. Buenos Aires: Amorrortu editores, 1973.

García-Gallo, Alfonso. *Los orígenes Españoles de las Instituciones Americanas: Estudios de Derecho Indiano*. Madrid: Real Academia de Jurisprudencia y Legislación, 1987.

230 Ernest Beaglehole, 'Ownership and Inheritance in an American Indian Tribe' (1935) 20 Iowa Law Review 316.

231 de Azcárate, *Ensayo sobre la historia del derecho de propiedad*, 352.

Guzmán Brito, Alejandro. *La codificación civil en Iberoamérica. Siglos XIX y XX*. Santiago: Editorial Jurídica de Chile, 2000.

Levaggi, Abelardo, ed. *El aborigen y el derecho en el pasado y el presente*. Buenos Aires: Universidad del Museo Social Argentino, 1990.

Levaggi, Abelardo. 'La réception du système juridique espagnol par les systèmes indigènes en Amérique.' In *La Réception des Systèmes juridiques: implantations et destins*, edited by Michel Doucet and Jacques Vanderlinden, 331–379. Brussels: Etablissements Emile Bruylant, 1994.

Mariluz Urquijo, José María. *El Régimen de la Tierra en el Derecho Indiano*. 2nd ed. Buenos Aires: Editorial Perrot, 1978.

Melleray, Fabrice (dir.). *Autour de Léon Duguit: Colloque commémoratif du 150e anniversaire de la naissance du doyen Léon Duguit. Bordeaux, 29–30 mai 2009*. Brussels: Bruylant, 2011.

Mirow, M.C. 'The Social-Obligation Norm of Property: Duguit, Hayem, and Others.' *Florida Journal of International Law* 22 (2010): 191–226.

Mirow, M.C. *Latin American Law: A History of Private Law and Institutions in Spanish America*. Austin: University of Texas Press, 2004.

Moréteau, Olivier, and Agustín Parise. 'Recodification in Louisiana and Latin America.' *Tulane Law Review* 83 (2009): 1103–1162.

Ots Capdequí, José María. *El régimen de la tierra en la América española durante el periodo colonial: Cursillo dictado en la Universidad de Santo Domingo del 27 de noviembre al 13 de diciembre de 1944*. Ciudad Trujillo [Santo Domingo]: Universidad de Santo Domingo, 1946.

Ots Capdequí, José María. *Manual de historia de derecho español en las Indias y del derecho propiamente indiano*. Buenos Aires: Editorial Losada, 1945.

Parise, Agustín. *Ownership Paradigms in American Civil Law Jurisdictions: Manifestations of the Shifts in the Legislation of Louisiana, Chile, and Argentina (16th-20th Centuries)*. Leiden: Brill, 2017.

Ramella, Susana T. 'Propiedad en función social en la Constitución de 1949: Una "mentalidad" del Antiguo Régimen representada en el constitucionalismo social de la época.' *Revista de Historia del Derecho* 35 (2007): 297–354.

Sánchez Bella, Ismael, Alberto de la Hera, and Carlos Díaz Rementería. *Historia del Derecho Indiano*. Madrid: Editorial MAPFRE, 1992.

CHAPTER 15

Commercial Law, Business, and Commerce

Óscar Cruz Barney

1 Development of Activity and Commercial Law in the Indies Law

Commercial law had from its origins, in the Late Middle Ages, a high degree of autonomy and specialty. It is considered an autonomous law because its norms were created with relative independence from the established powers, especially since its institutions were distinguished from similar ones, typical of property law.[1]

In the origins of commercial law, Phoenicians and Greeks were governed by custom in their maritime trade relations; these crystallized into a *Lex Rhodia*, considered originally for the island of Rhodes and which was recognized in the *Digest* as a *common law of the sea*. For its part, *ius civile* provided a series of principles that enriched the tradition of maritime trade; for example, that the sea is a free and universal space, open to common use, in which the ownership of ships and their goods must be respected, even in the event of shipwreck.[2]

After the fall of the Western Roman Empire, this principle of community and protection was broken, thus presenting the problem of piracy and the resurgence of territorial seas. However, the exclusive jurisdiction of the merchants was partly retained by the Germanic peoples, especially in the *Liber Iudiciorum*.

In the Mediterranean world, while commercial life was organized in Barcelona, customs and mercantile uses began to be collected in writing in private collections known as *Costums de la Mar*, which were later included in the *Libre del Consulat de Mar* or *Libro del Consulado del Mar* in the second half of the fourteenth century.[3] The *Libro* is a compilation of the mercantile naval tradition of the Mediterranean. It consisted of the *Costums de la Mar*, a procedural regulation for the consulate of Valencia, and provisions on discipline on board ships and armaments in privateering. A notary of the consulate of Mallorca,

---

1 Francesco Galgano, *Historia del derecho mercantil*, trans. Joaquín Bisbal (Barcelona: Ed. Laia, 1981), 23.

2 Santos M. Coronas González, *Manual de historia del derecho español* (València: Tirant lo Blanch, 1999), 347–348.

3 Its text in Spanish can be consulted in the edition of the Aseguradora Mexicana, México, 1983.

 | DOI:10.1163/9789004436091_017

Huguet Borras, was in charge of its drafting around 1345, and in 1370 it received the name by which it is known today, which is *Libro del Consulado del Mar*.[4] Its purpose was to offer a practical and easy-to-use work, in a clear and casuistic style, for all the consulates of the Mediterranean. The *Libro* was translated into Italian, Spanish, French, Dutch, German, and English.

In the Atlantic, in the twelfth century a text was drafted that collected the customary law of the North Atlantic, known as *Rooles d'Oleron*, in allusion to the decisions of the judges of the island of Oleron, in the French region of Bordeaux, center of extensive naval activity. The text is composed of twenty-four chapters written in Gascon, and deals with matters such as armaments, freight, seamanship, and piloting. It was widely disseminated in France, Holland, and England. In Spain a Castilian version was prepared in the thirteenth century with the name of *Fuero de Layrón*.

This set of uses, customs, laws, and judgments of the mercantile naval tradition made up the *ius mercatorum* as a medieval legal response to the needs of commercial traffic. The legal literature in Commercial Law during the American viceroyalty period has several representatives. In the Indies the works of Juan de Hevia Bolaños circulated with his *Curia Philippica*, published in Lima, Peru, in 1603. It is a treatise on procedural law that was widely disseminated in both the peninsula and the Indies; moreover, it was used until the codification in the nineteenth century. Fourteen editions of it were made in the seventeenth century, fifteen in the eighteenth and at least three in the nineteenth century to which is added his *Labyrinto del comercio terrestre y naval*, which deals with commercial law, published in Lima in 1617. This work was printed jointly with the *Curia Philippica* from the 1644 edition.

As for its content, the *Curia Philippica*, including the *Labyrinto*, is divided into two issues grouped in the same volume.[5] The first is divided into five books or parts; the first part deals with civil trials, the second with summary trials, the third with criminal trials, the fourth with the trial of residence, and the fifth with the appeal. The second volume is divided into three books or parts, which in turn are subdivided into chapters. It refers in general to land and maritime trade, and addresses issues such as merchants, exchanges, banks, companies, factors, shops, brokers, merchandise, weights and measures, fairs, markets, excise taxes, leases, mortgages, pledge, assignment, payments, settlements,

4 Aquilino Iglesia Ferreirós, 'Libro do Consulado da Mar' (1986) 56 Anuario de Historia del Derecho Español vol. 2, 231.

5 We consulted Juan de Hevia Bolaños, *Curia Philippica* (Madrid: Imprenta de Josef Doblado, 1783).

priority of debts, merchant consulates, naval trade, fleets, ships, charters, seizures, shipwrecks, insurance, betting, customs, registrations, etc.

The texts by Duarte Gómez Solís (Portuguese), with his *Discourso sobre los comercios de las Indias*, published in 1622, and by Fray Antonio Vázquez Espinosa, with the *Confesionario general con los contratos y tratos de las Indias*, published in 1624, as well as the work of Pedro de Oñate, *De contractibus*, published in Rome between 1646 and 1654, also circulated.

The work of Joseph de Veitia Linaje, who was an officer of the House of Contracting of Seville, and later Counselor of the Indies, author of the *Norte de la contratación de las Indias Occidentales*, printed in Seville in 1672, stands out for its importance.[6] For his part, Matías Lagunez, who was an *oidor* of the Audiencia of Quito, published in Madrid in 1686 the *Tractatus de fructibus tituli generali in quo selectiora quce ad rem fructuariam pertinentia iura expeduntur, difficiliora atque referentur*. These works provided the foundation for the subject.

Much has been written about the evolution of commercial law in general and in Latin America in particular, and recent works are listed in the references section of this chapter. The merchants were associated in large professional corporations that received the name of *Consulates* and defended the economic interests of their members. The membership was formed by the resident merchants who met the requirements of age, property, and occupation.[7] In addition, the Consulates acted as special courts to resolve commercial disputes arising between their members. The judges or consuls, the parish priest, and two or three elected members served on an annual basis. No jurists or professional judges intervened, only merchants knowledgeable about mercantile traffic and its problems and customs. Disputes were settled on the basis of *usus mercatorum* and the exclusive written rules of each Consulate.[8]

The first Consulate in Castile was in Burgos and was created by decree of the Catholic Monarchs given in Medina del Campo on July 21, 1494, at the request of local merchants. The decree was included in the *Nueva Recopilación*.[9] After

6 There are reissues, one by the Comisión Argentina de Fomento Interamericano, Buenos Aires, 1945; and another facsimile by the Instituto de Estudios Fiscales of the Ministry of Finance, an introductory study by Francisco de Solano, printed in the Fábrica Nacional de Moneda y Timbre, Madrid, 1981.

7 Robert Smith, José Ramírez Flores, and Leonardo Pasquel, *Los consulados de comerciantes en Nueva España* (México: Instituto Mexicano de Comercio Exterior, 1976), 15.

8 Francisco Tomás y Valiente, *Manual de Historia del derecho Español* (Madrid: Tecnos, 2001), 352–353; Coronas González, *Manual*, 353–354.

9 See *Ordenanzas del Consulado de Burgos*. About the Consulate of Burgos, see Eloy García de Quevedo, *Ordenanzas del Consulado de Burgos de 1538* (Burgos: Imprenta de la Diputación,1905), facsimile edition of the Hon. Diputación Provincial de Burgos

its initial charters and prior authorization granted by the emperor in 1520, the Consulate of Burgos saw its first ordinances confirmed in Valladolid on September 18, 1538.[10] The Consulate received its second ordinances in 1572, perfecting the previous ones by adding three forms of maritime insurance. In September 1511 the crown issued a general decree on the jurisdiction of the *Board of Trade in Seville*. This decree established that all processes relating to contracts and companies of American commerce, insurance, and freight would be governed by the rules and customs of the Consulate of Burgos.[11]

In 1511 the Consulate of Bilbao was created and was governed by the same provisions as that of Burgos. This consulate participated in trade with the Indies from its beginnings through the ports of Cádiz, Seville, the Canary Islands, and Lisbon until the uprising of Portugal.[12]

The third great Castilian Consulate was the Consulate of Shippers to the Indies of Seville, created on August 23, 1543 for trade with the Indies.[13] Its ordinances were approved by royal provision of July 14, 1556, and took into account the organization and operation of the Consulate of Burgos.[14] The ordinances established that the Consulate would have a Prior and two consuls elected from among the same merchants to hear any dispute related to the traffic of goods from or to the Indies, including freight, insurance, companies, contracts, and commissions.[15] García Fuentes divides the activities of this Consulate of Seville into three: judicial, commercial, and financial.[16] It heard lawsuits resulting from trade, loans and donations to trade with the Indies, delegation of the

---

V Centenerio de la Fundación del Consulado, Burgos, 1995. See also Manuel Basas Fernández, *El Consulado de Burgos en el siglo XVI* (Madrid: Consejo Superior de Investigaciones Científicas, 1963), facsimile edition of the Hon. Diputación Provincial de Burgos V Centenerio de la Fundación del Consulado, Burgos, 1994.

10 Basas Fernández, *El Consulado de Burgos*, 41.

11 Clarence H. Haring, *Comercio y navegación entre España y la Indias en la época de los Habsburgos* (México: Fondo de Cultura Económica, 1939), 51–52. This decree is essential for the study of marine risks and insurance in New Spain.

12 Lutgardo García Fuentes, *El comercio español con América 1650–1700* (Sevilla: Escuela de Estudios Hispano-Americanos, Consejo Superior de Investigaciones Científicas, 1980), 87.

13 For its creation Julián B. Ruiz Rivera and Manuela Cristina García Bernal, *Cargadores a Indias* (Madrid: Mapfre, 1992), 52–67.

14 Although José Luis Comellas notes that the final ordinances date from 1522. Jose Luis Comellas, *Sevilla, Cádiz, y América: El trasiego y el tráfico* (Madrid: Fundación Ignacio Larramendi, 2017), 63.

15 Robert Sidney Smith, *Historia de los Consulados de Mar, 1250–1700* (Barcelona: EDC Península, 1978), 121. On the subject of Hispanic-Indies business transactions see Óscar Cruz Barney, *El riesgo en el comercio hispano-indiano: préstamos y seguros marítimos durante los siglos XVI a XIX* (México: Instituto de Investigaciones Jurídicas, UNAM, 1998).

16 Garcia Fuentes, *El comercio español*, 23–25.

House of Contracting, traffic with the Indies, maritime insurance, tonnages, and fleet dispatch. The Consulate also set fees for sailors, wholesale markets, shipwrecks, and cargo.[17] Along with the Consulate there was another institution, the *Universidad de los Maestres e Pilotos de las Naos de la Navegación de las Indias.* This institution brought together owners of the ships and their captains who participated in the Indies convoy fleet. It also served for devotional purposes: chapel, festivals, and assistance.[18]

In New Spain, at the end of the sixteenth century a group of merchants formulated plans to organize their own guild separate from Seville. On June 15, 1592, the association charter of the first Spanish-American mercantile guild was issued. Royal privilege was granted to it on June 15, 1592, and was received by the guild on March 13, 1593, leading to the consulate and court.[19]

Without major opposition to the consulate project, on May 17, 1593, the *audiencia* authorized the creation of the guild court and provided for the formation of an appellate court administered by a treasury official as an appeals judge. On November 8, 1594, the *audiencia* was instructed to protect the new institution, and it issued its final accord on June 20, 1595.[20] The consulate's ordinances were ratified by the crown in 1604 and published in 1636. These ordinances provided that any matters not covered by them would be supplemented by those of Burgos and Seville.[21]

The next Indies consulate was in Lima and was incorporated by decree of December 29, 1593, although it did not begin its corporate life until February 21, 1613. Its first ordinances are from 1627.[22] Later, it was the Philippines's turn to

---

17 Ibid., 27.

18 Comellas, *Sevilla, Cádiz and America*, 64.

19 Robert Smith, 'Los consulados,' 16–17. See also Pablo Montero, *Ulúa, puente intercontinental en el sigo XVII* (México: Instituto nacional de antropología e historia: Internacional de contenedores asociados de Veracruz, 1997), 57. For the Consulate of New Spain see Rubén Ruiz Guerra, 'El Consulado de Comerciantes de la Ciudad de México' in *Memoria del IV Congreso de Historia del Derecho Mexicano*, ed. José Luis Soberanes (México: UNAM, 1984); and Ana Maria Barrero García, 'Notas para una nueva edición de las Ordenanzas del Consulado de la Universidad de Mercaderes de Nueva España' in *Memoria del IV Congreso de Historia del Derecho Mexicano*, ed. Beatriz Bernal (México: Instituto de Investigaciones Jurídicas, UNAM, 1988), vol. 1.

20 Robert Smith, 'Los consulados,' 4–10; Robert Smith, José Ramírez Flores, and Leonardo Pasquel, *Los consulados de comerciantes en Nueva España* (México: Instituto Mexicano de Comercio Exterior, 1976), 18.

21 Francisco R. Calderon, *Historia económica de la Nueva España en tiempos de los Austrias* (México: Fondo de Cultura Económica, 1995), 460.

22 On trade and the consulate of Lima see Manuel Moreyra Paz Soldán, 'El comercio de exportación en el Pacífico a principios del siglo XVIII' in *Estudios históricos*, ed. Grover Antonio Espinoza Ruiz (Lima: Pontificia Universidad Católica del Perú, Instituto Riva

have its consulate; the Consulate of Manila would be constituted in 1769, with jurisdiction over all the islands.[23]

With the *Regulation and royal tariffs for the free trade of Spain and the Indies of October 12, 1778*[24] issued by Carlos III, a second (late) stage in the creation of consulates is opened by ordering their formation in all the ports authorized in America for free trade. This measure sought to promote agriculture, industry, and navigation to the American domains.[25] These consulates were constituted as 'authentic administrative bodies, devoid of any initiative, and destined to develop the guidelines drawn up by the government.'[26]

Thus, the consulates of Seville were founded in 1784, also called *Nuevo de Sevilla* , to distinguish it from that of *Shippers to the Indies* of 1543; of Murcia in 1815; of La Coruña, Málaga, and Santander in 1785; of San Cristóbal de Tenerife in 1786; of Sanlúcar de Barrameda in 1806; of Granada in 1817; of Vigo in 1820, and of Madrid in 1827.[27] In the Indies, the Consulates of Lima and Mexico expressed their opposition. It was not until 1793 that Caracas[28] and Guatemala

---

Agüero, 1994); Paz Soldán 'El Tribunal del Consulado de Lima' in *Estudios históricos,* ed. Grover Antonio Espinoza Ruiz (Lima: Pontificia Universidad Católica del Perú, Instituto Riva Aguero, 1994); Carmen Parrón Salas, *De las reformas borbónicas a la República: el Consulado y el comercio marítimo de Lima, 1778–1821* (Murcia: Imprenta de la Academia General del Aire, 1995); Jesús Turiso Sebastian, *Comerciantes españoles en la Lima borbónica: Anatomía de una Elite de Poder* (*1701–1761*) (Valladolid: Universidad de Valladolid, Secretaría de Publicaciones e Intercambio Editorial, Instituto Riva-Agüero, 2002).

23 Carmen Yuste, 'La fundación de la Junta de Profesores Comerciantes o Consulado de Filipinas. Circunscripción, atribuciones y competencias' (2019) 38 Revista mexicana de historia del derecho 111–130.

24 *Reglamento y aranceles reales para el comercio libre de España y las Indias del 12 de octubre de 1778,* in the Imprenta de Pedro Marín, Madrid, 1778. General Archive of the Nation, Bandos, vol. 10, exp. 61, ff. 414–555. The work by Charles, roi d'Espagne, *Carlos III, la ilustración en las imprentas oficiales: 1759–1788* (Madrid: Departamento de programación editoriale del Boletín oficial del estado, 1989) can also be consulted. From now on it will be cited as *Reglamento de 1778* and article number. *The Reales Cédulas de Erección* of all the consulates of this new generation can be consulted in Óscar Cruz Barney, *El régimen jurídico de los consulados de comercio indianos: 1784–1795* (México: Instituto de Investigaciones Jurídicas, UNAM, 2001).

25 *Reglamento de 1778,* art. 53.

26 Enrique Gacto Fernandez, *Historia de la jurisdicción mercantil en España,* Series Anales de la Universidad Hispalense, Publicaciones de la Universidad de Sevilla, series Derecho numb. 11 (Sevilla: Publicaciones de la Universidad de Sevilla, 1971), 49.

27 Pere Molas Ribalta, *La burguesía mercantil en la España del antiguo régimen* (Madrid: Cátedra, 1985), 92–102.

28 For the Consulate of Caracas see Eduardo Arcila Farías, *El Real Consulado de Caracas* (Caracas: Universidad Central de Venezuela, 1957).

had their consulates; then, Buenos Aires[29] and Cartagena, Chile, Guadalajara, Havana, and Veracruz in 1795.[30]

Veracruz acquired relative commercial importance from the second half of the eighteenth century thanks to coastal trade with Yucatan and Guatemala, so that local merchants depended less on Mexico City.[31] In 1781 a group of merchants from the port of Veracruz requested the establishment of a consulate independent of that of the capital city, arguing that the port was key to the Kingdom of New Spain as a goal and anchorage of the fleets and ships from the peninsula and other American lands. Carlos IV, by decree of January 17, 1795, sanctioned the creation and organization of the Consulate of Veracruz, and it was inaugurated by the municipal council on April 25 of that year.[32] In the certificate of erection of the Consulate its creation is justified by the considerable increase of Indies trade with the freedom granted by Carlos III in the *Reglamento de 1778*.

In Guadalajara, a group of forty-eight merchants accompanied by two councilors and the *alcalde* met on July 12, 1791, and decided to request a license to found a consulate, a request they submitted to the general commander of Nueva Galicia, arguing that the Consulate of Mexico was too distant to resolve the commercial disputes of the merchants of Guadalajara. The crown, by decree of June 6, 1795, erected the Consulate of Guadalajara,[33] which was formally inaugurated in a council session of September 12 of that year.[34] This consulate was later extinguished by decree of the local congress on November 6, 1824.[35]

In independent Mexico, Emperor Agustín de Iturbide constituted the Consulate of Puebla on August 10, 1821, which used as its own the Ordinances of the Consulate of Guadalajara. After a short life, in which it heard more

29 Germán O.E. Tjarks, *El Consulado de Buenos Aires y sus proyecciones en la historia del Río de la Plata* (Buenos Aires: Universidad de Buenos Aires, 1962), vol. 1.

30 Robert Smith, 'Los consulados,' 27. The ordinances of the *Consulate of Veracruz* can be consulted in Cruz Barney, *El riesgo*, 214–232.

31 Robert Smith, 'Los consulados,' 26–28.

32 Ibid., 28–29.

33 Socorro Olguín Mosqueda, 'El Consulado de Guadalajara' (1953) 3(1) Historia Mexicana El Colegio de México 127.

34 Robert Smith, 'Los Consulados,' 28–31. José Ramírez Flores marks the 13th as the opening date. See José Ramírez Flores, 'El Real Consulado de Guadalajara, notas históricas' in *Los consulados de comerciantes en Nueva España* (México: Instituto Mexicano de Comercio Exterior, 1976), 74.

35 José Ramírez Flores, 'El Real Consulado,' 151.

than a hundred cases raised before its Court, it disappeared by decree of the Congress of Puebla in July 1824.[36]

Consular jurisdiction originated in the lack of specialization of judicial bodies in solving problems concerning trade, especially maritime trade. The merchants decided to entrust the resolution of their disputes to a colleague who acted as arbitrator and an expert in the subject matter of the conflict.[37] A fundamental characteristic of a consulate was the existence of its own independent court, empowered to decide the issues raised before it by the members of the commercial community.[38]

The Consulate of New Spain was governed 'by the Ordinances that have those of the said Cities of Burgos, and Seville.'[39] This happened during its first two years of life until the development of its own ordinances in 1603, confirmed by the king in 1604, printed for the first time in 1636, the second time in 1772, and the third and last time in 1816.[40] The *Ordinances of the Consulate of New Spain* addressed the election of the priest and consuls, and organization of the consulate, as well as its procedures. *The Ordinances of the Consulate of Seville and Burgos* were applied in a supplementary manner, in accordance with the provisions of the *Compilation of Laws of the Indies of 1680*.[41] In this sense, as Robert Smith points out, 'the only expressed purpose of the decrees that created the consulates of Mexico and Lima was to provide a mercantile court, but the structure of the *consulate court* presupposed the organization of a *merchants university*, or guild.'[42]

---

36 Ibid., 57–62. About the Consulate of Puebla see Óscar Cruz Barney, *El Consulado de Comercio de Puebla. Régimen Jurídico, Historia y Documentos 1821–1824* (México: Instituto de Investigaciones Jurídicas, UNAM, 2006); Robert S. Smith, 'The Puebla Consulado, 1821–1824' (1946) 21 Revista de Historia de América 19–28; Guy P.C. Thomson, *Puebla de los Ángeles. Industria y sociedad de una ciudad mexicana 1700–1850* trans. Carlos Avila Flores (Puebla: Benemérita Universidad Autónoma de Puebla, 2002), 278–279.

37 Enrique Gacto Fernández, *Historia de la jurisdicción*, 11.

38 Ibid., 29.

39 *Ordenanzas del Consulado de la Nueva España, Auto de el Acuerdo de la Real Audiencia de México, a veinte de junio de mil quinientos noventa y cinco*, 10. *Recopilacion de Indias* lib. IX, tit. 46 addresses the Consulates of Lima and Mexico.

40 Juan N. Rodríguez de San Miguel, *Pandectas hispano-megicanas* (México: New Edition, Librería de J.F. Rosa, 1852), vol. 3, 353. Also see *Reales cédulas y provisiones a que deben sujetarse los cónsules, licencia de S. M. para hacer las Ordenanzas del Consulado de la Nueva España, limitaciones de la póliza pasada y seguro de las naos de las Indias;* Archivo General de la Nación, Redes Cédulas Duplicadas, vol. 2, exp. 513, ff. 300–311 (June 15, 1592).

41 *Rec. Ind.*, lib. IX, tit. XXXXVI, ley 75.

42 Smith, Ramírez Flores, and Pasquel, *Los consulados*, 21.

Subsequently, on November 3, 1785, in a report submitted to the Viceroy of New Spain by the consulate on the application of the *Ordinances of Bilbao* in its transactions, it was indicated that 'this consulate observe, in the absence of its own ordinance, what is established by those of Bilbao in everything that is adaptable to the circumstances of the country and styles of this trade; which is very consistent with what the authors of the kingdom agree, who hold the first law of Toro, because they say unanimously, that when there is no law, statute or custom, it must be determined by the common opinion of the authors with much greater reason it must be resolved by what the sovereign has approved in similar cases and with respect to the same area, which is trade.'[43] In this regard the *Ordinances of Bilbao* 'became important and more respected in the peninsula than those of Burgos and Seville, and their use was introduced insensitively, and preference for them extended to America.'[44] In the *Consulate of Veracruz*, whose ordinances date from January 1795, the *Bilbao Ordinances* of 1737 were supplementarily applied.

As for commercial doctrine, it was not until the sixteenth century that professional jurists paid more attention to commercial problems. The jurists of the *mos italicus* who wrote on commercial law were Benvenuto Stracca with his *Tractatus de mercatura seu mercatore* (1576), Sigismund Scaccia and his *Tractatus de Commerciis et cambio* (1620), Carlos Targa with his *Reflexiones sobre los contratos marinos* translated into Castilian, Ansaldo Ansaldi with his *De commercio et mercatura discursus legales* (1689), and Francesco Rocco (1655) with a treatise on maritime law. Later important works include Giuseppe Lorenzo Maria Casaregi (1670–1737) with his *Discursus legales de comercio* (1740).

As Luisa Brunori points out, Benvenutto Stracca was not only a prominent lawyer, but also the first to make the conceptual separation among commercial, civil, and canon law. Thus, Stracca is considered to be the founder of modern commercial law. In his *De mercatura, seu Mercatore tractatus* (Venetiis, Paolo Manuzio, 1553), 'he was the first to consider commercial law as a complex of autonomous rules, distinct from those of civil law, offering a systematic exposition that took into account commercial uses and local institutions to satisfy the new demands of life of trade in the sixteenth century.'[45]

---

43 Rodríguez de San Miguel, *Pandectas*, 353–354.

44 Ibid., 354. Which at no time indicates that the *Ordinances of Burgos and of Seville* had not been applied before those of Bilbao and even less so when there is express reference to them in the text of the Ordinances of the Consulate of New Spain.

45 Luisa Brunori, 'Benvenuto Stracca: abogado y fundador del derecho comercial "científico" (1509–1578)' in *Historia del derecho y abogacía: Seminario Internacional; Histoire du droit et de la profession d'avocat; Séminaire International*, eds Óscar Cruz Barney and Serge

In Spain, other important works included Juan de Hevia Bolaños, author of the *Curia Philippica* in the seventeenth century and Francisco Salgado de Somoza, creator of the bankruptcy trial in his work *Labyrinthus creditorum concurrentium ad Litem per Debitorem communem inter illos causatam* (first edition, Lyon 1651 and last, Lyon, 1792).[46]

2 Commercial Law in the Nineteenth Century: Codification

After the independence of the Ibero-American nations and Mexico was achieved, the *Ordinances of Bilbao*, the 'true Spanish mercantile code, whose provisions were cited by the lawyers, and by which the courts ruled,' were constituted in the body of trade laws that governed the region,[47]
although other consular ordinances were applied (as is the case of Mexico), including the French and Spanish Commercial Code.
The Bilbao Ordinances remained in force until the promulgation of the respective commercial codes in several countries: Argentina, Colombia, Chile, Guatemala, Mexico, Peru (which adopted the Spanish Commercial Code), and Uruguay.

It was provided, in some cases such as Mexico, that lawsuits arising in federal territories in commercial matters would be determined by the *alcaldes* or judges in their respective cases; these would be associated with two colleagues who would choose between four proposed by the parties, arranged according to the laws in force in the matter.[48] In other cases the courts of the consulate were maintained as in the case of Peru and Chile until 1866, repealing the Ordinances of Bilbao. In yet others, commercial courts, or commercial judges were established as in Colombia, Argentina, Guatemala, and Uruguay.

Dauchy (México: Universidad Nacional Autónoma de México, Instituto de Investigaciones Jurídicas, Université de Lille, Centre d'Histoire Judiciaire, CNRS, Colección: Etudes comparatives de l'histoire du droit mexicain et français / Comparative Studies in Mexican and French Legal History / Estudios comparativos de historia del derecho mexicano y francés, 2020), no. 1, 1.

46 See Wolfgang Forster, *La invención del juicio de quiebra: Francisco Salgado de Somoza (1591–1665)* (Pamplona: Universidad de Navarra, 2017), 327.

47 In Spain they constituted the 'true Spanish commercial code, whose provisions were cited by lawyers, and by which the courts ruled.' José María Ros Biosca, *Código de Comercio reformado según el decreto-ley de 6 de diciembre de 1868; concordado y anotado* (Valencia: Librería de Pascual Aguilar 1878), 28.

48 See also Florentino Mercado, *Libro de los códigos, ó prenociones sintéticas de codificación romana, canónica, española y mexicana* (México: Imprenta de Vicente G. Torres, 1857), 565.

The commercial codification in Hispanic America started in Ecuador through Law of November 4, 1831, essentially adopting the Spanish Commercial Code of 1829, and entering into force on January 1, 1832. It was repealed in May 1882 by the Ecuadorian Commercial Code on April 27, 1882. Subsequently President Eloy Alfaro promulgated the Commercial Code on July 30, 1906, inspired by the Chilean and subsequent Venezuelan codes.[49] This was repealed by a new Code on August 20, 1960. Currently, the Commercial Code that governs is that of May 9, 2019.

This effort was followed by Bolivia, but in this case with an original code: the Mercantile Code of Santa Cruz, Bolivia, approved on November 12, 1834.[50] This Code was repealed by the Commercial Code of February 25, 1977.[51]

The codification effort in French America started in Haiti with its Commercial Code of 1826, very close to the French one of 1807. It was revised by Decree-Law of December 22, 1944.[52]

Some of the commercial codes were inspired by the Ordinances of Bilbao or by the Spanish Commercial Code of 1829: this is the case of Colombia, Costa Rica, Cuba, Chile, El Salvador, Guatemala, México, Nicaragua, Panamá, Paraguay, and Peru. The Spanish Commercial Code of 1829[53] was adopted by Costa Rica by Decree of June 6, 1853, adopting the first three books.[54] On August 10, 1961, a new Commercial Code was published, which repealed the previous one except for its Book III, referring to maritime trade. It entered into force on May 27, 1964. In a contrary move, the first Colombian Commercial Code was published on June 1, 1853, and explicitly repealed the Ordinances of Bilbao.

The Chilean Commercial Code of November 23, 1865 that came into force on January 1, 1867[55] was inspired by the Spanish Commercial Code of 1829, the French of 1807, the Ordinances of Bilbao, the Portuguese Commercial Code of 1833 and the Dutch Code of 1838; as well as the respective Hungarian, Prussian, Würtembourgean, and Buenos Aires codes.[56] This codification was

49 Ibid., 75.

50 Jose Rafael Canedo, *Código Mercantil de Bolivia* (*Vulgarizada para el uso del comercio y de los estudiantes*) (Cochabamba: Tip. Ponce de León, 1921).

51 Julio A. Olavarría, *Manual de Derecho Comercial* (Barcelona: Imprenta Clarasó, 1970), 74–76.

52 *Code of Commerce: Loi Du 27 Mars 1826 modifiée lar le Décret-Loi Du 22 Decémbre 1944* (Port-Au-Prince: Print of l'Etat, 1945).

53 *Código de Comercio, decretado, sancionado y promulgado en 30 de Mayo de 1829* (Madrid: Oficina de D.L. Amarita, 1829).

54 *Código de Comercio y otras leyes mercantiles* (San José: Tipografía Lehman, 1913).

55 *Código de Comercio de la República de Chile* (Santiago de Chile: Imprenta Nacional, 1866).

56 Olavarría, *Manual de Derecho*, 82.

adopted in Honduras: Olavarría maintains that Honduras adopted all Chilean codes, including the Commercial Code, by law of August 27, 1880, the date of its first Commercial Code, which was repealed by the Commercial Code of September 15, 1898, the work of Jerónimo Zelaya and Angel Ugarte inspired by the Guatemalan code of 1877.[57] It entered into force on February 1, 1899. Subsequently, a new Code inspired by the codes of Spain, Mexico, Costa Rica, Nicaragua, and the previous one of 1898 came into force.[58] This is the Commercial Code promulgated on March 5, 1940, of short validity and greatly criticized. It was subsequently repealed by Decree No. 73 of February 16, 1950, for a new code that is almost entirely the work of Spanish jurist Dr. Joaquín Rodríguez and the Honduran Lic. Roberto Ramírez.[59] Also, years later, Colombia finally adopted the Commercial Code of Chile, divided it into two books, and adopted and published them separately: the *Maritime Trade Code* adopted in 1870 corresponding to Book III of the Chilean Code, and the *Land Trade Code* adopted in 1887[60] from that of Panama. For Panama, originally the *Land Trade Code* and the Colombian *Maritime Trade Code* of 1870 governed until 1917. Subsequently, the Commercial Code promulgated on August 22, 1916, entered into force.

The first Commercial Code of El Salvador (1855) was also inspired by the Spanish one of 1829. It was repealed on May 1, 1882, by a new code that received important influences from the Chilean Code of 1865. The first Commercial Code of Guatemala was that of 1877[61] which repealed the Ordinances of Bilbao and the Spanish Commercial Code of 1829 that had been applied since 1839. Olavarría maintains that it is substantially the same text as the Chilean Code of 1865.[62] A new Code was issued on September 15, 1942 and was repealed by the current one which entered into force on January 1, 1971.

In the case on Mexico, on May 16, 1854, the first Mexican Commercial Code was published,[63] mainly inspired by the French

57 *Código de Comercio (1898)* (Tegucigalpa: Tipografía Nacional, 1898).

58 Roberto Ramírez, 'Historia del Derecho Mercantil Hondureño' (1947) 9(35–36) Revista de la Escuela Nacional de Jurisprudencia México 272.

59 Olavarría, *Manual de Derecho*, 75.

60 *Código Colombiano de Comercio Marítimo Expedido por el Congreso de 1870, adicionado con las leyes que lo complementan y reforman y anotado con las disposiciones análogas de varias legislaciones extranjeras por José Vicente Concha* (Bogotá: Librería Americana, 1907).

61 *Código de Comercio de la República de Guatemala* (Guatemala: Imprenta de Luna, 1877).

62 Olavarría, *Manual de Derecho*, 75.

63 About this, see Joseph J. Tornel and Mendívil, *Manual de derecho mercantil mexicano, o sea el Código de Comercio de México puesto en forma de diccionario* (México: Imprenta de Vicente Segura Argüelles, 1854).

Code,[64] and by the Spanish Code of May 30, 1829, of Sáinz de Andino.[65] It is known as the *Lares Code* and was put into force during the Second Mexican Empire (1863–1867) by decree of July 15, 1863. In the Republic, it was in force in some states such as Puebla and Mexico. Subsequently, the Commercial Code of 1854 ceased to be in force and the *Siete Partidas* and the Ordinances of Bilbao were again applied.

The first Commercial Code of Nicaragua was promulgated on February 2, 1869, based on the Spanish Code of 1829. On April 30, 1914, the current one was promulgated, prepared by the jurist Modesto Barrios, who, according to his statements, had as his inspiration the Chilean Code of 1865, the Italian Code of 1883, and the Spanish Code of 1885.[66]

In 1846 Paraguay adopted the Spanish Commercial Code of 1829; but by losing the war of the Triple Alliance, Paraguay became dependent on Argentine influence, successively adopting the codes of this republic. The reformed code of 1889, adopted by Paraguay by law of August 29, 1891, remained in force until 1987 when Civil and Commercial matters in relation to Obligations and Contracts were unified with the issuance of the civil code of that year. Previously by virtue of *Law No. 1034 of the Merchant*, on December 6, 1983, the First Book of the Commercial Code, then in force, was repealed except for Title III relating to stock exchanges and commercial markets. The promulgation of the Civil Code of 1987 unified civil and commercial matters.

Peru also adopted in 1853 the Spanish Commercial Code of 1829, with the modifications incorporated by the Council of State.[67] In the case of Venezuela, the first Commercial Code is from 1862, influenced by the French Code of 1807 and the Spanish Code of 1829, and was repealed by the Commercial Code of 1904. The current Commercial Code published on July 26, 1955, repealed the Commercial Code of April 8, 1904, the Stock Exchange Law of June 26, 1917, the Law on Cooperative Societies of May 29, 1917, and the Law of Companies Incorporated in foreign countries and having the main purpose of their exploitation, trade, or industry in Venezuela, June 4, 1918.

---

64 See the work of J.G. Locrè, *Esprit du Code de Commerce: Ou commentaire puisé dans les procès-verbaux du Conseil d'état, les exposés de motifs et discours, les observations du Tribunat, celles des Cours d'appel, Tribunaux et Chambres de Commerce* (Paris: Garnery, 1811), vol. 3.

65 *Código de Comercio Decretado, Sancionado y Promulgado en 30 de mayo de 1829* (Paris: Librería de Rosa, 1830).

66 Olavarría, *Manual de Derecho*, 75.

67 *Código de Comercio de la República del Perú* (Lima: Imprenta del Gobierno, 1853).

The Commercial Code for the State of Buenos Aires was drafted by the jurists Eduardo Acevedo, of Uruguayan nationality, and the Argentinian Dalmacio Vélez Sarsfield in 1857, and sanctioned in October 1859.[68] Inspired by the Spanish Code of 1829, it was applied in the State of Buenos Aires separated from the provinces gathered in the Argentine Confederation. The provinces adopted the code of Buenos Aires and others were governed by the Spanish one of 1829.

With the Argentine unification of 1862, the Code of 1859 was declared to be in force throughout the country by the National Congress. Reformed in 1889 and proposed as a new Commercial Code, it governed in Argentina from May 1, 1890[69] to August 1, 2015.

On May 26, 1865, the Commercial Code[70] of Uruguay was published which is the adoption of the Commercial Code for the province of Buenos Aires 'promulgated' (sic) on April 30, 1857. This was actually the adoption of the *Commercial Code for the Province of Buenos Aires Bill* by Vélez Sarsfield and presented on that date to the Chambers and approved in the Province of Buenos Aires on October 6, 1859.

Other codes as the Puerto Rico Code adopted the Commercial Code of Spain of 1885, which was repealed by the Code revised and published in 1932. On February 15, 1902, a new code was promulgated in Peru, currently in force, based on the Spanish Code of 1885. Also, the Mexican Commercial Code of 1889 was highly influenced by the Spanish Code of 1885, promulgated on September 15, 1889; it entered into force on January 1, 1890;[71] and in Cuba the Spanish Commercial Code of 1885[72] is applicable, with modifications and complementary laws.

---

68 *Código de Comercio para el Estado de Buenos Aires, sancionado por las honorables cámaras el 6 de octubre de 1859*, new corrected edition (Buenos Aires: Librería de la Victoria, 1860).

69 *Código de Comercio de la República Argentina: Sancionado por el Honorable Congreso Nacional el 5 de octubre de 1889; Reimpresión con las mismas planchas de la Edición Oficial con autorización del Superior Gobierno, fecha 2 de enero 1890* (Buenos Aires: Imprenta La Universidad, 1839).

70 *Código de Comercio para la República Oriental del Uruguay, promulgado por el Gobierno Provisorio el 26 de mayo de 1865* (Montevideo: Imprenta de la Tribuna, 1866).

71 On the centenary of the *Commercial Code* of 1889 a series of commemorative works contained in the *Centenario del Código de Comercio*, Instituto de Investigaciones Jurídicas, UNAM, México, 1991 were published. On the occasion of the 120th anniversary of the Code we published *120 años del Código de Comercio: Codificación y Descodificación Mercantil en México*, ed. Óscar Cruz Barney (México: Ilustre y Nacional Colegio de Abogados de México, Tribunal Superior de Justicia del D.F., Instituto de Investigaciones Jurídicas de la UNAM, 2009).

72 *Código de Comercio*, Official Edition (Madrid, 1885).

Other influences were received from the Italian Commercial Code of 1882 and the French Commercial Code of 1807: the Mexican Constitution was amended on December 14, 1883, to reserve to the federal government the legislative power in matters of trade.[73] A new Commercial Code was issued on April 20, 1884. It was elaborated on the basis of the two previous drafts of 1869 and 1880 and with great influence of the Italian Commercial Code of 1882. With important French influence, the Commercial Code by Decree of June 5, 1884, governs. It suffered derogations by virtue of the entry into force of the Labor Code, Law 146–02, on Insurance and Bonds and Law No. 479–08, General Law of Commercial Companies and Individual Limited Liability Companies, of December 11, 2008. In the case of El Salvador, the Code of 1904 was published with influences from both the Chilean Code and the Italian Code of 1883, the Spanish Code of 1885, and the Portuguese Code of 1888. On May 8, 1970, a new code came into force that repealed the First, Second, and Fourth Books of the 1904 Code. The Third Book of the Code of 1904 remains partially in force.

3 Conclusion

Commercial law had from its origins a high degree of autonomy and specialty. The uses, customs, laws, and judgments of the mercantile naval tradition made up an *ius mercatorum* as a medieval legal response to the needs of commercial traffic. Merchants were associated in large professional corporations that received the name of *Consulates* and defended the economic interests of their members in Seville, Burgos, Bilbao, and others in Spain; and in Mexico, Lima, Caracas, Guatemala, Buenos Aires, Chile, La Havana, Veracruz, Guadalajara in Spanish America.

As for commercial doctrine, it was not until the sixteenth century that professional jurists paid more attention to commercial problems. Commercial codification in Latin America was seen by the various nations as a necessity from the first years of independent life in the nineteenth century. The commissions appointed to draft such codes evince the attention and importance that Latin American countries placed on such legislation.

73 *Constitución Federal de los Estados Unidos Mexicanos, sancionada y jurada por el Congreso General Constituyente el 5 de febrero de 1857, adicionada por el 70. Congreso Constitucional el 25 de septiembre y 4 de octubre de 1873 y el 6 de noviembre de 1874, juntamente con las Leyes Orgánicas expedidas hasta hoy* (Imprenta del Gobierno, in Palacio, México, 1883), art. 72, sec. X; Jorge Barrera Graf, 'Codificación en México. Antecedentes. Código de comercio de 1889, perspectivas' in *Centenario del Código de Comercio* (México: UNAM, 1991), 16.

The task of codifying commercial law was considered necessary in order to make the action of justice faster, more energetic, and more effective, hence a lack of or delay in codification was considered to be one of the great evils that society suffered from the early days of independence. Some efforts crystallized early in countries like Bolivia and Ecuador. Some codes (not mentioning the Ordinances of Bilbao) have had an important influence on others, clearly the Spanish Codes of 1829 and 1885, the French Code of 1807, and the Chilean Code of 1865.

References

Brunori, Luisa. 'Benvenuto Stracca: abogado y fundador del derecho comercial "científico" (1509–1578).' In *Historia del derecho y abogacía: Seminario Internacional; Histoire du droit et de la profession d'avocat; Séminaire International*, edited by Óscar Cruz Barney and Serge Dauchy, Number 1. México: Universidad Nacional Autónoma de México, Instituto de Investigaciones Jurídicas, Université de Lille, Centre d'Histoire Judiciaire, CNRS, Collection: Etudes comparatives de l'histoire du droit mexicain et français / Comparative studies in Mexican and French legal history / Estudios comparativos de historia del derecho mexicano y francés, 2020.

Brunori, Luisa, Serge Dauchy, Olivier Descamps, and Xavier Prevost. *Le Droit face à l'économie sans travail*, 2 vols. Paris: Classiques Garnier, 2019–2020.

Calderón, Francisco R. *Historia económica de la Nueva España en tiempo de los Austrias.* México: Fondo de Cultura Económica, 1995.

Cruz Barney, Óscar. *El Consulado de Comercio de Puebla: Régimen Jurídico, Historia y Documentos 1821–1824*. México: Instituto de Investigaciones Jurídicas, UNAM, 2006.

Cruz Barney, Óscar. *El riesgo en el comercio hispano-indiano: préstamos y seguros marítimos durante los siglos XVI a XIX*. México: Instituto de Investigaciones Jurídicas, UNAM, 1998.

Cruz Barney, Óscar. *El régimen jurídico de los consulados de comercio indianos: 1784–1795*. México: Instituto de Investigaciones Jurídicas, UNAM, 2001.

Cruz Barney, Óscar. *Historia de la Jurisdicción Mercantil en México*. México: IIJ-UNAM, Universidad Panamericana, Porrúa, 2006.

Cruz Barney, Óscar. 'Operaciones mercantiles y consulados de comercio en el mundo hispano- indiano: notas sobre su estudio.' In *América Latina en la Historia Económica: Boletín de Fuentes*. México: Instituto de Investigaciones Dr. José María Luis Mora, January–December 2002, Numbers 17–18.

Dauchy, Serge, Heikki Pihlajamäki, Albrecht Cordes, and Dave De ruysscher. *Colonial Adventures: Commercial Law and Practice in the making*. Leiden, Brill, 2021.

Forster, Wolfgang. *La invención del juicio de quiebra. Francisco Salgado de Somoza (1591–1665)*. Pamplona: Universidad de Navarra, 2017.

Galgano, Francesco. *Historia del derecho mercantil*. Trans. Joaquín Bisbal. Barcelona: Laia, 1981.

Kozolchyk, Boris. 'El grado de avance del derecho mercantil al final del siglo XX.' In *El derecho comercial ante el libre comercio y el desarrollo económico*. Trans. Óscar Cruz Barney and Boris Kozolchyk. México: McGraw Hill, 1996.

Martínez Gijón, José. *Historia del Derecho Mercantil: Estudios*. Sevilla: Universidad de Sevilla, 1999.

Olavarría, Julio. *Manual de Derecho Comercial*. 3rd ed. Barcelona: Clarasó, 1970.

Petit, Carlos. *Historia del Derecho Mercantil*. Madrid: Marcial Pons, 2016.

Rubio, Jesús. *Sainz de Andino y la codificación mercantil*. Madrid: CSIC, 1950.

Santarelli, Umberto. 'La prohibición de la usura, de canon moral a regla jurídica. Modalidades y éxitos de un "transplante."' In *Del Ius Mercatorum al Derecho Mercantil*, edited by Carlos Petit. Madrid: Marcial Pons, 1997.

Szramkiewicz, Romuald, and Olivier Descamps. *Histoire du droit des affaires*. Paris, Domat, 2019.

Trakman, León E. *The Law Merchant: The Evolution of Commercial Law*. Littleton: Fred B. Rothman, 1983.

CHAPTER 16

Law and Labor Rights

Juan Manuel Palacio

Labor law, both as a set of positive laws and state institutions aimed at protecting and regulating labor, and as an autonomous field of law, has its historical origins in the Western world at the beginning of the twentieth century. It responded to a set of specific circumstances and processes such as the European Industrial Revolution and the emergence of the so-called 'social question' in the middle of the nineteenth century; the workers' movement and its growing organization and repertoire of struggle; and the emergence of an eclectic social reformism with strong roots, among others, in the Catholic Church and socialist thought. Additional factors include the First World War and the organizations resulting from the peace, especially the ILO in 1919; and the formation of an academic and university field around the law regulating labor relations, of international scope, what some academics called a 'new law,' with different bases than those of civil law, therefore claiming autonomy. This new law was expressed in the development of a set of specific norms, institutions, and jurisdictions since the last decade of the nineteenth century and throughout the twentieth century, reaching its peak towards the middle of that last century, together with the consolidation of the so-called Welfare State or 'social state.'

Although this set of circumstances allows us to locate historically the genesis of our object, the world knew before those years about laws regulating labor, that is, to a certain extent, about a series of labor law provisions. In fact, the regulation of work (understood in a broad sense, as a task that someone does for another, regardless of whether she does it freely or because she is bound by some kind of subjection), whether through written laws or conventions sanctioned by custom, is almost as old as work itself. And free labor being a relatively recent 'invention' in human history,[1] all other forms that predominated from earlier times had their regulation and contractual forms. For centuries, for example, specific laws ensured that labor contracts were complied with by workers, punishing violations if necessary. These were repressive laws,

1 Robert Steinfeld, *The Invention of Free Labor: The Employment Relation in Anglo-American Law and Culture* (Chapel Hill: University of North Carolina Press, 1991).

 | DOI:10.1163/9789004436091_018

designed to control and enforce servile labor, but they were nonetheless labor laws. Along with them, from ancient times, there were also laws protecting workers in a similar way to modern labor laws. Thus, as we shall see, in the dominions of the Iberian empires in America, an infinite number of regulations – which had their origins in the medieval legislation of the peninsula – were dedicated to the regulation and protection, sometimes meticulous, of the work of Indigenous people and slaves. The well-known fact that many of these laws were not obeyed does not undermine the importance of their existence as a legal precedent.

Labor, in any of its historical forms and manifestations, always had an inseparable relationship with the law. But then, what was 'new' about the 'new law' of the early twentieth century? At least four things. First, its exclusive object was the regulation of free labor (slavery and other forms of forced labor had already for the most part disappeared or had passed into the realm of the illegal, so the state could hardly engage in their regulation). Second, the new legislation was based on a different philosophy of the labor relationship and the employment contract than the one characterizing the liberal legal framework of the nineteenth century. In that tradition, enshrined in the civil codes of Latin American countries, the individualistic idea of the employment contract as a free relationship between equals prevailed. Now, conversely, the worker was considered to be structurally inferior to the employer, and therefore the primary meaning, and mission of the law was to protect the weaker party in the labor contract, trying to minimize the effects of this inequality. So to speak, the law was changing sides and was now decidedly on the side of the worker, to protect him from the employer's arbitrariness.

Third, the reformist legislation sought not only to protect the worker but also to guarantee rights, both those granted by the state and those earned by the workers through their historical struggles. The limitation of the working day; the prohibition of unhealthy work or that of women and children in certain activities; compensation for work accidents; weekly rest or vacations; and the freedom to organize and complain are some examples of those struggles. Modern labor law has enshrined these advances as workers' rights by setting them down in written laws.

Finally, what distinguishes the new labor legislation of the twentieth century is that it was accompanied by a well-defined state apparatus of intervention whose purpose was to guarantee the application of the laws and to punish their violation. Thus, simultaneously with the production of laws, specific state offices were created to deal with labor issues and to supervise compliance with the law such as labor departments or offices. Various mechanisms were created to resolve disputes between employers and workers too, including the creation of a new jurisdiction within the judicial organization, labor courts. The purpose of this chapter is to review the history of the development of labor law in Latin America from colonial times to the present, with a special focus on the peak period of that development, in the first two-thirds of the twentieth century.

1 *Derecho Indiano* and Workers

When the Europeans arrived in the Americas and subjugated the native population, they tried various methods to obtain labor. In the first decades after the conquest, the Spanish tried slave labor, especially in the Caribbean, while the Portuguese did the same in the sugar plantations of Bahia and Pernambuco. This was met with resistance from the Indigenous peoples many of whom experienced great mortality caused especially by diseases brought by the Europeans. Sectors of the Iberian courts, particularly the church, expressed strong opposition to coercion over Indigenous workers, which resulted in the legal prohibition of Indigenous slavery.

This did not put an end to slavery. Rather, it changed the subjects that embodied the institution: from then on, the slaves of Spanish America, as well as those of Brazil, would be Africans.[2] Slavery was an enduring institution. Although it was dominant as a labor system in some enterprises such as sugar plantations and gold mining, it was present in almost all sectors of the economy, from *haciendas* to domestic work, from textile mills to urban commerce. Omnipresent throughout Latin America's colonial geography, the enslavement of Africans transcended the crisis of independence and survived as an institution during parts of the nineteenth century in many countries, and in Cuba and Brazil until its last decades.

On the other hand, the fact that the Indigenous people were no longer slaves did not mean that they would not be forced to work, particularly in the Spanish domains. The systems of forced labor devised by the Spaniards varied over the

2 It is estimated that in Spanish America one million enslaved humans entered during the colony and 500,000 more after independence, while in Brazil there were 2.2 million during the colony and a million more in the nineteenth century until the end of the slave trade in 1850. See Manuel Lucena Salmoral, *Regulación de la esclavitud negra en las colonias de América Española (1503–1886): Documentos para su estudio* (Alcalá de Henares y Murcia: Universidad de Alcalá, 2005); Frederick P. Bowser, 'Africans in Spanish American Colonial Society' in *The Cambridge History of Latin America*, ed. Leslie Bethell (Cambridge: Cambridge University Press, 1984), vol. 2, 364.

centuries. Thus, the *encomienda* or *repartimiento* – the assignment of groups of Indians to colonists to obtain tribute and labor in exchange for Christian assistance – was dominant in the sixteenth century, but gradually disappeared at the end of that century due to a sharp decline in population, restrictive regulations also stemming from criticisms by Christian humanitarianism, and the crown's fear of fueling the growth of a powerful class of *encomenderos*.[3] The provision of labor was then left in the hands of the colonial authorities under the system of the *mita* or labor *repartimiento*, as it was known in Mexico, where each community had to provide an employer with part of its male population to work for a determined period of time, for which workers received a modest salary. Its most impressive manifestation was the Peruvian *mitas* for the mines of Potosí, which meant the transfer of thousands of people from sometimes remote places that were months of travel away from the mines. It was there, and in the other Peruvian mining centers, that the institution lasted until the end of the colonial period.[4]

Along with the implementation of these work systems, the Spanish crown sought to regulate them. Thus the *Recopilación de las leyes de las Indias* and its thousands of ordinances and edicts on the most diverse matters, generally written for specific situations and places in the extensive territory of the colonies, contained numerous provisions on Indigenous labor.[5] And to the extent that one of the explicit objectives of the colonizing task was evangelization and Indigenous conversion to the Catholic faith, a central chapter of this legislation was the defense of the Indigenous people, who, thanks to the humanist preaching of philosophers and religious figures such as Francisco de Vitoria, Antonio de Montesinos, and Fray Bartolomé de las Casas, were considered human beings with individual rights, on an equal legal footing with Europeans. For this reason, Indigenous slavery was explicitly prohibited, and some rights were recognized, such as the right to good treatment, marriage, or

3 Charles Gibson, 'Indian societies under Spanish Rule' in *The Cambridge History of Latin America*, ed. Leslie Bethell (Cambridge: Cambridge University Press, 1984), vol. 11, 386–387.

4 In New Spain, on the other hand, the *repartimiento* was quite ephemeral and never dominant in either the mining or agricultural sectors, being limited to large public works such as the drainage of the Valley of Mexico in the seventeenth century. Gibson, 'Indian Societies,' 404–405.

5 This work from 1680, consists of four volumes, nine books, and almost 6,500 laws. José María Ots Capdequi, *El Estado Español en las Indias* (México: El Colegio de México, 1941). See also, M.C. Mirow, *Latin American Law: A History of Private Law and Institutions in Spanish America* (Austin: University of Texas Press, 2004), 47–48.

judicial assistance if enslaved humans had well-founded complaints against their masters.[6]

Along with these general principles, the laws also regulated specific aspects of Indigenous labor. Thus, for example, they stipulated that wages should be 'fair and sufficient,' even establishing a minimum wage, equivalent to one and a half *reales* per day, to be paid weekly, in cash and not in kind. It was expressly forbidden to pay in wine, honey, chicha, or yerba mate, and payment had to be made 'in their own hands,' before the justices, the protector, or the parish priest.[7] Laws also expressed concern about the protection of women – they were forbidden to work in mines, *haciendas*, mills, and other workshops. They were also exempted from the *mita*, as well as working during pregnancy. Minors were forbidden to work in the mills or factories until they were eighteen years old and to carry excessive loads.[8] The working day should be eight hours, leaving Saturday afternoons for the payment of wages.

Colonial legislation was also concerned with the regulation and protection of slave labor. Although until the eighteenth-century norms were scarce, the project to promote sugar production in the Caribbean in the second half of that century, and the consequent need to increase the number of slaves, led the Spanish crown to establish freedom of trade in slaves in 1789, and also to concern itself with the regulation of that system of work.[9] Thus, that same year the crown issued the Royal Decree 'On the education, treatment and occupation of slaves' also known as the *Black Code*. Through its fourteen chapters, the code obliged masters to feed and clothe slaves in a way similar to that involving freed slaves or day laborers; established the working day 'from sunrise to sunset,' with two hours of rest; limited the working age from seventeen to sixty years old; and established that domestic slaves would be paid two pesos a year. It also ordered that unmarried slaves should have separate quarters by sex and that there should be an infirmary on each *hacienda*. It established the need to encourage marriage among slaves and to instruct them in the faith on Sundays and holidays (days on which it was forbidden to force them to work, except in times of harvest), attending Mass and doctrine. Although it admitted 'corrective' corporal punishments, the code limited it to twenty-five lashes and established sanctions for masters or stewards who caused enslaved humans serious contusions or mutilations.[10] However, while classical legal historians

6 Carlos Reynoso Castillo, 'La materia laboral en las Leyes de Indias' (2005) 61 Alegatos 615.

7 Idem., 617.

8 Ots Capdequi, *El Estado Español*, 87–88; Reynoso, 'La materia laboral,' 618.

9 Bowser, 'Africans,' 363.

10 Manuel Lucena Salmoral, 'La Instrucción sobre educación, trato y ocupaciones de los esclavos de 1789; una prueba del poder de los amos de esclavos frente a la debilidad de

emphasize the humanitarian nature of this legislation and its legal importance, more recent historiography highlights the distance between these norms and reality in the colonies, with the result that the treatment of enslaved humans truly remained a function of the masters' will.[11]

In the case of Brazil, the *Ordenações Filipinas*, of 1643, compiled under the reign of João VI, also brought together the legislation scattered in royal charters and ordinances that the Portuguese crown had produced since its occupation of the territory. And although to a lesser extent and without as much detail, the *Ordenações* also dealt with the labor of Indigenous and enslaved humans. In the case of the former, although it was forbidden to enslave them, except in exceptional cases such as '*la guerra justa*,' non-compliance with this precept was more the rule than the exception. It was only during the government of the Marquis of Pombal in the mid-eighteenth century that various decrees made this prohibition effective.[12] For its part, the regulation of black labor, despite its importance in the colonial economy, was quite scarce and nothing like the Spanish *Código Negro* ever existed for colonial Brazil. The *Ordenações*, in turn, only established some basic principles that established the legal relations between masters and slaves, but no section dealt specifically with the regulation of labor. The legislation was concerned with the practical aspects of controlling the trade, as well as the return of runaways (and penalizing those who helped them) or the nullity of the sale of sick or unusable slaves. In the words of one specialist, 'the legislation on African slaves and their descendants was especially careful not to interfere with the master's power and right of ownership over his slave.'[13]

Finally, 'free' labor coexisted in the Iberian colonies alongside Indigenous and slave labor. This was not exclusive to any one racialized group; it was practiced by whites, Indigenous, mulattos, blacks (freedmen), and mestizos. Nor was this modality exclusive to a region of the colony or to a productive activity: free labor was found in the Peruvian *haciendas*, in the Mexican mines, in the commerce of Buenos Aires or Bahia, or in the textile factories of Quito.

---

la corona española' (1996) 13 Estudios de historia social y económica de América 155–178; Salmoral, *Regulación*; see also José Torre Revello, 'Origen y aplicación del Código negrero en la América española (1786–1794)' (1932) 15 Boletín del Instituto de Investigaciones Históricas 53–54; Abelardo Levaggi, 'La condición jurídica del esclavo en la época hispánica' (1973) 1 Revista Historia del Derecho 83–176.

11 Bowser, 'Africans,' 369–370.

12 A.J.R. Russell-Wood, 'Iberian Expansion and the Issue of Black Slavery: Changing Portuguese Attitudes, 1440–1770' (1978) 83(1) The American Historical Review 40–41.

13 Silvia Hunold Lara, *Legislaçâo sobre escravos africanos na América portuguesa* (Madrid: Fundación Histórica Tavera, 2000), 38.

Colonial laws, or the historiography on the subject, seem to be silent on this free labor, which would indicate that such labor relations were left in private hands, with minimal state interference in rural areas or in the hands of the guilds through apprenticeship contracts in the cities.

2 Independence and the Formation of National States

The Spanish-American revolutions of independence did not substantially change the social and economic structures of the colony, nor, fundamentally, the prevailing labor systems. As for the legal structures, legal historians have long known that the normative frameworks of new Spanish-American republics and the Brazilian empire contained many survivals of colonial legislation, even well into the nineteenth century. The expression that best describes this legal framework seems to be that of 'juridical hybridity' in which diverse sources coexisted, such as *ius commune*, the new legislation generated by the revolutionary governments in the first decades, and laws belonging to the colonial normative framework.[14]

Independence did not, in fact, bring about any visible or sudden changes in labor systems. In fact, the coexistence of free labor, various forms of semi-servile labor, and slavery continued to be the general characteristic throughout Latin America for much of the nineteenth century. Colonial systems of forced labor such as the *mita* or the *encomienda* were for the most part abolished. In many cases, such as where they had never been important or had lost their validity, this abolition was symbolic to distance new nations from institutions too closely linked to colonial domination in the new imagery of the revolutions.

In the rural world, *haciendas* and plantations continued to use enslaved Africans until laws effectively prohibited the system in the different nations. Enslaved humans were used along with free or semi-free field workers, who were hired either permanently, in which case they generally lived on the *haciendas*, or temporarily for crops or specific jobs. Temporary workers were generally members of peasant communities in the area, often with origins in the old Indigenous villages. There also existed in some rural regions, although

14 Victor M. Uribe-Uran, 'The Great Transformation of Law and Legal Culture: "The Public" and "The Private" in the Transition from Empire to Nation in Mexico, Colombia, and Brazil, 1750–1850' in *Empire to Nation: Historical Perspectives on the Making of the Modern World*, eds Joseph W. Esherick, Hasan Kayali, and Eric Van Young (New York: Rowman Littlefield Publishers, 2005), 68–105; Tamar Herzog, 'Legal Pluralism,' Chapter 22 in this volume.

less widespread than the 'black legend' about the Latin American rural world would have us believe,[15] systems of 'debt peonage,' according to which workers were paid in advance, and thus became strongly tied to a specific employer or labor contractor.

Among the free workers, tasks were performed in exchange for remuneration, generally not in cash but under various forms of payments in kind, marginal benefits on the *hacienda* (i.e., housing or subsistence land), credits for purchases in nearby rural businesses, or contractual sharecropping arrangements. The other widespread form was unpaid family labor. This was practiced in rural areas by small landowners or settlers (*colonos*) and by peasant families of tenants within the *estancias*. Free labor was also characteristic in mining, in public works linked to transportation or urban infrastructure such as railroads and ports, and in general in the cities, in crafts, services, and domestic and export-related commerce.

From a strictly legal point of view, and despite the generalized absence of references to the subject in the historiography of the period, until the middle of the century there was no major innovation in labor regulations. Extant regulations remained scattered in municipal and local spheres and limited to some specific jobs or trades for artisans or rural laborers, often in the hands of policing institutions. Thus, the registration of contracts in notary's offices or before the police itself was sometimes required for fear that the employee, apprentice, or laborer would not comply with the agreed time or obligation.

This legal dispersion prevailed until the middle of the century, when political instability and civil wars gradually subsided and the new republics found a more or less stable constitutional framework. In fact, leaving aside the Brazilian empire's constitution of 1824 and the Uruguayan case, with only one constitution in 1830, in the nineteenth century other countries exhibited multiple and varied constitutional experiments since the dawn of independence. For example, Ecuador and Bolivia, had more than ten constitutional texts each, itself a clear expression of political instability. But around the middle of the century, when these political disagreements faded away and internationally recognized independence was achieved, more stable constitutional agreements were consequently reached. This happened earlier in some cases (Chile, 1833, Argentina, 1853, and Mexico, 1857), and somewhat later in others (Paraguay, 1870 and Peru, 1879). Together with constitutional organization, new states elaborated codes – laws systematizing all the essential normative

15 Gibson, 'Indian Societies,' 405–406; Arnold J. Bauer, 'Rural Workers in Spanish America: Problems of Peonage and Oppression' (1979) 59(1) The Hispanic American Historical Review 34–63.

regulations of a branch of law – especially in civil, commercial, procedural, and criminal matters. Some specific branches of economic activity were also codified as in the rural or mining codes. This process, which reached its peak between 1855 and 1875 throughout the region, was the necessary complement to constitutional organization.

The regulation of labor in new Latin American legal systems remained in the sphere of civil codes with common inspiration in the Napoleonic Code of 1804, more or less widely embraced by triumphant liberal leaders. In fact, this body of law, which in some cases, such as the early codes of Haiti of 1825 or the Dominican Republic's of 1845, was copied almost verbatim, had a direct influence on some emblematic Latin American codes, such as the Chilean Civil code of 1855, drafted by Andrés Bello, or that of Vélez Sarsfield in Argentina in 1869, which in turn inspired those of other countries in the region.

As in their common French source, the employment relationship in these new codes was included within the figure of service contracts, under the model of the *locatio* of the civil law tradition. Indeed, in line with the individualistic and egalitarian ideology of the French Revolution, the employment relationship was conceived as a service arrangement between entirely free persons with equal opportunities. This radically changed the nature of the *ancien régime* employer–worker relationship: it was now the service (work), not the person of the worker, that entered into the contract, as a commodity that the worker offered voluntarily to the employer in exchange for a payment in money.[16]

The 'labor contract,' thus conceived, theoretically dominated the relations between employers and workers in Latin America in the last third of the nineteenth century and during the first decades of the twentieth century. In these most dynamic years of export-led growth, this contractual model, under the civil code, guided the attitude of the state elites in labor issues. Consequently, this led to a more or less generalized abstention of the state from labor regulation beyond the few provisions contained in the codes governing different economic activities. Labor relations were to be left to private arrangements, with as little state regulation as possible and under the legal framework of civil law.[17]

16 Bruno Veneziani, 'The evolution of the contract of Employment' in *The Making of Labour Law in Europe: A Comparative Study of Nine Countries up to 1945*, ed. Bob Hepple (London: Mansell, 1986), 58.

17 In the words of Juan Bautista Alberdi, one of the most brilliant minds of Latin American liberalism, who inspired the Argentine Constitution of 1853: 'Free labor being the main source of wealth, to embarrass it by regulations is nothing other than to contradict and damage the progress of wealth in its purest and most abundant source.' Juan Bautista

Nonetheless, without departing from this general criterion, the provinces, municipalities, and police continued to dictate norms related to labor, in addition to those contained in the commercial, civil, mining, and rural codes. For example, the Argentine Commercial Code of 1859 imposed indemnities for work accidents, the Mining Code of 1887 contained provisions on safety and limitation of work for minors and women, and the Rural Code of 1865 required the signing of written contracts before the justice of the peace and provided for Sunday rest.[18] Even so, as was the case in the colonial period, and in some regions, even more so, the contrast between these regulations and what happened in real life was enormous. Apart from some exceptions that occurred in urban areas and in activities with a concentration of workers, such as railroads or food processing factories, where workers were already beginning to organize themselves, in the vast rural world of Latin America, where the bulk of the population lived and worked, the absence of state regulation was notorious.

3 The Shaping of Modern Labor Law

The emergence of the 'social question' in mid-nineteenth-century Europe, and only a few decades later in Latin America, brought the liberal ideology described above into crisis. The expression referred not only to the negative effects of the Industrial Revolution on the working conditions such as excessive working hours, low wages, unhealthy workplaces, exploitation of child labor, and precarious housing conditions, but also to the reaction that this situation generated among workers such as strikes, mobilizations, and union organization. It also referred to the debate that these circumstances triggered among various sectors of the political, academic, or religious world, as well as to the challenge they posed to governments increasingly confronted by the growing mobilizations and workers' protests. In sum, 'question' meant that the social issue had become a major problem and demanded attention.

The new situation gave rise to sociological, legal, political, and religious reflection in both Europe and America towards the end of the nineteenth century. Movements of social reformism had eclectic ideological bases from utopian socialism to Catholicism, passing through liberal reformism and revolutionary Marxism. All these perspectives coincided in their criticism of the

---

Alberdi, *Sistema económico y rentístico de la Confederación Argentina según la Constitución de 1853* (Buenos Aires: La Cultura Argentina, 1921). Cited in Abelardo Levaggi, 'Historia del derecho argentino del trabajo (1800–2000)' (2006) 3 Iushistoria Revista Electrónica 24.

18 Levaggi, 'Historia,' 26.

liberal order sanctioned by European and American constitutions modeled on liberal thought and agreed on the need for greater state intervention to counteract the 'social evils' caused by the development of capitalism. Individualism, freedom, and property as absolute values and the idea that the pursuit of individual interest led to collective welfare, the basis of *laissez-faire*, had been proven wrong and could no longer guide the social and normative order. It was then necessary to limit freedom by virtue of a greater interest, that of the social body, and private property should cease to be an absolute value and find its meaning and limits in its social function. Finally, because *laissez-faire* had led to all kinds of abuses by the powerful against the weaker, some kind of state tutelage of these unequal relations was needed. Social law thus laid its foundations in the region.[19]

As described by the first 'labor jurists' (*laboralistas*), such as the German Philipp Lotmar and his disciple Hugo Sinzheimer, considered the fathers of labor law in Europe,[20] or the Argentine Alfredo Palacios and the Chilean Moisés Poblete Troncoso, these new ideas translated into a critique of the labor contract, one of the founding institutions of liberal law, on which much of the capitalist economic and social order had been built. If the factory system had revealed anything, it was that far from being a relationship between entirely free equals with the same resources and opportunities, the labor relationship was essentially unequal, involving a weak, subordinate, and dependent party without power of decision over its working conditions.[21] Accepting this premise, the essential task of labor law was to regulate and control this subordinate relationship by protecting the weaker party.

These new ideas spread throughout the Western world very rapidly, thanks to the vehicle represented by international academic, political, and trade union networks, a process that was greatly facilitated by the creation of the ILO in 1919.[22] A climate of ideas was thus rapidly consolidated around the world

19 Gustav Radbruch is credited with the first conceptualization of this branch of law in his *Introduction to the Science of Law* (1929), although the concept had already been discussed in earlier works by him, as well as in those of Leon Duguit and in particular Georges Gurvitch. See Francois Ewald, 'El concepto de derecho social' (1997) Contextos, Revista crítica de derecho social 1.

20 Hepple, 'Introduction' in Hepple, *The Making*, 7–8.

21 Veneziani, 'The Evolution,' 63–67.

22 Juan Manuel Palacio, 'From Social Legislation to Labor Justice: The Common Background in the Americas' in *Labor Justice across the Americas*, eds Leon Fink and Juan Manuel Palacio (Urbana: University of Illinois Press, 2018), 16–43; *América Latina y la Organización Internacional del Trabajo: Redes, cooperación técnica e institucionalidad social, 1919–1950*, eds Fabián Herrera León and Patricio Herrera González (Morelia: UMSNH, Instituto de Investigaciones Históricas, 2013).

regarding the need for state intervention to regulate labor and contractual relations, which some authors have called the 'globalization of the social.'[23] For this reason, the way in which it developed also followed a similar trajectory in the Western world, varying only in chronology and sometimes in the pace or content of some laws.

In Latin America, the shaping of this 'new law' – a process that included not only the creation of legislation but also a state apparatus for intervention and enforcement of the new regulations – took the entire first half of the twentieth century, in which two moments can be defined. The first, comprising the first three decades of the century, corresponds to the period of export-led growth under liberal-conservative governments supported by a strong liberal consensus. In this 'early period,' thanks to the political and parliamentary action of some of the first labor activists – including 'reformist liberals'[24] such as Chile's Arturo Alessandri, Argentina's Joaquín V. González, the Colombian Rafael Uribe Uribe, or socialists like the Argentine Alfredo Palacios – the first labor laws were enacted. This happened in the face of the palpable threat of workers' activism that manifested itself in strikes and social outbursts throughout the region in the first two decades of the century. Such laws included benefits like Sunday rest, compensation for work-related accidents, limitations on the working day, and on the work of women and children, or the introduction of social insurance. These laws were not the result of a pre-designed legislative plan but rather reactions offered as responses to social challenges. Even so, with the passage of time they formed a corpus that constituted the first manifestation of modern labor law.[25]

Along with laws, the first state agencies to deal with social issues and labor legislation emerged in this period. Among the earliest undertakings were the Chilean Labor Office of 1907, the Mexican Labor Department of 1911, and the National Labor Department of Argentina of 1912. Somewhat later are the General Labor Office of Colombia of 1923, the Department of Labor of Bolivia of 1926, and the Secretariat of Labor and Social Security of Costa Rica of 1928. In their earliest versions, these agencies had the function of scientifically studying the situation of workers, compiling statistics on working conditions

23 Duncan Kennedy, 'Three Globalizations of Law and Legal Thought: 1850–2000' in *The New Law and Economic Development: A Critical Appraisal*, eds David M. Trubek and Alvaro Santos (Cambridge: Cambridge University Press, 2006), 19–73.

24 I use Eduardo Zimmermann term in *Los liberales reformistas: La cuestión social en la Argentina* (Buenos Aires: Sudamericana, 1995).

25 Oficina Internacional del Trabajo, *Legislación social de América Latina* (Ginebra: 1928), 2 vols.

in factories and working life, and advising governments on legal and labor matters. In some cases, they also inspected and controlled the application of the legislation and had capacity to sanction infractions of labor laws. Some agencies incorporated mechanisms of conflict resolution, generally under the system of conciliation and arbitration. They could also be responsible for the official recognition of labor unions and collective bargaining agreements between companies and workers.

Historiographic research on these early institutions is generally still scarce. Nonetheless, from existing studies it is known that, beyond their importance as agencies generating information and advice to governments on legal matters, their control and enforcement of labor legislation were limited, due to their scarce budgetary resources and limited territorial deployment. This reflected the lukewarm will of the conservative governments to supervise the application of the first labor laws and, in general, to commit themselves to the legislative program of the reformist ideology.

The crisis of 1930 and the Great Depression that followed inaugurated a second moment in shaping the state regulation of labor relations. The crisis provoked the revival of the 'workers' question' throughout Latin America and particularly in those countries where the strong impetus given to industrialization led to the concentration and growth of workers' organizations in the big cities. But the crisis also led to a profound revision of the liberal ideology, giving new vitality to preexisting ideas on the need for state intervention to regulate labor relations.

This second moment is characterized by a renewal, reinforcement, and expanded reproduction of all labor regulatory institutions. In the first place, laws multiplied exponentially and became more comprehensive and inclusive by reaching rural workers or Indigenous populations, and increasing regulation of labor contracts, collective bargaining agreements, the eight-hour workday, minimum wages, paid vacations, trade union organizations, labor courts, and agricultural workers, among other matters. Some countries went a step further and drafted labor codes, albeit with varying success and at different rates. Among the first were the Chilean code of 1931, the Mexican Federal Labor Law of the same year, and the codes of Ecuador and Bolivia, of 1938 and 1939, respectively. The codification process continued in the 1940s and 1950s with the Central American countries and Colombia. The most famous code for its comprehensiveness was the Consolidaçao das Leis do Trabalho (or CLT) of Brazil, approved under the Vargas regime in 1943. On the other hand, some countries such as Cuba, Peru, Uruguay, and Argentina, did not codify their labor laws in the first half of the twentieth century, in some cases in spite of having debated various projects to create them.[26]

Finally, Latin America participated in the movement known as 'social constitutionalism,' which had as a common feature the introduction in constitutional texts of a series of limitations to individual and property rights, inspired by the interests of the community, as well as the enumeration of fundamental social rights and a new role for the state in guaranteeing these rights. Although the Weimar Constitution of 1919 is often attributed as the starting point of this movement, this does not do justice to the precedent of the Mexican Constitution of 1917. Through Article 27, which establishes social aspects of land, and the monumental Article 123, which establishes a true legislative program for the protection of workers, the Mexican Constitution of 1917 was the first of its kind.[27] After the Mexican Constitution, there were other early manifestations, such as the constitutions of Peru in 1919 and Chile in 1925, but the culminating moment of this movement was between the mid-1930s – with the constitutions of Brazil in 1934 and 1937, which established the 'Estado Novo,' and those of Cuba and Paraguay, both in 1940. Guatemala in 1945, Ecuador and Brazil in 1946, Venezuela, the Dominican Republic and Nicaragua in 1947, and Argentina in 1949 joined these countries in the postwar period.[28]

In these years, state labor agencies were hierarchized, endowed with larger budgets and bureaucratic structures, real power of enforcement and sanction, and greater territorial deployment through regional and provincial delegations and offices. Thus, for example, in Chile the 1907 Office was transformed into a Ministry of Labor in 1932; in Mexico the Department of Labor became a Secretariat in 1940. Similar expansion occurred in Bolivia in 1936 and in Colombia in 1938; while in Brazil the Vargas government created the Ministry of Labor in 1931 and in Argentina the government of the June Revolution of 1943 converted the Department of Labor into a Secretariat in that year, and then the Perón government established a Ministry in 1949. This was not just a change of names. It was the material manifestation of a firmer purpose on the

---

26 Moisés Poblete Troncoso, *Evolución del Derecho Social en América* (Santiago: Editorial Nascimento, 1942), 157.

27 So much so that its text was one of the sources considered in the Commission on Labor Legislation of the Treaty of Versailles that designed the original structure and program of the International Labor Organization (ILO). See Fabián Herrera León, 'México y la Organización Internacional del Trabajo: los orígenes de una relación, 1919–1931' (2011) 51(2) Foro Internacional 341–342.

28 Segundo V. Linares Quintana, 'El derecho constitucional en la postguerra. El constitucionalismo social' (1946) 41 La ley 952–967; Poblete Troncoso, 'Evolución,' 119–120.

part of the governments of those years of state intervention in the economy and society and in the regulation of labor and control of industrial relations.

This second period also witnessed the creation of a specific jurisdiction within the judiciary to deal with conflicts between workers and employers: the labor courts. The matter was of great importance, since if the new legislation was to be recognized as 'special,' as an autonomous branch of law, it was therefore essential to have specialized courts, sensitive to the new philosophy that underpinned it. In fact, much of the justification for the new courts was based on the criticism of the ordinary courts (civil and commercial) by the promoters of labor law. The ordinary courts were criticized for class biases, lack of experience in labor matters, high costs, delays, and formalities that made the judicial process inaccessible and incomprehensible to the poor and illiterate. The ordinary jurisdiction presented serious limitations to the effectiveness of the new legislation.

In their first expressions, labor tribunals took the form of conciliation and arbitration systems modeled on those conceived early on in Europe and Oceania, that is, collegiate bodies with tripartite representation of workers, employers, and the state in the spirit of conciliation between the parties and peer arbitration.[29] These common antecedents gave rise, however, to important variations of this model in the different Latin American countries. The conciliation and arbitration systems were sometimes under state tutelage in the same labor agencies as those mentioned above, as in the cases of the Argentine and Chilean labor departments or the Technical Labor Office of Costa Rica, created in 1932. Sometimes they were independent institutions such as the Mexican Conciliation and Arbitration Boards or the Brazilian Juntas de Conciliação e Julgamento.[30] In turn, in some cases these conciliation systems evolved over time towards different forms of labor justice such as professional tribunals, as in the Chilean case. In other cases, they remained as the exclusive or predominant form of labor dispute resolution in the system, either within the executive branch, as in Mexico or as a new jurisdiction within the judicial branch, as in Brazil. In some countries, they survived as an administrative instance prior to

29 The oldest antecedent is the *Conseils de Prud'hommes*, existing in some French cities since the beginning of the nineteenth century, which spread towards the end of that century to other European countries. Also, those implemented in Australia and New Zealand since the first half of the nineteenth century served as a model for the design of the Brazilian courts. See Fernando Teixeira da Silva, 'The Brazilian and Italian Labor Courts: Comparative Notes' (2010) 55 International Review of Social History 381–412. Palacio, 'From Social.'

30 International Labor Office, *Labour Courts in Latin America* (Geneva, 1949).

the judicial one, thus coexisting with the professional labor courts of the judicial system, as in Argentina.[31]

At this time of greater intervention in labor regulation, the new labor courts were called upon to play a fundamental role in the application of the new labor laws. This rhetoric was also supported by the ILO, which, after the end of the Second World War, began to recommend more emphatically to its member countries the organization of specialized tribunals.[32] The labor courts, in their multiple forms, thus became the cornerstone of this second moment of expansion of state intervention in labor relations throughout the Americas. They would be responsible for the effective application of the legislation in accordance with the spirit of the 'new law.'

4 Crisis of Labor Law at the End of the Twentieth Century

> What meaning does labour law have if it is at most a law for an élite of workers, who have the good fortune to remain in work, if alongside the existence of labour law an economic graveyard of 'structural unemployment' opens up?
>
> HUGO SINZHEIMER, 1933[33]

The system just described regulated labor relations in Latin America during a good part of the twentieth century and, in many ways, still does so today. In particular, its fundamental principles and the rights they defend, such as the continuity of employment, compensation for dismissal or accidents, and the establishment of working conditions and working hours, among other protections and guarantees, are still fully in force. In sharp contrast, what has changed dramatically in the twilight of the twentieth century was the universe of labor relations.

Indeed, just as the civil law that emerged from the French Revolution assumed a society composed of free and equal citizens, founded on a social contract or 'common good,' the labor law that some jurists call 'classic,' included in

31 *Labor Justice across the Americas*, eds Leon Fink and Juan Manuel Palacio (Urbana: University of Illinois Press, 2018).

32 Thus, at the ILO conferences in Geneva (1947) and San Francisco (1948) and at the organization's Third and Fourth Regional Conferences of American Countries (Mexico City, 1946 and Montevideo, 1949). ILO, *Labour Courts*, 3. This publication is in fact the ad hoc study about the state of the tribunals in the Americas. It was prepared by the organization for the Montevideo meeting.

33 'Die Krisis des Arbeitsrechts,' quoted in Bob Hepple, 'Introduction' in *The Making*, 24.

the laws and codes enacted in the decades from 1920 to 1940, assumed an economy of full employment, dominated by formal and stable work as it existed in much of the Western world, including most of Latin America, during the 'thirty glorious years' from 1945 to 1975.[34] It regulated the relations between workers and employers that it presumed to be 'typical,' that is, those in which a worker had a *full-time* job under a contract in an establishment or industry, in a subordinate position to his employer, in exchange for which the worker expected to spend a large part of his working life in the company (perhaps performing the same tasks), receive protection against dismissal, a salary that would allow the support of family and eventually to make savings. In this way, the legal apparatus of the 'welfare' state served to protect individual workers from labor abuses or fraud, while it encouraged collective bargaining agreements between companies and unions to set wage scales, general working conditions, and guaranteed social security.

In contrast, the global economic crisis that followed the thirty glorious years began with the 1973 oil crisis and included diverse phenomena such as the increase in international competition, the digital revolution, the fall of the Iron Curtain, and the consolidation of regional markets. This crisis led to a redesign of the world economy and trade patterns, as well as to profound transformations in the organization of companies and labor. Thus, the last decades of the twentieth century and the beginning of the twenty-first century have witnessed new production processes and new forms of work organization that are more flexible and dynamic than the factory system, resulting in the substitution of stability for flexible forms of contracting, with temporary or task-based jobs and self-employed workers who frequently enter and leave the market. Also, with globalization, informal and unregistered work has grown exponentially throughout the world, reaching alarming levels in various parts of the world, including India, Mexico, Bangladesh, or Peru.[35] These changes have been so dramatic that some authors speak of the end of labor as a social class, as a category of analysis, and as an identity.[36]

Together with these global processes, which gradually transformed labor relations around the world, Latin America had its own crises. They included

34 The expression was coined by Jean Fourastié, in *Les Trente Glorieuses* (Paris: Editions Fayard, 1979).

35 Katherine V. Stone, 'Flexibilization, Globalization, and Privatization: Three Challenges to Labor Rights in Our Time' (2006) 44(1) Osgoode Hall Law Journal 77–104; Available at SSRN: https://ssrn.com/abstract=781249.

36 Harry Arthurs, 'Labour Law after Labour' in *The Idea of Labour Law*, eds Guy Davidov and Brian Langille (Oxford: Oxford University Press, 2013), 19–20.

both the 'lost decade' of the 1980s, which followed the debt crisis; and neoliberalism prevailing in the 1990s, with its state reforms and privatizations of public enterprises. These crises had a devastating social impact on the working classes, expelling a significant percentage from the formal economy and condemning them to various forms of precarious and casual employment, now a permanent feature of the social structure. Some authors mark this as the end of 'the wage society' because it places the 'typical' labor relationship model described in the previous section into crisis. The prior model has become far from the dominant relationship; it has become increasingly circumscribed to a privileged group of workers in certain formal sectors and with a high degree of organization.

Hand in hand with these profound transformations, labor law became the target of attacks from both the right and the left. On the right, since the 1980s and with greater force in the 1990s, the neoliberal consensus began to take shape in Latin America around the debt crisis and the recommendations of the so-called 'Washington Consensus.' This placed state interventionism in the economy in general at the center of criticism and especially targeted the state's regulation of labor. In particular, it criticized labor legislation and the courts that applied it, accusing them of excessive rigidity, an inability to adapt to new market conditions, increased labor costs, and decreased productivity and capital investment. Therefore, the generalized recipe of deregulation and flexibilization of economies had to reach labor relations. Thus, since the end of the 1970s in Europe and later in Latin America, a debate on 'labor flexibilization' was generated, which is still in force today and has inspired reform laws throughout the region.[37] In Latin America, labor reform processes in the form of draft laws and reforms to existing codes or norms were attempted in line with the recommendations of international organizations such as the IMF and the World Bank. Although with slight variations, the reforms included the limitation of severance payments, the incorporation of the figure of temporary work, the reduction of employer contributions, and the implementation of unemployment insurance. Even so, their success and depth varied from country to country, depending on the actual level of enforcement of labor laws in previous decades, the political will and strength of governments to implement the reforms, and the strength of trade union organizations to moderate or prevent them. Thus, there were profound reforms, as in the cases of Peru

37 Arturo Bronstein, *International and Comparative Labour Law: Current Challenges* (Geneva: International Labour Organization and Palgrave Macmillan, 2009).

and Chile, moderate reforms, as in Argentina and Brazil, and practically no reforms, as in Bolivia and Mexico.[38]

But criticism of labor law was also formulated in progressive academic and political circles. There, the arguments point to what Hugo Sinzheimer prophetically warned in 1933: the lack of flexibility of the law and the labor institutions responsible for the protection of workers to include the new forms of employment in their regulations, is leaving 'a cemetery' of thousands of workers helpless while only a privileged few enjoy established benefits. But the cemetery here and now, in Latin America, does not house the 'unemployed' – the greatest of evils that a European intellectual could foresee in the midst of the Great Depression – but thousands of informal and self-employed workers. These survive daily on the edge of poverty throughout the Latin American subcontinent thanks to various forms of temporary and precarious employment. These workers, increasingly numerous in absolute and relative terms, remain, by their very condition, outside the scope of labor legislation and the institutions for the protection and regulation of labor created in the mid-twentieth century, which are therefore increasingly irrelevant.[39] Along with labor law, these institutions are also subject to criticism from groups and organizations, such as the International Labor Organization (ILO), dedicated to promoting concerted global action patterns for the protection of labor.[40]

•••

In their various manifestations throughout history, the relations between owners and enslaved humans, lords and serfs, artisans and apprentices, industrialists and workers have been subject to some kind of regulation, whether by positive law, custom, or collective arrangements between parties. Even so, the legal corpus generated in the first half of the twentieth century separates itself from other regulations as a relatively autonomous branch of law, the only one that can claim for itself the denomination 'labor law.' As seen here, its philosophical pillars rest on the idea of the essential inequality inherent in the labor relationship and the consequent need for the intervention of law to

38 María Lorena Cook, *The Politics of Labor Reform in Latin America: Between Flexibility and Rights* (University Park: The Pennsylvania State University Press, 2006).

39 Kamala Sankaran, 'Informal Employment and the Challenges for Labour Law' in *The Idea of Labour Law*, eds Guy Davidov and Brian Langille (Oxford: Oxford University Press, 2013), 223–233.

40 Marcel Van der Linden, 'The International Labour Organization, 1919–2019: An Appraisal' (2019) 16(2) Labor 11–41.

compensate for that inequality by protecting the weaker party. It is also based on the fact that the protections it stipulates are workers' rights, which are also inalienable because they are matters of public interest and have been even enshrined in the constitution.

The golden age of modern labor law was actually quite brief. With variations from country to country, it would cover the years from the late 1930s to the mid-1970s, that is, a little more than thirty years. Even so, its impact on the legal tradition of each country, on the structure of the state, and on the legal culture of workers and employers was so great that its crisis, already longer than its golden years, has so far only managed to shake some of its postulates. As the body of legal and sociological literature increases, we learn that the future is uncertain, but the prognosis for labor law, and even for labor itself, does not appear to be good. Nonetheless, it is not evident that it will disappear, particularly because the golden years of labor law imprinted on workers a strong legal awareness of their rights, causing them, over time, indelibly to incorporate the law as a constituent part of their identity. And that imprint will not be easy to remove.

References

Bronstein, Arturo. *International and Comparative Labour Law: Current Challenges.* Geneva: International Labour Organization and Palgrave Macmillan, 2009.

Cook, Maria Lorena. *The Politics of Labor Reform in Latin America: Between Flexibility and Rights*. University Park: The Pennsylvania State University Press, 2007.

Davidov, Guy, and Brian Langille, eds. *The Idea of Labour Law*. Oxford: Oxford University Press, 2013.

Drinot, Paulo. *The Allure of Labor: Workers Race and the Making of the Peruvian State.* Durham: Duke University Press, 2011.

Fink, Leon, and Juan Manuel Palacio, eds. *Labor Justice across the Americas.* Urbana: University of Illinois Press, 2018.

French, John D. *Drowning in Laws: Labor Law and Brazilian Political Culture.* Chapel Hill: University of North Carolina Press, 2004.

Hepple, Bob, ed. *The Making of Labour Law in Europe: A Comparative Study of Nine Countries up to 1945*. London & New York: Mansell, 1986.

Hepple, Bob, and Bruno Veneziani, eds. *The Transformation of Labour Law in Europe: A Comparative Study of 15 Countries, 1945–2004*. Portland: Hart Publishing, 2009.

Herrera León, Fabián, and Patricio Herrera González, eds. *América Latina y la Organización Internacional del Trabajo: Redes, cooperación técnica e institucionalidad social, 1919–1950*. Morelia: UMSNH, Instituto de Investigaciones Históricas, 2013.

Hunold Lara, Silvia. *Legislaçâo sobre escravos africanos na América portuguesa*. Madrid: Fundación Histórica Tavera, 2000.

Kennedy, Duncan. 'Three Globalizations of Law and Legal Thought: 1850–2000.' In *The New Law and Economic Development: A Critical Appraisal*, edited by David M. Trubek and Alvaro Santos, 19–73. Cambridge: Cambridge University Press, 2006.

Mirow, Matthew. *Latin American Law: A History of Private Law and Institutions in Spanish America*. Austin: University of Texas Press, 2004.

Poblete Troncoso, Moisés. *Evolución del Derecho Social en América*. Santiago: Editorial Nascimento, 1942.

Steinfeld, Robert. *The Invention of Free Labor: The Employment Relation in Anglo-American Law and Culture*. Chapel Hill: University of North Carolina Press, 1991.

Suarez-Potts, William. *The Making of Law: The Supreme Court and Labor Legislation in Mexico, 1875–1931*. Stanford: Stanford University Press, 2012.

Van Daele, Jasmien, Magaly Rodríguez García, and Geert van Goethem eds. *ILO Histories: Essays on the International Labour Organization and Its Impact on the World during the Twentieth Century*. Bern: Peter Lang, 2011.

Van der Linden, Marcel. 'The International Labour Organization, 1919–2019: an Appraisal.' *Labor* 16(2) (2019): 11–41.

Van der Linden, Marcel, and Richard Price, eds. *The Rise and Development of Collective Labour Law*. Bern: Peter Lang, 2000.

CHAPTER 17

Criminal Law

Alejandro Agüero

1 Introduction

Writing on the history of Latin American 'criminal law' from the colonial period to the present requires some preliminary remarks. Leaving aside the nuances that may affect the geographical scope, and beyond the different ways of 'writing legal history' *tout court*, the very notion of 'criminal law' becomes problematic when dealt with historically through a *longue durée* period.[1] To avoid conceptual problems, 'criminal law' is used in a broad sense to refer to different forms of institutional punishments, to legal culture, and to authorities related to them. We will not address native customs assimilated to a form of intra-ethnic criminal justice, except when they are related to the colonial culture.

In the first part, we describe the general traits of the colonial criminal justice. We focus on secular justice, though we refer to other powers with punitive competence and some less formalized means of social discipline. Being impossible to give an account of every national development of criminal law throughout the nineteenth and twentieth centuries, the second part considers some common patterns at different moments. These moments in time move from the independence wars until the first criminal codes and from this point up to the present. We conclude with some remarks on the current challenges of Latin America criminal justice systems.

1 On the problems concerning the history of criminal law, Markus D. Dubber, 'European Criminal Law in the Nineteenth and Twentieth Centuries' in *The Oxford Handbook of European Legal History*, eds Heikki Pihlajamäki, Markus D. Dubber, and Mark Godfrey (Oxford: Oxford University Press, 2018), 1052–1072. On conceptual problems in legal history see Thomas Duve, 'European Legal History: Concepts, Methods, Challenges' in *Entanglements in Legal History: Conceptual Approaches*, ed. Thomas Duve (Frankfurt: Max Planck Institute for European Legal History, 2014), 29–66. For a social history perspective, see Carlos Aguirre and Ricardo Salvatore, 'Writing the History of Crime, Law, and Punishment in Latin America' in *Crime and Punishment in Latin America: Law and Society since Late Colonial Times*, eds Ricardo D. Salvatore, Carlos Aguirre, and Gilbert Joseph (Durham: Duke University Press, 2001), 1–32.

 | DOI:10.1163/9789004436091_019

2 Colonial Period

2.1 *General Traits*

War and enslavement were central to ruling colonial territories and their peoples, but in reproducing conquerors' Catholic cosmovision, law and justice played a significant role too. As legal historiography has shown, *iurisdictio* was the central concept of the *ancien régime* institutional structure. Drawn from Roman sources and reinterpreted by medieval jurists, it defined the power (*potestas*) to 'declare the law and establish fairness (*aequitas*).' It referred thus to a public power that encompassed both judicial competences (declaring the law) and legislative faculties (establishing fairness). In different degrees, all public authorities shared a portion of it, from the supreme royal jurisdiction exercised by the King, his Councils and Audiencias, to provincial officers (*gobernadores, corregidores, alcaldes mayores*), and local magistrates (*alcaldes ordinarios* yearly elected by cities). Hence, institutional authorities were expected to rule by doing justice, maintaining 'each one in his state' and 'giving to each his own,' according to a transcendent order revealed by sacred texts and the theological-legal tradition.[2]

We have begun by describing the so-called 'jurisdictional paradigm' to make it clear why we prefer to talk of 'criminal justice' rather than 'criminal law' for this period. In this way, we expect to avoid the bias of our contemporary rule-centered conception of the law to grasp the dynamics of a justice-centered legal culture. In criminal matters, alongside *iurisdictio*, the concept of *arbitrium* strengthened judicial discretion.[3] This does not mean that judges could act arbitrarily. Religion, theology, the Roman-canon tradition, and laws made up a textual universe that provided norms, examples, and reasons to be used in the courts. It supplied a limitless source of punishable conducts (sins and crimes, conceptually linked one to each other).[4] Under the hegemony of Catholicism and royal jurisdiction, local customary practices could make punishments suitable for every context. The legal order was thus flexible and adaptable. In turn, social hierarchies and local interests were often determinant in the courts.

2 Pietro Costa, *Iurisdictio: Semantica del potere politico medioevale, 1100–1433* (Milan: Giuffrè, 1969); António M. Hespanha, *La gracia del derecho: Economía de la cultura en la Edad Moderna* (Madrid: Centro de Estudios Constitucionales, 1993); Jesús Vallejo, *Ruda equidad, ley consumada: Concepción de la potestad normativa, 1250–1350* (Madrid: Centro de Estudios Constitucionales, 1992).

3 Massimo Meccarelli, *Arbitrium: Un aspetto sistematico degli ordinamenti giuridici in età di diritto comune* (Milan: Giuffrè, 1998).

4 Bartolomé Clavero, 'Delito y Pecado. Noción y escala de transgresiones' in *Sexo barroco y otras transgresiones premodernas* (Madrid: Alianza Universidad, 1990).

Punishment had diverse concurrent goals: restore order and peace, repair the damage caused to victims and the community, correct offenders, and serve as a deterrent to others. Punishing crimes and 'public sins' was regarded as a collective duty to prevent communitarian harms associated with God's displeasure. These diverse goals were consistent with a plural-jurisdictions structure (penitential, ecclesiastical, inquisitorial, secular, and military, for example). Procedural and substantive tenets were hardly discernible. Procedural issues could have substantive consequences and vice versa. For weak evidence could lessen punishment and the seriousness of the crime might allow overlooking formal proceedings or denying an appeal. Given these traits, a simple description of written laws would be biased and insufficient. Studies based on judicial records give us a more accurate insight into the administration of colonial criminal justice.[5]

2.2 *Law in Books, Law in Action*

If we had to identify a corpus of positive criminal law, construed as interpretation of transcendent principles, we would look at metropolitan laws. The *Siete Partidas* (thirteenth century) and the *Nueva Recopilación de Castilla* (1567), like the *Ordenações Filipinas* (1595) for the Portuguese dominions, established a positive law framework constantly referenced in colonial courts. In early colonial times, local authorities (city councils or magistrates) passed many criminal measures. As the colonial order consolidated, the crown sought to forbid this practice because enacting secular criminal laws was an exclusive competence of the royal jurisdiction. On this condition, at the request of local authorities, the Council of the Indies issued numerous criminal laws of regional validity until the end of the period. All this explains the relative dearth of criminal laws in the general body of laws for the Indies, *Recopilación de las leyes de Indias* (1680). A quick glimpse at its Seventh Book confirms this.

Among dispositions related to special judges (Title I), gamblers (II), husbands who left their wives in Spain (III), vagabonds and gypsies (IV), 'mulattos,

5 William B. Taylor, *Drinking, Homicide, and Rebellion in Colonial Mexican Villages* (Stanford: Stanford University Press, 1979); Charles Cutter, *The Legal Culture of Northern New Spain 1700–1810* (Albuquerque: University of New Mexico Press, 1995); Tamar Herzog, *La administración como un fenómeno social. La justicia penal de la ciudad de Quito, 1650–1750* (Madrid: Centro de Estudios Constitucionales, 1995); Tamar Herzog, *Upholding Justice: Society, State and the Penal System in Quito, 1650–1750* (Ann Arbor: University of Michigan Press, 2004); Alejandro Agüero, *Castigar y perdonar cuando conviene a la república: La justicia penal de Córdoba del Tucumán, siglos XVII y XVIII* (Madrid: Centro de Estudios Políticos y Constitucionales, 2008); Victor Uribe-Uran, *Fatal Love: Spousal Killers, Law and Punishment in the Late Colonial Spanish Atlantic* (Stanford: Stanford University Press, 2016).

blacks, Berbers, and children of Jews' (V), and jails (VI–VII), we find twenty-eight laws 'on crimes, punishments and their application' (Title VIII). Besides the general injunction to inquire and punish all crimes – particularly the 'public, atrocious, and scandalous offences' (law 1) – it includes some few norms about specific crimes (blasphemy, false testimony, adultery, concubinage) or about certain punishments (forced labor for Indians, galleys, fines, banishments). Finally, there are provisions that seem aimed at avoiding what most probably were everyday practices of colonial courts: judges should not moderate the legal penalties (law 15); they should execute the punishments according to the text of the laws, even the death penalty (law 16); and they should neither promote nor allow, in criminal cases, agreements among the parties 'except in particular cases' in which public vindication was not required (law 17).

Colonial justice records show that, in ordinary cases, judges tended to temper punishments, admitting pardons and agreements, and releasing prisoners during jail inspections. This was a common trait of a legal culture in which love and mercy had to guide, when possible, judicial decisions. Judges were aware that the severity of many laws was due to their antiquity, so they had to adjust them to the times and local circumstances. Likewise, they knew that many laws were issued *ad terrorem*, just to frighten, not to be literally applied except in extreme cases. Even so, as Cutter suggests, the colonial context contributed to stress that judicial performance, in that most people lived in small communities ruled by members of the local elite, away from the royal courts.[6]

Extreme cases, like crimes against the two majesties (divine or human *laesae maiestatis*), against religion (heresy, idolatry), or 'nature' (*contra naturam, nefando*), were punished in impressive punitive rituals: gallows or garrote executions, quartering the bodies and displaying their parts in public places, or burning at the stake for those 'relaxed' by the Inquisition (Courts of the Holy Office were established in Mexico and Lima in 1571). Although exceptional, these rituals wrote some of the darkest pages in the Latin America colonial history, like the Autos de Fe performed in Lima and Mexico in the seventeenth century or the executions of Tupac Amaru and his fellows in Peru at the beginnings of the 1780s.

Capital punishment was scarcely used in ordinary cases; gallows or garrote (this one reserved for noblemen), preceded by public humiliation, were the usual methods. Alongside reasons of mercy, the scarce use of capital

6 Charles Cutter, 'Judicial Punishment in Colonial New Mexico' (1995) 8 Western Legal History 122; Cutter, *The Legal Culture*, 5–6; Colin M. MacLachlan, *Spain's Empire in the New World: The Role of Ideas in Institutional and Social Change* (Berkeley: University of California Press, 1988), 12–13; Agüero, *Castigar y perdonar*, 256–272.

punishment is linked to a deep change in the paradigm of punishments. From the sixteenth century onwards, blood sentences were gradually replaced by utilitarian punishments. Penal servitude became a resource for galleys, arsenals, *presidios*, and mining work, throughout the Spanish Empire.[7] These punishments were generally reserved for serious crime, whereas whipping, public humiliation, and banishment were commonly applied to minor offenses. Incarceration was not a legal punishment (jails were just to assure the defendants), though it was a common practice to impose pre-trial imprisonment as a way to close a case.

Criminal procedure was based on the Roman-canon law tradition that inspired the development of inquisitorial proceedings, according to the *Decretals of Gregory IX* (Book V) and the *Siete Partidas* (Books III and VII). Notwithstanding, judicial practice was rather shaped by doctrinal books and manuals addressed at instructing magistrates to conduct legal process. The circulation of this literature was determinant for the observance of procedural forms in the vast colonial territories that were ruled to a great extent by lay judges. Except for the cities where royal courts were established, the lack of lawyers is a trait of the Spanish colonial experience.[8] However, judicial records show that local lay judges were generally able to formalize written criminal procedures according to the standards of the current legal culture. They could use the long ordinary mixed procedure (with *sumario* and *plenario*), or the summarized forms limiting the process to its essential formalities.[9] Some of these, such as the obligation of hearing the defendant, were regarded as commanded by the divine law.

Concerning evidence, confession on oath was the key (*regina probatorum*) to condemn. Many trials for lesser offenses were reduced to the indictment, confession, and sentence. Given the importance of confession, medieval and early modern laws minutely regulated the use of torture for cases deserving corporal or capital punishments (*Siete Partidas*, Book VII, Title 30; *Ordenaçoes Manuelinas,* Book V, Title 64; *Ordenaçoes Filipinas,* Book V, Title 133). Nonetheless, as blood sentences were gradually displaced, the use of

---

7 Ruth Pike, *Penal Servitude in Early Modern Spain* (Madison: University of Wisconsin Press, 1983); John Langbein, *Torture and the Law of Proof: Europe and England in the Ancien Règime* (Chicago: University of Chicago Press, 1977).

8 Víctor M. Uribe, 'Colonial Lawyers, Republican Lawyers and the Administration of Justice in Spanish America' in *Judicial Institutions in Nineteenth-Century Latin America*, ed. Eduardo Zimmermann (London: Institute of Latin American Studies, 1999), 25–48; Cutter, *The Legal Culture*, 3–6; Ricardo Levene, *Historia del Derecho Argentino* (Buenos Aires: Kraft, 1946), vol. 2, 435–466.

9 Herzog, *Upholding Justice*, 24–42; Agüero, *Castigar y perdonar*, 279–400.

torture also decreased. Judicial records show that it was not regularly used in first-instance secular courts. Despite legal restrictions, witness testimonies were widely admitted in colonial courts. The witness's social status usually determined the weight of his or her testimony; Solórzano Pereyra stated that six Indians were necessary to equal one qualified witness.[10]

Beyond procedural forms, judicial records show certain practices that are not usually associated with the inquisitorial model of criminal justice. It is not uncommon to find parties' agreements, peace deals, pardons deeds, or the suspension of the prosecution due to the intervention of a principal *vecino* who begs the judge to act with mercy. In a way, these practices reflected the cultural background that advised judges to avoid, when possible, long and harsh formal proceedings, acting as mediators in their communities. They were expected to fulfill their mission by 'punishing and forgiving when it is convenient for the Republic.'[11]

2.3 *Colonial Justices, Domestic Powers, and Police*

Jurisdictional pluralism was a useful tool for colonial cultures.[12] Diverse authorities had exclusive or concurrent competences in criminal issues. Indeed, a great deal of Indians' social practices, labeled as idolatry, sorcery, and bigamy, among others – was pursued by ecclesiastical courts. Due to their neophyte condition, Indians were excluded from the jurisdiction of the Inquisition so their crimes against Catholic doctrine were pursued by ordinary ecclesiastical courts. Campaigns of 'extirpation of idolatries' were undertaken in Peru and Mexico from the second half of the sixteenth century onwards.[13]

Regarding native peoples, in addition to some specific institutions (the General Indian Court in México and the *Protector de indios*),[14] special

10 Juan Solórzano Pereyra, *Política Indiana* (Madrid: Matheo Sacristán, 1736), Book II, Chap. XXVIII, § 35; Uribe-Uran, *Fatal Love: Spousal Killers*, 44.

11 Castillo de Bobadilla (1597), quoted in Agüero, *Castigar y perdonar*, 166.

12 Lauren Benton, *Law and Colonial Cultures: Legal Regimes in World History, 1400–1900* (New York: Cambridge University Press, 2002), 7–12.

13 Nicholas Griffiths, *The Cross and the Serpent: Religious Repression and Resurgence in Colonial Peru* (Norman: University of Oklahoma Press, 1996); Macarena Cordero Fernández, *Institucionalizar y desarraigar: Las visitas de idolatrías en la Diócesis de Lima, siglo XVII* (Lima: Instituto Riva-Agüero, 2016); Gabriela Ramos, 'Pastoral Visitations: Spaces of Negotiation in Andean Indigenous Parishes' (2016) 73 The Americas 1, 39–57; David Tavárez, 'Archivos, narrativas y silencios historiográficos sobre la extirpación de idolatrías en Nueva España' (2009) 46 Jahrbuch für Geschichte Lateinamerikas 43–60.

14 Woodrow Borah, *Justice by Insurance: The General Indian Court of Colonial Mexico and the Legal Aides of the Half-Real* (Berkeley: University of California Press, 1983); Constantino Bayle, *El Protector de Indios* (Sevilla: Escuela de Estudios Hispano-Americanos-CSIC,

provisions were applicable for them. These so-called 'privileges' encompassed norms for avoiding complex ordinary proceedings, for granting direct access to the high courts (Audiencias), making the rules of proof flexible, and allowing the suspects or witnesses to change their statements at any moment.[15] They could be subsumed in a general precept of tolerating misconducts derived, in the colonial view, from Indians' rusticity and weakness. They reflect thus the degraded condition of Indians who were regarded as perpetual minors, and miserable persons by colonial law.[16]

Judicial records show that even if these privileges were not strictly observed, Indians were not treated with special severity in common criminal cases. The crown sought to avoid, not always successfully, certain local punitive practices of the early colonization, such as whipping without trial, cutting hair, or forced labor (*servicio personal*). Recent studies have highlighted that Indians were not merely passive subjects of colonial justice, remarking on their ability to engage with Spanish institutions and use them strategically. How Indians contributed to shaping colonial law, mixing their own beliefs with the Catholic tradition, and how they exercised their local jurisdiction punishing minor crimes within their community, are some of the main concerns for current studies.[17]

This summary picture is incomplete if we do not consider an array of less formalized disciplinary devices that barely left written traces. Complaints for abuses of local authorities indicate that informal chastisement was a usual practice among lesser magistrates. Nonetheless, in many cases, it was an expression of a justified use of domestic power. For example, a theologian stated that a priest could impose up to twenty-five lashes without any formal proceeding because he was acting as 'a father would with his son.'[18] Local magistrates often invoked similar reasons to overlook formal proceedings in punishing minor offenses. Most of the population was subjected to a form of

1945); Charles Cutter, *The Protector de Indios in Colonial New Mexico, 1659–1821* (Albuquerque: University of New Mexico Press, 1986); Mauricio Novoa, *The Protectors of Indians in the Royal Audience of Lima: History, Careers and Legal Culture, 1575–1775* (Leiden: Brill, 2016).

15 Solórzano Pereyra, *Política Indiana*, Book II, Chap. XXVIII, § 25–27.

16 On the Indians' colonial law 'privileges,' see Paulino Castañeda, 'La condición miserable del indio y sus privilegios' (1971) *Anuario de Estudios Americanos* 28 245–335.

17 Yanna Yannakakis, 'Indigenous People and Legal Culture in Spanish America' (2013) 11 History Compass 931–947; Bianca Premo and Yanna Yannakakis, 'A Court of Sticks and Branches: Indian Jurisdiction in Colonial Mexico and Beyond' (2019) 124 American Historical Review 28–55.

18 Juan de Paz, *Consultas y resoluciones varias, theologicas, juridicas, regulares, y morales* (1687) (Tournes: Amberes, 1745), 426.

domestic power that encompassed disciplinary faculties exerted by the householders over wives, relatives, and servants; by landowners over peasants, and by slaveholders over slaves. Thus, widespread structures of micro-social discipline worked silently without leaving written traces.

The king was said to have a 'domestic power' (*potestas economica*) to apply executive or preventive measures without formal proceedings when necessary for the kingdom's protection. This patriarchal image of power would have two meaningful effects during the eighteenth century. On the one hand, it justified absolute obedience to the king, condemning scholastic theses on *tyrannicide*. On the other, it provided a conceptual ground for the development of police power.[19]

The Intendants Ordinances (Río de la Plata 1782, Lima 1784, New Spain 1786, and others), endowed Intendants and their delegates with a new competence for 'causes of police,' alongside the traditional faculties of justice, war, and public finances. Among the functions associated with the 'causes of police' (topography, roads, improvement of farmland, hygiene and decoration of cities, and public buildings), Intendants took over the repression of vagrants, an old function that gained increasing attention in the eighteenth century. Any vagrants, or people without 'application to work' should be sent to serve in 'military regiments, warship or merchant ships, or public works.' Furthermore, officers had to collect 'the useless' and the 'professional beggars' in hospices, whereas the 'restless, dangerous or wrongdoer' would be punished with forced labor in mines or *presidio*.[20]

According to the new police science, police measures were not deemed as punishments, but as 'paternal determinations to improve Citizens' customs'; therefore, they did not require ordinary justice proceedings.[21] Through an

---

19 Jesús Vallejo, 'Concepción de la policía' in *La jurisdicción contencioso-administrativa en España: Una historia de sus orígenes*, ed. Marta Lorente (Madrid: Consejo General del Poder Judicial, 2009), 117–144; Markus D. Dubber, *The Police Power: Patriarchy and the Foundations of the American Government* (New York: Columbia University Press, 2005); Alejandro Agüero, 'Republicanismo, Antigua Constitución o gobernanza doméstica. El gobierno paternal durante la Santa Confederación Argentina, 1830–1852' (2018) Nuevo Mundo Mundos Nuevos http://journals.openedition.org/nuevomundo/72795, 7–8; Agustín Casagrande, *Gobierno de la Justicia, poder de policía: La construcción oeconómica del orden social en Buenos Aires (1776–1829)* (Valencia: Tirant lo Blanch, 2018).

20 *Real Ordenanza para el Establecimiento é Instrucción de Intendentes de Exercito y Provincia en el Virreinato de Buenos Aires* (Madrid: Imprenta Real, 1782), § 55–56, 58–60; for New Spain, *Real Ordenanza para el Establecimiento é Instrucción de Intendentes de Exercito y Provincia en el Reino de la Nueva España* (Madrid: Ibarra, 1786), § 59–60, 68–70.

21 Isabel Ramos Vázquez, 'Policía de vagos para las ciudades españolas del siglo XVIII' (2009) 31 Revista de estudios histórico-jurídicos 217–258.

increasing network of lesser officers (subdelegates, *alcaldes de barrio, alcaldes de cuartel, and alcaldes pedáneos*), late colonial authorities sought to control a growing population using their policing jurisdiction. In Río de la Plata, a compulsory labor obligation (*conchabo*) could be imposed on any vagrants, or on those convicted who, after serving the penalty, had to undergo work for a landowner or an honorable man who would watch over them.[22] Similar compulsory labor obligations in bakeries, butcheries, and textile mills were also imposed in colonial Peru and New Spain.[23]

By the late decades of the colonial period, institutional punishment became less formalized and more utilitarian, providing soldiers and workers for public or private purposes. At the same time, military jurisdiction had a remarkable expansion. Privileges of high officers were extended to the lower ranks and militias. The boundaries between police powers, ordinary justice, and privileged *fueros* gave rise to endless jurisdictional competition.

2.4 *Criticism and Moderate Reformism*

Criticism against criminal justice administration was one of the leitmotivs of European Enlightenment thinkers. Beccaria's *On Crimes and Punishments* (1764) became the most influential work against *ancien régime* criminal justice. However, in the Spanish world, its reception was 'uneven and just moderately prolific in the short term.'[24] An academic debate on judicial torture had place in the late decades of the eighteenth century, but no legal reform was enacted. Catholic enlightened thinkers adhered to a historicist trend that led them to recognize the value of ancient laws, including criminal laws. Manuel de Lardizábal y Uribe, the so-called 'Spanish Beccaria,' stated that 'among all criminal legislations in Europe that have not been reformed yet there is not one less defective than ours'; he also stated that 'some maxims that today are adopted as useful and new, have been approved and enshrined from immemorial times in our homeland laws.'[25]

Beyond the historicist approach, the widespread confidence in religion kept the old connection between religious discipline and criminal law in force. In a

---

22 Alejandro Agüero, 'On Justice and "Home Rule" Tradition in the Spanish Colonial Order' (2012) 41 Quaderni Fiorentini 200–201.

23 Alberto Flores Galindo, *Aristocracia y plebe en Lima, 1760–1830 (Estructura de clase y sociedad colonial)* (Lima: Mosca Azul Editores, 1983); Samuel Kagan, *Penal Servitude in New Spain: The Colonial Textile Industry*, PhD Dissertation, City University of New York, 1976.

24 Francisco Tomás y Valiente, *La Tortura en España* (Barcelona: Ariel, 1994), 166.

25 Alejandro Agüero and Marta Lorente, 'Penal Enlightenment in Spain: From Beccaria's Reception to the First Criminal Code' in *The Spanish Enlightenment Revisited*, ed. Jesús Astigarraga (Oxford: The Voltaire Foundation, 2015), 246.

celebrated treatise on Spanish public law of 1800, Dou y Bassols wrote, 'there is no need for harsh penalties in Spain where a religion like ours rules and is professed, which forestalls an infinite number of crimes and makes men docile and obedient to its precepts.'[26] No wonder that Lardizábal had set crimes against religion in the first category within his classification of crimes, before crimes against customs, tranquility, and public or private security. The classification itself reveals the traditional values that inspired his thinking. Nonetheless, this moderate attitude was consistent with claims for humanizing punishments, for setting a proportional relationship between crime and punishment, and for reducing the use of corporal and capital punishment and abolishing judicial torture.[27]

Moderate reformers like Lardizábal pleaded for a gradual adjustment of the old laws to the new sensitivities and different conceptions of punishment. Still, more traditional thinking resisted. Inquisitorial courts surveilled the circulation of foreign books that challenged traditional doctrines. Beccaria's book was included in the Spanish Inquisition Index in 1777. The process of reform was further slowed down after the French Revolution, which meant a deterrent for Spanish reformism. Criminal trials for seditious rumors and high treason took place in different contexts from México to Río de la Plata. In New Granada, for instance, Antonio Nariño was convicted for translating into Spanish the French Declaration of the Rights of Man in 1794. Nonetheless, such episodes did not represent the general attitude of creole elites towards the colonial order and its criminal justice administration. This may explain the persistence of much of the colonial laws and practices after the imperial collapse.

3 Independence and Constitutional Culture

3.1 *New Constitutional Settings*

During the independence wars, new political doctrines spread throughout the region. American and French experiences inspired a new constitutional discourse characterized, however, by a mixture of liberal values and ancient legal tenets. Nonetheless, constitutional standards, such as popular or national sovereignty, separation of powers, civil rights, involved, theoretically, new conditions for criminal law. The Cádiz Constitution (1812) entered into force in most colonial dominions and influenced the drafting of constitutions in other

26 Ramón L. Dou y Bassols, *Instituciones de Derecho Público de España* (Madrid: Benito García y Cía., 1800), vol. 1, 35.

27 Alejandro Agüero and Marta Lorente, 'Penal Enlightenment in Spain,' 235–264.

territories as well.[28] It offers a good starting point for analyzing the new constitutional framework.

Despite its relative historicist tenor, the Constitution reveals 'new approaches in areas of criminal law, procedure, punishment, and detention.'[29] Whereas some constitutional provisions reflected ancient tenets (the need of a previous information of facts to impose a punishment, art. 287; or the personal responsibility of the judges, art. 254), others responded to reformers claims, such as the prohibition of torture (art. 303), the repealing of the requirement for the accused to confess on oath (art. 291), or the need for brief proceedings avoiding delays in justice administration (art. 286). Future legislation would provide a uniform procedural law with which neither the King nor the Cortes could dispense (art. 244). Although the Cortes failed in passing a draft for abbreviating criminal causes, its debate inspired new provisions issued for criminal procedure.[30] The constitution provided the possibility of introducing a form of jury (judges of facts) for criminal cases (art. 307). The Cortes could suspend some guarantees in case of extraordinary circumstances against state security (art. 308).

The constitutional settings implied an attempt to replace the jurisdictional paradigm for a law-centered one. The Cortes with the King would exert legislative power, confining King's competences in judicial matters (art.15). The magistrate's role was limited to the strict judicial application of the laws (arts. 17, 242, and 243). Judges could no longer pass general regulations for the administration of justice (art. 246). Furthermore, a system based on the legality principle required other conditions that the Constitution contemplated in its way: codifying the law and abolishing privileges. The civil, criminal, and commercial codes would be 'the same for the entire Monarchy, notwithstanding the variations that the Cortes may introduce due to particular circumstances' (art. 258).[31] And there would only be 'one jurisdiction (*fuero*) for all classes of persons' in 'common civil and criminal cases' (art. 248). However, the

28 M.C. Mirow, *Latin American Constitutions: The Constitution of Cádiz and Its Legacy in Spanish America* (Cambridge: Cambridge University Press, 2015).

29 M.C. Mirow, 'The Legality Principle and the Constitution of Cádiz' in *From the Judge's Arbitrium to the Legality Principle: Legislation as a Source of law in Criminal Trials*, eds Georges Martyn, Anthony Musson, and Heikki Pihlajamäki (Berlin: Duncker & Humblot, 2013), 191.

30 M. Paz Alonso Romero, *Orden procesal y garantías entre Antiguo Régimen y constitucionalismo gaditano* (Madrid: Centro de Estudios Políticos y Constitucionales, 2008), 330.

31 M.C. Mirow, 'Codification and the Constitution of Cádiz' in *Estudios Jurídicos en Homenaje al Profesor Alejandro Guzmán Brito*, eds Patricio-Ignacio Carvajal and Massimo Miglietta (Trento: Edizioni dell'Orso, 2014), vol. 3, 343–361.

ecclesiastical and military *fueros* were maintained (arts. 249–250). It was not clear which were the *uncommon* cases in which 'there could be many fueros for many different classes of persons' as a commentator would claim.[32]

Therefore, by admitting regional variations in the codes and preserving ecclesiastic and military *fueros*, the liberal ideal of one simplified law for all persons had two traditional limitations. Moreover, if we look at the jurisdictional structure, the Constitution stated that all civil and criminal cases should terminate in the territory of each court (Audiencia) (art. 262). No one instance for unifying and controlling the equal application of the law was established. Besides, the failure to pass the new legal codes in the short term implied keeping in force the old legal order, with its cumulative dynamics that relied necessarily on judicial discretion. In this context, and to the extent that no provision was adopted to oblige magistrates to ground their rulings (except in warrants for arrest), the effectiveness of the legality principle was rather illusory.[33]

The Cortes passed other reforms relevant to our discussion. The most important, perhaps, was in 1813 with the abolition of the Holy Inquisition whose activity in the latest times had been focused on controlling political propaganda and censoring foreign literature. Other than repairing the striking silence of the Constitution on this controversial institution, the decree of 1813 was in line with the secularization process of punishment driven by enlightened thinking. Alongside the repealing of manor jurisdictions, decreed in 1811, it also meant another step for jurisdictional unification, despite the aforesaid limitations.

3.2 *Insurgences, Restoration, Resiliencies (1810–1850)*

Cádiz's constitutional system had a relative success in changing institutional praxis. When Ferdinand VII recovered the crown, he repealed the Constitution and all the reforms (Decree of May 4, 1814). In the following years, traditional law coexisted with new provisions of revolutionary governments. Territories that remained outside the Cádiz system also passed symbolic reforms regarding punishment. In Rio de la Plata, revolutionary governments enacted new regulations on the separation of powers and the first Constituent Assembly abolished the Inquisition and judicial torture, commanding all instruments used for torment to be burned in public squares (1813).

Despite the liberal tenor of political discourse, independence declarations did not bring immediate effective changes in punitive practices. Amidst civil

32 Ramón de Salas, *Lecciones de Derecho Público Constitucional* (Madrid: Imprenta del Censor, 1821), vol. 1, 175.

33 Agüero and Lorente, 'Penal Enlightenment in Spain,' 259.

wars and political instability, traditional practices continued while the bulk of Spanish colonial law remained in force, in some cases until the last decades of the nineteenth century. We can outline some common traits of criminal justice administration in the new emerging countries during this period.

a) In line with the Constitution of Cádiz, early Latin American constitutions adopted the Roman Catholic religion as state creed with prohibitions of public worship of any other religions. Thus, the hegemonic and intolerant position of Catholicism conditioned the relationship between law and society, preserving traditional views on human conduct. It contributed to maintaining communitarian social structures and naturalized social hierarchies, hindering the emergence of an effective notion of individual rights. Moreover, it informed the interpretation of law and the function of punishment. It was also a limit for freedom of the press. In many countries, censorship juntas or juries were established to try press crimes and to protect Catholic morals from public writings.

b) The prevailing position of the Catholic Church, alongside the militarization of politics and wartime, discouraged attempts to abolish ecclesiastical and military *fueros*. According to the Mexican Constitutions of 1824, 1836, and 1843, for instance, ecclesiastic and military personnel had the right to be tried by their respective jurisdictions, even for ordinary crimes. Furthermore, civilians could be tried by those jurisdictions for breaching military or ecclesiastical laws.[34]

c) The continuation of Spanish colonial law made it impossible to accomplish the aims of the legality principle declared at the constitutional level. Some constitutions, for example the one enacted in Córdoba, Río de la Plata, in 1821, stated that provisions on the legality principle did not mean repealing the 'prudent discretion of the judges' to moderate punishments, according to circumstances of the crimes.

d) The inherited figure of strong provincial governors and the paternal conception of authority impeded the effective separation of powers. Whether through legal provisions or by concessions of extraordinary powers, in many regions governors continued to exercise multiple functions, including those of justice and police which often overlapped in repressive actions.[35] In addition to provisions aimed at pursuing political opponents, many local laws were passed with a twofold purpose: to

---

34 Elisa Speckman Guerra, *Del Tigre de Santa Julia, la princesa italiana y otras historias: Sistema judicial, criminalidad y justicia en la ciudad de México, siglos XIX–XX* (México: Instituto Nacional de Ciencias Penales, 2014), 9.

35 Agüero, 'Republicanismo, Antigua Constitución o gobernanza doméstica.'

shorten proceedings and increase penalties for the most frequent crimes, such as banditry and cattle rustling.[36]

e) Provisions against vagrants remained the main instrument of social discipline for the lower classes. A special court (*Tribunal de Vagos*) was established in Mexico in 1828. In the Argentine Confederation, provincial laws reinforced the practice of *conchabo* imposed on anyone who lacked property or a profitable occupation. A Colombian law systematized these practices setting up as penalties for vagrants: (a) to serve as '*concertado*' for individuals or public institutions or perform military service from two to six years, or (b) to be sent to new populations in desert lands (law of April 6, 1836). Many minor offenses against public order, such as drunkenness, gambling, and quarrels, broadened the scope of laws against vagrants. The repression of these offenses was assigned to police corps, generally subordinate to the executive branches. The Colombian case offers a paradigmatic example of this process. First-instance judges oversaw repression under the vagrancy law of 1836 (art. 3); however, the General Police Law of 1841 assigned that role to the police corps dependent on the executive power (additional law, June 1842, art. 1 and 12). A brief oral procedure to impose police sanctions took only twenty-four hours (General Police Law, 1841, art. 28).

f) Except for the main capital cities, the attempts to establish modern court structures faced the challenge of the shortages of qualified lawyers. The development of police institutions, however, strengthened social control in rural areas, often ruled by local agents who accumulated multiple functions including judicial and police procedures, tax collection, military recruitment, and the gathering of electoral rolls.

4 Towards a 'Modern' Criminal Law: Codification, Science, and Police Power

4.1 *Modernity's Double Face*

For a long time, codification was regarded as the best method for realizing modern ideas on criminal law. Newer approaches tend to remark that codification was not the only liberal way for replacing *ancien régime* practices and not all codes reflect the same values. Besides, codes also 'supplied the optimal

36 Águeda G. Venegas de la Torre, 'Nuevas Perspectivas sobre los Delitos y Castigos en México, 1824–1835' (2014) 2 Historia y Justicia 10.

method of legal control for the consolidation of political power.'[37] In line with Foucault's criticism on the hidden disciplinary face of enlightened reforms, other scholars have remarked on the fact that, alongside liberal tenets, modernity involved the development of powerful devices of social discipline.[38] As Dubber suggests, modernity encompassed not one but 'two foundational modes of governance' that have been in tension since the very beginning of the liberal project: *Rechtsstaat* versus *Polizeistaat*, the liberal ideal of law based on individual self-government against governance based on the state's police power.[39]

Similarly, Zaffaroni has pointed out the need to distinguish criminal law from what he calls 'punitive power.' While the latter refers to all agencies and forms, historical and present, of repressive powers, the first would denote the legal knowledge aimed at interpreting law and supplying guides to restrain the state's punitive power. These approaches convey the same concern for avoiding teleological narratives that read the history of criminal law as a story of evolution for humanizing punishments.[40] The history of modern criminal law in Latin America must not hide the parallel processes which led to reinforce police agencies, to exercise political control over judiciaries, and to resort systematically to states of exception or military governments.

4.2 *Criminal Law Codification: First Experiences*

The first criminal codification in Latin America did not replace the Spanish legal tradition overnight. New codes were often used as an additional text among other laws and doctrines. Indeed, following the Spanish code of 1822 (Preliminary Title, Chap. XIII), they provided that all crimes not included in the code should be punished by special laws still in force. The formal structure, taken from the Napoleonic *Code Pénal* (1810), set crimes against the state and public order in the first place in the Code's 'special section.' No wonder that the French code had been qualified as a law 'approved to ensure a despotic government.'[41] The Spanish code of 1822, 'a mixture of ancient laws (*fuero juzgo*

---

37 M.C. Mirow, *Latin American Law: A History of Private Law and Institutions in Spanish America* (Austin: University of Texas Press, 2004), 98.

38 Michel Foucault, *Discipline and Punish: The Birth of Prison* (New York: Random House, 1979).

39 Dubber, 'European Criminal Law,' 1065–1067.

40 E. Zaffaroni, A. Alagia, and A. Slokar, *Manual de Derecho Penal: Parte General* (Buenos Aires: Ediar, 2007), 165–166.

41 Aniceto Masferrer, 'The Myth of French Influence over Spanish Codification: The General Part of the Criminal Codes of 1822 and 1844' in *The Western Codification of Criminal*

and *Las Partidas*) wrapped in the character of Napoleon's Code,'[42] inspired the first Latin American criminal codification. Except for Haiti and the Dominican Republic which adopted the French code, the Spanish code was the main source for codification in Salvador (1826), Chihuahua (1827), Bolivia (1831/1834), Veracruz (1835), Ecuador (1837), and Colombia (1837). Despite their traditional traits, these codes attempted to systematize penal law and reduce judicial discretion.

Although the bulk of old penalties were maintained, some regarded ignominious, like whipping or the gallows, were excluded. Public executions were regulated in detail, and the garrote became the prevalent method for death penalties ('without any torture or maltreatment'). Infamy and deprivation of civil and political rights or office continued among the non-corporal punishments. The Spanish code, and most codes based on it, excluded public humiliation (*vergüenza pública*) as punishment, though the codes of El Salvador (arts. 31, 66) and Colombia (arts. 18, 51) included this punishment along with an exhaustive regulation on its execution.

An alternative stream, with more original notes, came up from two different sources. The Livingston draft for Louisiana (1825) which encompassed the reform of criminal, procedural, and penitentiary laws, was translated into Spanish and adopted in Guatemala and Nicaragua (1837). It has been said that this text was much more humanistic, technical, and liberal than its contemporaries.[43] For the first time, the death penalty was excluded from the list of punishments, which were mainly reduced to different forms of prison and fines (art. 100). On the other hand, the Brazilian code of 1830 which, although influenced by the French, Bavarian, and Spanish codes, has been qualified as an original, 'advanced and unique,' text for its time.[44] Beyond its technical innovations, it served as one of the main sources for the Spanish code of 1848 which, in turn, became a model for the next generation of Latin American codes.

Law: A Revision of the Myth of its Predominant French Influence, ed. Aniceto Masferrer (Cham: Springer, 2018), 210.

42 *El Código Penal concordado y comentado por D. Joachin F. Pacheco* (Madrid: Manuel Tello, 1871), vol. 1, liv. See also Masferrer, 'The Myth of French Influence,' 193–199.

43 Eugenio Raúl Zaffaroni, 'Los códigos penales de Latinoamérica' in *Códigos penales de los países de América Latina*, ed. Suprema Corte de Justicia de la Nación (México: ILANUD, 2000), 43.

44 Ignacio M. Poveda Velasco and Eduardo Tomasevicius Filho, 'The 1830 Criminal Code of the Brazilian Empire and Its Originality' in *The Western Codification of Criminal Law*, 365.

Thus, the first Brazilian code is a good example of the intense circulation of legal culture back and forth on both sides of the Atlantic Ocean.[45]

Drafted for societies in which slavery was in force, the Livingston project excluded crimes committed by slaves to be regulated by special laws (art. 64 Spanish version). The Brazilian preserved whipping (up to fifty lashes) as a punishment for slaves (art. 60) when not deserving death or galleys for insurrection (art. 113). These provisions were in line with a legal culture that still relied on domestic powers and the responsibility of fathers and masters or any other who had legitimate faculty 'to punish others by themselves' (Spanish Code, art. 607, Brazilian Code, art. 14 § 6). In exercising such powers, even the homicide of those being punished was always presumed as involuntary (Spanish Code, art. 625; Colombian Code, art. 606, § 6). Besides, a deep gap between formal law and punitive practices continued. According to Zaffaroni, the first Latin American criminal codes were a product of learned elites not much concerned with effective devices of social control.[46]

4.3 *Liberalism, New Codes, and Scholarship*

The last decades of the nineteenth century witnessed more political stability in the region, allowing elites to undertake deeper liberal reforms. A modern law was no longer just a matter of internal control but a requirement for inserting the new economies into the world market. In turn, criminal law became a specialized subject of the legal curriculum. This would intensify the circulation of ideas, while a growing number of lawyers was available to take over judicial structures. In this context, new European developments, the Italian and French doctrines, would reach the Hispanic world thanks to the works of Spanish scholars. Pacheco's *Studies on Criminal Law* (Madrid, 1842–1843) and his commentaries on the new Spanish penal code of 1848, for instance, would have a remarkable influence on Latin American scholars engaged in drafting new codes.[47]

The Spanish code of 1848, reformed in 1850 and 1870, was mainly inspired by the Brazilian code, and to a lesser extent by the Austrian (1803) and the Two Sicilies (1819) codes, all accompanied with original solutions and provisions

45 Bernardino Bravo Lira, 'La fortuna del código penal español de 1848. Historia en cuatro actos y tres continentes: de Mello Freire y Zeiller a Vasconcelos y Seijas Lozano' (2004) 74 Anuario de Historia del Derecho Español, 23–58.

46 Zaffaroni 'Los códigos penales de Latinoamérica,' 26.

47 Emilia Iñesta Pastor, 'La proyección hispanoamericana del código penal español de 1848' in XIII *Congreso del Instituto Internacional de Historia del Derecho Indiano*, ed. Luis E. González Vale (San Juan: Asamblea Legislativa de Puerto Rico, 2003), vol. 2, 494–495.

drawn from the Spanish tradition. It brought technical improvement in systematizing general principles and standards to graduate penalties and to reduce judicial discretion. Still, it contained a large list of minutely graduated punishments. Alongside the death penalty, whose public execution was slightly moderated, most punishments consisted of different forms of reclusion, *presidio*, banishment, disqualification, and civil interdiction. It expressly abolished the penalty of infamy (art. 23). In its 'special part,' before crimes against the state, it set a title on crimes against religion, punishing attempts to abolish Catholicism, the public worship of other cults, and public apostasy (Book II, Title I). These provisions would be replaced in 1870 with a title on crimes against 'freedom of worship' (Book II, Title II, Sec. III).

The Spanish text of 1848 influenced new code reforms in countries that had adopted the code of 1822. It had a direct influence on the first Chilean criminal code of 1874. In this case, alongside traditional laws, original solutions and adaptations, numerous provisions also evinced the influence of the Belgian code of 1867,[48] which, in turn, had been adopted in Ecuador in 1872. Along a more traditional Spanish line, the Ecuadorian code maintained a chapter on crimes 'against religion' aimed to protect Catholic intolerance (Book II, Chap. II). Also, in 1872 the first criminal code of Mexico's Federal District entered into force and was thereafter adopted in most states of the federation. Often associated with the Spanish criminal codification, it was based on many different sources and reflected the influence of scholars like Pacheco, Chauveau, and Hélie.[49] It is noteworthy that its special section departs from the French (and Spanish) model by setting crimes against property and persons in the first place (Book III, Chaps. I–III).

Setting 'private crimes' before crimes against the state (or public crimes) recalls Feuerbach's Bavarian code of 1813. Regarded as an alternative liberal model when compared to the Napoleonic Code, it had had little influence in Latin America until its translation into French in 1852 made it available in a more familiar language. In his draft of 1866–1867, for instance, Carlos Tejedor declared having taken the Bavarian code as the main source for the first Argentine criminal code.[50] His draft and commentaries reflected a

48 *Código Penal de la República de Chile comentado por Robustiano Vera* (Santiago de Chile: P. Cadot, 1883), 39–40; Iñesta Pastor, 'La proyección hispanoamericana del código penal español de 1848,' 511.

49 Óscar Cruz Barney, 'The Mexican Codification of Criminal Law: Its Foreign Influences' in *The Western Codification of Criminal Law*, 386.

50 Carlos Tejedor, *Proyecto de Código Penal para la República Argentina* (Buenos Aires: Comercio del Plata, 1866).

greater influence of the older laws and Spanish codes, alongside other South American codes of the time.[51] Challenged by an alternative project, Tejedor's draft was eventually passed in 1886. In the meantime, it had been adopted as provisional law in most Argentine provinces and in Paraguay (1880).[52] Latest codes of liberal inspiration followed the model of the first Italian code drafted by Zanardelli (1889). This work inspired reforms in newly republican Brazil (1890), Venezuela (1897), and Colombia (1922, though soon repealed).

This patchwork of nineteenth-century Latin American codes, inspired by mixed if not contradictory trends, says little about effective practice of punishment.[53] Structural challenges to uphold independent judiciaries, alongside an array of police regulations and special laws, weakened the pretended liberal standards. Consider, just as an example, the law restoring whipping for robbery and thefts in Chile (1876). Whipping had been abolished in 1852 and excluded from the criminal code. In 1876 it was restored 'with healthy profits.'[54] The need for old punishments and the death penalty were often justified through the lack of the type of penitentiaries required by the latest codes. Except for some early limited experiences (Brazil 1834, Chile 1844, and Peru 1862), the penitentiary would only become a generalized system of punishment in the twentieth century.[55]

Similar pragmatic and economic reasons were invoked to defer reforms on procedural laws. In 1891 a Chilean scholar claimed that the prohibition of torture and other constitutional guarantees were a 'dead letter' due to the lack of a procedural code and the impossibility to make judges responsible for their abuses during criminal prosecutions.[56] This picture may reflect the reality of procedural practice in most countries of the region at that time. Procedural codification came late, and it just systematized the slightly modified inquisitive model defined as 'mixt system.' It maintained the written procedure,

---

51 Thomas Duve, '¿Del absolutismo ilustrado al liberalismo reformista? La recepción del Código Penal Bávaro de 1813 de Paul J. A. von Feuerbach en Argentina y el debate sobre la reforma del derecho penal hasta 1921' (1999) 27 Revista de Historia del Derecho 125–152.

52 Alejandro Agüero and Matías Rosso, 'Coding the Criminal Law in Argentina: Provincial and National Codification in the Genesis of the First Penal Code' in *The Western Codification of Criminal Law*, 297–332.

53 Zaffaroni, 'Los códigos penales de Latinoamérica,' 22.

54 *Código Penal de la República de Chile comentado*, 70.

55 Ricardo Salvatore and Carlos Aguirre, 'The Birth of the Penitentiary in Latin America: Towards an Interpretative Social History of Prisons' in *The Birth of Penitentiaries in Latin America: Essays on Criminology, Prison Reform, and Social Control, 1830–1940*, eds Ricardo Salvatore and Carlos Aguirre (Austin: University of Texas Press, 1996), 1–43.

56 Robustiano Vera, 'El azote, la tortura y las incomunicaciones como medios de descubrir los delitos' (1891), 8 Revista forense chilena 586–591.

which followed the traditional division into *sumario* and *plenario*. The first phase, generally delegated to police corps, was decisive for the trial. One single judge was to carry out the entire procedure with scarce participation of prosecutors or complainants. Although most of the constitutions provided for the establishment of jury trials, only in very few cases, and for short periods, did they come into effect as ordinary system for common crimes, except for Brazil where they are in force since 1822. The long persistence of this model until the final decades of the twentieth century has led scholars to speak of an 'inquisitive culture' as an attribute of the history of Latin American procedure.[57]

5 The Twentieth Century and Contemporary Issues

5.1 *New Scientific Approaches, New Codes*

Since the last decades of the nineteenth century, the ideas of European positivist criminology began to spread in Latin America. The theories by Lombroso, Ferri, and Garofalo reoriented academic attention towards the study of crime and the delinquent as naturally or socially determined phenomena. This new approach prompted severe criticism of the liberal ideas that had inspired penal codification. In turn, it provided an allegedly 'scientific' explanation for their failure, evidenced by the perception of growing criminality and the glaring gap between liberal principles and effective practices. The racist episteme underpinning some of the new theories reinforced the prejudices of colonial times and provided an appropriate discourse to implement repressive policies based on dangerousness and racial discrimination. Subsequent medico-legal approaches encouraged the development of specific institutions for the surveillance, control, and treatment of potential criminals including members of the lower classes, ethnic groups, immigrants, and anarchists among others. Within this framework, penitentiaries acquired a new impulse as they became part 'of a common project aimed at normalizing, segregating, and correcting the subordinate.' However, due to regional economic and political circumstances, older prisons coexisted with modern penitentiaries.[58]

57 Alberto F. Binder 'La reforma de la justicia penal en América Latina como política de largo plazo' in *La reforma a la justicia en América Latina. Las lecciones aprendidas*, ed. Catalina Niño Guarnizo (Bogotá: Friedrich-Ebert-Stiftung, 2016), 53–103.

58 Robert M. Buffington, *Criminal and Citizen in Modern Mexico* (Lincoln: University of Nebraska Press, 2000); Zaffaroni, 'Los códigos penales de Latinoamérica,' 29, 76–77; Salvatore and Aguirre, 'The Birth of the Penitentiary,' 10; Ricardo Salvatore and Carlos Aguirre, 'Revisitando *El Nacimiento de la Penitenciaría en América Latina* veinte años después' (2017) 4 Revista de Historia de las Prisiones 7–42.

The reception of positivist criminology in criminal legislation was uneven. Its impact on scholarship and public policies is unquestionable, but it had a wavering influence in the new generation of penal codes. To a certain extent, positivist ideas meant altering the whole conceptual structure of criminal legal knowledge and abandoning deeply rooted tenets such as free will, not to speak of the legality principle and the separation of powers (as the treatment of criminals should be transferred onto police or expert boards). In this way, constitutional frameworks and institutional habits conditioned the legal impact of positive criminology. Thus, new codes based on 'the twofold notion of criminal liability and dangerousness' sought to harmonize liberal tenets with positivist claims for criminal treatment and social defense.[59] In line with the Stoos's draft (1893) for Switzerland, some new codes such as those of Argentina (1921) and Peru (1924), maintained the classical structure while introducing provisions related to positivist programs enunciating measures of security, indeterminate reclusion for recidivism, or dangerousness as a circumstance for graduating punishments or conceding conditional release.

A similar eclectic attitude is found in the new federal Mexican code of 1931, which replaced a recent one more committed to the positivist school of 1929.[60] By that time, the new Italian code of 1930, known as Rocco's Code, was also an expression of the 'two-track system.' Issued in the context of Italian fascism, it has been regarded as an expression of authoritarian criminal law.[61] While Ferri's positivist draft of 1921 had great influence on the codes enacted in Colombia (1936) and Cuba (1936, meaningfully titled Code of Social Defense), Rocco's text inspired new codes for Uruguay (1933) and Brazil (1940).[62] Despite his fascist inspiration, Rocco's methodological approach defined criminal law as a normative science in opposition to criminological perspectives. Some scholars have underlined Rocco's claims in support of a normative science, with an exegetical method, departed from the empirical sciences that had

59 Michele Pifferi, 'Global Criminology and National Tradition: The Impact of Reform Movements on Criminal Systems at the Beginning of the 20th Century' in *Entanglements in Legal History*, 543–564.

60 Speckman Guerra, *Del Tigre de Santa Julia*, 31–43.

61 Guido Neppi Modona 'Diritto e giustizia penale nel periodo fascista' in *Penale, Giustizia, Potere, Metodi, Ricerche, Storiografie: Per ricordare Mario Sbriccoli*, eds Luigi Lacchè, Carlotta Latini, Paolo Marchetti, and Massimo Meccarelli (Macerata, Università di Macerata, 2007), 341–378.

62 Zaffaroni, 'Los Códigos Penales de Latinoamérica,' 82, 90.

obscured (as had been the case of positivist criminology) the real task of criminal law jurist.[63]

Alongside Rocco's technical method, other Italian and Spanish scholars brought Latin American legal scholarship closer to German 'dogmatic' theories. In this process, the Spanish (exiled) jurist, Jimenez de Asúa has a prominent place. His translations into Spanish of von Liszt's works had begun as early as 1915. Thus, beyond his changing theoretical positions, he is said to have fostered a scientific revolution in criminal law studies in the Spanish-speaking world.[64] In Argentina, Sebastian Soler remarkably contributed to consolidate the 'German approach.' By 1929 he published a critical study against theories on 'the state of dangerousness'; in the following years, he translated into Spanish the works by Ernst von Beling. In 1940 Soler began publishing his treatise on penal law with the purpose of reinforcing respect for law through its 'dogmatic reconstruction.'[65] Five years later, in Caracas, appeared Jimenez de Asúa's 'Course on penal dogmatic.'[66]

An intense circulation of German theories would follow in later decades in Chile, México, Colombia, and Brazil. The consolidation of 'dogmatic' approaches by the mid-century led to a renewal of criminal law studies. In this context, between 1963 and 1979, several academic meetings, held in different countries, debated a project for a model *Latin American criminal code*. Though it never got official validity, it inspired reforms in Bolivia (1973), Panamá, and Central American countries. The debated drafts (1962, 1966) that preceded the German code of 1974 left their imprints in this process, whereas further developments of the German school influenced later Latin American reforms in codification in the decades of 1980–1990.[67]

Academic and legislative changes throughout the twentieth century ran parallel to, although not always in opposition to, political instability, coups d'état, and de facto governments. This involved, on the one hand, the enactment of numerous special laws and police regulations that strengthened provisions already contained in the codes to punish political crimes, as well as

63 Massimo Donini, 'El problema del método penal: de Arturo Rocco al Europeísmo judicial' (2011) 7 Revista Nuevo Foro Penal 76.

64 Enrique Bacigalupo Zapater, 'La recepción de la dogmática penal alemana en España y Latinoamérica' (2019) 2 InDret: Revista para el análisis del Derecho 1–22; Enrique Roldán Cañizares, *Luis Jiménez de Asúa: Derecho penal, República, Exilio* (Madrid: Dykinson, 2019).

65 Sebastián Soler, *Derecho Penal Argentino*, 5th ed. (Buenos Aires: Editora Argentina, 1992), prologue, v–x.

66 Luis Jiménez de Asúa, *La ley y el delito: Curso de dogmática penal* (Caracas: Editorial Andrés Bello, 1945).

67 Zaffaroni, 'Los Códigos Penales en Latinoamérica,' 91–97.

the application of martial law to the civilian population. On the other hand, in extreme cases, it meant deploying para-institutional practices that included illegal detentions, the systematic use of torture, and forced disappearance of persons. Repressive actions that breached any standard of the rule of law were justified through different versions of the national security doctrine.[68] These traumatic experiences, that in some cases continued up to the end of the century, would boost reforms aimed at preventing crimes against humanity. This historical background discourages any evolutionary reading. Still, we can outline some general features of Latin American criminal law in the twentieth century.

a) Despite the early irruption of positive criminology and its impact on scholarship and public policies, its influence on legal reforms was rather limited. From the third decade of the century on, legal studies and codes followed the trend of the dogmatic methods inspired by German, Italian, and Spanish scholars. Nonetheless, imprints of positive criminology persisted in some codified provisions, police regulations, and institutions created for research, prevention, and treatment of criminality.
b) Liberal principles recovered their theoretical relevance. They are enshrined in most constitutions, and criminal and procedural codes. They also involve provisions on the restrictive interpretation of criminal laws, forbidding application by analogy. Still, defective wording or the open texture of criminal definitions make their strict observance difficult. A certain degree of judicial discretion is lawfully admitted through provisions for aggravating or mitigating punishment within codified scales.
c) Gradually, the old wide-ranging catalog of penalties has been reduced to forms of imprisonment, fines, and disqualification. The generalization of penitentiary systems also contributed to the progressive abolition of the death penalty. By the end of the century, most countries had abolished the death penalty, persisting in some cases exclusively for wartime or within the military jurisdiction.
d) The American Convention on Human Rights (1969) that came into force in 1978 enshrined a set of guarantees regarding criminal justice, freedom from slavery, the right to a fair trial, and freedom from ex-post facto laws. It also set restrictive conditions on the death penalty, forbidding its extension 'to crimes to which it does not presently apply.' Likewise,

68 David Pion-Berlin, 'Latin American National Security Doctrines: Hard and Softline Themes' (1989) 15 Armed Forces & Society 411–429.

it stipulated that the death penalty 'shall not be reestablished in states that have abolished it' (art. 4, § 2–6). Reports and jurisprudence of the Inter-American Commission and Court of Human Rights have compelled reforms to improve state criminal justice systems, particularly in the aftermath of dictatorial governments. Among many protocols and additional conventions, those 'to Prevent and Punish Torture' (1987) and 'on Forced Disappearance of Persons' (1994) are noteworthy.

During the first half of the century as procedural law became a specialized field of legal studies, some procedural reforms were aimed at transforming the written inquisitive proceedings dominant in most countries. It was not until the 1980s that a movement driven by a network of intellectuals succeeded in promoting deeper procedural reforms. The objective was to design an accusatory model, based on oral trials, with adversarial control and the separation of the criminal investigation from the trial itself. In 1988, the Ibero-American Institute of Procedural Law elaborated a Model Code of Criminal Procedure, thus providing the main source for further procedural reforms. These reforms sought the dual purpose of improving efficiency of judicial systems and ensuring due process. They also prompted the adoption of alternative measures to punishment such as probations, plea bargain, and mediation. Different forms of jury trials were established in some cases (for instance, in several provinces in Argentina, Panamá, Nicaragua, El Salvador, Venezuela, and Bolivia).[69]

By the latest decades of the twentieth century, adopting a sociological perspective, a new 'critical criminology' showed how, behind the aseptic discourse of liberal law, the daily functioning of criminal justice selectively punished the lower classes, young people, and ethnic groups. Studies focused on prison conditions showed the failure of penitentiary systems denouncing overcrowding and mistreatment. Increasing rates of incarceration, the abuse of pre-trial detention, and delays in proceedings are still a matter of concern despite overall improvements in procedural laws.[70]

69 Máximo Langer, 'Revolution in Latin American Criminal Procedure: Diffusion of Legal Ideas from the Periphery' (2007) 55 American Journal of Comparative Law 617–676; Paul Hathazy, 'Punitivism with a Human Face: Criminal Justice Reformers' International and Regional Strategies and Penal-State Making in Argentina, Chile and Beyond' (2016) 48 Kriminologisches Journal 255–310; Andrés Harfuch and Cristian Penna, 'El juicio por jurados en el continente de América' (2018) 17 Sistemas Judiciales 21.

70 Eugenio R. Zaffaroni, *En busca de las penas perdidas. Deslegitimación y dogmática jurídico-penal* (Buenos Aires: Ediar, 2003); *Postneoliberalismo y penalidad en América del Sur*, ed. Máximo Sozzo (Buenos Aires: CLACSO, 2016).

5.2 *Contemporary Challenges*

Current developments in scholarship and legal reforms show contradictory trends. On the one hand, different versions of the 'dogmatic approach' have consolidated their role in legal analysis and teaching. On the other hand, phenomena such as terrorism, organized crime, and drug trafficking have promoted reforms that rely much more on policing aims of security and order than on liberal law tenets. In this sense, the notion of *policification* of criminal law, coined to highlight 'the dominance of police over law as model of penal governance,' is useful to describe our regional trends.[71] Besides, the proliferation of special laws passed to face new forms of criminality and increase punishments have led scholars to speak of de-codification, chaos, and inflation of criminal law.[72]

International legislation on human rights has also influenced this process, creating a new stage of multi-normativity that departs from the ideal of homogeneous national law. Regarding criminal law, the Inter-American system of Human Rights has had two opposite effects. On the one hand, it has reinforced citizens' guarantees curtailing the state's punitive power; on the other, it has compelled states to prosecute and punish human rights violations, stating that 'all amnesty' or 'provisions on statute of limitations' are inadmissible when they are intended to prevent punishment 'for serious human rights violations' (Barrios Altos v. Peru, 2001). Some scholars have pointed out that this kind of statements, other than expanding criminal law and judicial activism, undermine liberal guarantees and states' sovereignty.[73] Similar criticisms arose against the principle of universal jurisdiction derived from the Conventions on the crime of genocide (1948) and on War Crimes and Crimes Against Humanity (1968). Nonetheless, those standards have made it possible to, for example, try and punish crimes against humanity committed by military governments in Argentina, and to start prosecutions in other countries for the same reasons.[74]

Other postmodern developments have contributed to transform the idealized image of liberal criminal law. Consider the impact of gender perspectives in promoting the decriminalization of conducts related to sexual morality,

---

71 Dubber, 'European Criminal Law,' 1069–1070.

72 Daniel R. Pastor, *Recodificación penal y principio de reserva de código* (Buenos Aires: Ad-Hoc, 2005).

73 Ezequiel Malarino, 'Judicial Activism, Punitivism and Supranationalisation: Illiberal and Antidemocratic Tendencies of the Inter-American Court of Human Rights,' (2012) 12 International Criminal Law Review 665–695.

74 As examples of opposing views on this topic, see Malarino, 'Judicial Activism,' 665–695; Gabriel Pérez Barberá and Alejandro Agüero, 'Contrapunitivismo y neopunitivismo. Perspectiva histórica y moral' (2012) 2(2) Derecho Penal y Criminología 249–263.

on the one hand, and in passing new criminal types linked to gender-related offenses, on the other. By the Convention of Belem Do Para (1994), the States Parties agreed to pass provisions to prevent, to punish, and to eradicate violence against women (art. 7). Moreover, states must adopt measures to modify cultural patterns and practices based on the stereotyped roles for men and women that legitimize violence against women (art. 8, §b). By 2018, eighteen countries in the region have modified their penal codes or adopted special laws to punish femicide and other forms of gender violence.[75] Most importantly, the gender perspectives involve a need for reinterpreting the whole legal order to the extent that it was produced in a context in which patriarchy was a naturalized trait. Still, eradication of gender violence remains a pending issue, as is decriminalizing abortion, a subject of current reforms in some regions (Argentina, Chile, Uruguay, Mexico DF, Oaxaca).

Multiculturalism and decolonization represent other significative challenges to the liberal conception of criminal law. Since the mid-twentieth century, international law instruments have recognized Indigenous peoples' rights to self-determination and cultural identity. Regarding criminal law, Convention 169 of the International Labor Organization (1989) stated that in applying national laws to Indigenous and tribal peoples 'due regard shall be had to their customs or customary laws.' It also states that their customary methods 'for dealing with offences committed by their members shall be respected' (to the extent they are compatible with the national legal system and human rights). Moreover, it provides that 'in imposing penalties laid down by general law on members of these peoples, account shall be taken of their economic, social and cultural characteristics,' and that 'preference shall be given to methods of punishment other than confinement in prison' (art. 10). In parallel, many constitutions in the region have assumed the pluricultural and multiethnic composition of the nations (Bolivia, Colombia, Ecuador, Guatemala, México, Nicaragua, Panamá, Paraguay, Peru, and Venezuela).[76]

The UN Declaration on the Rights of Indigenous Peoples (2007) meant a decisive step in this process. It enshrines the right to promote, to develop, and to maintain Indigenous peoples' institutional structures and traditions and, in the cases where they exist, their juridical systems or customs under

75 Alicia Deus and Diana Gonzalez, *Analysis of Femicide/Feminicide Legislation in Latin-America and the Caribbean and a Proposal for a Model Law*, UN-Women Report 2018: https://lac.unwomen.org/en/digiteca/publicaciones/2018/12/analisis-legislacion-feminicidio-femicidio-modelo-de-ley.

76 S. James Anaya, *Indigenous Peoples in International Law* (Oxford: Oxford University Press, 2004).

international human rights standards (art. 34). Jurists trained in the Western tradition have shown reluctance to recognize Indigenous jurisdiction in criminal matters.[77] Conditions, however, have been set for the development of plural legal systems, giving rise to different experiences ranging from limited jurisdictions to settle intra-ethnic disputes under state supervision to autonomous Indigenous jurisdictions as a part of plurinational state organizations (Ecuador 2008, and Bolivia 2009). Still, to what extent it is possible to harmonize Indigenous peoples' rights with dominant western-colonial conceptions on constitutional law and human rights is a question that remains open.[78]

References

Agüero, Alejandro, and Marta Lorente. 'Penal Enlightenment in Spain: From Beccaria's Reception to the First Criminal Code.' In *The Spanish Enlightenment Revisited*, edited by Jesús Astigarraga, 235–264. Oxford: The Voltaire Foundation, 2015.

Agüero, Alejandro. *Castigar y perdonar cuando conviene a la república: La justicia penal de Córdoba del Tucumán, siglos XVII y XVIII*. Madrid: Centro de Estudios Políticos y Constitucionales, 2008.

Aguirre, Carlos, and Ricardo Salvatore. 'Writing the History of Crime, Law, and Punishment in Latin America.' In *Crime and Punishment in Latin America: Law and Society Since Late Colonial Times*, edited by Ricardo D. Salvatore, Carlos Aguirre, and Gilbert Joseph, 1–32. Durham: Duke University Press, 2001.

Anaya, S. James. *Indigenous Peoples in International Law*. Oxford: Oxford University Press, 2004.

Bacigalupo Zapater, Enrique. 'La recepción de la dogmática penal alemana en España y Latinoamérica.' *InDret* 2 (2019): 1–22.

Binder, Alberto F. 'La reforma de la justicia penal en América Latina como política de largo plazo.' In *La reforma a la justicia en América Latina: las lecciones aprendidas*, edited by Catalina Niño Guarnizo, 53–103. Bogotá: Friedrich-Ebert-Stiftung, 2016.

Borah, Woodrow. *Justice by Insurance: The General Indian Court of Colonial Mexico and the Legal Aides of the Half-Real*. Berkeley: University of California Press, 1983.

Buffington, Robert M. *Criminal and Citizen in Modern Mexico*. Lincoln: University of Nebraska Press, 2000.

77 Idón Moisés Chivi Vargas, 'El largo camino de la jurisdicción indígena' in *Justicia indígena, plurinacionalidad e interculturalidad en Bolivia*, eds Boaventura de Sousa Santos and José Luis Exeni Rodríguez (Quito: Fundación Rosa Luxemburg/Abya-Yala, 2012), 275–379.

78 Bartolomé Clavero, *Derecho de otras gentes entre genocidio y constitucionalidad* (Santiago de Chile: Olejnik, 2019).

Casagrande, Agustín. *Gobierno de la Justicia, poder de policía. La construcción oeconómica del orden social en Buenos Aires (1776–1829)*. Valencia: Tirant lo Blanch, 2018.

Cordero Fernández, Macarena. *Institucionalizar y desarraigar: Las visitas de idolatrías en la Diócesis de Lima, siglo XVII*. Lima: Instituto Riva-Agüero, 2016.

Cutter, Charles. *The Legal Culture of Northern New Spain 1700–1810*. Albuquerque: University of New Mexico Press, 1995.

Cutter, Charles. *The Protector de Indios in Colonial New Mexico, 1659–1821*. Albuquerque: University of New Mexico Press, 1986.

Dubber, Markus D. 'European Criminal Law in the Nineteenth and Twentieth Centuries.' In *The Oxford Handbook of European Legal History*, edited by Heikki Pihlajamäki, Markus Markus D. Dubber, and Mark Godfrey, 1052–1072. Oxford: Oxford University Press, 2018.

Griffiths, Nicholas. *The Cross and the Serpent: Religious Repression and Resurgence in Colonial Peru*. Norman: University of Oklahoma Press, 1996.

Herzog, Tamar. *Upholding Justice: Society, State and the Penal System in Quito, 1650–1750*. Ann Arbor: University of Michigan Press, 2004.

Hespanha, Antonio M. *La gracia del derecho Economía de la cultura en la Edad Moderna*. Madrid: Centro de Estudios Constitucionales, 1993.

Langer, Máximo. 'Revolution in Latin American Criminal Procedure: Diffusion of Legal Ideas from the Periphery.' *American Journal of Comparative Law* 55(4) (2007): 617–676.

Masferrer, Aniceto. 'The Myth of French Influence over Spanish Codification: The General Part of the Criminal Codes of 1822 and 1844.' In *The Western Codification of Criminal Law: A Revision of the Myth of its Predominant French Influence*, edited by Aniceto Masferrer, 193–242. Cham: Springer, 2018.

Mirow, M.C. *Latin American Constitutions: The Constitution of Cádiz and Its Legacy in Spanish America*. Cambridge: University of Cambridge Press, 2015.

Mirow, M.C. *Latin American Law: A History of Private Law and Institutions in Spanish America*. Austin: University of Texas Press, 2004.

Mirow, M.C. 'The Legality Principle and the Constitution of Cádiz.' In *From the Judge's Arbitrium to the Legality Principle: Legislation as a Source of law in Criminal Trials*, edited by Georges Martyn, Anthony Musson, and Heikki Pihlajamäki, 189–205. Berlin: Duncker & Humblot, 2013.

Novoa, Mauricio. *The Protectors of Indians in the Royal Audience of Lima: History, Careers and Legal Culture, 1575–1775*. Leiden: Brill, 2016.

Pike, Ruth. *Penal Servitude in Early Modern Spain*. Madison: University of Wisconsin Press, 1983.

Speckman Guerra, Elisa. *Del Tigre de Santa Julia, la princesa italiana y otras historias: Sistema judicial, criminalidad y justicia en la ciudad de México, siglos XIX–XX*. México: Instituto Nacional de Ciencias Penales, 2014.

Taylor, William B. *Drinking, Homicide, and Rebellion in Colonial Mexican Villages.* Stanford: Stanford University Press, 1979.

Uribe, Víctor M. 'Colonial Lawyers, Republican Lawyers and the Administration of Justice in Spanish America.' In *Judicial Institutions in Nineteenth-Century Latin America*, edited by Eduardo Zimmermann, 25–48. London: Institute of Latin American Studies, 1999.

Uribe-Uran, Victor M. *Fatal Love: Spousal Killers, Law and Punishment in the Late Colonial Spanish Atlantic.* Stanford: Stanford University Press, 2016.

Yannakakis, Yanna. 'Indigenous People and Legal Culture in Spanish America.' *History Compass* 11 (2013): 931–947.

Zaffaroni, Eugenio R. 'Los códigos penales de Latinoamérica.' In *Códigos penales de los países de América Latina*, edited by Suprema Corte de Justicia de la Nación de México, 15–35. México: ILANUD, 2000.

Zaffaroni, Eugenio R., Alejandro Alagia, and Alejandro Slokar. *Manual de Derecho Penal: Parte General.* Buenos Aires: Ediar, 2007.

CHAPTER 18

Filiation, Marriage, Family, and Domestic Conflicts

Victor M. Uribe-Uran

This chapter considers the legal history of family formation and marriage, family relations, and family conflicts in both colonial and modern Latin America and the Caribbean. First, it must be noticed that the history of colonial Latin American and Caribbean families and family relations came of age in the mid-1980s, following the footsteps of research published a few years before by American and Latin American scholars on topics such as the history of slavery,[1] demography,[2] landownership and business,[3] power networks,[4] sexuality,[5] and the institution of marriage itself.[6] Pioneering research done after 1985,

---

1 Verena Martínez-Alier, *Marriage, Class and Colour in Nineteenth-Century Cuba: A Study of Racial Attitudes and Sexual Values in a Slave Society* (Cambridge: Cambridge University Press, 1974).

2 Silvia Arrom, 'Marriage Patterns in Mexico City, 1811' (1978) 3(4) Journal of Family History 23–36; *Studies in Spanish American Population History*, ed. David Robinson (Boulder: Westview Press, 1981); Robert McCaa, *Marriage and Fertility in Chile: Demographic Turning Points in the Petorca Valley, 1840–1976* (Boulder: Westview Press, 1983); Robert McCaa, 'Calidad, Clase, and Marriage in Colonial Mexico: The Case of Parral, 1788–1790' (1984) 64(3) Hispanic American Historical Review 477–501.

3 David Brading, *Miners and Merchants in Bourbon Mexico, 1763–1810* (Cambridge: Cambridge University Press, 1971); Charles H. Harris III, *A Mexican Family Empire: The Latifundio of the Sánchez Navarros, 1765–1867* (Austin: University of Texas Press, 1975); Susan M. Socolow, *The Merchants of Buenos Aires 1778–1810: Family and Commerce* (Cambridge: Cambridge University Press, 1978); Ann Twinam, *Miners, Merchants, and Farmers in Colonial Colombia* (Austin: University of Texas Press, 1982); John E. Kicza, *Colonial Entrepreneurs: Families and Business in Bourbon Mexico City* (Albuquerque: University of New Mexico Press, 1983).

4 Diana Balmori, Stuart F. Voss, and Miles Wortman, *Notable Family Networks in Latin America* (Chicago: University of Chicago Press, 1984).

5 Serge Gruzinski, 'Matrimonio y sexualidad en México y Texcoco en los albores de la conquista o la pluralidad de los discursos' in *Seis ensayos sobre el discurso colonial relativo a la comunidad doméstica*, ed. Solange Alberro (México: INAH, 1980), 16–74; *Simposio de Historia de las Mentalidades: Familia y Sexualidad en Nueva España*, INAH (México: Fondo de Cultura Económica, 1982).

6 Silvia Arrom, *La mujer mexicana ante el divorcio eclesiástico, 1800–1857* (México City: SepSetentas, 1976); Daisy Rípodas Ardanaz, *El matrimonio en Indias: Realidad social y regulación jurídica* (Buenos Aires: Fundación para la Educación, la Ciencia y la Cultura, 1977); Maria Beatriz Nizza da Silva, *Sistema de casamento no Brasil colonial* (Sao Paulo: Editoria da Universidade de São Paulo, 1984). For a historiographical essay produced at the time see Elizabeth Kuznesof and Robert Oppenheimer, 'The Family and Society in Nineteenth-Century

 | DOI:10.1163/9789004436091_020

gradually put marriage, family, sexuality and related relations and conflicts at the center of historical debates concerning not only racial relations, population trends, economic relations, culture, political power, and daily life in colonial and modern Latin America but also law and justice.

Whereas at least some authors had previously embraced an institutional perspective, addressing in particular the legal dimensions of marriage, as Argentine Daisy Rípodas Ardanaz and Brazilian Beatriz Niza da Silva did in their seminal works of 1977 and 1984 respectively, a new wave of mature historical works touched on law and justice but privileged social and cultural aspects.[7] Eventually, another surge of innovative research combined more

---

Latin America: An Historiographical Introduction' (1985) 10(3) Journal of Family History 215–234.

7 Silvia Arrom, *The Women of Mexico City, 1790–1857* (Stanford: Stanford University Press, 1985); Sergio Ortega, *De la santidad a la perversión, o de porqué no se cumplía la ley de Dios en la sociedad novohispana* (México: Grijalbo, 1986); Elizabeth Kuznesof, *Household Economy and Urban Development: Sao Paulo, 1765 to 1836* (Boulder: Westview Press, 1986); *Mulheres, adúlteros e padres: história e moral na sociedade brasileira*, eds Lana Lage da Gama Lima and Raymundo Paula de Arruda (Rio de Janeiro: Dois Pontos Editora, 1987); Linda Lewin, *Politics and Parentela in Paraiba: A Case Study of Family-Based Oligarchy in Brazil* (Princeton: Princeton University Press, 1987); Sandra Lauderdale Graham, *House and Street: The Domestic World of Servants and Masters in Nineteenth-Century Rio de Janeiro* (Cambridge: Cambridge University Press, 1988); Patricia Seed, *To Love, Honor and Obey in Colonial Mexico: Conflicts over Marriage Choice, 1574–1821* (Stanford: Stanford University Press, 1988); Asunción Lavrin, 'Sexuality in Colonial Mexico: A Church Dilemma' in *Sexuality and Marriage in Colonial Latin America*, ed. Asunción Lavrin (Lincoln: University of Nebraska Press, 1989), 47–92; Carmen Castañeda García, *Violación, estupro y sexualidad: Nueva Galicia, 1790–1821* (Guadalajara: Editorial Hexágono, 1989); Eduardo Cavieres F. and René Salinas Meza, *Amor, sexo y matrimonio en Chile tradicional: La sociedad colonial vista desde la vida cotidiana* (Valparaíso: Instituto de Historia Universidad Católica de Valparaíso, 1991); Alexandra Parma Cook and Noble D. Cook, *Good Faith and Truthful Ignorance: A Case of Transatlantic Bigamy* (Durham: Duke University Press, 1991); Ramon Gutiérrez, *When Jesus Came, the Corn Mothers Went Away: Marriage, Sexuality, and Power in New Mexico, 1500–1846* (Stanford: Stanford University Press, 1991); Muriel Nazzari, *Disappearance of the Dowry: Women, Families, and Social Change in São Paulo, Brazil, 1600–1900* (Stanford: Stanford University Press, 1992); Ana Maria Alonso, *Thread of Blood: Gender, Colonialism and Revolution on Mexico's Northern Frontier* (Tucson: University of Arizona Press, 1995); Richard Boyer, *Lives of the Bigamists: Marriage, Family and Community in Colonial Mexico* (Albuquerque: University of New Mexico Press, 1995); Steve J. Stern, *The Secret History of Gender: Women, Men and Power in Late Colonial Mexico* (Chapel Hill: University of North Carolina Press, 2000); Richard C. Trexler, *Sex and Conquest: Gendered Violence, Political Order, and the European Conquest of the Americas* (Ithaca: Cornell University Press, 1995); *Sentimientos y Vida Familiar en el Nuevo Reino de Granada*, ed. Pablo Rodríguez (Bogotá: Editorial Ariel, 1997); Pilar Gonzalbo Aizpuru, 'Violencia y discordia en las relaciones personales en la ciudad de México a fines del siglo XVIII' (2001) Historia Mexicana 233–259; Clara López Beltrán, *Alianzas familiares: Élite, género y negocios en La Paz, s. XVII* (Perú: Instituto de Estudios Peruanos, 1998); *The Faces*

evenly the two dimensions, the legal/judicial and sociocultural, yielding a picture more comprehensive yet nuanced than we had ever had before.[8] An additional layer added to this combined socio-legal history involved the discussion of domestic violence and divorce, angles that had received little attention and to this day continue to require further exploration.[9] For the sake of clarity,

---

of Honor: Sex, Shame and Violence in Colonial Latin America, eds Lyman Johnson and Sonya Lipsett-Rivera (Albuquerque: University of New Mexico Press, 1999); Susan M. Socolow, *The Women of Colonial Latin America* (Cambridge: Harvard University Press, 2000).

8 Susan Kellogg, *Law and the Transformation of Aztec Culture, 1500–1700* (Norman: University of Oklahoma Press, 1995); Ann Twinam, *Public Lives, Private Secrets: Gender, Honor, Sexualty, and Illegitimacy in Colonial Spanish America* (Stanford: Stanford University Press, 1999); Ann Twinam, *Purchasing Whiteness: Pardos, Mulattos, and the Quest for Social Mobility in the Spanish Indies* (Stanford: Stanford University Press, 2015); Linda Lewin, *Surprise Heirs II: Illegitimacy, Inheritance Rights, and Public Power in the Formation of Imperial Brazil, 1822–1900* (Stanford: Stanford University Press, 2003); Arlene Díaz, *Female Citizens: Patriarchs and the Law in Venezuela, 1786–1904* (Lincoln: Nebraska University Press, 2004); Ana Lidia García Peña, *El fracasodel amor: Género e individualismo en el siglo XIX mexicano* (México: El Colegio de México, 2006); Catalina Villegas del Castillo, *Del hogar a los juzgados: Reclamos familiares en los juzgados superiores en el tránsito de la Colonia a la República, 1800–1850* (Bogotá: Universidad de los Andes, 2006); Nara Milanich, *Children of Fate: Childhood, Class, and the State in Chile, 1850–1930* (Durham: Duke University Press, 2009); Kimberly Gauderman, *Women's Lives in Colonial Quito* (Austin: University of Texas Press, 2003); Chad Thomas Black, *The Limits of Gender Domination: Women, the Law and Political Crisis in Quito, 1765–1830* (Albuquerque: University of New Mexico Press, 2010); Laura M. Shelton, *For Tranquility and Order: Family and Community in Mexico's Northern Frontier, 1800–1850* (Tucson: University of Arizona Press, 2010); Camillia Cowling, *Conceiving Freedom: Women of Color, Gender and the Abolition of Slavery in Havana and Rio de Janeiro* (Chapel Hill: North Carolina University Press, 2013); Nicole von Germeten, *Violent Delights, Violent Ends: Sex, Race, and Honor in Colonial Cartagena de Indias* (Albuquerque: University of New Mexico Press, 2013); Sarah Chambers, *Families in War and Peace: Chile from Colony to Nation* (Durham: Duke University Press, 2015); Michelle McKinley, *Fractional Freedoms: Slavery, Intimacy, and Legal Mobilization in Colonial Lima, 1600–1700* (Cambridge: Cambridge University Press, 2016).

9 Christine Hunefeldt, *Liberalism in the Bedroom: Quarreling Spouses in Nineteenth-Century Lima* (University Park: Pennsylvania State University Press, 2000); Eugenia Rodríguez Sáenz, *Hijas, novias y esposas: familia, matrimonio y violencia doméstica en el Valle Central de Costa Rica (1750–1850)* (Heredia: Editorial de la Universidad Nacional, 2000); Viviana Kluger, *Escenas de la vida conyugal: los conflictos matrimoniales en la sociedad virreinal rioplatense* (Buenos Aires: Ed. Quorum, 2003); Tanja Christiansen, *Disobedience, Slander, Seduction and Assault: Women and Men in Cajamarca, Peru, 1862–1900* (Austin: University of Texas Press, 2004); Francisca Rengifo, *Vida conyugal, maltrato y abandono: El divorcio eclesiástico en Chile, 1850–1890* (Santiago de Chile: Centro de Investigaciones Diego Barrios Arana (DIBAN): Editorial Universitaria, 2011); Nicholas A. Robins, *Of Love and Loathing: Marital Life, Strife, and Intimacy in the Colonial Andes, 1750–1825* (Lincoln: University of Nebraska Press, 2015); Victor M. Uribe-Uran, *Fatal Love: Spousal Killers, Law and Punishment in the Late Colonial Spanish Atlantic* (Stanford: Stanford University Press, 2015); Bianca Premo, *Enlightenment on Trial: Ordinary Litigants and Colonialism in the Spanish Empire* (Oxford: Oxford University Press, 2017).

the discussion below follows a life cycle approach whereby the legal history of family relations will be examined chronologically, that is from inception to rupture, looking also at antecedents and processes in between family formation and its dissolution.

1 Sex and Procreation before Marriage

For over three decades comprehensive historical research has established that in Spanish America and Brazil since colonial times intimate sexual relations between men and women predating marriage, or taking place on its side, were plentiful and had all kinds of legal consequences and judicial ramifications, even more so if offspring resulted from them. A series of pioneering works explored the frequency with which single parents gave birth to illegitimate offspring, *hijos naturales* (in Brazil, *filhos naturais*); or, a married parent, to illegitimate children out of wedlock, *hijos adulterinos*. In the case of parents who refused to identify themselves, such spurious children could be designated in baptismal records as foundling or abandoned, *hijos expósitos* or of unknown parentage, *de padres no conocidos*, or unknown, *desconocidos*.[10] In Portuguese and Brazilian law the latter, children of a publicly unknown father, were designated *quaesitos*. Finally, if the father of any illegitimate children happened to be a priest, the offspring carried perhaps the greatest dishonor and were legally known as *hijos sacrilegos*.[11]

Some of the sexual transgressions addressed in the historical works available about colonial times, by the authors listed and others, took the form of clandestine consensual unions and cohabitation among single folk. In Portuguese legal culture such informal conjugal unions were known as *mancebia* and were widely tolerated and acceptable since, in many instances, they occurred

10 In the early seventeenth-century Lima even created the *Casa de Niños Expósitos*, a special institution to house abandoned white children. By the mid-seventeenth century a school to educate the female ones (*expósitas*) was also created. See Emma Mannarelli, *Private Passions and Public Sins: Men and Women in Seventeenth-Century Lima*, translated by Sidney Evans and Meredith D. Dodge (Albuquerque: University of New Mexico Press, 2007), 153–154, 160–168.

11 Ann Twinam, 'Honors, Sexuality, and Illegitimacy in Colonial Spanish America' in *Sexuality and Marriage in Colonial Latin America*, ed. Asunción Lavrin (Lincoln: University of Nebraska Press, 1989), 118–155; Ann Twinam, 'Honors, Sexuality'; Maria Mannarelli, *Private Passions and Public*; Guiomar Dueñas-Vargas, *Los hijos del pecado: Ilegitimidad y vida familiar en la Santafé de Bogotá colonial* (Bogotá: Editorial Universidad Nacional de Colombia, 1997); Lewin, *Surprise Heirs II*.

due to canonical impediments for the parents to marry or their reluctance to contravene social or racial boundaries.[12] Other sexual transgressions resulted rather from occasional sex extracted by means of abduction (*rapto de seducción*) or elopement, whether under the pretense of an imminent marriage or not. Even more common was sex obtained through unfulfilled marriage promises, a sexual criminal violation known as *estrupro*. Yet other transgressions, the ones involving a married person and a lover, might have constituted the crime of *adulterio*, but only if the unfaithful spouse happened to be a woman.[13] Unfaithful husbands could not be accused of adultery, a clear expression of dominant patriarchal principles, legal and otherwise. For instance, several laws in the *Siete Partidas*, a renowned legal text originally issued in the thirteenth century (1251–1265) and based on Roman, canon, and feudal law, dealt with marriage-related criminal behaviors, including adultery. They made clear that this conduct only harmed married men and the female culprit's close kin and, therefore, only these men (the woman's husband, father, brothers, and uncles) could denounce it because only they suffered 'damage' (*daño*) and 'dishonor' (*desonrra*).[14] As a result, for example, a husband had the right to kill the man he found in bed with his wife. However, unlike the woman's father, who could kill both lovers, the husband could not kill her but had to let judges handle the matter. Justice officials would flog the offender and lock her in a convent for no less than two years, even for life. In addition, she would lose her wedding tokens (*arras*) and dowry, which would revert to the husband.[15]

Apart from the consequences of illegitimacy in terms of a person's diminished social hierarchy and lower stratification, and blemished public morality and honor, values of considerable significance in colonial times, inheritance and their distribution suffered direct impact as well. In Spanish America during early colonial times, for example, children of unknown parents could not inherit entailed estates (*mayorazgos*) or estates and could not have one established in their name. Those born out of wedlock could not inherit *encomiendas*, neither could they succeed to a *mayorazgo* without a father's express stipulation which was also required for them to use his surname or coat of arms. A noble father's natural children could inherit his estate only

12 Ibid., vol. 1.

13 *Recopilación de leyes de estos reinos*, 3 vols. Lib. 8, tit. 20 (Madrid, 1723), vol. 2, 347.

14 Credit for its enactment went to King Alfonso X of Castile, who was unable to enforce it at the time, however, due to noble resistance. See 'Siete Partidas,' Partida 7, Tit. XVII, Ley 1 and 2, in *Códigos Antigüos de España*, ed. Marcelo Martínez Alcubilla (Madrid: J. López Camacho Impresor, 1895), vol. 1, 645.

15 Ibid., Ley 13, 14 and 15, vol. 1, 647.

if they enjoyed his recognition and social position.[16] However, in Brazil, once natural offspring received recognition, frequently within a will, they enjoyed equal succession rights, except that for this to happen, those of noble parents had to be legitimated directly by the crown.[17]

Besides potential criminal accusations and effects on property rights, another major legal dimension worth addressing concerns avenues for illegitimate offspring to gain recognition. An intriguing legal situation in Spanish America, especially by the eighteenth century, consisted of the opportunity for illegitimates to embark on lengthy and costly administrative proceedings before the Council of the Indies to request a royal dispensation (*cédula de gracias al sacar*). With it, qualified petitioners could change their birth status and receive legitimation through the payment of a special fee, thus enhancing prospects to restore their honor, improve their social standing or public condition, and have greater prospects for social mobility, for themselves or their descendants, through better marriages, public appointments, and access to a university or the sacred orders. For example, Twinam provides a masterful analysis of social, cultural, and legal aspects surrounding colonial illegitimacy, that also examines in detail the history of applications for royal legitimation in Spanish America, highlights the tensions between private realities and public reputation, and establishes the centrality of law and justice to broker and overcome such conflicts.[18]

Two other circumstances making it possible to change one's illegitimate status were a consequence of voluntary acts from both parents, or one of them. First was the case of the parents' subsequent marriage, not uncommonly deathbed marriage, as a mechanism to legitimize illegitimate offspring.[19] The second consisted of fathers who had refused to do so formally before but eventually recognized their illegitimate children when they made their wills, thus transforming them into natural descendants. Both instances gave newly legitimized children the opportunity to gain access to inherit a particular bequest or, in the case of non-testamentary or *ab intestato* succession, a portion of the parents' property, except in the case of Spanish America certainly a restricted share relative to that of their legitimate half-siblings, if there were any.[20] Other than voluntary recognition, the possibility for offspring to demand the judicial

16 Mannarelli, *Private Passions and Public Sins*, 74.

17 Lewin, *Surprise Heirs II*, vol. 1.

18 Twinam, *Public Lives*.

19 Christiansen, *Disobedience*, 50.

20 Mannarelli, *Private Passions*, 11, 89–96; Christiansen, *Disobedience*, 50.

investigation of paternity was a more complicated proposition and would become yet more so in postcolonial times.

Despite continuing social obsession over honor, restrained female sexuality, and the preservation of virginity before marriage, premarital sex remained widespread after political independence from Spain. Studies of nineteenth-century Peru and Mexico, for example, have established that seduction of single women continued to be frequent, sometimes taking the customary form of *estupro*, elopement, *rapto* or bride stealing.[21] Whereas voluntary legitimation of offspring born out of such circumstances stayed as a possibility, one of the major legal transformations in postcolonial legal regimes was the closure of administrative avenues for offspring to request legitimation through the payment of special fees; or to demand judicial investigation of paternity to compel reluctant fathers to recognize them. This has been well established in, for example, the cases of Brazil and Chile.

In Brazil over the course of the nineteenth century the generous norms on heirship for natural offspring characteristic of the colonial period, gave way in 1847 to a more restricted system where succession rights became entirely dependent on paternal recognition before a notary prior to marriage. This made it virtually impossible for most natural offspring with legitimate half-siblings to become heirs in their father's *ab intestato* succession. In this way children of a publicly unknown father, the *quaesitos*, were effectively disinherited.[22] In Chile, also as a seemingly paradoxical result of the 'liberalization of kinship' the legal and social rights of illegitimate offspring were substantially eroded. Under the prevailing liberal logic illicit sex and illegitimate kinship were to be considered a 'private' subject and thus paternity investigations ('filiation suits') were eventually rendered illegal. Parental recognition became entirely a 'free and voluntary act' as of 1857.[23] The legally acceptable formation of family was through formal marriage.

2 Family Formation and Marriage in Colonial Society[24]

In colonial times there were two separate bodies of legislation on marriage and family/sexuality relations and conflicts. The first was royal or 'civil law,' enacted

21 Kathryn Sloan, *Runaway Daughters: Seduction, Elopement, and Honor in Nineteenth-Century Mexico* (Albuquerque: University of New Mexico Press, 2008); Christiansen, *Disobedience*, 50.

22 Lewin, *Surprise Heirs II*, vol. 2, XIII, 303.

23 Millanich, *Children of Fate*, Chapter 1.

24 Portions of the text in the following sections come from Uribe-Uran, *Fatal Love*, Chapter 1.

by the crown and thus secular. The other, canon law, originated in the Catholic Church and had a religious character. It was made up of the orders, rules, and commentaries – variously referred to as bulls or briefs, edicts, decrees, letters, sanctions, constitutions, and laws – issued by popes, councils (meetings of the high clergy, especially archbishops and bishops, of an ecclesiastical province), diocesan synods (meetings of the priests and clerics of a diocese, presided over by their bishop), archbishops and bishops. The most important collections of ecclesiastical regulations (the *Decretum* of Gratian, *Decretals* of Gregory IX, and Boniface VIII's *Sextus* or *Liber Sextus Decretalium*) were compiled in the twelfth and thirteenth centuries. The Council of Trent (1545–1563) introduced major additions and reforms dealing particularly with various aspects of marriage, especially the formalization of its sacramental nature, its indissoluble character, the exclusion of priests from contracting it, the series of impediments hindering or dissolving it, and the exclusive jurisdiction of ecclesiastical authorities over all matters pertaining to it. Similar other ecumenical councils (meetings of the bishops of the world, presided over by the Pope), provincial councils, and diocesan synods produced other relevant additions and binding commentaries to canon law.[25]

Spain, Portugal, and their American domains commonly observed and enforced all the laws and regulations made or adopted by ecclesiastical authorities, and lawyers and priests studied them avidly. Law schools and ecclesiastical seminaries in the Iberian Peninsula and Spanish America systematically taught canon law.[26] The crown's authorities and its subjects recognized its legitimacy and were generally willing to uphold and follow its precepts. With the crown's acquiescence, and following the mandates of the Council of Trent, the church maintained registries (of births, baptisms, marriages, and deaths), authorities and institutions – not only missions, parish priests, bishops, and archbishops, but also ecclesiastical courts of justice. As early as the fifteenth century, the church also established the tribunals of the Inquisition, which, along with ecclesiastical judges, kept track of and policed the observance of canon law and other religious precepts throughout the kingdom. All these organs enforced legal prescriptions on marriage and other aspects of Christian life.

25 Rípodas Ardanas, *El matrimonio en Indias*; R.H. Helmholz, *The Spirit of Classical Canon Law* (Athens: University of Georgia Press, 1996); James Muldoon, *Canon Law, the Expansion of Europe, and World Order* (Aldershot: Ashgate, 1998).

26 Victor Uribe-Uran, *Honorable Lives: Lawyers, Family, and Politics in Colombia, 1780–1850* (Pittsburgh: University of Pittsburgh Press, 2000), Chapter 4.

In the words of any standard legal manual, marriage was a spiritual and legal bond, joining a man and a woman together for life. St. Paul arguably considered it to represent the union between divine and human nature.[27] In contrast to later Protestant views of marriage as a worldly institution, the Catholic Church's approach was founded on the late medieval notion of the marital union as one of the Seven Sacraments of Evangelical Law instituted by Jesus Christ, equivalent in significance to baptism, confirmation, the Holy Eucharist, orders, extreme unction, and confession.[28] All these sacraments were under the exclusive jurisdiction of the church, which regulated the various conditions and formalities of their attainment.

For instance, the church established the minimum legal age (fourteen for males, twelve for females) and mutual free consent of the parties contracting marriage; required both parties to have been previously admitted into the church through baptism; and precluded any impediments (i.e., consanguinity, affinity, a valid previous marriage, the killing of one's former spouse) to an intended marriage, prescribing the need for banns (public announcement of the names of the contracting parties in church during Mass by their own parish priest on three consecutive Holy Days) to learn if any such impediments existed. One of the main objectives of marriage was procreation, and husband and wife had the obligation to be faithful to each other and to always live together, for the church considered marriage 'perpetual and indissoluble.'[29] More important, canon law also stressed patriarchal (male) authority as the guiding principle of social life, marriage, and family relations. This fundamental 'truth,' allegedly based on divine will as expressed in biblical precepts, legitimated the differential treatment afforded to men and women, most evident, for example, with the inconsistent approach to battery.[30]

---

27 Archivo Histórico Nacional (hereafter AHN), Madrid, Consejos, Alcaldes de Casa y Corte, Legajo 9344, no folio.

28 Manuel Silvestre Martínez, *Librería de Jueces, Utilísima y Universal* (Madrid: Imprenta de la Comisaria de Cruzada, 1764–1772), 7 vols, 1–10.

29 *Council of Trent*, 'Doctrine and Canons.' Available at http://www.thecounciloftrent.com/ch24.htm.

30 Charles J. Reid Jr., *Power over the Body, Equality in the Family: Rights and Domestic Relations in Medieval Canon Law* (Grand Rapids: William B. Eerdmans Publishing Company, 2004), esp. Chapters 2 and 3; A. Brundage, *Law, Sex, and Christian Society in Medieval Europe* (Chicago: University of Chicago Press, 1987), 92, 115, 122, 236, 254; Marie A. Kelleher, *The Measure of Woman Law and Female Identity in the Crown of Aragon* (Philadelphia: University of Pennsylvania Press, 2010), 25–26; Domingo Cavallario, *Instituciones del Derecho Canónico* (Madrid Imprenta de Gómez Fuentenebro, 1843); Adhémar Esmein *Le mariage en droit canonique* (New York: Burt Franklin, 1968); Seed, *To Love, Honor, and Obey*; Ripodas Ardanas, *El matrimonio en Indias*.

Nevertheless, canon law was by nature controversial and malleable. Jurists offered diverse and at times conflicting interpretations of its prescriptions on marriage and heatedly debated the crown's authority to modify them and supervise the clergy in charge of enforcing them.[31] Over time, some exceptions (*privilegios* and *dispensas*) to the general requirements for entering marriage became possible. These were especially common in the case of the subaltern ethnic groups (blacks and Indians) that fell under the domination of Europeans during the fifteenth century. The exceptions were intended to facilitate unions blessed by the church among 'primitive' cultures.[32] Other significant changes concerned an opposite trend, greater restrictions to marry socially or racially inferior individuals. This was done, for instance, in 1778 through a Spanish royal order (Royal Pragmatic on Marriages) that gave parents more control over their children's marriage to maintain social and racial equality.[33] Some principles surrounding marriage remained absolute.

Patriarchal authority and indissolubility, for example, were absolute rules for everyone entering Catholic marriage, irrespective of social origin or cultural affiliation. The church regarded husbands as heads of family, dominant over wives, children, and others in the household. It also encouraged and ordered husband and wife to remain together for life, in good times and bad, 'in sickness and in health.' Members of the clergy, especially parish priests and confessors, received instructions to mediate to heal marital disagreements and reunite couples in distress. Still, conflictive marriages were not at all uncommon and many faced separation.

3 Domestic Violence, Divorce, and Civil Law Reform

Ecclesiastical judges frequently reviewed incidents of 'divorce' in colonial times.[34] Divorce was in practice a generic expression used at the time to refer

31 Even before the fourteenth-century *Ordenamiento de Alcalá*, the crown was understood to have *patronato* or supervision over the church and was entitled, for instance, to authorize the election of bishops and archbishops. See *Novisima Recopilación*, Book 1, tit. 17.

32 Juan de Solorzano y Pereyra, *Política indiana* (Madrid: Compañía Iberoamericana de Publicaciones, 1972), vol. 1, chapter 29; Paulino Castañeda, 'La Condición Miserable del Indio y sus Privilegios' (1971) 28 Anuario de Estudios Americanos 67–75; Ripodas Ardanas, *El matrimonio en Indias.*

33 Seed, *To Love, Honor and Obey.*

34 Kluger, *Escenas de la vida conyugal*; Silvia Mallo, 'Justicia, divorcio, alimentos y malos tratos en el Río de la Plata, 1766–1857' (1992) 42 Investigaciones y Ensayos 373–400; Mendoza, 1998; María Teresa Pita Moreda, 'Conflictos familiares y tribunales de justicia a finales de la colonia: algunos casos novohispanos' in *Familia y vida privada en la historia de*

to, on the one hand, petitions for annulment (divorce *quoad vinculum*), after which either spouse could usually marry someone else; and, on the other, requests for physical separation (divorce *quoad thorum et cohabitationem* or *quoad thorum et mensam*), also known as 'bed and table' divorce, which did not free spouses to enter into a new marriage but did at least legitimate their living apart.[35] The first type of divorce was based upon the demonstration that some essential requisite for a valid marriage such as free will, legal age, absence of kinship, no valid previous marriage, or baptism had been lacking. This was not thus generally related to domestic conflicts and violence, except in the case of attempts to marry an accomplice by someone guilty of having killed his/her former spouse.

The second type of divorce, physical separation involved domestic disputes of different types, some of which even culminated in a spouse's murder. For instance, *sevicia* or battery constituted a justifiable cause for physical separation from one's spouse and could help prevent more tragic results. Adultery and drinking could also lead to *quod thorum et mensam* divorce.[36]

According to contemporary legal and religious manuals that reflect the gender ideology and inequalities of the period, wives could file for ecclesiastical divorce only in cases of 'cruel and atrocious battery' (*malos tratamientos graves y atroces*). Both civil and canon law considered it permissible for a husband to practice 'discreet and moderate' or 'reasonable' punishment, but they did not provide a clear definition of these open-ended expressions. The provision allowed men to claim that they had merely been trying to 'correct' an unruly spouse and make her 'change her ways' (*enmendar*).[37] Furthermore,

---

Iberoamérica, eds Pilar Gonzalbo Aizpuru and Cecilia Rabell Romero (México: El Colegio de México, Universidad Nacional Autónoma de México, 1996), 341–358; Juan Javier Pescador, 'Entre la espada y el olvido: pleitos matrimoniales en el provisorato eclesiástico de México, siglo XVIII' in *La familia en el mundo iberoamericano*, eds Pilar Gonzalbo Aizpuru and Cecilia Rabell, 202–205 (Mexico City: UNAM, 1998), 202–205; René Salinas Meza, 'Uniones ilegítimas y desuniones legítimas. El matrimonio y la formación de la pareja en el Chile colonial' in *La familia en el mundo Iberoamericano*, eds Pilar Gonzalbo Aizpuru and Cecilia Rabell (México, UNAM, 1994), 173–192; Gonzalbo Aizpuru, 'Violencia y discordia,' 233–259; Arrom, *La mujer mexicana*.

35 Edward Behrend-Martínez, *Unfit for Marriage: Impotent Spouses on Trial in the Basque Region of Spain, 1650–1750* (Reno: University of Nevada Press, 2007), 1–10; Kluger, *Escenas de la vida conyugal*.

36 Lourdes Villafuerte García, Teresa Lozano Armendares, Sergio Ortega Noriega, and Rocío Ortega Soto, 'La sevicia y el adulterio en las causas matrimoniales en el Provisorato de México a fines de la era colonial. Un estudio de la técnica procesal jurídica' (2008) 38 Estudios de Historia Novohispana 91.

37 See AGN, Mexico, Criminal, Vol. 108, Case 10, fols. 264–277, esp. fol. 273.

for light battery to be a sufficient cause for divorce under canon law it had to be 'chronic' (*cotidiano*) and without any 'just cause,' both vague conditions.[38]

Limited though the possibilities for divorce may have been, evidence exists, for instance, of as many as 300 divorce petitions filed with Mexico City's ecclesiastical judge (*Provisor Eclesiastico*) in the eighteenth century. A telling number, ninety-four (31.3 percent of the total), were based on *malos tratos* inflicted by husbands against their wives. These cases represented only three-quarters of the battery-related divorce suits; the remaining quarter involved thirty-one husbands (10.3 percent of the total) who reported being verbally and physically abused by their wives, situations that were probably underrepresented in the records.[39] An average of just a little more than one abuse-related petition for divorce per year seems rather insignificant for as densely populated a region as central Mexico.[40] This figure most likely does not reflect the true magnitude of domestic conflicts but merely some of its extreme manifestations.

Unlike battery, which tended to be mainly a male offense, adultery had a broader meaning under canon law. Whereas royal law considered adultery a crime only when committed by females, under canon law either spouse could cite it as a reason for ecclesiastical divorce. In the eyes of the church, such behavior was a mortal sin irrespective of gender. Furthermore, from early on canon law opposed private vengeance (murder) against adulterous spouses, for it viewed adultery not as an offense against male honor but as a gender-neutral, individual sin that violated marital obligations. The behavior revealed the existence of lies, lust, infidelity, and a violation of a spouse's exclusive sexual power over his or her partner's body, part of the conjugal or marital debt (*debito*) that included the obligation to give one's spouse sex on demand.[41] Mexico City's archbishopric recorded forty-two of these allegations in the eighteenth century; wives filed twenty-three of them and husbands, the other nineteen. The

38 Francisco Antonio de Elizondo y Alvarez, *Practica universal forense de los tribunales de España y de las Indias*, 6th ed. (Madrid: Imprenta de Ramón Ruíz, 1796), 7 vols, vol. 1, 351, vol. 3, 359–361, vol. 7, 161–185.

39 Tomás Mantecón, 'Hogares infernales: una visión retrospectiva sobre la violencia doméstica en el mundo moderno' in *La familia en la historia*, ed. Francisco J. Lorenzo Pinar (Salamanca: Ediciones Universidad de Salamanca, 2009), 197.

40 Dora Teresa Dávila Mendoza, 'Hasta que la muerte nos separe (el divorcio eclesiástico en el arzobispado de México, 1702–1800)' PhD diss. (México: Departamento de Historia, Colegio de México, 1998), 236–237.

41 Thomas Sánchez, *Compendium Totius Tractatus de Sancto Matrimonij Sacramento* (Hispali ex officina Franciscum Lyra: vendese en casa de Francisco Toro, 1623), 3–6, 62–71; Brundage, *Law, Sex, and Christian Society*, 93, 241–248; Elizondo, *Practica universal forense*, vol. 7, 162; Lavrin, 'Sexuality in Colonial Mexico,' 72–80.

men in question seemed to be searching for a solution rather more peaceful than the one favored by longstanding codes of honor sanctioned into royal law; that is, the legitimate killing of wives caught having intercourse with their lovers. Archival records of adultery-related complaints reveal a low average number of annual petitions (0.4), but at least some instances were being tried. This almost never happened with drinking, another common form of misconduct.

Drinking was admissible grounds for divorce only if it was habitual and represented a 'grave danger' to the wife. Divorce requests were rarely, if ever, based upon this sole motive. More likely they resulted from the drinker's inability to provide for his family and/or problems with vagrancy.[42]

Divorce, therefore, was a potential remedy under canon law for some serious marital tensions and disputes. In practice, however, the provision was neither widely available to most people nor a popular means for resolving family feuds. Mediation by relatives, neighbors, priests, and civil authorities to discourage breakups, lack of money, insufficient access to legal advice, geographical obstacles, fear, or a combination of these circumstances made many spouses, especially modest Indian and peasant women, generally unwilling or unable to sue for divorce. They were more likely to use de facto remedies, including abandoning their spouses.

Despite ecclesiastical admonishments and *censura* (mainly excommunication) of spouses who separated informally, civil provisions ordering the reunification of estranged couples, and even criminal sanctions, abandonment was a common recourse in, for instance, late colonial Colombia, Mexico, and Spain.[43] In some instances, recurrent abandonment, followed by unification mandated by ecclesiastical or civil authorities or achieved under family mediation and persuasion, resulted in escalating tensions, even murder.[44]

More accessible and inexpensive than divorce was the option of denouncing one's spouse as a criminal to *justicias mayores* or local magistrates (*alcaldes* and *corregidores*).[45] Except in cases in which religious asylum was an issue,

---

42 Elizondo, *Practica universal forense*, vol. 7, 160–185; Juan Alvarez Posadilla, *Practica Criminal por Principios*, 3rd ed. (Madrid: En la Imprenta que fue de García, 1815 [1794]), vol. 3, 186–191; Brundage, *Law, Sex, and Christian Society*, 511.

43 René De La Pedraja, 'La mujer criolla y mestiza en la sociedad colonial, 1700–1830' (1984) 13 Desarrollo y Sociedad, 215–217; *Sentimientos y Vida Familiar*, 237–253; Dueñas-Vargas, *Los hijos del pecado*, 182–187; María Himelda Ramírez, *Las mujeres y la sociedad colonial de Santafé de Bogotá, 1750–1810* (Bogotá: Instituto Colombiano de Antropología e Historia, 2000), 151–160; Behrend-Martínez, *Unfit for Marriage*, 113; Catherine Komisaruk, *Labor and Love in Guatemala: The Eve of Independence* (Stanford: Stanford University Press, 2013), 192–196.

44 Uribe-Uran, *Fatal Love*.

45 Elizondo, *Practica universal forense*, vol. 3, 351.

many crimes were neither regulated by canon law nor investigated by ecclesiastical authorities, falling instead under the crown's own body of secular laws and judges who generally upheld patriarchal authority, and made manifest and 'natural' other contemporary social biases and hierarchies.

Mainly over the course of the nineteenth century marriage underwent a significant transformation in Latin America: its secularization. This corresponded to the general weakening of the church after independence through, among others, the abolition of the tithe, a key source of ecclesiastical revenue, and the closure of small convents and monasteries. The main expression of the new trend was the recognition of civil marriage as indispensable for a union to produce legal effects, thus divesting the church of its exclusive control over marriage. Despite failed or short-lived attempts in Central America during the 1830s, the first lasting reforms took place in liberal Colombia and Mexico during the 1850s and in Venezuela during the early 1870s. In the last quarter of the nineteenth century several other countries also introduced civil marriages. This was the case of Chile (1884), Uruguay (1885), Argentina (1888–1889), and Brazil (1890). More countries followed suit and introduced civil marriages in the early twentieth century. This was, for example, the case of Ecuador (1902), Cuba (1918), and Peru (1931).[46]

In parallel, various countries also introduced measures that promoted legal equality within marriage, thus reversing the dominant trend that had resulted from the adoption of civil codes from the 1850s to the 1870s throughout the region. Inspired by the *Code Napoléon*, such codes had restricted the rights of married women and sanctioned the dominant authority of fathers and husbands, including their administrative control over a wife's property, whether acquired before or after marriage. An illustrative and well-documented case of efforts to reform civil codes and make women equal to men before the law occurred in the Southern Cone where between the 1920s and 1940s, to greater or lesser extent, different countries endowed women with enhanced civil rights. They granted them, for instance, *patria potestad* under some circumstances, the ability to administer their earning and property, and the capacity to intervene in civil and criminal suits without their husband's permission.[47]

46 Asunción Lavrin, *Women, Feminism & Social Change in Argentina, Chile & Uruguay, 1890–1940* (Lincoln: University of Nebraska Press, 1995), 227; Fernando Arlettaz, 'Laicidad y Matrimonio' in *Escenarios actuales de la laicidad en América Latina*, eds Pauline Capdevielle and Fernando Arlettaz (México: Universidad Nacional Autónoma de México, 2019), capítulo 6.

47 Lavrin, *Women, Feminism & Social Change*, chapter 6.

Another important component of civil reformism impacting marriage concerned the enhancing of the limited 'divorce' legislation already available in colonial times and during the nineteenth century.[48] Since secular marriage was a civil contract, its possible termination like any other civil contract was a logical next step. Yet debates over the indissolubility of marriage, naturally fueled by the embattled Catholic Church, lingered on. Eventually, sooner or later, all countries but Chile, where it would happen just in 2004, introduced 'complete dissolution' divorce bills over the course of the twentieth century, typically on grounds such as adultery, grave physical injury, criminal violations by one spouse resulting in penal sentences, protracted abandonment or desertion, and even mutual consent.[49] The most advanced reform, even by world standards, took place in Uruguay where starting in 1913 divorce could take place by the sole will of the woman.[50] Further reforms involving domestic violence are worth examining separately.

4 From the Domestic to the Public, and the International[51]

In colonial times violence against women did not have a separate status but was just part of the larger legal category of physical injury ('*lesiones*'). Eventually, to differentiate it from aggressions occurring in other contexts, in the modern era, after independence from Spain, it came to be generally designated as 'domestic violence,' a widespread situation impacting all sorts of households. A rapid overview of the situation during various historical sub-periods helps us understand the phenomenon.

A first sub-period could be designated as 'liberal patriarchy.' Overall, the mostly qualitative information available leads to the conclusion that, despite the enactment of 'modern' civil and criminal codes, as well as some

48 Rengifo, *Vida conyugal, maltrato y abandono.*

49 A partial chronological list of the introduction of enhanced divorce legislation in Latin America suggests great variation. The list includes, for instance, Venezuela (1904), Uruguay (1913), Mexico (1914, 1928), Peru (1930), Argentina (1888, 1954), Brazil (1977), Colombia (1992), and Chile (2004).

50 Lavrin, *Women, Feminism & Social Change*, chapter 7.

51 Information in this section is taken from Victor M. Uribe-Uran, 'Physical Violence against Wives and the Law in the Spanish American World, 1820s-2000s' in *Murder and Violence in Modern Latin America*, eds Eric A. Johnson, Ricardo D. Salvatore, and Pieter Spierenburg (London: Wiley-Blackwell, 2013), 49–80; and Victor M. Uribe-Uran, 'From "Domestic Violence" to Violence(s) against Women in Modern Mexico and Latin America' (2013) 22 Hemisphere 5–13.

secularization in the treatment of family relations and domestic disputes, there was more continuity than change in these areas relative to colonial times. Domestic violence continued to be a common feature of everyday family life, was perceived as an entirely private matter, and elicited a mild response from justice officials. Husbands continued to exert *patria potestad* over their children or *potestad marital* over their wives. They proclaimed and enforced their right to reprehend disobedient wives and mete out 'moderate' punishment (whatever this meant). They continued to excuse themselves by citing insolence, attacks against their honor, alleged infidelity, or simply uncontrollable passion or confusion, all regarded as extenuating circumstances under the law.

Mexico affords us valuable historical evidence of the situation during the liberal nineteenth century, a time during which this and other regions in Latin America continued to be predominantly agrarian and livestock-based economies, with some mining, internal trade, and very limited industry. During the 1830s, for instance, in portions of northern Mexico such as Laredo and Matamoros, some Catholic clergymen were in favor of separating married couples in cases of pervasive domestic violence. When some of these regions, including Texas, were incorporated into the United States in the late 1840s, women seem to have found it much easier to have violent husbands punished. In a rich study relying on more than 500 judicial cases from the 1850s to the 1890s, including 292 incidents of divorce, most instances (more than 50 percent) involved the middle classes, a minority the wealthy, and an intermediate figure, about one-quarter, the poor. Abusive husbands were the main reason wives sought divorce during these four decades. For the entire century, this complaint accounted for about two-thirds of petitions. Husbands alleged abuses by their wives in less than 10 percent of cases.[52]

Semantic and rhetorical debates persisted in Mexico in the second half of the nineteenth century over what constituted abuse and what was just acceptable 'correction' of insubordinate wives. Husbands kept on battering their wives and claimed the authority to reprehend allegedly insolent, disobedient, and irresponsible behavior.[53] An important change in most regions of Mexico during the 1850s, however, was the secularization of divorce proceedings. Instead of ecclesiastical tribunals, civil judges were charged with hearing divorce cases. In the portions of Mexico annexed to the United States in the late 1840s, women experienced this change a decade earlier, when American civil officials rather than the Catholic Church began hearing divorce cases

52 Omar Valerio Jimenez, 'New Avenues for Domestic Disputes and Divorce Lawsuits along the U.S.-Mexico Border, 1834–1893' (2009) 21(1) Journal of Women's History 16, 25.

53 García Peña, *El fracaso del amor*, 88–89, 94, 121–123.

and resolving domestic disputes. By mid-century, therefore, the mores and beliefs of Catholic priests ceased to be the driving force in resolving battery and domestic disputes with secular magistrates deciding how to resolve such cases.[54]

More than a decade later, in the 1870s, divorce petitions in Mexico soared suddenly. Divorce suits jumped from an average of sixty annually to almost twice that number, a total of 104. Although this could be a function of irregular records, the increment has been attributed to the enactment of new legal reforms, including the July 23, 1859, law of civil marriage; and the new pro-divorce civil code introduced in 1866 under Emperor Maximilian. In 1871, after Maximilian had been deposed, a new code prohibited civil divorce forcing spouses once more into conciliation.[55] Still, although it did not necessarily bring greater equality for women, liberalism did increase the 'criminalization of domestic violence.' In places like the rural pueblo of Namiquipa, Chihuahua, men accused of domestic violence were arrested and many were reprimanded by judges and sentenced to eight to thirty days in the local jail. Not a few were recidivists, however, and persisted in asserting their right to 'correct' their wives. The judicial authorities also continued to favor women who showed 'subordination to domestic patriarchy.'[56]

The enactment of republican constitutions, modern civil and criminal codes, and some pro-divorce and secularizing legislation did not seem to have had significant effect on the way civil and ecclesiastical authorities approached the problem of intimate partner violence. Battered women continued to face major difficulties when seeking redress, not only because of the persistence of deeply entrenched cultural values and social practices but also because the law left open various avenues for husbands to justify their conduct. Even when physical, psychological, or sexual harm resulted to one of the parties, the authorities maintained the perception that family relations were a fundamentally private matter.

The second sub-period could be labeled 'modernized patriarchy.' In the last quarter of the nineteenth century, many Latin American nations experienced a major economic and social transformation because of the boom in the export of agrarian and mining products. Industrialization, led by export growth, also entered the scene, mostly represented by food processing plants, breweries, textile mills, and railroad expansion. This all came along with the growth of cities and population in general, a growth sometimes driven by internal migration

54 Jimenez, 'New Avenues,' 10–33.

55 García Peña, *El fracaso del amor*, 109.

56 Alonso, *Thread of Blood*, 41.

or massive foreign immigration. Material progress and demographic growth, as could be expected, brought about changes in the shapes and dynamics of households, but, unfortunately, these do not appear to have included a reduction in the incidence of domestic violence. In some places more than others, however, patriarchy was 'modernized,' and women were given additional legal tools to fight against it.

In Mexico, as a detailed local study demonstrates, women continued to experience a high incidence of domestic abuse and other forms of violence during the long early twentieth century, on the eve of the Mexican Revolution. In the rural peasant district of Tenango, in central Mexico, women were the regular victims of various forms of violence at the hands of men, including both individual and collective rape, battery, and deadly attacks. Of a sample of 138 cases of physical violence in the region over a thirty-year period, husbands or intimate partners of the victims committed 80 percent of these acts. Three-quarters of all cases of male violence against women involved aggression against intimate female partners by formal or common-law husbands who accused them of failing to prepare meals on time or serve them politely, leaving the house without permission, or disobeying their orders.[57]

It was not just in rural Mexico that domestic violence continued to haunt women. Recent research demonstrates the 'systemic and systematic' nature of such violence throughout the entire country, although, unless it led to death, bloodshed, or excessive publicity, both the press and the judicial system minimized its seriousness. Domestic violence against women was not only widespread and neglected by authorities and the media, but also was considerably underreported. Public opinion considered it a normal aspect of domestic life and, with a large part of the problem remaining in the private sphere, judicial activity did not reflect its true magnitude. The available statistics are therefore defective, but they are enough to indicate that women rather than men denounced most cases (80 percent of a sample of 113 cases of injuries and homicides committed between 1900 and 1930). The women in these cases were battered for reasons that should by now seem familiar such as not delivering meals appropriately, speaking disrespectfully, being suspected of infidelity, or leaving the home without authorization.[58]

57 Soledad González Montes and Pilar Iracheta Cenegorta, 'La violencia en la vida de las mujeres campesinas: El Distrito de Tenango, 1880–1910' in *Presencia y transparencia: La mujer en la historia de México*, ed. Carmen Ramos E. (México: El Colegio de México, 1987), 128–129.

58 Pablo Piccato, *City of Suspects: Crime in Mexico City, 1900–1931* (Durham: Duke University Press, 2001), chapters 4 and 5.

The criminal legislation in place at the time, the Code of 1871, afforded men several valid excuses or extenuating circumstances. The main excuse was the defense of one's honor. For instance, husbands who found their wives committing adultery would receive one-sixth of the regular sentence for battery and a shorter sentence for homicide. There would be no punishment at all for battery if it was performed in 'the exercise of the right to punish the victim, even if the correction is excessive.'[59] Detailed research on 'crimes of passion' in Guanajuato and Queretaro has found that consideration of men's honor and 'justifiable' jealousy and rage meant that spousal murder was punished rather lightly, with death sentences commuted for jail terms, which were further reduced upon completion of one-quarter of the penalty. Punishment was also waived in cases of drunkenness, a relatively common circumstance among abusive husbands. And while passion and rage were invoked as a valid excuse to explain male violence against intimate partners, women who committed similar crimes were censored and, with a few notable exceptions motivated by a desire to protect female honor, condemned. Women could not even press charges against adulterous husbands unless the adultery was committed in the couple's home, caused scandal, or involved a steady concubine. In other words, material progress and the claim to 'modernity' had not been accompanied by significant changes in the way domestic violence was approached in Mexico.

Even after the enactment of revolutionary leader Venustiano Carranza's 1914 decree legalizing divorce, the pro-divorce provisions of the February 1917 Constitution, and the egalitarian Law of Family Relations (April 9, 1917), double sexual standards and patriarchal practices continued in Mexico. To be sure, modernized *patria potestad* was now shared by husband and wife, women were given the right to administer their property and enter contracts without their husbands' authorization, divorce by mutual consent became possible, adultery became illegal irrespective of gender, and, since it rendered marital life 'impossible,' battery was also a gender-neutral cause for divorce (art. 76, no. VII). However, women needed their husbands' permission to work outside the home and were charged exclusively with the care of the household (*asuntos domésticos*). Furthermore, whereas female adultery was 'always' a cause for divorce, the same was true of male adultery only when it took place in the family home or was combined with concubinage, public scandal, insult, or ill treatment of the wife, either by the husband or his lover (art. 77). Finally, divorced men were allowed to marry much sooner than divorced women, who had to

59 Ibid., 82.

wait 300 days after the dissolution of their first marriage (art. 140). Not even the Mexican Revolution, therefore, truly put an end to paternalistic rule.[60]

The long early twentieth century witnessed some important changes in the regulation of patriarchy, marriage, and domestic violence. In addition to the further secularization of family relations, including the widening of civil marriage rights and full divorce in at least some countries of the region, gender-neutral language found its way into some criminal codes, most notably in Argentina (1886) and Puerto Rico (1902). These codes outlawed male adultery for the first time in each country's history. As in Brazil a few decades later, these statutes also made it illegal for husbands to kill their wives. They did not bring an end to patriarchy – not only because patriarchal customs trumped formal legal changes but also because, under civil legislation men continued to enjoy various legal powers over women – but they did modernize it by providing women with some additional tools to defend their rights and fight back. And fight they did.

It is impossible to neglect the significance of events in Brazil during the period under consideration. Public sentiment against the law's tolerance for domestic violence, in particular the large number of legally acceptable wife-killings, reached a peak in the early twentieth century. The result was the beginning of a collective 'social hygiene' campaign sparked by middle-class female writers who published angry pieces demanding change. In early 1925, a group of male professionals followed suit with an organization, the Brazilian Council on Social Hygiene, with the goal of ending impunity and complacency for men accused of crimes of passion. 'In courtrooms, public lecture halls, legal journals, books, professional organizations, and the popular press,' one study notes, they fought against the legal protections for wife-killers and managed to bring about the revision of the Penal Code. Starting in 1940, criminal legislation ceased to accept emotion or passion as a justification for killing one's spouse. Prior to this time, as was the case elsewhere in Latin America, Brazilian women had little protection against violent outbursts from their husbands.[61]

Even though the period from the 1940s to the 1970s witnessed the rise in industrialization in the bigger countries of Latin America, a period during which the participation of women in the labor market increased considerably, the legal treatment of domestic violence did not experience any truly

60 Sandra McGee Deutsch, 'Gender and Sociopolitical Change in Twentieth-Century Latin America' (1991) 71(2) Hispanic American Historical Review, 266–271.

61 Susan K. Besse, 'Crimes of Passion: The Campaign against Wife Killing in Brazil, 1910–1940' (1989) 22(4) Journal of Social History, 654.

significant legal changes. It was only during the 1990s when dramatic transformations took place at last as a product of feminism and globalization.

Finally, the last sub-period could be termed 'globalized patriarchy.' Latin American societies experienced watershed historical changes in this period. As a result of the 'debt crisis' in the 1980s, most of the region's economies, to a greater or lesser extent, introduced wide-ranging trade reforms, deregulation of labor markets, and the large-scale privatization of utilities, banks, energy production and supply, transportation, and other formerly state-owned sectors. This led to increasing 'globalization' and deindustrialization of economies throughout the subcontinent. In parallel, political systems experienced an uncontainable expansion of democratic government, intense feminist organizing, and progressive constitutional and legal reforms. Some of these touched on family relations, gender equality, and women's rights. The most significant legal reforms took place in the international arena in response to long simmering pressures from feminist movements, among others. One could even argue that concerns over human rights and, later, public health led to a true globalization of policies toward patriarchy.

In 1962, under the leadership of the Dominican Republic, the women's movements of Latin America and the Caribbean selected November 25 as the day to denounce violence against women. On that day two years earlier, three Dominican women activists (the Mirabal sisters: Patricia Mercedes, Minerva Argentina, and María Teresa) had been killed by the Trujillo dictatorship. Three and a half decades later, in 1997, the General Assembly of the United Nations passed a formal resolution recognizing that same day as the 'International Day to Eliminate Violence Against Women.' Even though it was political violence in the Spanish Caribbean that prompted the earlier marker, various forms of gender violence, including intimate partner violence, were unquestionably central to explaining the second landmark. During this period, intimate partner and other modalities of gender violence had become a matter of increasing concern for the women's movement, the international community, and individual states in the region and elsewhere. From 1975 to 1985, the United Nations Decade for Women, numerous feminist conferences, encounters, and campaigns were organized around the world. Research and writing on gender increased dramatically along with information about the condition of women and families. As we have seen, by 1997 many Latin American countries had compiled statistics and evidence of the human rights and public health significance of intimate partner violence. A host of international actions and policies on this issue were implemented. Much as in the case of protective international policies in favor of ethnic minorities, numerous countries gradually endorsed these international rules which became binding and determined the passage of copycat legislation in country after country.

The international feminist movement gained strength thanks to a series of world women's conferences, starting with the one in Mexico in 1975 to mark the start of the 'UN Decade for Women.' This conference led to the establishment of the International Research and Training Institute for the Advancement of Women (INSTRAW) and the United Nations Development Fund for Women (UNIFEM), designed to provide the institutional framework for research, training, and operational activities around women and development. Follow-up conferences were held in Copenhagen (1980), Nairobi (1985), and Beijing (1995), and there is now pressure for a fifth world conference in the future. All these conferences served to push forward 'global' efforts to promote the advancement of women and opened a worldwide dialogue on gender equality. They each developed strategic objectives and platforms culminating in a World Plan of Action that addresses a variety of gender equality fronts targeting governments, international organizations, communities, and individuals. An important component of the platforms and the World Plan is the issue of gender violence, starting with intimate partner violence, which has rightly come to be understood as a 'global problem.'

Intimate partner violence has gained increasing recognition in contemporary societies. At least since the UN Convention on the Elimination of All Forms of Discrimination Against Women (CEDAW) entered into force in 1981, and explicitly in the 1993 World Conference on Human Rights in Vienna, the world community began framing these behaviors as discriminatory and a major human rights violation. In the last decade, the World Health Organization also elevated physical, psychological, and sexual violence against women to the category of a grave public health problem.

By 1992, all countries in Latin America and the Caribbean had ratified the UN Convention on the Elimination of All Forms of Discrimination Against Women (CEDAW). Then came the Organization of American States' Inter-American Convention to Prevent, Punish and Eradicate Violence against Women (also called the Convention of Belém do Pará) in June 1994. By 1998, this multilateral treaty had been ratified by almost all countries in the region. Three Caribbean nations did it later, namely, Grenada (2000), Suriname (2002), and Jamaica (2005). Following ratification, numerous signatory nations passed their own national laws on intimate partner violence. At no other time in the history of Latin America had intimate partner violence been considered a human rights or public health problem of global dimensions worth addressing through comprehensive legislation, specialized state and civil society institutions, and mass campaigns.

Not having declined significantly, if at all, from the 1940s to 1980s, domestic violence continued to be pervasive in several Spanish American nations during the 1990s too. Nevertheless, thanks to the mentioned international developments there has been a dramatic increase in the amount of attention paid to domestic violence on the part of legal, human rights, and public health activists in virtually every nation of Latin America over the last three decades. Attention has been accompanied with the establishment of new gender-sensitive and women-focused public institutions, protective policies, awareness campaigns, service guidelines, and action plans ('*rutas críticas*').[62] Puerto Rico was the first Latin American country to enact comprehensive laws against violence within the family, in 1989, followed by Trinidad and Tobago (1991), Argentina (1994), Bolivia (1995), Chile (1994), Colombia (1996), Costa Rica (1996), Ecuador (1995), El Salvador (1996), Guatemala (1996), Honduras (1997), Mexico (1996), Nicaragua (1996), Panama (1995), Peru (1993, 1997), and Venezuela (1998). The same trend, because of the listed international pressures, was occurring in other parts of the world, including Europe – Austria (1996), Belgium (1997), Great Britain (1996), Ireland (1996), Northern Ireland (1998), and Portugal (1995, 1999) – New Zealand (1995) and South Africa (1998).

This is the general context to better understand individual Latin American examples. For instance, the case of Mexico. In April 1996, the Mexico City government passed the 'Law of Attention to and Prevention of Intra-familial Violence,' the country's first. In December 1997, related reforms were introduced to the country's civil, civil procedural, criminal, and criminal procedural codes. Later, in early 2000, Mexico issued an official national statute (Official Mexican Norm or ONM-190-SSA-1999) to orient health services in the prevention and treatment of domestic violence. The norm required health services to report cases to the judicial authorities. Finally, as a culmination of thirty years of feminist struggle, in December 2006 the Mexican legislature passed a norm to protect women from violence in general, the *Ley General de Acceso a Una Vida Libre de Violencia*, the first comprehensive legislation to combat gender violence in the country. The law created, among other things, a national system to prevent violence against Mexican women and girls and to assist and protect victims (*Sistema Nacional de Prevención, Protección, Asistencia y Erradicación de la Violencia contra las Mujeres y las Niñas*).

---

62 On '*rutas críticas*' see the comparative study of ten Latin American countries by Montserrat Sagot et al., *Ruta crítica de las mujeres afectadas por la violencia intrafamiliar en América Latina* (Washington, DC: Organización Panamericana de la Salud. Programa Mujer, Salud y Desarrollo, 2000).

It seems clear that social and official attitudes toward domestic violence have changed considerably in the land of the Aztecs. As indicated, similar trends can be observed in other countries of the region, as well since the 1990s at least. Now, if the 1990s brought a long series of anti-domestic violence laws to various parts of Latin America, the start of the new century witnessed yet another wave of legal reform, this time integral laws concerning violence in general against women and girls, such as the one enacted in Mexico in 2006. Rather than a coincidence, this was in great measure the result of not only local feminist movements but also developments in international law, through which the regulation of patriarchy reached truly global dimensions.

The passage of patriarchy from private to global regulation is a truly structural transition likely to have greater impact on patterns of gender relations than liberal and modernized versions had in the past. Still, one must not forget that patriarchy and the violence associated with it have been structural (cultural, social, economic, political) circumstances of world societies for centuries and shall remain an enduring condition.

5 Conclusion

Legal norms concerning filiation, marriage, family relations, and domestic conflicts have evolved significantly over the last five centuries in Latin America and the Caribbean. The forces behind such transformation have been quite diverse, including European colonial powers, the Catholic Church, legal scholars, and individual family members, women being perhaps the most prominent. International actors such as the global feminist movement and multilateral organizations like the United Nations have played a key role as well. As a matter of fact, one of the most notable trends has been precisely the transition of family norms from the private to the international sphere. Still, amidst the significant changes, patriarchal forces have exhibited considerable resilience. Even the transit from colonial to independent national legal regimes in the family arena, and the experiences with liberalism, modernization, and globalization, suggest that the ongoing transition to more egalitarian norms is likely to be protracted and face all kinds of hurdles, because structural situations, including *habitus*, are hard and costly to break.

References

Hunefeldt, Christine. *Liberalism in the Bedroom: Quarreling Spouses in Nineteenth-Century Lima*. University Park: Pennsylvania State University Press, 2000.

Lavrin, Asunción. 'Sexuality in Colonial Mexico: A Church Dilemma.' In *Sexuality and Marriage in Colonial Latin America*, edited by Asunción Lavrin, 47–92. Lincoln: University of Nebraska Press, 1989.

Lavrin, Asunción. *Women, Feminism & Social Change in Argentina, Chile & Uruguay, 1890–1940*. Lincoln: University of Nebraska Press, 1995.

Lewin, Linda. *Surprise Heirs II: Illegitimacy, Inheritance Rights, and Public Power in the Formation of Imperial Brazil, 1822–1900*. Stanford: Stanford University Press, 2003.

Mannarelli, Maria Emma. *Private Passions and Public Sins: Men and Women in Seventeenth-Century Lima*. Albuquerque: University of New Mexico Press, 2007.

McKinley, Michelle. *Fractional Freedoms: Slavery, Intimacy, and Legal Mobilization in Colonial Lima, 1600–1700*. Cambridge: Cambridge University Press, 2016.

Milanich, Nara. *Children of Fate: Childhood, Class, and the State in Chile, 1850–1930*. Durham: Duke University Press, 2009.

Nizza da Silva, Maria Beatriz. *Sistema de casamento no Brasil colonial*. Sao Paulo: Editoria da Universidade de São Paulo, 1984.

Rípodas Ardanaz, Daisy. *El matrimonio en Indias. Realidad social y regulación jurídica*. Buenos Aires: Fundación para la Educación, la Ciencia y la Cultura, 1977.

Rodríguez Sáenz, Eugenia. *Hijas, novias y esposas: familia, matrimonio y violencia doméstica en el Valle Central de Costa Rica (1750–1850)*. Heredia: Editorial de la Universidad Nacional, 2000.

Seed, Patricia. *To Love, Honor and Obey in Colonial Mexico: Conflicts over Marriage Choice, 1574–1821*. Stanford: Stanford University Press, 1988.

Socolow, Susan M. *The Women of Colonial Latin America*. Cambridge: Harvard University Press, 2000.

Stern, Steve J. *The Secret History of Gender: Women, Men and Power in Late Colonial Mexico*. Chapel Hill: University of North Carolina Press, 2000.

Twinam, Ann. *Public Lives, Private Secrets: Gender, Honor, Sexuality, and Illegitimacy in Colonial Spanish America*. Stanford: Stanford University Press, 1999.

Uribe-Uran, Victor M. 'Physical Violence against Wives and the Law in the Spanish American World, 1820s-2000s.' In *Murder and Violence in Modern Latin America*, edited by Eric A. Johnson, Ricardo D. Salvatore, and Pieter Spierenburg, 49–80. London: Wiley-Blackwell, 2013.

Uribe-Uran, Victor M. *Fatal Love: Spousal Killers, Law and Punishment in the Late Colonial Spanish Atlantic*. Stanford: Stanford University Press, 2015.

CHAPTER 19

The Church

M.C. Mirow

1 Introduction

After the arrival of Spaniards and Portuguese in the Americas, Catholic Christianity and its institutions spread rapidly.[1] From colonial to recent times, the church addressed spiritual, political, governmental, educational, charitable, and medical needs through a variety of actors, structures, and institutions. Apart from the crown and succeeding independent governments, the church was the largest and best-organized institution throughout the region and vied for political and social prominence with secular institutions. In the colonial period and often through the nineteenth century, church and state overlapped in complex legal and political relationships that were defined by law and customary practices. Coexistence was shattered at times through political dissonance leading to the separation of church and state and new constellations of legal and political competencies. Law was central to these developments throughout the centuries, and the church's legal weight has been a considerable force in the structure and development of law from questions of the status of Indigenous peoples to relatively recent challenges to dictatorship and abuses of human rights.

2 The Royal Patronage and Colonial Law

A complex and carefully negotiated set of principles governed the relationship between the church and royal authorities during the colonial period. These principles were incorporated into Spanish colonial law, or *derecho indiano*. The delegation of authority and activities from the church to the Spanish crown became the cornerstone of this relationship expressed as crown's Royal Patronage (*Patronato Real*) of the church. In exchange for Spain's assuming the evangelization and associated costs in its newly found lands in the Americas,

1 David Thomas Orique, Susan Fitzpatrick-Behrens, and Virginia Garrard, *The Oxford Handbook of Latin American Christianity* (Oxford: Oxford University Press, 2020), 'Introduction,' 2–4 (hereinafter *OHLAC*).

 | DOI:10.1163/9789004436091_021

the crown was granted substantial independent rights that had formerly been exercised exclusively by the church. These included the collection of tithes and the right to present bishops.[2] Indeed, the general structures of the patronage were set as early as 1508 by Pope Julius in the bull *Universalis ecclesiae regimini* that

> Granted to the Spanish kings the exclusive privilege of building and endowing church, benefices, and other pious activities. Through these powers, the kings could appoint and nominate candidates to serve the newly created bishoprics, ecclesiastical dignities, and benefices forever. Offices in the lower clergy were left to the local bishop, while appointments within the religious orders were subject to the international approval processes of the orders. In the last of his bull, Julius granted to the monarch the perpetual right to collect and enjoy the tithe on gold, silver, and other precious metals. With these grants the papal legislation creating the Patronato Real essentially was complete.[3]

By the mid-sixteenth century, the Pope had granted Spain universal patronage in the Americas and the power to modify ecclesiastical jurisdictions.[4] Ecclesiastics required royal license through the Board of Trade (*Casa de Contratación*) to travel to the Americas.[5] In Brazil a similar but less structured form of Royal Patronage developed from the negotiations between the Portuguese crown and the Pope.[6]

In 1574, Spanish Royal Patronage was expressed in royal legislation known as the Ordinance of Patronage (*Ordenanzas del Patronazgo*). Amongst many broad provisions assigning royal control of the church, these royal laws

2 Although entitled to tithes from the early sixteenth century, the crown often donated most of these funds to bishops and ecclesial institutions. J. Lloyd Mecham, *Church and State in Latin America: A History of Politico-Ecclesiastical Relations*, rev. ed. (Chapel Hill: University of North Carolina Press, 1966), 25.

3 John Frederick Schwaller, *The History of the Catholic Church in Latin America: From Conquest to Revolution and Beyond* (New York: New York University Press, 2011), 48–49. See also, Mecham, *Church*, 16.

4 Ricardo Levene, *Manual de historia del derecho argentino*, 5th ed. (Buenos Aires: Depalma, 1985), 58–59; Robert C. Padden, 'The Ordenanza del Patronazgo of 1574: An Interpretive Essay' in *The Church in Colonial Latin America*, ed. John F. Schwaller (Wilmington: Scholarly Resources, 2000), 27–47; John F. Schwaller, *The Church and Clergy in Sixteenth Century Mexico* (Albuquerque: University of New Mexico Press, 1987); John F. Schwaller, 'The Ordenanzas del Patronazgo in New Spain, 1574–1600' in *The Church in Colonial Latin America*, 49–69.

5 Mecham, *Church*, 23.

6 Schwaller, *History*, 48–50.

required competitive examinations for parish priests. They also sought the removal of regular clerics in rural parishes and their replacement with secular priests more closely controlled by the crown. This moved many regular clerics from rural settings to urban centers with their related institutions.[7]

The justification for such grants of ecclesiastical power was the evangelization of the Indigenous populations of the Americas. Spain, Portugal, papal power brokers, theologians, and canon lawyers applied their arguments and positions to establish the right of the European powers to preach to native inhabitants and consequently to obtain their lands.[8] The legal and theological status of Indigenous peoples was at the forefront of the evangelization and Spain's claims. Spanish theologians and canonists considered such questions fully and repeatedly decided that Indigenous people had intellects and souls receptive to permanent conversion to Christianity.[9]

Debates included notions of the 'just war' and legal notice, the *Requerimiento*, a declaration of the right to spread the claims of the Pope and the crown.[10] As Schwaller writes: 'The existence and occasional use of the Requirement indicates that the Spaniards seriously thought about their legal claim to the New World, which claim was intimately related to the Christianizing mission.'[11]

---

7 Mecham, *Church*, 32–33; Schwaller, *History*, 88.

8 José Luis Egío and Christiane Birr, 'Before Vitoria: Expansion into Heathen, Empty, or Disputed Lands in Late-Mediaeval Salamanca Writings and Early 16th-Century Juridical Treatises' in *A Companion to Early Modern Spanish Imperial Political and Social Thought*, ed. Jörg Alejandro Tellkamp (Leiden: Brill, 2020), 53–77; Miguel Anxo Pena González, 'The "School of Salamanca" and the American Project' in *A Companion to Early Modern Spanish*, 78–101; Luis N. Rivera, 'The Theological Juridical Debate' in *The Church in Colonial Latin America*, ed. John F. Schwaller (Wilmington: Scholarly Resources, 2000); Schwaller, *History*, 40–41.

9 Felipe Castañeda, 'Spanish Colonialism as Perpetual Dominion in the Writings of Juan Solórzano Pereira' in *A Companion to Early Modern Spanish*, 273–294; M.C. Mirow, *Latin American Law: A History of Private Law and Institutions in Spanish America* (Austin: University of Texas Press, 2004), 13; M.C. Mirow, 'Juan Solórzano Pereira' in *Great Christian Jurists in Spanish History*, eds Rafael Domingo and Javier Martinez-Torrón (Cambridge: Cambridge University Press, 2018), 240–257. In 1537, the Pope determined that natives were fully human and therefore capable of conversion to Christianity. Schwaller, *History*, 45–46. See also, Lewis Hanke, *The Spanish Struggle for Justice in the Conquest of America* (Philadelphia: University of Pennsylvania Press, 1949); David M. Lantigua, 'Scholastic Theology, Justice, and the Conquest of the Americas' in *OHLAC*, 39–56; James Muldoon, *The Americas in the Spanish World Order: The Justification for Conquest in the Seventeenth Century* (Philadelphia: University of Pennsylvania Press, 1994).

10 Christian Schäfer, '*Conquista* and the Just War' in *A Companion to Early Modern Spanish*, 199–221; Schwaller, *History*, 42. For the *Requerimiento* see Lantigua, 'Scholarly Theology,' 45; Mirow, *Latin American Law*, 13–14.

11 Schwaller, *History*, 42.

With the success of his discoveries and although he obtained substantial rights to extract wealth and to exercise political power, Columbus sought, but was not granted, the right to control the church in the new territories. Subsequent voyages seeking discovery, conquest, political control, and settlement often included priests, particularly members of religious orders that exercised relatively loose supervision of their members when far from central authorities. For example, both Cortés's expedition to Mexico and Pizarro's expedition to Peru included diocesan or secular and regular clergy.[12]

Spanish and Portuguese systems of enslaving humans and forced labor were part of the colonial enterprise. Although Spanish theologians and canon lawyers debated the legal status and proper treatment of Indigenous people, there was less intellectual and human concern for enslaved humans.[13] Under colonial law, enslaved people were permitted to marry and might bring actions in ecclesiastical courts for legal determinations of free status. Nonetheless, enslaved Africans and their descendants were subject to heightened scrutiny for heterodox practices such as witchcraft and sorcery.[14]

The first missionaries to Indigenous communities were relatively unsupervised by their religious orders or by bishops whose ecclesiastical and regional hierarchy was yet to be constructed. As the European presence in Mexico, Peru, and Brazil consolidated over the sixteenth century, waves of regular clergy and some secular clergy arrived to maintain the religious life of Spaniards and to spread the gospel to Indigenous people. Although many different religious orders were involved in this process, the Franciscans (with broad grants of power in the Americas through the papal letter *Omnimoda* of 1522), Dominicans, Jesuits, Carmelites, Mercedarians, and Augustinians were active in establishing communities and evangelizing native people. In Brazil, the Jesuits established important institutions of learning and wildly successful agricultural estates. Regular orders were also able to establish hierarchical structures such as provinces in the Americas to monitor better their activities.[15]

12 Ibid., 37, 46, 55–59.

13 Luis Perdices de Blas and José Louis Ramos Gorostiza, 'The Debate over the Enslavement of Indians and Africans in the Sixteenth- and Seventeenth-Century Spanish Empire' in *A Companion to Early Modern Spanish*, 295–317.

14 Rachel Sarah O'Toole, '(Un)making Christianity: The African Diaspora in Slavery and Freedom' in OHLAC, 101, 108, 111–112.

15 Schwaller, *History*, 7, 59–70. As monasteries and houses were established, America also gained cloistered spaces for religious women and religious institutions for lay women. Some of these institutions were wealthy and engaged in loans, mortgages, and other dealings in property. Schwaller, *History*, 89–93. See also, John F. Schwaller, 'The Making of Colonial Christianity in Hispanic America' in OHLAC, 9–14.

In the seventeenth century, regular orders not only reached into new areas to bring Christianity to Indigenous peoples but also established substantial urban institutions such as convents, friaries, and monasteries, to further the goals of the orders. These were based on the particular rule and organizational structure of the order.[16]

The church while exploiting methods of collecting and applying Indigenous labor also stepped in to provide moral guidance, supervision, and legal critique of these institutions called *encomiendas* and *repartimientos*. Indeed, Bartolomé de las Casas's ownership of an *encomienda* and his subsequent critique of the institution and Spain's enterprise in the Americas, particularly as it related to the treatment of Indigenous peoples, is well known.[17]

The Royal Patronage was woven into the primary sources of *derecho indiano* and found its provisions in the *Ordenanzas del Patronazgo* (The ordinances of the patronage, 1574) and the first book of the *Recopilación de las Leyes de las Indias* (The compilation of laws of the Indies, 1680).[18] In this way the Royal Patronage was a regular aspect of Spanish colonial law, and Latin American jurists of succeeding generations viewed this allocation of power as part and parcel of the legacy of the *derecho indiano* in succeeding centuries.

The Royal Patronage had substantial effects on the traditional ecclesiastical jurisdiction as it was applied in the Americas. For example, testamentary causes, a mainstay of ecclesiastical jurisdiction, were heard in royal rather than church courts.[19] Royal courts reviewed ecclesiastical judgments, taxed ecclesiastical corporations, and enforced financial obligations on church officials.[20] This meant that much of the canon law as applied in medieval and early modern Spain was adapted and modified to the colonial setting.[21] Nonetheless, the

---

16 Schwaller, *History*, 74–76.

17 Ibid., 39, 43–46; Lantigua, 'Scholastic Theology,' 49–53; Kenneth Pennington, 'Bartolomé de Las Casas' in *Great Christian Jurists in Spanish History*, 98–114. For a recent study of Las Casas's well-known debate with Juan Ginés de Sepúlveda on this topic see Francisco Castilla Urbano, 'The Debate of Valladolid (1550–1551): Background, Discussions, and Results of the Debate between Juan Ginés de Sepúlveda and Bartolomé de las Casas' in *A Companion to Early Modern Spanish*, 222–251.

18 M.C. Mirow, *Latin American Law*, 48.

19 Abelardo Levaggi, *Manual de historia del derecho argentino* (Buenos Aires: Depalma, 1987), vol. 2, 34–35; Levene, *Manual*, 60, 121; José Luis Soberanes Fernández, *Los tribunales de la Nueva España* (México: Universidad Nacional Autónoma de México, 1980), 148–149, 159–160.

20 Jorge Adame Goddard, 'Asimilación y rechazo en México del sistema de relaciones entre la iglesia y el estado contemplado en la Constitución de Cádiz' (2010) 22 Anuario Mexicano de Historia del Derecho 61–65.

21 Aniceto Masferrer, *Spanish Legal Traditions: A Comparative Legal History Outline*, 2nd ed. (Madrid: Dykinson, 2012), 129–136, 232–246; Antonio Padoa-Schioppa, *A History of Law*

church's corporate nature and framework continued to impact Latin American social and political arrangements.

The church's special jurisdiction in ecclesiastical matters and over ecclesiastical persons was also recognized. Peninsular Spanish law and *derecho indiano* recognized *fueros*, collections of rights and privileges attached to individuals with a particular status, such as a member of the military or clergy, or to a specific town or region as a reward by the king for exemplary service to the crown. For our purposes, the ecclesiastical *fuero* was particularly important. It gave special substantive rules of law and jurisdictional advantages to individuals who successful established that they were covered by the *fuero* under *derecho indiano*.[22]

The disputes entered into by Juan de Palafox y Mendoza, Bishop of Puebla in the mid-seventeenth century, illustrate the conflicts that could result under ecclesiastical jurisdiction. Palafox y Mendoza arrived in Puebla in 1640 and subsequently removed regular clergy from thirty-six parishes. He substituted secular clergy in their place. Under the provisions of the Council of Trent, he then required Jesuits to obtain a license to administer sacraments. When the Jesuits resisted, Palafox y Mendoza doubled down to argue that if Jesuits were not under his supervision, then they should pay the tithe on their vast agricultural holdings. A new viceroy sided with the Jesuits and ordered the bishop's arrest. In the end, the crown supported Palafox y Mendoza's position, and the Jesuits had to obtain licenses, but the conflict was only resolved after Palafox y Mendoza had returned to Spain in 1649.[23]

Ecclesiastical courts heard causes of purely spiritual matters, and the church decided questions of civil status such as espousals, matrimony, and their dissolution. Valid marriage or legitimacy, and thus rights to property, hinged on these areas of canon law and their resolution in ecclesiastical courts.[24] Furthermore, churches and other buildings tied to the church provided sites of sanctuary for criminal defendants.[25]

---

in Europe: From the Early Middle Ages to the Twentieth Century (Cambridge: Cambridge University Press, 2017), 95–113, 193–211; Francisco Tomás y Valiente, *Manual de historia del derecho español*, 4th ed. (Madrid: Tecnos, 2009), 180–193, 325–245.

22 Schwaller, *History*, 15–16.

23 Joel M. Cruz, *The Histories of the Latin American Church: A Handbook* (Minneapolis: Fortress Press, 2014), 415; Schwaller, *History*, 89; Schwaller, 'The Making,' 19–20.

24 Mirow, *Latin American Law*, 28.

25 Michelle A. McKinley, 'Standing on Shaky Ground: Criminal Jurisdiction and Ecclesiastical Immunity in Seventeenth-Century Lima, 1600–1700' (2014) 4 U.C. Irvine Law Review 141–174; Victor M. Uribe-Uran, '"*Iglesia me Llamo*": Church Asylum and the Law in Spain and Colonial Spanish America' (2007) 49, 2 Comparative Studies in Society and History 446–472.

The ecclesiastical jurisdiction was exercised by the bishop and clerics appointed by him to serve as ecclesiastical judges called *vicarios*.[26] On the diocesan level, these usually included a court for Spaniards, a court of Indigenous people, and a court administering charitable activities and church property and revenues. Ecclesiastical jurisdiction was generally limited to Catholic litigants and extensively exercised over clergy and other religious. Appeals to Rome from the Americas were curtailed in 1606, and in the later colonial period, in 1795, royal courts seized jurisdiction over serious offenses by ecclesiastics. Disputes over the patronage were heard in royal rather than ecclesiastical courts.[27]

An important institution that bridged areas of royal and ecclesiastical concern was the Holy Office of the Inquisition, established by the Pope and placed under Spanish royal control in 1478 as part of the apparatus of Christian reconquest of the Iberian peninsula. Although originally under the supervision of the bishop within each diocese, the Inquisition was transferred by 1570 to the Spanish crown to exercise the function of investigating religious orthodoxy.[28] Inquisitors included priests or those trained in canon law. Two inquisitors were established in Lima in 1570, and two more in Mexico a year later.[29] Indigenous people were exempt from the jurisdiction of the Inquisition. Foreign residents, however, might find themselves before the tribunal. The Inquisition investigated cases of heresy, violation of the sacraments, bigamy, sexual solicitation by priests, witchcraft, divination, idolatry, and similar offenses.[30] The Inquisition reported to a Council of the Inquisition in Spain, and royal government in the Americas executed the tribunal's judgments.[31]

With the stability of urban centers in the sixteenth century, archdioceses and dioceses were erected for the organizational support of the secular clergy and this wing of the church. New dioceses followed the expansion of the Spanish and Portuguese empires in the Americas.[32] The diocese was headed by the bishop who 'was responsible for supervising the secular clergy within his territory, the administration of the sacraments, the collection of the ecclesiastical tax (the tithe), and the execution of ecclesiastical justice (the enforcement of

26 Schwaller, *History*, 78.

27 Mecham, *Church*, 29–30, 78.

28 Schwaller, *History*, 19, 77.

29 Mecham, *Church*, 34.

30 Schwaller, *History*, 86. See generally, Boleslao Lewin, *La inquisición en Hispanoamérica: Judíos, Protestantes, Patriotas* (Buenos Aires: Editorial Proyección, 1962).

31 Mecham, *Church*, 35.

32 Schwaller, *History*, 76–77.

the ecclesiastical [canon] law).'[33] Various members of the bishop's cathedral chapter (*cabildo eclesiástico*) took on supporting functions under canon law.

The chapter collected the tithe on one-tenth of agricultural production. In a complex set of fractions from the total amount, the king received one-ninth, the parish clergy (at first just the clergy of the cathedral parish) got two-ninths, and the rest, after substantial portions for the bishop and members of the cathedral chapter, was given for the maintenance of the building, supplies needed for the liturgy, and a hospital.[34] Indigenous people, subject to tribute payments, were generally not subject to the tithe.[35]

Ecclesiastical finances were not solely dependent on the tithe. The church played an important function in economic affairs in colonial society. It was a main lender and used complex legal structures to secure the payments on its loans including interests in agricultural estates. The church provided pious works and chantries where clergy prayed for the souls of the endowing family and its deceased members. Land might be given for this purpose or used as the basis for various complex forms of loans and mortgages. These activities were so lucrative and complex that bishops supervised these investments through a Court of Chantry and Pious Works, *Juzgado de capellanías y obras pías*.[36]

Lay sodalities or confraternities, *cofradías*, under clerical supervision provided social and devotional community, support, piety, charity, and burial assistance. Many of these organizations held land in their own right and extended mortgages and loans related to this real property.[37]

In sum, the church's wealth was based on several sources of income including the tithe, rents from land, interest from mortgages and loans, parochial dues, alms, and small customary payments. Riches were amassed not only by secular institutions; some religious orders also exhibited great wealth. Although the economic successes of the Jesuits on large estates are well known, the Augustinians and Benedictines successfully entered agriculture and commerce.[38] Individual members of the regular clergy also amassed considerable fortunes represented in land, livestock, and commercial establishments.[39]

33 Ibid., 77.
34 Ibid., 79–81.
35 Schwaller, 'The Making,' 14.
36 Schwaller, *History*, 82–83.
37 Ibid., 84–85.
38 Ibid., 98–106.
39 Charles Harris III, *A Mexican Family Empire: The Latifundio of the Sánchez Navarro Family 1765-1867* (Austin: University of Texas Press, 1975).

Such material success, social importance, and political independence led the church to scrutiny by jealous royal minds. In a broad sweep to strengthen royal government, increase tax collection and revenues, channel trade, and bolster military defense, the Spanish and Portuguese crowns examined the church's wealth and power. Spanish Bourbon and Portuguese Pombaline reforms subjected the church to greater royal control and substantially limited its landholding and lending activities. The crowns reinvigorated existing sources of controls under the Royal Patronage and sought greater power to appoint local parish priests and to diminish the activities of the orders by restricting buildings, the acquisition of land, and the admission of new members. From the 1740s, a program of secularization was effected to limit the independence of regular clergy so that they did not expand beyond their present spheres of influence, houses in urban areas and rural missionary activity. As another avenue of control, religious clerics were required to obtain a license from the bishop to administer sacraments. The crown asserted its right of *pase regio*, the practice of reviewing and approving papal communications before their dissemination in the colony. The crown continued to extract wealth from the church during the late eighteenth century by confiscating chantries and assuming mortgages and investments formerly owned by church entities. Under Pombal's guidance, the Jesuits were expelled from Portugal and its colonies. They left Brazil in 1759. Expulsion of the Jesuits had devastating effects for the persons involved, higher education in the Americas, the colonial economy, and land values as Jesuit lands flooded the market for large agricultural estates. The Jesuits were expelled from Spanish America in 1767.[40]

Royal courts exercised greater appellate jurisdiction over ecclesiastical tribunals. Appointments to church offices were properly contested in royal courts if the actions were under the Royal Patronage. Many aspects of tithe disputes were heard in royal courts because the crown had the right to collect tithes, although it had granted this activity back to the church. In the eighteenth century, some members of the clergy effectively challenged the bishop's jurisdiction through the use of the *recurso de fuerza*, a means of removing a case from a jurisdiction because proper procedures were not used. This oddly left religious clergy opting out of an ecclesiastical court to have their cases reviewed and perhaps heard in a royal court.[41]

---

40 Schwaller, *History*, 3, 107–108, 112–115.

41 María Teresa Bouzada Gíl, *La vía de fuerza: La práctica en la Real Audiencia del Reino de Galicia; Siglos* XVII–XVIII (Santiago de Compostela: Xunta de Galicia, 2001); Schwaller, *History*, 107, 109.

Actions like these destabilized the traditional economic and political arrangements between the Spanish crown and the church in the late colonial period.[42] Reliant on the crown for their appointments, bishops were predominantly aligned with royal government. Nonetheless, the crown moved away from financially supporting parish priests and had substantially curtailed the position of the church.[43]

3 Independence

Independence from Spanish rule in the Americas did not happen all at once. The French invasion of Spain in 1808 resulted in Fernando VII's exile and in loyal peninsular Spaniards fleeing to the south to set up a government in the name of the king in Cádiz. Many regions of the Americas participated in this government that resulted in the first Spanish nation composed of Spaniards in Europe and America, 'Spaniards of both hemispheres' as the resulting Spanish Constitution of 1812 declared.[44] This constitution, also known as the Constitution of Cádiz, established Roman Catholicism as the official religion of the state and applied widely in the American provinces that remained loyal to the royal government in Spain. Its prologue begins, 'In the name of God Almighty, Father, Son, and Holy Spirit, author and supreme legislator of society.'[45] Often associated with Spanish liberalism, the Constitution of Cádiz provided for electoral representation at different levels of the polity, constrained the power of the king, protected individual property and contractual rights, protected the criminally accused, and did away with seigniorial structures for wealthy landholders, and tribute payments and forced labor by Indigenous people.[46] Nonetheless, the Constitution was grounded in a Roman Catholic worldview.[47]

The Royal Patronage continued. The king's constitutional power included the right 'to present all bishoprics and all ecclesiastical dignitaries and benefices under the Royal Patronage of the church, at the proposal of the Council of

42 Fredrick B. Pike, 'Latin America' in *The Oxford Illustrated History of Christianity*, ed. John McManners (Oxford: Oxford University Press, 1990), 422–423.

43 Schwaller, *History*, 114–115.

44 M.C. Mirow, *Florida's First Constitution, The Constitution of Cádiz: Introduction, Translation and Text* (Durham: Carolina Academic Press, 2012), 15.

45 Ibid., 15.

46 M.C. Mirow, *Latin American Constitutions: The Constitution of Cádiz and Its Legacy in Spanish America* (Cambridge: Cambridge University Press, 2015), 31.

47 Ibid., 62.

State.'[48] Under the constitution, The Supreme Tribunal's jurisdiction included the power 'to hear all disputed matters pertaining to the Royal Patronage of the church' and 'to hear appeals removing cases from ecclesiastical courts to royal courts.'[49] Although often exercised by the Cortes in the name of the king for the nation, the Royal Patronage endured the empire's transfer from absolute monarchy to constitutional monarchy with substantial limitations on royal power.[50]

Independence of Latin American colonies resulted from a lack of effective control by a weakened Spain and the eventual rebellion of towns, regions, and provinces that moved towards greater autonomy. Allegiance to the vacant Spanish throne led to new institutions that displaced traditional royal control and that asserted mediating powers in relationship to the church. If new or expanded institutions represented the crown, then they now could represent the king in his exercise of the Royal Patronage.[51] In keeping with the church's long-standing cooperation with the Spanish crown, it was highly reluctant to recognize independent movements and nascent breakaway countries in the Americas.[52] The wealth of the church and its control of the economic life of the colonies made it a particularly important actor and target in the independence process.[53]

One of the first cries for independence from Spain was raised by a priest, Father Miguel Hidalgo y Costilla, who in 1810 objected to increasing reforms against the independence of the church in Mexico with 'Long live Our Lady of Guadalupe, down with bad government, death to Spaniards.'[54] The uprising was put down quickly, and Father Hidalgo was subsequently defrocked and executed.[55] This presence as a voice of independence no doubt reflected clerical disaffection with the successes of the Bourbon reforms that left the church and its members to fend for themselves in many ways.[56] Hidalgo was not the only cleric who rose up in these nascent acts of Mexican independence.[57] Rebellions were eventually successful leading to independence in Mexico and elsewhere.

48 Constitution of Spain (1812), art. 171(6); Mirow, *Florida's First Constitution*, 37.
49 Constitution of Spain (1812), art. 261(7) and (8); Mirow, *Florida's First Constitution*, 47.
50 Mirow, *Latin American Constitutions*, 120.
51 Ibid., 25.
52 Mecham, *Church*, 52–58.
53 Ibid., 38–41.
54 Pike, 'Latin America,' 424.
55 Ibid.
56 Schwaller, *History*, 118.
57 Mecham, *Church*, 50–56.

New countries claimed the rights and privileges afforded under the Royal Patronage as the national successors to imperially negotiated relationships over the church, its appointments, personnel, property, finance, privileges, and status.[58] An effective National Patronage required an agreement between the new independent sovereigns and the Holy See. Although new countries might claim National Patronage as the successors of the Spanish crown, papal recognition of this assertion was lacking. 'To the Spanish Americans ... the pope announced that the patronage had reverted to the papacy, its original source.'[59] Newly independent countries went into a period of protracted negotiation with the Vatican and its highest representatives in the Americas.[60] Despite these conflicts, many lay people and priests found that their Catholic faith and call to citizenship in new republics were not inconsistent.[61] For example, with the Constitution of Cádiz in mind, the Mexican Constitution of Apatzingán of 1814 continued Roman Catholicism as the official religion of the state. Political participation was afforded only to Roman Catholics, and apostates and heretics lost citizenship. Freedom of the press was permitted only when consonant with Roman Catholicism.[62] And a subsequent Plan of Three Guarantees for Mexican independence in 1821 declared independence from Spain, the equality of peninsular and American Spaniards (similar to the Constitution of 1812), and the centrality of Catholicism in the new nation.[63]

The first and perhaps fullest enunciation of a new National Patronage of the church was enacted by Gran Colombia in 1824, in opposition to clerical pronouncements that the patronage came to an end on independence. Key portions of this *Ley de Patronato* signaled Gran Colombia's expectation that the Holy See would confirm the country's rights as successor to the patronage, and that the country would control the creation, reorganization, and supervision of dioceses, monasteries, confraternities, fees, tithes, exterior discipline of the church, missions, and the presentation and nomination of bishops and archbishops, among many other areas. The nation would exercise its right to

---

58 See, e.g., Javier Francisco Infante Martin, 'Mariano Egaña (Chile, 1793–1846)' in *Law and Christianity in Latin America: The Work of Great Jurists*, eds M.C. Mirow and Rafael Domingo (London: Routledge, 2021), 81, 83.

59 Mecham, *Church*, 62.

60 Ibid., 48–50, 62–63.

61 Cristóbal García-Huidobro Becerra, 'Justo Donoso Vivanco (Chile, 1800–68)' in *Law and Christianity*, 89.

62 Mirow, *Latin American Constitutions*, 134–135.

63 Schwaller, *History*, 124.

review and prohibit publication of various kinds of communications from the Vatican.[64]

Independence in Latin America left the Catholic hierarchy in disarray. Many top ecclesiastical offices were vacant, and countries' hopes to fill vacant sees were stymied by their assertions of the National Patronage before an entrenched papacy unwilling to recognize such national rights.[65] In some regions, such as Argentina, Paraguay, Uruguay, and Bolivia, independence disrupted the cohesiveness of the church when former administrative subdivisions of the church now crossed international borders and where vacant positions of the higher clergy evaded quick solutions to the question of who had power to fill them.[66] Similar desires for archdioceses matching new political boundaries arose in Central America as republics gained their independence.[67] In other areas, such as Peru and Chile, the church viewed independence as unsanctioned challenges to established authority and opposed such movement.[68]

Brazil was unique. Crown prince Dom Pedro rebelled against Portugal and led Brazil to an independent monarchy. The church moved fluidly from one monarchy to the other with little disruption although it was faced with the challenges of having its wealth raided by the government and regional pressures to abandon the monarchy in favor of a republic. The Vatican recognized Dom Pedro's rule of Brazil in 1823 but questions regarding the Royal Patronage sullied the possibilities of cordial and supportive relations.[69]

Elected Pope in 1831, Gregory XVI was the first to recognize independent Latin American countries. Although battles over the validity of the patronage continued, vacant sees were filled over the next decade.[70]

4 Nations, Liberalism, and Conservatism

Two groups emerged in new nations and reflected the distinction between those supporting the church, conservatives, and those seeking to reduce greatly its place in society and government, liberals. Conservatives sought to continue the privileges of the church and its special place in society consistent

---

64 Mecham, *Church*, 92–94, 99, 101.

65 Ibid., 70–84, 95, 346.

66 Schwaller, *History*, 126.

67 Mecham, *Church*, 311–313, 323, 332.

68 Schwaller, *History*, 128.

69 Ibid., 128, 129.

70 Mecham, *Church*, 85–87, 118.

with the colonial church before the Bourbon reform.[71] Liberals sought to remove the ecclesiastical *fuero* and Roman Catholicism from its favored status, to limit the ownership of church property, to reduce the number and extent of religious orders and their members, to control the appointment of clergy and ecclesiastical officials, to separate church and state, to abolish tithes, and to secularize education, cemeteries, and marriages and associated recordkeeping for these and other events such as births and deaths. These goals could be effected through skillful liberal exercise of the National Patronage of the church and ensconced in legislative and constitutional texts. Thus, conservative or liberal national constitutions addressed a range of issues that crossed secular and religious boundaries: the status of religious individuals, ecclesial institutions, public and religious education, voting and who voted, civil registers and their coexistence with or exclusivity from religious registers, marriage laws, cemeteries for Catholics and non-Catholics, the National Patronage of the church, the ecclesiastical *fuero*, and the place of the church in the constitution, if at all.[72]

Despite their admiration of Spain, conservatives sought to shed the restrictions of the Royal Patronage and to provide the church, its institutions, and its clergy with absolute freedom from state intervention. They argued that the Royal Patronage was unique to the crown and not transmitted to succeeding independent nations. Oddly enough, then, liberals generally argued in favor of the continuity of the colonial relationship established by the Royal Patronage. If new nations inherited rules and practices that led to the national control of the church, politicians could mold the National Patronage to liberal ends with little interference from resident clergy or papal assertions of power. Over time, both conservative and liberal arguments for independent nations as successors of the patronage were ineffective as the church moved for greater centralized control throughout the world including the Americas.[73]

In early independence acts and constitutions the Inquisition was abolished. Ecclesiastical jurisdictions were severely limited to exclusively spiritual matters such as the discipline of clergy. For example, Colombia's *Ley de Patronato* of 1824 gave the national High Court of Justice jurisdiction over archbishops and bishops who violated the patronage, territorial disputes between dioceses, and the interpretation of concordats. The Superior Courts had jurisdiction

71 Schwaller, *History*, 140.

72 Mirow, *Latin American Constitutions*, 146.

73 Schwaller, *History*, 132, 135, 142.

over the violation of the patronage by other ecclesiastics and the conflict of jurisdictions between national and ecclesiastical tribunals.[74]

A significant arena of contention between the governments of new countries and the Vatican was the right to appoint high-level clergy such as bishops and archbishops. After independence, many of these positions were empty, and only bishops could ordain priests, leading to a long-standing problem for the church, a paucity of well-trained and able priests on the lower levels of the church. This challenge was exacerbated by the common practice of suppressing religious orders, an alternative source for parish-level priests, in the decades following independence.[75]

By the middle of the nineteenth century as liberalism and conservatism became defining philosophies of political parties, liberalism moved toward religious toleration and anticlericalism. Indeed, 'by the 1850s (and considerably earlier in Mexico and a few other republics), the clergy had rallied around the banner of conservatism.'[76] Liberal principles including the separation of church and state were resoundingly rejected by Catholics in 1864 in Pius IX's *Syllabus of Errors*.[77] Thus, with liberal thought officially banned from the church, the church moved forward with a new-found impetus for consolidation in the second half of the nineteenth century.[78] Where nations maintained the *fuero*, usually under conservative governments, the church and clergy continued to hold separate rights and jurisdiction over their affairs.

Consistent with the principles of liberalism, the abolition of the ecclesiastical *fuero* immediately reduced the power and privilege of the church. Removing special legal status from clergy made them citizens with the same rights, duties, rules, tribunals, and punishments as any other citizen under legislation and the constitution. Liberals sought and often accomplished the suppression of convents, monasteries, and religious houses.[79] While closing monastic houses, liberal practices forced many regular clergy to become secular clergy, left dioceses without bishops required for ordaining new priests, and depleted the financial stability and reduced the number of available priests for parishes and sacraments. Many areas suffered from a lack of priests and in rural areas popular religions and practices increased.[80]

---

74 Mecham, *Church*, 59, 90, 94.
75 Pike, 'Latin America,' 427.
76 Ibid., 428.
77 Ibid., 431; Schwaller, *History*, 186.
78 Schwaller, *History*, 186.
79 Mecham, *Church*, 96, 107, 123.
80 Schwaller, *History*, 152, 165, 179, 180.

Nations expelled or welcomed back Jesuits according to shifts in political leanings. For example, in 1844 New Granada was the first to welcome back the Jesuits, originally expelled by Spain in 1767. A few years later, in 1850, the same country expelled the Jesuits with two days to depart. In the same period, Jesuits were welcomed to and then expelled from Ecuador. Similarly, the Jesuits were expelled from Uruguay in 1859 and permitted to return in 1865.[81]

Liberals pushed for the abolition of the tithe and the independence of the state from tithe collection and from ecclesiastical finances.[82] In many countries, tithes were abolished, and the church obtained other forms of support such as fixed salaries from the government.[83]

Liberalism was also associated with Freemasonry, and Masons sometimes visibly clashed with the church or governments over their status, over anticlericalism, and religious restrictions on membership.[84] For the most part, 'it is impossible to ascertain to what extent Freemasonry, which was introduced into Latin America in the early years of the nineteenth century, was an antagonist of the Catholic organization.'[85] Nonetheless, Mexican liberal and conservative parties in the early nineteenth century were marked by allegiances to either the Scottish (conservative) or York (liberal) Rites of Masonry. A telling example is found in Brazil in reaction to the Pope's *Syllabus of Errors* and other writings that condemned Freemasonry. The Pope excommunicated any Catholic who joined a Masonic order. Such orders were favored institutions of the country's wealthy and powerful citizens and membership included clergy as well. On the practical level, many Brazilians simply ignored this papal guidance. On the governmental level, because Dom Pedro had the power to approve papal communications before their circulation, called the *exequatur*, he simply did not allow publication of the communications. There were several other clashes between the church and Freemasonry in mid-nineteenth-century Brazil.[86]

Liberalism also played out on the level of private law. The most important battlefield was the law of marriage where ecclesiastical institutions sought to maintain complete control as liberal actors sought to secularize marriage by defining it in contractual terms subject to provisions in the civil code.[87] The

81 Mecham, *Church*, 120, 123, 142, 254–255.

82 Schwaller, *History*, 132.

83 Mecham, *Church*, 204, 209, 211, 226.

84 Pike, 'Latin America,' 428.

85 Mecham, *Church*, 60.

86 Mecham, *Church*, 270–273, 345; Schwaller, *History*, 161–162.

87 Mecham, *Church*, 113. See also Juan Carlos Frontera, 'Eduardo Acevedo Maturana (Uruguay, 1815–63)' in *Law and Christianity*, 210; Viviana Kluger, 'Tristán Narvaja (Argentina and Uruguay, 1819–77)' in *Law and Christianity*, 247; Agustín Parise, 'José Manuel Estrada

Mexican reform law of September 25, 1873, stated succinctly 'Marriage is a civil contract.'[88] Argentina, Chile, and Uruguay, for example, adopted civil marriage in the 1880s but the nature of marriage continues to be contested in the region to this day.[89] Individuals seeking to marry were at times caught in competing jurisdictions risking either excommunication for yielding to state structures or non-recognition of their marriages for yielding to church structures. Liberal attempts could go too far; Venezuelan liberal dictator Antonio Guzmán Blanco's attempt to legalize marriage of clerics was foiled by public outrage. There were also battles over registries for births and deaths and the regulation of cemeteries. Codes of civil law or other provisions under liberal guidance might also provide for divorce and rights to inheritance for children born out of wedlock, also areas of significant debate.[90] Quotidian life was subject to political and jurisdictional battles.

Most countries experienced oscillations between liberal and conservative governments and political regimes. Argentina, Chile, Peru, Bolivia, Venezuela, Colombia are cases in point, where fluctuations were fairly similar. The countries of Central America can be viewed as a laboratory for the implementation of liberal ideas and their rejection under various conditions and circumstances.[91] For the purposes of this study, Mexico in the nineteenth century serves as a clear example. The early constitutions of Mexican independence recognized the Roman Catholic Church as the official state religion.[92] Mexican independence was recognized by Spain and the Vatican in 1836. During the conservative period when Antonio López de Santa Anna was in power, the church benefitted greatly from his support.[93] The loss of large portions of northwest Mexico to the United States led to popular reaction against his leadership. In the first half of the nineteenth century, the church in Mexico was a significant political and economic force.[94]

The pendulum swung towards liberalism in the years leading up to the Mexican Reform of 1854 and the restrictions on the church ushered in by Benito Juárez. Three important sets of reforms dramatically reshaped the contours

---

(Argentina, 1842–94)' in *Law and Christianity*, 316–317; José de la Puente Brunke, 'José de la Riva-Agüero y Osma (Peru, 1885–1944)' in *Law and Christianity*, 397.

88 Mirow, *Latin American Law*, 148.

89 Ibid.

90 Mecham, *Church*, 107, 173, 187, 198, 213, 246, 383. See also Kluger, 'Tristán Narvaja,' 247–248.

91 Schwaller, *History*, 151–165.

92 Mecham, *Church*, 341–448; Mirow, *Latin American Constitutions*, 136–142.

93 Mecham, *Church*, 353–358; Schwaller, *History*, 139.

94 Michael P. Costeloe, *Church Wealth in Mexico: A Study of the 'Juzgado de Capellanías' in the Archbishopric of Mexico 1800–1856* (Cambridge: Cambridge University Press, 1967).

of the relationship between the church and the state in this period. First, the Laws of Juarez (*Ley Juárez*) abolished the ecclesiastical *fuero* and removed the ecclesiastical jurisdiction from any dispute that was not entirely within the church. Second, the Laws of Lerdo (*Ley Lerdo*) went after the church's wealth. Corporations (such as the church) could not hold any property beyond that necessary for their central purposes, so the church could only hold the church and monastery buildings themselves, and no interests in real property as investments.[95] Wealthy investors swooped in to buy up the available lands. This affected not only the church but also Indigenous communal holders of land who saw their lands similarly subject to speculators and investors.[96] Third, the Laws of Iglesias (*Ley Iglesias*) restricted the customary amounts priests could charge for activities or some sacraments.[97]

These reforms were folded into similar provisions found in the Constitution of 1857.[98] Thus, leading Mexican bishops forbade Catholics from swearing to the constitution.[99] Additional reforms confiscated church property, captured marriage under the civil law and established civil registers, and suspended religious holidays. They dissolved religious communities and secularized hospitals and other charities formerly run by the church.[100]

These extreme positions led to a civil war, the War of the Reform; liberals were victorious in 1860.[101] Conservative hopes for change grew with the short-lived French monarchy from 1862 to 1865 but were ultimately frustrated because it adopted many of the liberal reforms.[102] Emperor Maximillian was executed, and Mexico turned again to the Constitution of 1857.[103]

During the last quarter of the nineteenth century until the Revolution in 1910, Mexico was led by Porfirio Díaz whose less rigorous application of the reform laws permitted a long period of toleration of the church in which it was able to recover much of its property and wealth confiscated during more strident reformist times.[104] Díaz also consulted with the Vatican on appointments

95 Mecham, *Church*, 361–362; Schwaller, *History*, 146.
96 Schwaller, *History*, 147, 189.
97 Mecham, *Church*, 363–364; Schwaller, *History*, 147.
98 Mecham, *Church*, 364; Mirow, *Latin American Constitutions*, 198; Mirow, *Latin American Law*, 113.
99 Mecham, *Church*, 365.
100 Mirow, *Latin American Constitutions*, 183; Schwaller, *History*, 148.
101 Mecham, *Church*, 161; Schwaller, *History*, 148.
102 Mecham, *Church*, 369–374; Schwaller, *History*, 149.
103 Schwaller, *History*, 150.
104 Mecham, *Church*, 376–379; Schwaller, *History*, 174, 190–191.

of bishops. These reforms and economic advances benefitted only the few, and Indigenous groups who lost their land and the poor opposed the status quo.[105]

In the face of mounting armed revolts, Díaz resigned and left Mexico in 1911. Opposition leader Francisco Madero, a follower of French spiritist doctrines, called for elections and won, but the rate of his reforms was too slow for many, or they were simply unacceptable to members of the old guard. He was ousted in 1913 by one of them, General Victoriano Huerta, who staged a coup supported by the church. After the regional and internal struggles of different rebel groups, Venustiano Carranza surfaced as a leader and in an attempt to consolidate power called for a constitutional convention in 1917.[106]

If the reforms of Juarez and Lerdo in Mexico serve as an example of liberal success, then the late nineteenth-century movement called the Regeneration in Colombia illustrates conservative triumph in reaction to previous liberal regimes from the 1850s through the 1880s.[107] The subsequent conservative Constitution of 1886 reinstated the Roman Catholic Church as a privileged actor in the country and permitted censorship of the press. The new regime signed a concordat with the Holy See in 1887.[108] It provided for the privileged status of Roman Catholicism, the recognition of ecclesiastical law and jurisdictional safeguards for clergy, the economic and property rights of the church, the stability of religious orders and their institutions, the cooperation of the church in education, the Holy See's right to fill archdioceses and dioceses, the religious nature of matrimony, and the recognition of debts, mortgages, and loans held by ecclesiastical institutions.[109] The resolution of these issues was not permanent and Colombia experienced violent clashes between liberals and conservatives in the twentieth century.[110]

Another example of conservative victory was Gabriel García Moreno's control of the Ecuadorian government in 1860 that led to, in the words of Mecham, 'the nearest approach to a theocracy in the western world' until the mid-1870s.[111] García Moreno entered into a extensive concordat in 1862 protecting the ecclesiastical *fuero* and abandoning any glimmer of National Patronage.[112]

105 Schwaller, *History*, 175, 191.

106 Ibid., 191–192.

107 Ibid., 154–155.

108 Mirow, *Latin American Constitutions*, 153–154. See Eduardo Herrera and M.C. Mirow, 'Miguel Antonio Caro Tobar (Colombia, 1853–1909)' in *Law and Christianity*, 328–337.

109 Mecham, *Church*, 131.

110 Mirow, Latin American Constitutions, 216–220.

111 Mecham, *Church*, 142. See generally, Peter V.N. Henderson, 'Gabriel García Moreno (Ecuador, 1821–75)' in *Law and Christianity*, 252–267.

112 Mecham, *Church*, 143–152.

Over the decades following the 1870s, the concordat was suspended, restored, amended, and supplemented. In 1899, a liberal president reinstated traditional assertions of the patronage.[113] Similarly, strong dictators might capture the national church and its hierarchy, as in the case of Paraguay during the first part of the nineteenth century.[114] Likewise, in Argentina, 'under the dictatorship of Juan Manuel de Rosas (1835–1852) the Catholic Church was converted into a servile instrument of the tyranny.'[115]

While associated with liberal reforms, freedom of religion was often the result of a much narrower desire to accommodate foreign traders and commercial actors. For example, Juan Bautista Alberdi, drafter of the Argentine Constitution of 1853, wanted to attract 'beneficial,' although not necessarily Catholic immigrants to the country to improve trade and commerce.[116] Consequently, more than fifteen Latin American constitutions from the nineteenth century had provisions allowing the freedom of public religious worship. Still, these constitutions and their provisions of toleration could easily be swept aside with a change of the political winds toward conservatism and Roman Catholic exclusivity.[117]

In addition to questions of constitutional and private law, the official relationship of new nations with the Holy See through concordats was another issue for resolution. Some concordats were lasting; others were not. In 1852, Costa Rica, Guatemala, and Honduras signed concordats with the Holy See, and Nicaragua entered into a concordat ten years later, in 1862. Conservatives in several Central American republics remained in power for many decades of the nineteenth century until liberal views led to attacks against the church and opened avenues for the relatively early growth of Protestantism in the region.[118] Also in 1862, Venezuela negotiated and signed a concordat with the Holy See under General José Antonio Páez, but it was rejected by the next president.[119]

Nonetheless, even before or without concordats, 'governments would routinely forward commendations for episcopal appointments to the pope.'[120] Without concordats, the Vatican was able to instruct and to communicate with bishops without the permission or oversight of the state. And much was done

113 Ibid., 152–154.

114 Ibid., 190–194.

115 Ibid., 232.

116 Mirow, *Latin American Law*, 198.

117 Brian Loveman, *The Constitution of Tyranny: Regimes of Exception in Spanish America* (Pittsburgh: University of Pittsburgh Press, 1993), 372–373.

118 Schwaller, *History*, 164, 179–181.

119 Mecham, *Church*, 104–105; Schwaller, *History*, 157.

120 Schwaller, *History*, 131.

informally without concordats. For example, without an agreement with the Vatican, Argentina recommended appointments for bishops and was able to create an archdiocese of Buenos Aires, while the Vatican extracted the right to create new dioceses and to appoint bishops and other higher clergy. In the mid-nineteenth century, Peru and the Vatican lacked a concordat but consulted informally for over three decades on the appointment of bishops. Peru established a clear working agreement with the Vatican through a papal bull issued in 1874.[121] In the meantime, a new modality of law took shape.

A distinct form of canon law developed in the new republics leading to what some have called a Latin American canon law. For example, by the mid-nineteenth century, the Chilean priest and jurist Justo Donoso was able to produce a manual for Latin American priests and a comprehensive treatment of canon law in Spanish America.[122] And the famous Argentine codifier Dalmacio Vélez Sarsfield spent much of his professional life advising and writing about the legal relationship between the church and state.[123]

5 The Twentieth Century, Revolution, and the Rise of the Social

Commencing in 1910, the Mexican Revolution led to years of physical and political battles. The resulting constitutional consensus, the Mexican Constitution of 1917, submitted the church and religious affairs to state control. Article 130 of the Constitution:

> gave federal authorities an exclusive jurisdiction in religious affairs, prohibiting Congress from establishing or prohibiting any religion, placed determinations of civil status within civil authorities, removed the legal personality of churches, gave local legislatures the power to determine the number of priests and ministers in each state, required members of religious orders to be Mexican by birth, prohibited religious officials from voting, removed official recognition from seminary studies, prohibited religious publications from commenting on political affairs, prohibited political meetings in religious buildings, and prohibited religious officials

121 Ibid., 150, 151, 153, 183–184. The bull was accepted by the Peruvian government in 1880. Ibid., 181, 182–183.

122 García-Huidobro Becerra, 'Justo Donoso' in *Law and Christianity*, 91–99.

123 Abelardo Levaggi, 'Dalmacio Vélez Sarsfield (Argentina, 1800–1874)' in *Law and Christianity*, 105–113. E.g., Dalmacio Vélez Sarsfield, *Derecho público eclesiástico. Relaciones del Estado con la Iglesia en la Antigua América Española* (Buenos Aires: J.A. Bernheim, 1854).

> from inheriting unless the bequest came from a family member within the fourth degree, among other restrictions and prohibitions.[124]

The new government prohibited religious ceremonies in public places, and primary education was removed from the church.[125] Several subsequent legislative acts whittled away at the church as an institution, property owner, and educator.[126] In 1924, a vehemently anticlerical period followed under President Plutarco Elias Calles. A rift between the government and the church widened and even produced a clerical strike from mid-1926 to mid-1929.[127] In 1926 the Archbishop of Mexico announced that Catholics did not recognize and ought to combat the anticlerical provisions of the Constitution.[128] Violence ensued as the church was supported by guerilla groups rallying to 'Viva Cristo Rey' Long Live Christ the King, the source of the name to this civil war as the Cristero Revolt.[129] In the civil war between 1926 and 1929, hundreds of priests fled the countryside, and approximately ninety were murdered.[130] Although violence was diminished through negotiations that included the U.S. government and Catholic leaders, the resulting peace was religiously and politically unstable.[131] Nonetheless, even under such conditions, the church and its individuals raised powerful but hidden voices for legal and political change.[132]

Although Mexico, for example, provides a nineteenth-century example of the separation of church and state and the disestablishment of the church from the governmental sphere, this change became more sweeping through the region in the twentieth century. For example, the separation of church and state was established in Uruguay in 1917 and Chile in 1925.[133] After a liberal victory in Colombia in 1930, more moderate factions negotiated a new concordat for Colombia in 1942.[134] From 1946 to 1957, liberal and conservative violence escalated to a point where this period is know as *La Violencia*, The Violence, in

124 Mirow, *Latin American Constitutions*, 209.
125 Ibid., 209–210.
126 Schwaller, *History*, 192.
127 Mecham, *Church*, 392–399, 403; Schwaller, *History*, 193.
128 Mecham, *Church*, 391–392.
129 Mecham, *Church*, 399; Schwaller, *History*, 193.
130 Stephen J.C. Andes, 'Catholicism, Revolution, and Counter-Revolution in Twentieth-Century Latin America' in *OHLAC*, 179.
131 Schwaller, *History*, 194.
132 Peter Lester Reich, *Mexico's Hidden Revolution: The Catholic Church in Law and Politics since 1929* (Notre Dame: University of Notre Dame Press, 1995).
133 Mecham, *Church*, 418.
134 Schwaller, *History*, 194–195.

which the church was seen as strongly aligned with the conservative party and anticlericalism a tenet of liberal factions.[135]

By the middle of the twentieth century, Mecham observed that 'Argentina, Bolivia, Colombia, Costa Rica, Dominical Republic, El Salvador, Haiti, Paraguay, Peru, and Venezuela' exhibited union between church and state, while 'Brazil, Chile, Cuba, Ecuador, Guatemala, Honduras, Mexico, Nicaragua, Panama, and Uruguay' exhibited their separation.[136] But beyond separation of church and state, new perspectives on religion and society surfaced.

In addition to shifting the place of the church in the Mexican state, the Constitution of 1917 ushered in important new perspectives on labor and property. The Constitution called for fair wages, safe working conditions, and unions of workers and their rights. It called for new visions of property and land, the nationalization of natural resources and oil. These new stances evinced a new turn to what has been labeled 'the social.' Nonetheless, the Mexican Constitution, like the Revolution, was unique, and it had less influence in the region than one might expect. A turn to 'the social' elsewhere in Latin America obeyed other factors.

Movement towards the social was guided by two related streams of thought: European legal sociology found in thinkers like Léon Duguit who gave a series of influential lectures on private law in Buenos Aires in 1911; and, Catholic social doctrine attempting to find a Christian middle way between the harshness of unbridled capitalism and the loss of private property under socialism. The papal encyclicals *Rerum Novarum* (1891) and *Quadragesimo Anno* (1931) served as important sources in the construction of the social from the religious perspective.[137] Influenced by the social doctrine of the church and by the writings of more secular European legal sociologists, drafters of Latin American constitutions in the twentieth century incorporated ideas of the social function of property, land reform, and social solidarity.[138]

Numerous jurists were influenced by the church's ideas of property and labor. For example, from the 1910s to the 1950s Ecuadorian jurist Julio Tobar Donoso wrote several books on these and related themes.[139] Chilean scholar and law professor Pedro Lira Urquieta was similarly influenced by these

135 Mecham, *Church*, 134–135; Schwaller, *History*, 195–197.

136 Mecham, *Church*, 420–421.

137 M.C. Mirow, '*Rerum Novarum*: New Things and Recent Paradigms in Property Law,' 47 (2016) University of the Pacific Law Review 188–196.

138 Mirow, *Latin American Constitutions*, 221–222.

139 Álvaro R. Mejía-Salazar, 'Julio Tobar Donoso (Ecuador, 1894–1981)' in *Law and Christianity*, 438–442.

developments. Villalonga writes that Lira Urquieta's 'relentless reflections on law and social affairs constitute, to a great extent, a particular form of engagement with Catholicism after *Quadragesimo Anno* (1931).'[140] In Venezuela, Rafael Caldera was similarly influenced by Catholic social doctrine in his work and teaching.[141]

Furthermore, some leaders of the twentieth century carved out new forms of political spirituality that appropriated religion. There were certainly Christian aspects of Argentine Juan Perón's political, social, and religious amalgamation of *justicialismo*.[142] And Perón's chief legal adviser within this movement, Arturo Enrique Sampay, was highly influenced by Catholic thought.[143] Nonetheless, the last days of Perón's dictatorship in 1954 and 1955 were marked by a clear split from the Catholic Church.[144] Pike finds the best example of this spiritual eclecticism in Peru's Víctor Raúl Haya de la Torre in the 1930s:

> Finding his inspiration in the early Mexican Revolution, in Anarchism, in social gospel Protestantism, and the Book of Revelation, in Anatoli Lunacharsky's interpretation of the Bolshevik revolution and in Romain Rolland's brand of spiritualism, in symbolic Masonry and pre-conquest Inca religious beliefs, in Heraclitus and Pythagoras and other exemplars of esoteric enlightenment, and in hazy concepts of raising consciousness to the fourth dimension purportedly deriving from Albert Einstein, Haya de la Torre proclaimed that only his religio-political movement could bring redemption to Peru.[145]

The church also served in transition from autocratic rule. In Brazil, under the dictatorship of the generals from the mid-1960 to the latter 1970s increased possibilities for democracy led to improved relations with the church and the election of General João Batista Figueiredo in 1979.[146] In Chile, in reaction to the election of Marxist President Salvador Allende in 1970 and his party's gain in congressional seats in 1973, General Augusto Pinochet staged

140 Cristián Villalonga, 'Pedro Lira Urquieta (Chile, 1900–81)' in *Law and Christianity*, 455. See Id., 460–466.

141 Carlos García-Soto, 'Rafael Antonio Caldera Rodríguez (Venezuela, 1916–2009)' in *Law and Christianity*, 483–495.

142 Mecham, *Church*, 246–248; Pike, 'Latin America,' 440–441.

143 Susana T. Ramella, 'Arturo Enrique Sampay (Argentina, 1911–77)' in *Law and Christianity*, 470–482.

144 Mecham, *Church*, 249–250; Schwaller, *History*, 218–220.

145 Pike, 'Latin America,' 440.

146 Schwaller, *History*, 234–236.

a coup. The country entered into a military dictatorship and when a return to democracy appeared unlikely, 'the Catholic Church then became one of the many voices calling for a return to democracy, finding partners in sometimes strange places.'[147] Other factions of the church and several bishops supported Pinochet. After a papal visit of Pope John Paul II in 1987, pressure from the church's opposition gained steam. Under the Vicariate of Solidarity and center parties, and through the intermediation of Chilean Cardinal Juan Francisco Fresno, Archbishop of Santiago, the regime slowly accepted a transition that led to a plebiscite on the political future of the country in 1988 and the subsequent election of President Patricio Aylwin in 1990. Variations of similar political changes occurred in Argentina and Peru.[148]

Changes in ecclesial perspective led to grassroots Catholic lay groups that reshaped the way the Catholic Church interacted with the people of Latin America. In the first part of the twentieth century, Catholic Action produced organizations for discrete groups: students, women, union members, and peasants, for example.[149] In the 1950s and 1960s, Base Ecclesial Communities (CEBs as they are commonly known for *Comunidades Eclesiales de Base*) grew to promote lay-level spirituality combined with direct social and political action in accordance with the social doctrine of the church. It is estimated that by the late 1970s there were as many as 200,000 CEBs in Latin America.[150]

6 Recent Times

In the latter half of the twentieth and the first decades of the twenty-first centuries, countries have experienced wide variations in democratic, populist, and authoritarian governments. The church has almost always played a role or had a voice in these events to support, to intervene, to mediate, to critique, and to resist depending on the time and place. Even non-believing leaders often recognized the Catholicism of their populations and recognized the importance of the church in maintaining stable polities.[151]

---

147 Ibid., 241.

148 Ibid., 241–243.

149 Nick Rowell, 'Activist Christians, the Human Rights Movement, and Democratization in Latin America' in *OHLAC*, 219.

150 Andes, 'Catholicism,' 185; Robert S. Pelton, 'Catholic Laity in the Latin American Church' in *OHLAC*, 507–511; Rowell, 'Activist Christians,' 220.

151 Schwaller, *History*, 206–207.

Members of the clergy have stood up to military and authoritarian actors who have ignored human rights or violently suppressed opposition. In other instances the church and religious leaders have fallen into worrisome complicity or willful ignorance with military, authoritarian, and dictatorial regimes.[152] After surveying the horrors of political violence in twentieth-century Mexico, Cuba, Chile, Argentina, Guatemala, Nicaragua, and Peru, Stephen Andes notes:

> Catholics were integral participants in the bloodbath. The Catholic Church shaped, and was shaped by, the cycles of insurgency, counter-insurgency, and state terror, which defined Latin America's twentieth-century violence. ... Catholics took up all sides in twentieth-century conflict, from revolutionary priests, accommodationist bishops, and lay counter-revolutionaries, to Catholic generals who massacred their own citizens with state-sponsored death squads.[153]

Often at the same time, the church has worked quietly in the shadows or loudly in the open to maintain peace and to spare lives. The church, despite the dangers involved to its individual members, advanced human rights in the face of repression and was often the main institution to lead opposition to violence and state oppression.[154] As Rowell observes, 'In many highly repressive environments, the Catholic Church was the only segment of civil society that was allowed to continue operating with relative autonomy.'[155] The ability to survive in repressive environments enabled the church to act. It was not without a high cost: 'Between 1968 and 1990, over a thousand priests and nuns were exiled, imprisoned, tortured, or killed in Latin America by authoritarian governments.'[156]

For example, Christian and Catholic human rights actions against the Pinochet regime are well known, and the Catholic Church's Vicariate of Solidarity documented abuses, aided families, and gathered facts.[157] The Medellín Conference of bishops established a Commission of Peace and Justice in Rio de Janeiro that documented human rights abuses.[158] Nonetheless, as

152 Amy Edmonds, 'The Ambivalence of Catholic Politics in Latin America: Ideology, Interests, and Institutions' in *OHLAC*, 258; Mecham, *Church*, 295–297.
153 Andes, 'Catholicism' in *OHLAC*, 176.
154 Rowell, 'Activist Christians,' 221.
155 Ibid.
156 Edward Brett, 'Prophetic Martyrdom in Modern Latin America' in *OHLAC*, 252.
157 Rowell, 'Activist Christians,' 224.
158 Edmonds, 'The Ambivalence,' 260.

authoritarian regimes fell in Latin America the church's engagement with human rights declined both on the lower levels as CEBs shifted away from social action and on the higher levels as Pope John Paul II appointed more conservative bishops to Latin American dioceses. Secular social movements and NGOs filled the void.[159]

In the second half of the twentieth century, Latin American bishops' conferences led to a distinctly Latin American Roman Catholicism both in relation to Rome and to Latin America.[160] Especially the conferences in Medellín, Colombia (1968) and in Puebla, Mexico (1979) coupled with the rise of liberation theology led the church's religious and lay members to focus on poverty, the lived experiences of the faithful, and appropriate responses to oppressive or distant governments. With these issues in the forefront, the Medellín Conference sought ways of implementing Vatican II in Latin America. In Puebla, the bishops continued their dedication to Vatican II and the Medellín Conference emphasizing the importance of small groups within the church and of the centrality of poverty and human rights.[161] At this conference 'the bishops articulated the now-famous "preferential option for the poor."'[162]

Liberation theology grew from a variety of external and internal critiques that drew from the fields of economics, sociology, political science, and notions of dependency theory as these intellectual trends reached theological training in the 1960s and 1970s.[163] A theological commitment to the poor meant taking action on levels above the individual or locality. Indeed, the church forged new tools and methods to protect human dignity and recognized human rights.[164] In the following decade, these ideas pushed many clergy towards militancy and direct conflict with opposing governments.[165] Some clergy became revolutionaries who argued for the 'theological correctness of armed struggle.'[166]

In 1984, the Vatican, through the Congregation of the Doctrine of the Faith led by Cardinal Ratzinger, issued an 'Instruction on Certain Aspects of the Theology of Liberation.'[167] Although it bolstered many of the social and

159 Rowell, 'Activist Christians,' 225–226.

160 The conferences, usually referred to as CELAM for Consejo Episcopal Latinoamericano, were in Rio de Janeiro (1955), Medellín (1968), Puebla (1979), Santo Domingo (1992), and Aparecida, Brazil (2007). Erika Helgen, 'Bishops, Priests, and CELAM' in *OHLAC*, 195–216.

161 Schwaller, *History*, 246–248, 259–260.

162 Ibid., 260.

163 Pike, 'Latin America,' 443. See generally, Phillip Berryman, 'Liberation Theology: History and Trends' in *OHLAC*, 157–174.

164 Schwaller, *History*, 249.

165 Pike, 'Latin America,' 445; Schwaller, *History*, 220–227.

166 Schwaller, *History*, 243.

167 Ibid., 261.

economic concerns of the church, the document critiqued the overall trajectory of liberation theology.[168] Liberation theology was linked, especially by its opponents, to Marxism and communism.[169] The Vatican turned to appointing more conservative bishops who supported other avenues of local religious formation with more moderate theological foundations.[170]

Because of the region's lack of economic development, Central America and its countries proved to be fruitful ground for the application of liberation theology from the 1960s to the 1990s.[171] In El Salvador, for example, Óscar Romero was appointed archbishop of San Salvador in 1977 and was expected to maintain a conservative position. He soon became a prominent voice of the poor and spoke against the military. In 1980 he was murdered while celebrating Mass.[172] In Nicaragua, although the church was on good terms with the Somoza dictatorship, the Sandinista opposition contained many members of the clergy and the Sandinistas were not hostile to the church. In fact, at one point there were five priests who had taken official positions in the Sandinista government with Vatican permission.[173] 'This broad support in the Church, nearly half of all priests, made the Sandinista experiment in Nicaragua far different from any other communist or Marxist government.'[174]

While liberation theologians and clergy continued in resistance, or were brought back to orthodoxy or excommunicated, the call for social justice and human rights by the church continued, particularly in light of Vatican II (1962–1965) and its movement from ecclesial hierarchy to a religious and lay body of believers protecting the rights of all persons as human beings.[175]

Recent efforts by the church have been to hold the line on encroachments into orthodoxy on areas related to family, sexuality, reproduction, clerical celibacy, divorce, and male priesthood.[176] And the church has taken on newer

168 Ibid.

169 Berryman, 'Liberation Theology,' 166–168.

170 Schwaller, *History*, 262–263.

171 Ibid., 250–258.

172 Ibid., 254; Rafael Domingo, 'Óscar Arnulfo Romero y Galdámez (El Salvador, 1917–1980)' in *Law and Christianity*, 496–510.

173 Schwaller, *History*, 254–257; Andes, 'Catholicism,' 186–189.

174 Schwaller, *History*, 256.

175 Andes, 'Catholicism,' 189; Pike, 'Latin America,' 446; Schwaller, *History*, 227–230, 249–250.

176 Edmonds, 'The Ambivalence,' 265–266; Pike, 'Latin America,' 447; Marta Rodriguez de Assis Machado, Ana Luisa Villela de Viana Bandeira, and Fernanda Emy Matsuda, 'Law, Gender, and Social Movements in Latin America: Moral Negotiations and Uneven Victories in Feminist Legal Mobilization' in *Routledge Handbook of Law and Society in Latin America*, eds Rachel Sieder, Karina Ansolabehere, and Tatiana Alfonso (Abingdon: Routledge, 2021), 358, 360–364, 367.

areas of concern: gang violence, Indigenous rights, women and children's rights, immigration, bioethics, and the environment.[177]

Approximately 40 percent of the world's Roman Catholics are Latin Americans, and the present Pope is an Argentine. Nonetheless, Protestant Christianity has made substantial gains in the region since the mid-twentieth century.[178] Of these Protestants in Latin America, it is estimated that over 70 per cent are Pentecostals who form a highly impactful religious minority in several regions of Latin America, such as Guatemala and Brazil.[179] Apparently in response to the immediacy of religious experience found in Pentecostal worship, a movement of Catholic Charismatic Renewal has gained adherents in the region.[180] Religious voices continue to influence the region's politics and law.

7 Conclusion

Apart from royal or national government, the Catholic Church has been the most cohesive and assertive institution of social, political, and legal action in Latin America. Royal governments looked to theologians, canon lawyers, and papal officials to justify and to affirm imperial enterprises that implicated both violent and peaceful interactions with new populations. The legal and spiritual status of Indigenous populations was at the intellectual center of imperial action.

In the colonial period, an unusual collaboration formed between the church and royal government under the Royal Patronage of the church. Through this arrangement, the Pope transferred considerable ecclesiastical power to the crown and its operation in the Americas based on the royal assumption of evangelization to Indigenous peoples in the new expanses under crown

177 Robert J. Cottrol, 'Carlos Alberto Menezes Direito (Brazil, 1942–2009)' in *Law and Christianity*, 544–546; Christine Kovic, 'Rights, Religion, and Violence at Mexico's Borders' in OHLAC, 273–288; Lois Ann Lorentzen, 'Christianity and Ecology in Latin America' in OHLAC, 459–472; Rowell, 'Activist Christians,' 226–229.

178 Pike, 'Latin America,' 448–451; Pew Research Center, 'Religion in Latin America: Widespread Change in a Historically Catholic Region' November 13, 2014, https://www.pewforum.org/2014/11/13/religion-in-latin-america/.

179 Virginia Garrard and Justin M. Doran, 'Pentecostalism and Neo-Pentecostalism in Latin America: Two Case Studies' in OHLAC, 293–307; Henry Gooren, 'Conversion Processes and Social Networks in Latin America' in OHLAC, 309–327.

180 Brenda Caranza, 'Preferential Option for the Spirit: The Catholic Charismatic Renewal' in OHLAC, 393–410.

control. This led to new legal institutions and structures for these activities promoted by both royal and ecclesiastical officials. Although governed through the Royal Patronage, the church became a central spiritual, social, political, and economic force in colonial America with its own canon law and institutions.

Religious concerns and the place of the church in government and society arose in the context of independence. While higher-level ecclesiastical officials were generally sympathetic with the crown and resisted independence, many priests and lower-level officials supported new governments, particularly in light of royal limitations on the church imposed during the decades leading up to independence. Many independence leaders and early constitutions sought to continue the privileged status of the church in their new constitutional structures. The Spanish Constitution of 1812, the Constitution of Cádiz, was an important model in this regard.

On independence, national attempts to transfer the Royal Patronage to new countries led to conflicts between the church and governments creating schisms between liberal and conservative thinkers. Political groups and parties reflected different views of the role of the church in society and government. These tensions led to national conflicts and even wars as liberal and conservative forces asserted their views of the place of the church in government, education, marriage, records of civil status, and cemeteries to name a few common areas of heated disagreement. Church wealth, its participation in the economic life of the nation, and its ability to hold property beyond that strictly necessary for worship were also subject to political contention.

In more recent times, often as the sole dissenting voice under repressive regimes, the church has turned to political action, social justice, and human rights. The church has monitored human rights abuses of military and autocratic regimes, publicized such activities, and aided victims. With a theological turn towards the poor and a wide ecclesial net, the church has taken direct action and supported legal reforms to improve the condition of the poor. With the rise of Protestant denominations in the region, the Roman Catholic Church has lost its monopoly as the singular voice of Christianity in Latin America. Nonetheless, the religious, cultural, and political influences of Catholicism and other forms of Christianity presently constitute an essential aspect of the region and its legal development.

References

Bouzada Gíl, María Teresa. *La vía de fuerza: La práctica en la Real Audiencia del Reino de Galicia. Siglos XVII–XVIII*. Santiago de Compostela: Xunta de Galicia, 2001.

Cruz, Joel M. *The Histories of the Latin American Church: A Handbook*. Minneapolis: Fortress Press, 2014.

Duve, Thomas, and Otto Danwerth, eds. *Knowlege of the* Pragmatici: *Legal and Moral Theological Literature and the Formation of the Early Modern Ibero-America*. Leiden: Brill, 2020.

Dussel, Enrique. *Historia general de la Iglesia en América Latina*. 11 vols. México: Ediciones Paulinas, 1981–1985.

Lynch, John. *New Worlds: A Religious History of Latin America*. New Haven: Yale University Press, 2012.

Masferrer, Aniceto. *Spanish Legal Traditions: A Comparative Legal History Outline*. 2nd ed. Madrid: Dykinson, 2012.

McManners, John, ed. *The Oxford Illustrated History of Christianity*. Oxford: Oxford University Press, 1990.

Mecham, J. Lloyd. *Church and State in Latin America: A History of Politico-Ecclesiastical Relations*. Rev. ed. Chapel Hill: University of North Carolina Press, 1966.

Mirow, M.C., and Rafael Domingo, eds. *Law and Christianity in Latin America: The Work of Great Jurists*. London: Routledge, 2021.

Orique, David Thomas, Susan Fitzpatrick-Behrens, and Virginia Garrard, eds. *The Oxford Handbook of Latin American Christianity*. New York: Oxford University Press, 2020.

Padoa-Schioppa, Antonio. *A History of Law in Europe: From the Early Middle Ages to the Twentieth Century*. Cambridge: Cambridge University Press, 2017.

Pike, Fredrick B. 'Latin America.' In *The Oxford Illustrated History of Christianity*, edited by John McManners, 420–454. Oxford: Oxford University Press, 1990.

Reich, Peter Lester. *Mexico's Hidden Revolution: The Catholic Church in Law and Politics since 1929*. Notre Dame: University of Notre Dame Press, 1995.

Schwaller, John Frederick. *The History of the Catholic Church in Latin America: From Conquest to Revolution and Beyond*. New York: New York University Press, 2011.

Tellkamp, Jörg Alejandro, ed. *A Companion to Early Modern Spanish Imperial Political and Social Thought*. Leiden: Brill, 2020.

Tomás y Valiente, Francisco. *Manual de historia del derecho español*. 4th ed. Madrid: Tecnos, 2009.

CHAPTER 20

The Welfare State

Eduardo Zimmermann

One obstacle to be faced when writing a history of the Welfare State in Latin America from the perspective of legal history is the almost absolute predominance of studies from the social sciences – economics, political science, sociology – in the existing literature on the subject. Almost always, these studies have emphasized the centrality of very general processes in their explanations such as industrialization, urbanization, democratization, and pressure-group participation. One of the pioneering works on the subject, published by Carmelo Mesa-Lago almost half a century ago, illustrated well the foundations of what was to become a recurrent trend. The 'traditional' perspectives, Mesa-Lago suggested, provided 'superficial' explanations of the origins of social security in the region, taking as causes humanitarian motivations, or processes of 'diffusion' and 'demonstration' effects of nations with more advanced programs, or the influence of international organizations, or idiosyncratic traits of officials or political leaders who launched these programs from a paternalistic attitude, or as an instrument to soften or contain social conflict. Although these factors could be taken into account to explain some particular cases, Mesa-Lago emphasized, 'a more refined position' explained these processes as the result of a particular 'socio-political-economic structure.' Thus, it was industrialization, urbanization, and modernization, with the consequent erosion of traditional forms of social protection (extended families, parishes, guilds or cooperatives), that gave birth to public social protection systems.[1]

Some of the advantages of this 'structuralist' approach, which would inspire most social science studies in the following decades, were evident; they explained why in Latin America, for example, social security protection was extended to urban workers in formal employment while rural workers or those employed in informal markets were left aside for a long time. Nonetheless, as Peter Baldwin rightly pointed out some years ago, some of these interpretations of the origin and evolution of the Welfare State in general present certain problems of particular importance when thinking about developments

1 Carmelo Mesa-Lago, *Social Security in Latin America: Pressure Groups, Stratification, and Inequality* (Pittsburgh: University of Pittsburgh Press, 1978), 5–7.

 | DOI:10.1163/9789004436091_022

in Latin America. The first is the problem of 'unilinearity' as an implicit methodological presupposition. This is the assumption that, given certain initial conditions, levels of industrial development, degrees of democratization, and articulation of certain pressure groups, societies advance in a similar way in the institutionalization of their social policies. This approach tends to sacrifice a more detailed contextualization of the different national cases in pursuit of the establishment of common regularities. The second problem arises as a variant of what Butterfield called 'the *Whig* interpretation of history' in which the advance towards socialization and the establishment of social security policies is seen as an inherent attribute of the historical development of societies, with a character of inevitability that eventually imposes itself once the obstacles posed by certain interests have been overcome.[2]

In Latin American history, the scheme proposed by T.H. Marshall in 1950 concerning three successive phases in the construction of the idea of citizenship through the extension of civil, political, and social rights between the eighteenth and twentieth centuries, offers a case in point. This scheme frequently encouraged a teleological reading in which the reforms of the mid-twentieth century, the conquest of social rights, and the genuine attainment of citizenship became a reality, a perspective that greatly undervalues previous historical experiences in this area.[3]

More recent studies on Latin America coming from the social sciences have mitigated these dangers, offering in some cases studies of longer duration, in which the differences between traditional forms of social welfare are seen as antecedents of the processes of construction of the modern Welfare State.

2 Peter Baldwin, 'The Welfare State for Historians' (1992) 34(4) Comparative Studies in Society and History 695–707. In the same critical position of Baldwin to the 'assumptions about the evolutionary nature of the welfare state and the socioeconomic roots of political processes,' see Theda Skocpol, *Protecting Soldiers and Mothers: The Political Origins of Social Policy in the United States* (Cambridge: Harvard University Press, 1992), 39. For the analysis of some difficulties surrounding 'the modernization hypothesis' and comparative studies of social policies see Edwin Amenta, 'What We Know about the Development of Social Policy: Comparative and Historical Research in Comparative and Historical Perspective' in *Comparative Historical Analysis in the Social Sciences*, eds James Mahoney and Dieter Rueschemeyer (Cambridge: Cambridge University Press, 2003), 91–130.

3 This perspective is also centered on a definition of citizenship focused almost exclusively on the possession of rights, which takes little account of other perspectives aimed at emphasizing the presence of certain virtues and attitudes as defining elements of citizenship. About this see Will Kymlicka and Norman Wayne, 'Return of the Citizen: A Survey of Recent Work on Citizenship Theory' (1994) 104 Ethics 352–381.

These also provide a more careful reconstruction of the specificities of the different national cases.[4]

These studies, however, still often tend to undervalue some of those variables that Mesa-Lago described as 'traditional' and that now return in a new body of literature that has given the history of social policies a 'global and transnational turn.'[5] In this new historiography the accent is placed on the weight of the transnational circulation of doctrines and institutional mechanisms, and on the construction of networks of experts, bearers of new 'social knowledge' and drivers of social policy models.[6] This perspective is of particular importance for approaching the construction of the *welfare state* from the point of view of *legal history*. In the following sections, I will first describe the general evolution of 'social states' in Latin America, from the first expressions of social policies to the construction of contemporary welfare states. Then, I will analyze the processes of circulation of legal doctrines and their inscription in constitutional texts that served as intellectual support for this evolution.

1 From the 'Social Question' to the 'Truncated Welfare State' in Latin America

There is a general consensus in locating the starting point of social policy-making processes in Latin America in the so-called 'social question' of the early twentieth century. In all national cases, the convergence of workers'

---

4 Emily J. Brearley, 'A History of Social Protection in Latin America: From Conquest to Conditional Cash Transfers' (2016) 56 Revue Interventions économiques 1–27; Francisco H.G. Ferreira and David Robalino, 'Social Protection in Latin America. Achievements and Limitations' (2010) 5305 The World Bank Policy Research Working Paper 1–39; Sonia Fleury, 'The Welfare State in Latin America: Reform, Innovation and Fatigue' (2017) 33 Cadernos de Saúde Pública 1–10; Evelyne Huber, 'Options for Social Policy in Latin America: Neoliberal versus Social Democratic Models' in *Welfare States in Transition: National Adaptations in Global Economies*, ed. Gøsta Esping-Andersen (London: Sage, 1996), 141–191; James M. Malloy, *The Politics of Social Security in Brazil* (Pittsburgh: University of Pittsburgh Press, 1979); Tomoko Murai, 'The Foundation of the Mexican Welfare State and Social Security Reform in the 1990s' (2004) 42(2) The Developing Economies 262–287; Francisca Rengifo, 'Desigualdad e inclusión. La ruta del Estado de seguridad social chileno, 1920–1970' (2017) 97 Hispanic American Historical Review 485–522; Alex Segura-Ubiergo, *The Political Economy of the Welfare State in Latin America: Globalization, Democracy, and Development* (Cambridge: Cambridge University Press, 2007).

5 Daniel T. Rodgers, 'Bearing Tales: Networks and Narratives in Social Policy Transfer' (2014) 9 Journal of Global History 301–313.

6 *States, Social Knowledge, and the Origins of Modern Social Policies*, eds Dietrich Rueschemeyer and Theda Skocpol (Princeton: Princeton University Press, 1996).

activism and the perception of new problems generated by demographic change, urbanization, and economic modernization prompted the enactment of legislation to regulate social conflicts and improve the living conditions of the neediest sectors. That common starting point generates two other shared features. First, the evolution in the political scenarios of a particular 'climate of ideas' favorable to the advancement of new regulations, fueled by different reformist strands: conservative, Catholic, socialist, liberal. Second, a similar chronology marked by two distinctive initial moments: the first, the aforementioned 'social question' of the early twentieth century; and second, the Great Depression of 1929–1930 and its social consequences.[7] If the first stage was characterized by the early forms of a social reformism expressed within the framework of the liberal institutions in force, the second stage was marked by a profound revision and a constant challenge to that inherited institutional framework, and by the search for models inspired by quite different ideological currents that mixed different doses of corporativism and forms of authoritarian populism.

From its beginnings, state intervention in social matters could include not only the construction of sanitary works and drainage, vaccination campaigns, and the improvement of urban housing but also eugenic measures to control reproduction, moralizing campaigns against alcoholism and prostitution, and the restriction of immigration. This last element was implemented when immigration was considered 'undesirable' from a racial point of view or the opposite, when it was seen as a factor in improving the biological composition of the local population. Such implementation might be mirrored in public education to consolidate the identity of a national 'race.' In this sense, concerns about the 'whitening' or miscegenation of the population in Brazil, Cuba, or Colombia, were parallel to concerns about the supposed 'degenerative' effects that Italian immigrants, especially in cases involving urban criminality or anarchist protest, produced in Argentina at the turn of the century.[8] It was this kind of knotting of social welfare concerns with the defense of 'national interests' that centralized the authority of the new institutions and mechanisms of intervention, and that frequently overruled objections arising from the defense of individual rights, voluntary associations, or the autonomy of local governments and their police power. In 1892, a report of the Argentine

7 Juan Manuel Palacio, 'From Social Legislation to Labor Justice' in *Labor Justice across the Americas*, eds Leon Fink and Juan Manuel Palacio (Urbana: University of Illinois Press, 2018), 16–43.

8 Eduardo Zimmermann, 'Racial Ideas and Social Reform: Argentina, 1890–1916' (1992) 72 Hispanic American Historical Review 23–46.

National Department of Hygiene summarized this philosophy well: 'Hygiene does not admit the principle that an individual is the master of disposing of his person or property to the point of causing harm to public health, nor that local powers proceed in sanitary matters independently of the central power.'[9]

This preference for the centralization of state authority in its social interventions was accompanied by a more profound change, which ended up driving the transformation of isolated social policies towards the first steps of a 'social state.' These steps were the growing acceptance of a new relationship between state and society based on the preeminence of interdependence links and an objective to guarantee to all individuals the development of their faculties, and the removal of obstacles opposed to development.[10] As we will see in the next section, certain changes in legal thinking at the turn of the century were key to sustain and to expand these new conceptions of social relations.

From the beginning of the twentieth century, it was the countries of the Southern Cone – Argentina, Brazil, Chile, and Uruguay – that first introduced social legislation such as insurance against work accidents and pension systems. From those very beginnings, a feature that would last for a long time in Latin American social security systems was present: benefits granted depended on labor status. Benefits were granted to those who maintained a formal labor relationship, and this generally led to the exclusion of vast sectors of informal workers and rural laborers, who often constituted the majority of the economically active population. The persistence of this exclusionary dimension of social policies has been described as the construction of a 'truncated welfare state' in which the distribution of benefits took place among those who were better positioned in the labor force.[11]

The most advanced case of transformation of the state in the face of the new economic and social reality in Latin America was that of Uruguay under the presidencies of José Batlle y Ordoñez (1903–1907 and 1911–1915) who laid

---

9 Departamento Nacional de Higiene, 'Higiene administrativa. Deberes y derechos de las autoridades sanitarias' (1892) vol. 2 Anales del Departamento Nacional de Higiene 18–27.

10 Rengifo, 'Desigualdad,' 491; Huber, 'Options for Social Policy,' 142.

11 This reproduced features of the evolution of the Welfare State in general. As Daniel Rodgers rightly pointed out: 'The emotional center of contemporary social politics is "welfare," but it is a concept of welfare narrower than any known in the past ... In fact, none of the so-called welfare states constructed before the last third of the twentieth century was focused on the poor. From Bismarck's to Beveridge's, their target population was the working class, those who worked with their hands for wages, not the destitute with no work at all.' Rodgers, *Atlantic Crossings*, 209; Ferreira and Robalino, 'Social Protection,' 5–6, 10; Brearley, 'A History of Social Protection,' 2; Fleury, 'The Welfare State,' 2; Huber, 'Options for Social Policy,' 142.

the foundation for what could be called the first Welfare State in the region. Coming from the Colorado Party, Batlle launched an ambitious program of reforms aimed at social matters, the expansion of public education, the enactment of legislation on the maximum working day, minimum wage, right to strike, the establishment of a national pension system, and compensation for industrial accidents.[12] In this case, the process of advancing social legislation seems to have been the result of government initiatives rather than a response to pressure from organized groups. In the following decades, however, the expansion of the Welfare State in Uruguay responded to the pressures and influences of an organized and mobilized labor movement.[13]

Chile, on the other hand, presents a case of interaction between government initiatives and pressures from the labor movement from the beginning of the first social legislation measures. The military and some sectors of the organized labor movement, such as railroad workers, obtained old-age pensions in the early years of the twentieth century. In 1924, social laws were passed that established the regulation of the labor contract, mandatory insurance against the risk of illness, compensation for work accidents, and pensions for disability and old age. The *Caja de Seguro Obligatorio* regulated the extension and administration of social insurance, and the advance towards 'social constitutionalism' was reflected in the 'social rights' of the Constitution of 1925.[14]

In Argentina, President Yrigoyen, of the Radical Civic Union, promoted in the first postwar years the expansion of social legislation, which had begun in the early years of the twentieth century under liberal and conservative governments, measures that largely benefited the new middle sectors that constituted his electoral base. In Brazil, the first signs of modern social and labor legislation originated in the political conflicts of the 1920s, when components of the political elite designed a reformist program. The Lei Eloy Chaves, the basis of the general system of *previdência social* reflected, in the words of James Malloy, 'a paternalistic approach to social reform flowing from a deeper sense of social control and enlightened self-interest.'[15]

The 1930s and 1940s would bring more profound transformations, in part driven by the crisis and replacement of the model of economic development prevailing in the previous period. The development of import substitution

12 Fernando López-Alves, 'State Reform and Welfare in Uruguay, 1890–1930' in *Studies in the Formation of the Nation State in Latin America*, ed. James Dunkerley (London: Institute of Latin American Studies, 2002), 94–111.

13 Segura-Ubiergo, *The Political Economy*, 57–59.

14 Rengifo, 'Desigualdad e inclusión,' 489–490.

15 Malloy, *The Politics of Social*, 49; Segura-Ubiergo, *The Political Economy*, 62–64.

industrialization (ISI) was carried forward in several countries by military governments that combined political authoritarianism with the expansion of social policies. These policies were based on a widespread consensus on the need for state intervention in the regulation of the economy, new relations between capital and labor, and the sanctioning of new social protection mechanisms. The examples of the military governments of Ibáñez in Chile and Uriburu in Argentina would be followed in the following years by those of Getúlio Vargas in Brazil and Perón in Argentina. Both arising from military movements, they laid the foundations for a profound transformation of state structures of their respective countries. This transformation included a corporate strategy of co-optation of the labor movement and the development of social legislation arising from processes of direct intervention between the state and social actors that weakened the institutions of previous liberal constitutionalism.[16]

The expansion of social programs in the region in the 1930s and 1940s, under Lázaro Cárdenas and Manuel Ávila Camacho, was also part of other political processes of those years, such as the revitalization of the social policies of the Mexican Revolution, based on the Constitution of 1917. Under the presidency of Avila Camacho, the Social Security Law (*Ley del Seguro Social*) was enacted in 1943. This law which aimed at providing comprehensive social security coverage for industrial workers by integrating them into the corporate structure of the Mexican state developed by the PRI.[17] In Colombia, the so-called *Revolution on the March*, under the liberal president López Pumarejo, promoted social policies based on the new conceptions regarding the 'social function of property,' and the role of the state as provider of 'social assistance,' established in the constitutional amendment of 1936.[18]

In addition to European corporatist experiments that gave ideological impetus to these processes in Latin America, President Roosevelt's *New Deal* in the United States and the so-called *Beveridge Report* of 1942 in Great Britain served as inspiration for these social reforms. Common features included the global ambition to eradicate backwardness and poverty through economic

16 For labor policy see the cases studied in Fink and Palacio, 'From Social Legislation.'

17 Murai, 'The Foundation,' 262–87.

18 Sandra Botero, 'La reforma constitucional de 1936. El Estado y las políticas sociales en Colombia' (2006) 33 Anuario Colombiano de Historia Social y de la Cultura 85–109; Juan David Restrepo Zapata, 'Aportes para una historia del constitucionalismo social en Colombia: la reforma liberal de 1936' (2019) 57 Revista de Historia del Derecho 157–183; Álvaro Tirado Mejía, 'La economía y lo social en la reforma constitucional de 1936' (1986) 21 Lecturas de Economía 81–98.

development accompanied by social reform programs. Organizations such as ECLAC (Economic Commission for Latin America) and the ILO (International Labor Organization), and their experts, played a central role in this process in the years following the second postwar period. These actions initiated a period of modernization of Latin American state structures that would last until the mid-1970s.[19]

The specialized literature has grouped Latin American social security regimes, created during that period, using different typologies. Some studies accentuate the features of stratification and exclusion in different countries (inclusive, universalist, stratified, exclusionary, dual); other studies take as variables the sources of provision of social protection (state, market, community, mixed). All these systems would undergo further changes in the following two decades. The transitions to democracy in the 1980s, which followed the cuts introduced by the military dictatorships of the previous decade, and the structural reform programs of the 1990s generated strong pressures to reform these social coverage models, which were seen as inefficient and as reproducing mechanisms of exclusion and social stratification. Some of these reforms aimed at designing new social policies with a double objective: on the one hand, to universalize coverage, and, on the other, to target extreme poverty.[20]

If the first concern about the 'truncated' character of the Latin American Welfare State was its exclusionary or differentiating character in the granting of benefits, the last decades of the twentieth century made visible a new problem, which has also been explored in considerable detail by social sciences and which has seriously deformed the evolution of social policies in the region. The expansion of political clientelism and corruption tended to displace programmatic commitments in the distribution of benefits.[21]

As mentioned earlier, the literature produced by the social sciences transformed from the markedly 'structuralist' approach of its beginnings and gradually incorporated a greater historical sensitivity to other factors analyzed in

19 Joseph Love, 'CEPAL as Idea Factory for Latin American Development: Intellectual and Political Influence, 1950–1990' in *State and Nation Making in Latin America and Spain*, eds Agustín Ferraro and Miguel Centeno (Cambridge: Cambridge University Press, 2019), 29–50; Amy C. Offner, *Sorting out the Mixed Economy: The Rise and Fall of Welfare and Developmental States in the Americas* (Princeton: Princeton University Press, 2019), 3–10; Juan Carlos Yáñez Andrade, 'Moisés Poblete Troncoso y su aporte a la recopilación de la legislación laboral' (2018) 40 Revista de Estudios Histórico-Jurídicos 385–386.

20 Fleury, 'The Welfare State,' 2–3; Ferreira and Robalino, 'Social Protection,' 5–10.

21 For a detailed analysis of different national cases, see the articles collected in *Clientelism, Social Policy, and the Quality of Democracy*, eds Diego Abente Brun and Larry Diamond (Baltimore: Johns Hopkins University Press, 2014).

greater detail by the new strands of transnational and global history. The following section analyzes some of these changes, in particular the way the circulation of new currents of legal thought facilitated ideological and political consensus around many projects of the new social states.

2 Circulation of 'Social Legal Thought' and the Construction of the Welfare State in Latin America

More recent historiography on the origin and development of the social policies that built the Welfare State has focused on the circulation of new forms of 'social knowledge': statistics and specialized reports on material living conditions, hygiene, housing, and public health, produced by a new class of 'experts' guided by the principles of the new social sciences, in particular sociology and 'social economics.'[22] The transnational circulation of experts, ideas, institutional models for the development of social policies, especially the 'Atlantic Crossings' analyzed masterfully in Rodgers in 1998, were also an important key in the process of formation of the Latin American Welfare State.

In the previous section, Carmelo Mesa-Lago's work from the 1970s was mentioned as a pioneering study of Latin American social states in the second postwar period. Something similar could be said of the Chilean Moisés Poblete Troncoso's work for the first half of the twentieth century. His studies *Instituciones de previsión social* (1920) and *Evolución del Derecho Social en América* (1942) were pioneering essays compiling various existing social security regimes. In his narrative, Poblete Troncoso highlighted not only the role fulfilled by the social content of some new constitutions in the region, but also the numerous instances of international cooperation that since the beginning of the century had focused on the development of social policies.[23] In Santiago de Chile the first Pan American Scientific Congress in 1908, passed several resolutions concerning new social problems and the organization and regulation of industrial relations. Some years later, in 1916, as part of the celebrations for the centenary of the Declaration of Independence, the Argentine government organized an American Congress of Social Sciences in Tucumán. In the section on 'Labor, Welfare and Social Assistance,' the commission in charge dedicated itself to the study of the standard of living of the 'working class' and its improvement through social legislation. Among topics such as

22 See the works compiled in Rueschemeyer and Skocpol, *States, Social Knowledge*.

23 Yáñez Andrade, 'Moisés Poblete Troncoso,' 386.

workers' housing, the problem of unemployment, strikes, and conciliation and arbitration mechanisms, participants highlighted the role that mutual aid societies and compulsory social insurance could play as social policy tools.[24] This was followed by the Social Welfare Congress in Rio de Janeiro (1923), the Social Economy Congress in Buenos Aires (1924), and especially the Inter-American Conference on Social Security held in Santiago de Chile in 1942. This Santiago conference clearly expressed the role of the network of specialists in social insurance that populated a good number of private and governmental agencies; and, of technicians from international bodies such as the International Labor Organization, reflecting the parallelism of the discussion concerning social security with that regarding the new labor law.[25]

In general, these initiatives concentrated more on the political and institutional aspects of the new social security systems than on legal thought and its evolution in the matter. Towards the end of the nineteenth century, the Spanish reformer Adolfo Posada drew attention to this relative lack of interest in the legal foundations of the approach to the social question: 'one of the clearest defects of modern *social* doctrines, as they are formulated by economists and anarchist socialists, is that they are formulated by people who have hardly realized that the law is something that inevitably has to be encountered every time one wants to transform and improve the condition of men.' Posada analyzed the phenomenon in an essay entitled 'Law and the Social Question,' inserted as a preliminary study to his translation of the Austrian jurist Anton Menger's work, *Civil Law and the Poor* (*Das Bürgerliche Recht und die besitzlosen Volksklassen*, 1890), a detailed critical analysis of the draft German civil code which, as we shall see, would have a strong influence on Latin American jurists as they considered the social question.[26] Menger's text would quickly become a reference for several Latin American jurists oriented to the discussion of the new social problems and to the renewal of the methods and contents of the new law. His work became part of what Duncan Kennedy described as the 'second globalization' of legal thought, which displaced the era of classical liberal

24 'Las cuestiones sociales en el Congreso Científico Panamericano' (1909) 8 Boletín del Departamento Nacional del Trabajo 95–97; 'Congreso Americano de Ciencias Sociales' (1915) 11 Revista Argentina de Ciencias Políticas 169–172; (1915) 32 Revista Jurídica y de Ciencias Sociales 630; (1916) 33 Revista Jurídica y de Ciencias Sociales 508–509; Eduardo Zimmermann, *Los liberales reformistas: La cuestión social en la Argentina, 1890–1916* (Buenos Aires: Editorial Sudamericana, 1995), 94–96.

25 Yáñez Andrade, 'Moisés Poblete Troncoso,' 371–390; Fink and Palacio, 'From Social Legislation,' 16–43.

26 Anton Menger, 'El derecho y la cuestión social' in *El derecho civil y los pobres*, ed. Adolfo Posada (Madrid: Librería General de Victoriano Suárez, 1898), 8.

thought. In this second globalization, the extremely formalistic character and individualistic contents of classical legal thought were criticized leading to a true 'crisis of legal orthodoxy,' soon to spread in Latin America, informing the modernization of private law.[27]

In addition to Menger's text, the writings of Rudolf von Jhering proved to be a second source. This had happened in the United States where Roscoe Pound tried to apply Jhering's 'social theory of law' to displace the 'individualistic' interpretations that still marked American law, and thus formulate a new 'sociological jurisprudence.'[28] In Latin America, jurists such as the Chileans Valentín Letelier and Arturo Contreras, and the Brazilian Augusto Viveiros absorbed those principles of Jhering, redefining the meaning of justice in 'social' terms. They thus contributed to the foundations of the new social constitutionalism that would make its appearance in the first postwar period. This trend was also oriented towards legal education with a demand for introducing historical and comparative perspectives and the new knowledge coming from the social sciences. The Chilean Alejandro Álvarez and the Argentine Ernesto Quesada are examples of this renewal produced in the classrooms of Latin American law schools. They intertwined the demand for new pedagogical methods with new contents provided by the social sciences for the creation of a 'new law.'[29]

The French jurist Léon Duguit is the third notable name in this circuit of European juridical references in Latin America that grounded the new perspective of 'social' law. Duguit, professor at the Faculty of Law of the University of Bordeaux, whose prestige would increase in the following years, became in the 1930s one of the most renowned figures in the legal world.[30] The lectures

27 Duncan Kennedy, 'Three Globalizations of Law and Legal Thought: 1850–2000' in *The New Law and Economic Development: A Critical Appraisal*, eds David Trubek and Álvaro Santos (Cambridge: Cambridge University Press, 2006), 19, 37; *Derecho privado y modernización: América Latina y Europa en la primera mitad del siglo XX*, eds María Rosario Polotto, Thorstein Keiser, and Thomas Duve (Frankfurt am Main: Max Planck Institute for European Legal History, 2015).

28 David M. Rabban, *Law's History: American Legal Thought and the Transatlantic Turn to History* (Cambridge: Cambridge University Press, 2013), 453–459.

29 Manuel Bastías Saavedra, 'Jehring and the Working Class. Law and Labor in Turn-of-the-Century Latin America, 1890–1930' paper presented at the Conference *Social Policies and the Welfare State in the Global South (19th – 20th Century)* (Bremen: University of Bremen, 2017); Eduardo Zimmermann, 'Intellectuals, Universities and the Social Question' in *Essays in Argentine Labour History 1870–1930*, ed. Jeremy Adelman (London: Macmillan, 1992), 199–216.

30 M.C. Mirow, 'Léon Duguit (1859–1928)' in *Great Christian Jurists in French History*, eds Olivier Descamps and Rafael Domingo (Cambridge: Cambridge University Press, 2019), 358–371.

given at the Law School of the University of Buenos Aires in 1911, which had as their theme the reconfiguration of private law, became a manifesto of the new principles that would guide the transformation of civil law in Latin America. 'The Declaration of the Rights of Man, the *Code Napoléon* and all modern codes that proceed more or less from those two acts, rest on a purely individualistic conception of law ... The legal system of modern peoples tends to be established on the verification of the fact of social function, imposing itself on individuals and groups,' Duguit said in Buenos Aires.[31] This formula generated a new interpretation of the social function of property justifying new forms of property regulation.[32] This concept was transferred to some of the constitutional texts of the first postwar period, as we shall see. This perspective also synthesized the idea of social interdependence as the foundation of the new law, which would support the construction of new Latin American social states in the following decades.

After World War I, this trend calling for the modification of certain classical institutions of civil law deepened and continued along the path marked by those who had adapted the ideas of Jhering, Menger, and Duguit since the beginning of the century. In 1919 the Chilean jurist Alejandro Álvarez summarized the elements giving rise to a 'new law.' In civil law, said Alvarez, 'the transformations of an economic nature ... have broken the unity of legislation, creating in many matters a special and entirely particular nature, which affects a whole category of persons – the workers – and is inspired by their interests.' For Alvarez, who would become one of the most prestigious Latin American jurists of the twentieth century, the convergence of these new trends suggested

31 Facultad de Derecho y Ciencias Sociales de la Universidad de Buenos Aires, *Discursos Académicos 1911–1921* (Buenos Aires, 1921), 117. The Buenos Aires conferences were published in France under the title *Les transformations générales du Droit privé depuis le Code Napoléon* (Paris: Librairie Félix Alcan, 1912) and in Spain as *Las transformaciones generales del Derecho privado desde el Código Napoleón* (Madrid: F. Beltrán, 1912), in addition to its later translation in *Discursos Académicos 1911–1921* (Buenos Aires: Facultad de Derecho y Ciencias Sociales de la Universidad de Buenos Aires, 1921). About Duguit, the conferences in Buenos Aires, and his influence in the Latin American legal thought see M.C. Mirow, 'The Social-Obligation Norm of Property: Duguit, Hayem, and Others' (2010) 22 Florida Journal of International Law 191–226; M.C. Mirow, 'Origins of the Social Function of Property in Chile' (2011) 80 Fordham Law Review 1183–1217; Eduardo Zimmermann, '"Un espíritu nuevo": la cuestión social y el Derecho en la Argentina, 1890–1930' (2013) 73 Revista de Indias 81–106; Carlos Miguel Herrera, 'Léon Duguit en Buenos Aires: Sociabilidad y política en la recepción de una teoría jurídica' (2014) 8 Problema. Anuario de Filosofía y Teoría del Derecho 147–177.

32 *Léon Duguit and the Social Obligation Norm of Property: A Translation and Global Exploration*, eds Paul Babie and Jessica Viven-Wilksch (Cham: Springer, 2019).

an inevitable result: 'the new conception of the State and its attributes ... the principles that inspire workers' legislation ... trace the new conception of Law and its future orientation. This new conception is inspired by *solidarity*, by virtue of which legal relations must be regulated not as a function of individual interest, but of that of the collectivity.'[33]

In a similar vein, the Argentine Alfredo Palacios published in 1920 *El nuevo derecho* incorporating arguments put forward by Adolfo Posada, Anton Menger, and Léon Duguit, together with the work of Jean Jaurés – closer to Palacios's partisan socialist convictions – to describe the process that had led to the transformation of civil law, then underway in Argentina as well. Palacios, the first socialist deputy elected in America by popular vote, had been a precursor of the enactment of the first social laws in Argentina. In particular, the enactment of the first law on liability for industrial accidents, promoted by Palacios and enacted in 1915, revealed the depth of the changes in civil law that the new social reality demanded. The elaboration of the notions of 'social obligation' and 'professional risk' by French jurists such as Maurice Hauriou and Raymond Saleilles, which would culminate in the French law of 1898 on employers' liability based on the concept of *risques professionels*, was an important precedent for Argentine doctrine. The concept of professional risk meant that liability for accidents in the workplace was not interpreted as the result of fault on the part of the employer or employee but as a consequence of the inevitable insecurity and unpredictability introduced by the industrial era. The solution thus lay in a compensation system that recognized liability without attributing fault. Palacios was proud to have contributed to this transformation: 'Our code thus reproduced the Roman theory of fault, which no longer responds to the current needs of our country, created by the modifications of industrial life. And I am proud to have incorporated into our legislation the principle of professional risk, a principle that was considered as unlawful, claiming that it had no basis in law, since it came from the economic sciences, without remembering that law, which is part of the superstructure of societies, frequently follows the transformations of the economic base, that is, of the structure.'[34] In the same sense, a year later, Alfredo Colmo, commemorating the fiftieth anniversary of the entry into force of the Argentine Civil Code, criticized the 'individualism taken to the pinnacle' and the code's 'very notion of contract, rudimentarily Romanist.' This had led the code to leave

33 Alejandro Álvarez, *De la necesidad de una nueva concepción del Derecho* (Chile: Memoria de incorporación del Miembro Académico de la Facultad de Leyes, Universidad de Chile, 1919).

34 Alfredo L. Palacios, *El nuevo derecho* (Buenos Aires: Editorial Claridad, 1960), 87–88.

aside the adequate regulation of important aspects that the new social reality of the twentieth century demanded: on the one hand, everything concerning modern labor relations; on the other hand, in a clear allusion to Duguit's ideas, the inclusion as a general criterion of '*sociality*, instead of individualism, so that rights are a function rather than a power.'[35]

The circulation of texts and authors and the creation of professional networks with shared understandings were an important factor in promoting the creation of the 'new law' with a 'social' orientation that would facilitate not only the sanctioning of the first traces of social legislation but also the advance towards a conception of the state that would gradually incorporate among its functions the idea of social interdependence, an ideological basis of the Welfare State. The inclusion of many of these principles in the constitutional texts of the region would be the other great renovating current that would sustain these changes as discussed in the following section with a selection of case studies, for reasons of space limitation.

3 Latin American Social Constitutionalism

There is a general consensus in considering the Mexican Constitution of 1917 as the first example of 'social constitutionalism' in the world. The focus has been particularly on the content of Articles 27, on the land tenure regime, and 123, on the regulation of labor relations and workers' rights. The text sanctioned in Querétaro is seen as the strongest sign of the beginning of the transition from liberal constitutionalism to the new social constitutionalism that would ideologically sustain the evolution towards social states in the region. That perception was fueled in part by the revolutionary governments that sought to construct a narrative as propaganda for their social action and its identification as a cause rooted in nationality itself. It was also partly fueled by Latin American progressive intellectual and political elites. Sensitized by other contemporary events of great impact such as the end of World War I and the sense of an 'end of the epoch' that accompanied it, the success of the Bolshevik Revolution, and the beginning of the university reform movement, these elites were particularly receptive to this interpretation.[36]

---

35 Alfredo Colmo, 'El Código Civil en su cincuentenario' (1921) 7 Revista de Filosofía 321–338.

36 Catherine Andrews, *De Cádiz a Querétaro: Historiografía y bibliografía del constitucionalismo mexicano* (México: Fondo de Cultura Económica, 2017), 94–101; Ricardo A. Ortega Soriano, 'La construcción del Estado social a partir de la Constitución de 1917' in *La herencia del constitucionalismo social mexicano y sus desafíos* (México: DR Suprema Corte de Justicia de la Nación, 2017), 37–42; Pablo Yankelevich, 'La Constitución de 1917 en

More recent historiography has somewhat qualified this interpretation, offering a complex and multidimensional interpretation of the constitutional process of 1917 and its immediate consequences on the social policies of the revolutionary governments. On the one hand, it is clear that the tradition of liberal constitutionalism was not extinguished, but rather coexisted both at the Convention of Querétaro, and for quite some time afterwards, alongside new trends that for many were not opposed to but reconcilable with that liberal tradition.[37] On the other hand, research more focused on jurisprudential sources, and not only on legislative antecedents, has shown that in the years following the sanctioning of the constitution one of the most serious obstacles to the implementation of the new socioeconomic rights sanctioned in the two articles mentioned was the role of the Mexican Supreme Court, which followed a long jurisprudential tradition of granting writs of amparo protecting the individual rights of employers and landowners. It would be only after the constitutional reforms of 1928 that allowed the renewal of the members of the Court, and the amendments of 1931 and 1934, when the Court's jurisprudence was aligned with the progressive purposes of the Executive.[38] Only gradually, and with jurisprudential interpretations that varied, a 'post-revolutionary social jurisprudence' was established that would introduce important changes both in the world of workers' rights and in land regulation in rural and urban areas.[39]

The Mexican Civil Code of 1928 is seen as another derivation of the 'social' legal thinking of the revolution. The considerations of the Mexican jurists who worked in the codification process have been analyzed as the result of the interaction between the reception of the aforementioned European doctrines that upheld the introduction of 'the social' in civil law, the regulations of the 1917 Constitution, and the particular circumstances of the post-revolutionary

América Latina' in *De Cádiz al Siglo XXI: Doscientos años de constitucionalismo en México e Hispanoamérica (1812–2012)*, eds Adriana Luna-Fabritius, Pablo Mijangos y González, and Rafael Rojas Gutiérrez (México: Taurus/CIDE, 2012), 321–341.

37 Luis Barrón, 'Del constitucionalismo liberal al constitucionalismo social' in *De Cádiz al Siglo XXI: Doscientos años de constitucionalismo en México e Hispanoamérica (1812–2012)*, eds Adriana Luna-Fabritius, Pablo Mijangos y González, and Rafael Rojas Gutiérrez (México: Taurus/CIDE, 2012), 293–319.

38 Timothy M. James, *Mexico's Supreme Court: Between Liberal Individual and Revolutionary Social Rights, 1867–1934* (Albuquerque: University of New Mexico Press, 2013), 51, 75–76, 101–102.

39 Rodrigo Meneses Reyes, 'Los efectos materiales del constitucionalismo social mexicano. Una perspectiva de la sociología del derecho' in *La herencia del constitucionalismo social mexicano y sus desafíos* (México: DR Suprema Corte de Justicia de la Nación, 2017), 301–329.

political-social context. The exposition of motives of the Code stated that 'socializing law means extending the sphere of law from rich to poor, from owner to worker, from industrialist to wage earner, from man to woman, without any restriction or exclusivism.'[40]

Despite the centrality that the Mexican Constitution of 1917 acquired as a precedent in Latin American social constitutionalism, it was not the only precedent taken into account by the constitutions that followed a similar line in other countries of the region. Moreover, in the case of the Chilean Constitution of 1925, another early example of Latin American social constitutionalism, the Mexican precedent does not seem to have been a relevant reference. In its Article 10, the Chilean text guaranteed to all inhabitants the protection 'to work ... to social welfare works ... in order to provide each inhabitant with a minimum of welfare' and ordered the state to promote 'the appropriate division of property.' This last reference was reinforced in President Alessandri's speech to the commission in charge of debating the constitutional draft: 'One may say that in fact the concept of property as a subjective right disappears, to be replaced by the concept of property as a social function,' a statement which, as M.C. Mirow has pointed out, was a verbatim quotation from the legal writings of Léon Duguit. This central idea of 'the social function of property,' although not expressed literally in the constitutional text, was interpreted as the lynchpin that would conceptually organize many of the debates on social policies in Chile, from the right to housing, to public health policies, to the conception of 'welfare,' during almost the entire twentieth century. Here again we see the weight of a particular cultural context: as in the discussions of the Argentine jurists Palacios or Colmo, the intellectual references of the Chilean case seem to have been more closely aligned with the discussions of European thought, in particular Duguit and his doctrine of the 'social function of property,' than with the Mexican antecedent.[41]

The transformation of the basis of land ownership was also one of the central axes of the Colombian constitutional reform of 1936, the result of the so-called 'Revolution on the March' led by the liberal president Alfonso López Pumarejo. In the final part of its Article 10, the constitutional text stated that, if the rights of private individuals came into conflict with the need established by law, they should yield to the 'public or social interest.' And, again making visible echoes of Duguit's thought, it culminated by stating 'Property is a social

40 Thorsten Keiser, 'Social Conceptions of Property and Labour – Private Law in the Aftermath of the Mexican Revolution and European Legal Science' (2010) 20 Rg. Rechtsgeschichte-Legal History 261–263.

41 Mirow, 'Origins of the Social Function,' 1183, 1214–1215.

function that implies obligations.' Articles 16 ('public assistance is a function of the state') and 17 ('work is a social obligation and shall enjoy the special protection of the state') completed this advance towards a new notion of 'social security' provided by the state.[42]

That same year of 1936, the Argentine jurist Rafael Bielsa clearly summarized how much this process of abandoning the liberal legal thinking inherited from the nineteenth century had spread throughout the region in favor of a legal philosophy that expanded the radius of action of the state. The mission of the jurist, said Bielsa, was 'to collaborate in the work of integration of public law, abandoning somewhat the overly broad formulas of that liberal political philosophy that has dominated the last century, formulas that served for the great proclamations stamped on constitutions, but which have not proved very efficient in the domain of the *concrete activity of the state*.'[43] And a few years later, another Argentine jurist, Arturo Sampay, announced through the title of his book, *The Crisis of the Liberal-Bourgeois Rule of Law*. Sampay analyzed possible variants in detail: the fascist state, the Russian Soviet state, the national-socialist state, and the corporative state of Portugal. Regarding the latter, which Sampay analyzed very favorably, the author quoted Mihail Manoilesco: 'the twentieth century will be the century of Corporatism, as the nineteenth century has been the century of Liberalism.'[44]

The preference for corporatist formulas at the time of thinking up new 'social' constitutions was most fully manifested in the regimes of Getúlio Vargas in Brazil and Juan Domingo Perón in Argentina. The Brazilian constitutions of 1934 and 1937 strongly exhibited this tendency towards the corporatist structuring of social interests with a high concentration of authority in the national executive. As regards the social content, a repeated reference as inspiration was the 1919 Weimar Constitution, a source that would also be present in the convention that would sanction the Argentine Constitution of 1949 during the presidency of Juan Perón. References to this source happened, though, through selective readings and appropriations that clearly reflected

42 Botero, 'La reforma constitucional,' 85–109; Restrepo, 'Aportes para una historia,' 157–183; Tirado Mejía, 'La economía,' 81–98.

43 Rafael Bielsa, 'El desarrollo institucional del derecho administrativo y la jurisdicción contenciosa. Discurso de incorporación a la Academia Nacional de Derecho y Ciencias Sociales, 20 de agosto de 1936' in *Estudios de Derecho Público: Derecho Administrativo* ed. Rafael Bielsa (Buenos Aires: Editorial Depalma, 1950).

44 Arturo Sampay, *La crisis del estado de derecho liberal-burgués* (Buenos Aires: Losada, 1942), 353. See also, Susana T. Ramella, 'Arturo Enrique Sampay (Argentina, 1911–77)' in *Law and Christianity in Latin America: The Work of Great Jurists*, eds M.C. Mirow and Rafael Domingo (London: Routledge, 2021), 470–482.

the central role that Peronist jurists such as Sampay, Joaquín Díaz de Vivar, or Rodolfo Valenzuela played as translators and mediators in the adaptation of external influences.[45]

Peronism effectively meant the most significant break in the relationship between the new Argentine state and the judicial institutions inherited from the liberal era. This challenge went through several stages, beginning with the creation of a network of 'para-judicial' administrative bodies that promoted the new social policies of the regime. It continued with the impeachment of members of the Supreme Court of Justice and culminated with the enactment of a new constitution in 1949. Driven by General Perón's intention to make possible his reelection as president, the constitutional reform began under the shadow of doubt. The opposing parties challenged the lack of compliance with requirements established by the constitution regarding the computation of the qualified majority of the Congress to declare the need for the reform. The following debates showed that the purpose of the reform went much further, confirming that the ideological inspiration of the new text would be to consecrate the absolute expiration of the individualistic liberal regime which, according to the advocates of the project, had been embodied in the Constitution of 1853. The reform would provide a legal framework to the new political, social, and economic order headed by General Perón. The new constitution sanctioned an ambitious program of expansion of new social and labor rights,[46] and reinforced the majoritarian character of the electoral regime. It expanded the powers of the president of the nation with respect to the other powers in matters such as the legislative veto and the use of emergency powers and increased the predominance of the national government over the provinces, strongly

45 Leticia Vita, 'Weimar in Argentina: A Transnational Analysis of the 1949 Constitutional Reform' (2019) 27 Rg. Rechtsgeschichte-Legal History 176–183.

46 It is on these norms that the Peronist Welfare State project was based: Art. 37, inc. 6 and 7: 'Right to welfare – The right of workers to welfare, the minimum expression of which is the possibility of having adequate housing, clothing and food, of satisfying without anxiety their needs and those of their families in a way that allows them to work with satisfaction, rest free of worries and enjoy measured spiritual and material expansion, imposes the social need to raise the standard of living and work with the direct and indirect resources that economic development allows. Right to social security – The right of individuals to be protected in cases of diminution, suspension or loss of their capacity for work promotes the obligation of society to unilaterally take charge of the corresponding benefits or to promote schemes of compulsory mutual aid intended, one or the other, to cover or complement the insufficiencies or inabilities proper to certain periods of life or those resulting from misfortunes arising from eventual risks.' Art. 38: 'Private property has a social function and, consequently, is subject to the obligations established by law for the common good.'

accentuating the centralizing elements already present in the Constitution of 1853. It added authoritarian features of militarist nationalism, present even in some conservative groups that had supported the military coup of 1930.[47]

4 Conclusions

'What was modern was social, and what was social was modern.'[48] The phrase succinctly captures the spirit of conceptual innovation that drove the doctrinal changes in the law surrounding the new social policies. The overcoming of formalism and the individualistic spirit, both in private and public law, was sustained by the belief that the new social realities produced by modernization in Latin America demanded new state structures to deal with them. In civil law, the arrival of 'the social' was embodied in three major innovations: on the one hand, the conceptual renewal of the nature of the labor contract in which modern industrial relations were framed. The classical figures of the contract theory of the existing civil codes based on the idea of equality of the parties were insufficient and were replaced by new formulas. Second, the transformation in the notion of individual liability brought about by the concept of 'professional risk' and the consequent imputation of 'liability without fault' of employers for accidents at work (a transformation parallel to that of the meaning of punishment in positivist criminology at the beginning of the twentieth century). Finally, the concept of the 'social function of property' that consecrated the subordination of private property rights to social interests, a principle that would be interpreted as the most complete synthesis of the arrival of a new legal paradigm.[49] In public law, the advance of administrative law and the science of public administration gradually broke down the barriers that classical liberal constitutionalism erected to obstruct the advance of state action over private interests.

---

47 Gabriel L. Negretto, 'El populismo constitucional en América Latina. Análisis crítico de la Constitución Argentina de 1949' in *De Cádiz al Siglo XXI: Doscientos años de constitucionalismo en México e Hispanoamérica (1812–2012)*, eds Adriana Luna-Fabritius, Pablo Mijangos y González, and Rafael Rojas Gutiérrez (México: Taurus/CIDE, 2012), 343–376, 362–368; Roberto Gargarella, *Latin American Constitutionalism, 1810–2010: The Engine Room of the Constitution* (Oxford: Oxford University Press, 2013), 119–121; Carlos Miguel Herrera, 'En los orígenes del constitucionalismo social argentino: discursos en torno a la constitución de 1949' (2014) 15 Historia Constitucional 391–408.

48 Keiser, 'Social Conceptions,' 260.

49 M.C. Mirow, *Latin American Constitutions: The Constitution of Cádiz and Its Legacy in Spanish America* (Cambridge: Cambridge University Press, 2015), 202, 217, 221, 225.

These changes, which were mainly due to the circulation and appropriation of European doctrines by Latin American jurists, and their expression in university chairs, treatises and essays, and parliamentary debates, began the path towards a more profound transformation: a redefinition of the way of thinking about the relationship between the state and society. The very idea of citizenship reflected a situation of social interdependence produced and guaranteed by the state. Thus, as we have seen, some of the first examples of social constitutionalism in the region guaranteed forms of public assistance and the right to shared levels of 'welfare' provided by the state.

In the process, Latin American legal frameworks and state institutions were far from being simply the result of a passive appropriation of foreign models. In all cases, the circulation and reception of legal doctrines, social policies, and institutional structures were mediated and 'translated' by local interpreters, who had to respond to the needs presented by the political, economic, social, and cultural context of each country. Thus, the results tended to show hybrid forms of assimilation of legal doctrines and the construction of new 'social states.'[50]

These processes of 'hybridization' reflected some of the legacies of the state-building development in Latin America. The long history of political and institutional instability, economic stagnation, and the persistence of profound inequality in Latin American societies left their mark on the evolution towards what has been called the Latin American 'truncated welfare state.' In addition to the initial differentiation in access to benefits for different social groups that marked the new social security systems, two other features were added in the second half of the twentieth century that are still present today. The first feature was the systematic appearance of political clientelism schemes that distorted the functioning of the social assistance systems and introduced serious problems of corruption. The second feature, and this is a point closer to *legal history*, was the way in which the gradual increase in the generation of new social rights with constitutional status was accompanied by an equivalent process of concentration of authority in what Roberto Gargarella called the 'engine room of the constitution': 'the reforms seemed to have concentrated their energies in the section of rights, without taking into account the impact that the organization of power tends to have upon those very rights that were then (extra) protected.'[51]

50 Vita, 'Weimar in Argentina,' 177; Keiser, 'Social Conceptions,' 271.

51 Gargarella, *Latin American Constitutionalism*, 185.

In short, these processes point to the importance of writing the history of the Welfare State in Latin America not only as a history of the new forms of state intervention driven by the structural changes produced by modernization in the region, but also as a reconstruction of the changes in legal thinking and resulting normative frameworks. Emphasis should be placed on the study of the historical processes through which those conceptual changes accelerated the process of institutional transformation. This opens up a very interesting collaborative research agenda for historians of law and students of history, society, economics, politics, and intellectual change, with the purpose of reconstructing the permanent interaction between the global and the local, the traditional and the modern, and the legal world and the broader contexts of change in the region.

References

Abente Brun, Diego, and Larry Diamond, eds. *Clientelism, Social Policy, and the Quality of Democracy*. Baltimore: Johns Hopkins University Press, 2014.

Amenta, Edwin. 'What We Know about the Development of Social Policy. Comparative and Historical Research in Comparative and Historical Perspective.' In *Comparative Historical Analysis in the Social Sciences*, edited by James Mahoney and Dieter Rueschemeyer, 91–130. Cambridge: Cambridge University Press, 2003.

Andrews, Catherine. *De Cádiz a Querétaro: Historiografía y bibliografía del constitucionalismo mexicano*. México: Fondo de Cultura Económica, 2017.

Baldwin, Peter. 'The Welfare State for Historians.' *Comparative Studies in Society and History* 34(4) (1992): 695–707.

Barrón, Luis. 'Del constitucionalismo liberal al constitucionalismo social.' In *De Cádiz al Siglo XXI: Doscientos años de constitucionalismo en México e Hispanoamérica (1812–2012)*, edited by Adriana Luna-Fabritius, Pablo Mijangos y González y Rafael Rojas Gutiérrez, 293–319. México: Taurus/CIDE, 2012.

Bastías Saavedra, Manuel. 'Una nueva generación de estadistas. Derecho, Universidad y la Cuestión Social en Chile, 1860–1925.' *Revista Austral de Ciencias Sociales* 29 (2015): 33–47.

Bastías Saavedra, Manuel. 'Jehring and the Working Class. Law and Labor in Turn-of-the- Century Latin America, 1890–1930.' Paper presented at the Conference *Social Policies and the Welfare State in the Global South (19th – 20th Century)*. University of Bremen, 2017.

Botero, Sandra. 'La reforma constitucional de 1936. El Estado y las políticas sociales en Colombia.' *Anuario Colombiano de Historia Social y de la Cultura* 33 (2006): 85–109.

Brearley, Emily J. 'A History of Social Protection in Latin America: From Conquest to Conditional Cash Transfers.' *Revue Interventions économiques* 56 (2016): 1–27.

Ferreira, Francisco H.G., and David Robalino. 'Social Protection in Latin America. Achievements and Limitations.' *The World Bank Policy Research Working Paper* 5305 (2010): 1–39.

Fleury, Sonia. 'The Welfare State in Latin America: Reform, Innovation and Fatigue.' *Cadernos de Saúde Pública* 33 (2017): 1–10.

Gargarella, Roberto. *Latin American Constitutionalism, 1810–2010: The Engine Room of the Constitution*. Oxford: Oxford University Press, 2013.

Herrera, Carlos Miguel. 'En los orígenes del constitucionalismo social argentino: discursos en torno a la constitución de 1949.' *Historia Constitucional* 15 (2014): 391–414.

Herrera, Carlos Miguel. 'Léon Duguit en Buenos Aires: Sociabilidad y política en la recepción de una teoría jurídica.' *Problema: Anuario de Filosofía y Teoría del Derecho* 8 (2014): 147–177.

Huber, Evelyne. 'Options for Social Policy in Latin America: Neoliberal versus Social Democratic Models.' In *Welfare States in Transition: National Adaptations in Global Economies*, edited by Gøsta Esping-Andersen, 141–191. London: Sage, 1996.

James, Timothy M. *Mexico's Supreme Court: Between Liberal Individual and Revolutionary Social Rights, 1867–1934*. Albuquerque: University of New Mexico Press, 2013.

Keiser, Thorsten. 'Social Conceptions of Property and Labour – Private Law in the Aftermath of the Mexican Revolution and European Legal Science.' *Rg. Rechtsgeschichte-Legal History* 20 (2012): 258–273.

Kennedy, Duncan. 'Three Globalizations of Law and Legal Thought: 1850–2000.' In *The New Law and Economic Development: A Critical Appraisal*, edited by David Trubek and Álvaro Santos, 19–73. Cambridge: Cambridge University Press, 2006.

Kymlicka, Will, and Wayne Norman. 'Return of the Citizen: A Survey of Recent Work on Citizenship Theory.' *Ethics* 104 (1994): 352–381.

López-Alves, Fernando. 'State Reform and Welfare in Uruguay, 1890–1930.' In *Studies in the Formation of the Nation State in Latin America*, edited by James Dunkerley, 94–111. London: Institute of Latin American Studies, 2002.

Love, Joseph. 'CEPAL as Idea Factory for Latin American Development: Intellectual and Political Influence, 1950–1990.' In *State and Nation Making in Latin America and Spain*, edited by Agustín Ferraro and Miguel Centeno, 29–50. Cambridge: Cambridge University Press, 2019.

Malloy, James M. *The Politics of Social Security in Brazil*. Pittsburgh: University of Pittsburgh Press, 1979.

Marshall, T.H. *Citizenhip and Social Class and Other Essays*. Cambridge: Cambridge University Press, 1950.

Meneses Reyes, Rodrigo. 'Los efectos materiales del constitucionalismo social mexicano. Una perspectiva de la sociología del derecho.' In *La herencia del constitucionalismo social mexicano y sus desafíos*, 301–329. México: DR Suprema Corte de Justicia de la Nación, 2017.

Mesa-Lago, Carmelo. *Social Security in Latin America. Pressure Groups, Stratification, and Inequality*. Pittsburgh: University of Pittsburgh Press, 1978.

Mirow, M.C. *Latin American Constitutions: The Constitution of Cádiz and Its Legacy*. Cambridge: Cambridge University Press, 2015.

Mirow, M.C. 'The Social-Obligation Norm of Property: Duguit, Hayem, and Others.' *Florida Journal of International Law* 22 (2010): 191–226.

Mirow, M.C. 'Origins of the Social Function of Property in Chile.' *Fordham Law Review* 80 (2011): 1183–1217.

Murai, Tomoko. 'The Foundation of the Mexican Welfare State and Social Security Reform in the 1990s.' *The Developing Economies* 42(2) (2004): 262–287.

Negretto, Gabriel L. 'El populismo constitucional en América Latina. Análisis crítico de la Constitución Argentina de 1949.' In *De Cádiz al Siglo XXI: Doscientos años de constitucionalismo en México e Hispanoamérica (1812–2012)*, edited by Adriana Luna-Fabritius, Pablo Mijangos y González, and Rafael Rojas Gutiérrez, 343–376. México: Taurus/CIDE, 2012.

Offner, Amy C. *Sorting out the Mixed Economy: The Rise and Fall of Welfare and Developmental States in the Americas*. Princeton: Princeton University Press, 2019.

Ortega Soriano, Ricardo A. 'La construcción del Estado social a partir de la Constitución de 1917.' In *La herencia del constitucionalismo social mexicano y sus desafíos*, 1–48. México: DR Suprema Corte de Justicia de la Nación, 2017.

Palacio, Juan Manuel. 'From Social Legislation to Labor Justice.' In *Labor Justice across the Americas*, edited by Leon Fink and Juan Manuel Palacio, 16–43. Urbana: University of Illinois Press, 2018.

Polotto, María Rosario, Thorstein Keiser, and Thomas Duve, eds. *Derecho privado y modernización: América Latina y Europa en la primera mitad del siglo XX*. Frankfurt am Main: Max Planck Institute for European Legal History, 2015.

Rabban, David M. *Law's History: American Legal Thought and the Transatlantic Turn to History*. Cambridge: Cambridge University Press, 2013.

Rengifo, Francisca. 'Desigualdad e inclusión. La ruta del Estado de seguridad social chileno, 1920–1970.' *Hispanic American Historical Review* 97 (2017): 485–522.

Restrepo Zapata, Juan David. 'Aportes para una historia del constitucionalismo social en Colombia: la reforma liberal de 1936.' *Revista de Historia del Derecho* 57 (2019): 157–183.

Rodgers, Daniel T. *Atlantic Crossings: Social Politics in a Progressive Age*. Cambridge: Harvard University Press, 1998.

Rodgers, Daniel T. 'Bearing Tales: Networks and Narratives in Social Policy Transfer.' *Journal of Global History* 9 (2014): 301–313.

Rueschemeyer, Dietrich, and Theda Skocpol, eds. *States, Social Knowledge, and the Origins of Modern Social Policies*. Princeton: Princeton University Press, 1996.

Segura-Ubiergo, Alex. *The Political Economy of the Welfare State in Latin America: Globalization, Democracy, and Development*. Cambridge: Cambridge University Press, 2007.

Skocpol, Theda. *Protecting Soldiers and Mothers: The Political Origins of Social Policy in the United States*. Cambridge: Harvard University Press, 1992.

Tirado Mejía, Álvaro. 'La economía y lo social en la reforma constitucional de 1936.' *Lecturas de Economía* 21 (1986): 81–98.

Vita, Leticia. 'Weimar in Argentina: A Transnational Analysis of the 1949 Constitutional Reform.' *Rg. Rechtsgeschichte-Legal History* 27 (2019): 176–183.

Yankelevich, Pablo. 'La Constitución de 1917 en América Latina.' In *De Cádiz al Siglo XXI: Doscientos años de constitucionalismo en México e Hispanoamérica (1812–2012)*, edited by Adriana Luna-Fabritius, Pablo Mijangos y González, and Rafael Rojas Gutiérrez, 321–341. México: Taurus/CIDE, 2012.

Yáñez Andrade, Juan Carlos. 'Moisés Poblete Troncoso y su aporte a la recopilación de la legislación laboral.' *Revista de Estudios Histórico-Jurídicos* 40 (2018): 371–390.

Zimmermann, Eduardo. 'Racial Ideas and Social Reform. Argentina, 1890–1916.' *Hispanic American Historical Review* 72 (1992): 23–46.

Zimmermann, Eduardo. 'Intellectuals, Universities and the Social Question.' In *Essays in Argentine Labour History 1870–1930*, edited by Jeremy Adelman, 199–216. London: Macmillan, 1992.

Zimmermann, Eduardo. *Los liberales reformistas: La cuestión social en la Argentina, 1890–1916*. Buenos Aires: Editorial Sudamericana, 1995.

Zimmermann, Eduardo. '"Un espíritu nuevo": la cuestión social y el Derecho en la Argentina, 1890–1930.' *Revista de Indias* 73 (2013): 81–106.

CHAPTER 21

Constitutions, Rights, and Government

Marta Lorente Sariñena

1 Introduction

1.1 *Latin American Constitutionalism: Between History and Historiography*

After the first modern constitutional experiences, the triumph of the emancipatory revolution in Haiti gave way to a third Atlantic constitutional cycle.[1] The French armies were more successful in the Iberian Peninsula (1808), where the occupation forced the hitherto-bearers of the sovereignty – the monarchs – to flee. The king's absence enabled some simultaneous constituent processes with very different and conflicting territorial claims. While *Ibero-American* constitutions were conceived for the former subjects of the Iberian Monarchies, *Latin American* constitutions were based not only on the break from the Iberian metropolis but also on the collapse of the empire's territorial integrity.[2] The subsequent achievement of independence put an end to the constitutional duplicity in Ibero/Latin America (1824).

Hundreds of constitutions have been debated, adopted, amended, and abrogated since then in Latin America. The sheer number of texts shows that constitutionalism did not take hold in the region. Wars, revolutions, *pronunciamientos, caudillismos*, reforms, abrogations, and dictatorships – de facto or in law – point to a congenital disease of Latin American constitutionalism. Lack of continuity has undermined these constitutional processes from the outset, but something similar could be said of European continental constitutionalism. Since the French Revolution almost to the present day, most constitutional experiences have been plagued by discontinuity.[3] This explains why a

---

1 See generally Bernard Baylin, *Atlantic History: Concept and Contours* (Cambridge: Harvard University Press, 2005).

2 Hispanic American constitutional texts are available at www.cervantesvirtual.com/portales/constituciones_hispanoamericanas/. The Haitian Constitutions and Luso-Brazilian texts can be found at http://www.modern-constitutions.de/nbu.php?page_id=8294b7496ae06609fa222b156332446b.

3 Maurizio Fioravanti, *Los derechos fundamentales: Apuntes de historia de las constituciones* (Madrid: Editorial Trotta, 1996).

 | DOI:10.1163/9789004436091_023

significant part of EU Member States are young or very young constitutional democracies. With a hint of exaggeration, we could conclude that the history of Latin American constitutionalism is as old and torn as continental Europe's. But let us leave aside far-fetched musings and focus instead on historiographic facts: in spite of the emergence of global history, very few scholars study the experiences of Ibero/Latin America under the light of modern constitutional history.

As a fact, the historiographic invisibility of Latin American constitutionalism has become an object of study in itself guided by the well-known question *À qui la faute?*[4] In my understanding, this invisibility may respond to the expulsion of America from the narratives of modernity that underlie and shape an enlightened intellectual tradition still alive today.[5] The famous 'scientific' reflection on the American nature, which according to Buffon was inferior to the Old World's, was assumed and further spread by renowned authors in the nineteenth and twentieth centuries. Latin America was portrayed in a childish light: just like lions transformed into jaguars and men became beardless in the New World, constitutionalism degraded beyond recognition when it set foot on American soil.

Nevertheless, it is worth noting that the first to denounce the weakness of American constitutions were not Eurocentric intellectuals but Latin American revolutionaries. The best example is Bolivar's assertion that American constitutions were 'pieces of paper' only suitable for 'ethereal republics.'[6] Since then, the list of constitutional frustrations only increased. In the words of the extraordinary Mexican writer Octavio Paz, 'the liberal and democratic ideology, far from expressing our concrete historical situation, obscured it. The political lie installed itself almost constitutionally in our countries. The moral damage has been incalculable and reaches into deep layers of our character.'[7] There are few doubts that an equation of hope and frustration has marked the life of constitutions in Latin America to the present.

4 The expression was first coined by Victor Hugo in *Les Misérables* (available at: http://dans.mon.cartable.free.fr/Primaire/poesie/La_chanson_de_Gavroche.pdf).

5 Antonello Gerbi, *The Dispute of the New World: The History of a Polemic, 1750–1900* (Pittsburg: University of Pittsburgh Press, 1973). See also Jorge Cañizares Esguerra, *How to Write the History of the New World? Histories, Epistemologies, and Identities in the Eighteenth-Century Atlantic World* (Stanford: Stanford University Press, 2001).

6 Manifiesto de Cartagena (Cartagena de Indias, 1812). A good electronic version is available at 1232.pdf (biblioteca.org.ar).

7 Octavio Paz, *El laberinto de la soledad* (México: FCE, 1984), 110–111. For an English version, see Octavio Paz, *The Labyrinth of Solitude and Other Writings* (New York: Grove Press, 1994).

Today, however, Latin American constitutionalism is in fashion for two reasons. First, this renewed interest has been stimulated by the emergence of a 'new political history' that has overcome both traditional historiography and economic historiography dominant until recently. Second, the explosion of Latin American constitutionalism after the fall of regional dictatorships has caught the eye of researchers around the world, since it has not only recovered representative democracy but also introduced far-reaching constitutional innovations.[8] In short, everything suggests that the history of Latin American constitutionalism will no longer be invisible.

1.2 *Some Methodological Remarks*

At least as problematic as the above is the methodological approach to the object of study. It is therefore essential to identify the obstacles that have undermined Latin American legal history in general and constitutionalism in particular.[9] In my opinion, the most important are the following.

First, the 'nationalist straitjacket' woven by traditional historiography, which regarded nations as the subject instead of the object of history. Constitutions were conceived as an attribute of preexisting nations, even those that did not exist or consolidate until their adoption. For instance, the 'Political Constitution of the Spanish Monarchy' (1812) was seen as merely Spanish, when it actually was European, American, Philippine, and somewhat African. The same can be said of the first Latin American constitutions since those developed in the area of Rio de la Plata were not Argentinean but from Córdoba (1821) or Santa Fe (1819), just as 'Neogranadina' ones were not Colombian or Ecuadorian but from Cundinamarca (1811) or Quito (1812). The nationalization of constitutions stimulated nation-building rather than historical study.

The second obstacle has a neocolonial flavor. The study of Latin American constitutionalism has been driven by some sort of 'comparative obsession.' Latin American texts and experiences were invariably studied by reference to foreign equivalents in order to determine their originality or similarity. Although the literature on foreign influence or borrowed elements from other

---

8 There is abundant literature on these issues. New political history, significantly influenced by the work of François X. Guerra, has been profusely analyzed. See *Ensayos sobre la nueva historia política de América Latina, s. XIX*, ed. Guillermo Palacios (México: El Colegio de México, 2007). The same can be said of new constitutionalism. See *New Constitutionalism in Latin America: Promises and Practices*, eds. Deflet Nolte and Almut Schilling-Vacaflor (Farnham: Ashgate, 2012).

9 *New Horizons in Spanish Colonial Law: Contributions to Transnational Early Modern Legal History*, eds Thomas Duve and Heikki Pihlajamäki (Frankfurt am Main: Max Planck Institute for European Legal History, 2015).

experiences has contributed to the understanding and knowledge of Latin American constitutional history, it should not be forgotten that experiences elsewhere can be very helpful to build one's own. That is why the excessive focus on these constitutional references reveals a conscious or unconscious Eurocentric framework that retrospectively belittles Latin American constitutional drafters and constrains the analysis of their work. Hence the many studies on the influence of the Cádiz or the U.S. Constitutions on the Federal Mexican Constitution of 1824 – and the scarce literature on the latter's relation with State constitutions adopted thereunder.[10]

These obstacles have been overcome today. The current process of denationalization underpins the most recent and significant works on Latin American constitutionalism, focused on constitutional issues rather than nation-building. The present contribution is deeply indebted to such an approach.[11]

2 The Crisis of Iberian Monarchies and Catholic Constitutionalism

2.1 *Setting the Grounds for Latin American Constitutionalism: History vs. Constituent Will*

Even if dissatisfaction had spread widely in the Iberian Empires before 1808, the opening of the constitutional cycle was due more to alien imposition than to self-will. An external cause, the French invasion of the Iberian Peninsula, triggered the crisis. It is therefore not surprising that the same (or very similar) constitutional issues emerged over and over again between 1808 and the central decades of the nineteenth century.

Leaving aside some strained interpretations, the truth is that the personal behavior of the monarchs in 1808 determined the course of constitutional processes in Latin America. The transfer of the Portuguese court to Brazil saved the dignity of the royal family and fostered territorial unity: after Brazil's independence, both remained as a constitutional empire (1824–1889). By contrast,

10 Beatriz Rojas, *Procesos constitucionales mexicanos: la Constitución de 1824 y la antigua constitución* (México: Instituto Mora, 2017).

11 I have especially used the following works: Roberto Gargarella, *Latin American Constitutionalism, 1810–2010: The Engine Room of the Constitution* (Oxford: Oxford University Press, 2013); M.C. Mirow, *Latin American Constitutions: The Constitution of Cádiz and Its Legacy in Spanish America* (Cambridge: Cambridge University Press, 2015); José María Portillo, *Historia mínima del constitucionalismo en América latina* (México: El Colegio de México, 2016).

the shameful behavior of the Spanish Bourbons, who surrendered the crown to Napoleon 'without asking anyone,'[12] not only ruined any potential future of the Monarchy in America but triggered an unstoppable process of territorial dispersion.

However, the events of 1808 brought a new tune to a recurring issue that affected both monarchies and called into question the constitutional status of their fundamental laws.[13] The meaning of the term 'constitution' had changed only recently, when the North Americans and the French decided that neither the revered English constitution nor the fundamental laws of the Kingdom of France could be considered true constitutions.[14] The new formal constitutions emanating from the constituent power were regarded as the negative of historical-material constitutions.[15] Their basic features were thus defined as opposed to the latter's. In this regard, new constitutions are often described as legal texts instead of a state of affairs; an obligation rather than a situation; prescriptive rather than descriptive. They did not refer to external elements but were self-referential, and they did not reflect a previous order but founded a new one based on political participation and the recognition of individual rights – the guarantee of which was the main driver and purpose of institutional power.[16]

However, early Ibero-American constitutionalism does not fit well into such a dichotomous framework. History and volition cohabited rather than opposed each other; the conceptual and institutional heritage of the old Iberian Monarchies found accommodation in the emerging Ibero-American constitutionalism. History legitimized monarchy's survival before and after independence, as illustrated by the Ibero-American constitutions (Spain 1812, Portugal 1822), some Hispanic American constitutions (Cundinamarca 1811), the Brazilian Imperial Constitution (1824), or even most of the failed monarchical projects in Hispanic America.[17]

---

12 See Conde de Toreno, *Historia del levantamiento, guerra y revolución de España: 1807–1814* (Astorga: Akron, 2008), vol. 1, 169–170.

13 António M. Hespanha, 'Qu'est-ce que la "Constitution" dans les Monarchies Ibériques de l'Époque Moderne?' (2000) 1–2 Themis 5–18.

14 Gerald Stourzh, *From Vienna to Chicago and Back: Essays on Intellectual History and Political Thought in Europe and America* (Chicago: University of Chicago Press, 2007), 80–99.

15 Charles H. McIlwain, *Constitutionalism: Ancient and Modern* (available at https://constitution.org/cmt/mcilw/mcilw.htm).

16 See generally Dieter Grimm, *Constitucionalismo y derechos fundamentales* (Madrid: Trotta, 2006).

17 Edmundo O'Gorman, *La supervivencia política novo-hispana: Reflexiones sobre el monarquismo mexicano* (México: Fundación Cultural de Condumex, S.A., Centro de estudios de historia de México, 1969).

But history played an even more relevant role in the early constitutionalism in Hispanic America. The concept of constitution itself was at stake. Many in the Hispanic World argued that the absence of the King called not only for the 'devolution of sovereignty' to the different bodies so that they keep it in their 'custody,' but also and more importantly for recovering the fundamental laws in all their essence.[18] The historicist discourse articulated in the metropolis by Jovellanos or Martínez Marina was certainly enshrined in the Preamble of the Spanish Constitution of 1812,[19] but was also replicated in Hispanic America. Servando Teresa de Mier, who would later support independent movements, argued that the charter of rights and freedoms of Americans was already embedded in the Laws of the Indies promulgated by the Spanish crown.[20] Nevertheless, the historicist argument became ineffective since it did not answer an urgent question: who was the sovereign after 1808? So-called historic freedoms could only be restored if it was previously determined who was to carry out that task and how, which in turn implied a voluntarist conception of the constituent power. Not by chance, the modern concept of constitution spread quickly throughout Ibero-America, fostering the discussion and adoption of numerous constitutions before and after the final independence.

In the Hispanic World, 1808 entailed the breakup of the Monarchy *and* the Empire. In the absence of the king new political bodies – the *Juntas* – were formed both in the Iberian Peninsula and in America, proclaiming themselves as successors and depositaries of the Monarch's sovereignty. These new subjects triggered contradictory constitutional logics: on the one hand, the 548unitary and peninsular logic, which attempted to prevail by convening bicontinental Cortes; on the other, a pro-independence logic in Hispanic America, whose most prominent leaders ignored the call from the metropolis or quickly became disappointed. In any case, the American territories adopted their own constitutions before and after 1824.

The Portuguese Empire faced a similar scenario but with a rather different outcome. Until the 1850s, many revolts called into question the unity of the Brazilian territory. But unlike what happened in Hispanic America, the centrifugal forces did not achieve their goal and the Monarchy survived the dissolution of the Portuguese Empire in America. The Brazilian Emperor self-limited

18 José María Portillo, *Crisis atlántica: Autonomía e independencia en la crisis de la monarquía* (Madrid: Marcial Pons, 2006).

19 Francisco Tomás y Valiente, *Génesis de la Constitución española: De muchas leyes fundamentales a una sola Constitución* (Pamplona: Urgoiti, 2013).

20 José Guerra, *Historia de la Revolución de Nueva España, antiguamente Anahuac* (London: Guillermo Glindon, 1813).

its power by granting a charter – the Political Constitution of the Empire of Brazil – that preserved slavery and turned the Monarch into the fourth power, a sort of moderator. This Constitution remained in force for an exceptionally long period from 1824 to 1889.

Disaggregation of men and territories was the first problem faced by Ibero-American constitutionalism. Hence their attempt to impose cluster logics – most of them destined to fail. In this frail context, the problematic 'devolution of sovereignty' could only be carried out under the modern concept of constitution as emanated from the constituent power, thus without a historic break *à la française*.

2.2 *The Constitutions*

Among the other constitutions of the period, the Political Constitution of the Spanish Monarchy of 1812 (the Constitution of Cádiz) stands out, also inspiring the Political Constitution of the Portuguese Monarchy (1822). Both were frustrated by the American independence movements and were abrogated or suspended by their respective monarchs (the Spanish Constitution by Fernando VII in 1814 and 1823, and the Portuguese Constitution by João VI in 1823). Nevertheless, the Cadiz Constitution was neither the first nor the only one.

The Constitution of 1812 was preceded by Neogranadian constitutions (Socorro, 1810; States of Venezuela, 1811; Cundinamarca, 1811; Tunja, 1811; Quito, 1812), Chilean constitutional regulations (1811, 1812), or failed statutes in Rio de la Plata (1811). Furthermore, its promulgation in the 'Spanish realms' did not prevent constitutional dispersion even in those territories where it was in force. In this regard, the Mexican case is very significant. Just when the authorities and new Hispanic corporations swore allegiance to the 1812 Constitution, the outbreak of an Indigenous insurrection (1810) started a process that ended with the promulgation of the famous 'Constitutional Decree for the Liberty of Mexican America' (Apatzingán, 1814). Nevertheless, the implementation of the Constitution of 1812 was the first constitutional experience for many territories – including some Indigenous ones. Cádiz constitutionalism cast a long shadow over Hispanic America, thus becoming a key milestone in the study of Latin America constitutional history.[21]

Neither the independence of Brazil (1822) nor the defeat of the Spanish army in Ayacucho (1824) solved the issue of the replacement or devolution of sovereignty. This explains why Latin American political processes had such diverse constitutional outcomes, especially in terms of stability. The first period of

21 Mirow, *Latin American Constitutions*.

Brazilian constitutionalism remained in force for many decades (1824–1889) and can be compared with the Chilean experience, embodied after some failures in a long-lived conservative centralist and authoritarian Constitution from 1833 to 1925. The Uruguayan Constitution (1830–1918) cannot be included in this group because it was repeatedly suspended. The same can be said of Dr. Francia's dictatorship in Paraguay; he governed the country from its independence in 1814 until his death in 1840 without any constitution.

In the rest of the Hispanic World, constitutionalism followed a different path. The total failure of the first Mexican Empire (1821–1823), with the participation of Central America, launched a constituent process that ended with the adoption of the Federal Constitution of the United Mexican States (1824). Its abrogation in 1835 gave way to a period of instability until 1857. The area of the former Viceroyalty of Rio de la Plata saw the failure of all centralist constitutional projects (1819, 1826) and the (dis)united provinces of Rio de la Plata, with their respective Constitutions, underwent a convoluted political process until the promulgation in 1853 of a Constitution for the Argentine Federation – endorsed by Buenos Aires seven years later. By contrast, the failure of the Constitution of the Republic of Colombia (Venezuela, Ecuador, and Colombia) gave way to the Venezuelan Constitution (1830), the Ecuadorian Constitution (1830), and the Neogranadian Constitution (1832). The same occurred with the Constitution of the Federal Republic of Central America (1824–1838) or the short-lived Constitution of the North and South Peruvian States and Bolivia (1837–1838). In both cases, different provinces or states either embarked on an independent constitutional journey (Guatemala, Honduras, El Salvador, Nicaragua, and Costa Rica) or resumed their separate paths (Peru and Bolivia).

2.3 *Basic Features of Early Latin American Constitutionalism*

In spite of their large number, the first Ibero-Latin American constitutions have a certain family resemblance not simply explained in terms of cross-influences. They arose from the voluntarism of political actors and their management of a heavy heritage of concepts, institutions, and practices developed in the Iberian Monarchies. The main features of this constitutionalism – some sort of modern constitutionalism's third way – can be summarized as follows.[22]

22 Marta Lorente, 'Catholic Constitutionalism in the Hispanic World (1808–1826) ' (2013) 130 Zeitschrift der Savigny-Stiftung für Rechtsgeschichte Germanistische Abteilung 326–347. This work summarizes the findings of a collective research: *El momento gaditano: La Constitución en el orbe hispánico, 1808–1826*, eds Marta Lorente and José María Portillo (Madrid: Congreso de los Diputados, 2013).

First, its inherent Catholicism – including but not limited to banning other religions, even if that curtailed individual or collective freedoms. This early constitutionalism reproduced in different terms the Catholic understanding of society as the sum of communities (families, religious or secular corporations, villages, towns, or republics) rather than individuals.[23] This may explain the limitations and exclusions underlying the configuration of the new subjects' rights. They conformed to the model of a Catholic *pater familias* whose domestic power allowed him to manage the 'natural' subordination of slaves, serfs, workers, relatives, women, and dependent children. They were based on corporatist representative mechanisms such as indirect suffrage with varying degrees, or imperative mandate. Even the territorial organization in terms of federalism versus centralism actually responded to old logics based on a jurisprudential conception of political power.

At a different level, early Ibero-American constitutionalism assumed symbolic and institutional religious devices, such as the constitutional collective oath conceived as the foundation of political obligation. Regulated for the first time in the Cádiz Constitution, it survived in Hispanic America for decades. The failure of this constitutional option, which turned the clergy into public servants, led to major and well-known conflicts between the church and state in the second half of the century. Nonetheless, even if individuals were accorded little weight, the introduction of representative mechanisms disrupted the unanimity of the classic version of Catholic republics regarded as perfect communities.[24] This new constitutionalism brought a new factionalism that was visible from the outset in elections and assemblies, and undermined confidence in the constitution's thaumaturgical power to articulate society in political terms.

Second, all the above affected the complex issue of replacement and reformulation of sovereignty. With the king no longer on the scene, conflicting sovereignties ensued, in the words of Annino.[25] The 'peoples' in plural opposed the 'people' represented by General Assemblies before and after independence. People's *pronunciamientos* became a common instrument, understood as the gathering of the former republic's populations of cities, towns, and Indigenous villages to decide the termination and renewal of their contract

23 José María Portillo, 'Repúblicas. Comunidades perfectas, colonias. La crisis de la Monarquía Hispana como laboratorio conceptual' (2004) 28 Historia Contemporánea 157–184.

24 Antonio Annino, coord., *Historia de las elecciones en Iberoamérica, Siglo XIX* (Buenos Aires: Fondo de Cultura Económica, 1995).

25 Antonio Annino, *Silencios y disputas en la Historia de Hispanoamérica* (Bogotá: Taurus, 2014).

with new national, federal, or confederal bodies. This explains the mostly pactist nature of early Latin American *caudillismo* and the constitutional hyperactivity of this period. Given that constitutions did not vanish altogether from the political horizon, some authors use the expression 'constitutional *caudillismo*' to describe political regimes that distinguished between areas governed by the constitution and those under the *caudillo*'s executive government. The shifting holders of sovereignty believed they needed a constitution to justify de facto situations or to impose their governments, with examples ranging from Páez and the Monagas in Venezuela to Melgarejo in Bolivia, Santa Anna in Mexico, or Rosas and Bustos in the provinces of Buenos Aires and Córdoba, respectively.

Instability, however, was not only caused by *pronunciamientos* and *caudillo*-led governments. From the beginning, many thought that the first constitutions had designed a very unstable institutional framework, mainly due to the fact that they identified the state with political participation. Indeed, the elections not only had a mobilizing effect on many sectors of the old American societies that until then had not enjoyed any prominence but also endowed the constitutional institutions with a new legitimacy based exclusively on the fiction of consensus. This explains why the Bolivian constitution drafted by Simón Bolívar himself (1826) not only confined a reduced bill of rights to a brief final chapter but also established a lifelong presidency not subject to the whims of representation. The experiment lasted barely two months, but the problem of governance continued to beset most of Latin America – hence the tendency to enhance the role of the executive at the expense of the other branches of government. Nevertheless, neither emperors, presidents, or *caudillos*, nor provincial or state Parliaments, and much less parochial republics could get rid of the legacy of the Iberian Monarchies when it came to organizing the life of American societies.[26]

2.4 *Civilization or Barbarism*

Since the second half of the century, some Latin American political leaders subscribed to the theories of Domingo Faustino Sarmiento, future President of Argentina, in *Civilization and Barbarism* (1845). Republished countless times, this work outlined a political program based on reformulating an old antinomy. According to Sarmiento, barbarism thrived in the Latin American rural world, populated by gauchos, Indigenous peoples, and *caudillos* oblivious to

26 Marta Lorente, 'More than just Vestiges: Notes for the Study of Colonial Law History in Spanish America after 1808' in *New Horizons in Spanish Colonial Law*, 193–254.

the law, while civilization stemmed from *European cities* governed by law and order. The desire to *civilize* Latin American in this specific sense opened a new constitutional cycle.

3 Liberal Constitutionalism and Oligarchic Republics

3.1 *The Individual and the State*

The constitutional accommodation of premodern institutional devices and concepts, such as religious legitimation, personal and territorial plurality of legal orders, corporatist and community networks, did not serve to stabilize political life in Latin American societies. Even if a significant part of the leaders committed to state-building, these processes depended more on the recovery of regional economies than on the will of political elites.[27]

The second Latin American constitutional cycle developed between the central decades of the nineteenth century and the first decades of the twentieth century. It was defined by the assimilation of the liberal discourse. As is well known, the most prominent liberal thinkers in Europe and North America at the time, whose works were eagerly devoured by an important sector of the Latin American elites, argued that individual rights were only ensured if the role of the State was limited to (i) guaranteeing the functioning of the market by protecting property-related freedoms; and (ii) maintaining social order, based in turn on limited political participation and a certain morality. State-building in Latin America, which entailed the emergence of individuals, was generally slow and territorially diverse. Nonetheless, it is possible to identify some constitutional elements common to the whole region.

Latin American morality was essentially Catholic. Nevertheless, the conflict between church and state broke out precisely during this second period and extended throughout practically all Latin America. In Mexico, for example, the conflict manifested itself brutally, but interestingly the strengthening of the State ran parallel to the progressive weakening of the corporatist fabric affecting ecclesiastical, professional, territorial, or cultural collectives alike.[28] State-building favored the individualization of rights, but it did not lead to the abolition of slavery in Brazil, or even less of the innumerable personal servitudes particularly prevalent in the Latin American rural environment. Among the

27 Tulio Halperin Donghi, *The Contemporary History of Latin America* (Durham: Duke University Press, 1993).

28 Brian Connaughton, *Entre la voz de Dios y el llamado de la patria: Religión, identidad y ciudadanía en México, siglo XIX* (México: FCE, 2011).

rights advocated by liberalism stands out individual property as well as those which are instrumental to the former. Finally, the right to individual property almost completely determined political rights.

State-building was also expressed in terms of the international positioning of Latin American political formations, which were forced to define internally and externally the 'national' territory. All this resulted in many conflicts, including those caused by the military, political, administrative, and cultural occupation of border areas in order to annex or sell territories that were either unoccupied or populated by Indigenous communities. The conquest of the Argentinean desert, the march towards the Brazilian West, the Chilean conquest of the Araucania, or the sale of Mexican state lands served not only the individualization of the right to property through the distribution of enormous extensions among a chosen few but also the whitening of the population. A two-pronged policy was implemented to this end: the expulsion of the Indigenous element and the promotion of European immigration. On the other hand, the effective control of the 'national territory' turned out to be a cause and consequence of the professionalization of the military, whose increasing political prominence would determine the course of Latin American constitutionalism in the twentieth century.

The constitutions adopted throughout this second period attest to this process of state-building and individualization, which relied on the pact between conservative and liberal political formations that monopolized the political arena for decades. It is not by chance that scholars use the expressions liberal or 'fusion' constitutionalism to account for this second stage of Latin American history as noted by Argentine political scientist Roberto Gargarella.[29]

3.2 *The Constitutions*

The constitutional texts adopted throughout this second cycle can be grouped into different categories. The first and most representative period is defined by the Constitution of the Argentine Confederation (1853), amended in 1860 upon the accession of Buenos Aires, and the Political Constitution of the Mexican Republic (1857), and the Constitution of the United States of Colombia (1863). The three texts placed a broad catalogue of individual rights and guarantees above the law. These were contrary to slavery and privileges of blood or birth. These texts enshrined equality before the law, separated church from state (although with different intensity), declared the separation of powers opting

29 Gargarella, *Latin American Constitutionalism*, chapter 2.

for presidential systems, and further elaborated on the design and organization of the Federation.

The second group is comprised of the constitutions adopted in regions where the most radical version of liberalism was defeated, which entailed the abrogation of many previous constitutions. For example, the long-lived Political Constitution of the Republic of Colombia (1886–1991) was a very conservative and centralist text that returned power to the Catholic Church, imposed a strict censorship on the press, and limited political participation. The moderate and long-lived Constitution of the Republic of Peru (1860–1920) declared the primacy of Catholicism, restricted representation through certain requirements (education, property, and taxes), and recovered indirect suffrage. Finally, the Constitution of Guatemala (1879–1944) put an end to the Catholic-inspired paternalistic government of the last old-style *caudillo* Rafael Carrera (1844–1865), but it also excluded a large majority from the rights of citizenship and opened the door to what would become the foremost problem of Central America – surrendering entire sectors of the economy to foreign companies or individuals.

The amendments to previous constitutions (for example Chile in 1833) also illustrate this particular constitutionalism: extension of freedom of religion, limitations to the reelection of the President, and protections of the rights of association and peaceful assembly. Something similar can be said of the long and unequal life of the first and supposedly liberal Brazilian Constitution. While it allowed a certain freedom of worship and included some individual rights and freedoms, it fully tolerated slavery until 1888 and imposed indirect and censitary suffrage. From 1850 onwards, Brazilian political life stabilized, as the pact between liberals and conservatives ensured the functioning of a system of domination based on power sharing between economic and territorial elites. However, the accumulation of unresolved problems led to a military coup, with little or no popular support, that destroyed the imperial Constitution and replaced it with the first republican one in 1891.

3.3 *Oligarchic Republics: Basic Features of Liberal Constitutionalism*

State-building processes had very disparate outcomes. In the field of civil rights, constitutions typically included a detailed list of negative freedoms with particular emphasis on individual property rights. Some of them established previously designed guarantee instruments, such as the famous Mexican '*amparo*,' which inspired others such as the '*mandato de segurança*' in Brazil or the '*tutela*' action in the Colombian Constitution of 1991. However, in most of Latin America, a wide variety of situations of personal dependency still questioned the effectiveness of the individual freedoms enshrined in the constitutions.

Moreover, the limitation of political rights, which not only affected suffrage but also a good part of what we now understand as labor or social rights, expelled a large portion of the population from that state-building community. The individualization of civil rights, combined with the limitation of political rights, led to the unilateral imposition of a political, economic, social, and cultural system completely oblivious to the heterogeneous nature of Latin American populations.[30]

These constitutions provided different check-and-balance systems between the three traditional powers. Most of them gradually evolved towards strengthening the executive. In particular, presidents tended to accumulate exceptional powers and perpetuated in office by virtue of consecutive terms and electoral corruption – although the latter was common to almost all constitutional experiences at the time. The same cannot be said about the establishment of a judiciary system based on the rule of law. Indeed, a truly independent and accountable third power took a long time to settle in Latin America. The extremely slow replacement of the old legal bodies of the Iberian monarchies by a new regulation did not contribute to the transformation of colonial judges and their submission to the law. This in turn allowed the reproduction of old judicial procedures and customs for a long time.

In terms of territorial organization, most of these constitutions favored federalism, with significant exceptions such as Colombia. Undoubtedly, the U.S. constitution served as a reference on many occasions, but the truth is that Latin American federalism was managed more by power groups than by states. Finally, liberal constitutionalism was unable to compensate institutionally for the loss of the thaumaturgical nature of the first Latin American constitutionalism. The basic principles enshrined in the constitutions such as a declaration of rights, separation of powers, and territorial organization were regulated by subsequent lower-ranking norms, including codes, laws, regulations, and ministerial orders, without establishing institutions or procedures to guarantee and to defend the constitution. The problem was clearly identified, but Latin American constitutionalism (just like continental European constitutionalism at the time) did not want to or failed to solve it.

3.4 *Imaginary Citizens, Failed Nations*

Liberal constitutionalism failed or perhaps did not even attempt to create equal citizenship. The excluding element of the liberal political imaginary,

30 Bartolomé Clavero, *Freedom's Law and Indigenous Rights: From Europe's Oeconomy to the Constitutionalism of the Americas* (Berkeley: University of California-Robbins Collection, 2005).

tinged with racism, took on extraordinary dimensions in Latin America. This undoubtedly tainted the whole field of rights. In fact, inequality was simultaneously the foundation and the goal of nineteenth-century Latin American constitutionalism.[31] Even where universal male suffrage took root, liberal constitutionalism only created *imaginary citizens*.[32] In this sense, Latin American communities were *barely* imagined towards the end of the century.[33] Many contemporaries warned of the scale of the problem. For instance, the Peruvian communist intellectual and politician, José Carlos Mariátegui, talking about his home country, stated in 1928: 'It is a country in which Indians and foreign conquerors live side by side but do not mingle with or even understand one another ... The feelings and interests of four-fifths of the population play almost no role in the formation of the national identity and institutions.'[34]

Liberal constitutionalism was at the same time the cause and consequence of state-building processes which left little room to integration policies for an economically, socially, racially, and culturally heterogeneous population. Not surprisingly, Latin American oligarchic republics fell into crisis in the first decades of the twentieth century.

4 The Constitution in the Twentieth Century

4.1 *Back and Forth in the Chronology: Mexican Revolution and the History of Constitutionalism*

Establishing or proposing chronologies is often risky, since the main threads of any particular history – economic, social, cultural – do not usually coincide in time and space. Many historians point out that the 1929 crash marked a watershed in the life of Latin American political communities, even if most of the conflicts that erupted at that time had been brewing long before then. For many scholars, however, the true turning point in the history of Latin American constitutionalism was the promulgation of the Political Constitution of the United Mexican States (1917).

31 Roberto Gargarella, *The Legal Foundations of Inequality: Constitutionalism in the Americas, 1776–1860* (Oxford: Oxford University Press, 2010).

32 Fernando Escalante, *Ciudadanos imaginarios* (México: Colegio de México, 2011).

33 Benedict Anderson, *Imagined Communities: Reflections on the Origen and Spread of Nationalism* (London: Verso, 1983).

34 José Carlos Mariátegui, *7 Ensayos de interpretación de la realidad peruana* (Lima: Librería Editorial Minerva, 2007), 105, originally published in 1928. Here I use the 79th edition, which was translated into many languages. For an English version, see *Seven Interpretative Essays on Peruvian Reality* (Austin: University of Texas Press, 1971).

After a long and conflictive revolution, the Mexican Constitution of 1917 brought a new version of constitutionalism to Latin America. Without breaking with the foundations and the structure of the liberal Constitution of 1857, the revolutionary constitution introduced major amendments to all its chapters, including the one on rights and guarantees of freedoms. Thus, both the social question and to a lesser extent the Indigenous one were present in the Constitution. It addressed the problem of land ownership and its distribution in the chapter on individual guarantees, dedicating one of its titles to work and social security. The Constitution of 1917, still in force although reformed on countless occasions, is one of the most notable products of the Latin American constitutional laboratory. However, Mexico's constitutional model did not spread widely. The crisis of liberal constitutionalism that affected almost all Latin America in the first years of the twentieth century manifested itself in very different ways that did not conform to the Mexican chronology. Therefore, we can only identify some factors that may help understand the twentieth-century Latin American constitutional conundrum.

4.2 *New Actors: Personal Leadership and Political Parties*

Liberal constitutionalism managed to introduce major reforms without abrogating the nineteenth-century constitutions, some of which turned out to be real time bombs. For instance, the gradual implementation of universal male suffrage – and women for the first time in Uruguay in 1927 – changed the basic rules that had ensured the reproduction of elite control of the political life of the oligarchic republics. The emergence of new leaders and formations completely transformed the political scene, until then occupied exclusively by conservatives and liberals. The new actors channeled political, economic, and social demands from broad sectors of the population so that a series of previously invisible issues acquired constitutional resonances. The protection of workers or Indigenous people reinforced their legal presence: the Mexican Constitution of 1917 included social and labor rights, becoming a reference in this regard, while the Peruvian (1920) and Ecuadorian (1928) Constitutions recognized the Indigenous component of their respective nations and acknowledged the need to protect it by means of special laws.

Immersed in a spectacular process of social change, Latin American republics tried to face the new challenges by resorting to legal and constitutional reforms: for example, the reform of the Chilean Constitution of 1925 entailed the 'constitutionalization' of some previously recognized rights including the freedom of conscience, assembly, and association. The Uruguayan case was similar, with a program of reforms set in motion under its old Constitution (1830) – thus modernizing different economic sectors, consolidating secularism, achieving a real democratization of the country, and seeking to address the social issue from the state administration. In contrast to Chile, a new Constitution (1919) harvested the fruits of the Uruguayan reformism promoted by President Batlle.

Other countries did not curb this process of political 'aristocratization' rooted in liberal constitutionalism. The case of the first Brazilian republic (1889–1930) is significant in this regard. On one hand, it affirmed the state's secularity, consolidated some rights such as expression, association, and peaceful assembly, and developed certain guarantees such as habeas corpus and judicial tenure. On the other, the first republican Constitution (1891) designed a quasi-confederal system in which states and even municipalities had ample margin to manage their particular interests, often identified with those of their regional elites and local chiefs.

Despite its enormous significance, the consolidation, extension, or expansion of rights and guarantees was not the only constitutional innovation at the turn of the century. Previously, a different problem had arisen in Latin America since the new international order established at the Berlin Conference (1885) had region-wide constitutional effects of great relevance.

4.3 *International Order and Latin American Constitutionalism*

After its victory in the Spanish–American War and the Treaty of Paris of 1898, the U.S. imposed a new order in Latin America based on a novel reading of the 'Monroe doctrine.' It was now obliged to intervene in any country where the rights and property of U.S. citizens were in danger. The appendix added to the Cuban Constitution (1902), known as the Platt Amendment, was the first embodiment of this doctrine limiting Cuban sovereignty in terms of U.S. interests. This neocolonial framework can be illustrated by cases such as the dismemberment of Colombia, which led to the creation of Panama (1904 Constitution), or by very personal dictatorships such as that of the Somoza family in Nicaragua (1937–1979) or Trujillo in Santo Domingo (1930–1961). Also paradigmatic is the coup that overthrew Guatemalan President Jacobo Árbenz in 1954, whose constitutional reform program included the expropriation of the extensive territories owned by the United Fruit Company. It is not by chance that Central American republics came to be referred to as 'banana republics,' an expression that hints at their limited sovereignty.[35]

35 The expression was coined in 1904 by William Sidney Porter in his work *Cabbages and Kings* (available at: http://www.gutenberg.org/ebooks/2777).

Later, the fight against communism justified interventions that altered the Latin American constitutional course giving rise to very different political regimes. Originally, nationalism and anti-imperialism underpinned the Cuban Revolution, which finally assumed a dictatorial regime constitutionally enshrined in 1976. At the other end of the political spectrum was the also dictatorial Chilean regime presided over by Augusto Pinochet (1973–1990), resulting from a coup against President Allende with the support of the United States. This same interventionist logic was present in the Sandinista Revolution (Political Constitution of the Republic of Nicaragua, 1986), or in the civil war that devastated El Salvador (1980–1992), which after resorting to the UN to settle the conflict ended up enacting a new Constitution in 1983.

The above and other similar cases help us to understand an essential characteristic of the twentieth-century history of Latin America: left-wing or right-wing nationalism that took on anti-democratic overtones from the 1920s onwards. Nonetheless, international interference is insufficient to explain the dramatic upheavals of Latin American constitutions between the first and last decades of the century.

4.4 *Constitutional Decline in Latin America: Populist Authoritarianism and Military Dictatorships*

The first decades of the last century witnessed the awakening of authoritarianism in Latin America, which adopted very different languages and institutional forms. In some cases, such as Peru, authoritarianism served to eradicate what was left of the aristocratic republics: a coup brought Augusto Bernardino Leguía to power, which he retained for eleven years (1919–1930) during which he developed a program based on the democratization of political life, the education of the masses, public works, the industrialization of the country, and the opening up of its economy. Regardless of its results, Leguía's authoritarian regime – oriented towards a 'New Fatherland' or '*Patria Nueva*' – was endowed with a constitution in 1920. Indeed, even if most Latin American countries entered into a dynamic that swept away liberal constitutionalism, their authoritarian regimes somehow coexisted with constitutions – unlike military dictatorships.

Again, the Mexican case is paradigmatic. The entry into force of the Constitution of 1917 did not put an end to the violence unleashed by the revolution. Beyond the murders of revolutionary leaders such as Zapata and Villa, or of presidents such as Carranza and Obregón, there were also significant armed conflicts. The *Cristero* War of 1926, for instance, had its roots in the virulent rejection of a law that implemented in radical terms the anticlerical Article 130 of the 1917 Constitution. Hence the widespread consideration that the pacification of Mexican political life was due not so much to the entry into force of the Constitution as to the creation of the National Revolutionary Party (*Partido Nacional Revolucionario*) in 1929, which after several (re)foundations eventually adopted its current name: Institutional Revolutionary Party (PRI). However, the pacification came at a great democratic cost, since the political regime designed by the Constitution was managed exclusively by the PRI for seventy consecutive years (1929–2000). Given that political parties were not banned, and elections were not cancelled, PRI's success did not lie in its monopolization of the political arena but in its identity as a mass party designed to protect the interests of the workers. This explains the creation of powerful trade union organizations linked to the party and their central role in the Mexican political life for decades. In short, the 1917 Constitution laid the foundation for a very powerful presidential regime. Limited at times by the federal structure, it created, fueled, and used corporatism – conceived as a conflict resolution framework parallel or superior to political representation.

Other Latin American authoritarian regimes were at the opposite ideological extreme. In this regard, Brazil and Argentina also adopted corporatist foundations and institutions, as exemplified by the incorporation of trade union organizations to the political and institutional life. Based on European experiences – mainly Italian fascism and Spain's Falange – some charismatic leaders such as Getulio Vargas in Brazil or Juan Domingo Perón in Argentina resorted to military coups to take power but held on to it thanks to massive popular support expressed, among other things, in elections. The Brazilian and Argentinian regimes were authoritarian, organicist, nationalist, and partly religious, but they were also progressive in terms of labor legislation. They eventually adopted constitutions that did not establish democratic political systems but rather provided cover to fascist or semi-fascist ideologies. For instance, in 1937 the constitution granted by Vargas established the *Estado Novo* in Brazil (1937–1945). Along the same lines, the Argentinian Constitution of 1949, based on Peronist *justicialism*, legitimized Perón's first government until he was overthrown in 1955 by a coup that restored the liberal Constitution of 1853.

The professionalization of the military throughout the twentieth century facilitated its participation in Latin American politics. Military officials holding institutional positions was not a new phenomenon, but from the 1930s onwards the Army took it upon itself to save the country through dictatorships. It is impossible to give an account of the Latin American regimes arising from coups between 1930 and 1980, but one thing can be said for certain: military dictatorships did away with the very idea of Constitution in Latin America.

5 Concluding Remarks: Present and Future of Latin American Constitutionalism

From the 1980s onwards, dictatorships gradually disappeared from the Latin American political scenario. Almost all the countries of the region have adopted new charters that are particular versions of democratic and social constitutionalism. Based on the recognition of prior rights and the principle of separation of powers, they establish mechanisms that ensure the primacy of the constitution over the rest of the legal system. This explains, for example, the creation of constitutional courts or the strengthening of constitutional review mechanisms. Up to this point, the new Latin American constitutionalism does not differ much from continental Europe's – conceived in the interwar period and reformed after World War II. Nevertheless, recent Latin American constitutions such as the ones enacted in Brazil and Ecuador in 1988 and Colombia in 1991 have brought a great novelty, namely the recognition of the 'plurinational' character of their populations. Understood as a starting point rather than as a concession, this recognition completely transforms the basic characteristics of democratic constitutionalism. It not only opens the door to a new generation of collective rights individually held, such as the right to the environment or to one's own culture, but also transforms the institutional design of the State.

Nevertheless, this new Latin American constitutionalism has opened the way to the strengthening of an essentially charismatic presidentialism. Political leaders have often advocated constitutional interpretations or reforms mainly oriented towards extending their time in office. The general crisis undergone by traditional political parties and social organizations has reinforced such charismatic drift. Nonetheless, this has not served to consolidate a new institutional framework – rather the opposite. Given that new Latin American constitutionalism has so far failed to meet popular expectations, frustration has once again set in. In short, everything points to the fact that Latin America is on the threshold of a new cycle in which constitutions have no assured place.

References

Annino, Antonio. *Silencios y Disputas en la Historia de Hispanoamérica*. Bogotá: Taurus, 2004.

Anderson, Benedict. *Imagined Communities: Reflections on the Origin and Spread of Nationalism*. London: Verso, 1983.

Baylin, Bernard. *Atlantic History: Concept and Contours*. Cambridge: Harvard University Press, 2005.

Duve, Thomas, and Heikki Pihlajamäki, eds. *New Horizons in Spanish Colonial Law: Contributions to Transnational Early Modern Legal History*. Frankfurt am Main: Max Planck Institute for European Legal History, 2015.

Duve, Thomas, ed. *Entanglements in Legal History: Conceptual Approaches, Global Perspectives on Legal History*. Frankfurt am Main: Max Planck Institute for European Legal History, 2014.

Fioravanti, Maurizio. *Los Derechos Fundamentales*. 6th ed. Madrid: Trotta, 2016.

Gargarella, Roberto. *The Legal Foundations of Inequality: Constitutionalism in the Americas, 1776–1860*. Cambridge: Cambridge University Press, 2010.

Gargarella, Roberto. *Latin American Constitutionalism, 1810–2010: The Engine Room of the Constitution*. Oxford: Oxford University Press, 2013.

Gerbi, Antonello. *The Dispute of the New World: The History of a Polemic, 1750–1900*. Pittsburgh: University of Pittsburgh Press, 1973.

Halperin Donghi, Tulio. *The Contemporary History of Latin America*. Durham: Duke University Press, 1993.

Lorente, Marta. 'Catholic Constitutionalism in the Hispanic World (1808–1826).' *Zeitschrift der Savigny-Stiftung für Rechtsgeschichte Germanistische Abteilung* 130 (2013): 326–347.

Mirow, M.C. *Latin American Constitutions: The Constitution of Cádiz and Its Legacy in Spanish America*. New York: Cambridge University Press, 2015.

Portillo, José María. *Historia Mínima del Constitucionalismo en América Latina*. México: El Colegio de México, 2016.

CHAPTER 22

Legal Pluralism

Tamar Herzog

Legal pluralism is a term many scholars now use to describe the coexistence of various competing legal spheres within a single polity. Yet, what they mean by it and what they seek to demonstrate differ dramatically from case to case. In what follows, I uncover some of the many ways in which the term is currently employed. Mostly seeking to place European and American, as well as historical and legal scholarship in dialogue, I ask what we stand to gain from having a longer and a wider perspective.

1 Early Modern Legal Pluralism and Empire

Current-day scholarship mostly associates early modern legal pluralism with empire. According to the most frequent narrative, colonial domains featured a legal structure where colonists and colonized were each subjected to a different legal regime, and also to different authorities and courts.[1] This division facilitated domination as it legally sanctioned a political project seeking to privilege one sector over the other. Because classification into groups determined the rights and obligations of individuals, all actors had powerful motives to care about how both they and others were classified, and they constantly debated who should benefit from which treatment. The result was frequent discussions regarding what the various categories meant, who belonged in them, and how they should be implemented.

Historians who have studied these processes suggested that, because the classification of individuals into groups depended on a multiplicity of factors and because the definition of the groups themselves was often unclear, actors frequently strove to influence the way they were classified to obtain membership in the group that best suited their interests. Identifying these activities as 'forum shopping,' a term currently used to describe attempts by litigants to choose the courts they believe will treat their case most favorably, scholars

1 Lauren Benton, *Law and Colonial Cultures: Legal Regimes in World History, 1400–1900* (Cambridge: Cambridge University Press, 2002).

DOI:10.1163/9789004436091_024

of empire likewise suggested that legal pluralism generated endless conflicts among the authorities who could disagree as to who had power over which individual or case. Actors could use these tensions to their benefit, adopting a behavior that some identified as 'jurisdictional politics,' or 'jurisdictional jockeying.'

Imperial legal pluralism (as this reality came to be called) thus featured various legal universes, each with distinct laws and authorities that applied to different segments of the colonial world. This structure provided individuals, collectivities, and institutions with reasons to engage in protecting or subverting the existing order, as well as interpreting and manipulating the classificatory system to their advantage. Thus, if actors, who struggled to improve their standing, sometimes obeyed existing divisions and power relations, on other occasions they strove to re-structure and change them. Because the various concurring legal spheres were not neatly distinguished or stacked, the same individuals could on occasions be ascribed to more than a single group. Border crossing between groups was frequent, and the groups themselves constantly changed shape. The result was a highly mobile legal universe, in which the coexistence of concurring legal systems required the permanent elaboration and re-elaboration of categories of belonging, which were constantly invented, employed, re-employed, challenged, interpreted, and subverted.

Applied to early modern colonial Spanish America, this analysis sought to explain how Spaniards and Indigenous persons were identified and how distinctions between them became legally meaningful. According to a well-known narrative, Spaniards distinguished themselves from the Indigenous, among other things, by creating two separate legal and political structures. These structures, identified as *repúblicas*, mandated that, while Spaniards would be members of a 'Spanish republic' and would be placed under obedience to Spanish law and Spanish authorities and judges, natives would belong to an Indigenous republic, and would be subjected to Indigenous laws, authorities, and judges. Although the two republics were in theory separate, given the colonial context, the liberty of Indigenous authorities and judges was not absolute, and neither was all Indigenous law upheld.[2] Indigenous communities received judicial autonomy to settle their affairs according to their 'laws

2 Miguel Ángel González de San Segundo, *Un mestizaje jurídico: el derecho indiano de los indígenas* (Madrid: Universidad Complutense, 1995); Juan Manzano Manzano, 'Las leyes y costumbres indígenas en el orden de prelación de fuentes del derecho indiano' in *Actas del Primer Congreso del Instituto Internacional de Historia del Derecho Indiano* (Buenos Aires: Instituto Internacional de Historia del Derecho Indiano, 1967), 65–71; Margarita Menegus Bornemann, 'La costumbre indígena en el derecho indiano, 1529–1550' (1992) 4 Anuario Mexicano de Historia del Derecho 151–159. See also Karen Graubart, 'Learning from

and good customs,' only as long as these were not repugnant to Spanish law and morality.[3]

As happened elsewhere, the application of a different regime to Spaniards and Indigenous individuals led to frequent conflicts regarding who was who. If, initially, the task of distinguishing colonizers from colonized seemed self-evident, as the colonial period advanced, clarity dissipated. The vicinity and frequent blending of peoples of different origins, the rise of miscegenation, and substantial processes of acculturation and hybridity led to constant questioning. At stake were basic questions such as whether the distinction between Spaniards and Indigenous individuals was based on origin, descent, race, culture, or place within the colonial order. When classification had important legal implications, both Spaniards and the Indigenous took active part in these discussions. Sometimes being classified as Indigenous was a result that individuals and groups sought to avoid, as during campaigns to collect *tributo*, a tax mostly associated with natives.[4] On other occasions, this status was deliberately pursued, for example, in order to benefit from legal representation by a court appointed official (*protector de indios*). Taking advantage of such debates, the Tlaxcalans of New Spain (present-day Mexico), argued that they were conquistadors rather than vanquished and therefore Spanish rather than Indigenous.[5] Many native nobles followed the same road, pointing out that their privileged situation assimilated them to Spaniards rather than confirmed their nativeness. Even as late as the end of the eighteenth century, Indigenous rebels adopted this analysis, which had them classify all acculturated Indigenous persons as Spanish rather than Indigenous.[6] Particularly

---

the Qadi: The Jurisdiction of Local Rule in the Early Colonial Andes' (2015) 95(2) Hispanic American Historical Review 195–228.

3 The jurisdiction of Indigenous authorities and submission to Indigenous law were recognized in a variety of royal orders, among them the *Recopilación de Indias*, 2.1.4, 4.7.2, and 4.7.13.

4 Martin Minchom, *The People of Quito 1690–1810: Change and Unrest in the Underclass* (Boulder: Westview Press, 1994), 153–171.

5 Ruth Hill, 'Teaching the Pre-history of Race along the Hispanic Transatlantic' (2007) 30(1) Dieciocho 105; Laura E. Matthew, 'Whose Conquest? Nahua, Zapotec, and Mixteca Allies in the Conquest of Central America' in *Indian Conquistadors: Indigenous Allies in the Conquest of Mesoamerica*, eds Laura E. Matthew and Michel R. Oudijk (Norman: University of Oklahoma Press, 2007), 119.

6 Jan Szeminski, 'Why Kill the Spaniard? New Perspectives on Andean Insurrectionary Ideology in the Eighteenth-Century World' in *Resistance, Rebellion and Consciousness in the Andean Peasant World: Eighteenth to Twentieth Centuries*, ed. Steve Stern (Madison: University of Wisconsin Press, 1987), 166, 191.

troublesome was the identification of liminal individuals who did not fully exhibit the characteristics usually associated with either group.[7]

Although historians of empire usually affirmed that legal pluralism implied the application of a distinct set of rules by a distinct set of authorities, this was not always the case. Contrary to present-day 'forum shopping,' in colonial Spanish America, the choice of court did not necessarily imply the choice of law and vice versa.[8] Indigenous individuals were indeed subjected to Indigenous law as implemented by their authorities, but they were also subjected to Indigenous law as applied by Spanish judges, and to Spanish law as applied by both Indigenous and Spanish authorities. Emblematic in this regard was the *Juzgado General de Indios* of New Spain where, as part of their duty to adjudicate conflicts, Spanish judges oversaw cases involving Indigenous litigants by using both Indigenous and Spanish law. Other Spanish judges were also under the same obligation, and habitually considered Indigenous law, or creatively combined it with Spanish law, for example, when they ruled on native land rights or when they decided on the identity of Indigenous leaders (*caciques*).[9]

The blurring of legal spheres also transpired in Indigenous jurisdictions. Indigenous authorities, who were to apply Indigenous law, were deeply affected by Spanish law, from which they borrowed, or which they blended with their own laws, sometimes even rejecting the 'old' (Indigenous) law in favor of the 'new' (Spanish) law.[10] Furthermore, although during the colonial period Indigenous communities maintained some measure of political and

---

7 Joanne Rappaport, *Disappearing Mestizo: Configuring Differences in the Colonial New Kingdom of Granada* (Durham: Duke University Press, 2014).

8 Thomas Duve, 'Indigenous Rights: Latin America' in *The Oxford Handbook of Legal History*, eds Markus D. Dubber and Christopher Tomlins (Oxford: Oxford University Press, 2018), 833–834.

9 Woodrow Borah, *Justice by Insurance: The General Indian Court of Colonial Mexico and the Legal Aids of the Half-Real* (Berkeley: University of California Press, 1983); Max Deardorff, 'Republics, Their Customs, and the Law of the King. *Convivencia* and Self-Determination in the Crown of Castile and Its American Territories, 1400–1700' (2018) 26 Rechtsgeschichte 162–199; Carlos J. Díaz Rementería, *El cacique en el virreinato del Perú, estudio histórico-crítico* (Sevilla: Universidad de Sevilla, 1977); Tamar Herzog, 'Colonial law and "Native Customs": Indigenous Land Rights in Colonial Spanish America' (2013) 63(3) The Americas 303–321.

10 José Carlos de la Puente Luna, 'That Which Belongs to All: Khipus, Community, and Indigenous legal Activism in Early Colonial Andes' (2015) 72(1) The Americas 19–54; Yanna Yannakakis and Martina Schrader-Kniffki, 'Between the "Old Law" and the New: Christian Translation, Indian Jurisdiction, and Criminal Justice in Colonial Oaxaca' (2016) 96(3) Hispanic American Historical Review 517–548.

juridical autonomy, they nevertheless gradually took on Spanish forms and assimilated them. This transformed communities, mostly defined by descent, and run by traditional authorities, into Spanish-styled municipalities defined by residence and governed by local councils (*cabildos*).[11] Changes were also evident in Indigenous law, which gradually absorbed colonial standards.[12] As a result, if the initial wish was to create two separate republics, one Spanish and the other Indigenous (and this conclusion has been questioned, even discredited, in recent years), it soon became clear that separation would be impossible. Instead, both the Spanish and the Indigenous legal spheres constantly dialogued with one another as Indigenous authorities also applied Spanish law and Spanish magistrates took Indigenous law into consideration.

Colonial legal pluralism, in short, was much murkier than previously described because, in most instances, the identity of the authority applying the law and the law itself were not identical. Furthermore, during the colonial period, the Indigenous were placed under both Indigenous and Spanish law as applied by both Indigenous and Spanish authorities. Within Spanish law, they were sometimes relegated to a particular status that implied a different set of rights and obligations and, possibly, subjection to a different authority. For example, the Indigenous could be identified as 'neophytes' (new converts to Christianity) or *miserables* (defenseless individuals who required special royal protection).[13] The Indigenous shared these statuses – neophytes and *miserables* – with many non-Indigenous individuals: all those recently converted to Christianity and all those considered 'miserable' (orphans, minors, widows, the poor, and so forth). As a result, while the Indigenous belonged to an Indigenous republic, and were subjected to Indigenous laws and Indigenous authorities,

---

11 Tamar Herzog, *Defining Nations: Immigrants and Citizens in Early Modern Spain and Spanish America* (New Haven: Yale University Press, 2003), 61–62.

12 Alcira Dueñas, *Indians and Mestizos in the 'Lettered City': Reshaping Justice, Social Hierarchy, and Political Culture in Colonial Peru* (Boulder: University Press of Colorado, 2010); Alcira Dueñas, 'Indian Colonial Actors in Lawmaking of the Spanish Empire of Peru' (2018) 65(1) Ethnohistory 61, 63.

13 Paulino Castañeda Delgado, 'La condición miserable del indio y sus privilegios' (1971) 28(1) Anuario de Estudios Americanos 245–335; Caroline Cunill, 'El indio miserable: Nacimiento de la teoría legal en América colonial del siglo XVI' (2011) 8(9) Cuadernos intercambios 229–248; Thomas Duve, 'La condición jurídica del indio y su condición como persona miserabilis en el Derecho indiano' in *Un giudice e due leggi: Pluralismo normativo e conflitti agrari in Sud America*, ed. Mario G. Losano (Milan: Giuffrè, 2004), 3–33; Thomas Duve, 'Derecho canónico y la alteridad indígena: los indios como neófitos' in *Esplendores y miserias de la evangelización en América: Antecedentes europeos y alteridad indígena*, eds Wulf Oesterreicher and Roland Schmidt-Riese (Berlin: De Gruyer, 2010), 73–94.

they were also members of the Spanish republic (because subjected to Spanish law and Spanish authorities), the 'republic' of neophytes, and the 'republic' of miserable individuals, to mention but a few examples. Furthermore, there was no single Spanish nor single Indigenous republic. Instead, multiple Spanish and multiple Indigenous republics coexisted because each community, each city, and each group, had its own manifestations of these republics. Society was profoundly plural and polyvalent; a multiplicity of powers operated at different levels, over different (or the same) individuals, with different ends.

Under Spanish American colonial conditions, in short, law (a particular regime of rights and obligation) and jurisdiction (subjection to particular authorities) sometimes coincided but sometimes did not. Furthermore, all individuals always pertained to more than a single republic and the republics themselves did not necessarily correspond to a division between conquerors and conquered. These observations clarify, among other things, the legal status of individuals of African descent. Historians have long argued that in colonial Spanish America there was no African republic with legitimate African authorities, applying African law. Nonetheless, even if this was true – and recent research indicates it might not have been wholly correct – Africans, both enslaved and free, were discriminated against by a particular legal regime, applied to them by the Spanish authorities. In other words, they were relegated to a separate legal sphere, at least in some respects, without a separate legal jurisdiction. Here too, the question who was African could become a major issue as actors often fought to obtain the classification that suited their interests best. As happened with members of other groups, those classified as Africans could claim that they were not Africans or they could argue that, despite their origins, their situation justified a different treatment.[14]

1.1 *Legal Pluralism – from the Colonies back to Europe*

The coexistence of several legal systems and (sometimes) distinct jurisdictions in the colonial world was often said to reproduce divisions already present in medieval Europe. The most cited example is the treatment of Iberian Jews and Muslims.[15] According to this narrative, members of these religious minorities

---

14 Tamar Herzog, 'The Colonial Expansion and the Making of Nations: The Spanish Case' in *Cambridge History of Nationhood and Nationalism*, eds Cathie Carmichael, Matthew D'Auria, and Aviel Roshwald (Cambridge: Cambridge University Press, 2023), vol. 1, 145–162.

15 Benton, *Law and Colonial Cultures*, 2. Because of this understanding, Benton considers James Muldoon's *Popes, Lawyers, and Infidels: The Church and the Non-Christian World, 1250–1550* (a study of how canon law defined the relations between Christians and non-Christians) as a 'fundamental work on the legal pluralism in early European expansion

were allowed to follow their own laws, which were implemented by their own authorities. These arrangements recognized cultural distinctions as legally and politically meaningful and supplied the perfect precedent, so it is argued, for defining and administrating colonial differences. They provided a technology, legal pluralism, that could be implemented overseas and facilitate imperial rule by enabling a discriminatory regime that gave different people a distinct treatment. In Spain, legal pluralism allowed a measure of autonomy to Jews and Muslims yet placed them under Christian control. In Spanish America, it would do the same with the Indigenous.

This narrative, which imagined legal pluralism as a mechanism specifically devised to administer religious, cultural, or ethnic differences, has been questioned in recent years.[16] The most salient criticism came from scholars who pointed out that, until the French Revolution (and perhaps beyond), European societies were plural rather than singular, and so were their authorities and laws. Plurality was not restricted to religious, ethnic, or cultural differences. Instead, it permeated society and was embedded in the very nature of the early modern state, which was a 'jurisdictional state.'[17] This state, rather than a unitary structure headed by a king as nineteenth-century thinkers imagined it to have been, was a conglomerate made of a plurality of republics, that is, communities, each with its own legal regime and sometimes authorities. Among these communities (also identified as 'corporations') were families, guilds, cities, religious orders, the church, and the military. During this period, public authority was diffused rather than concentrated, because it was divided among

---

into the Atlantic.' Benton, *Law and Colonial Cultures*, 15 n. 8. Benton again insists on privileging religious and cultural differences in Lauren Benton 'Historical Perspectives on Legal Pluralism' (2011) 3 Hague Journal on the Rule of Law 50. It is clear, however, that by the early fourteenth century Jews and Muslims retained (to some degree) their laws but no longer had a separate jurisdiction: Deardorff, 'Republics,' 170.

16 Tamar Herzog, '*Law and Colonial Cultures* by Lauren Benton. Review' (2002) 26(2) Itinerario 149–150; Richard Ross and Philip J. Stern, 'Reconstructing Early Modern Notions of Legal Pluralism' in *Legal Pluralism and Empires, 1500–1850*, eds Lauren Benton and Richard J. Ross (New York: New York University Press, 2013), 109–141.

17 These ideas can be traced back to Otto von Gierke and Otto Brunner. Historians have since insisted that these structures persisted throughout the early modern period. Bartolomé Clavero, *Tantas personas como estados: Por una antropología política de la historia europea* (Madrid: Tecnos, 1986); António Manuel Hespanha, 'A historiografia jurídico-institucional e a morte do estado' (1986) 3, Anuario de Filosofía del Derecho 191–227. For more recent reiteration of these ideas see Maurizio Fioravanti. 'Stato e costituzione' in *Lo Stato moderno in Europa: Istituzioni e diritto*, ed. Maurizio Fioravanti (Roma: Laterza, 2002), 4–36; Carlos Garriga, 'Orden jurídico y poder político en el antiguo régimen' (2004) 4(16) Istor: Revista de Historia Internacional 1–21.

the various corporations. The king was not a sovereign. He was an arbiter and a mediator, his duty mainly consisting of resolving conflicts between the various communities with the aim of guaranteeing social harmony. Government was jurisdictional in the sense that its main task was, literally, to *iuris-dictio*, that is, to both announce and apply the law.

Radically unequal and fragmented, the early modern European state was an incredibly messy arrangement. It featured multiple parallel jurisdictions, that is, a plurality of authorities with power over people and things, each with a relatively autonomous sphere of activity and each constantly contending with the others. Competition was intense, not because individuals either belonged to one corporation or the other, but because they all belonged to more than a single category and were simultaneously subjected to multiple jurisdictions. They were, for example, contemporaneously under the regulation and government of a *pater familias*, a municipality, a guild, and an estate. There was no clear distribution of tasks among the distinct corporations, as the authority and rules of the *pater familias*, for example, were not restricted to the domestic sphere but could oversee issues also belonging to other spheres. And, because the privileges of one authority could challenge the privileges of others, they constantly engaged in rendering decisions that, rather than applying a phantasmagorical law, sought to implement justice. Under this system, all normative solutions (whether inspired in doctrine, customs, legal enactments, or religious duties) were but options meant to guide actors to an ultimate goal of doing the right thing.

Early modern actors could attempt to choose in each case the most convenient forum and could try to affect the way they were classified, but this so-called jockeying was neither exceptional nor detrimental. It was part of the way things habitually operated. That is, the legal posturing colonial historians attributed to empire and the jurisdictional conflicts they described were an inherent and constitutive part of the time period, not overseas expansion. To paraphrase the words of António Manuel Hespanha, the Old Regime existed not only in Europe but also in the Tropics.[18]

If so, then there is no reason to look back to the administration of religious differences and minorities in Spain as a privileged site to explain how empires functioned. A greater familiarity with the literature on the early modern European state would also raise the question of whether the legalities of Europe differed from the legalities of empire and why legal pluralism should

18 António Manuel Hespanha, 'Antigo Regime nos trópicos? Um debate sobre o modelo político do Império colonial português' in *Na trama das redes*, eds João Fragoso and Maria de Fátima Gouvêa (Rio de Janeiro: Civilização Brasileira, 2010), 43–94.

feature so massively in narratives of colonial domination as if it was exclusive to these political formations.

Taking a step back, those who advocated identifying early modern legal pluralism with empire responded to such criticism by arguing that legal pluralism, already existing in 'core regions' became 'more complex' in the colonial setting because of the existence of Indigenous, enslaved, and conquered peoples.[19] In empire, they contended, struggle over plurality made plurality more explicit because the cultural significance of legal boundaries was central to colonial legal politics. In overseas territories, in other words, legal differentiation became a routine for organizing cultural differences, indeed a means to administer multiculturalism. But this response rarified colonial struggles without proving that they were truly distinct. It anachronistically presupposed that cultural differences were the most salient differences in the early modern period, and it falsely assumed that adherence to a family, or an estate, was substantially different (and by implication less important) than ethnic or religious classifications.[20] This response also silenced the fact that tying legal pluralism to empire had less to do with imperial specificity than with the genealogy of how legal pluralism emerged as an academic pursuit in English-speaking scholarly circles in the first place. Originally proposed by anthropologists with the aim of demonstrating the persistence of Indigenous legal structures despite colonialism, legal pluralism was soon taken up by scholars who wished to render manifest the incapacity of states to monopolize the creation and application of norms.[21] Inspiring legal historians of empires, both these quests were extremely presentist and both were geared towards vindicating cultural and ethnic particularities. Thought important for comprehending present-day conditions, they had no pretention to understand (or explain) the past and indeed cannot operate there the way historians of empire pretended.

1.2 *Legal Pluralism and Modernity*

The various legal regimes that applied to individuals by virtue of their classification in groups that could be distinguished according to religion, ethnicity,

---

19 Lauren Benton and Richard J. Ross, 'Jurisdiction, Sovereignty and Political Imagination in the Early Modern World' in Benton and Ross, *Legal Pluralism*, 1.

20 Peter Burke, 'Foundation Myths and Collective Identities in Early Modern Europe' in *Europe and the Other and Europe as the Other*, ed. Bo Strath (Brussels: Peter Lang, 2000), 113–122.

21 Sally Engle Merry, 'Legal Pluralism' (1988) 22(5) Law and Society Review 869–896; Brian Tamanaha, 'The Folly of the Social Scientific Concept of "Legal Pluralism"' (1993) 20(2) Journal of Law & Society 192–217.

race, gender, professional activities, residence, estate, or family membership, those typical of the *ancien régime*, came under attack in the eighteenth century. They were first questioned by monarchs, who wished to create a new type of polity where citizens would be directly tied to kings rather than to intermediate bodies (corporations). Monarchs also sought to subject all legal orders and authorities to their jurisdiction and assert their sovereignty, that is, their superiority with regard to the law.[22] Following such ambitions, across Europe as well as in Spain, Portugal, and their overseas domains, royal officials strove to limit the autonomy and jurisdiction of communities and corporations.[23]

Although they managed to introduce important changes, it was not until the French Revolution that the elimination of pluralism was truly envisioned, as was the invention of a single, undivided sovereignty that would no longer tolerate other powers but instead declare itself both exclusive and monopolistic. French revolutionaries who proposed these radical moves also declared legislation the only legitimate legal source. According to this proposal, either norms were expressed in legislation, or they were not legally binding. Thereafter, government would no longer exercise jurisdiction, that is, the power to tell and apply the law. Instead, legislators would create norms; administrators would enforce them.

To enable these truly remarkable transformations, the first step French revolutionaries took was to imagine a new legal subject, which would be equal to all others.[24] Abandoning the existing axiom that insisted that all humans were dissimilar because distinguished by birth, occupation, and residence, French revolutionaries moved to invent abstract individuals who, regardless of their distinct traits, would be considered identical to all others. This new individual would be decontextualized by way of a legal fiction that, in the name of legal equality, would imagine identical individuals who could benefit from the same treatment by the same authorities.

---

22 Jean Bodin (1530–1596) was the most famous proponent of the idea of sovereignty, though, when he authored *The Six Books of the Republic* (1576), his proposals were revolutionary and thus largely rejected. On the birth of absolutism during the French Revolution (but not before) see Matteo Sanfilippo, 'Alcune note sul concetto di assolutismo nella storiografia europea' in *L'Europa di Giovanni Sobieski: cultura, politica, mercatura e società*, ed. Gaetano Platania (Viterbo: Sette Città, 2005), 479.

23 Airton Cerqueira-Leite Seelaender. 'A longa sombra da casa. Poder doméstico, conceitos tradicionais e imaginario jurídico na transição brasileira do antigo regime à modernidade' (2017) 178 (473) Revista Instituto Histórico e Geográfico Brasileiro 342–343.

24 Tamar Herzog, *A Short History of European Law: The Last Two and a Half Millennia* (Cambridge, MA: Harvard University Press, 2018), 183–203.

The need to create a new legal subject was seconded by the necessity of inventing a new public authority.[25] Instead of a state made of a conglomerate of republics, each with its own authorities and laws, French revolutionaries imagined a single sovereign that created law though legislation. To achieve this end, they introduced a new distinction between the making and the application of norms. Thereafter, reasonable and responsible legislators, elected by the nation, would create norms that would be applied universally by an executive branch with the help of a judiciary. The old jurisdiction, that combined declaring and implementing the law, would thereafter cease to exist.

Put together, these new ideas implied the ambition to abandon the old system that bestowed rights and privileges on individuals according to who they were by their authorities that governed by both declaring and applying norms. Instead, the new regime no longer acknowledged the appropriateness of distinctions in estate, profession, ethnicity, race, or place of residence and only recognized a single authority that oversaw the affairs of everyone equally. The result was a new type of state, a new legitimacy, and a new legality. The promise of legal equality, however, was not complete. While some distinctions were abolished or deliberately ignored, others, such as those based on gender (the different treatment of men and women), civic state (slavery or freedom), and religion (the discrimination of non-Christians) survived. The equal citizen envisioned by the French Revolution, in other words, was a free Christian male.

1.3 *Latin American Modernity*

These revolutionary ideas, typified by the French Revolution but germinating in worldwide conversations and experiences, gradually travelled the globe. Among the many polities that fell under their influence were the new Latin American states. Having gained their independence in the early nineteenth century, most Latin American states moved to institute legal equality among their citizens, give the state a monopoly over legal creation, and equate law with legislation. As elsewhere, these moves required the eradication of *ancien régime* corporations and the monopolization of all power by a single sovereign. Abolished were the rights of many communities and corporations, as well as the legal distinctions between the Indigenous, Spaniards, and individuals of African descent. Particularly heralded were proclamations such as the declaration of 1821 according to which 'henceforth the aborigines will not be called Indians or natives; they are sons and citizens of Peru and will be known as

25 Rafe Blaufarb, *The Great Demarcation: The French Revolution and the Invention of Modern Property* (Oxford: Oxford University Press, 2016), 15–47.

Peruvians' or the decision in 1857 that Indigenous peoples would be 'made equal with the rest of Ecuadorians with regards to duties and rights granted and imposed by the constitution.'[26]

The abolition of *ancien régime* structures affected both privileges and duties. It led to the abandonment of impositions specifically levied on the Indigenous (*tributo* and *mita*) but it also brought the dismantling of Indigenous communal structures, alongside their particular authorities and rights, most importantly, the right to communal lands. Also abolished were judicial instances such as the *Juzgado General de Indios* of Mexico or the understanding that the Indigenous would be protected from military draft. In the aftermaths of these developments, in most Latin American states, the only classification that was deemed legally pertinent was the distinction between nationals and non-nationals, citizens and non-citizens, free or enslaved. Heralded as a move to improve the status of Indigenous peoples, now allegedly liberated from colonial subjection and discrimination, and made equal citizens, these measures nonetheless often led to the hardening of burdens, the loss of important immunities, and subsequent dispossession and marginalization.

Theoretical blindness to differences, at any rate, did not guarantee de facto equal treatment. In some Spanish American republics, taxes levied on the Indigenous during the colonial period were initially abolished but were soon reintroduced under a host of different names.[27] Reintroduction led to new classificatory efforts, aimed at identifying who the Indigenous were in order to decide who should pay these tributes. In some cases, the new taxes were individually levied and thus eroded communal structures. In others, they reinforced these structures as, in practice, communal authorities administered these new fiscal and labor obligations, as well as many related questions, such as land distribution.[28] Paradoxically, the final abolition of Indigenous duties across the continent, starting in the mid-nineteenth century, led to the intensification, rather than the waning, of labor extraction, land dispossession, and violence though, here again, response to these pressures sometimes manifested the persistence of communal authorities, which adhered to an Indigenous law.[29]

---

26 Mark Van Aken, 'The Lingering Death of Indian Tribute in Ecuador' (1981) 61(3) Hispanic American Historical Review 439, 454.

27 Carlos Contreras, 'Estado republicano y tributo indígena en la sierra central en la post independencia' (1988) 48(182–183) Revista de Indias 517–550; Cecilia Sanhueza Tohá 'Ser "indio" en el siglo XIX: Categorías fiscales y discurso social del estado boliviano en la provincia de Atacama' (2015) 47(3) Arica 507–519.

28 Andrés Guerrero, 'Curagas y tenientes políticos: La ley de la costumbre y la ley del estado' (1989) 14(2) Revista Andina 329–336.

29 Brooke Larson, *Trials of Nation Making: Liberalism, Race and Ethnicity in the Andes, 1810–1910* (Cambridge: Cambridge University Press, 2004), 249, 252.

An emblematic example of the half-hearted abolition of *ancien régime* categories were the early twentieth-century Peruvian Penal Codes, which defined some locals as limited in their understanding of the 'dominant morality' and prescribed for them a distinct penal procedure and punishment. Aimed at 'civilizing' rather than penalizing, these arrangements limited the criminal responsibility of some Peruvians in ways not dissimilar to colonial law.[30] In other words, the move to create a single citizen accomplished a re-definition of what being Indigenous meant. Having been understood as a corporate identity during the colonial period, in the nineteenth and twentieth centuries it became a racial classification that, albeit including individuals recognized as 'nationals,' identified some of these individuals as members of groups that were considered inferior and therefore unfit to comply with the demands of citizenship.[31]

Experience in nineteenth- and early twentieth-century Latin America, therefore, demonstrated the persistence of a grey zone between an officially sanctioned Indigenous republic (which was abolished) and the promise of equality (that never materialized). And, despite the creation of nations with legally (though never politically, socially, economically, or culturally) equal citizens and a monopolistic sphere of legality controlled by the state, as the anthropologists who coined 'legal pluralism' in the early twentieth century pointed out, in practice, legal equality and state monopoly were merely orienting principles. In Latin America as elsewhere, Indigenous communal structures and legal orders often persisted and they continued to shape daily experiences in communities where state normativity and state authorities were sometimes supplemented, sometimes replaced, by local authorities and norms.

1.4 *Present-Day Legal Pluralism*

The realization that the project of constructing a single decontextualized equal citizen was not necessarily successful led to the quest to recognize formally that the body of nationals was made of distinct, rather than similar, individuals. From the 1980s to the present, most Latin American states embraced

30 Tamar Herzog, 'Percibir el otro: El código penal de 1924 y la división de los peruanos en personas "civilizadas," "semi-civilizadas" y "salvajes"' in *Observation and Communication: The Construction of Realities in the Hispanic World*, eds Johannes Michael Scholz and Tamar Herzog (Frankfurt: Vittorio Klostermann, 1997), 399–414; José Hurtado Pozo, 'Derecho penal y derechos culturales' in *Derechos Culturales* ed. Marco Borgui (Lima: Pontificia Universidad Católica del Perú, 1997), 105–127.

31 Larson, *Trials of Nation*, 246–247.

such recognition either in their constitutions, or through laws that instituted at least some measure of plurality. Although the arrangements they adopted were profoundly diverse, currently, Guatemala, Nicaragua, Argentina, Bolivia, Brazil, Colombia, Ecuador, Mexico, Panama, Paraguay, Peru, and Venezuela all have provisions that upend the idea of a single citizen led by a single authority and subjected to a single legal regime. In some countries, this entails recognizing communal structures and communal authorities. This usually results in the recuperation of important collective rights, such as the right to land. In others, this involves acknowledging the existence of legal spheres, other than those monopolized by the state. Part of a larger universal trend to uphold Indigenous rights, most particularly, the right to a distinct culture, these developments justify not only reintroducing differentiations among citizens by recognizing that not all are the same but also adding Indigenous notions to state law. The most noteworthy example in this regard is the Ecuadorian Constitution of 2008, which confers rights on nature, identified by the traditional Andean appellation of *Pacha Mama*.

Currently, throughout Latin America, there is a growing conviction that different communities should be allowed to submit to different laws, but this recognition is not absolute. The constitution of Indigenous jurisdictions – such as mandated for example by the Colombian Constitution of 1991 that recognizes the right of Indigenous authorities to exercise jurisdictional functions within their territories in conformity with their own norms and procedures – nevertheless limits this exercise to what is 'not contrary to the constitution and the laws of the republic.'[32] While the Colombian Constitutional Court, seeking to allow the greatest autonomy possible, has tended to give this clause a restrictive interpretation according to which Indigenous legality would not have to comply with all national legislation (or else Indigenous legality would be a charade), it set limits that could not be violated. According to the judges, these were to be defined by a 'true intercultural consensus' or include a 'core of untouchable rights' such as 'the right to life, the prohibition of slavery

32 Colombian Constitution (1991), art. 246. Somewhat similar were arts. 84 and 191 of the Ecuadorian Constitution of 1998 and arts. 57 and 171 of the Ecuadorian Constitution of 2008. Article 344 of the Código Orgánico de la Justicia, Ecuador, also defined the scope of Indigenous jurisdiction and its interaction with state authorities. An early reflection on how state law and Indigenous law can live side by side is Raquel Yrigoyen Fajardo, *Pautas de coordinación entre el derecho indígena y el derecho estatal* (Guatemala: Fundación Myrna Mack, 1999). The Indigenous and Tribal Peoples Convention of 1989 by the International Labor Organization already placed limits on Indigenous jurisdiction. Art. 8 of the Convention determined that Indigenous law cannot violate fundamental rights as defined by the national legal system as well as internationally recognized human rights.

and torture, and some measure of due process.'[33] In other cases, such as the Bolivian Constitution of 2009, legal pluralism is guaranteed through a plurinational constitutional court, which includes judges representing 'indigenous native peasants.'[34]

Although Colombia and Bolivia now guarantee some measure of legal pluralism, state normativity remains superior. In other words, the legal pluralism these states allow is 'weak' according to some, 'asymmetrical,' according to others.[35] This form of legal pluralism distinguishes what some scholars have categorized as the 'permissible' Indigenous (whose distinct culture and normativity could be tolerated) from the non-permissible Indigenous (whose norms must be rejected).[36] Scholars also denounced the absence, in most countries, of legislation necessary to transform constitutional arrangements into actual practices.

As happened during the *ancien régime*, the re-emergence in late twentieth century of new jurisdictions that were to apply Indigenous norms to Indigenous individuals led to continuous processes of identification. Now that Indigenous identity carried important legal consequences, the question who was who again became a contentious issue. Questions asked during the colonial period also re-surfaced: would indigeneity be a category based on descent, culture, place of residence, or self-identification? Because answering these questions was difficult, most Latin American countries shied from defining indigeneity in a clear and conclusive manner. Yet, historians have observed that the renewed powers of Indigenous communities as well as their re-found jurisdiction led to the assumption of Indigenous identity by individuals and groups who previously had not been identified as such, or had abandoned this identification but now found it useful again. In late twentieth-century Latin America, group identity was often the result of complex interactions between

33 Felipe Gómez Isa, 'Cultural Diversity, Legal Pluralism, and Human Rights from an Indigenous Perspective: The Approach of the Colombian Constitutional Court and the Inter-American Court of Human Rights' (2014) 36(4) Human Rights Quarterly 737–739.

34 Bolivian Constitution (2009), art. 1 and Ley del Tribunal Constitucional Plurinacional, Law 027, July 6, 2010, art. 3.

35 Almut Schilling-Vacaflor and René Kuppe, 'Plurinational Constitutionalism: A New Era of Indigenous-State Relations?' in *New Constitutionalism in Latin America: Promises and Practices*, eds Detlef Nolte and Almut Schilling-Vacaflor (Farnham: Ashgate, 2012), 352. See also Anna Barrera, 'Turning Legal Pluralism into State-Sanctioned Law: Assessing the Implications of the New Constitutions and Laws in Bolivia and Ecuador' in *New Constitutionalism*, 371–390. On weak versus strong legal pluralism see John Griffiths 'What Is Legal Pluralism?' (1986) 24 Journal of Legal Pluralism and Unofficial Law 1–55.

36 Charles R. Hale, 'Neoliberal Multiculturalism: The Remaking of Cultural Rights and Racial Dominance in Central America' (2005) 28(1) Political and Legal Anthropology Review 24.

locals, state, and international norms, governmental agencies, missionaries, anthropologists, the church, and international organizations.[37]

Initially, the new Latin American legal pluralism mostly centered on protecting Indigenous rights. Recently, however, there is a growing awareness that individuals of African descent also form groups that have a distinct take on legality and that they too deserve both group recognition and a legal autonomy. As a result, in some countries, the rights of Afro-descendants were lumped together with those of Indigenous peoples. This was the case, for example, in Article 56 of the Ecuadorian Constitution of 2008, which recognized 'indigenous communities, peoples and nations, the Afro-Ecuadorian people, the back-country people of the inland costal region, and commune' as forming populations belonging to the nation. Article 60 determined that 'ancestral, Afro-Ecuadorians, and coastal back-country people' can 'establish territorial districts for the preservation of their culture and or establish communities with collective land ownership.' Yet, even when the sameness of difference is recognized, the rights granted to Afro-descendants are not as extensive as those given to Indigenous peoples. Thus, while Article 57 of the Ecuadorian Constitution extensively dealt with the rights of Indigenous communities, including among them the right to 'keep their own forms of peaceful coexistence,' to institute authorities, and move to self-determination, Article 58 dealing with Afro-descendants only recognized their 'collective rights.' There was no clause similar to Article 171 dealing with the Indigenous that would allow Afro-nationals to have their own norms or give their authorities the power to perform jurisdictional duties in internal disputes.

According to scholars, this differential treatment can be explained by history. Colonial structures recognized the existence of an Indigenous but not an African republic.[38] Afro-descendants, it is also argued, were mostly imagined as belonging to a racial rather than an ethnic community and, presently, the rights of ethnic communities are more easily accepted than the rights of racial groups. Also detrimental to Afro-descendants was the fact that, traditionally,

---

37 Jean Jackson, 'Being and Becoming Indian in the Vaupés' in *Nation-States and Indians in Latin America*, eds Greg Urban and Joel Sherzer (Austin: University of Texas Press, 1991), 131–155.

38 Juliet Hooker, 'Indigenous Inclusion/Black Exclusion: Race, Ethnicity and Multicultural Citizenship in Latin America' (2005) 37 Journal of Latin American Studies 285–310; *Política e identidad afrodescendientes en México y América Central*, ed. Odile Hoffmann (México: UNAM, 2010); Esther Ojulari, 'The Social Construction of Afro-Descendant Rights in Colombia' in *Contemporary Challenges in Securing Human Rights*, ed. Corinne Lennox (London: Institute of Commonwealth Studies, 2015), 19–28.

Indigenous groups had a greater public visibility and a greater degree of activism. They seemed, in most countries, more present.

Although in most Latin American countries Afro-nationals have not yet achieved the same recognition as Indigenous peoples, in some places, their communities nevertheless managed to win important gains, among them at least some measure of legal autonomy. Honduras, for example, moved in the 1990s to apply most policies to both Indigenous and Afro-hondureños.[39] Somewhat similarly, the Chilean parliament recently recognized the existence of 'the tribal people' (*pueblo tribal*) of African descent, alongside its cultural, linguistic, historical, institutional, and normative particularities.[40] Regardless of such exceptional cases, differences between the autonomy granted to Indigenous and African communities tend to be great. Scholars argue that the conferral of communal rights, including legal rights, to Afro-Latin Americans usually succeeded only after they (or their advocates) adopted the language of 'ethnic rights.' Afro-hondureños, for example, who received a measure of legal autonomy, were classified as belonging to autochthonous ethnic groups (*etnias autóctonas*). In 1993, the Colombian authorities followed the same road when they moved to recognize Afro-Colombian communities, which possessed their own culture, shared a common history, had their own traditions and customs, and 'revealed and preserved a consciousness of identity that distinguished them from other ethnic groups.'[41] The tendency to demand (or to give) rights to Afro-Latin American communities on the basis of their ethnicization led to important processes of ethnogenesis that had blackness 'look increasingly like Indianness.'[42]

As happened with natives, the allocation of rights and jurisdiction on the basis of communal belonging led to the emergence of new or renewed identities among individuals of African descent. In Brazil, where the Federal

39 Mark Anderson, 'When Afro Becomes (like) Indigenous: Garifuna and Afro-Indigenous Politics in Honduras' (2007) 12(2) Journal of Latin American and Caribbean Anthropology 384–413.

40 https://www.elciudadano.cl/chile/congreso-despachado-a-ley-proyecto-que-otorga-reconocimiento-legal-al-pueblo-afrodescendiente-chileno/03/07/, consulted on March 29, 2019.

41 Ley 70, 1993, art. 2, para. 5, cited in Ojulari, 'The Social,' 22.

42 Peter Wade, *Race and Ethnicity in Latin America* (Chicago: Pluto Press, 1997), 37, 117–119; Jean Muteba Rahier and Mamyrah Dougé Prosper, 'Afrodescendants, the Multicultural Turn and the "New" Latin American Constitutions and Other Special Legislations: Particularities of the Andean Region' in *Blackness in the Andes: Ethnographic Vignettes of Cultural Politics in Times of Multiculturalism*, ed. Jean Muteba Rahier (New York: Palgrave-Macmillan, 2014), 90.

Constitution of 1988 recognized ownership over land to members of ancient runaway enslaved communities (*quilombos*), the promise of rights led to the emergence of many new groups.[43] According to researchers, it entailed identity reconfiguration by rural communities who had extensive population of African descent but who previously did not identify as such.

1.5 *The New Latin American Legal Pluralism: Old or New?*

Despite formal resemblance to colonial categories, the legal pluralism that emerged in Latin America in the late twentieth century is new. While *ancien régime* pluralism recognized the particularities not only of ethnic groups but also of cities, professional associations, estates, and families, the new pluralism restricts what can and should be recognized as a right-bearing group. Indeed, the new legal pluralism is so adamant that only some groups, basically ethnic groups, can have their own legal sphere, that Afro-Latin Americans must model their demands accordingly. And, while some ethnic groups can have their authorities and (sometimes) their own law, current developments include no true questioning of state monopoly, nor is there a suggestion to replace state-sanctioned law in any meaningful way. The new pluralism is also different from the old because it tends to combine law and jurisdiction, a combination that was unusual during the early modern period. The current legal pluralism, reversing some of the propositions made by French revolutionaries but not all, also finds it difficult to justify the coexistence of legal equality with the emergence of distinct legal personalities and distinct sets of rules. Furthermore, while the opportunities opened to some communities led to the emergence of new or renewed identities, they also entailed soul searching. Must communities who demand rights as well as their norms be fossilized as relics of the past, or can they be recognized as dynamic entities that experience internal change and constant mutations because of interaction with other groups? Must Indigenous law be oral and customary, as anthropologists often assume, or can it take on other forms? Must it stand in opposition to, indeed be used as

43 Sérgio Costa, 'Freezing Differences: Politics, Law and the Invention of Cultural Diversity in Latin America' in *Legitimization in World Society*, eds Aldo Mascareño and Kathya Araujo (Farnham: Ashgate, 2012), 148–151. This right was recognized in Articles 215 and 216 of the constitution. The Colombian Constitution of 1991, art. 55, also included arrangements allowing recognition of the collective rights of Black communities to certain lands. These issues are also explored in Jan H. French, *Legalizing Identities: Becoming Black or Indian in Brazil's Northeast* (Chapel Hill: University of North Carolina Press, 2009), 13; Manuel Góngora Mera, Rocío Vera Santos, and Sérgio Costa, *Entre el Atlántico y el Pacifico Negro: Afrodescendencia y regímenes de desigualdad en Sudamérica* (Madrid: Iberoamericana Editorial Vervuert, 2019), 508–511.

a vehicle to resist, the imposition of state law? In practice, research indicates that, despite the constant invocation of historical normativity, the emergence of new legalities led to massive changes. In many cases, communal authorities allowed the co-penetration of their own law and state law, co-opting what they found useful and adapting to the requirements of multiculturalism even within their own autochthonous sphere, which was just as pluralistic as the state. In some places, newly empowered Indigenous authorities abandoned their own law altogether and instead adopted written codes. These codes were the result of lengthy negotiations among various groups and involved input from non-native individuals.[44] The legitimization of an Indigenous legal sphere also introduced important changes in Indigenous normativity such as, for example, improving the status of women.[45]

While the realization that not all nationals are similar is both pertinent and important, as is the desire to enable some degree of communal autonomy, the main question facing Latin American jurists today is how to generate and protect consensus despite diversity. Can there be an equality of conditions that is not based on abstract and decontextualized individuals who have no group identifiers?[46] Can the guarantee of rights coexist with diversity, or must there be limits to what is permitted even in a multicultural and legally plural universe? Must differentiation be based on the essentialization of who people are or are there ways we have not yet imagined, to recognize diversity without pretending that some identities are fixed while others are contingent, some are singular, while others are plural?

References

Benton, Lauren. 'Historical Perspectives on Legal Pluralism.' *Hague Journal of the Rule of Law* 3 (2011): 57–69.

44 Marcela Velasco, 'Multiculturalism, Legal Pluralism, and Local Government in Colombia: Indigenous Autonomy and Institutional Embeddedness in Karmata Rúa, Antioquia' (2017) 50 Journal of Latin American Studies 517–547.

45 Rachel Sieder and Anna Barrera, 'Women and Legal Pluralism: Lessons from Indigenous Governance Systems in the Andes' (2017) 49 Journal of Latin American Studies 633–658. On such processes, which some legal scholars have identified as 'interlegality,' see, for example, Marc Simon Thomas, *The Challenge of Legal Pluralism: Local Dispute Settlement and the Indian-State Relationship in Ecuador* (New York: Routledge, 2017).

46 António Manuel Hespanha, *Pluralismo jurídico e direito democrático: Prospetivas do direito no século XXI* (Brazil: Annablume Editora, 2013).

Benton, Lauren, and Richard J. Ross, eds. *Legal Pluralism and Empires, 1500–1850*. New York: New York University Press, 2013.

Costa, Sérgio. 'Freezing Differences: Politics, Law and the Invention of Cultural Diversity in Latin America.' In *Legitimization in World Society*, edited by Aldo Mascareño and Kathya Araujo, 139–159. Farnham: Ashgate, 2012.

Deardorff, Max. 'Republics, Their Customs, and the Law of the King: Convivencia and Self- Determination in the Crown of Castile and Its American Territories, 1400–1700.' *Rechtsgeschichte* 26 (2018): 162–199.

Duve, Thomas. 'Indigenous Rights: Latin America.' In *The Oxford Handbook of Legal History*, edited by Markus D. Dubber and Christopher Tomlins, 817–838. Oxford: Oxford University Press, 2018.

Garriga, Carlos. 'Orden jurídico y poder político en el antiguo régimen.' *Istor: Revista de Historia Internacional* 4(16) (2004): 1–21.

Herzog, Tamar. 'Percibir el otro: El código penal de 1924 y la división de los peruanos en personas "civilizadas," "semi-civilizadas" y "salvajes."' In *Observation and Communication: The Construction of Realities in the Hispanic World*, edited by Johannes Michael Scholz and Tamar Herzog, 399–414. Frankfurt: Vittorio Klostermann, 1997.

Herzog, Tamar. *Defining Nations: Immigrants and Citizens in Early Modern Spain and Spanish America*. New Haven: Yale University Press, 2003.

Herzog, Tamar. 'Colonial Law and "Native Customs": Indigenous Land Rights in Colonial Spanish America.' *The Americas* 63(3) (2013): 303–321.

Herzog, Tamar. *A Short History of European Law: The Last Two and a Half Millennia*. Cambridge, MA: Harvard University Press, 2018.

Hooker, Juliet. 'Indigenous Inclusion/Black Exclusion: Race, Ethnicity and Multicultural Citizenship in Latin America.' *Journal of Latin American Studies* 37 (2005): 285–310.

Larson, Brooke. *Trials of Nation Making: Liberalism, Race and Ethnicity in the Andes, 1810–1910*. Cambridge: Cambridge University Press, 2004.

Merry, Sally E. 'Legal Pluralism.' *Law and Society Review* 22(5) (1988): 869–896.

Puente Luna, Jose Carlos de la. 'That Which Belongs to All: Khipus, Community, and Indigenous legal Activism in Early Colonial Andes.' *The Americas* 72(1) (2015): 19–54.

Schilling-Vacaflor, Almut, and René Kuppe. 'Plurinational Constitutionalism: A New Era of Indigenous-State Relations?' In *New Constitutionalism in Latin America: Promises and Practices*, edited by Detlef Nolte and Almut Schilling-Vacaflor, 347–370. Farnham: Ashgate, 2012.

Yannakakis, Yanna, and Martina Schrader-Kniffki. 'Between the "Old Law" and the New: Christian Translation, Indian Jurisdiction, and Criminal Justice in Colonial Oaxaca.' *Hispanic American Historical Review* 96(3) (2016): 517–548.

Index

www.ingramcontent.com/pod-product-compliance
Lightning Source LLC
LaVergne TN
LVHW010637300926
849161LV00005B/965